W9-CNX-907

ENCYCLOPEDIA OF
KNOWLEDGE

ENCYCLOPEDIA OF

KNOWLEDGE

First published in 2017 by Miles Kelly Publishing Ltd
Harding's Barn, Bardfield End Green, Thaxted, Essex, CM6 3PX, UK

This edition printed 2019

4 6 8 10 9 7 5

Publishing Director Belinda Gallagher
Creative Director Jo Cowan
Editorial Director Rosie Neave
Proofreaders Teri Putnam, Jenni Rainford
Cover Designers Rob Hale, Simon Lee
Designers Jo Cowan, Warris Kidwai, Venita Kidwai, Sally Lace, Peter Radcliffe
Indexers Helen Snaith, Marie Lorimer
Image Manager Liberty Newton
Production Elizabeth Collins, Jennifer Brunwin-Jones
Reprographics Stephan Davis,Callum Ratcliffe-Bingham
Assets Lorraine King

Planners, Authors and Consultants Simon Adams, Sue Becklake, Clive Carpenter, Stuart Cooper, Camilla de la Bedoyere, Fiona MacDonald, Rupert Matthews, Steve Parker, Stephen Setford, Clint Twist, Brian Williams

ISBN 978-1-78617-326-3

Printed in China

British Library Cataloguing-in-Publication Data
A catalogue record for this book is available from the British Library

Made with paper from a sustainable forest

www.mileskelly.net

CONTENTS

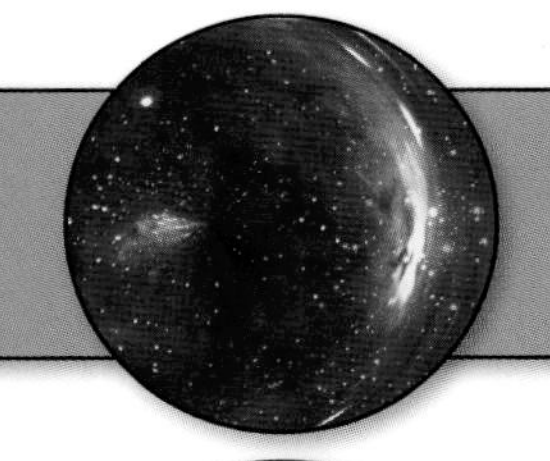

UNIVERSE  10

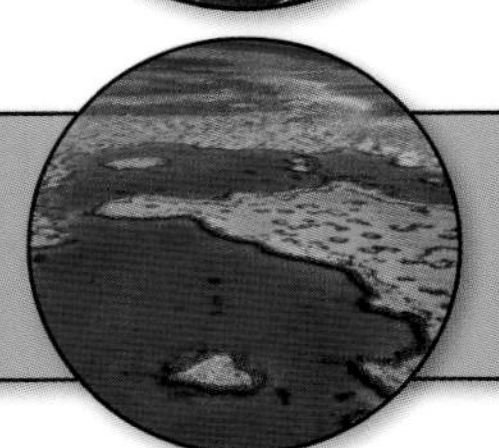

PLANET EARTH  70

LIFE ON EARTH  130

HISTORY 190

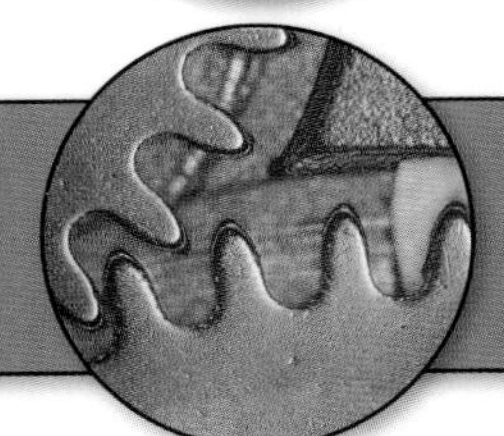

SCIENCE & TECHNOLOGY 250

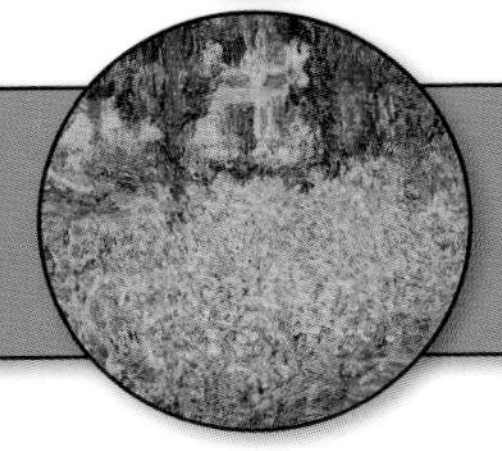

ARTS & CULTURE 310

INDEX 370

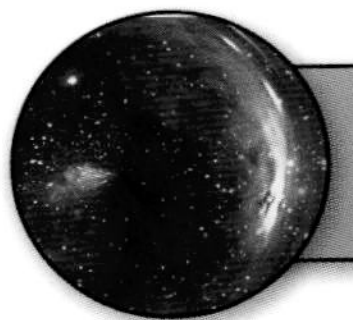

UNIVERSE

The Big Bang 12
Stars 14
Constellations 16
Galaxies 18
The Milky Way 20
Nebulae 22
Black Holes 24
The Solar System 26
The Sun 28
The Earth 30
The Moon 32
Mercury 34
Venus 36
Mars 38
Jupiter 40
Saturn 42
Uranus 44
Neptune 46
Pluto and the Dwarf Planets 48
Comets 50
Asteroids and Meteorites 52
Astronomy 54
Telescopes and Observatories 56
Space Probes 58
Artificial Satellites 60
Man on the Moon 62
The Space Shuttle 64
Space Stations 66
Glossary 68

PLANET EARTH 70

The Formation of Earth	72
Spinning Earth	74
Ages of the Earth	76
Inside the Earth	78
Rocks	80
Gemstones	82
Fossils	84
Continents	86
Islands	88
Drifting Continents	90
Volcanoes	92
Earthquakes	94
Landscapes	96
Mountains	98
Glaciers and Ice Ages	100
Rivers	102
Lakes	104
Oceans and Seas	106
Caves	108
Deserts	110
Forests	112
The Atmosphere	114
Clouds	116
Weather	118
Climate	120
Global Warming	122
Resources	124
Maps and Mapmaking	126
Glossary	128

LIFE ON EARTH 130

Origins of Life	132
The Plant Kingdom	134
Parts of a Plant	136
Food Factory	138
Plant Reproduction	140
How Plants Grow	142
Plants on our Planet	144
The Animal Kingdom	146
Invertebrates	148
How Animals Move	150
Fish	152
How Animals Feed	154
Amphibians	156
How Animals Breed	158
Reptiles	160
Dinosaurs	162
Communication	164
Birds	166
Mammals	168
Animals in Danger	170
The Human Body	172
Bones and Joints	174
Muscles and Moving	176
Lungs and Breathing	178
Eating and Digestion	180
Heart and Blood	182
The Nervous System	184
Reproduction	186
Glossary	188

HISTORY

The Ancient World	192
The Fertile Crescent	194
Ancient Greece	196
The Roman Empire	198
China and Japan	200
The Barbarians	202
New States	204
Feudal Europe	206
Indian Empires	208
Medieval Asia	210
The Americas	212
New Learning	214
Age of Explorers	216
Religion and Wars	218
Beyond Europe	220
1600–1800	222
Expanding World	224
Asia in Decline	226
A Europe of Ideas	228
The Industrial Revolution	230
The Age of Revolutions	232
Europe in Revolution	234
Europe Supreme	236
World Wars	238
The Cold War	240
The Changing World	242
History Timeline	244
Glossary	246

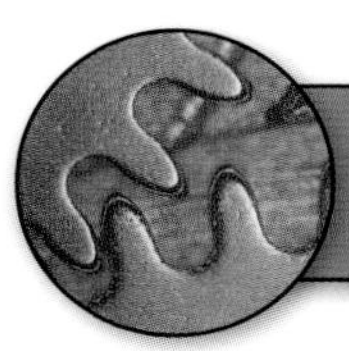

SCIENCE & TECHNOLOGY 250

Atoms and Molecules 252
Solids, Liquids and Gases 254
The Periodic Table 254
Chemicals and Materials 258
Carbon Chemicals 260
Electricity and Magnetism 262
Energy 264
Force and Motion 266
Heat and Temperature 268
Light 270
Sound 272
Air and Water 274
Early Inventions 276
Machine Power 278
Construction 280
Bridges 282
History of Rail Transport 284
History of Road Transport 286
History of Water Transport 288
History of Air Transport 290
Computers 292
Telecommunications 294
The Internet 296
Audiovisual Technology 298
Power 300
Medicine 302
Numbers and Shapes 304
Glossary 308

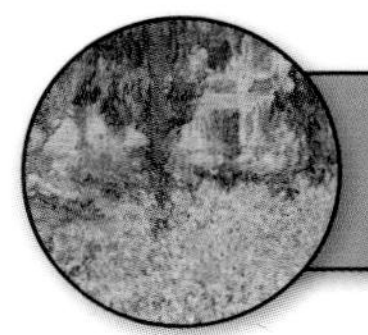

ARTS & CULTURE 310

The First Artists 312
Old Masters, New Ideas 314
Art Techniques 316
Art around the World 318
Modern Art 320
Making Music 322
Classical Music 324
Musical Instruments 326
Popular Music 328
The Origins of Drama 330
World Theatre 332
Modern Theatre 334
Moving to Music 336
Ballet 338
Dance 340
Words and Writing 342
Scriptures and Sacred Writing 344
Poems and Novels 346
Printing and Publishing 348
Beginnings of Broadcasting 350
Home Entertainment 352
The First Films 354
Making Movies 356
Special Effects and Superstars 358
Buildings Great and Small 360
Modern Architecture 362
History of Culture 364
Glossary 366

UNIVERSE

The Big Bang

The Universe is everything that we can ever know – all of space and all of time. It is almost entirely empty, with small clusters of matter and energy. The Universe is about 13.8 billion years old, but estimates vary. The Big Bang explosion is how scientists think the Universe began 13.8 billion years ago.

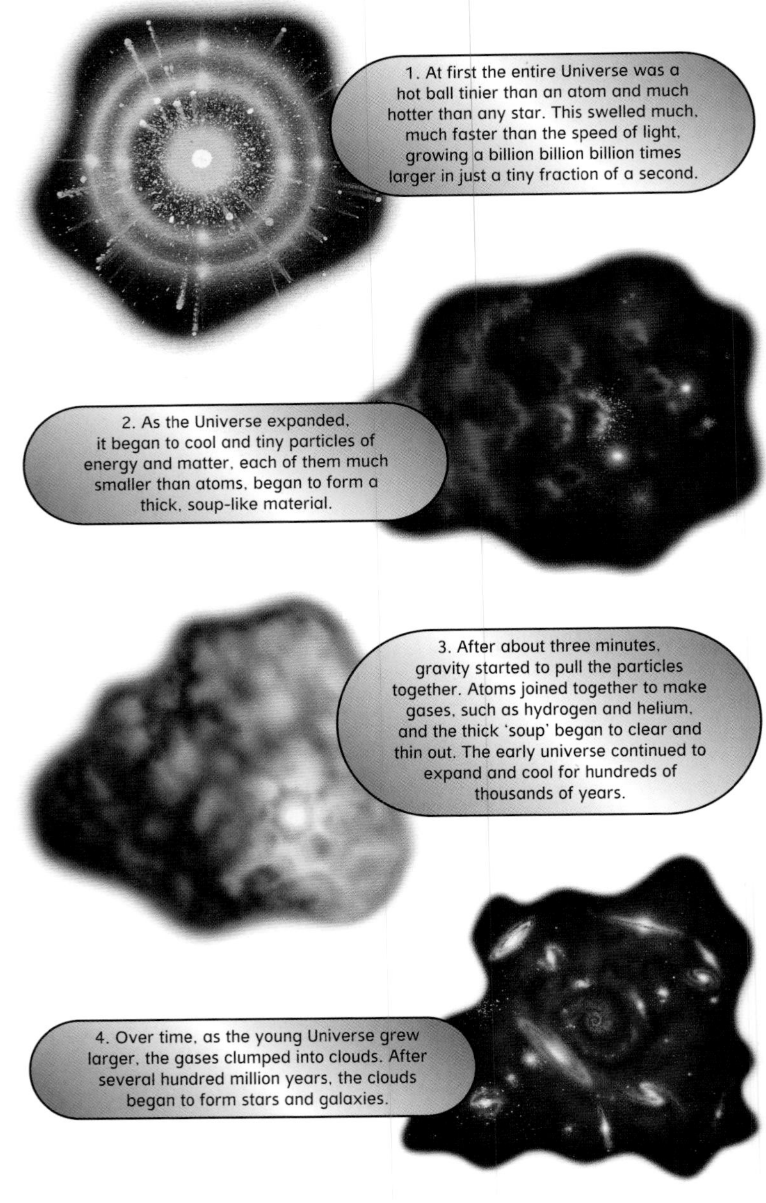

1. At first the entire Universe was a hot ball tinier than an atom and much hotter than any star. This swelled much, much faster than the speed of light, growing a billion billion billion times larger in just a tiny fraction of a second.

2. As the Universe expanded, it began to cool and tiny particles of energy and matter, each of them much smaller than atoms, began to form a thick, soup-like material.

3. After about three minutes, gravity started to pull the particles together. Atoms joined together to make gases, such as hydrogen and helium, and the thick 'soup' began to clear and thin out. The early universe continued to expand and cool for hundreds of thousands of years.

4. Over time, as the young Universe grew larger, the gases clumped into clouds. After several hundred million years, the clouds began to form stars and galaxies.

The Universe after the Big Bang. Although the Big Bang took place in just a fraction of a second, the explosion was strong enough to send energy and matter flying out at great speed in all directions. No one is able to explain yet what might, if anything, have come before the Big Bang.

- First there was a hot ball tinier than an atom. Its temperature and density were too high to be understood by modern science.
- A split second after the Big Bang, a super-force swelled the infant Universe a thousand billion billion billion times. Scientists call this inflation.
- As it mushroomed out, the Universe was flooded with energy and matter, and the super-force separated into forces such as electricity and gravity.
- There were no atoms at first, just tiny particles, such as quarks, in a dense soup a trillion trillion trillion trillion trillion times denser than water.
- There was also antimatter, the mirror image of matter. Antimatter and matter destroy each other when they meet, so they battled it out. Matter won – but the Universe was left almost empty.

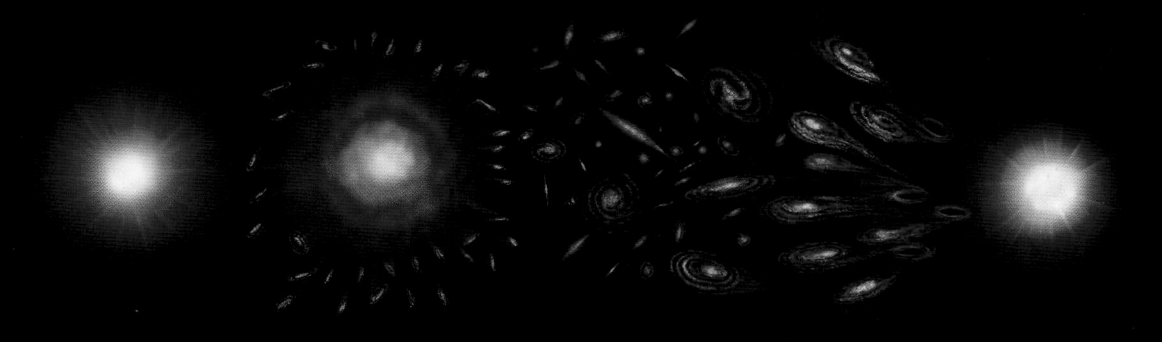

- After three minutes, quarks started to fuse (join) to make the smallest atoms, hydrogen. Then hydrogen gas atoms fused to make helium gas atoms.
- After millions of years the gases began to curdle into strands with dark holes between them.
- After 300 million years, the strands clumped into clouds, and then the clouds clumped together to form stars and galaxies.
- The afterglow of the Big Bang can still be detected as microwave background radiation coming from all over space.

The Universe is expanding, with all the galaxies rushing away from each other. Astronomers do not know if this will go on forever. If it stops, and the Universe starts to contract, the galaxies would rush towards each other. Then the Universe might end in a Big Crunch, the opposite of the Big Bang. This might set off another Big Bang and a brand new Universe.

- The Universe may have neither a centre nor an edge, because according to Einstein's theory of relativity, gravity bends all of space-time around into an endless curve.
- The furthest galaxies yet detected are about 13 billion lightyears away.

Hot ball

Scientists have calculated that the hot ball just after the Big Bang must have swelled at a much faster rate than even the speed of light. The hot ball would have grown at least a billion billion billion times larger within a fraction of a second.

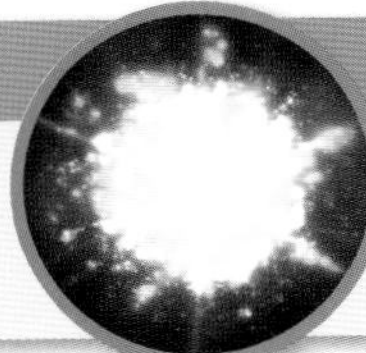

History of the Universe

Time after Big Bang	*Era*	*Description*
10^{-43} seconds	Planck era	Temperatures and pressures too high for scientists to understand
10^{-6} seconds	Hadron era	Fireball in which protons and neutrons formed from quarks
3 minutes	Radiation era	First atoms of hydrogen and helium form as fireball cools
30,000 years	Matter era	Matter dominates over radiation
300,000 years	Decoupling era	Particles and radiation no longer interact. Background radiation starts to cool
300 million years	Formation of galaxies and stars	Ripples in the Universe result in galaxy formation. Stars and galaxies bring light to the Universe and create the elements from which people and planets are made

Amazing

Scientists believe that because both space and time began with the Big Bang, there may possibly be no time 'before' it occurred.

Lightyears and parsecs

Earth distances are measured in miles or kilometres, but these units are too small to be useful in space. Scientists measure the Universe in lightyears or parsecs. Light is the fastest thing in the Universe, so by measuring in lightyears scientists are able to get a better idea of such great distances. A lightyear is the distance that light travels in one year – about 10 million million km. A lightyear is roughly 3.26 parsecs. Light from even the closest star takes years to reach us. The nearest star is over four lightyears away, so this means that when astronomers look at it through a telescope, they are actually looking back into the past – seeing the star as it was four years ago. Light from the most distant galaxies takes about 13,000 million years to reach us. The Universe may go on expanding forever. Or it may eventually stop and collapse in on itself to possibly even start all over again.

Stars

A star is a ball of gas so hot that it shines brightly. The temperatures of stars range from 2500°C to about 50,000°C. The colour of a star is an indication of how hot it is. White stars are hotter than red ones, but some stars become even hotter and shine with a blue light.

Stars begin in giant clouds of dust and gas called nebulae where material gathers into thicker clumps or globules, which collapse to become stars.

Clusters

A swarm or large cluster of stars known as M80 (NGC 6093), is found in the Milky Way galaxy. This swarm, 32,600 lightyears from Earth, contains hundreds of thousands of stars, 'attracted' to each other by gravity.

Amazing

It is estimated that there are about 50,000 billion billion stars in the Universe, more than all the grains of sand on all the beaches of the Earth.

❍ Stars are balls of mainly hydrogen and helium gas.

❍ Nuclear reactions in the heart of stars, like those in atom bombs, generate heat and light.

❍ The centre of a star reaches 16 million°C. A grain of sand this hot would kill someone 150 km away.

❍ The gas in stars is in a hot state called plasma, which is made of atoms stripped of electrons.

❍ Stars twinkle because we see them through the wafting of the Earth's atmosphere.

❍ In the core of a star, hydrogen nuclei fuse (join together) to form helium. This nuclear reaction is called a proton-proton chain.

❍ Astronomers work out how big a star is from its brightness and temperature.

❍ The size and brightness of a star depends on its mass – that is, how much gas it is made of. Our Sun is a medium-sized star, and no star has more than 100 times the Sun's mass or less than 6–7 per cent of its mass.

❍ The few thousand stars visible to the naked eye are just a tiny fraction of the trillions in the Universe.

❍ The coolest stars, such as Arcturus and Antares, glow reddest. Hotter stars are yellow and white. The hottest are blue-white, like Rigel and Zeta Puppis.

❍ The blue supergiant Zeta Puppis has a surface temperature of 42,000°C.

Life cycle of a star

The 'life cycle' of a star: gases and dust collect (1) and form a hot core, a new star (2). A 'main sequence' star (3), like our Sun, shines for 10 billion years. This cools to a red giant (4), which leaves a smaller, hotter white dwarf (5).

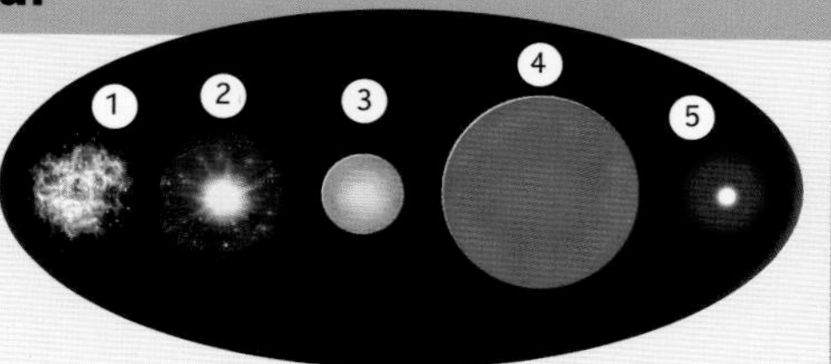

Brightest stars

	Star of constellation	Apparent magnitude	Distance
Sirius	Alpha Canis Major	–1.46	8.6 lightyears
Canopus	Alpha Carinae	–0.72	310 lightyears
	Alpha Centauri	–0.27	4.37 lightyears
Arcturus	Alpha Bootis	–0.04	36 lightyears
Vega	Alpha Lyrae	+0.03	26 lightyears
Capella	Alpha Aurigae	+0.08	45 lightyears
Rigel	Beta Orionis	+0.12	850 lightyears
Procyon	Alpha Canis Minoris	+0.38	11.4 lightyears
Achernar	Alpha Eridani	+0.46	140 lightyears

Note: the lower the magnitude, the brighter the star.

Not all of these stars can be seen in the Northern Hemisphere

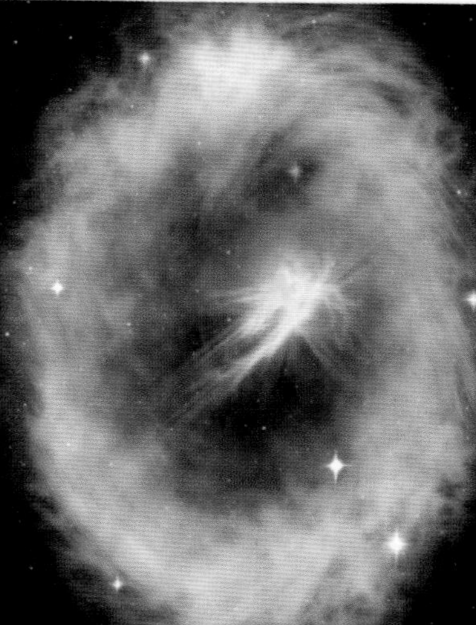

Once a supergiant's core turns to dense iron at the end of its life, gravity squeezes it so hard that it collapses in just a few seconds, then blows itself to bits in a gigantic explosion called a supernova (plural supernovae). Gases are thrown out thousands of kilometres in a fraction of a second and huge amounts of light, heat and X-rays radiate out. Supernovas rarely last for more than a few months, but in that brief time they can burn brighter than a billion suns.

Constellations

Constellations are patterns of stars in the sky that astronomers use to help them pinpoint individual stars among the thousands in the night sky. Astronomers today divide the whole sky into 88 different constellations, and at different times of year you can see different constellations.

❍ Most of the constellations were identified long ago by the stargazers of ancient Babylon and Egypt.

❍ Constellations are simply patterns – there is no real link between the stars.

❍ Southern Hemisphere constellations are different from those in the Northern Hemisphere.

❍ Heroes and creatures of Greek myth, such as Orion the Hunter and Perseus, provided the names for many constellations, although each name is usually written in Latin form, not Greek.

❍ The stars in each constellation are named after Greek alphabet letters.

❍ The brightest star in each constellation is called the Alpha star, the next brightest Beta, and so on.

The three Giza pyramids in Egypt seem to be positioned in such a way as to mirror the pattern of the three bright stars in the constellation Orion.

In the middle of the constellation of Orion (the Hunter), a row of three bright stars marks his belt and the smaller row is his sword.

Seven bright stars in the constellation of the Great Bear in the northern sky make a familiar shape called the Plough or Big Dipper.

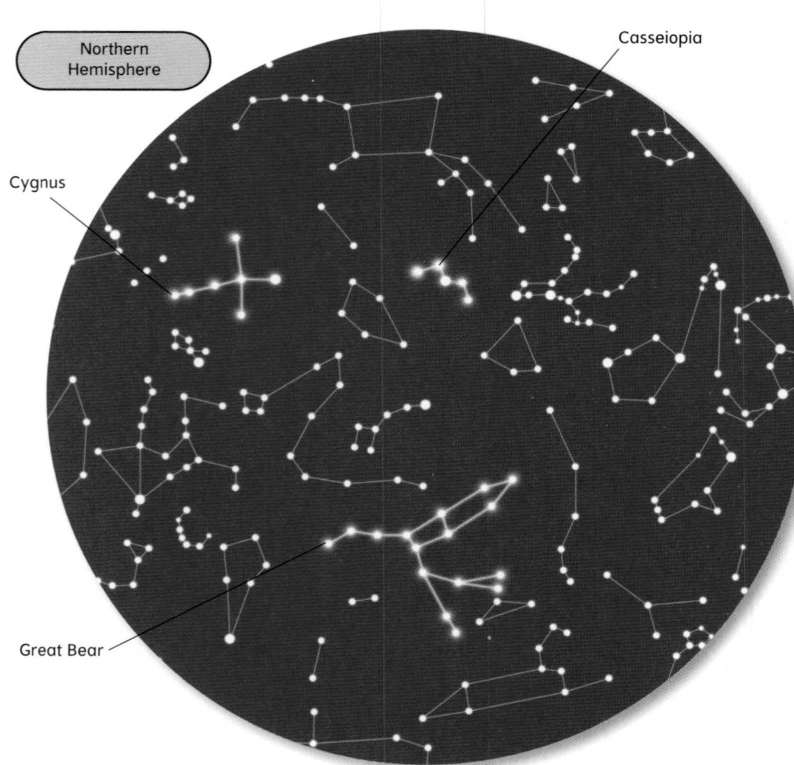

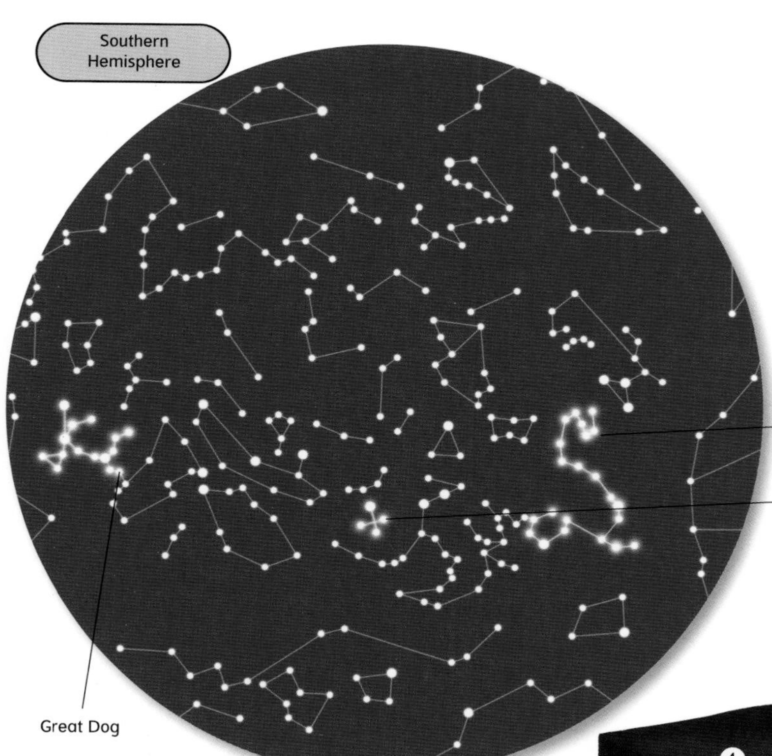

Nebulae

If you look at the sky through binoculars you can see some fuzzy patches between the pinpoint stars. Some are nebulae, others star clusters or distant galaxies.

The Big Dipper seen in the Northern hemisphere is made up of seven stars that are at different distances from Earth. The farthest star in the Big Dipper, Alkaid, is three times farther away than the nearest, Megrez.

KEY
1. Alkaid
2. Mizar
3. Alioth
4. Phecda
5. Megrez
6. Merak
7. Dubhe

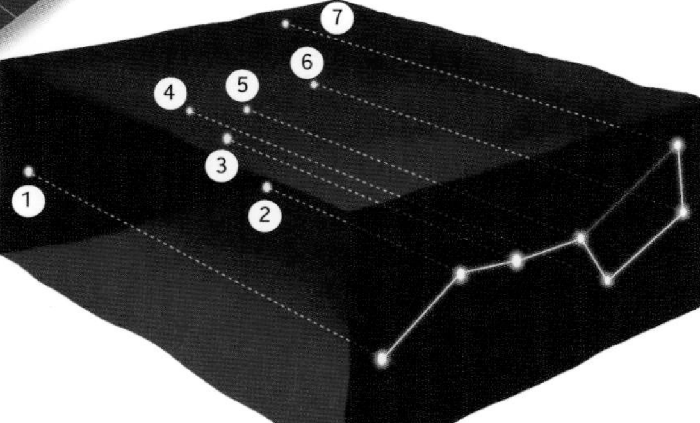

The star groups seen in the Northern Hemisphere are not the same as those seen south of the Equator, in the Southern Hemisphere. Stars are best seen on a clear, moonless night away from the glare of city lights.

Constellation shapes

The patterns the stars make in the sky do not change from night to night. We see the same constellations that the ancient Greeks did thousands of years ago. However, the constellations appear to move slowly across the sky from east to west during the night. This is because the Earth is always spinning round.

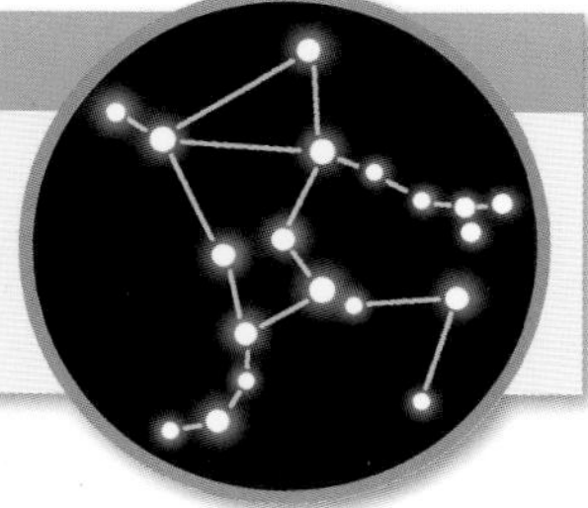

❍ For thousands of years, sailors used the stars to navigate. Studying the constellations could tell them which way was north, for example.

❍ Different constellations become visible at different times of the year, as the Earth travels around the Sun.

Galaxies

Galaxies are giant groups of millions or even trillions of stars. Our local galaxy is the Milky Way. There may be many billions of galaxies in the Universe.

❍ Only three galaxies are visible to the naked eye from Earth besides the Milky Way – the Large and Small Magellanic Clouds, and the Andromeda Galaxy.

❍ Although galaxies are vast, they are so far away that they look like fuzzy clouds. Only in 1916 did astronomers realize that they are huge star groups.

❍ Spiral galaxies are spinning, Catherine-wheel-like galaxies with a dense core and spiralling arms.

❍ Irregular galaxies are galaxies with no obvious shape. They may have formed from the debris of galaxies that crashed into each other.

❍ Elliptical galaxies are vast, very old, egg-shaped galaxies, made up of as many as a trillion stars.

❍ Barred spiral galaxies have just two arms. These are linked across the galaxy's middle by a bar from which they trail like water from a spinning garden sprinkler.

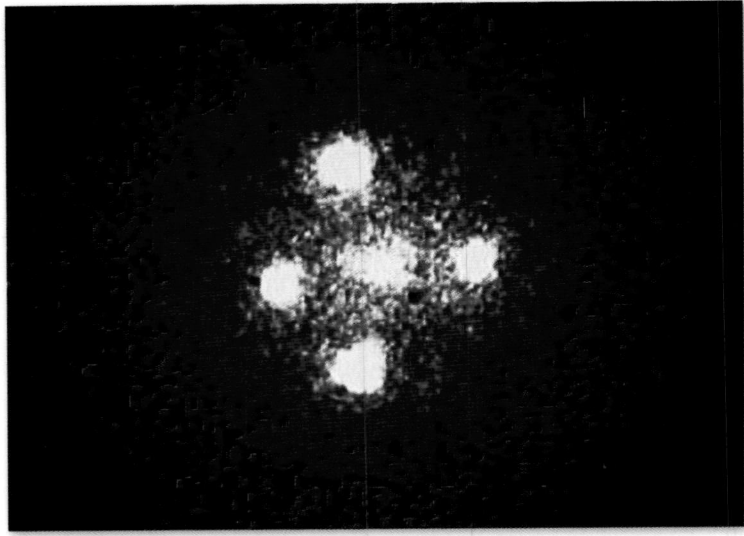

Quasars are luminous objects at the centre of some distant galaxies. Most are the size of the Solar System and glow with the brightness of 100 galaxies.

Galaxies are incredibly vast. Even travelling at lightspeed, a spacecraft would take 100,000 years to cross the Milky Way.

Sucked in

Spiral galaxies may have a giant black hole at the centre, which sucks in stars like water spiralling down a plug hole.

The main galaxy shapes are spiral, irregular and elliptical. The smallest galaxies contain only a few million stars, while the super-galaxies are giants with many billions of stars. There are about 200,000 million stars in our own galaxy, the Milky Way.

Spiral | Irregular | Elliptical | Barred spiral

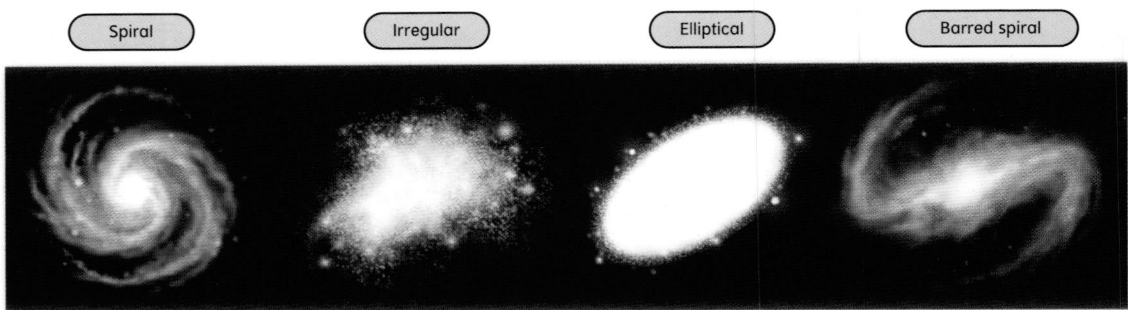

Magellanic clouds

In the night sky of Earth's Southern Hemisphere, two blurry shapes can be seen with the naked eye. These are the Magellanic Clouds – small galaxies lying relatively near to our own galaxy, the Milky Way. The Magellanic Clouds are irregular galaxies, having no distinct pattern or shape.

Amazing

When galaxies get too near they pull each other into weird shapes, often with a long tail or a bright ring. Large galaxies swallow up small ones that get too close.

Some galaxies in the Local Group

The Milky Way is part of a group of galaxies held together by gravity, called the Local Group.

	Type	*Distance*
Milky Way	Spiral	–
Andromeda	Spiral	2.5 million lightyears
Triangulum	Spiral	2.7 million lightyears
Large Magellanic Cloud	Irregular spiral	160,000 lightyears
Small Magellanic	Irregular	200,000 lightyears

Plus at least 20 other very small galaxies

The Milky Way

The Milky Way is the faint, hazy band of light that you can see stretching right across the night sky. It is the galaxy we live in. Looking through binoculars, you would see that the Milky Way is made up of countless stars.

❍ A galaxy is a vast group of stars.

❍ There are billions of galaxies located in space. The centres of large elliptical and spiral galaxies are believed to contain vast black holes.

We cannot see the spiral shape of the Milky Way Galaxy because we are inside it. We see it as a hazy band so faint that you can only see it on very clear nights.

If you could fly out of the Milky Way galaxy in a spaceship and see it from the side, it would look like this – very flat with a bulge in the middle.

❍ The Milky Way is 100,000 lightyears across and 1000 lightyears thick. It is made up of 200 billion stars.

❍ All the stars are arranged in a spiral (like a giant Catherine wheel), with a bulge in the middle.

❍ Our Sun is just one of the billions of stars on one arm of the spiral.

❍ The Milky Way's stars are all whirling rapidly around the centre. Our Sun is moving at 800,000 km/h.

❍ The Sun travels around the galaxy once every 230 million years – a journey of about 170,000 lightyears.

❍ The huge bulge at the centre of the Milky Way is about 20,000 lightyears across and 3000 thick. It contains only very old stars and little dust or gas.

❍ There may be a huge black hole in the very middle of the Milky Way.

❍ In the spiral arms are mostly young stars and clouds of dust and gas where new stars are born.

Factfile

Diameter	100,000 lightyears
Thickness (disc)	1000 lightyears
Mass	140 billion solar masses
Age	About 13 billion years
Distance of Sun from centre	27,000 lightyears

The word galaxy comes from the ancient Greek word for milk,* gala. *The Greeks saw a hazy belt in the night sky, which reminded them of a trail of spilt milk. They made up a story to explain that the heavenly milk had been spilt by the baby Heracles (Hercules). The galaxy came to be known as the 'road of milk', or Milky Way. The centre of the Milky Way is the core or nucleus of the galaxy, with a dense mass of stars. The Sun is about halfway out from the centre, on one of the spiral arms of the galaxy.

Round or elongated?

The Milky Way looks different seen from above (showing the spiral arms) and from sideways on, when it looks like a flying saucer.

Black hole

A two-week observation using the Chandra X-Ray Observatory revealed several explosions occurring in the super massive black hole at the Milky Way's centre, known as Sagittarius A. Huge lobes of 20 million°C gas flank both sides of the black hole and extend over dozens of lightyears indicating that enormous explosions have occurred several times over the last 10,000 years.

Amazing

If the Sun were the size of a baseball, the density of the stars in the Milky Way would be comparable to scattering 80 baseballs across the USA.

Nebulae

Nebula (plural – nebulae) was the word once used for any fuzzy patch of light in the night sky. Today nebulae are giant clouds of dust and gas where new stars are born and old ones die.

Nebulae types

There are three main types of nebula – glowing, reflection and dark nebulae. Out in space are huge invisible clouds of dust and gas. Nebulae are the parts of these clouds that we can see, as they either glow or reflect starlight, or block out light.

- Nebulae are gigantic clouds of gas and space dust.
- Glowing nebulae are named because they give off a dim, coloured light, as the gases in them are heated by radiation from nearby stars.
- The Great Nebula of Orion is a glowing nebula just visible to the naked eye.
- Reflection nebulae have no light of their own. They can only be seen because starlight shines off the dust in them.
- Not only do dark nebulae not have any light of their own, but they block out all other light. They can only be seen as patches of darkness, blocking out light from the stars or bright nebulae behind them.

This is a glowing nebula called the Trifid nebula, which glows as gases in it are heated by radiation from new young stars.

Amazing

The Crab Nebula is the remains of a supernova that exploded in AD 1054.

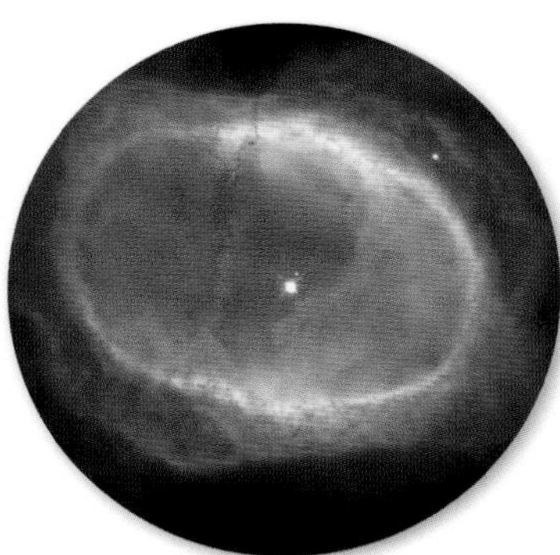

Pictures of planetary nebulae, as observed by the Hubble Space Telescope.

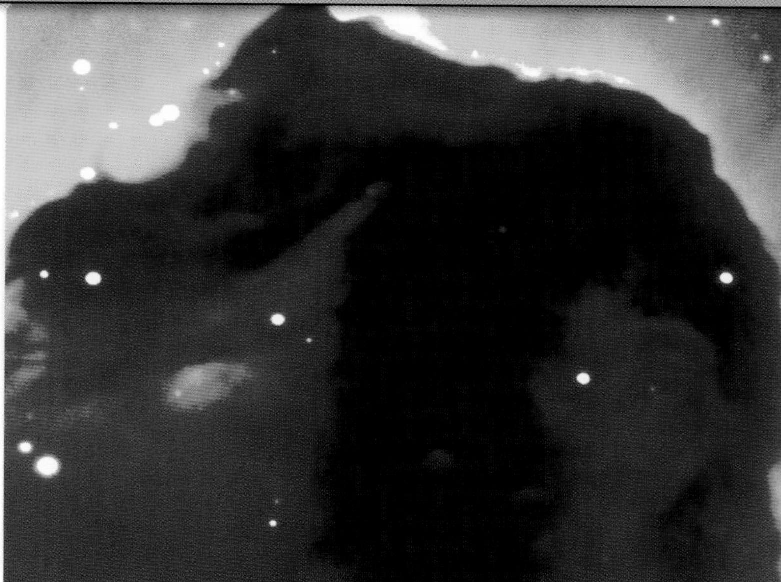

The Horsehead Nebula in Orion is the best-known dark nebula. As its name suggests, it is shaped like a horse's head.

An example of a 'butterfly' or a bipolar planetary nebula. Glowing gas streaming from the star in the centre looks like a pair of exhausts from a jet engine. Because of the nebula's shape and the velocity of the gas, in excess of 200 km/sec, astronomers believe that the description as a super-super-sonic jet exhaust is very suitable.

- Planetary nebulae are thin rings of gas cloud, which are thrown out by dying stars. Despite their name, they have nothing to do with planets.

- The Ring nebula in Lyra is the best-known of the planetary nebulae.

- Inside nebulae, gravity creates dark clumps called dark nebulae, each clump containing the seeds of a family of stars.

Orion's nebula

The Great Nebula of Orion is the nearest star formation region to Earth, about 1300 lightyears away. It is visible to the naked eye as a fuzzy patch of light near the centre of Orion's sword, in the same spiral arm of the Milky Way as the Sun. With a cloud that spans some 30 lightyears, it is one of the most visually stunning objects in space.

Black Holes

Black holes are places where gravity is so strong that it sucks everything in, including light. Black holes form when a star or galaxy gets so dense that it collapses under the pull of its own gravity.

Amazing

If you were sucked into a black hole, your body would be stretched out like a piece of spaghetti.

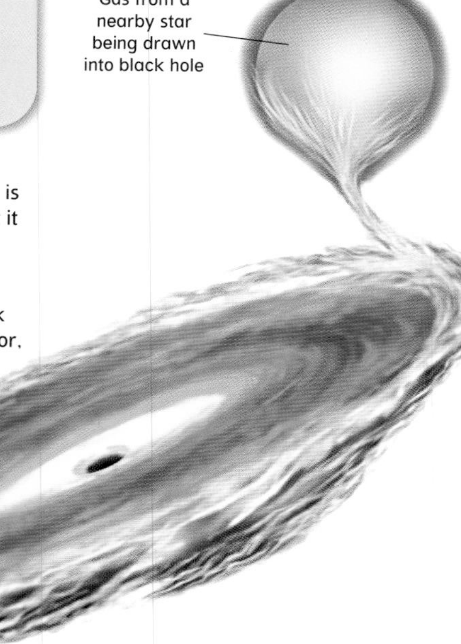

- Black holes may exist at the heart of every galaxy.

- Gravity shrinks a black hole to an unimaginably small point called a singularity.

- Around a singularity, gravity is so intense that space-time is bent into a funnel.

- Matter spiralling into a black hole is torn apart and glows so brightly that it creates the brightest objects in the Universe – quasars.

- The swirling gases around a black hole turn it into an electrical generator, making it spout jets of electricity thousands of light years out into space.

No light is able to escape from a black hole. Scientists can find them because gas swirling around them gets so hot it gives out x-rays.

This X-ray image shows the central part of the Andromeda Galaxy. The blue dot in the centre shows a supermassive black hole. The gas swirling into it has a temperature of 1 million°C.

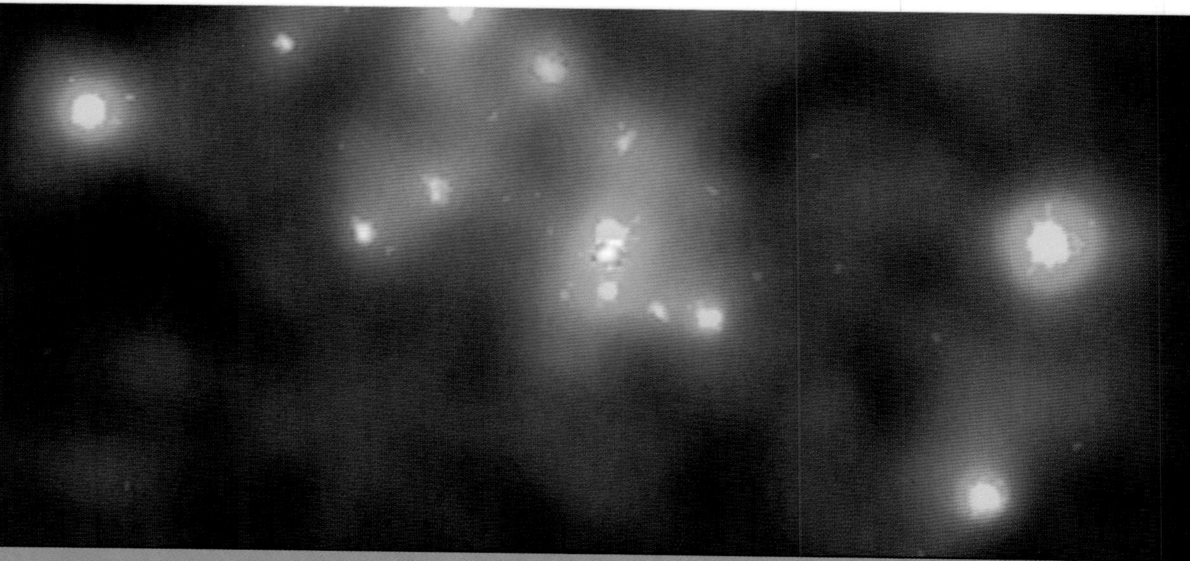

White holes and wormholes

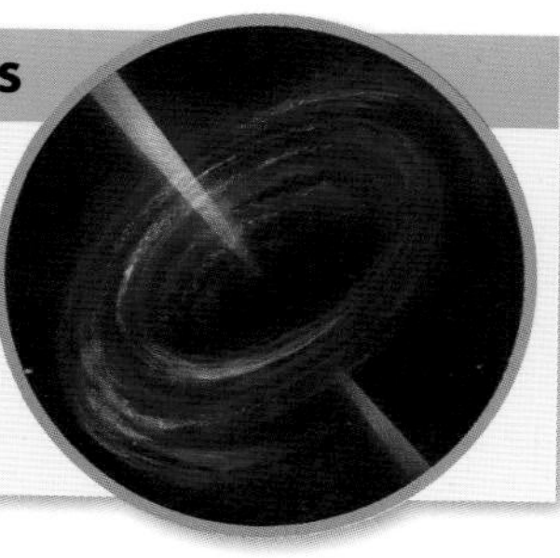

Some scientists believe in the existence of white holes, which are the opposite of black holes because they spray out matter and light rather than sucking it in. Some also think that black holes and white holes may join to form tunnels called wormholes – and these may be the secret to time travel. However, white holes have not been proved to exist, and they may violate one of the fundamental laws of physics.

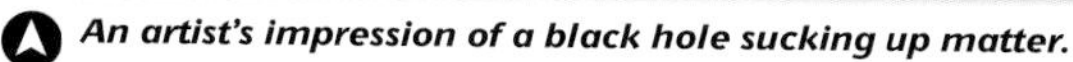

An artist's impression of a black hole sucking up matter.

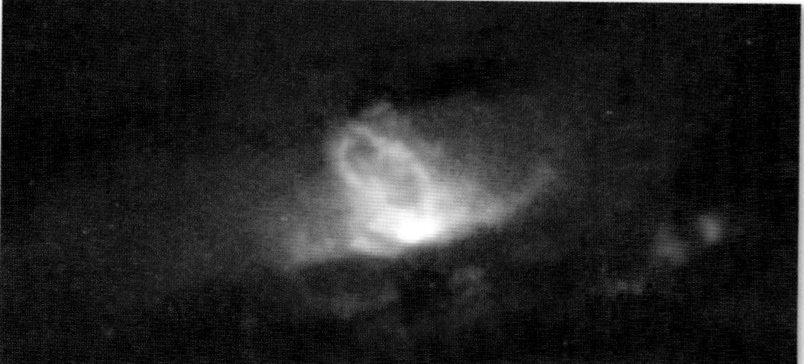

A supermassive black hole blows bubbles of hot gas into space. Known as the peculiar galaxy because of its unusual shape, NGC4438 is 50 million lightyears from Earth. One bubble rises from a dark band of dust while another emanates from below the band of dust showing up as dim red blobs in the close-up. These exceedingly hot bubbles are caused by the voracious eating habits of black holes.

The Swift spacecraft was launched on 20 November 2004 by a Delta II rocket. It carried a multi-wave space observatory, and was sent to monitor gamma-ray bursts that are thought to occur when a black hole forms.

Black holes and electricity

An artist's impression of what a black hole might look like, with jets of electricity shooting out from either side.

The Solar System

The Solar System is made up of the Sun, the eight planets and over 160 known moons, plus asteroids, comets, dust and gas. The planets, moons, asteroids and comets travel around the Sun, the centre of our Solar System.

❍ Most of the bodies in the Solar System travel around the Sun along nearly circular paths or orbits, and all the planets travel around the Sun in an anticlockwise direction (when viewed from above).

❍ Solar System formation began billions of years ago, when gases and dust began to come together to form the Sun, planets, and other bodies of the Solar System.

❍ The Sun is a medium-sized star measuring 1,392,000 km across – 109 times the diameter of the Earth.

❍ Mercury is the nearest planet to the Sun – during its orbit it is between 45.9 and 69.7 million km away.

❍ Venus is the nearest of all the planets to Earth in size, measuring 12,104 km across its diameter.

❍ Mars is the nearest planet to Earth after Venus, and its temperature is the closest of any of the planets to the Earth's, although it is much colder.

❍ Jupiter is the biggest planet in the Solar System – twice as heavy as all the other planets put together.

❍ Saturn is the second biggest planet in the Solar System – 764 times as big in volume as the Earth, and measuring 120,000 km around its equator.

❍ Uranus is the seventh planet out from the Sun. Its orbit keeps it a distance of 2870 million km away on average and takes 84 years to complete.

❍ Neptune is the eighth planet out from the Sun, varying in distance from 4450 to 4550 million km.

❍ Pluto was discovered in 1930. It is much smaller than any of the other planets and is now classified as a 'dwarf planet'. There are now five dwarf planets in total.

The inner Solar System planets are Mercury, Venus, Earth and Mars. They are all terrestrial (made of rock). The outer Solar System planets are Jupiter, Saturn, Uranus and Neptune. They are substantially bigger than the inner, terrestrial planets.

Amazing

The distance across the Solar System is estimated to be over 30 billion km.

Moons in our Solar System

To date there are over 160 known moons orbiting planets in our Solar System.

Venus

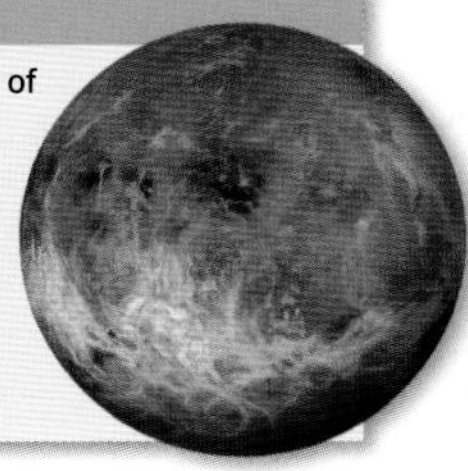

Venus is the hottest of the Sun's planets, even hotter than Mercury. Temperatures on Venus can reach 470°C, which is hot enough to melt some metals.

Planets in the Solar System

	Discovered	*Distance from Sun*	*Diameter*
Mercury	Ancient times	57.9 million km	4879 km
Venus	Ancient times	108.2 million km	12,104 km
Earth	–	149.6 million km	12,756 km
Mars	Ancient times	227.9 million km	6794 km
Jupiter	Ancient times	778.6 million km	142,984 km
Saturn	Ancient times	1433.5 million km	120,536 km
Uranus	1781	2872.5 million km	51,118 km
Neptune	1846	4495.1 million km	49,528 km

The Sun

The Sun is the Earth's nearest star, about 150 million km away. It is a medium-sized star, and belongs to a group of star types that astronomers call 'main sequence' stars. Most of these, including the Sun, will shine for about ten billion years before expanding and cooling to become red giants, ultimately using up all their fuel. The Sun is about halfway through its lifetime.

❍ The Sun weighs 2000 trillion trillion tonnes – about 300,000 times as much as the Earth – even though it is made almost entirely of hydrogen and helium, the lightest gases in the Universe.

❍ The Sun's interior is heated by nuclear reactions to temperatures of 15 million°C.

❍ The visible surface layer of the Sun is the photosphere. This sends out the light and heat we see and feel on Earth.

❍ Above the photosphere is the chromosphere, a layer through which dart flames called spicules, making the chromosphere look like a flaming forest.

❍ Above the chromosphere is the Sun's halo-like corona.

❍ The Sun gets hot because it is so big that the pressure in its core is huge – enough to force the nuclei of hydrogen atoms to fuse to make helium atoms. This nuclear fusion releases huge amounts of energy.

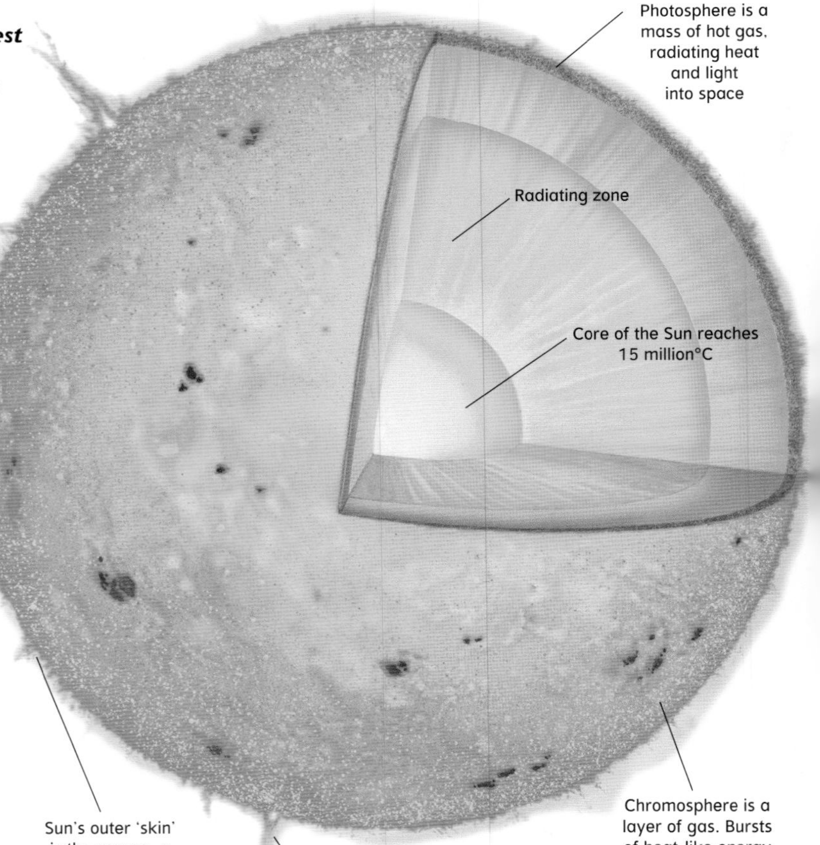

This cutaway of the Sun shows its different parts. The energy that is created inside the core takes many thousands of years to pass through its many layers and reach the surface.

Factfile

Diameter	1,392,000 km
Mass	333,000 times Earth's mass
Volume	1.3 million times Earth's volume
Density	1408 kg/m^3 (1.4 times density of water)
Average rotation period	25.4 days
Surface temperature	6000°C
Distance from Earth	149.6 million km

When the Moon passes between the Earth and the Sun, it causes a solar eclipse, that blocks out the light from the Sun momentarily.

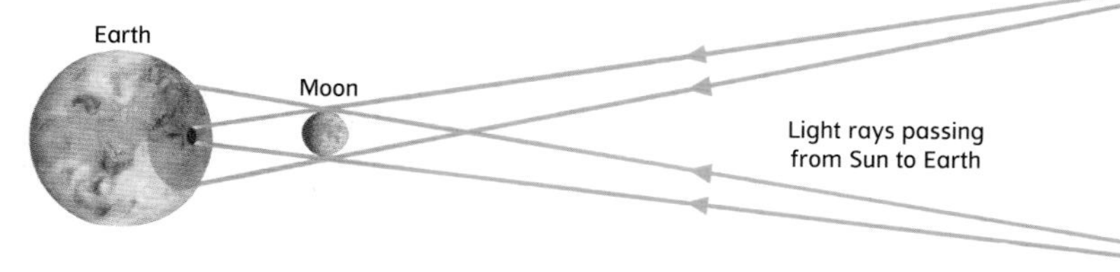

❍ The heat from the Sun's interior erupts on the surface in patches called granules and in gigantic, flame-like tongues of hot gases called solar prominences.

❍ Halfway out from its centre to its surface, the Sun is about as dense as water. Two-thirds of the way out from its centre, it is as dense as air.

❍ The nuclear fusion reactions in the Sun's core send out billions of energy photons every single minute – but they take many thousands of years to reach its surface.

❍ Space observatories like SOHO (Solar and Heliospheric Observatory) have revealed a great deal about the Sun to astronomers.

Warning

Never ever look directly at the Sun. It can damage your eyes.

Sunspots

Astronomers viewing the Sun through special filters can detect dark spots called sunspots on the Sun's surface. The sunspots are caused by changes to the magnetic field surrounding the Sun. As the Sun spins round, the magnetic field becomes tangled. Sunspots develop in places where the magnetic force has become up to 3000 times stronger than normal. The Sun's surface is cooler at these places, so the sunspots appear darker than the surrounding surface.

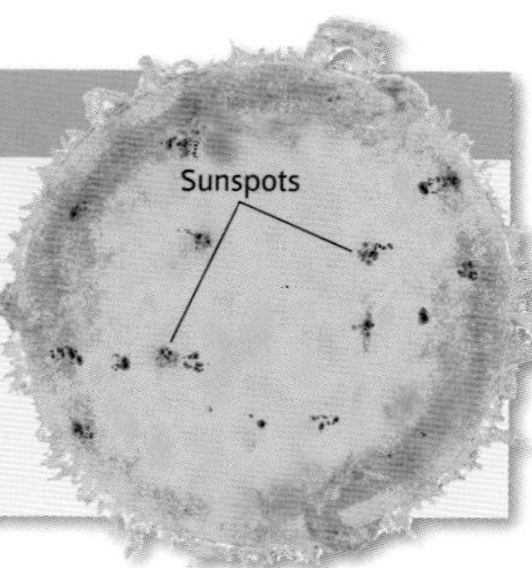

Tilting Earth

As the Earth tilts on its axis and spins around the Sun, the Sun warms different parts of the planet. The Earth is the third planet out from the Sun, on average 149.6 million km away. On 3 January, at the nearest point of its orbit (called the perihelion), the Earth is 147,097,800 km away from the Sun. On 4 July, at its furthest (the aphelion), it is 152,098,200 km away.

Sun
Earth

Solar eclipses

	Type of eclipse	*Visible from where in the world*
15 February 2018	Partial	Antarctica, South America
13 July 2018	Partial	Australia
11 August 2018	Partial	North Europe, North Asia
6 January 2019	Partial	North Asia, North Pacific
2 July 2019	Total	South Pacific, Australia
26 December 2019	Annular	Asia, Australia
21 June 2020	Annular	Africa, Europe, Asia
14 December 2020	Total	Pacific, South America, Antarctica
10 June 2021	Annular	North America, Europe, Asia
4 December 2021	Total	Antarctica, South Africa, southern Atlantic
30 April 2022	Partial	Southeast Pacific, South America

Amazing

The temperature at the Sun's surface is 6000°C. Each centimetre of the Sun's surface burns with the brightness of 250,000 candles.

The Earth

The Earth is the fifth largest planet in the Solar System, with a diameter of 12,756 km and a circumference of 40,075 km at the Equator.

❍ The Earth is one of four rocky planets, along with Mercury, Venus and Mars. It is made mostly of rock, with a core of iron and nickel.

❍ No other planet in the Solar System has water on its surface, which is why Earth is uniquely suitable for life. Over 70 per cent of Earth's surface is under water.

❍ The Earth's atmosphere is mainly nitrogen and life-giving oxygen, and it is over 100 km deep. The oxygen has been made and maintained by plants over billions of years.

❍ The Earth formed 4.65 billion years ago from clouds of spacedust whirling around the Sun. The planet was so hot that it was molten at first. Only slowly did the surface cool into a hard crust.

❍ The Earth's orbit around the Sun is 940 million km long and takes 365.2 days.

❍ The Earth is tilted at an angle of 23.5°. Even so, it orbits the Sun in a level plane, called the plane of the ecliptic.

❍ The Earth is made up of the same materials as meteorites and the other rocky planets – mostly iron (35 percent), oxygen (30 percent), silicon (15 percent), magnesium (13 percent) and nickel (2.7 percent).

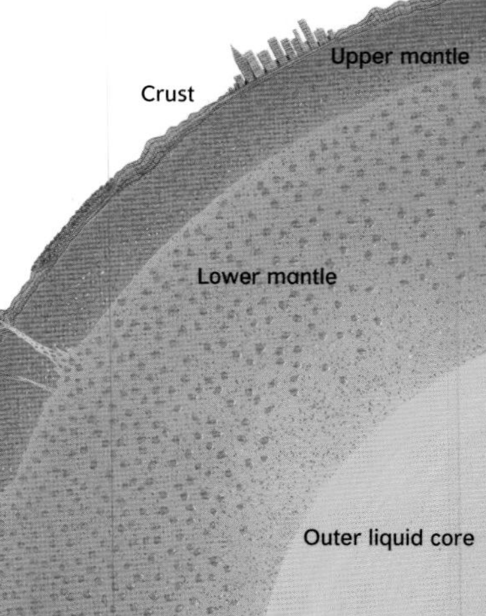

Central Sun

People used to think that the Sun moved round the Earth until the Polish scientist Nicolaus Copernicus realized in the 1500s that the Earth and all the planets in the Solar System moved around the Sun.

Amazing

Because the Earth rotates and is more flexible than you might think, it bulges in the middle like a pumpkin. The bulge was lessening for centuries, but now, suddenly, it is growing again because of accelerated melting of the glaciers.

Factfile

Diameter	12,756 km
Planetary mass	6×10^{24} kg
Average distance from Sun	149.6 million km
Length of day	23 h 56 min
Length of year	365.2 days
Number of moons	1
Planetary ring system	0
Average temperature	15°C
Atmospheric composition	21% oxygen, 78% nitrogen, many other minor trace elements

Scientists call planet Earth the geosphere. The outer rocky part on which we live is the biosphere. Surrounding this is the atmosphere in layers. The inside of the Earth is also in layers. At the centre is a solid inner core made of an alloy of nickel and iron squeezed together under pressure. The rocks surrounding the core are hot and liquid.

Life planet

Earth is the only planet we know of that can support life because of a remarkable set of conditions. The Sun is a stable star with a constant temperature. Earth's temperature is high enough for liquid water to occur, and for oxygen-producing organisms to thrive in the liquid oceans, but not so hot that all the water vapour evaporates (as in the case of Venus). The presence of the Moon helps to preserve liquid water. Large gas giants in the Solar System help to draw a lot of earthbound asteroids away from our planet.

Viewed from space, the Earth, which is mainly covered by oceans, appears mostly blue. Cloud formations swirl above the familiar shapes of the continents. Earth is protected from the Sun's radiation by a magnetic field that stretches over 60,000 km out into space.

UFO sightings

Who?	*When?*	*Where and what?*
Betty and Barney Hill	September 1961	From New Hampshire, USA, the couple reported a close sighting of a UFO. They underwent hypnosis and claim to have been abducted and probed.
Frederick Valentich	October 1978	Australian pilot disappeared over the Bass Strait between Tasmania and Australia after reporting he saw a UFO.
Travis Walton	November 1975	Woodcutter who disappeared for a few days and claimed to have been abducted and probed at a secret UFO base.
Airmen	December 1980	Airmen at a USAF base in Suffolk, England, claimed to have had encounters with a UFO.
Linda Cortile	November 1989	Cortile claims to have been beamed from her apartment in New York and transported to a UFO that plunged into the Hudson River, near Brooklyn Bridge.

The Moon

The Moon is 384,400 km from the Earth and about 25 per cent of Earth's size. The Moon orbits the Earth once every month and each orbit takes 27.3 days. It also spins on its axis every 27.3 days.

The Moon may have formed when a smaller, newly formed planet collided with the Earth early on in the formation of the Solar System.

❍ The Moon is the brightest object in the night sky, but it does not give out any light itself. It shines only because its light-coloured surface reflects sunlight.

❍ Only the side of the Moon lit by the Sun is bright enough to see. As it travels round the Earth we see different amounts of the sunlit side so the Moon seems to change shape from a slim crescent to full disc.

❍ During the first half of each monthly cycle, the Moon waxes (grows) from a crescent-shaped New Moon to a Full Moon. During the second half, it wanes (dwindles) back to a crescent-shaped Old Moon.

❍ A lunar month is the time between one Full Moon and the next. This is slightly longer than the time the Moon takes to orbit the Earth because the Earth is also moving.

❍ The Moon has no atmosphere and its surface is simply grey dust, pitted with craters created by meteorites smashing into it early in its history.

❍ On the Moon's surface are large, dark patches called seas – because that is what people once believed they were. They are, in fact, lava flows from ancient volcanoes.

❍ One side of the Moon is always turned away from us and is called its far side. This is because the Moon spins round on its axis at exactly the same speed that it orbits the Earth.

Lunar eclipses 2017–2021

Each eclipse of the Moon can be seen from about half of the Earth's surface.

Date	Type	Date	Type
11 February 2017	Penumbral	10 January 2020	Penumbral
7 August 2017	Partial	5 June 2020	Penumbral
31 January 2018	Total	5 July 2020	Penumbral
27 July 2018	Total	30 November 2020	Penumbral
21 January 2019	Total	26 May 2021	Total
16 July 2019	Partial	19 November 2021	Partial

Monthly Full Moons

January	Moon after Yule
February	Wolf moon
March	Lenten moon
April	Egg moon
May	Milk moon
June	Strawberry moon
July	Hay moon
August	Green corn moon
September	Harvest moon
October	Hunter's moon
November	Beaver's moon
December	Moon before Yule

The Moon is relatively close to the Earth and therefore seems much larger than the stars.

Amazing

The Moon's gravity is 16 per cent of the Earth's, so astronauts in space suits can jump 4 m high.

The changes from New to Full Moon and back again are called the phases of the Moon. The full cycle from New to Full and back to New again takes one month.

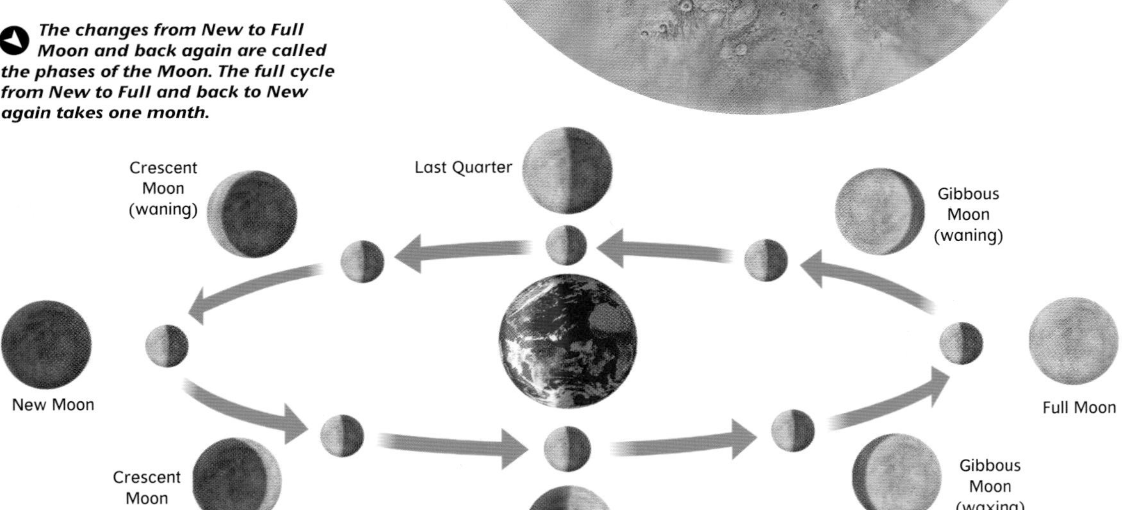

10 seas on the Moon

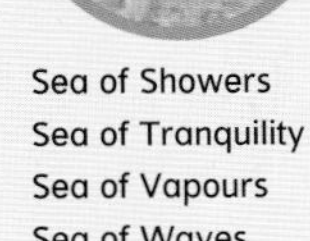

- Sea of Cleverness
- Sea of Clouds
- Sea of Islands
- Sea of Moisture
- Sea of Nectar
- Sea of Serenity
- Sea of Showers
- Sea of Tranquility
- Sea of Vapours
- Sea of Waves

Moon crater names

All moon craters are named after people

Aldrin	Edwin (Buzz) Aldrin
Babbage	Charles Babbage
Cook	Captain James Cook
Darwin	Charles Darwin
Edison	Thomas Alva Edison
Freud	Sigmund Freud
Gagarin	Yuri Gagarin
Harvey	William Harvey
Icarus	Greek mythological character
Jenner	Edward Jenner
Kepler	Johannes Kepler
Lindberg	Charles Lindberg
Morse	Samuel Morse
Newton	Sir Isaac Newton
Oppenheimer	Robert Oppenheimer
Pasteur	Louis Pasteur
Quetelet	Adolphe Quetelet
Rutherford	Ernest Rutherford
Scott	Robert Falcon Scott
Tereshkova	Valentina Tereshkova
Urey	Harold Urey
Van de Graaff	Robert van de Graaff
Watt	James Watt
Xenophon	Greek historian
Young	Thomas Young

Mercury

Mercury, named after the Roman messenger god, is the smallest planet in the Solar System, and the closest to the Sun. This makes observations very difficult as it is lost in the Sun's glare at least half of the time. It can be observed for only a brief period in the morning or early evening.

❍ Mercury is the fastest orbiting of all the planets, travelling around the Sun in just 88 days.

❍ Mercury takes 58.65 Earth days to rotate once, but from sunrise to sunrise is 176 Earth days, so a 'day' on Mercury is twice as long as its year.

❍ Temperatures on Mercury range from –180°C at night to over 430°C during the day (enough to melt lead).

❍ The crust and mantle are largely rock, but the core (75 per cent of its diameter) is solid iron.

❍ Mercury's dusty surface is pocketed by craters made by space debris crashing into it.

❍ With barely 20 per cent of Earth's mass, Mercury is so small that its gravity is too weak to hold on to a permanent atmosphere.

❍ Mercury is so small that its core has cooled and solidified. As this happened, Mercury shrank, and its surface wrinkled like the skin of an old apple.

❍ Craters on Mercury are named after famous writers, artists and musicians like Bach, Beethoven, Wagner, Shakespeare and Tolstoy.

Mercury is a tiny planet with a very thin atmosphere and a solid core.

Sunrise, sunset

If you could stand on the surface of Mercury in certain places you would see the Sun rise about halfway, then reverse and set, then rise again, all within the same day.

❍ Mercury's surface is wrinkled by long, low ridges, which probably formed as the core cooled and shrank.

❍ The largest feature on Mercury is a huge impact crater called the Caloris Basin, which is about 1300 km across and 2 km deep.

Amazing

Twice during its orbit, Mercury gets very close to the Sun and speeds up so much that the Sun seems to go backwards in the sky.

Messenger mission to Mercury

***Messenger** was the second spacecraft to visit Mercury and the first to orbit the planet. Launched in August 2004, it went into orbit round Mercury in March 2011, and has sent back over 250,000 images covering the whole planet.*

Messenger *spacecraft*

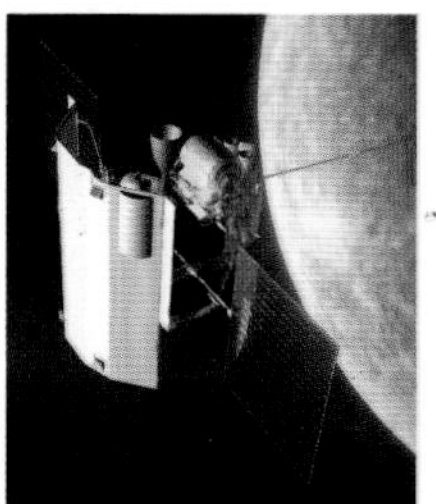

This artist's impression shows the *Messenger* spacecraft close to Mercury. Its sunshade protects it from the intense heat of the Sun, which is 11 times brighter at Mercury than at Earth. From orbit the craft studied the surface composition and even found water ice in deep craters where the Sun never shines.

Volcanism on Mercury

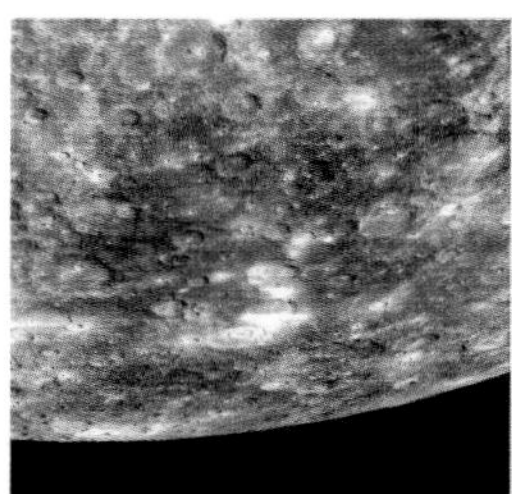

In this view looking towards the edge of the planet, the brighter yellow areas are volcanic vents where ash and gas exploded from beneath the surface. Unlike Earth's volcanoes, those on Mercury look like irregular shaped craters.

Ridge and crater

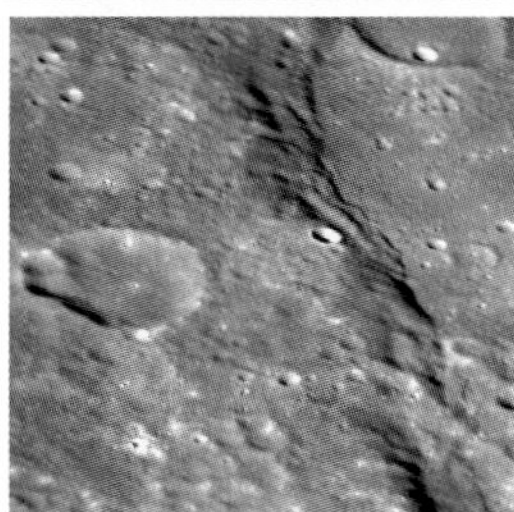

A dark ridge runs from top to bottom of this image. It was probably formed when Mercury's core cooled and shrank, pushing one part of the surface up and over another. The crater on the left is 20 km across.

Blue-rayed crater

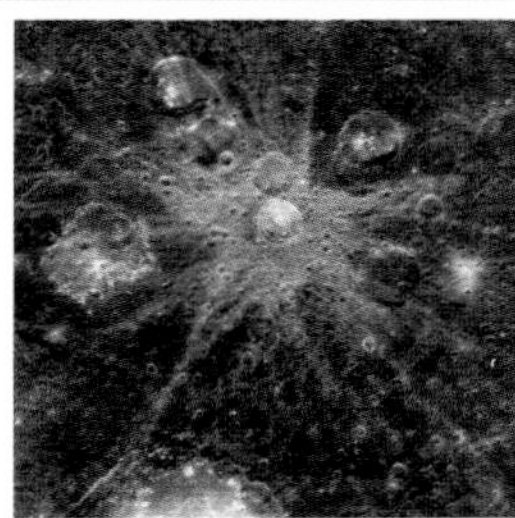

The crater in the middle of this image, called Bek, is 32 km across. It is surrounded by rays of bluish material thrown outwards by the impact of the space rock that formed the crater. The new material has fallen across older craters nearby.

Mariner 10

Mariner 10, launched in November 1973, was the first probe to visit Mercury. It flew past Venus on its way, then past Mercury three times in 1974 and 1975. Each time the same side of the planet was facing the probe so it sent back images of about half the surface. These showed a surface very like the Moon, pockmarked with craters.

Factfile

Diameter	4879 km
Mass	0.33×10^{24} kg
Time to spin once	58.65 days
Average distance from Sun	57.9 million km
Time for one orbit	88 days
Average temperature	167°C
Number of moons	0
Ring system	No

Venus

Venus is named after the Roman goddess of love and beauty. It orbits at a distance of between 107.4 and 109 million km and is the second planet from the Sun. Venus is also known as the Evening Star, because it can be seen from Earth in the evening, just after sunset. Venus can also be seen before sunrise.

❍ Venus shines very brightly because its thick clouds reflect sunlight amazingly well. It is the brightest object in the night sky after the Sun and the Moon and can even be seen in daylight.

❍ Venus's cloudy atmosphere is a thick mixture of carbon-dioxide gas and sulphuric acid.

Almost three-quarters of the surface of Venus is covered by plains. These were mostly formed by volcanic processes and are marked by impact craters and flows of lava. They have features that have been sculpted by the winds on Venus. Ridges rise for several hundred metres and can stretch for hundreds of kilometres across the Venus plains.

This is what Venus would look like if you could see through the thick clouds that hide the surface. Space probes have mapped the whole of Venus using radar that can penetrate the clouds, to reflect off the volcanoes and craters on the surface.

❍ Venus is the hottest planet in the Solar System, with a surface temperature of over 464°C.

❍ Venus is so hot because the carbon dioxide in its atmosphere works like the panes of glass in a greenhouse to trap the Sun's heat. This overheating is called a runaway greenhouse effect.

❍ Venus's thick clouds hide its surface so well that until space probes detected the very high temperatures some people thought there might be rainforests beneath the clouds.

Pressured planet

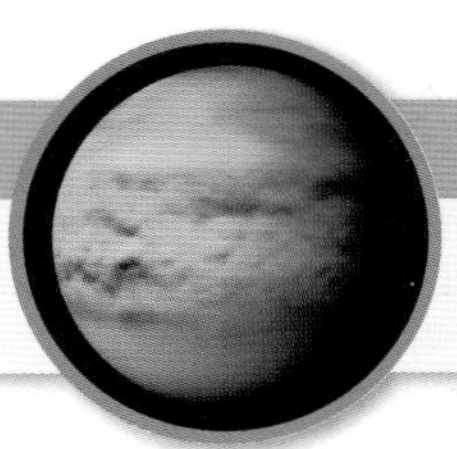

The pressure at the surface of Venus is so strong that the first spacecraft that tried to land there was crushed before it even reached the surface.

Maat Mons

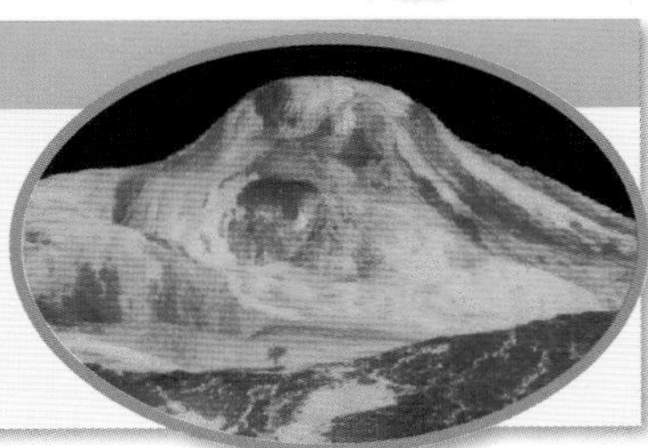

This is a view of a 6 km high volcano on Venus's surface called Maat Mons. It is not an actual photograph but was created on computer from radar data collected by the *Magellan* orbiter, which reached Venus in 1990. The colours are what astronomers guess them to be from their knowledge of the chemistry of Venus.

- Venus's day (the time it takes to spin round once) lasts 243 Earth days – longer than its year, which lasts 224.7 days. But because Venus rotates backwards, the Sun actually comes up twice during the planet's yearly orbit – once every 116.8 days.

- Venus is the nearest of all the planets to Earth in size, measuring 12,104 km across its diameter.

- Pressure on the surface of Venus is 90 times greater than that on Earth.

- Periodically the planet Venus passes directly between the Earth and the Sun, appearing as a small black dot on the Sun's disk. These 'transits of Venus' are extremely rare. The first was studied in 1639 and helped astronomers accurately measure the distance to the Sun. The last occurred on 6 June 2012 but the next will not be until December 2117.

Amazing

All the planets in the Solar System rotate anticlockwise, except Venus. It is the only planet that rotates clockwise.

Factfile

Diameter	12,104 km
Mass	4.87×10^{24} kg
Time to spin once	243 days (retrograde)
Average distance from Sun	108.2 million km
Time for one orbit	224.7 days
Average temperature	464°C
Number of moons	0
Ring system	No

Mars

Mars, named after the Roman god of war, is the fourth planet out from the Sun, and the nearest planet to Earth after Venus. Its temperature is closer to Earth's than any other planet and a Martian day is almost the same as an Earth day.

Deimos and Phobos are the two satellites (moons) that orbit Mars. They are named after the two companions of the Roman god, Mars.

❍ Mars is called the red planet due to its rusty red colour. This comes from oxidized (rusted) iron in its soil.

❍ Mars orbits the Sun at an average distance of 227.9 million km. It takes 687 days to complete its orbit.

❍ Mars is 6794 km in diameter and spins round once every 24.6 hours – almost the same time as the Earth takes to rotate.

❍ Mars's volcano Olympus Mons is the biggest in the Solar System. It covers the same area as Ireland and is three times higher than Mount Everest.

❍ In the 1890s, the American astronomer Percival Lowell was convinced that the dark lines he could see on Mars's surface through his telescope were canals built by Martians.

Amazing

Two rovers called *Spirit* and *Opportunity* landed on Mars in 2004 and spent over five years exploring. They analysed the rocks, looking for evidence of a watery past.

The 3-metre-long, six-wheeled* Curiosity *rover landed in Gale Crater on Mars in August 2012. It crawls slowly across the surface stopping to drill into rocks and scoop up and analyze soil. It has found evidence that there was water on Mars millions of years ago.

Factfile

Diameter	6794 km
Mass	0.642×10^{24} kg
Time to spin once	24.6 hours
Average distance from Sun	227.9 million km
Time for one orbit	687 days
Average temperature	–65°C
Number of moons	2
Ring system	No

❍ Evidence is growing that Mars was warmer and wetter in the past. There are dried up river and lake beds on the surface, and rocks that only form in water.

❍ Mars has two tiny moons called Phobos and Deimos. Phobos is just 27 km across, while Deimos is just 15 km across and has so little gravity that you could reach escape velocity riding a bike up a ramp!

❍ The 1997 Mars *Pathfinder* mission showed that many of the rocks on Mars's surface were dumped in their positions by a huge flood at least two billion years ago.

Viking looks for life in Mars

In 1976 the two Viking landers became the first spacecraft to land safely on Mars. Their mission was to look for signs of life. The Viking spacecraft consisted of two orbiters each with a lander, which they released to touch down in different areas. As well as cameras, the landers had instruments to analyze the soil and to monitor the Martian weather. A scoop at the end of an extending arm took samples of the soil to test for signs of life. The results were puzzling but scientists concluded that there was no evidence of life at the landing sites.

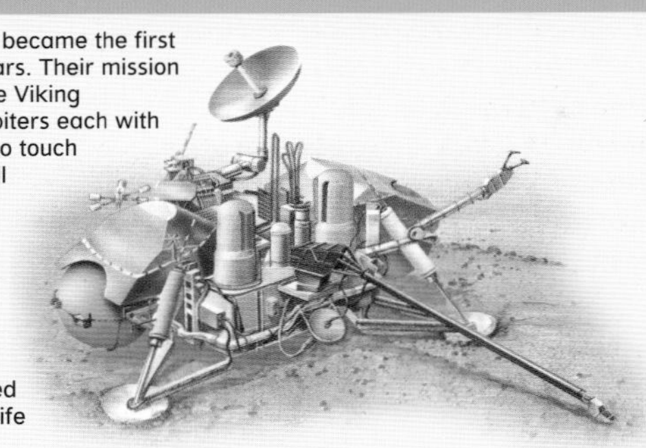

Giant valley

Mars's surface is cracked by a valley called the Vallis Marineris – so big that it makes the Grand Canyon look tiny. It appears to cut Mars in half. Dark areas cover about one-third of the planet. They have historically been called *maria* (meaning seas), even though they do not contain any amount of water that can be measured. These *maria* change colour at different times of the year. During the Martian autumn and winter parts of them become lighter or disappear. In spring and summer they become darker and larger.

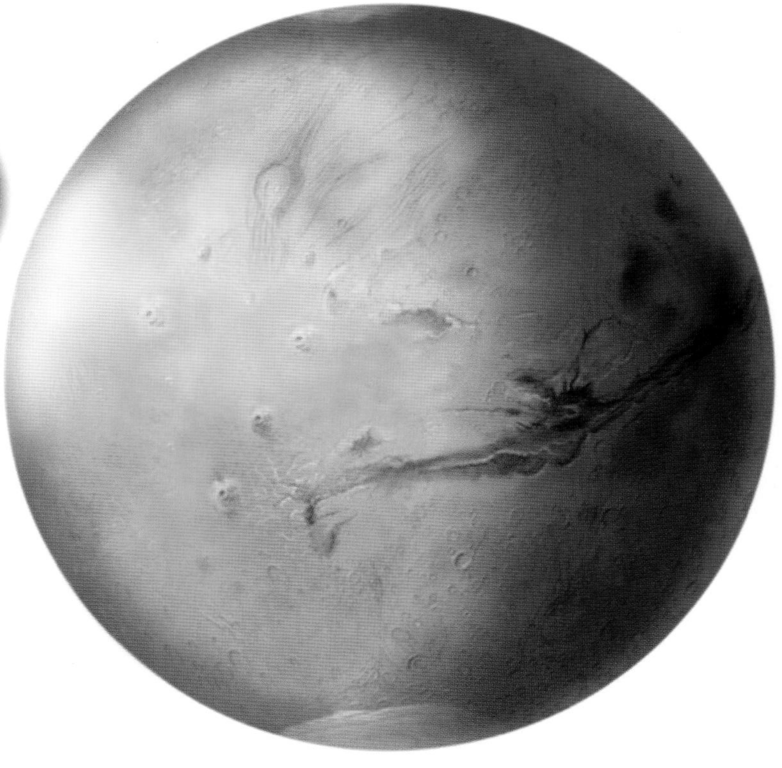

➤ ***Winds on Mars whip up huge dust storms that can cover the whole planet. Mars is very dry, like a desert, and covered in red dust. It has giant volcanoes, valleys, ice caps and dried-up river beds.***

Jupiter

Named after the Roman god of the skies and the supreme ruler of all the gods, Jupiter is the biggest planet in the Solar System. It is twice as heavy as all the other planets put together and has over 60 known moons. Jupiter is the fifth planet out from the Sun.

- Towards Jupiter's core, immense pressure makes the hydrogen gas behave like a liquid.
- The ancient Greeks originally named the planet Zeus, after the king of their gods. Jupiter was the Romans' name for Zeus.
- Jupiter spins right round in less than ten hours, which means that the planet's surface is moving at nearly 50,000 km/h.
- Jupiter's speedy spin makes its middle bulge out. It also churns up the planet's metal core until it generates a hugely powerful magnetic field, ten times as strong as the Earth's.
- Jupiter has a Great Red Spot – a huge swirl of red clouds measuring up to 40,000 km across. The scientist Robert Hooke may have first noticed the spot in 1644.
- Jupiter's four biggest moons were first spotted by Galileo in the 17th century. Their names are Ganymede, Callisto, Io, and Europa.

Jupiter is a gigantic planet, 142,984 km across. Its orbit takes 11.86 years and varies between 740.5 and 816.6 million km from the Sun. Its surface is often rent by huge lightning flashes and thunderclaps, and temperatures here plunge to –110°C. Jupiter's surface is a swirling mass of red, brown and yellow clouds stretched out into coloured bands because the planet spins round so fast.

Jupiter's largest moons

Metis	**Leda**
Adastrea	**Himalia**
Amalthea	**Lysithea**
Thebe	**Elara**
Io	**Ananke**
Europa	**Carme**
Ganymede	**Pasiphae**
Callisto	**Sinope**

plus at least 50 other smaller moons

❍ Jupiter also has at least 60 other smaller moons. Most are tiny and some have been discovered so recently that they have not yet been named.

❍ Jupiter is so massive that the pressure at its heart makes it glow very faintly with invisible infrared rays. Indeed, it glows as brightly as four million billion 100-watt lightbulbs. But it is not big enough for nuclear reactions to start, and make it become a star.

Life on Europa?

Jupiter's moon Europa may have oceans of water beneath its icy surface, and it is a major target in the search for life in the Solar System.

❍ Jupiter's rings consist of three different types. The inner halo is a faint ring about 20,000 km thick that is thought to extend down to the top of the clouds. The second is the main ring, 7000 km wide and about 30 km thick. The third is the gossamer ring that extends out to 200,000 km.

Amazing

The Great Red Spot is a huge storm about twice the size of planet Earth that has lasted for over 300 years.

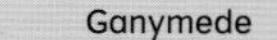

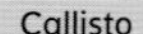

Io

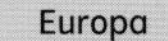

The largest of Jupiter's Galilean moons is Ganymede, with a diameter of 5262 km. It is bigger than the planet Mercury and is the largest moon in the Solar System. Callisto (4821 km in diameter) is scarred with craters from bombardments in the Solar System's early life. Io's surface (3643 km diameter) is a mass of volcanoes, caused by Jupiter's massive gravity. Europa, the smallest Galilean moon (3122 km in diameter), is covered in ice.

Gas planet

Jupiter has no surface for a spacecraft to land on because it is made mostly from hydrogen and helium gas. The massive pull of Jupiter's gravity squeezes the hydrogen so hard that it is liquid.

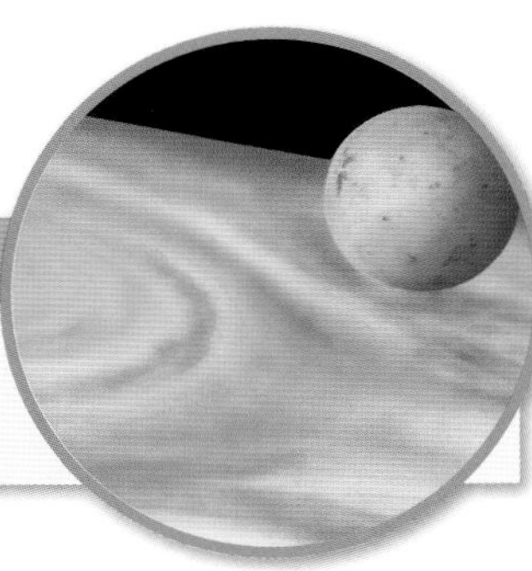

Factfile

Diameter	142,984 km
Mass	1899 x 10^{24} kg
Time to spin once	9.9 hours
Average distance from Sun	778.6 million km
Time for one orbit	11.86 years
Average temperature	–110°C
Number of moons	67
Ring system	Yes

Saturn

Saturn is the second biggest planet in the Solar System after Jupiter, and is easily recognized by its distinctive, shimmering rings. The sixth planet out from the Sun, it was named after Saturnus, the Roman god of seed sowing, who was celebrated in the Roman's wild festival of Saturnalia.

❍ Saturn takes 29.46 years to travel round the Sun, so Saturn's year is 29.46 Earth years. The planet's complete orbit is a journey of more than 4.5 billion km.

❍ Winds ten times stronger than a hurricane on Earth constantly swirl around Saturn's equator, reaching up to 1800 km/h.

❍ Saturn is not solid but is made of hydrogen and helium, both as gasses and liquids. Only in the planet's very small core is there any solid rock.

❍ Because Saturn is so massive, the pressure at its heart is enough to turn hydrogen liquid.

❍ Around Saturn's inner core of rock, pressure is so great that the liquid hydrogen behaves like a metal.

❍ Saturn is one of the fastest spinning of all the planets. Despite its size, it rotates in just 10.7 hours – which means it turns round at over 30,000 km/h.

❍ Saturn's surface appears to be almost completely smooth, though *Voyager 1* and *2* did photograph a few swirling storms when they flew past.

Saturn is almost as big as Jupiter, and made largely of liquid hydrogen and helium. Saturn is stunningly beautiful, with a smooth, pale-butterscotch surface (clouds of ammonia) and a shimmering halo of rings. Telescopes have never pierced its upper atmosphere, and data from the fly-bys of the* Voyager *probes focused on its rings and moons. The* Cassini *probe that went into orbit round Saturn in 2004 spotted a huge storm in 2010 even larger than Jupiter's Great Red Spot.

Saturn's moons

Pan
Atlas
Prometheus
Pandora
Epimetheus
Janus
Mimas
Enceladus
Tethys
Telesto
Calypso
Dione
Helene
Rhea
Titan
Hyperion
Iapetus
Phoebe

plus at least 16 other smaller moons

Saturn's rings are made up of millions of fragments of ice, dust and tiny rocks, which orbit the planet around the equator. The main rings measure over 270,000 km across but are very thin – only 100 m or less. They may be fragments of a moon that was torn apart by Saturn's gravity before it could form properly. There are three main rings, called A, B and C, that can be seen through a telescope but the Voyager space probes found other fainter rings.

Amazing

Saturn is so low in density that if you could find a bath big enough, you would be able to float the planet in water.

Saturn's rings

Saturn's rings may be fragments of a moon that was torn apart by Saturn's gravity before it formed properly. Since the 1980s, space probes revealed many other rings and 10,000 or more ringlets, some just 10 m wide.

Factfile

Diameter	120,536 km
Mass	568 x 10^{24} kg
Time to spin once	10.7 hours
Average distance from Sun	1433.5 million km
Time for one orbit	29.46 years
Average temperature	–140°C
Number of moons	62
Ring system	Yes

Titan

Saturn has more than 62 moons – new tiny ones are still being discovered. One of its moons, Titan, is one of the few moons with an atmosphere. Its sky is a mass of yellowish clouds.

Uranus

Uranus is the seventh planet out from the Sun and is the third largest in the Solar System. It is only just visible from Earth, looking like a star, but a telescope shows it as a small greenish spot. Uranus was named after the Greek god of the heavens.

❍ When Herschel first spotted Uranus in 1781 he thought he had found a new comet, even though it had no tail. However, astronomers soon realized that its orbit was round like a planet's and not long and thin like a comet's.

❍ Uranus tilts so far on its side that it seems to roll around the Sun like a gigantic bowling ball. The angle of its tilt is 98°, so its equator runs top to bottom. This tilt may be the result of a collision with another planet a long time ago.

❍ In summer on Uranus, the Sun does not set for 20 years. In winter, darkness lasts for over 20 years. In autumn, the Sun rises and sets every nine hours.

❍ Because Uranus is so far from the Sun, it is very, very cold, with surface temperatures dropping to –210°C. Sunlight takes just eight minutes to reach Earth, but 2.5 hours to reach Uranus.

❍ Uranus's icy atmosphere is made of hydrogen and helium. Winds whistle around the planet at more than 900 km/h – five times as fast as hurricanes on Earth.

❍ Uranus doesn't have a solid surface. Around its small rocky core is the mantle, a thick liquid layer containing water and ammonia. At the bottom of this there may be an ocean of liquid diamond. Above it is a deep gassy layer and an outer atmosphere with methane clouds which give it its beautiful colour.

These two images of Uranus were put together from pictures taken by Voyager 2 in 1986 when the spacecraft was 18 million kilometres from the planet. The image on the left shows Uranus as the human eye would see it from the spacecraft. The image on the right is an exaggerated false-colour view, obtained by using different colour filters, that shows details not visible to the human eye. The blue-green appearance of Uranus is a result of the methane in the atmosphere.

Uranus's moons

All named after Shakespeare characters

Ariel	**Oberon**
Belinda	**Ophelia**
Bianca	**Portia**
Caliban	**Puck**
Cordelia	**Rosalind**
Cressida	**Sycorax**
Desdemona	**Titania**
Juliet	**Umbriel**
Miranda	

plus at least 10 other smaller moons

Moons

Uranus has 27 moons, all named after characters in William Shakespeare's plays. There are five large moons – Ariel, Umbriel, Titania, Oberon and Miranda. The smaller ones were discovered by the *Voyager 2* space probe in 1986. Uranus's moon Miranda (shown here) is the weirdest moon of all. It looks as though it has been blasted apart, then put itself back together again.

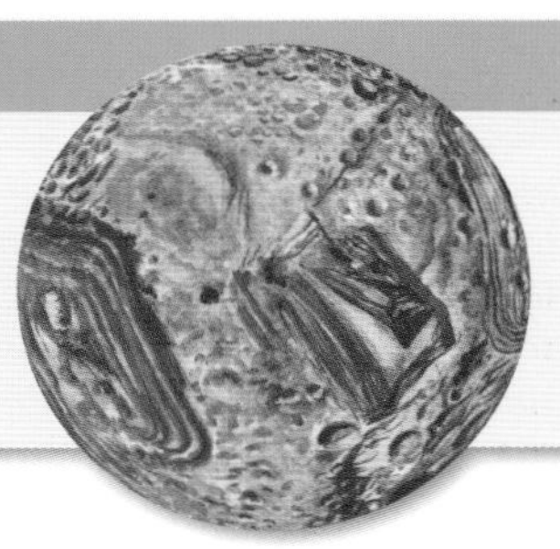

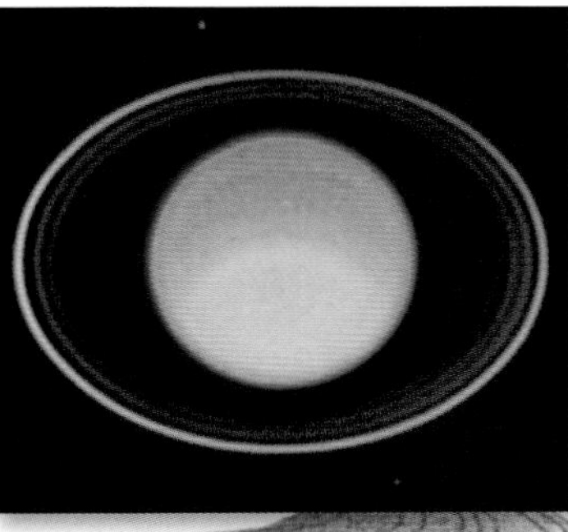

In 1995, the Hubble Space Telescope peered deep into Uranus's atmosphere to see clear and hazy layers created by a mixture of gases, and identified features of three different atmospheric layers. The red rim around the planet's edge represents a very thin haze at a high altitude. The haze is so thin that it can only be seen by looking at the edges of the disc, and is similar to looking at the edge of a soap bubble. The yellow near the bottom is another hazy layer. The deepest layer, the blue near the top of Uranus, shows a clear atmosphere. Image processing was used to brighten Uranus's rings. In reality, the rings are the colour of black lava or charcoal.

Uranus is the third largest planet in the Solar System – 51,118 km across and with a mass 14.54 times that of Earth. The planet spins round once every 17.2 hours, but because it is lying almost on its side, this has almost no effect on the length of its day. Instead, this depends on where the planet is in its orbit of the Sun. Like Saturn, Uranus has rings, but they are much thinner and were only detected in 1977. They are made of an extremely dark material.

Amazing

Uranus's 11 narrow rings were discovered when an astronomer saw a star 'wink' on and off on either side of the planet when the star went behind Uranus.

Studying the night sky

Uranus was not discovered until 1781. It was identified by the German-born astronomer William Herschel who used a telescope to make a thorough study of the night sky.

Factfile

Diameter	51,118 km
Mass	86.8×10^{24} kg
Time to spin once	17.2 hours retrograde
Average distance from Sun	2872 million km
Time for one orbit	83.75 years
Average temperature	–195°C
Number of moons	27
Ring system	Yes

Neptune

Neptune is the fourth largest planet, and the eighth out from the Sun. Like its neighbour Uranus it has no solid surface but is made of gases and icy liquids with a small rocky core and an atmosphere of hydrogen and helium. It is named after the Greek god of the sea.

❍ Like Uranus, Neptune is mostly made of water, ammonia and methane ices, and is very cold, only –200°C at the top of the atmosphere.

❍ Unlike Uranus, which is almost perfectly blue, Neptune has white clouds, created by heat inside the planet.

❍ Neptune was discovered in 1846 by two mathematicians, John Couch Adams in England and Urbain le Verrier in France.

❍ Adams and le Verrier worked out that Neptune must be there because of the effect of its gravity on the movement of Uranus.

❍ Neptune is so far from the Sun that its orbit lasts 164.8 years.

❍ Neptune has the strongest winds in the Solar System, blowing at up to 600 m/sec.

❍ The *Voyager 2* encounter confirmed that Neptune has three distinct rings, with a diffuse ring of material.

❍ Neptune's moon Triton is the coldest place in the Solar System, with surface temperatures of –236°C.

❍ Triton is the only large moon to orbit backwards.

At 49,528 km across, Neptune is slightly smaller than Uranus – but it is actually a little heavier. Like Uranus, methane in the atmosphere gives it a beautiful shiny blue colour although Neptune is a deeper blue than Uranus. Again like Uranus, Neptune has a thin layer of rings. There are swirling storms in Neptune's clouds. In 1989* Voyager 2 *spotted one called the Great Dark Spot. Then in 1994 the Hubble Space Telescope found a new storm, but the Great Dark Spot had disappeared.

Factfile

Diameter	49,528 km
Mass	102 x 10^{24} kg
Time to spin once	16.1 hours
Average distance from Sun	4495.1 million km
Time for one orbit	164.8 years
Average temperature	–200°C
Number of moons	14
Ring system	Yes

Magnetism

Neptune and Uranus are unusual planets because, unlike other planets' magnetic fields, theirs do not line up with their axis of rotation (the angle at which they spin).

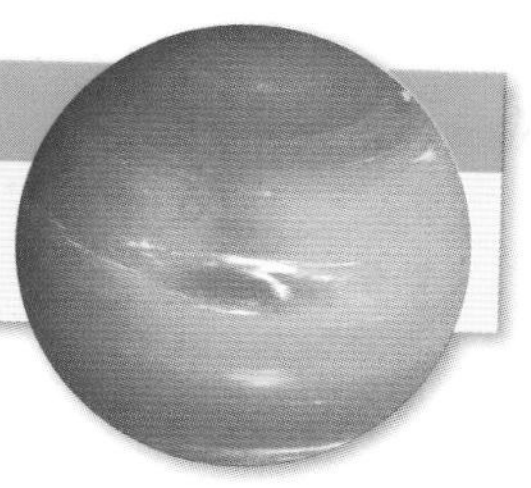

Amazing

Neptune has only completed a single orbit of the Sun since it was first discovered in 1846!

Neptune's biggest moon is Triton, with a diameter of 2700 km. It looks like a green melon, while its icecaps of frozen nitrogen resemble pink ice cream. Triton is gradually spiralling towards Neptune and in 10 million to 100 million years time it will break up and form rings around the planet. Triton's geysers shoot out freezing nitrogen gas.

Aerial view

The Great Dark Spot, and the little white tail of clouds, named Scooter by astronomers, are clearly visible in photographs of Neptune taken from *Voyager 2* in 1989.

Neptune's largest moons

Despina
Galatea
Larissa
Naiad
Nereid
Proteus
Thalassa
Triton

plus at least six other smaller moons

Pluto and the Dwarf Planets

Pluto was discovered in 1930 and until 2006 was considered to be the ninth planet in our Solar System. It was by far the smallest – smaller than the Earth's moon! Since 2006, Pluto has been classified as a dwarf planet by the International Astronomical Union (IAU). This means it fails to dominate its orbit around the Sun.

❍ Pluto was only found because astronomers thought there was another planet disturbing the orbits of Uranus and Neptune.

❍ The path of Pluto's orbit makes its distance from the Sun vary from 4435 to 7375 million km.

❍ Its orbit is so far from the Sun that Pluto takes 248 Earth years just to travel once around it. This means that a year on Pluto lasts two and a half centuries. A single day on Pluto lasts 6.4 days.

❍ Pluto has a strange elliptical (oval) orbit which actually brings it closer to the Sun than Neptune for about 20 years every few centuries.

❍ Unlike the main planets, which orbit on exactly the same plane (level) as the Earth, Pluto's orbit tilts at an angle to all the other orbits.

❍ Four other dwarf planets have been named – Eris, Ceres, Haumea and Makemake. Ceres is the largest asteroid and orbits between Mars and Jupiter. The others are all further from the Sun than Pluto.

❍ While studying a photograph of Pluto in 1978, American astronomer James Christy noticed a bump. This turned out to be a large moon, which was later named Charon.

❍ Charon is about half the size of Pluto and they orbit one another, locked together like a weightlifter's dumbbells.

❍ Charon always stays in the same place in Pluto's sky, looking three times as big as our Moon.

❍ Pluto is made from rock, covered in water and ice. Daytime temperatures on Pluto's surface are –225°C or lower, so the surface is thought to be coated in frozen nitrogen and methane.

❍ The name Pluto comes from the name of the god of the Underworld in Roman mythology. Pluto was named after him because it is so far from the Sun that it is in perpetual darkness.

This picture of Pluto is based entirely on guesswork, since the planet is so small and so far away that even photographs from the Hubble Space Telescope show only fuzzy dark and light patches on Pluto's surface, with no detail at all. However, a twinkling of starlight around the edge of the dwarf planet shows that it must have some kind of atmosphere.

Amazing

When Pluto was discovered in 1930, many names were considered. The name Pluto was a suggestion submitted by Venetia Burney, an 11-year-old schoolgirl from Oxford, England.

Factfile: Pluto

Diameter	2306 km
Mass	0.0125×10^{24} kg
Time to spin once	6.39 days
Average distance from Sun	5870 million km
Time for one orbit	248 years
Average temperature	–225°C
Number of moons	5
Ring system	No

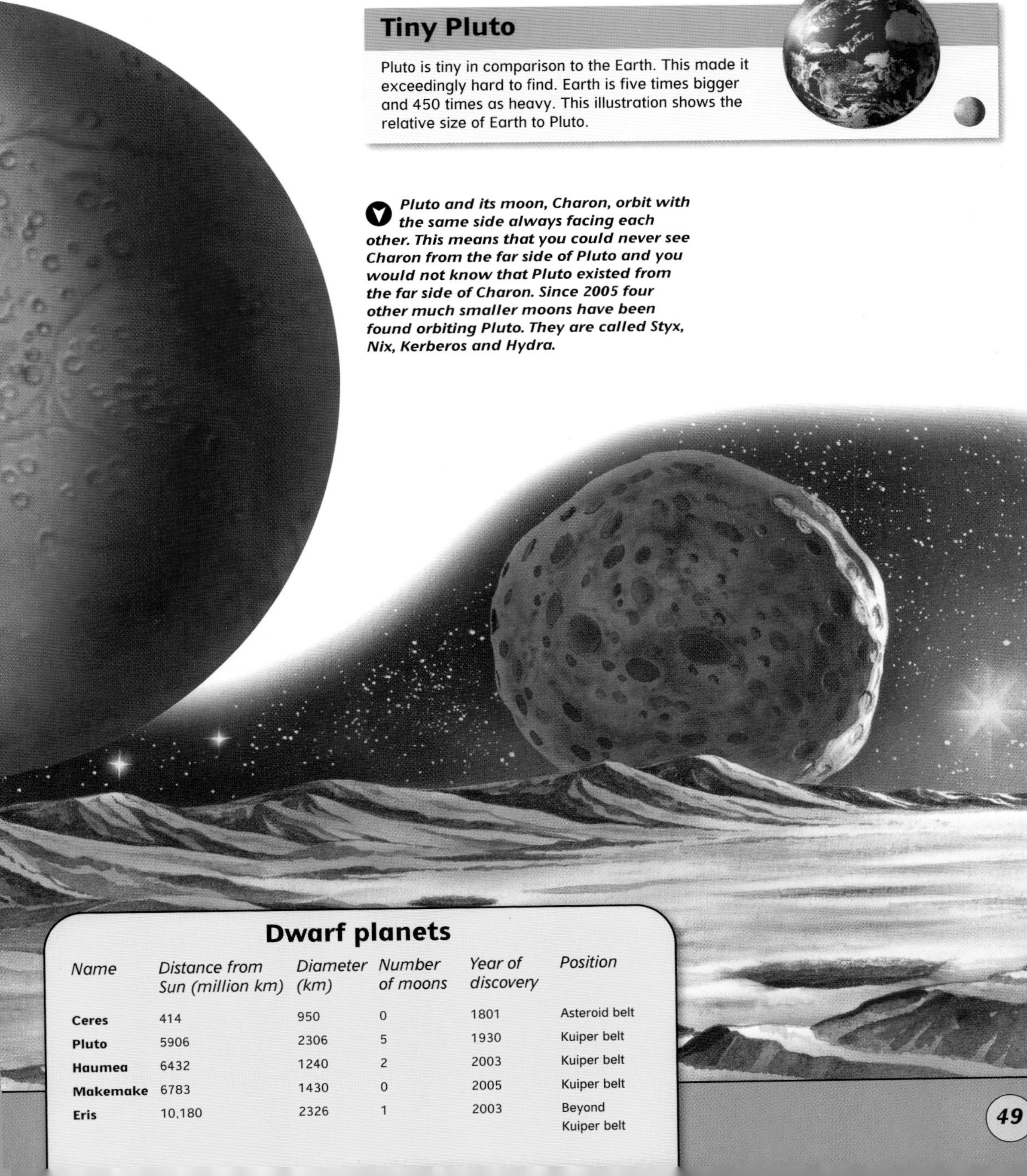

Tiny Pluto

Pluto is tiny in comparison to the Earth. This made it exceedingly hard to find. Earth is five times bigger and 450 times as heavy. This illustration shows the relative size of Earth to Pluto.

Pluto and its moon, Charon, orbit with the same side always facing each other. This means that you could never see Charon from the far side of Pluto and you would not know that Pluto existed from the far side of Charon. Since 2005 four other much smaller moons have been found orbiting Pluto. They are called Styx, Nix, Kerberos and Hydra.

Dwarf planets

Name	*Distance from Sun (million km)*	*Diameter (km)*	*Number of moons*	*Year of discovery*	*Position*
Ceres	414	950	0	1801	Asteroid belt
Pluto	5906	2306	5	1930	Kuiper belt
Haumea	6432	1240	2	2003	Kuiper belt
Makemake	6783	1430	0	2005	Kuiper belt
Eris	10,180	2326	1	2003	Beyond Kuiper belt

Comets

Comets are bright objects with long tails, which we sometimes see glowing in the night sky. They may look spectacular, but a comet is actually just a dirty ball of ice a few kilometres across.

❍ Many comets orbit the Sun, but their orbits are very long and they spend most of the time in the far reaches of the Solar System. We see them when their orbit brings them close to the Sun for a few weeks.

❍ A comet's tail is made as it nears the Sun and begins to melt. A vast plume of gas millions of kilometres long is blown out by the solar wind. The tail is what you see, shining as the sunlight catches it.

The Kohoutek comet was first seen on 7 March 1973 by Czech astronomer Lubos Kohoutek. The period when it could be seen with the naked eye was from the end of November 1973 until late January 1974. Initially labelled the 'Comet of the Century' it actually proved to be disappointing in putting on a poor display.

Amazing

The comet with the longest-ever recorded tail is probably Hyakutaye, discovered in 1996. Its tail stretched over 500 million km.

This photograph of Halley's Comet was taken when it last came close to Earth in 1986. The comet comes back close to Earth within visible range, roughly every 76 years.

Comet orbits

	Orbital period
Encke	3.30 years
Grigg-Skjellerup	5.09 years
Honda-Mrkos-Pajd	5.28 years
Wirtanen	5.46 years
Wild 2	6.17 years
Kohoutek	6.24 years
Giacobini-Zinner	6.52 years
Crommelin	27.89 years
Tempel-Tuttle	32.92 years
Chiron	50.7 years
Halley	76.1 years
Hale-Bopp	4000 years
Hyakutake	65,000+ years

How did life begin on Earth? One idea was that life did not start here. Simple life-forms appeared somewhere else in the Universe, and travelled to Earth on a long-distance space wanderer such as a comet or asteroid.

What is a comet?

The nucleus of a comet (the tiny dark spot in the centre) is usually just a few kilometres across. Jets of gas burned off by the Sun form the coma, or cloud of gas, and the tail.

Ancient comet

The most famous comet is named after the British scientist Edmund Halley (1656–1742). He accurately predicted that this particular comet would be seen in the night sky in 1758, which was 16 years after his death. He was the first person to predict when a comet would arrive. Halley's comet orbits the Sun every 76 years. It was last seen in 1986 and its next visit will be in 2061. The Chinese described a visit from the comet as long ago as 240 BC. King Harold of England saw it in 1066, and it is embroidered on the Bayeux Tapestry, which shows Harold's defeat by William the Conqueror.

- Some comets are bright enough to be seen with the naked eye, while others can only be seen with the aid of a telescope. You will not be able to see comets moving, but over a period of time their progress can be charted.
- Comets called periodics appear at regular intervals.
- Some comets reach speeds of 2 million km/h as they near the Sun.
- Far away from the Sun, comets slow down to 1000 km/h or so – that is why they stay away for so long.
- The visit of the comet Hale-Bopp in 1997 was spectacular. It was bright enough to be seen from cities and visible for 18 months.
- The Shoemaker-Levy 9 comet smashed into Jupiter in July 1994, with the biggest crash ever witnessed.

Comets travel through the inner Solar System and after about 100 orbits usually lose all their gas and dust and die. However, sometimes comets die more spectacularly, such as these seen being pulled apart by Jupiter's gravity. In July 1994, 21 pieces crashed into Jupiter's atmosphere.

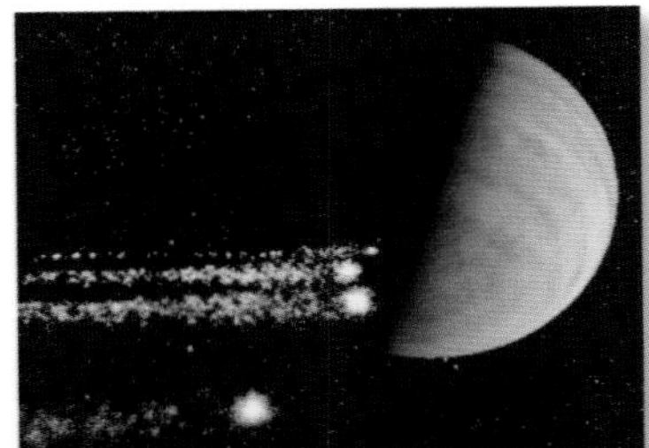

Halley's Comet

1682	British astronomer Edmund Halley saw it and worked out that the comet (now named after him) would return in 76–77 years.
1759	Great excitement: the comet returned as predicted.
1835	Comet was seen again, but was not so bright.
1910	Despite scientific progress, some superstitious people still feared that the reappearance of the comet heralded the end of the world.
1986	Several spacecraft flew close to the comet.
2061	Next time Halley's Comet is due to return.

Asteroids and Meteorites

Asteroids are lumps of rock that orbit the Sun. When asteroids collide, small chunks of rock and dust called meteoroids zoom off into space. If these enter the Earth's atmosphere they burn up, leaving a streak of light called a meteor or shooting star. Those that survive and fall to the ground are called meteorites.

❍ Most asteroids travel within the Asteroid Belt, which lies between Mars and Jupiter.

❍ Some distant asteroids are made of ice and orbit the Sun beyond Neptune.

❍ A few asteroids come near the Earth. These are called Near Earth Objects (NEOs).

❍ The first asteroid to be discovered was Ceres in 1801. It was detected by Giuseppi Piazzi. It is now also called a dwarf planet.

❍ Ceres is the biggest asteroid – 950 km across, and about a quarter of the size of the Moon.

❍ The *Galileo* space probe took close-up pictures of the asteroids Ida and Gaspra in 1991 and 1993.

❍ The Trojan asteroids are groups of asteroids that follow the same orbit as Jupiter.

❍ Many of the Trojans are named after warriors from the ancient Greek tales of the Trojan Wars.

This crater in Arizona, measuring 1.2 km in diameter, is the first to be identified as an impact crater, proved to be such by the discovery of fragments of the Canyon Diablo meteorite. Between 20,000 and 50,000 years ago this small asteroid, about 50 m in diameter, hit Earth.

Amazing

Once every 50–100 million years the Earth is hit by an asteroid measuring over 10 km in diameter.

Largest asteroids in the Asteroid Belt

These are still much smaller than the Moon. Collectively, the asteroids probably only weigh about one-twentieth of the Moon's weight.

	Discovered	*Discoverer*	*Diameter*	*Distance from Sun*
Ceres	1801	G. Piazzi	952 km	413.9 million km
Pallas	1802	H. Olbers	545 km	414.5 million km
Vesta	1807	H. Olbers	530 km	353.4 million km
Hygiea	1849	A. de Gasparis	408 km	470.3 million km
Davida	1903	R. Dugan	326 km	475.4 million km
Interamnia	1910	V. Cerulli	316 km	458.1 million km
Europa	1858	H. Goldsmith	302 km	463.3 million km
Juno	1804	K. Harding	268 km	399.4 million km
Sylvia	1866	N. Pogson	260 km	521.5 million km
Euomnia	1851	A. de Gasparis	256 km	395.5 million km
Euphrosyne	1854	J. Ferguson	256 km	472.1 million km
Psyche	1852	A. de Gasparis	254 km	437.1 million km
Cybele	1867	E. Tempel	240 km	513.0 million km
Bamberga	1892	J. Palisa	230 km	401.4 million km
Patentia	1899	A. Charlois	226 km	458.2 million km
Doris	1857	H. Goldschmidt	222 km	465.5 million km
Camilla	1968	N. Pogson	222 km	521.8 million km
Herculina	1904	M. Wolf	222 km	414.7 million km
Eugenia	1857	H. Goldschmidt	214 km	407.1 million km

Earthbound

Most meteoroids burn away in the atmosphere, but some come crashing down to Earth as meteorites.

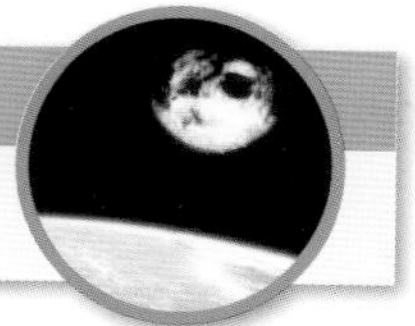

Small asteroids are burnt up by the Earth's atmosphere every day. The chances of a big one colliding with us and destroying the Earth, like in this illustration, are remote.

- A meteoroid that strikes Earth is called a meteorite. It can create a huge hole or crater.

- Scientists believe that a huge meteorite, possibly the size of an asteroid, crashed to Earth 65 million years ago and sent up a huge dust cloud that caused the extinction of the dinosaurs.

Meteors are mostly caused by dust smaller than a grain of sand, much too small to be seen, even with a telescope.

The Asteroid Belt

Millions of asteroids can be found in the Asteroid Belt, which lies between the orbits of Mars and Jupiter. They range in size from Ceres, which is about one quarter of the diameter of our Moon, to bodies that are less than one kilometre across, and many smaller ones. Spacecraft that have travelled through the Asteroid Belt have found that it is actually quite empty and that asteroids are separated by large distances.

10 large meteorite craters on Earth

	Diameter
Vredefort South Africa	300 km
Sudbury Ontario, Canada	250 km
Chicxulub Yucatan, Mexico	170 km
Popigai Russia	100 km
Manicouagan Quebec, Canada	100 km
Acraman Australia	90 km
Chesapeake Bay Virginia, USA	90 km
Puchezh-Katunki Russia	80 km
Morokweng South Africa	70 km
Kara Russia	65 km

Astronomy

Astronomy is the study of the night sky – from the planets and moons to the stars and galaxies. It is the most ancient of sciences, dating back thousands of years. The word astronomy comes from the Greek* astro*, meaning 'star' and* nomia*, meaning 'law'.

- The ancient Egyptians used their knowledge of astronomy to work out their calendar and to plant their crops. The great Egyptian pyramids at Giza are said to have been positioned to align with certain stars.

- Astronomers use telescopes to study objects far fainter and smaller than can be seen with the naked eye.

- Space objects give out other kinds of radiation besides light, and astronomers have special equipment to detect this.

- Professional astronomers study photographs and computer displays instead of staring through telescopes, because most faint space objects only show up on long-exposure photographs.

Most astronomers work far from city lights in observatories where they can get a very clear view of the night sky and sights such as this supernova.

Amazing

In 2003, NASA's WMAP satellite took images of the most distant parts of the Universe observable from Earth. Nearly 14 billion lightyears away, it showed the Universe long before the stars and galaxies formed.

Astrology

The Zodiac is the band of constellations the Sun appears to pass in front of during the year, as the Earth orbits the Sun. It lies along the ecliptic, which is the plane (level) of the Earth's orbit around the Sun. The Moon and all planets lie in the same plane. The ancient Greeks divided the Zodiac into 12 parts, named after the constellation they saw in each part. These are the signs of the Zodiac. The Zodiac signs are imaginary symbols that ancient astronomers linked to star patterns. Astrologers believe that the movements of planets and stars have an effect on people's lives. They are not scientists, like astronomers. A 13th constellation, Ophiuchus, now lies within the Zodiac but astrologers ignore it.

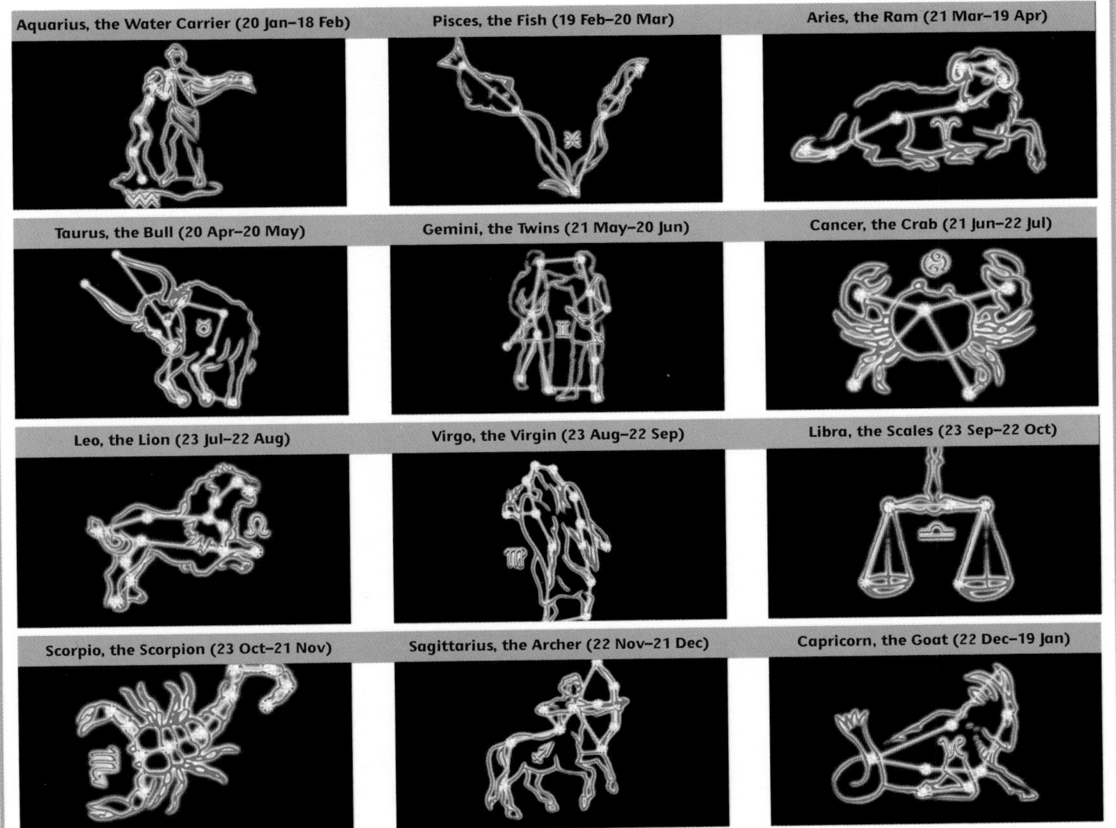

Telescopes and Observatories

The most important tool for studying the skies is the telescope. Today, there are several different types of telescope, ranging from simple ones used by amateur star-gazers to immensely powerful space telescopes that allow astronomers to see into the furthest reaches of the Universe. Observatories are special places where astronomers study space and, to give the best view of the night sky, most are built on mountain tops far from city lights.

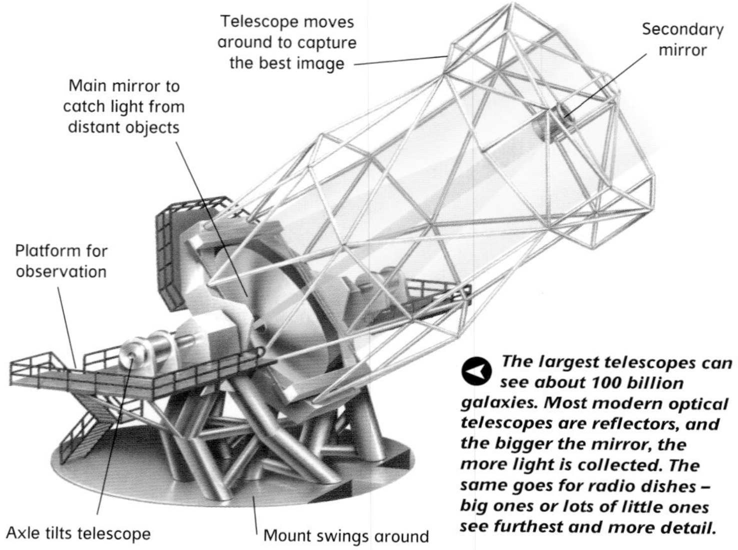

The largest telescopes can see about 100 billion galaxies. Most modern optical telescopes are reflectors, and the bigger the mirror, the more light is collected. The same goes for radio dishes – big ones or lots of little ones see furthest and more detail.

- Optical telescopes magnify distant objects by using lenses or mirrors to refract (bend) light rays so they focus (come together).
- Other telescopes detect radio waves, X-rays, or other kinds of electromagnetic radiation.
- Refracting telescopes are optical telescopes that use lenses to refract the light rays.
- Another type of optical telescope is a reflecting telescope. These use curved mirrors to reflect and focus the light.
- Because the light rays are folded, reflecting telescopes are shorter and fatter than refracting ones.
- Most professional astronomers do not gaze at the stars directly, but pick up what the telescope shows with light sensors called Charge-Coupled Devices (CCDs).

Galileo Galilei

The great Italian mathematician and astronomer, Galileo Galilei (1564–1642), studied the skies through his telescope, which he demonstrated to members of the Venetian senate. Learning of the invention of the telescope, Galileo made his own to look at the Moon, Venus and Jupiter. Through his telescope, he discovered four of Jupiter's moons and studied the phases of Venus.

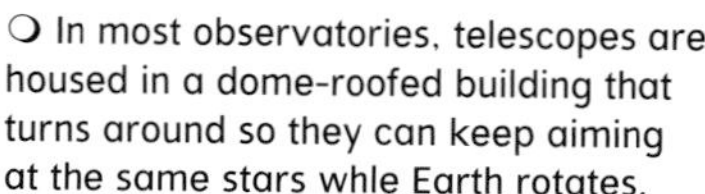

- In most observatories, telescopes are housed in a dome-roofed building that turns around so they can keep aiming at the same stars whle Earth rotates.
- The mirrors of big modern telescopes are often made of hexagons of coated glass or metal fitted tightly together.
- The highest observatory on Earth is 5640 m above sea level, in the Atacama desert in Chile.
- Some observatories are deep underground. Instead of telescopes they use huge tanks of water or cleaning fluid to trap neutrinos (tiny particles) from the Sun.
- The first astronomical photograph was taken in 1840. Nowadays astronomers rely on CCD images which can record much fainter and more distant objects than the naked eye.

Observatories

The most powerful optical telescopes are housed in observatories – specially designed buildings which allow astronomers to study space in comfort. To give the best view of the night sky, most observatories are built on mountaintops far away from city lights. They generally have domed roofs that can turn around in order to aim at the same stars as the Earth rotates. One of the largest observatory complexes (part of which is shown here) is 4200 m above sea level, in the crater of the extinct Hawaiian volcano, Mauna Kea. It has 13 telescopes, including one radio telescope, operated by 11 different countries.

Amazing

Telescope dishes have to be made accurate to within 2 billionths of a millimetre.

❍ Astronomical photographs are made using sensors called Charge-Coupled Devices (CCDs), which give off an electrical signal when struck by light.

❍ Astronomers can spot new objects in the night sky by comparing images taken at different times and looking for differences.

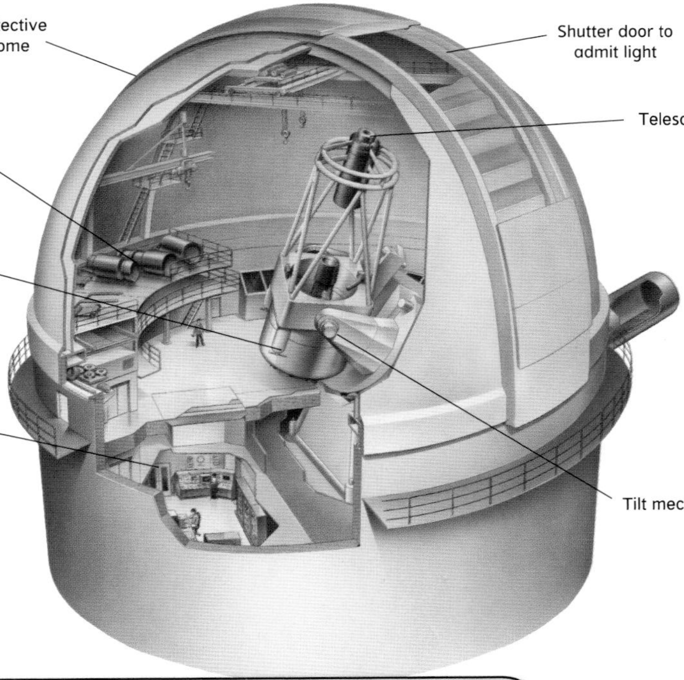

Protective dome

Shutter door to admit light

Alternative mirror cages

Telescope

Primary mirror in base

Control room

Tilt mechanism

A huge dome protects this large telescope. It opens to let the telescope point at the sky, and both the dome and telescope can turn to look at any part of the sky.

Major radio telescopes

		Size of array
VLA (Very Large Array)	New Mexico, USA	27 x 25 m dishes
Effelsberg Radio Telescope	Effelsberg, Germany	100 m
Arecibo Observatory	Puerto Rico	305 m diameter
Green Bank Telescope	West Virginia, USA	100 x 110 m
ALMA (Atacama Large Millimetre Array)	Atacama, Chile	66 x 12 m and 7 m dishes

Space Probes

A space probe is an unmanned spacecraft controlled remotely by computer. Most probe missions are 'fly-bys' – a few days spent passing a target and sending data back to Earth – although some land on the surface of planets, moons and asteroids.

❍ In 1976, *Vikings 1* and *2* were the first spacecraft to return images from Mars' surface. Their experiments looked for signs of life in the soil but found none.

❍ *Voyagers 1* and *2*, launched in 1977, flew past Jupiter (1979) and Saturn (1980–1). *Voyager 2* went on to Uranus (1986) and Neptune (1989). *Voyager 1* entered interstellar space in 2012.

❍ The *Galileo* space probe circled Jupiter for nearly eight years. It arrived in 1995 and dropped a small probe into Jupiter's clouds. *Galileo* took pictures of the planet and its largest moons. From this it was discovered that two of them may have water hidden under ice thicker than the Arctic ice on Earth.

❍ *Cassini* has orbited Saturn for more than 10 years, exploring the planet's rings, moons and cloudy surface. It arrived in 2004 and dropped a probe onto Titan, the largest moon, revealing its hidden surface.

❍ *Messenger*, the first spacecraft to orbit Mercury, arrived in 2011. It sent back images of the whole surface, analyzed the surface rocks and measured the magnetic field.

❍ *New Horizons* is the first spacecraft to visit Pluto, flying past in 2015 and sending back close-up images of the dwarf planet. It is then expected to explore the Kuiper Belt.

❍ To save fuel on journeys to distant planets, space probes may use a nearby planet's gravity to catapult them on their way. This technique is known as a slingshot.

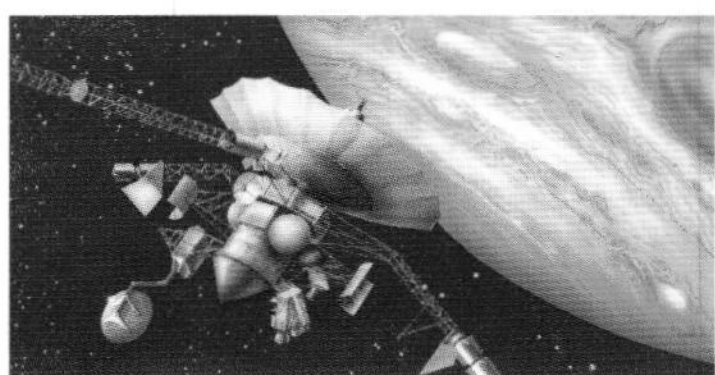

In September 2003, Galileo was sent into Jupiter's atmosphere.

Probes to the planets

MERCURY	LAUNCH DATE	MISSION
Mariner 10	3 November 1973	Three fly-bys in March and September 1974 and March 1975
MESSENGER	3 August 2004	Fly-by January 2008. Orbit from March 2011

VENUS	LAUNCH DATE	MISSION
Venera 4-16	1967–1983	Series of entry probes, landers and orbiters. *Venera 7* was first successful lander
Pioneer Venus	May/August 1978	One orbiter and four atmospheric probes
Magellan	4 May 1989	Orbiter – radar mapped surface
Venus Express	9 November 2005	Observation of Venusian atmosphere from April 2006

MARS	LAUNCH DATE	MISSION
Mariner 9	30 May 1971	Orbiter – first to orbit another planet
Viking	August/September 1975	Two orbiters with two landers – tested soil for life
Mars Global Surveyor	7 November 1996	Orbiter
Mars Pathfinder	4 December 1996	Lander with *Sojourner* rover
Mars Odyssey	7 April 2001	Orbiter
Mars Express	1 June 2003	Orbiter with *Beagle 2* lander (failed)
Mars Exploration Rovers	June/July 2003	Rovers, *Spirit* and *Opportunity*, explored surface and continue to send data back to Earth
Mars Reconnaissance Orbiter	12 August 2005	Orbiter
Mars Curiosity Rover	26 November 2011	Rover landed 6 August 2012

JUPITER	LAUNCH DATE	MISSION
Voyager 1	5 September 1977	Fly-by March 1979
Voyager 2	20 August 1977	Fly-by July 1979
Galileo	18 October 1989	Orbited December 1995–September 2003 Dropped small probe into atmosphere
Juno	5 August 2011	Orbiter, arrival July 2016.
New Horizons	19 January 2006	Fly-by July 2015

SATURN	LAUNCH DATE	MISSION
Voyager 1	5 September 1977	Fly-by November 1980
Voyager 2	20 August 1977	Fly-by August 1981
Cassini	15 October 1997	Orbiter plus *Huygens* probe that landed on Titan January 2005

URANUS	LAUNCH DATE	MISSION
Voyager 2	20 August 1977	Fly-by January 1986

NEPTUNE	LAUNCH DATE	MISSION
Voyager 2	20 August 1977	Fly-by August 1989

Amazing

In January 2005 the *Huygens* probe, launched from the *Cassini* spacecraft, landed on Saturn's moon, Titan. It is the furthest from Earth a spacecraft has ever landed, about 1.3 billion km away.

❍ Sample return missions bring space material back to earth. In 2004 *Genesis* returned solar wind particles, *Stardust* collected comet particles in 2006 and *Hayabusa* brought back asteroid rock in 2010.

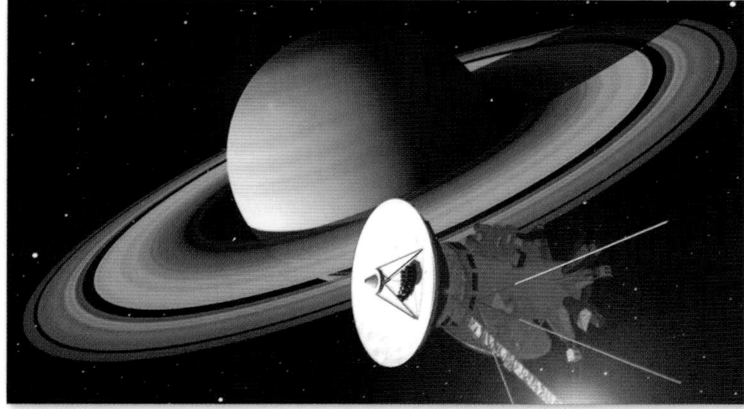

***Cassini* flew close to Saturn's moon Enceladus, discovering icy fountains and possibly an ocean of water beneath its surface.**

Voyagers

The Voyagers are a pair of unmanned US space probes, launched to explore the outer planets. The Voyagers used the 'slingshot' of Jupiter's gravity to hurl them on towards Saturn. The probes revealed volcanoes on Io, one of Jupiter's Galilean moons. *Voyager 2* also found ten unknown moons around Uranus and six unknown moons and three rings around Neptune. *Voyager 2* will beam back data until 2020 as it travels beyond the edges of the Solar System.

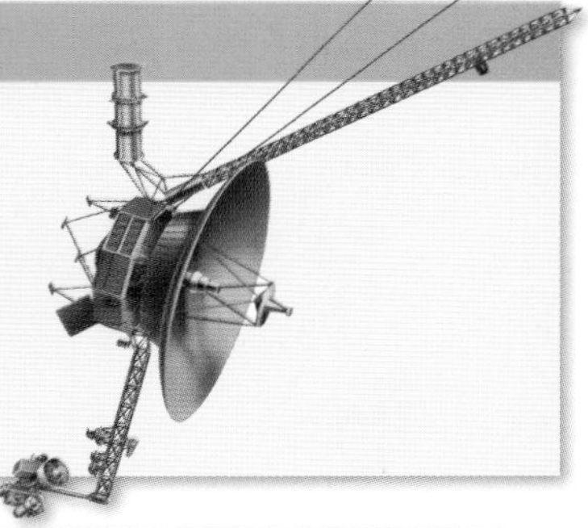

On 5 September 1977,* Voyager 1 *was launched aboard the* Titan III/ Centaur. *It was sent to join its sister spacecraft, the* Voyager 2, *on a mission to the outer planets.

Probes to comets and asteroids

PROBES	LAUNCH DATE	MISSION
Vega 1	15 December 1984	Russian probe flew past comet Halley
Vega 2	21 December 1984	Russian probe flew past comet Halley
Sakigake	8 January 1985	Japanese probe flew past comet Halley
Suisei	18 August 1985	Japanese probe flew past comet Halley
Giotto	2 July 1985	Flew past comet Halley, closest approach 1986
NEAR	17 February 1996	Orbited asteroid Eros then landed on it, 2001
Deep Space 1	24 October 1998	Flew past asteroid Braille July 1999 Flew past comet Borrelly September 2001
Stardust	7 January 1999	Flew past comet Wild 2, collected sample. Return to Earth January 2006
Genesis	8 August 2001	Collected sample of solar wind. Crash landed on return to Earth, some samples saved
Hayabusa	9 May 2003	Sample return from asteroid Itokawa 2005
Rosetta	2 March 2004	Orbit comet Churyumov-Gerasimenko, drop lander 2014
Deep Impact	12 January 2005	Launch impactor at comet Tempel 1, July 2005
Dawn	27 September 2007	Asteroid orbiter, Vesta 2011-2012, Ceres 2015

Artificial Satellites

Natural satellites are objects such as moons that orbit planets and other bodies in space. Artificial satellites are devices that are launched to orbit around the Earth. The signals they transmit are picked up by radio telescopes and other equipment, providing us with useful information about the Earth and space, and enabling us to communicate over long distances.

❍ The first artificial satellite, *Sputnik 1*, was launched on 4 October 1957.

❍ About 80 artificial satellites are now launched every year. A few of them are space telescopes.

Communications satellites beam everything from TV pictures to telephone calls around the world.

❍ Observation satellites scan the Earth and are used for purposes such as scientific research, weather forecasting and map-making.

❍ Navigation satellites, such as the Global Positioning System (GPS), are used to pinpoint a user's position and provide directions to a destination.

❍ Satellites are launched at a particular speed and trajectory (path) to place them in just the right orbit.

❍ A geostationary orbit is 35,786 km above Earth. Satellites in geostationary orbit over the Equator always stay in exactly the same place above the Earth.

❍ Polar orbiting satellites circle the Earth from pole to pole about 1000 km up, covering a different strip of the Earth's surface on each orbit.

❍ Geostationary orbit gets crowded so when a geostationary satellite fails, it is pushed into another orbit to make room for others.

The most famous space telescope is the Hubble, launched from a space shuttle in 1990. The diameter of its main light-gathering mirror measures 2.4 m. It is controlled by NASA and transmits data by radio waves to astronomers on the ground. The Hubble orbits about 570 km above the Earth, thus escaping the effects of the Earth's atmosphere, which bends light from the stars and thus blurs images.

Modern navigation instruments use signals from several satellites to pinpoint their position. A hand-held instrument, called a GPS receiver, receives signals from satellites in space. It shows your position within a few metres. These receivers can be built into cars, planes – even mobile phones.

Satellite orbit

Global Positioning Satellite (GPS)

Sputnik

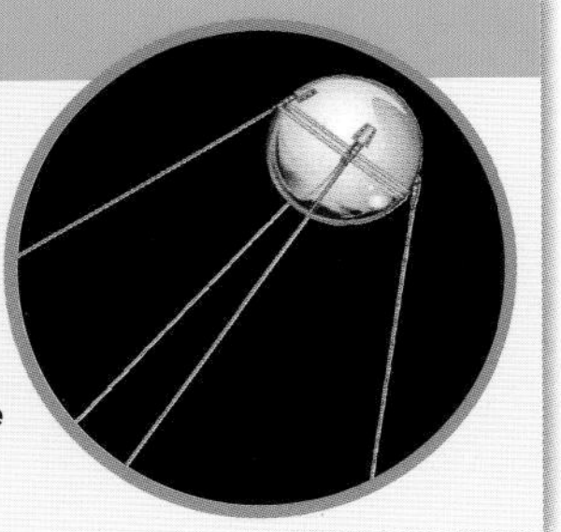

Sputnik 1 was the world's first artificial satellite, sent into orbit by the USSR on 4 October 1957. The word *sputnik* means 'fellow-traveller' in Russian, and the satellite weighed 84 kg and was about the size of a basketball. It took about 96 minutes to orbit Earth on its elliptical path, and transmitted a 'beep-beep' signal for 21 days before the chemical (silver-zinc) batteries ran down. The launch of *Sputnik 1* marked the start of the space age and the battle for dominance in space exploration between the United States and Russia, which was known as the 'space race'.

Satellite speed

The lower a satellite's orbit, the faster it must fly to avoid falling back to Earth. Most satellites fly in low orbits, 500 km above the Earth.

Amazing

Over 6000 satellites have been launched since *Sputnik 1*, by a total of 12 countries including China, France, India, Israel, Japan, Russia, UK and USA.

Satellite orbits

	Earth-observation/ scientific	*Communication/ weather*	*Navigation*
Orbit	Low Earth	Geostationary	Mid Earth
Height	200–2000 km	35,780 km	2000–35,780 km
Speed of satellite	27,000 km/h	11,000 km/h	Variable
Time to orbit Earth	Once every 90 min	Once a day	Variable

Man on the Moon

As the largest object in the night sky, the Moon has held a fascination for humans since the earliest times. It was not until the late 1960s, however, that the technology was developed to send a person to the Moon.

❍ The first unmanned Moon landing was the Soviet probe *Lunar 9*, which touched down on the Moon in 1966.

❍ The first men to orbit the Moon were the astronauts on board the US *Apollo 8* in 1968.

❍ On 20 July 1969 the manned American mission *Apollo 11* landed on the Moon. Astronauts Neil Armstrong and Edwin (Buzz) Aldrin stepped from the *Eagle* landing craft and became the first men ever to walk on the Moon.

❍ When the first astronauts landed on the Moon they found a landscape of cliffs and plains, completely covered in many places by a fine white dust.

❍ Twelve men landed on the Moon between 1969 and 1972.

Space suits protect astronauts outside their spacecraft. The suits are also called EMUs (Extra-vehicular Mobility Units). The outer layers of a space suit protect against harmful radiation from the Sun and bullet-fast particles of spacedust (micrometeoroids). The clear, plastic helmet also protects against radiation and micrometeoroids. Oxygen is circulated around the helmet to stop the visor misting.

❍ The Moon astronauts brought back 380 kg of Moon rock.

❍ A mirror was left on the Moon's surface to reflect a laser beam, which measured the Moon's distance from Earth with amazing accuracy.

❍ Laser measurements showed that, on average, the Moon is 384,467 km away from the Earth.

❍ Gravity on the Moon is so weak that astronauts can leap high into the air wearing their heavy space suits.

❍ Temperatures reach about 110°C at midday on the Moon, but plunge to below –150°C at night.

Apollo 13

On 11 April 1970 the third Apollo mission, *Apollo 13*, blasted off and started its journey to the Moon. However, halfway there disaster struck. A big explosion onboard the spacecraft left the three astronauts with little air or power. Landing on the Moon was out of the question. The problem now was devising a way to get the crew back to Earth. To save energy, they turned the heating off and travelled in the cramped Lunar Module. They had to go round the Moon before they could swing back to Earth, but eventually they landed safely on 17 April.

The 12 men who have walked on the Moon

Neil Armstrong
Edwin 'Buzz' Aldrin
Charles Peter Conrad
Alan Bean
Alan Shepard
Edgar Mitchell
David Scott
James Irwin
John Young
Charles Duke
Eugene Cernan
Harrison Schmitt

An astronaut's footprint left on the Moon will remain there for centuries because there is no wind or erosion to disturb it.

On 20 July 1969 the American astronauts Neil Armstrong and Edwin (Buzz) Aldrin (seen here) became the first people ever to walk on the Moon. When Neil Armstrong stepped on the Moon for the first time, he uttered these now famous words: "That's one small step for man; one giant leap for mankind".

Amazing

Even though only 12 people have walked on the Moon, 24 people have actually travelled to it.

Neil Armstrong

Before becoming an astronaut, Neil Armstrong flew over 78 combat missions over Korea as a Navy fighter pilot, then joined NASA as a civilian test pilot. He was accepted into the astronaut corps in 1962 and piloted the *Gemini 8* mission, launched in 1966. Named commander for the *Apollo 11* mission, he was the first to step onto the Moon's surface.

Apollo missions to the Moon

Mission	*Dates*	*Time on Moon*	*Rock collected*
Apollo 11	16–24 July 1969	22 hours	22 kg
Apollo 12	14–24 November 1969	32 hours	35 kg
Apollo 14	31 January–9 February 1971	34 hours	42 kg
Apollo 15	26 July–7 August 1971	67 hours	78 kg
Apollo 16	16–27 April 1972	71 hours	98 kg
Apollo 17	7–19 December 1971	76 hours	115 kg

The Space Shuttle

The space shuttle was a reusable craft, able to land on a runway and then blast off again on another mission. From the launch of the first shuttle,* Columbia, *in 1981, until the last flight in 2011, astronauts from many countries worked together on missions to launch, repair and retrieve satellites, take photos of Earth and deep space, and carry out experiments.

❍ The space shuttle was made up of a 37.2-m-long orbiter with three main engines, two big solid fuel rockets (SRBs), and a huge fuel tank.

❍ The shuttle orbiter was launched into space upright on the SRBs, which fell away to be collected for reuse. When a mission was over the orbiter landed like a glider.

The biggest problem when launching a spacecraft is overcoming the pull of Earth's gravity. To escape Earth's gravity, a spacecraft must be launched at a particular velocity (speed and direction). A spacecraft cannot use wings to lift it off the ground, as wings only work in the lower atmosphere. Instead, launch rockets must develop a big enough thrust to power them straight upwards, overcoming gravity with a mighty blast of heat. Three rocket engines and two huge booster rockets were used to launch the spacecraft.

❍ The orbiter could only go as high as a near-Earth orbit, some 300 km above the Earth.

❍ The maximum crew was eight, and a basic mission was seven days, during which the crew worked in shirtsleeves.

❍ Orbiter toilets used flowing air to suck away waste.

❍ The orbiter could carry up to a 25,000 kg-load in its cargo bay.

Amazing

The shuttle orbiter was covered with over 24,000 special tiles that protected it from temperatures that could reach 1650°C when it re-entered Earth's atmosphere.

Landing

Unlike other spacecraft, the space shuttle could land like an aeroplane ready to be used again for another mission. The shuttle landed back on Earth on a long runway. It did not use any engines for the landing, unlike an aircraft. It touched down so fast, the pilot used a parachute as well as brakes to stop it on the runway.

Orbiter factfile

Length 37.24 m
Height 17.27 m
Wingspan 23.79 m
Capacity of cargo bay 24,990 kg
Crew size 2–8
Endurance up to 16 days in space
Power 3 main engines plus 44 smaller rockets for orbital manoeuvring
Fuel supercold liquid oxygen and liquid hydrogen
Capacity of external fuel tank over 2 million l
Speed in orbit 28,000 km/h
Maximum landing speed 415 km/h
Cost to build *Endeavour*, built in 1991, cost approximately $1.7 billion

❍ The first four orbiters were named after old sailing ships – *Columbia*, *Challenger*, *Discovery* and *Atlantis*.

❍ The three main engines were used only for lift-off. In space, the small Orbital Manoeuvring System (OMS) engines took over. The Reaction Control System (RCS) made small adjustments to the orbiter's position.

❍ In 1986 the shuttle programme suffered a major setback when the *Challenger* space shuttle exploded shortly after launch, killing its crew of seven. Tragedy struck again in 2003, when the shuttle *Colombia* broke up as it returned from a 16-day mission, killing the seven astronauts on board.

❍ Until shuttle flights ended in 2011, the space shuttle played an important part in the development of the International Space Station (ISS), delivering parts and transporting crew to-and-from the station.

Orbiter goes into orbit around the Earth

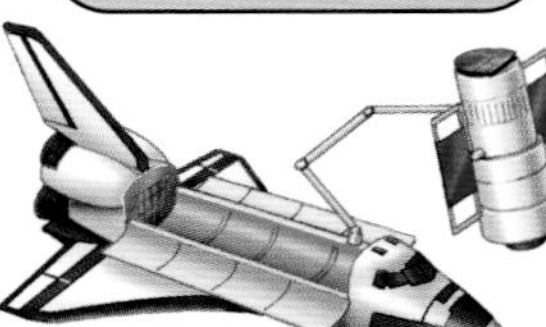

Orbiter crew place satellite in space

Main fuel tank falls away 110 km up

Powerful rockets are needed to boost a spacecraft to the speed it needs to break away from the Earth's gravity. But once it is out in space, these rockets are no longer needed, so spacecraft are launched by a series of rockets or stages that drop away once their task is done and their fuel is spent.

Orbiter positions itself to re-enter the Earth's atmosphere

Solid fuel rocket burners fall away 45 km up

Orbiter lands like a glider

Shuttle blasts off using its own engines and two solid rocket boosters

Cargo bay

The entire centre section of the orbiter was a cargo bay, which could be opened in space so that satellites could be placed in orbit.

Firsts in space

Man in space	Yuri Gagarin	1961
American in space	Alan Shepard	1961
American to orbit the Earth	John Glenn	1962
Woman in space	Valentina Tereshkova	1963
Space walk	Alexei Leonov	1965
American woman in space	Sally Ride	1983
Woman to pilot a spacecraft	Eileen Collins	1995

Space Stations

A space station is a structure designed for human beings to live on in outer space, for periods of weeks, months, or even years. They are used to study the effects of long-term space flight on the human body and to carry out scientific experiments in space. Space stations do not have a major propulsion system and are unable to land back on Earth. Instead, other vehicles are used to transport crew, equipment and supplies to-and-from the station.

The first US space station, **Skylab,** *was launched in 1973. It was visited three times in 1973 and 1974 by crews of three astronauts who spent up to 84 days on board. It stayed in orbit until 1979 when it fell back to Earth.*

- The first space station was the Soviet *Salyut 1*, launched in April 1971. Its low orbit meant it stayed up for only six months.
- The first US space station was *Skylab*. Three crews spent a total of 171 days in it in 1973–1974.
- All the air, food and water that the astronauts need to live on a space station must be supplied regularly by spacecraft from Earth.
- Weightlessness can make an astronaut grow several centimetres taller during a long mission in space.
- There is neither an up nor a down in a space station, but *Mir* had carpets on the 'floor', pictures on the 'wall' and lights on the 'ceiling'.
- Cosmonaut Valery Polyakov spent a record 437 consectutive days in space on board *Mir*.
- The giant International Space Station (ISS) was built between 1998 and 2011. Each part was launched from Earth and added to the station in orbit. It has grown to 108 m long and 73 m wide, almost four times as large as *Mir*.

Mir

Mir was a Russian space station, and the first large station built in orbit. It was launched in 1986 and made more than 86000 orbits of the Earth. The last crew left it in 1999. *Mir* was built in stages. It weighed 130 tonnes and had six docking ports and two living rooms, plus a bathroom and two small cabins. It was crashed into the Pacific Ocean in March 2001.

International Space Station factfile

Length	108 m
Width	73 m
Weight	454 tonnes
Living space	373 m^3 (a bit bigger than a three-bedroom house)
Average altitude	415 km
Average speed	27,724 km/h
Time to orbit Earth	Once every 91 min
Power	Electricity (250 kilowatts) provided by eight giant solar arrays
Crew number	3–7
Crew changeover	Every 90 days
Ground crew	More than 100,000 people in 16 countries

Life on board

Some inhabitants of the *Mir* space station spent more than a year on board. The station experienced power failures and crashes with ferry craft bringing supplies. The large panels shown here are solar cells used to make electricity from sunlight.

Amazing

The ISS travels at 27,700 km/h and completes almost 16 orbits every 24 hours.

Sixteen countries are taking part in the International Space Station project, including the USA, Russia, Japan, Canada, Brazil and other European countries. The 15 separate modules (sections) were fitted together by ISS astronauts using the shuttle's robot arm. With all its sections in place the ISS looks like this as it circles the Earth.

❍ The ISS began with an agreement between the US and Russia to combine their separate planned space stations *Freedom* and *Mir-2*.

❍ A robot arm mounted on the outside of the International Space Station helps astronauts build the space station and keep it in good repair.

❍ The ISS has been occupied since the first crew went aboard in November 2000.

❍ The ISS sinks downwards about 2000 m each month. It has to be pushed back up again using small booster rockets on its visiting spacecraft.

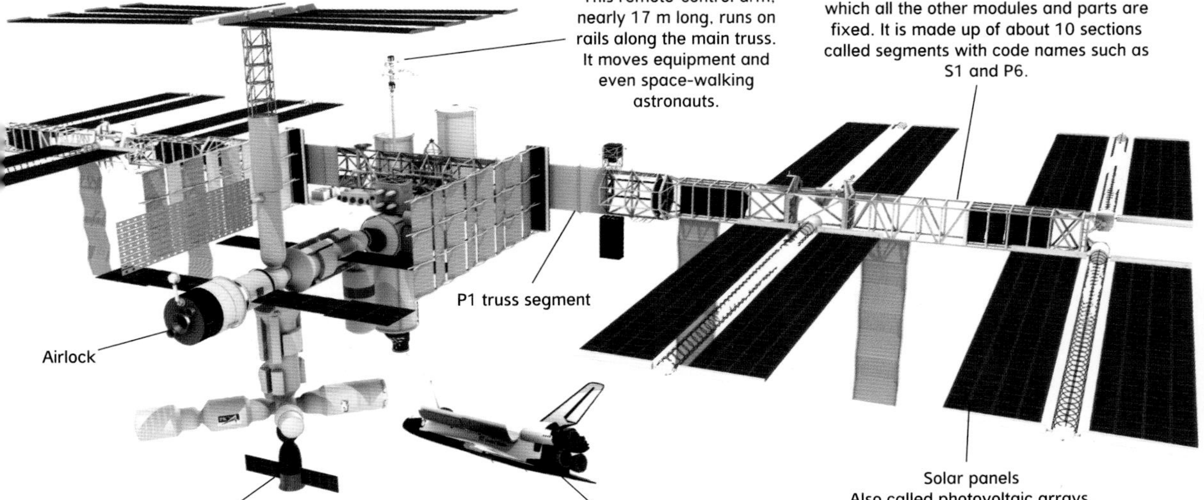

Canadarm2
This remote-control arm, nearly 17 m long, runs on rails along the main truss. It moves equipment and even space-walking astronauts.

Main truss
The truss is the 'backbone' of the ISS to which all the other modules and parts are fixed. It is made up of about 10 sections called segments with code names such as S1 and P6.

P1 truss segment

Airlock

Soyuz
There is always at least one Russian Soyuz spacecraft docked at the ISS as a 'lifeboat' in case of an emergency, such as crew illness. Soyuz takes almost two days to launch and chase after and link onto the station, but it can be back down on Earth in less than four hours.

Space shuttle
Visiting spacecraft join the ISS at docking ports. The connection is airtight so that the crew can enter the ISS through an airlock.

Solar panels
Also called photovoltaic arrays, the solar panels swivel as the ISS orbits so they point at the Sun. Each panel is about 34 m long.

Most experienced in space

Sergei Krikalev	USSR/Russia	803.4 days	6 missions
Sergei Avdeyev	Russia	747.59 days	3 missions
Valery Poliakov	USSR/Russia	678.69 days	2 missions
Anatoli Solovyov	USSR/Russia	651.11 days	5 missions
Aleksandr Kaleri	Russia	609.9 days	3 missions

Glossary

Antimatter Atomic particles that are the exact opposite of normal particles. If a particle meets its antiparticle they cancel each other out releasing huge amounts of energy.

Asteroid Small rocky body circling the Sun usually in a region between Mars and Jupiter called the asteroid belt.

Atmosphere Layer of gas around a planet, moon or star. Usually a mixture of different gases thinning out further from the planet until it merges into space.

Atom The smallest particle of any element that can exist on its own.

Big Bang The event that happened at the beginning of the Universe when time and space began and the Universe started expanding.

Black hole An object that has a pull of gravity so strong that nothing, not even light, can escape so it cannot be seen.

CCD (charge coupled device) A computer chip that can detect light falling on it and convert it into an electrical signal. Telescope cameras use CCDs to produce an image instead of photographic film.

Chromosphere The region of the Sun's atmosphere just above its visible surface made of very hot gas.

Cluster A group of stars or galaxies that are all held together by the pull of gravity between them.

Comet A tiny icy body that circles the Sun in a long thin orbit bringing it from the Solar System edge to swing close by the Sun. Near the Sun it forms a huge glowing tail that astronomers can see.

Constellation A pattern made by stars in the night sky.

Corona The thin outer atmosphere of the Sun made of very hot gas. It can be seen as a glowing halo during an eclipse of the Sun.

Eclipse This happens when one body passes in front of another hiding it from view. During an eclipse of the Sun, the Moon hides the Sun. In an eclipse of the Moon, the Earth blocks the sunlight that would fall on the Moon.

Galaxy A huge family of stars, gas and dust held together by gravity.

Geostationary orbit An orbit above the Earth's Equator where a satellite moves round the Earth at the same pace as the Earth spins. So the satellite appears to stay fixed in the sky always above the same point on the Earth.

Gravity A force that pulls bodies towards each other. The Earth's gravity pulls us all down onto the ground and the Sun's gravity holds everything in the Solar System in orbit around it.

Jet A thin stream of high speed particles and radiation coming from a galaxy, quasar or young star.

Lightyear The distance that light travels in one year, used to measure the vast distances in space. One lightyear is 9.5 million million kilometres.

Local Group of galaxies The small cluster of galaxies that contains the Milky Way galaxy. There are over 30 members, mostly very small.

Magellanic Clouds The two small galaxies closest to the Milky Way galaxy. They are called the Large Magellanic Cloud and the Small Magellanic Cloud. They can be seen from the Southern Hemisphere as faint fuzzy patches.

Meteor A streak of light seen in the night sky when a small piece of space rock burns up in the atmosphere.

Meteorite A space rock that falls to the ground because it is too large to burn up when it hits the atmosphere. A meteorite often forms a crater when it lands.

Meteoroid A small rock speeding through space.

Micrometeoroid A tiny particle of dust speeding through space.

Microwave background radiation Weak radio waves that come from all directions in the sky. Astronomers think this is a residue of the Big Bang.

Milky Way Galaxy The galaxy that the Sun belongs to. It is a spiral galaxy but we see it as a very faint band of light across the sky.

Moon An object that circles round a planet. Most of the planets in the Solar System have moons and the Earth has one, called the Moon.

Near Earth Object An asteroid that does not orbit in the asteroid belt but comes nearer the Sun. Some pass quite close to the Earth.

Nebula A cloud of gas and dust in space where new stars are born. A planetary nebula is a shell of gas thrown off by a dying star. The gas reflects starlight or glows when heated by nearby stars, making the nebula visible through a telescope.

Observatory A place or site where telescopes are built and astronomers study the Universe. They are mostly on mountaintops above the clouds to get a clearer view of the Universe.

Orbit The path of a planet round the Sun, or a moon or satellite round a planet. An orbit can be almost circular like a planet or very long and thin like a comet, or anything in between.

Parsec A measure of distances in space. One parsec is 3.26 lightyears or 31 million million kilometres.

Phases Changing shape of the Moon during a month. As the Moon orbits the Earth we see different amounts of its sunlit side, from a tiny crescent increasing to a whole disc at Full Moon and then back to nothing at New Moon.

Photosphere The surface of the Sun that gives out the heat and light that reaches the Earth. It is hot churning gas with no solid surface.

Planet A large body circling the Sun or another star. Some are small and rocky like the Earth, others are large and made of gas and liquid with no solid surface, like Jupiter.

Planetary rings Flat rings stretching round the equator of a large planet, made of millions of icy or dusty particles all orbiting the planet.

Prominence A huge loop or tail of hot gas reaching out from the Sun's surface. These prominences can last for a few days or months.

Quasar A very bright but very distant object that looks like a star but is probably the centre of a young energetic galaxy.

Radar Radio waves bounced off an object like the surface of a planet to map its landscape.

Radiation Particles or energy like heat or light that travel through space. X-rays, gamma rays, radio waves, infrared and ultraviolet radiation are all types of radiation similar to light.

Radio telescope A telescope that collects radio waves from distant objects in space often using a large metal dish. It produces an image of the Universe as seen in radio waves.

Retrograde Movement along an orbit in a clockwise direction as seen from above, i.e. in the opposite direction to most planets and moons in the Solar System. It also applies to the spin of a planet or moon.

Satellite Anything that circles round another object in space. Moons are called natural satellites. Artificial satellites are manufactured objects usually circling the Earth.

Shooting star A popular name for a meteor.

Singularity A point with temperatures and pressures too enormous for scientists to explain. The Universe is thought to have started from a singularity, and there is a singularity at the centre of a black hole.

Solar System The family of planets, moons, comets and asteroids orbiting the Sun, held together by the Sun's pull of gravity.

Space probe Robot spacecraft sent to explore other planets and moons. A probe can fly past, go into orbit or land on the surface of the planet or moon.

Space shuttle Reusable spacecraft that carried astronauts into Earth orbit or to a space station and returned to Earth for repeat trips.

Space station A home and workplace for astronauts, usually in orbit round the Earth, containing everything needed to keep them alive and well.

Space telescope A telescope launched into space to orbit the Earth or the Sun. Most collect radiation like X-rays that cannot get through the atmosphere to telescopes on the ground.

Star A ball of hot glowing gas. Nuclear reactions in its centre make the energy that it gives out as light and heat.

Sun The nearest star to the Earth, an ordinary star of average size and temperature. It is made mostly of hydrogen and helium, and has many layers. It has a core where its energy is made.

Sun spot A darker area on the Sun, that is cooler than the rest of the surface.

Supernova Explosion of a giant star that has collapsed at the end of its life. It shines very brightly for a short time then may leave a glowing nebula with a tiny neutron star or a black hole at the centre.

Telescope An instrument that collects light or other radiation and forms images of stars, galaxies or nebulae.

Universe Everything that exists out in space and here on Earth.

Weightlessness Floating in space and feeling as if you weigh nothing when in an orbiting space station or shuttle.

PLANET EARTH

The Formation of Earth

The story of the Earth began about 4.54 billion years ago when dust whirling around the newborn Sun started to clump into lumps of rock called planetesimals. Pulled together by their mutual gravity, these planetesimals then clumped together to form the Earth and other planets.

❍ The Solar System was created when the gas cloud left over from a giant supernova explosion started to collapse in on itself and spin.

❍ Clumps of gas and dust formed in the collapsing cloud and grew bigger as gravity pulled more and more gas and dust towards them. A dense mass formed at the centre, which eventually became our Sun. The remaining gas and dust flattened into a rotating disc, later forming the planets.

❍ When the Earth first formed, it was little more than a red-hot ball of churning molten rock.

❍ After 50 million years a giant rock cannoned into the newborn Earth. The impact melted the rock into a hot splash, which cooled to become our Moon.

❍ The Earth was so shaken by the impact that all the elements in it separated. The dense metals, iron and nickel, collapsed to the centre to form the Earth's core.

❍ The molten rock formed a thick mantle about 3000 km thick around the metal core. The core's heat keeps the mantle warm and churning, like boiling porridge.

❍ After about 100 million years the surface of the mantle cooled and hardened to form a thin crust.

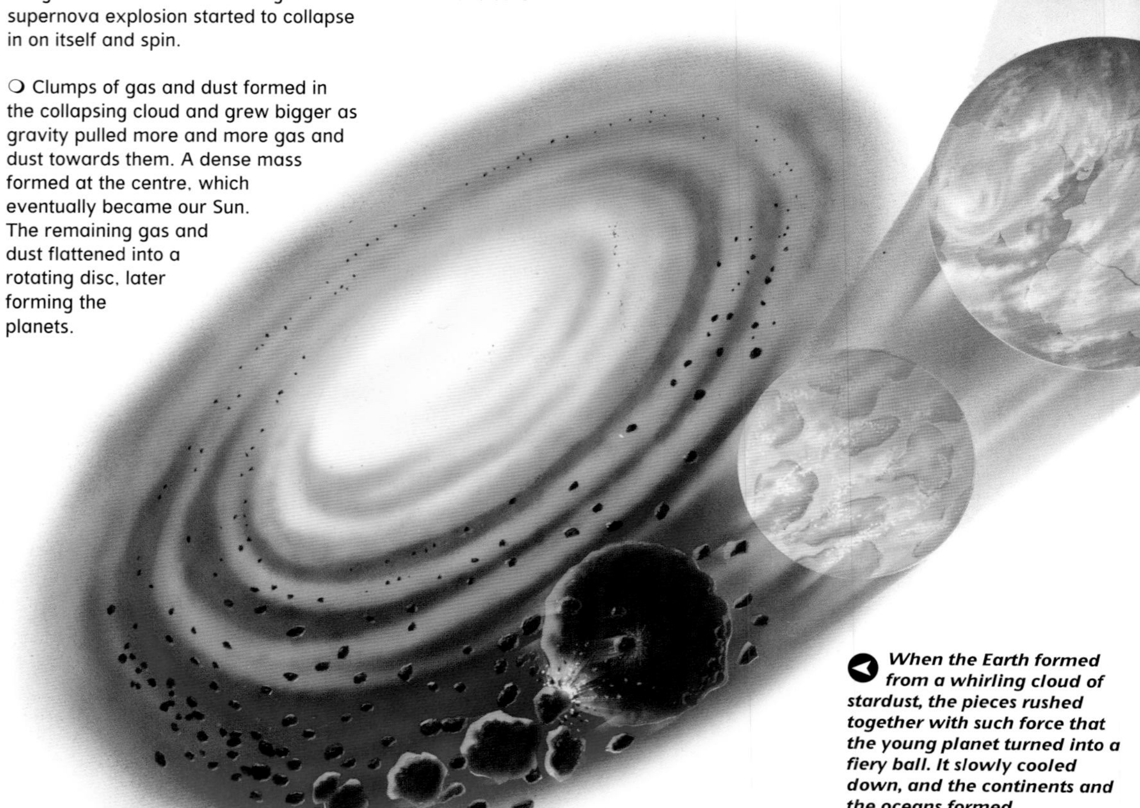

When the Earth formed from a whirling cloud of stardust, the pieces rushed together with such force that the young planet turned into a fiery ball. It slowly cooled down, and the continents and the oceans formed.

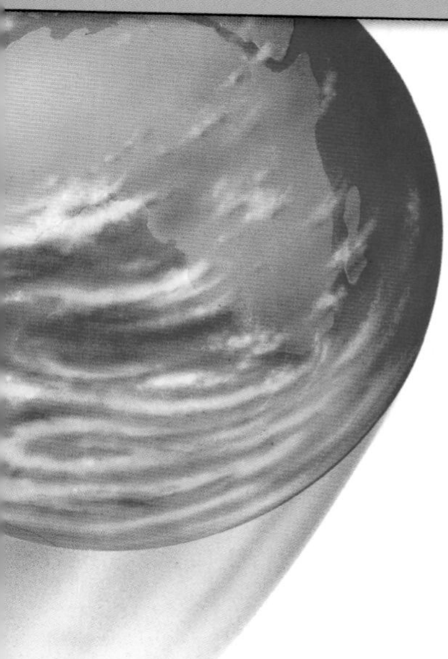

Early volcanoes

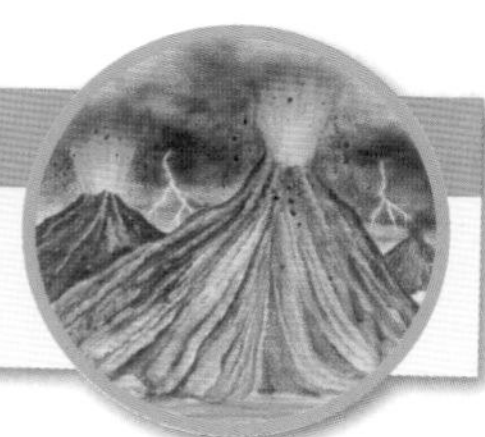

A mass of erupting volcanoes and smoke appeared on the young Earth. Streams of lava (molten rock) turned the Earth's surface into churning, red-hot oceans.

Watery planet

The Earth is unique in the Solar System because it is the only planet with running water on the surface and life. Seen from space, the Earth is a planet of oceans. Only about 29 per cent is land. Earth is home to a huge variety of living things that can only survive here because of all this water.

- An atmosphere containing poisonous gases, such as methane and hydrogen, soon wrapped around the planet, rising from volcanoes on the surface.

- After about 500 million years, the air began to clear as water vapour that had gathered in the clouds fell as rain, to create the oceans.

Amazing

Earth's first atmosphere would have been poisonous to animals. Early microscopic plants gradually converted carbon dioxide gas into oxygen gas for animals to breathe.

History of the Earth

4600 mya	Sun formed
4600–4500 mya	Earth formed
4500 mya	Moon formed
3500 mya	Life appeared in oceans
400 mya	Life started on land
3–2 mya	Humans appeared

mya approximate million years ago

The Moon was also hit by rocks in space. These made huge craters, and mountain ranges up to 5000 m high.

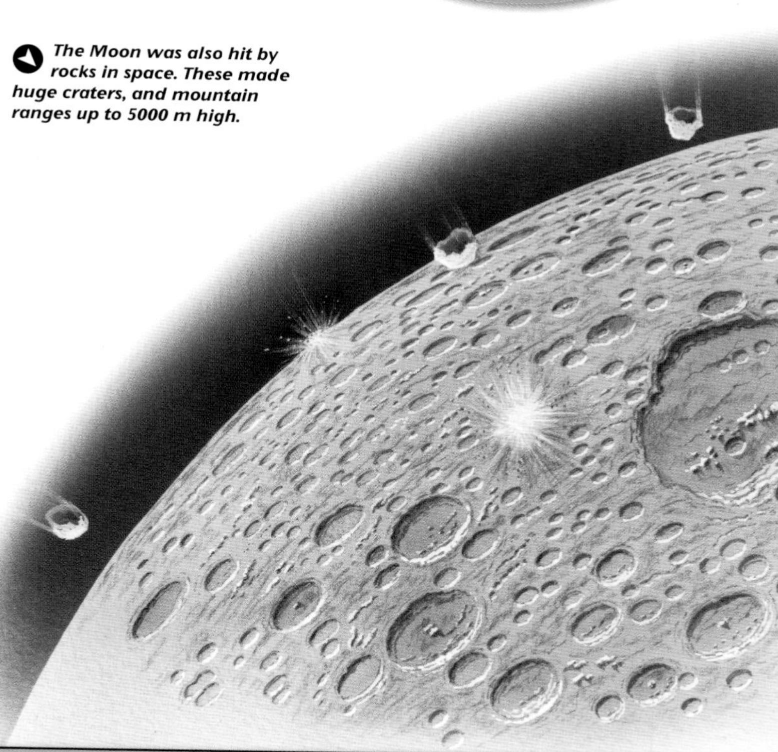

Spinning Earth

Though it seems perfectly still, the Earth is actually spinning around at an average speed of more than 1600 km/h at the Equator. We are unaware of this movement because we are locked firmly to the ground by gravity.

❍ As the Earth spins and whirls through space, the view of the Sun from different places on the Earth is constantly changing, bringing not only day and night but all the seasons, too.

❍ At any one time, half the Earth is facing towards the Sun and is brightly lit, while the other half is facing away from the Sun and is in darkness.

❍ As the Earth turns, the dark and sunlit halves move around the world, bringing day and night to different parts of the world.

❍ Because the Earth turns eastwards, we see the Sun rising in the east as the Earth turns our part of the world towards it, and setting in the west as it turns us away from the Sun.

❍ The Earth turns completely around about once every 24 hours, which is why there are 24 hours in every day.

❍ The Earth does not spin upright, but is tilted at an angle of 23.5°, which always remains the same.

❍ When the Earth is on one side of the Sun, and the Northern Hemisphere (the world north of the Equator) is tilted towards it, it receives more sun, bringing summer.

❍ At the same time, the Southern Hemisphere is tilted away from the Sun, bringing winter.

❍ Six months later when the Earth is on the other side of the Sun, the Northern Hemisphere tilts away from the Sun and so there is less sunlight and it is winter here.

❍ The Southern Hemisphere now gets more heat and light from the Sun and has its summer time.

❍ The part of the Earth close to the Equator is never tilted far away from direct sunlight so it is always hot and there is little change in the seasons.

❍ In between, as the Earth moves around the Sun and neither hemisphere is tilted more towards it, we have spring and autumn.

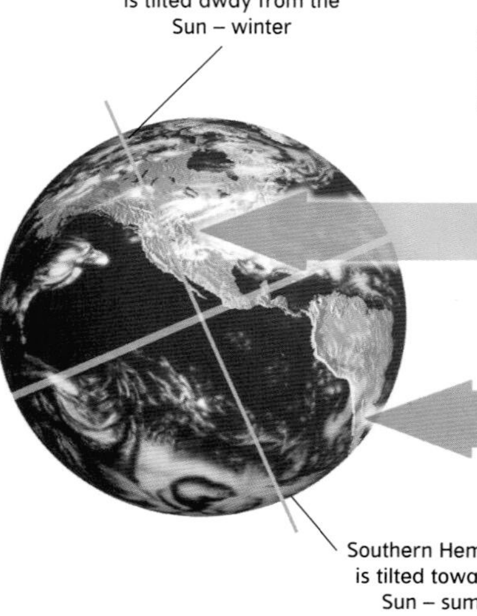

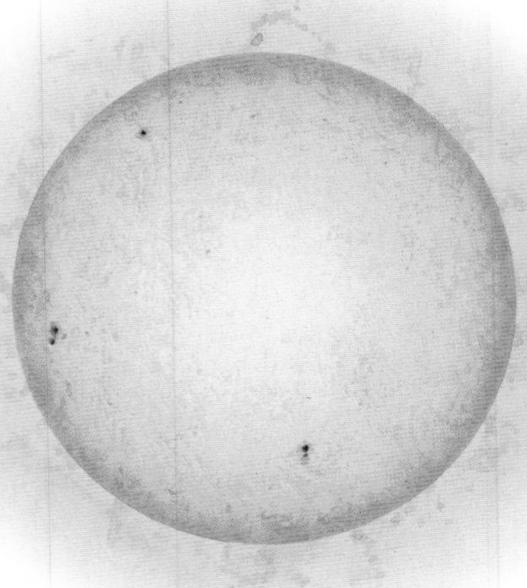

We have different seasons because the Earth is tilted as it spins round.

❍ The Earth takes 0.242 days longer than a calendar year to complete its orbit. To make up for this, an extra day is added to the end of February every four years. This is called a leap year.

Time zones

As the Earth rotates, the Sun rises in one place and sets in another so time is not the same everywhere. So that noon is always at the middle of the day wherever you are, the world is divided into 24 time zones, one for each hour of the day. So at noon in London, it is 7 a.m. in New York. Some countries like Russia are so large that they have several time zones. The western side of Russia can be up to 11 hours different from the eastern side.

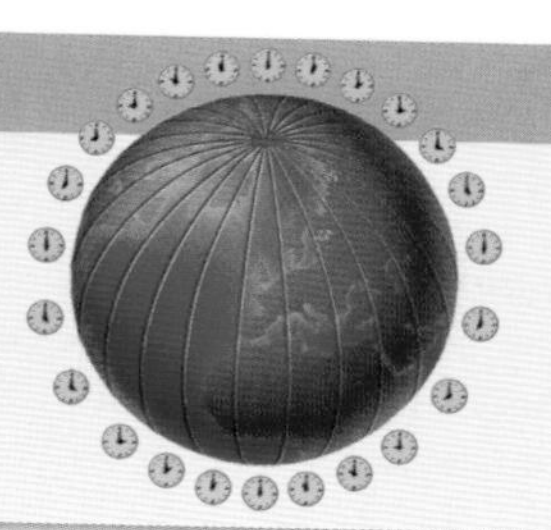

Axis

North Pole

South Pole

❍ Near the North and South poles the Earth's tilt means that the Sun never rises in the middle of winter, and night can last for several weeks.

❍ In the middle of summer at the poles the Sun never sets and there is daylight all the time.

Amazing

The spin of the Earth is very gradually slowing down, but only by less than two thousands of a second in every hundred years.

❍ Around 21 March and 21 September, the night is exactly 12 hours long all over the world. These times are called the vernal (spring) equinox and the autumnal equinox.

The Earth spins on its axis – an imaginary line between the poles.

What's the time?

When it is 12 noon Greenwich Mean Time (GMT) in London, the time in other cities is:

3 p.m.	Moscow, Russia
5 p.m.	Karachi, Pakistan
8 p.m.	Beijing, China
9 p.m.	Tokyo, Japan
10 p.m.	Sydney, Australia
12 a.m.	Auckland, New Zealand
4 a.m.	Los Angeles, USA
6 a.m.	Mexico City, Mexico
7 a.m.	New York, USA
9 a.m.	Buenos Aires, Argentina

Earth speed

As the Earth spins around every 24 hours, places near the poles barely move at all, while places at the Equator whizz around at more than 1600 km/h. The extra speed of the Earth at the Equator flings it out in a bulge.

Ages of the Earth

The Earth was formed 4540 million years ago (mya) but the first animals with shells and bones appeared less than 600 mya. It is mainly with the help of their fossils that geologists have learned about Earth's history. We know very little about the 4000 million years before, known as Precambrian Time.

❍ Just as days are divided into hours and minutes, so geologists divide the Earth's history into time periods. The longest are eons, thousands of millions of years long. The shortest are chrons, a few thousand years long. In between come eras, periods, epochs and ages.

❍ The years since Precambrian Time are split into three eras: Palaeozoic, Mesozoic and Cenozoic.

❍ Different plants and animals lived at different times, so geologists can tell from the fossils in rocks how long ago the rocks formed. Using fossils, they have divided the Earth's history since Precambrian Time into 12 periods. Layers of rock form on top of each other, so the oldest rocks are usually at the bottom and the youngest at the top, unless they have been disturbed. The order of layers from top to bottom is known as the geological column.

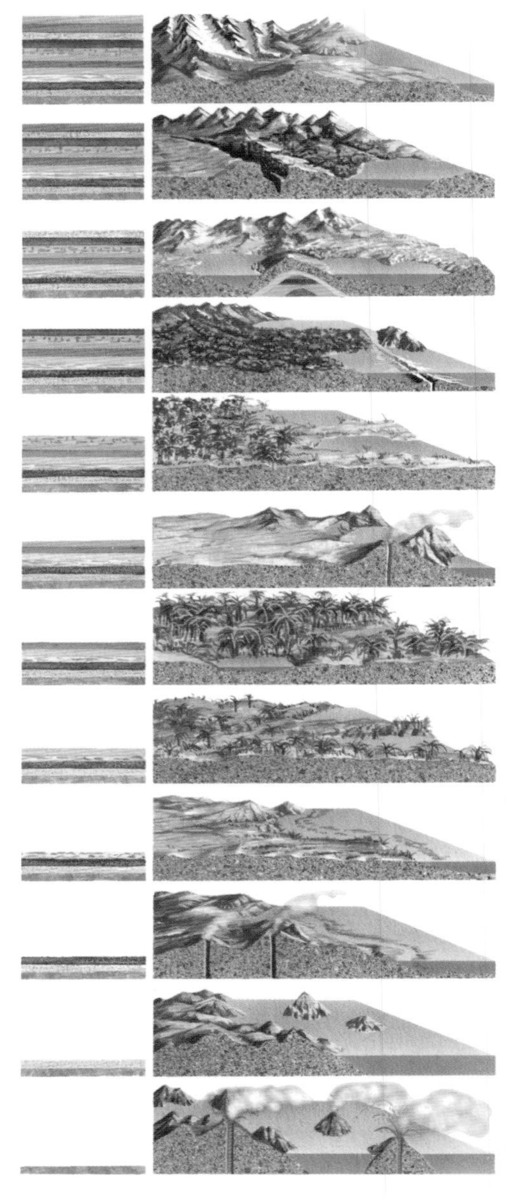

Quaternary 2.6–0 mya
Many mammals die out; humans evolve

Neogene 23–2.6 mya and Paleogene 65.5–23 mya
First large mammals appear; birds thrive; grasslands spread

Cretaceous 145.5–65.5 mya
Dinosaurs die out; first flowering plants

Jurassic 200–145.5 mya
Age of the dinosaurs; some dinosaurs evolve into birds

Triassic 251–200 mya
Mammals and seed-bearing plants appear

Permian 299–251 mya
Conifers appear; many animals die out as deserts spread

Carboniferous 359–299 mya
Reptiles evolve; vast areas of swampy fern forests

Devonian 410–359 mya
Insects and amphibians evolve; ferns and mosses as big as trees

Silurian 435–410 mya
Plants appear on land and fish in rivers

Ordovician 488–435 mya
Sahara is covered in ice; fish-like creatures evolve in the sea

Cambrian 540–488 mya
No life on land but shellfish thrive in the oceans

Precambrian Time before 540 mya
First micro-organisms appear, give atmosphere the oxygen larger animals need to breathe

➤ ***Experts use clues about fossils of particular animals or plants to divide the last 541 million years of the Earth's history into 12 units of time called Periods, each lasting many millions of years.***

Amazing

The earliest evidence of living things on Earth are tiny threadlike fossils in rocks from 3.5 billion years ago, visible only under a microscope.

Megazostrodon ***probably fed like the shrews of today.***

Archaeopteryx ***could probably glide well, swoop and turn as it pursued flying prey, such as dragonflies. However, its long, strong legs suggest that it was also an able walker and runner. So it may have chased victims such as baby lizards and cockroaches on the ground.***

- By looking for certain fossils geologists can tell if one layer of rock is older than another, and so place it within the geological column.
- Fossils can only show if a rock is older or younger than another; they cannot give a date in years. Also, many rocks, such as igneous rocks, contain no fossils. To give an absolute date, geologists may use radiometric dating.
- Radiometric dating allows the oldest rocks on Earth to be dated. After certain substances such as uranium and rubidium form in rocks, their atoms slowly break down into different atoms. As atoms break down they send out rays, or radioactivity. By assessing how many atoms in a rock have changed, geologists work out the rock's age.
- Breaks in the sequence of the geological column are called unconformities. They help to create a picture of the geological history of an area.

Indricotherium ***was three times bigger than elephants of today.***

The ammonite's body was covered by a spiral shell. The body rotted while the shell became a fossil.

Inside the Earth

The Earth is not a solid ball. Vibrations from earthquakes and volcanic explosions have revealed a complex internal structure. The Earth's crust rests on a layer of hot, partly molten rock called the mantle, which in turn surrounds the two cores, one inside the other.

The main layers inside the Earth from the boiling hot core to the hard rocky surface.

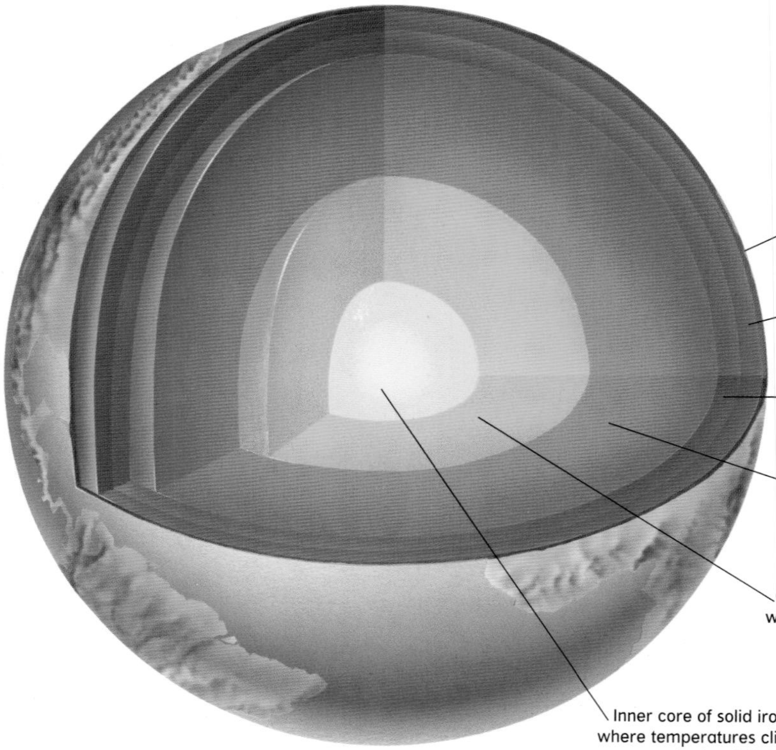

❍ The Earth's crust is a thin hard outer shell of rock which is a few dozen kilometres thick. Its thickness in relation to the Earth is about the same as the skin on an apple.

❍ There are two kinds of crust: oceanic and continental.

❍ Oceanic crust is the crust beneath the oceans. It is much thinner – just 7–10 km thick on average. It is also young, with none being more than 200 million years old.

❍ Continental crust is the crust beneath the continents. It is up to 50 km thick and mostly old.

❍ The mantle makes up the bulk of the Earth's interior. It reaches from about 10–90 km to 2950 km down.

❍ Temperatures in the mantle climb steadily as you move through the mantle, reaching over 4000°C.

❍ Mantle rock is so warm that it churns slowly round like very, very thick treacle boiling on a stove. This movement is known as mantle convection currents. Beneath the mantle is a core of hot iron and nickel. The outer core is so hot – climbing from an amazing 4500°C to 5900°C – that it is always molten. The inner core is about 5400°C but it stays solid because the pressure is 6000 times greater than on the surface.

Hot material from the Earth's interior often bursts onto the surface from volcanoes.

Earth's weight

The inner core contains 1.7% of the Earth's mass, the outer core 30.8%; the core-mantle boundary 3%; the lower mantle 49%; the upper mantle 15%; the ocean crust 0.099% and the continental crust 0.374%.

Earthquake waves

Our knowledge of the Earth's interior comes mainly from studying how earthquake waves vibrate right through the Earth. Analysis of how earthquake waves are deflected reveals where different materials occur in the interior. S (secondary) waves pass only through the mantle. P (primary) waves pass through the core as well. P waves passing through the core are deflected, leaving a shadow zone where no waves reach the far side of the Earth. Love, or Q, waves shake the ground from side to side in a jerky movement. Rayleigh, or R, waves shake the ground up and down, often making it seem to roll.

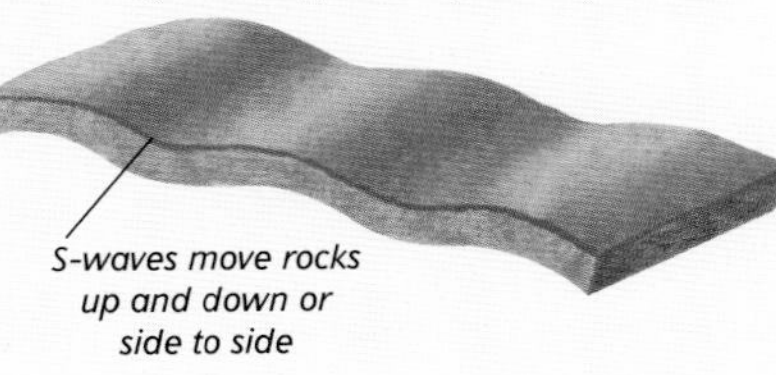

S-waves move rocks up and down or side to side

Amazing

In 1989 scientists in Russia drove one of the deepest boreholes into the Earth's crust. It was 12,261 m deep. The temperature of the rocks at the bottom was 180°C.

❍ The only time we see the hot molten rock of the mantle is when it bursts out through the crust in a volcanic eruption.

❍ Hot spots are places on Earth's crust where the hot mantle rock wells up nearer to the surface and breaks through to form volcanoes.

Rocks

Rocks are the hard mass of the Earth's surface. Some are just a few million years old, while others formed almost 4 billion years ago. They are always changing as new rock forms and old rocks wear away.

❍ There are three main kinds of rock: igneous rock, sedimentary rock and metamorphic rock.

❍ Igneous rocks are formed from molten rock called magma, deep inside the Earth.

❍ At over 1000°C, magma is so hot that it is molten rock. It is also crushed by enormous pressure. When magma gets pushed to the surface by volcanic action it becomes lava and cools to form igneous rocks.

❍ Sedimentary rocks such as shale and sandstone are made by the action of wind and water, which grind other rocks into sand and mud, carried by rivers until they are deposited as sediments.

❍ Sediment piles up in layers, and is squeezed hard by the pressure of layers on top, until it becomes rock.

❍ Metamorphic rocks are formed when other rocks are changed by extreme heat and pressure (but not melted), such as limestone, which nearby hot magma turns to marble.

❍ Limestone and chalk are sedimentary rocks made mainly from the remains of sea creatures. All rocks are made of tiny crystals or grains of naturally occurring chemicals called minerals. Some rocks are made from just one mineral; others contain six or more.

❍ There are more than 2000 different kinds of mineral, but only 30 or so occur commonly.

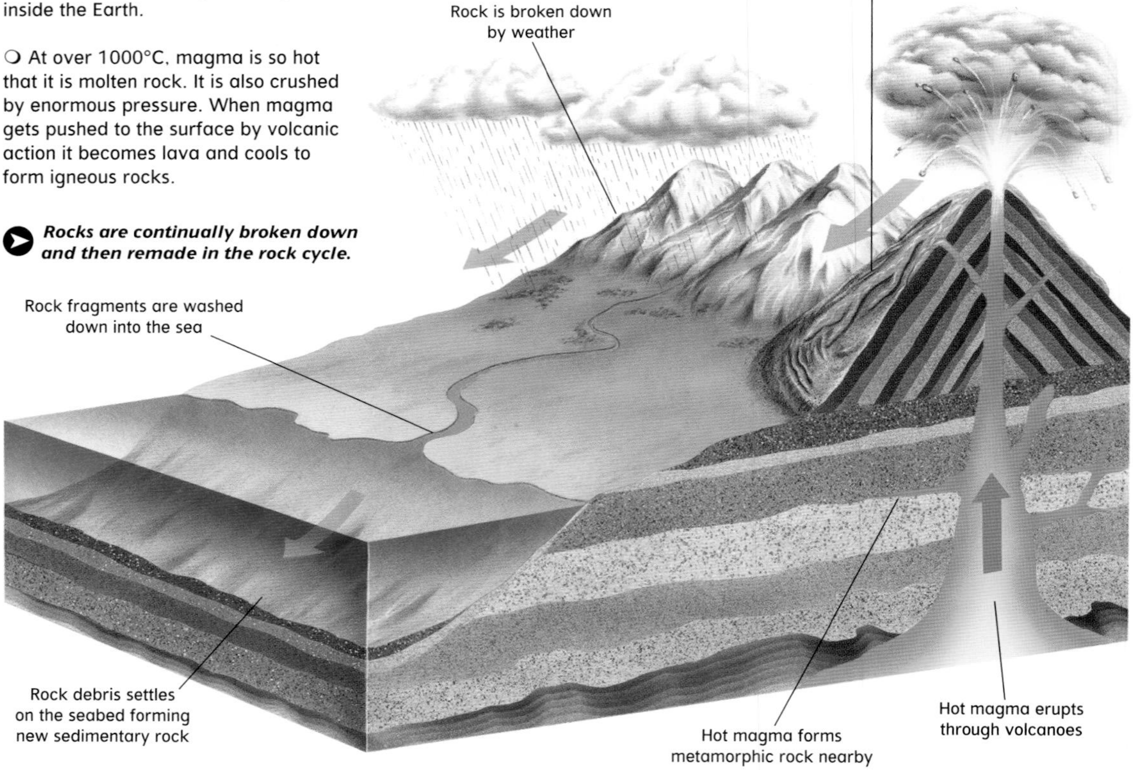

Lava cools to form igneous rock

Rock is broken down by weather

Rocks are continually broken down and then remade in the rock cycle.

Rock fragments are washed down into the sea

Rock debris settles on the seabed forming new sedimentary rock

Hot magma forms metamorphic rock nearby

Hot magma erupts through volcanoes

Rock cycle

Rocks are continually recycled. Whether they form from volcanoes or sediments, all rocks are broken down into sand by weathering and erosion.The sand is deposited on seabeds and riverbeds where it hardens to form new rock. This process is the rock cycle.

Most chalk was formed at the time of the dinosaurs but chalk is still forming in some places today.

The rich range of colours in each layer is evidence of traces of different minerals within the rocks. Many minerals found in rocks contain useful materials like metals.

Scientists study the Earth's history to understand how it has changed, and is still, as natural forces reshape it.

Chemical elements

Most of the Earth is made from just four chemical elements: iron, oxygen, silicon and magnesium. Much of its rocky crust is made from combinations of two of these elements: oxygen and silicon, known as silicates. But there are small quantities of many other elements, such as aluminium and calcium.

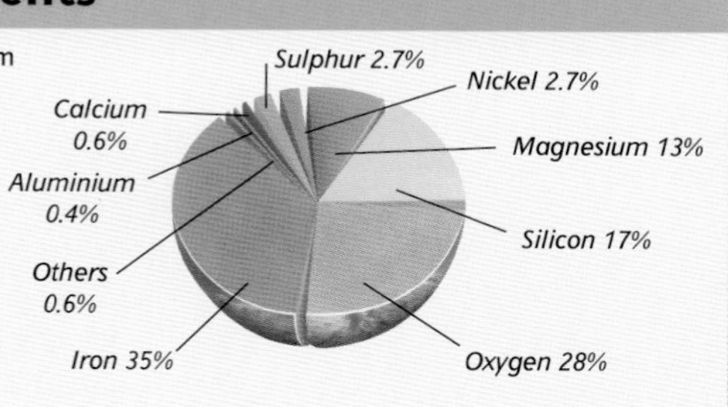

Amazing

The oldest rocks found on Earth are just over four billion years old, discovered in Canada. Some older crystals of zircon, 4.4 billion years old, have been discovered in Western Australia.

Gemstones

The Earth is full of natural riches. Most metals are found in rocks called ores – mixtures of different substances, of which metal is one. Beautiful crystals grow in lava bubbles. There are more than 100 kinds of gemstone – coloured rocks that are cut and polished. Gems, such as topaz, emerald and garnet, formed in hot rocks that rose to the Earth's crust and cooled. Most are found as small crystals. Some are associated with different months of the year and are known as 'birthstones'.

Silver forms branching wires in rock. It does not shine in its natural state like jewellery, but is covered in a black coating called tarnish.

Quartz is a very common mineral. Occasionally it forms beautiful purple amethyst. Minute traces of iron in the rock turn the quartz to amethyst.

This is bauxite, which is the ore of aluminium. Heat, chemicals and electricity are used to get the metal out of the rock. Aluminium is used to make all kinds of things, from kitchen foil to aeroplane parts.

A number of colour varieties of beryl are known, many of which are gemstones. Emerald is the rich green variety of beryl, heliodor is yellow, morganite is a pink form and aquamarine is greenish-blue.

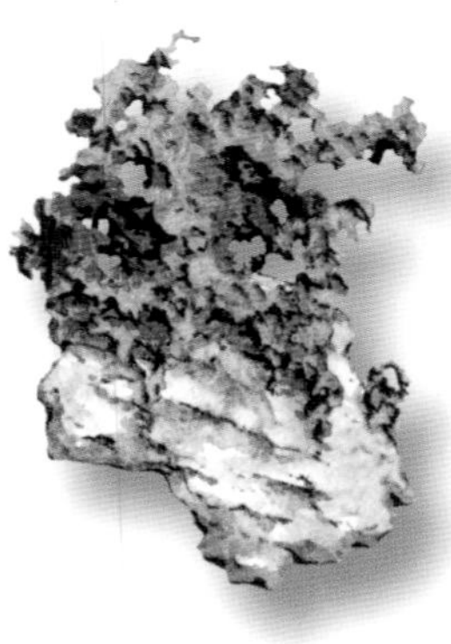

Gold forms in small grains or large nuggets or veins in rocks. It can be melted and moulded to form all kinds of jewellery.

Gemstones

Name	*Type*	*Hardness*	*Colour*
Diamond	Carbon	10	Colourless
Ruby	Corundum	9	Red
Sapphire	Corundum	9	Blue
Emerald	Beryl	7.5–8	Green
Aquamarine	Beryl	7.5–8	Greenish-blue
Garnet	Garnet	6.5–7.5	Dark red
Jade	Jade	6.5–7	Green
Lapis lazuli	Lapis lazuli	5–6	Deep blue
Opal	Opal	5.5–6.5	Milky white, blue or green
Peridot	Peridot	6.5–7	Olive green
Amethyst	Quartz	7	Purple, violet
Topaz	Topaz	8	Yellow, brown
Tourmaline	Tourmaline	7–7.5	Pink, green + wide range
Zircon	Zircon	7.5	Green, brown
Turquoise	Turquoise	5–6	Blue-green
Amber	Fossilized resin	2–2.5	Orange, brown
Pearl	Oyster shells	3–4	White, cream, black

Amazing

Quartz is thought to have great healing properties. This may stem from its ability to vibrate consistently. A perfect quartz crystal can allow meditation at a deep level.

Birthstones

For nearly 2000 years, crystals and precious stones have been linked with months of the year. Different religious and cultural groups have associated different stones with different months. Those popular in western culture today are shown here, together with their different characteristics. According to tradition, a person's birthstone brings them good luck. Gemstones also correspond to the signs of the Zodiac, although the birth dates for each month do not exactly match the beginning and end of each month. Birthstones may originate from a story in the Bible about Aaron, first high priest of the Israelites, whose breastplate is described as being decorated with 12 precious stones.

January, Garnet, Constancy

February, Amethyst, Sincerity

March, Aquamarine, Courage

April, Diamond, Innocence

May, Emerald, Love

June, Pearl, Health

July, Ruby, Contentment

August, Peridot, Married happiness

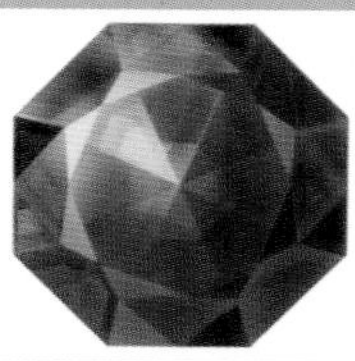

September, Sapphire, Clear thinking

October, Opal, Hope

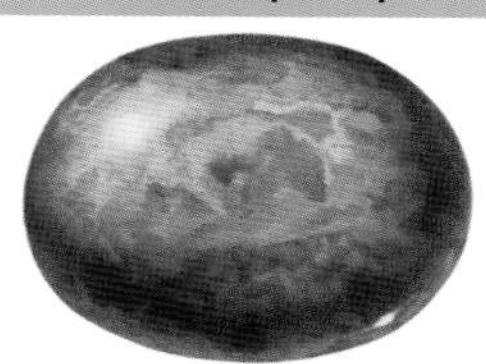

November, Topaz, Faithfulness

December, Turquoise, Wealth

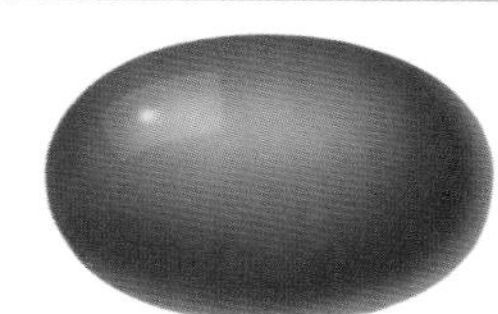

Fossils

Fossils are the remains of once-living things that have been preserved in rocks and turned to stone, usually over millions of years. Many kinds of living things from prehistoric times have formed fossils, including mammals, dinosaurs and birds, lizards, fish, insects and plants such as ferns and trees.

➤ ***Fossils usually form when animal remains are quickly covered by sediments, such as sand, silt or mud, especially along the bank of a river or lake, on the seashore or on the sea bed.***

❍ When an animal dies, its soft parts rot away quickly. If its bones or shell are buried quickly in mud, they may turn to stone over time.

❍ When a shellfish dies and sinks to the seabed, its shell is buried. Over millions of years, water trickling through the mud may dissolve the shell, but minerals in the water fill its place to make a perfect cast.

❍ Fossil formation is a very long process and extremely prone to chance and luck. Only a tiny fraction of animals that ever lived have left remains preserved by this process.

❍ Because of the way fossils are formed, animal remains located in water or along banks and shores were most likely to become fossilized.

❍ It is very rare to find all parts of an animal arranged as they were in life. Much more often, parts have been separated, jumbled, broken, crushed and distorted.

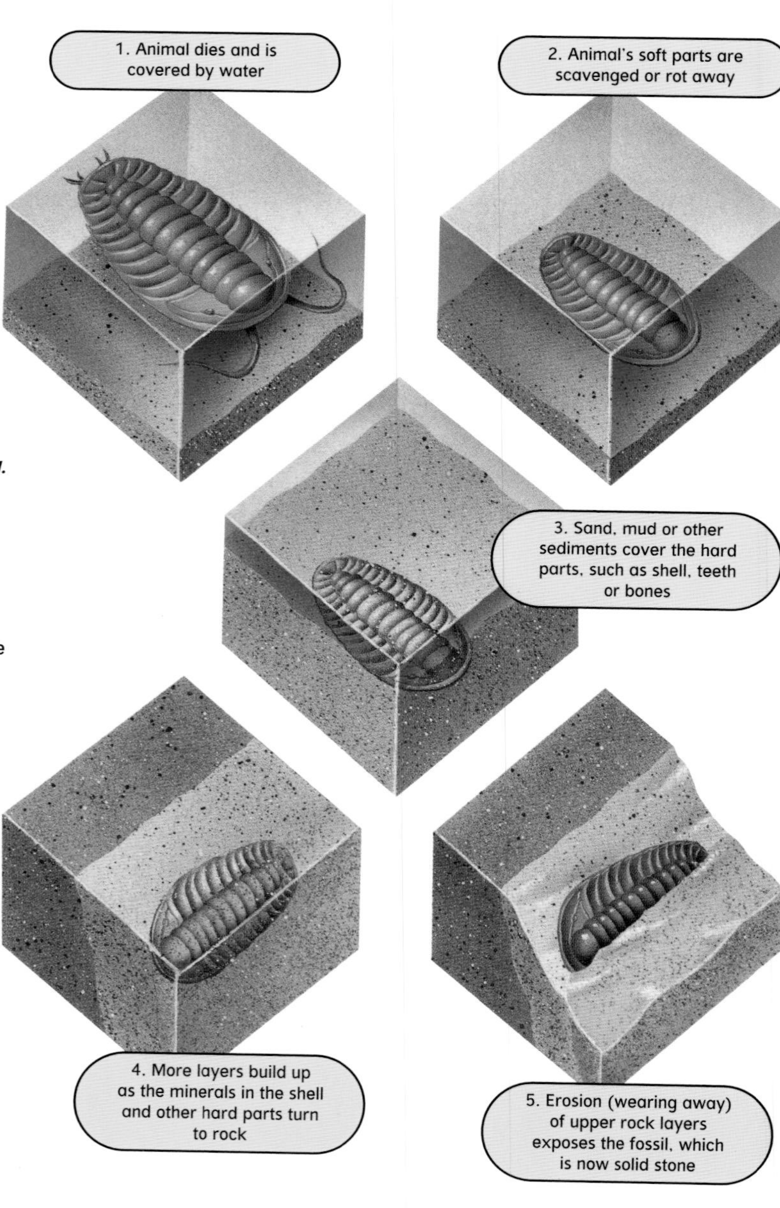

❍ Many insects have been preserved in amber, the solidified resin of ancient trees.

❍ Certain widespread, short-lived fossils are very useful for dating rock layers. These are known as index fossils. They include ancient shellfish such as trilobites, belemnites, ammonites and brachiopods, also graptolites and crinoids.

This fossil ammonite is a mollusc that swam in prehistoric seas. The soft body parts decayed millions of years ago but the impression of the animal's shell is preserved.

Fossilized footprints

Thousands of fossilized animal footprints have been found all over the world. Some animals left footprints when they walked on the soft mud or sand of riverbanks. Then the mud baked hard in the sun, and was covered by more sand or mud, which helped preserve the footprints as fossils. Some fossil footprints were made when animal feet left impressions in soft mud or sand that was then covered by volcanic ash, which set hard. The relative positions of footprints indicate how an animal stood or moved.

❍ 'Trace' fossils were not actual parts of bodies, but other items or signs of their presence. Trace fossils include egg shells, footprints and marks made by claws and teeth.

❍ Not all fossils are composed of stone. Mammoths have been preserved by being frozen in the permafrost of Siberia.

Fossil of a* Tyrannosaurus rex *skull, a dinosaur that lived on Earth about 66–70 million years ago.

Amazing

Some of the largest dinosaur footprints were found near Salt Lake City in the USA. They are 1.36 m long and 81 cm wide.

Fossil discoveries

Sometimes scientists find a whole skeleton, which can be removed bone by bone and carefully reconstructed for scientific analysis or exhibition.

Continents

Emerging above the Earth's oceans are seven masses of land. These are the continents of North and South America, Oceania, Antarctica, Africa, Asia and Europe. The continents are made of very old rocks, dating back some 3800 million years.

❍ Africa is a vast, warm, fairly flat continent covered in savannah, desert and tropical forest.

❍ Africa is the world's warmest continent. It lies almost entirely within the tropics or subtropics. The very hot temperatures in the Sahara Desert are among the highest on Earth, often soaring to over 50°C.

❍ Oceania is a vast region that includes islands spread over much of the Pacific Ocean as well as Australia and New Zealand. Australia is the only large land mass in Oceania.

❍ Oceania is mostly tropical, with temperatures averaging 30°C in the north of Australia, and slightly lower on the islands where the ocean keeps the land cool.

❍ Europe is one of the smallest continents, with an area of just 10,200,000 sq km. For its size Europe has an immensely long coastline. Europe is joined to Asia and some people think that they should be one continent, Eurasia.

❍ North America is the oldest continent on Earth. It has rocks that are almost 4000 million years old.

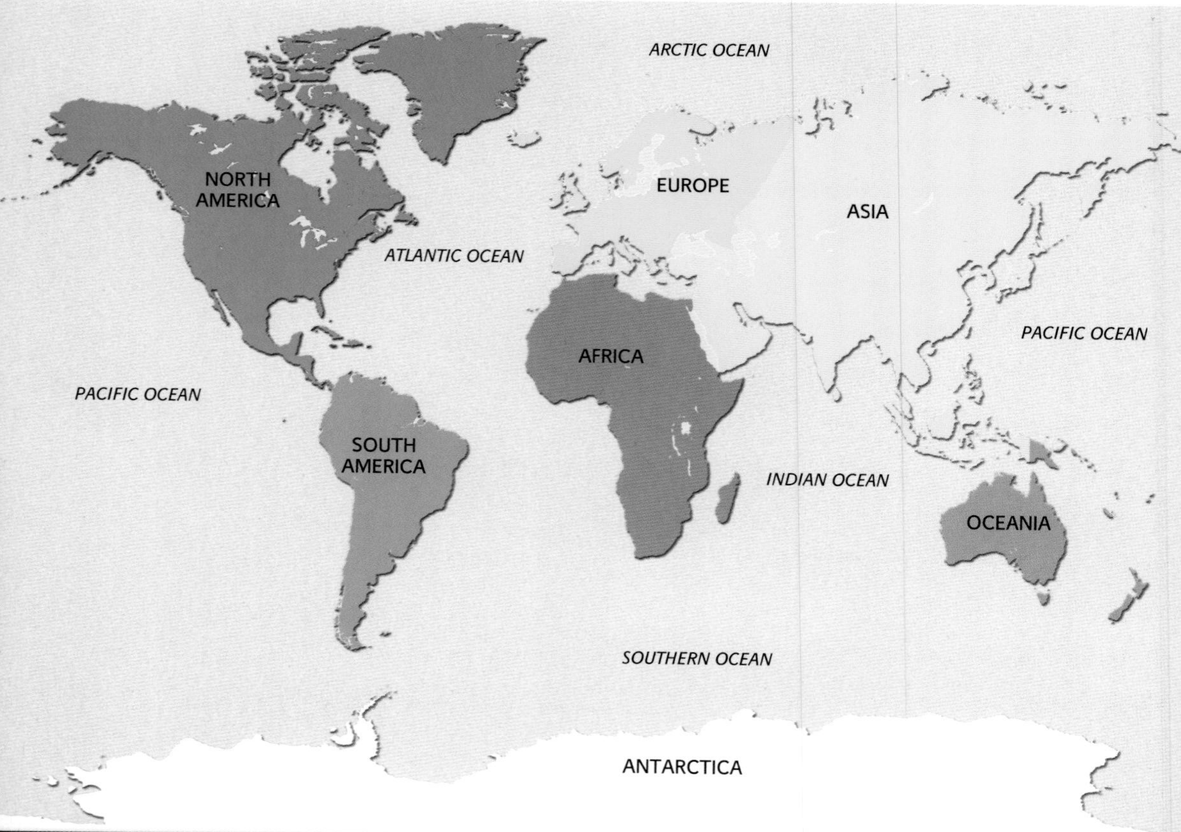

The seven continents include Antarctica, which has land beneath its thick ice, but not the Arctic, which is mostly frozen ocean.

❍ The north of North America lies inside the Arctic Circle and is icebound for much of the year. Death Valley, in the southwestern desert in California and Nevada, is one of the hottest places on the Earth.

❍ The heart of South America is the vast Amazon rainforest around the Amazon River and its tributaries. No other continent reaches so far south. South America extends to within 1000 km of the Antarctic Circle.

Asia

Asia is by far the biggest continent. The total land area of Asia is 44 million sq km, which is four times bigger than Europe and nearly twice as big as North America. Asia includes the biggest country by land area (Russia) and the two biggest by population (China and India).

Many penguins such as the emperor, the world's largest penguin, live on the ice floes of the Southern Ocean. Antarctica is so cold that few land animals live there, only sea creatures like penguins.

This tree in the Namib Desert of southwestern Africa manages to survive, even growing in such a hostile, dry environment.

Antarctica

Antarctica is the ice-covered continent at the South Pole. It is the coldest place on Earth. Even in summer, temperatures rarely climb over –25°C. On 21 July 1983, the air at the Vostok science station plunged to –89.2°C. Antarctica is also one of the driest places on Earth, with barely any rain or snow. It is also very windy. Antarctica does not belong to any one nation. Under the Antarctic Treaty of 1959, 12 countries agreed to use it only for scientific research.

Amazing

The continents are made of very old rock, some over 4000 million years old. They are much older than the rocks that are found underneath the oceans.

The spectacular Iguacu Falls lie on the border between Brazil and Argentina in South America. Water thunders over 275 falls cascading 82 m down into a gorge formed 100 million years ago. The horseshoe shape of the Falls is 3 km wide.

The seven continents

Asia	44,500,000 sq km
Africa	30,200,000 sq km
North America	24,700,000 sq km
South America	17,800,000 sq km
Antarctica	14,000,000 sq km
Europe	10,200,000 sq km
Oceania	8,500,000 sq km

Islands

Islands are made in different ways. Some are the tops of undersea mountains or volcanoes. Others, such as the British Isles, were once part of a large landmass, but became surrounded by sea when the water level rose.

❍ A chain of islands is called an archipelago. The world's biggest archipelago is Indonesia, with more than 13,000 islands.

❍ New islands can appear out of the sea. Surtsey Island off Iceland rose from the waves following a volcanic eruption as recently as 1963.

Surtsey Island, off Iceland, grew to a height of 170 m in three years as lava and ash from repeated volcanic eruptions piled up above sea level.

❍ Reefs are made from the bodies of millions of tiny coral animals. In warm seas they often form rings around small islands.

❍ Coral is the skeletons of tiny sea animals called polyps. Some larger polyps can grow to be 10 cm across.

❍ A coral reef is a rich habitat for wildlife. It provides food and shelter for all kinds of tropical fish.

❍ There are thousands of tiny islands in the Pacific Ocean. Many are ringed by coral reefs.

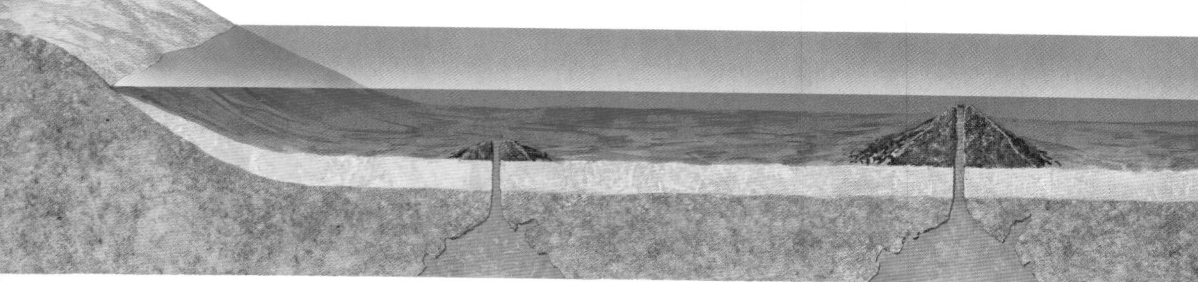

When volcanoes erupt under the sea, new islands may appear.

Molten rock breaks through Earth's crust

As more lava is deposited on the seabed, a cone shape builds up

5 largest islands in the world

Greenland	Atlantic/Arctic Ocean	2,130,000 sq km
New Guinea	Pacific Ocean	786,000 sq km
Borneo	South China Sea	748,000 sq km
Madagascar	Indian Ocean	588,000 sq km
Baffin	Arctic Ocean	507,000 sq km

▲ ***Sometimes a volcanic island sinks, and all that is left is a ring of coral, called an atoll.***

Great Barrier Reef

The biggest coral reef on Earth is the Great Barrier Reef off eastern Australia. It is 2000 km long, and is made from over 400 different corals. The reef has taken more than 2 million years to form.

Amazing

One of the newest islands on Earth is Niijima near Japan, which appeared in the Pacific Ocean in 2013.

When this breaks the water's surface, a new island appears. The volcano may go on erupting

Greenland

The biggest island in the world is Greenland, at 2670 km long and 1210 km wide. It is owned by Denmark, but is 50 times bigger. Greenland is 85 per cent covered by ice and has very little greenery!

▶ ***The Indian Ocean is scattered with thousands of tropical islands such as the Seychelles and Maldives. Many of the Indian Ocean's islands have shining coral beaches.***

Different types of islands

Volcanic islands	Islands that appear when an undersea volcano grows tall enough to emerge above the surface of the sea
Archipelago	Group of islands close together or an area of the ocean that has many islands in it
Coral islands	Islands in warm tropical waters that have built up from coral reefs
Freshwater islands	Islands in inland lakes or rivers where the water is fresh, rather than salty

Drifting Continents

Slowly, slowly, the Earth's surface is moving around beneath our feet. About 220 million years ago (mya) all the world's continents were joined together in one huge landmass that geologists call Pangaea. Pangaea gradually split up into today's continents.

The continents drifted to where they are today (continental drift) and are still moving.

❍ Continental drift is the name for the slow movement of the continents around the world.

❍ It is not just the continents that are moving. The ocean beds are also moving. In fact, the whole of the Earth's surface is on the move.

❍ The Earth's crust is made of curved rocky plates, which float like pieces of gigantic jigsaw on the molten layer of hot rocks in the mantle.

Amazing

Scientists know that the continents were once all joined up because identical fossils of prehistoric plants and reptiles have been found in Africa, India, South America and Antarctica. These continents have now moved away from each other to form separate continents.

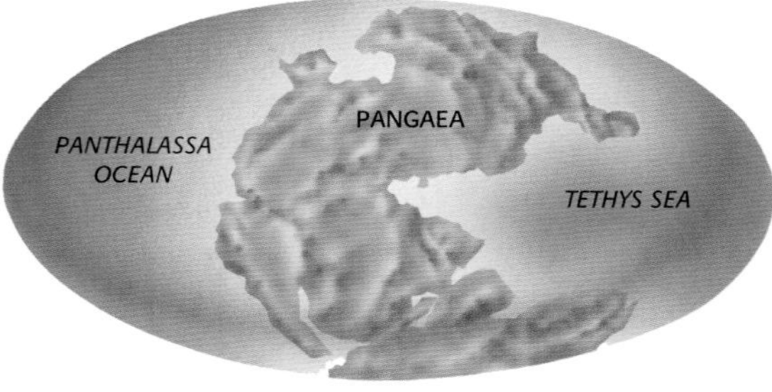

220 million years ago (mya)
There was just one giant land mass, called Pangaea (meaning 'all Earth'), and one giant ocean, known as Panthalassa. But a long arm of the ocean, the Tethys Sea, stretched into the heart of Pangaea

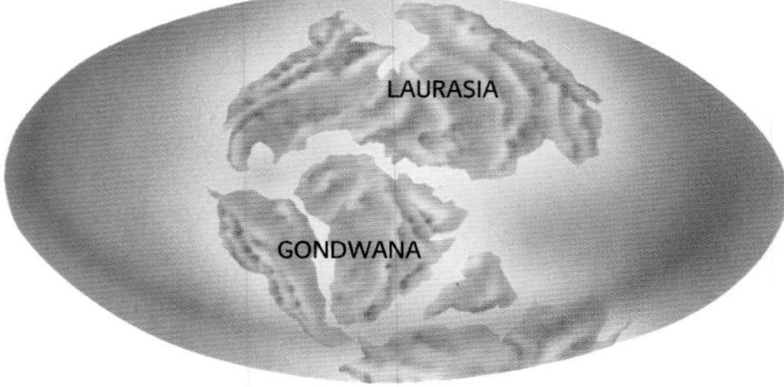

190 mya
Pangaea split either side of the Tethys Sea. To the north was Laurasia, including North America, Europe and most of Asia. To the south was Gondwana, including South America, Africa, Australia, Antarctica and India

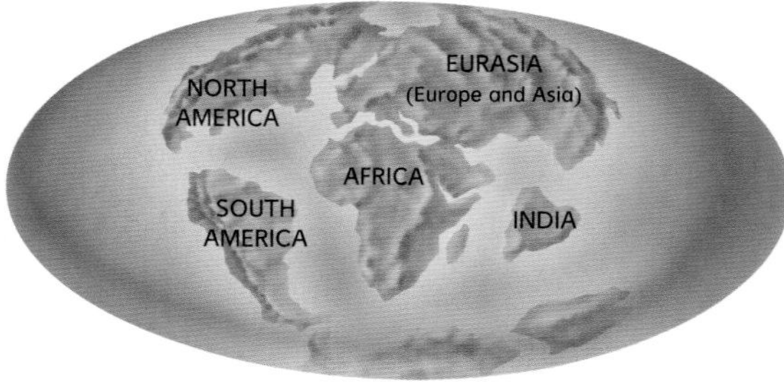

135 mya
The South Atlantic Ocean opened up between the continents of Africa and South America. India broke off from Africa and drifted towards Asia. Europe and North America were still joined

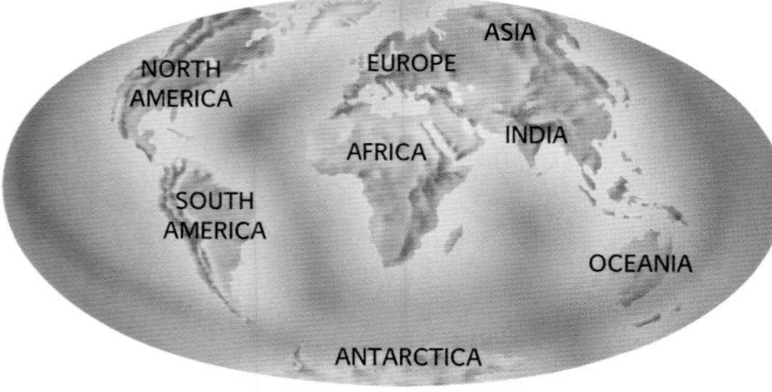

Today
North America and Europe are widely separated, having split 60 mya. India has crunched into Asia, Australia is moving into the tropics and Antarctica has moved to the South Pole

❍ Over millions and millions of years, the continents that rest on top of these plates also move.

❍ There about 10 large plates and some 20 smaller ones, and they move very slowly (between 1 and 10 cm every year) on currents circulating within the mantle.

❍ Strong evidence of continental drift has come from similar ancient fossils found in separate continents, such as the *Glossopteris* fern found in both Australia and India; the Diadectid insect found in Europe and North America; and *Lystrosaurus*, a tropical reptile from 200 million years ago, found in Africa, India, China and Antarctica.

Tectonic plates

In some places, tectonic plates are crunching together. Where this happens, one of the plates – typically the one carrying a continent – rides over the other and forces it down into the Earth's interior. This process is called subduction. Where one plate dives beneath the other, there is often a deep trench in the ocean floor.

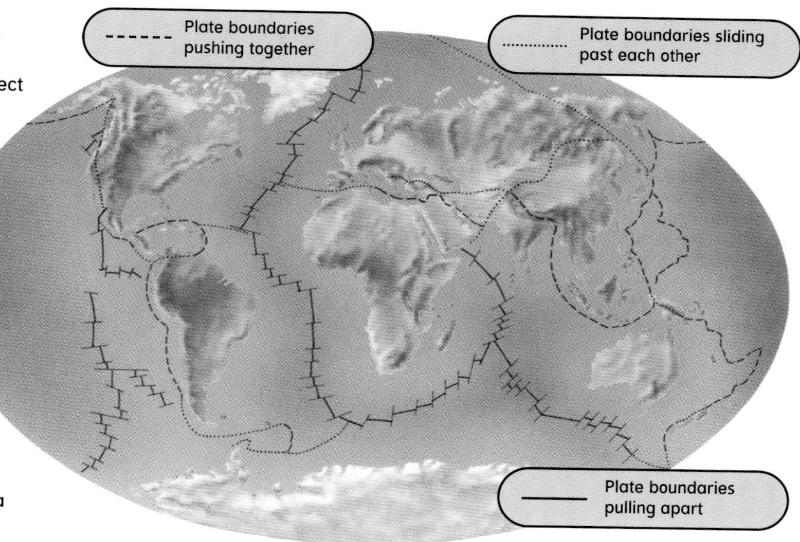

The jagged boundaries between the plates of the Earth's surface. Along these boundaries where the plates push together or slide past each other earthquakes and volcanoes occur.

❍ Rates of continental drift vary. India drifted north into Asia very quickly. South America is moving 20 cm farther from Africa every year. On average, continents move at about the same rate as a fingernail grows.

❍ Some tectonic plates have moved so far, they have travelled half way around the globe.

Diverging plates

In some places, usually in the mid-ocean on the seabed, tectonic plates move apart or diverge. As they move apart, hot molten magma from the Earth's interior wells up through the gap and solidifies on the exposed edges. So the seabed grows wider and wider. The floor of the Pacific Ocean is becoming wider by about 20 cm every year.

Major tectonic plates

Pacific plate
North American plate
South American plate
Antarctic plate
African plate
Eurasian plate
Indian plate

Volcanoes

Volcanoes are places where hot molten rock or magma wells up to the surface from deep within Earth's interior. In a volcanic eruption, molten magma explodes from the main vent as lava. Ash and lava pour out and flow down the side of the volcano. Gas, dust and rock 'bombs' are thrown into the sky.

➤ ***The biggest volcanic eruptions are powered by a combination of steam and carbon dioxide gas. They remain dissolved in the magma inside the volcano because of the extreme pressure. But as the plug of magma breaks, the pressure is suddenly released, creating an explosion big enough to send chunks of rock the size of houses many thousands of metres up into the air.***

Amazing

The most active volcano in the world is Kilanea on Hawaii in the Pacific Ocean. It has erupted continuously since 1983 and produced lava at a rate of 5 cu m every second.

❍ Eruptions begin with a build-up of pressure in the magma chamber beneath the volcano.

❍ Bubbles of steam and gas form and swell rapidly inside the magma, and burst out like the froth from a violently shaken bottle of fizz.

❍ As the steam and gas jet out, they carry clouds of ash and larger fragments of the broken plug of magma, called volcanic bombs. This ejected material is called tephra.

❍ With the volcanic plug out of the way, magma surges up and out of the volcano, and flows down as lava.

❍ All the magma does not gush up the central vent. Some exits through branching side vents, often forming their own smaller cones on the side of the main one.

❍ Successive eruptions can build up such a huge cone of ash and lava around the volcano that it becomes a mountain.

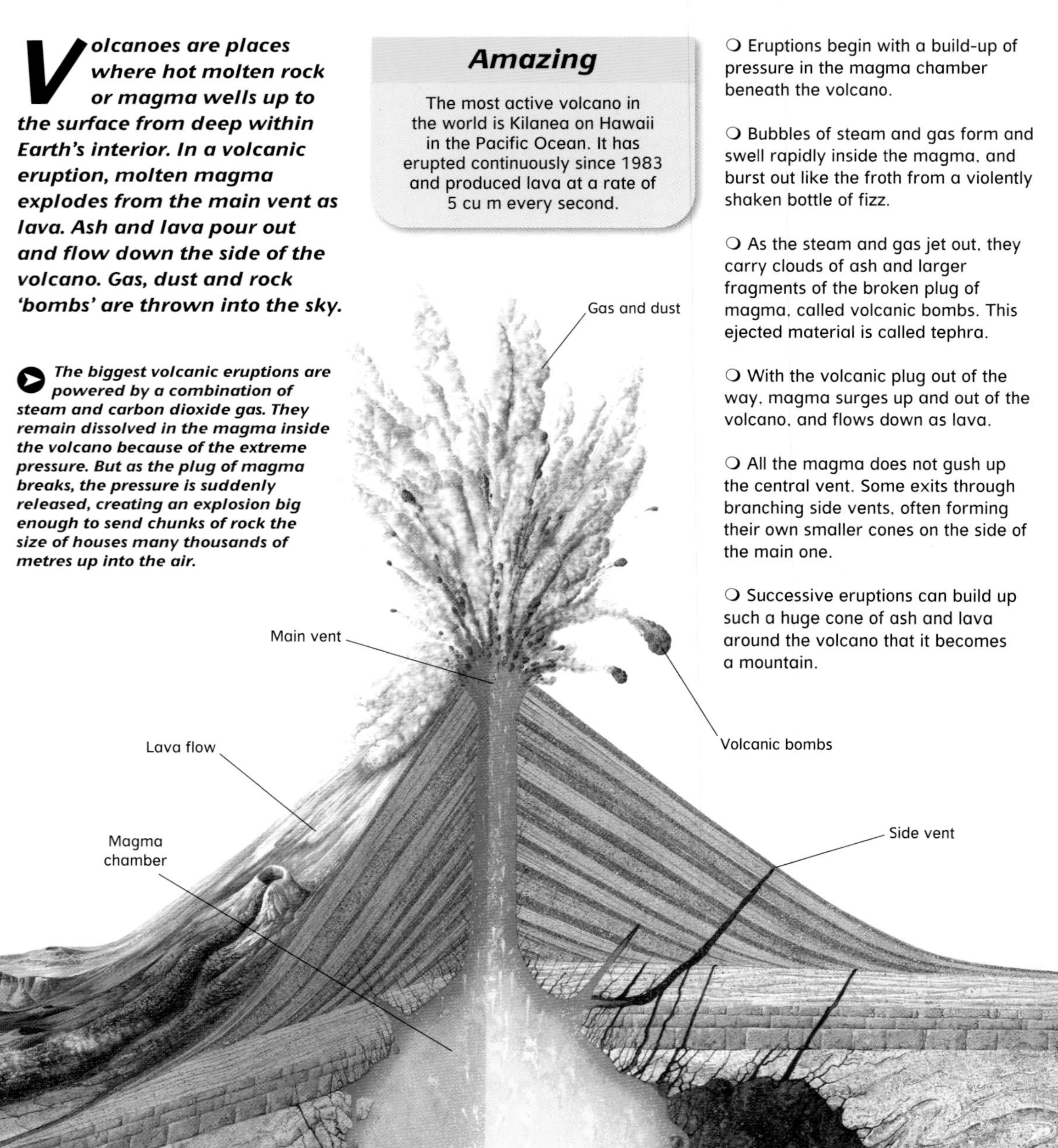

Every now and then, mantle rock melts into floods of magma, which collects along the edges of tectonic plates. It then rises to the surface and erupts as a volcano.

❍ If the level of magma in the magma chamber drops, the top of the volcano's cone may collapse into it, forming a giant crater called a caldera.

❍ Where the magma is runnier, it reaches the surface easily and floods out steadily as lava to form a gentle slope that looks like an upturned shield, known as a 'shield' volcano. Kilauea volcano on the island of Hawaii is a typical shield volcano.

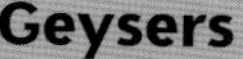

Geysers

Geysers are spouts of steam and hot water. They are found in volcanically active regions. In 1903 a New Zealand geyser spurted to 460 m high – the highest ever measured. The tallest geyser 'blowing' today is Steamboat Geyser in Yellowstone National Park, USA (see above). Hot steam rises to a height of 115 m.

❍ The lava that gushes from the Hawaiian volcanoes in the Pacific is very runny. Because of this, the explosive gases leak out, and so the lava rarely bursts out in a huge explosion. Instead, it tends to spray out frequently in fiery fountains, or well out in slower streams of molten rock.

❍ Active volcanoes erupt often. Dormant volcanoes do so only occasionally. Extinct volcanoes are safely dead and will not erupt again.

❍ The biggest volcano is Mauna Loa in Hawaii, with a crater 10 km wide and 180 m deep. More than 80 per cent of this volcano is beneath the ocean.

❍ There are more than 800 active volcanoes in the world. The country with the most is Indonesia, which has about 200.

Volcanoes in the Pacific spray out fiery lava fountains.

Ring of Fire

Most volcanoes occur near cracks between the giant tectonic plates that make up the Earth's surface. Around the Pacific there is a ring of explosive volcanoes called the Ring of Fire. It includes Mount Pinatubo in the Philippines and Mount St Helens in Washington State, USA. There are about 60 major volcanic eruptions a year, including two or three huge, violent eruptions.

Major volcanic eruptions

Location	*Date*	*Casualties*
Santorini, Greece	c.1500 BC	Unknown, but probably destroyed the Minoan civilization
Tambora, Indonesia	1815	92,000
Krakatoa, Indonesia	1883	50,000 (the eruption was heard 4000 km away)
Mount Pelée, Martinique	1902	30,000
Mount St Helens, USA	1980	Over 100
Mount Pinatubo, Philippines	1991	Number of deaths estimated at around 800

Earthquakes

Earthquakes are a shaking of the ground. Some are slight tremors that barely rock a cradle. Others are so violent they can tear down mountains and cities. Small earthquakes may be set off by landslides, volcanoes or even just heavy traffic. Bigger earthquakes are set off by the grinding together of the vast tectonic plates that make up the Earth's surface.

❍ Tectonic plates are moving all the time, radiating minor tremors as they grind past each other.

❍ Every now and then they get jammed. Then the pressure builds up until they suddenly lurch on again, sending out vibrations, called shock waves, in all directions and creating major earthquakes.

❍ Tectonic plates typically slide 4–5 cm past each other in a year. In a slip that triggers a major quake they can slip more than 1 m in a few seconds.

❍ In an earthquake, shock waves radiate out in circles from its origin or hypocentre (focus).

❍ Shock waves vibrate throughout the ground, but it is at the surface that they do most damage.

❍ Damage is most severe at the epicentre – the point on the surface directly above the focus – where the shock waves are strongest. But they can often be felt up to thousands of kilometres away.

During an earthquake, shock waves radiate in circles outwards and upwards from the focus of the earthquake. The damage caused is greatest at the epicentre, where the waves are strongest, but vibrations may be felt 1000 km away.

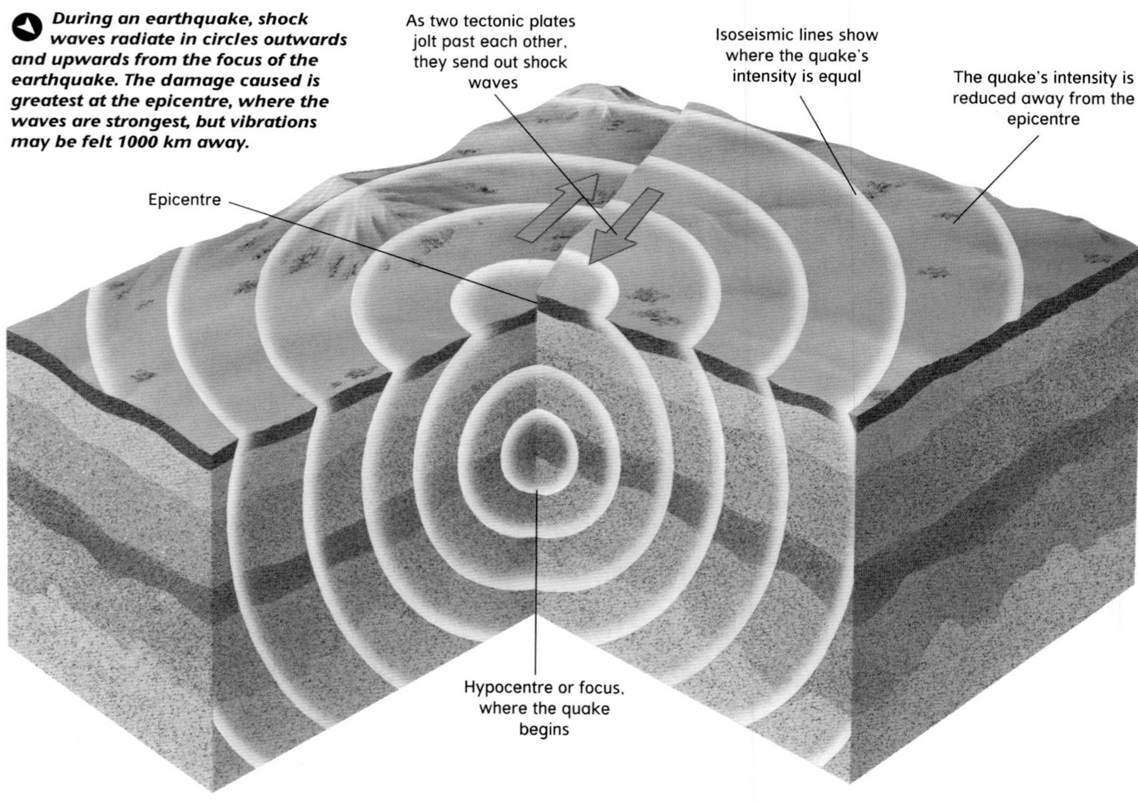

Moment Magnitude Scale

This scale indicates how much energy an earthquake has and thus how big it is.

2.5	Usually not felt, but can be recorded by a seismograph
2.5–5.4	Often felt, but only causes minor damage
5.5–6.0	Slight damage to buildings and other structures
6.1–6.9	May cause a lot of damage in very populated areas
7.0–7.9	Major earthquake. Serious damage
8.0 or more	Great earthquake. Can totally destroy communities near the epicentre

Seismometer

Seismologists (scientists who study earthquakes) measure the strength of the shock waves with a device called a seismometer. They then grade the severity of the quake on the Moment Magnitude Scale (see box left). Experts also rate an earthquake on the Mercalli scale, which assesses the damage on a scale of one (barely noticeable) to 12 (total destruction).

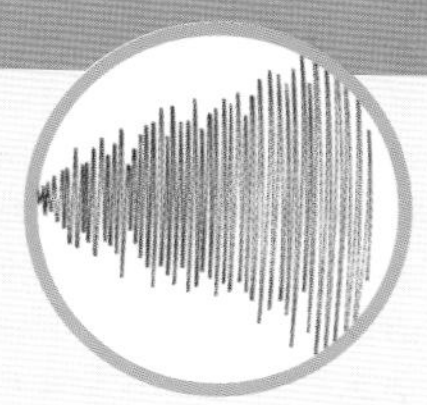

Tsunamis

Undersea earthquakes can produce huge waves, called tsunamis. These waves move at up to 800 km/h but may not be noticed in the open sea. In shallow waters however, the wave builds into a colossal wall of water up to 30 m high, which rushes inland, drowning everything in its path.

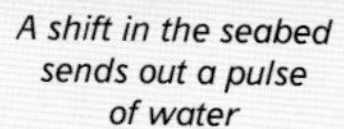

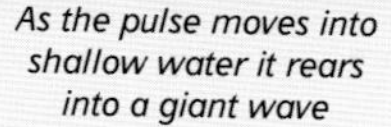

A shift in the seabed sends out a pulse of water

As the pulse moves into shallow water it rears into a giant wave

Amazing

Each year around 800,000 earthquakes are detected by sensitive instruments worldwide. About 40,000 to 50,000 can be felt but don't do any damage, and less than 1000 actually cause damage.

In 1906, San Francisco in California, USA, was shaken by an earthquake that lasted three minutes. The earthquake started fires that burned the city almost flat. The earthquake was so strong that its effects were detected thousands of miles away. More than two-thirds of San Francisco's population were left homeless.

❍ In most quakes a few minor tremors (foreshocks) are followed by an intense burst lasting just one or two minutes. A second series of minor tremors (aftershocks) occur over the next few hours. While aftershocks are less powerful than the main quake they can often add to the damage.

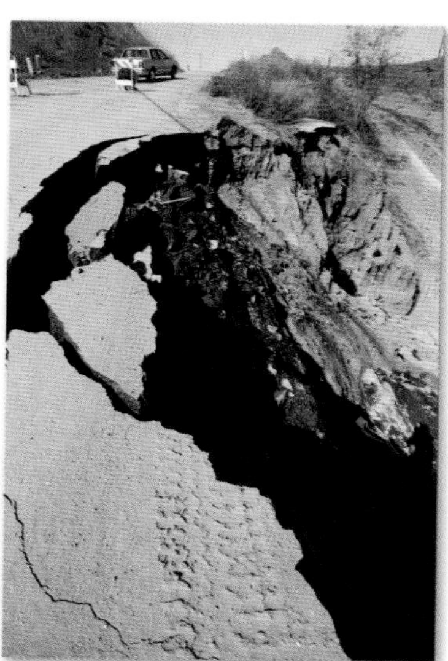

The Moment Magnitude Scale tells us how much energy an earthquake has – but the damage it does depends on how far the place is from the centre of the earthquake.

Major earthquakes of the 20th and 21st centuries

Place	*Date*	*Moment Magnitude Scale*
San Francisco, USA	1906	7.9
Gansu, China	1920	8.0
Kanto Plain, Japan	1923	8.0
Assam, India	1950	8.7
Aleutian Islands, USA	1957	8.7
Tangshan, China	1976	8.0
Léogâne, Haiti	2010	7.0

Landscapes

The Earth's surface changes all the time. Most changes take millions of years. The surface is distorted and re-formed from below by the huge forces of the Earth's interior. The landscape is moulded from above by waves, weather, water, ice, wind and other agents of erosion.

Weathering

Weathering is the gradual breakdown of rocks when they are exposed to air and water. Weathering works chemically and mechanically. Chemical weathering is when gases dissolve in rain to form weak acids that corrode rocks, such as limestone. The main form of mechanical weathering is frost shattering – when water expands as it freezes in cracks in the rocks and so shatters the rock. The landscape is shaped by the weather often into formations like this rock arch.

Rivers are one of the most powerful agents of erosion. The Colorado River in the USA has worn away tonnes of rock, creating a huge canyon that extends for 446 km.

Amazing

The Grand Canyon shows the power of flowing water that has cut through rock to a depth of 1600 m in places and to a width of 16 km.

❍ Mountains are made by movements of the Earth's rocky crust, pushed up by enormous pressure deep inside the Earth.

❍ The Earth's landscape is changing all the time because of erosion, which is the wearing away of rocks and soil by 'scouring' forces, such as wind, water, ice and frost.

❍ Most landscapes, except deserts, are moulded by running water, which explains why hills have rounded slopes. Dry landscapes are more angular, but even in deserts water often plays a major shaping role.

❍ Over thousands of years a river carves out a course through the rocks and soil, as it flows towards the sea or into lakes. These river courses create valleys and canyons.

❍ In winter, water trapped in cracks in rock freezes, expands and causes chunks of rock to split off.

Cold conditions have a dramatic effect on the landscape.

Glaciers

Glaciers move slowly but their sheer weight and size give them enormous power to shape the landscape. Over tens of thousands of years glaciers carve out winding valleys into huge, straight U-shaped troughs. Glacier lakes are created by glacial erosion, which deepens the valley floor. Water fills these valleys and moraine debris falls from the glacier to form a dam to keep the water in.

The desert heat means that both the chemical and the mechanical weathering of the rocks is intense.

❍ When water freezes in cracks in rocks, it expands and splits the rock with an estimated force of 3000 kg on an area the size of a postage stamp.

❍ Heavy rain can quickly wash soil down a slope, especially if there are no trees on the slope to 'bind' the soil.

❍ The wind can make a mountain of sand. The Dune of Pilat on the French Atlantic coast has been created by wind and waves piling up sand from the bay over the last 200 years. The dune is 110 m high, 500 m wide and nearly 3 km long.

The contours of hills in damp places have often been gently rounded over long periods by a combination of weathering and erosion by running water.

Mountains

Mountains look solid and unchanging, but they are being built up, then worn away by the weather, all the time. The Himalayas, for instance, were built up in the last 40 million years, and are still growing.

❍ All the world's great mountain ranges, such as the Andes and Rockies, were made by the crumpling of rock layers as tectonic plates pushed against each other. Such mountains are called fold mountains.

❍ A few mountains, such as Washington's Mount St Helens, are volcanoes – tall cones built up by successive eruptions of lava and ash.

❍ Fault block mountains are made when a section of rock tilts or is pushed up during a tremor. This happens along faults or breaks in the Earth's crust.

❍ The Himalayan range in Asia has the world's 20 highest mountains, including Mount Everest, which rises to 8848 m.

❍ The most ancient mountain ranges have long been worn flat, or reduced to hills, such as New York's Adirondacks, which are now over 1 billion years old.

❍ The Andes is the longest mountain range, stretching for 7240 km along the western side of South America. The highest peak is Mount Aconcagua in Argentina. It is 6961 m high.

❍ One side of a mountain range is often very wet. Approaching winds rise over the mountains, cooling and dropping rain on the windward side. The other side gets very little rain and often becomes a desert.

The highest mountain in the world, Mount Everest, is surrounded by other mountains that are almost as tall.

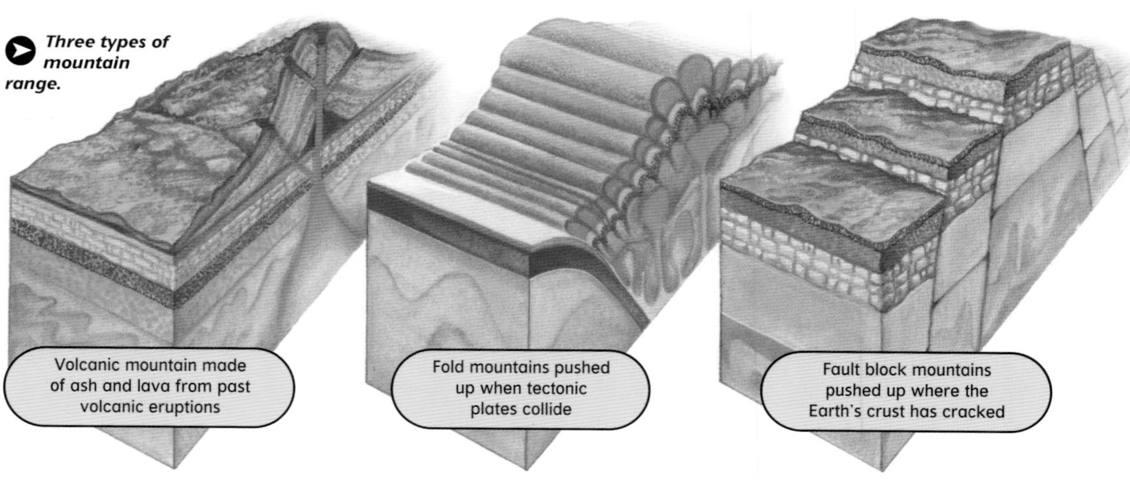

Three types of mountain range.

10 highest mountains

Everest	8848 m
Tirich Mir (K2)	8611 m
Kangchenjunga	8586 m
Lhotse	8516 m
Makalu	8485 m
Cho Oyu	8188 m
Dhaulagiri	8165 m
Manaslu	8163 m
Nanga Parbat	8125 m
Annapurna	8091 m

Thin air

The air is thinner on mountains, so the air pressure is lower. Climbers may need oxygen masks to breathe. Temperatures drop 0.6°C for every 100 m you climb, so mountain peaks are very cold and often covered in snow.

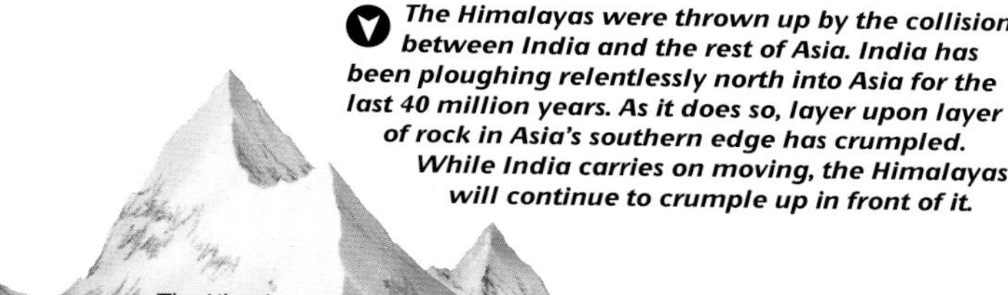

The Himalayas were thrown up by the collision between India and the rest of Asia. India has been ploughing relentlessly north into Asia for the last 40 million years. As it does so, layer upon layer of rock in Asia's southern edge has crumpled. While India carries on moving, the Himalayas will continue to crumple up in front of it.

Fold mountains

Most rocks form in flat layers called strata. Fold mountains build up where the movement of the Earth's crust tilts, crumples and squeezes, and lifts these flat layers.

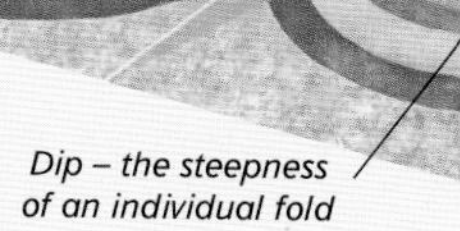

Amazing

The tallest mountain measured from its base under the sea is Mauna Kea in Hawaii. From base to tip it measures 10,000 m but only 4205 m is above the sea.

10 longest mountain ranges on land

The Andes	7240 km
Rocky Mountains	4827 km
Himalayas	3861 km
The Great Dividing Range	3620 km
The Transantarctic Range	3540 km
Brazilian Coastal Range	3057 km
Sumatra-Java Range	2896 km
Aleutians	2574 km
Tien Shan	2252 km
New Guinea Range	2011 km

The Andes mountain range is being pushed up along the western side of South America.

Glaciers and Ice Ages

Glaciers are rivers of slowly moving ice. Nowadays, glaciers only form in the highest mountains and in polar regions. But in the past, in cold periods called ice ages, glaciers were far more widespread.

❍ Glaciers begin in small hollows in the mountain called cirques, or corries. They flow downhill, gathering huge piles of debris called moraine on the way.

❍ Glaciers form when new snow, or névé, falls on top of old snow. The weight of the new snow compacts the old snow into denser snow called firn.

❍ In firn snow, all the air is squeezed out so it looks like white ice. As more snow falls, firn gets more compacted and turns into glacier ice that flows slowly downhill.

❍ When a glacier goes over a bump in the rock below it, or round a corner, the ice often breaks making deep cracks in the ice. These cracks are called crevasses.

❍ Ice ages are periods lasting millions of years when the Earth is so cold that the polar ice caps grow huge.

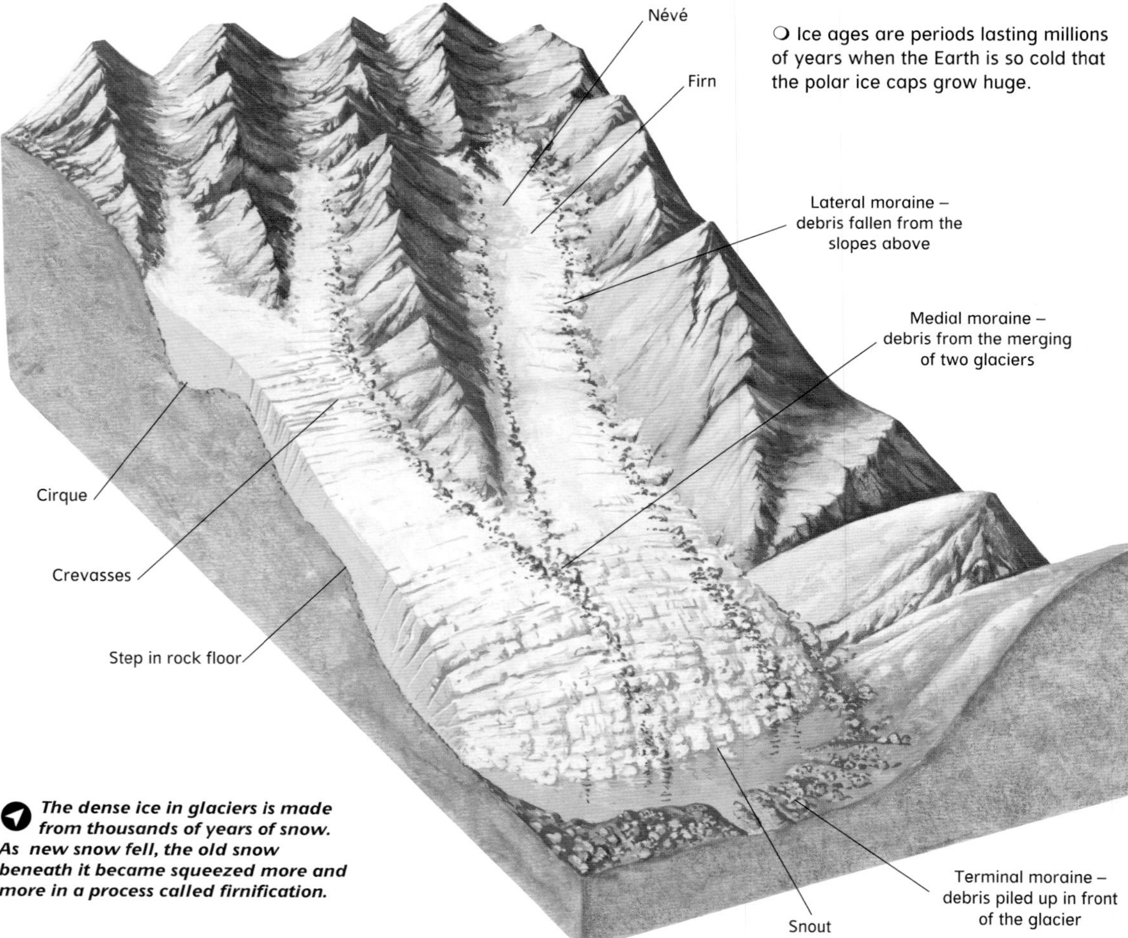

The dense ice in glaciers is made from thousands of years of snow. As new snow fell, the old snow beneath it became squeezed more and more in a process called firnification.

Long glaciers

Lambert, Antarctica	400 km
Fedchenko, Tajikstan	77 km
Jostedalsbreen, Norway	60 km

❍ There have been four ice ages in the last 1000 million years, including one which lasted 100 million years.

❍ The most recent ice age – called the Pleistocene Ice Age – began about 2.5 million years ago.

❍ Ice covered 40 per cent of the world and glaciers spread over much of Europe and North America 18,000 years ago. Ice caps grew in Tasmania and New Zealand. About 18,000 years ago there were glaciers in Hawaii.

❍ Where Washington, USA, and London, England, are today, the ice was 1.5 km thick 18,000 years ago.

Snowflake crystals

Snowflakes are made of masses of tiny crystals. These crystals grow together in an infinite variety of shapes and no one has ever found an identical pair. They fall from clouds in cold weather when the air is too cold to melt ice or rain.

Around 15,000 icebergs calve each year in the Arctic.

Floating ice

Icebergs are big lumps of floating ice that calve, or break off, from the end of glaciers or polar ice caps. This often occurs when tides and waves move the ice up and down. Arctic icebergs vary from car-sized ones called growlers to mansion-sized blocks. A huge Arctic iceberg, 11 km long, was spotted off Baffin Island in 1882. Antarctic icebergs are much bigger than Arctic ones. One of the biggest, at 300 km long, was spotted in 1956 by the icebreaker USS *Glacier*. About 11 per cent of a tall iceberg shows above water, the rest is submerged.

Icebergs float out to sea where they can be a danger to shipping because nine-tenths of the iceberg is hidden beneath the water.

Amazing

The Columbia Glacier in Alaska, USA, once reached speeds of 35 m per day but has recently slowed to less than half this.

Sizes of icebergs

Category	*Height*	*Length*
Growler	Less than 1 m	Less than 5 m
Bergy Bit	1–4 m	5–14 m
Small	5–15 m	15–60 m
Medium	16–45 m	61–122 m
Large	46–75 m	123–213 m
Very large	over 75 m	over 213 m

Rivers

Rivers are filled with water from rainfall running directly off the land, from melting snow or ice or from a spring bubbling out water that is soaked into the ground. Whenever there is enough rain or melting snow to keep them flowing, rivers run down to the sea or to lakes.

Amazing

The world's rivers carry about 10,000 million tonnes of sediment, tiny particles of rock and debris, into the oceans every year.

A river changes in many ways as it flows from its source high up in the hills downwards to the sea.

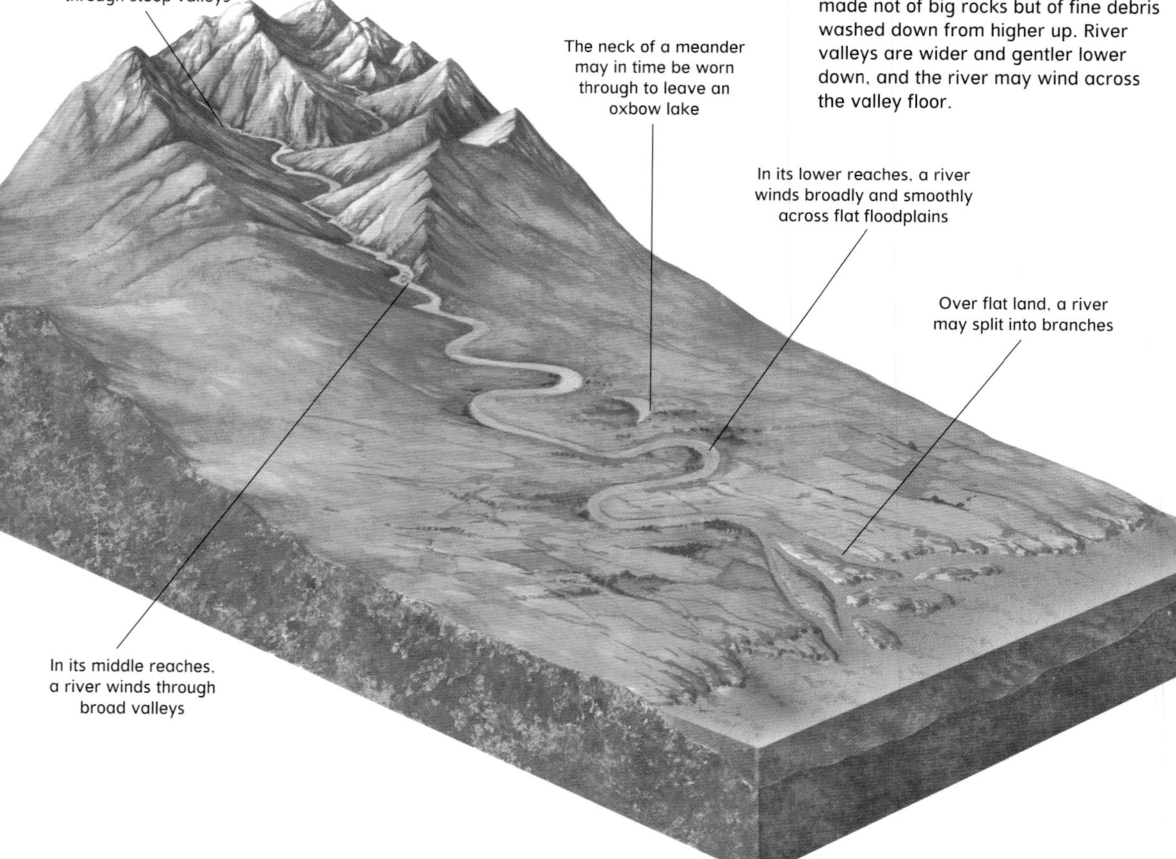

- High up in mountains near their source (start) rivers are usually small. They tumble over rocks through narrow valleys, which they carved out over thousands of years.
- All the rivers in a certain area flow down to join each other, like branches on a tree. The branches are called tributaries. The bigger the river, the more tributaries it is likely to have.
- As rivers flow downhill, they are joined by tributaries and grow bigger. They often flow in smooth channels made not of big rocks but of fine debris washed down from higher up. River valleys are wider and gentler lower down, and the river may wind across the valley floor.

Longest rivers

Nile, Africa	6670 km
Amazon, South America	6448 km
Chang Jiang (Yangtze), China	6380 km
Mississippi, Missouri, USA	6020 km
Yenisey, Russia and Mongolia	5540 km

❍ Rivers wear away their banks and beds, mainly by battering them with bits of gravel and sand and by the sheer force of the moving water.

❍ Every river carries sediment, which consists of large stones rolled along the riverbed, sand bounced along the bed and fine silt that floats in the water.

❍ In its lower reaches a river is often wide and deep. It winds back and forth in meanders across broad floodplains made of silt from higher up.

❍ A river slows down as it flows into the sea, so it can no longer carry the load of silt it has collected along the way. Often, the silt is dumped in a fan-shape, or a delta.

❍ The Amazon River carries more water than any other river. It pours 770 billion litres of water into the Atlantic Ocean every hour.

❍ Oxbow lakes form when a river meanders (changes course) cutting off patches of water before linking back up.

❍ The discharge of a river is the amount of water flowing past a particular point each second.

❍ The world's rivers wear the entire land surface down by an average of 8 cm every 1000 years.

10 highest waterfalls

Angel	Venezuela
Tugela	Africa
Utigård	Norway
Mongefossen	Norway
Yosemite	USA
Ostre Mardola Foss	Norway
Mutarazi	Zimbabwe
Espelands	Norway
Mara Valley	Norway
Tyssestrengene	Norway
Cuquenan	Venezuela

Waterfalls

Waterfalls occur when a river flows over a band of hard rock, and then over softer rock, which is more quickly worn away by the water. The hard rock forms a step over which the river pours, creating a waterfall. The highest falls are the Angel Falls in Venezuela, South America, with a drop of 979 m.

Near its source, the river tumbles over the rocks wearing them away to smooth pebbles.

Water cycle

All the water on Earth is constantly recycled. The warmth of the sun makes water in the oceans 'evaporate' or turn into water vapour in the air. The water vapour is blown over land by the wind. As the moist air rises over hills, it cools and turns into water droplets that fall as rain or snow. The rainwater finds its way into streams and rivers, which return it to the oceans.

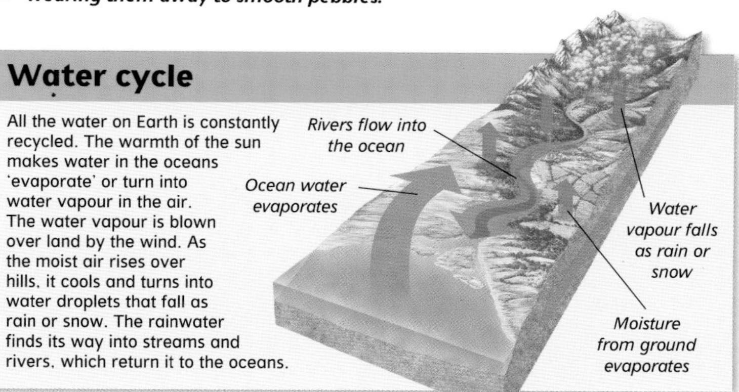

Lakes

A lake is a big expanse of water surrounded by land. Some lakes are so big they are called inland seas. Most lake water is fresh rather than salty, but in some lakes so much water evaporates that the remaining water tastes very salty.

❍ Most of the world's great lakes lie in regions that were once glaciated. The glaciers carved out deep hollows in the rock in which water collected. The Great Lakes of the USA and Canada are partly glacial in origin.

❍ The world's deepest lakes are often formed by faults in the Earth's crust, such as Lake Baikal in Siberia and Lake Tanganyika in East Africa.

❍ Most lakes last only a few thousand years before they are filled in by silt or drained by changes in the landscape.

Many of the world's great lakes were formed by glaciation, and will eventually disappear.

A salt island of crystal formations in the Dead Sea, a saltwater lake, in Israel. It is almost impossible to sink in the Dead Sea because of the amount of salt produced by scorching temperatures and high evaporation.

Salt and freshwater

There is a huge amount of water in the world – over 525 million cubic km – but 97 per cent is saltwater in the sea. The other 3 per cent is freshwater, but most of this is frozen in ice sheets at the poles, or deep underground. Only a very tiny portion moves round in the water cycle.

Amazing

The Aral Sea, a large lake in central Asia, is rapidly shrinking because the rivers that feed it have been diverted to irrigate farmland. The water level has dropped by over 12 m since 1960 and its area has shrunk by over three quarters.

❍ Lake Baikal in Siberia, Russia, is about 25 million years old. It is 1642 m deep and contains about one-fifth of ali the world's freshwater. The water is carried there by 336 rivers that flow into it.

❍ The Dead Sea in Israel and Jordan is well named. This saltwater lake is the lowest lake on Earth – about 400 m below sea level. In summer, scorching heat causes high evaporation, making the water so salty that a person cannot sink, and any fish entering the lake from the Jordan River die instantly. Only bacteria can survive.

❍ The Caspian Sea is the biggest lake in the world. But it is getting smaller because more water is being taken out for irrigation than flows into it from rivers.

❍ High in the Andes Mountains of Peru, straddling the border with Bolivia, is Lake Titicaca – the highest navigable lake in the world. It is 3810 m above sea level.

❍ The largest underground lake in the world is Drauchen-hauchloch, which is inside a cave in Namibia.

❍ The construction of dams creates large artificial lakes called reservoirs.

Lake Titicaca is a vast expanse of blue water surrounded by snow-capped peaks. It is home to the native Indians, who live in floating villages made from huge reed rafts.

❍ Some lakes, called crater lakes, form as water collects in the hollow of an old volcano, like Crater Lake in Oregon, USA, which is 9 km across.

Great Lakes

Canada and the United States share the five Great Lakes, so named because they are the biggest group of freshwater lakes in the world. They are: Lake Superior (the world's biggest freshwater lake by area), Lake Huron (the fourth largest lake in the world), Lake Michigan (the fifth largest lake), Lake Erie and Lake Ontario. Canada has the most freshwater (by area) – twice as much as any other country.

❍ During the colder winter months, powerful icebreakers are used to keep the Great Lakes free of ice so that the shipping routes remain navigable throughout the icy period.

Largest lakes by area

Superior, North America	82,350 sq km
Victoria, Africa	69,484 sq km
Huron, North America	59,600 sq km
Michigan, USA	57,800 sq km
Tanganyika, Africa	32,900 sq km
Baikal, Russia	31,499 sq km
Great Bear, Canada	31,328 sq km
Malawi, Africa	29,600 sq km

Oceans and Seas

Viewed from space, the Earth looks like a planet of blue ocean – more than 70 per cent is water. About 97 per cent of all the Earth's water is in the oceans, which cover more than 360 million sq km of the planet.

Surveys undertaken with sound equipment and computerized underwater craft have revealed a hugely varied landscape on the oceanbed, with high mountains, wide plains and deep valleys.

❍ There are five oceans, which all connect to make one vast body of water. The three biggest oceans are the Pacific, Atlantic and Indian oceans. They meet in the Southern or Antarctic Ocean. The Pacific and the Atlantic also meet in the smaller Arctic Ocean.

❍ Seas, such as the Baltic Sea, are smaller areas of saltwater, but most seas are joined to an ocean, such as the Mediterranean Sea, which is linked to the Atlantic Ocean at the Strait of Gibraltar.

❍ The Pacific is the world's largest ocean. It is twice as large as the Atlantic (the next largest) and covers an area of 165 million sq km – one-third of the world.

❍ Around the edge of the ocean is a shelf of shallow water called the continental shelf.

❍ At the edge of the shelf, the oceanbed plunges steeply to the deep ocean floor – the 'abyssal plain'.

❍ This plain is vast, but not completely flat. In the Pacific especially, it is dotted with huge mountains, called seamounts.

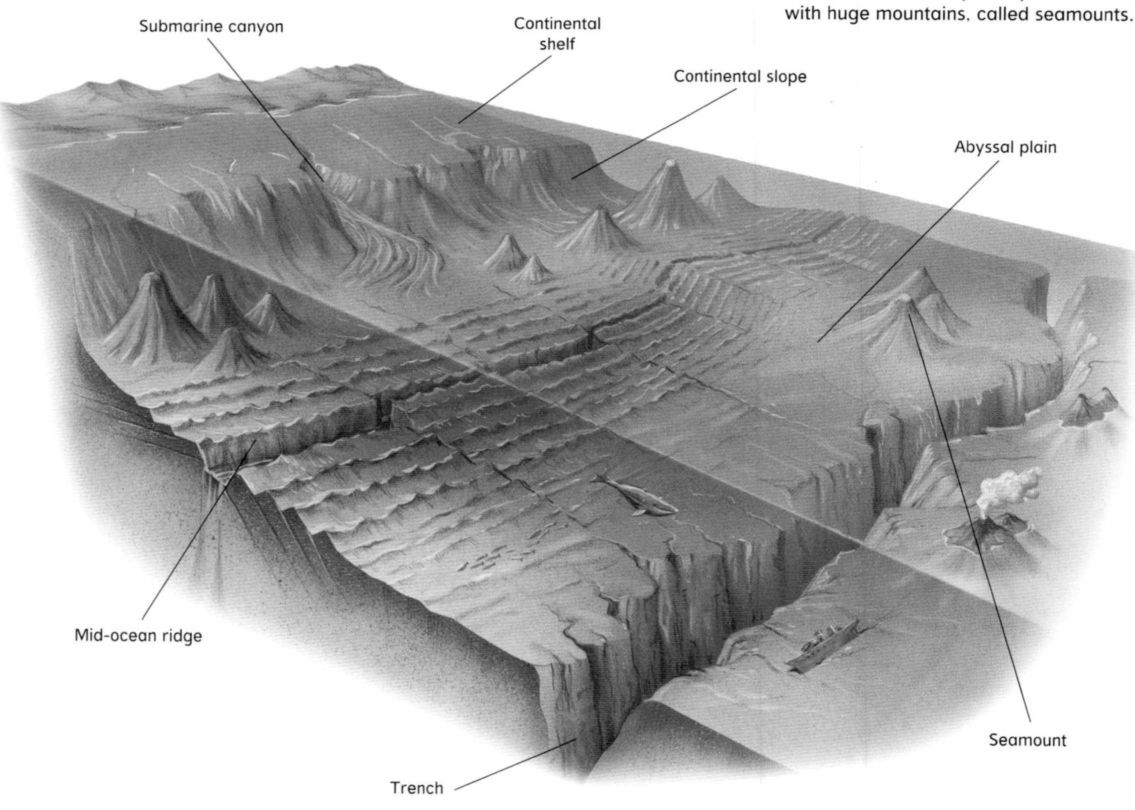

10 large seas

South China Sea
Caribbean Sea
Mediterranean Sea
Bering Sea
Sea of Okhotsk
Gulf of Mexico
Arabian Sea
Sea of Japan
Hudson Bay
East China Sea

Where the ocean meets the land, waves batter the coast wearing it away and forming strange rock shapes. When a sea arch collapses, it leaves behind tall pillars called stacks.

Amazing

Deep under the ocean where sunlight never reaches are black smokers, springs of water heated by volcanic rocks. Strange tube worms and blind crabs live there.

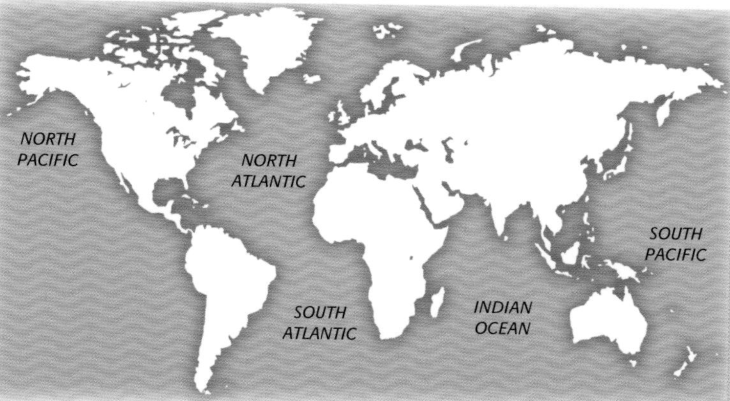

Some maps name the North and South Pacific, and the North and South Atlantic separately, but the Pacific and Atlantic are each one ocean.

Arctic Ocean

Most of the Arctic Ocean is permanently covered with a vast floating raft of sea ice. Temperatures are low all year round, averaging –30°C in winter and sometimes dropping to –70°C. During the long winters, which last more than four months, the Sun never rises above the horizon. The seal is one of the few creatures that can survive the bitter cold of the Arctic winter.

Tides

All around the world, the sea rises and falls slightly twice every day in 'tides'. Tides are caused by the pull of the Moon's gravity on the oceans' waters as the Earth spins around. Spring tides (high tides) happen twice a month. They occur as the Moon and Sun line up with each other, combining their gravitational pull.

The sea moves or 'flows' upwards and inland as the tide rises

The sea ebbs, sinking and retreating, as the tide drops

Ocean depths

	Deepest point
Pacific	10,911 m
Atlantic	8380 m
Indian	8045 m
Southern	7236 m
Arctic	5450 m

Caves

Caves are holes in the ground, usually hollowed out by water. Rainwater trickles down through the ground and dissolves the minerals in rocks, such as limestone, forming hollows and tunnels.

Amazing

One of the longest underwater cave systems in the world is the Nohoch Nah Chich system in Mexico. Over 65 km of underwater passages have been mapped by cave-diving teams.

Cave animals

Cave animals include bats, birds and even fish. Bats roost in caves, often in huge numbers, sleeping upside-down by day and leaving the cave at dusk to feed. Rarely disturbed by people, some caves have been home to bat colonies for thousands of years. Many cave species are blind and so rely on smell, touch or echolocation (using echoes from sound to judge distances and obstacles) to find their way around in the darkness.

❍ Soft rock in limestone caves is worn away by 'chemical weathering'. In the limestone, calcium carbonate reacts with rainwater to form a weak acid, which gradually dissolves rock. Water seeping down the rock forms cracks and potholes that open into caverns.

Limestone caverns and cave systems are eroded (worn away) by chemical weathering.

Stream flows underground

Underground waterfall

Limestone rock worn away to form cavern

Stalactites

Stalagmites

Water emerges into an underground lake

Prehistoric cave paintings

Prehistoric people lived in caves, and some caves contain pictures of animals made by these cave-dwellers. Stone Age people drew cave paintings of hunting scenes at Lascaux in France more than 17,000 years ago.

- Some caves are very long passages, and some are huge open spaces called caverns.
- Much more common are 'pot-holes', which are deep, narrow passages, sometimes leading to caverns. Explorers crawl through pot-holes, or even swim through flooded sections of a cave, using flashlights to penetrate the gloom.
- Stalactites hang down like huge icicles from the roofs of caves. They form as water drips down and deposits calcium carbonate.
- Stalagmites grow up from the floors of caves as water drips down from the roof and deposits calcium carbonate.
- The world's longest caves are the Mammoth Caves of Kentucky in the USA, first explored in 1799. This system has 650 km of caves and passages.
- The biggest cave chamber is called the Sarawak Chamber, in a cave system in Sarawak, Malaysia. It is 700 m long, has an average width of 300 m and is about 70 m from floor to roof.
- One of the longest stalactites on record measured more than 12 m long. It was in a cave in Brazil.

Some cave systems contain huge caverns, large enough for people to stand in. Others are cramped and narrow, and can only be crawled through by cave explorers.

A stalagmite more than 30 m tall – higher than a house – was measured insidea cave in Slovakia.

Deep caves

Krubera, Georgia	2190 m
Gouffre Mirolda/ Lucien Bouclier, France	1733 m
Lamprechtsofen-Vogelshacht, Austria	1632 m
Reseu Jean Bernard, France	1602 m
Shakta Pantujhina, Georgia	1508 m
Sistema Huautla, Mexico	1475 m
Sistema del Trava, Spain	1441 m
Vercors, southeast France	1271 m

Deserts

Dry desert, where the land gets less than 250 mm of rainfall in a year, covers almost one eighth of the Earth's land surface. Many are hot, but one of the biggest deserts is Antarctica.

❍ The driest place on Earth is the Atacama Desert in Chile, South America. Intervals between showers may be as long as 100 years, and in some areas it has not rained for more than 400 years!

❍ The biggest desert is the Sahara in north Africa, at 5000 km across and up to 2250 km north to south.

❍ The vast Sahara takes in 12 countries of northern Africa, including Algeria and Tunisia, where there are 'seas of sand', called ergs.

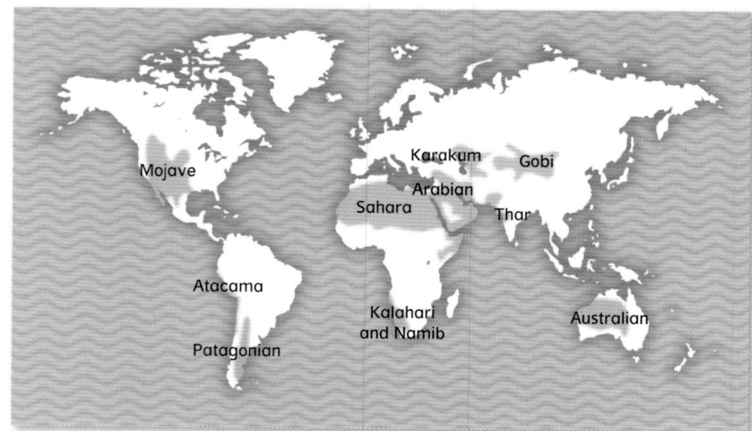

❍ The Sahara desert has some of the world's biggest sand dunes, some more than 200 m high.

❍ In the Arabian Desert is the world's biggest area of sand dunes – the Rub' al-Khali, which means 'Empty Quarter' in Arabic.

Hot dry deserts occur in warm areas where cool air sinks, warms up and absorbs moisture from the land. The world's biggest deserts are shown here.

Amazing

Dallol, Ethiopia, is known as the hottest place on Earth, with an average temperature of 34°C. The hottest temperature ever measured was 56.7°C in Death Valley, California in 1913.

Wind and sand have eroded, or worn away, these famous desert rocks in Monument Valley, Arizona, USA, giving them strange shapes.

Temperatures in the desert can be scorching hot by day and near-freezing at night.

❍ Only about 20 per cent of the Earth's deserts are sandy. The rest are rocky, stony, covered by scrub and bush, or ice-covered.

❍ An oasis is a green 'island' in the desert, a haven for thirsty travellers. Plants can grow there by tapping water from a well or underground spring. Even beneath the Sahara Desert a lot of water is trapped deep in the rock strata (layers).

Sand dunes

Loose sand is blown by the wind and piles up in wave-shaped formations called dunes. Sand is made up of tiny mineral grains, less than 2 mm across. Like waves of water, sand is blown up, rolls over the crest of the wave and down the steeper far side. Dunes move across the desert in this way.

Desert animals

Desert animals are able to go for days without water, getting most of the moisture they need from their food. These animals include mammals, such as antelope, camels, foxes and rodents, as well as birds and insects. Other animals, such as desert frogs, go into a state of suspended animation in burrows until the next rain.

Largest deserts

Sahara North Africa, 9 million sq km
Australian Australia, 3.8 million sq km
Arabian Southwest Asia, 1.3 million sq km
Gobi Central Asia, 1 million sq km
Kalahari Southern Africa, 520,000 sq km

Forests

Many trees covering an area of land create a forest. A wood is a smaller area of trees. There are different types of forest around the world, depending on the climate in the world's vegetation zones.

Amazing

Tropical rainforests cover less than 8 per cent of Earth's surface, but contain one third of the world's growing wood and provide a home for 40 per cent of all plant and animal species.

❍ In the warm tropics there are rainforests, seasonal forests (where trees lose leaves during the dry season) and savanna (warm grassland) forests.

❍ Rainforests are abundant with wildlife. There are more species of animals and plants in the Amazon rainforest than anywhere else on Earth.

❍ Tropical rainforests grow luxuriantly because the rainfall is heavy and regular – often more than 2000 mm of rain in a year.

❍ A rainforest has different levels, like floors in a building. The thickest part is the main canopy, about 30 m high, where most animals live. Taller trees emerge from the canopy.

❍ The world's biggest rainforest is the Amazon rainforest of South America, which stretches from the foothills of the Andes Mountains in the west to the Atlantic Ocean in the east.

❍ Rainforests also grow in cooler zones, where there is a lot of rainfall.

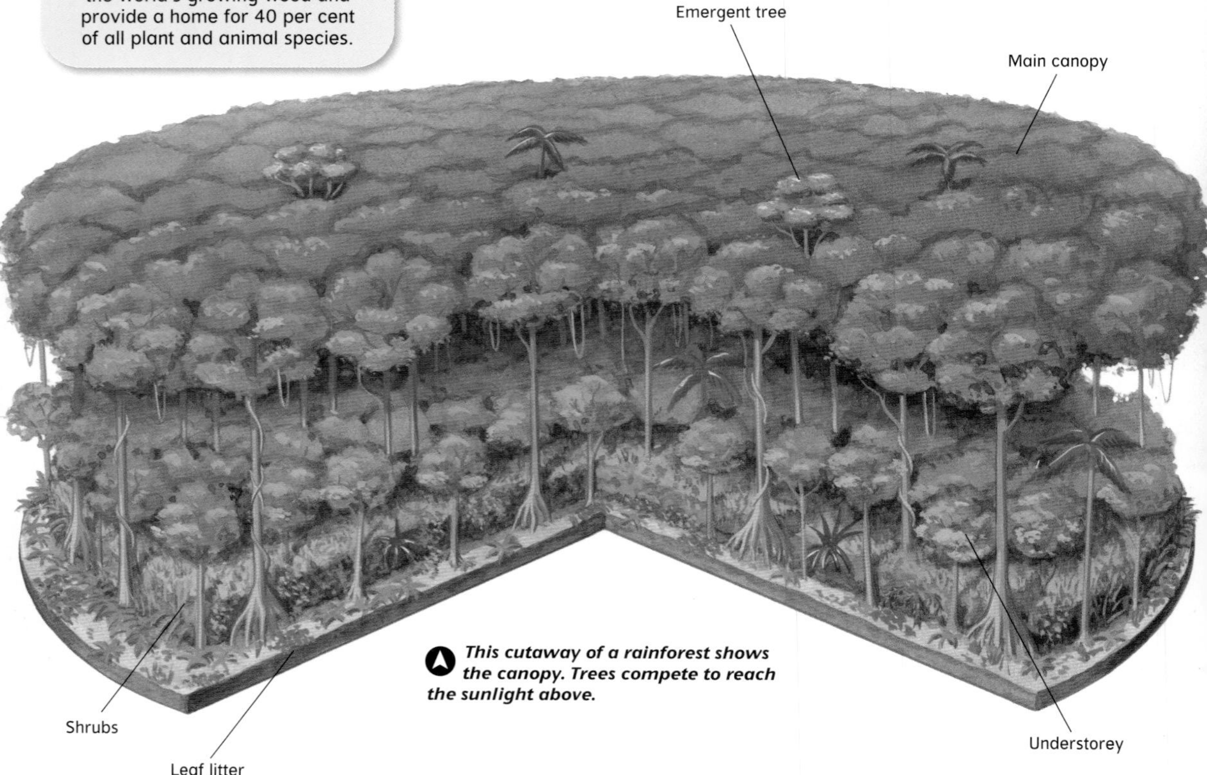

This cutaway of a rainforest shows the canopy. Trees compete to reach the sunlight above.

Forest fires

Forest fires can begin naturally, when vegetation is very dry after months without any rain. Often humans are responsible for starting the fires carelessly. Many forest trees and other plants regenerate quickly after a fire, but wildlife can be seriously affected. Forest fires can spread rapidly. Firefighters often cut trees to create a firebreak (strip of open ground) to stop flames spreading.

❍ In cooler zones, there are forests of mixed deciduous trees (which shed their leaves before winter), and of evergreen conifers, such as fir and pine.

❍ Trees in a deciduous forest shed their leaves to save water, because their roots cannot soak up water very well from cold soil. Deciduous forests grow in countries with warm summers and cool winters.

With high temperatures and heavy rain the tropical rainforest air is always moist and misty. Vegetation and plants thrive in this atmosphere, growing rapidly. The different levels within the rainforest support many animals.

Tropical rainforests

Many tropical rainforests are being destroyed to clear the land for farming and ranching. Felled trees are not replaced, leaving a stump-littered wasteland. Widespread deforestation can have devastating effects on the landscape. Tropical soil rapidly loses fertility. Rain washes off the topsoil, and once-lush forest becomes scrubland or desert.

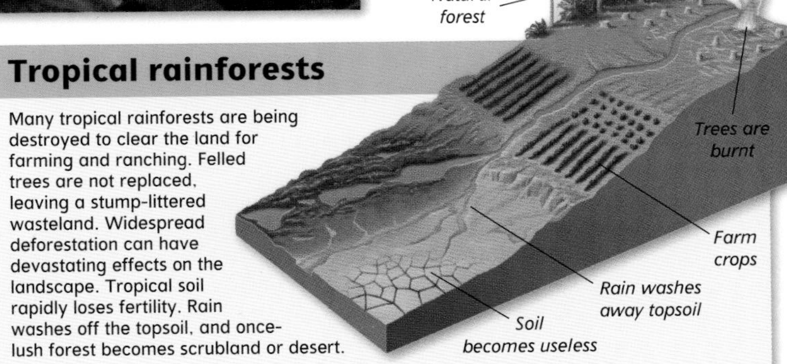

Types of forest

Tropical rainforest Hot and wet regions, supporting a huge variety of plant and animal species

Deciduous forest Regions with warm summers and colder winters; trees lose their leaves in winter

Cool evergreen forest Cold climates; trees such as pines with narrow needles that lose less moisture and shed snow; supports fewer different species

The Atmosphere

The atmosphere is the layer of gases that surround the Earth. It is held in place by the Earth's gravity, which keeps most of the gases in the atmosphere close to the ground.

❍ The atmosphere contains oxygen, nitrogen and tiny amounts of other gases – argon, carbon dioxide, carbon monoxide, hydrogen, ozone, methane, helium, neon, krypton and xenon.

❍ The most important gas in the atmosphere is oxygen, because people and animals need to breathe it. When we breathe, we take in oxygen and breathe out carbon dioxide. Green plants, such as trees, take in carbon dioxide and give off oxygen during their food-making process (photosynthesis).

❍ The atmosphere can be divided into five main layers: troposphere (the lowest), stratosphere, mesosphere, thermosphere and exosphere.

Amazing

The atmosphere protects the Earth from space rocks. About 100 tonnes of rocks and dust enters the atmosphere every day but almost all of it burns up when it hits the atmosphere at high speed.

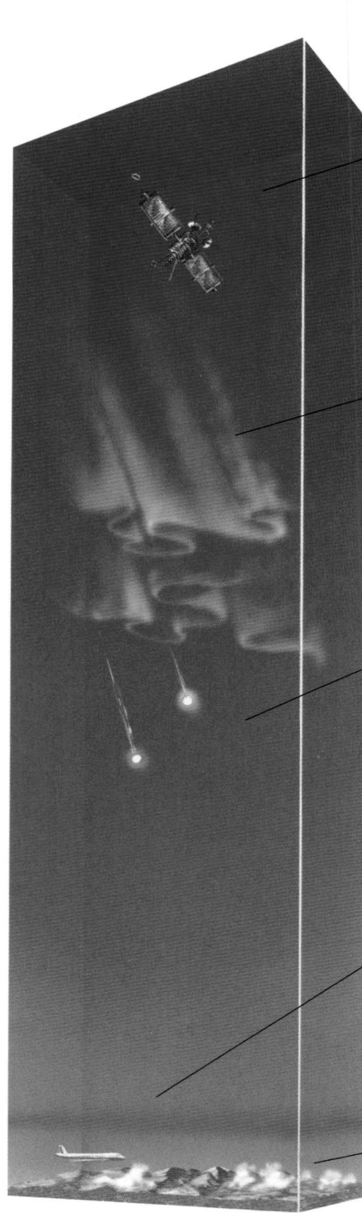

Exosphere 500–1000 km
Contains hardly any gas; low-level satellites orbit here

Thermosphere 80–500 km
Becomes roasted by the Sun to up to 1800°C, but is so thin in gases that it contains little real heat

Mesosphere 50–80 km
Is too thin to soak up much heat, but is thick enough to stop meteorites that burn up leaving fiery trails in the sky

Stratosphere 10–50 km
Contains the ozone layer and becomes hotter higher up; little water and no weather; airliners cruise here in the still air

Troposphere 0–10 km
Contains three-quarters of the atmosphere's gases and nearly all its water; temperatures drop by about 6.5°C every kilometre upwards

➤ ***The atmosphere absorbs the Sun's warmth, yet shields the Earth from its most harmful rays. It gives us fresh, clean water to drink and provides us with the air that we, and most other animals, need to breathe.***

In the Northern Hemisphere, winds spiral clockwise away from areas where the air pressure is high.

Winds spiral anticlockwise in towards low-pressure areas where the air is rising. In the Southern Hemisphere the directions are reversed.

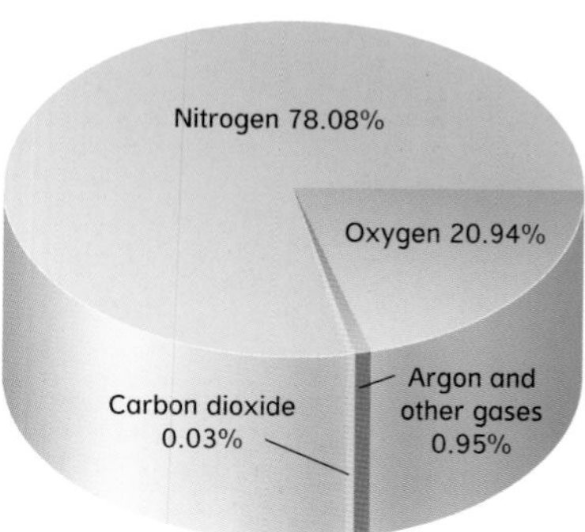

Nitrogen and oxygen together make up about 99 per cent of the Earth's atmosphere.

❍ At the bottom is the troposphere – only 10 km thick, but containing over 70 per cent of the atmosphere's gases by weight.

❍ All of Earth's weather, including clouds, is produced in the lowest layer of the atmosphere, called the troposphere.

Northern Lights

The Aurora Borealis, or Northern Lights, makes the night sky glow green, gold, red or purple. The effect is caused by solar wind – radiation from the Sun – hitting Earth's atmosphere.

❍ In the upper levels of the atmosphere is a layer of ozone (a form of oxygen), which forms a protective layer blocking out harmful ultraviolet rays from the Sun.

❍ The gases become thinner and thinner with each layer, until at about 1000 km up, they are so thin or 'rarified' that it is hard to tell where the atmosphere ends and where empty space begins.

❍ Air pushes in all directions at ground level with a force of over 1 kg per sq cm – that is the equivalent of an elephant standing on a coffee table.

Blue sky

The sky looks blue because light from the Sun is scattered by tiny particles of dust and moisture in the air. This breaks up the sunlight into its rainbow colours. The blue rays scatter most, so we see blue more and the sky looks blue.

Clouds

Clouds are dense masses of water drops and ice crystals that are so tiny they float high in the air. Most clouds eventually turn to rain, which falls back to the ground. This is called precipitation.

Amazing

Lenticular clouds form when the wind blows like a wave over the top of a mountain. Lenticular means that it looks like a lens but some could be mistaken for flying saucers.

❍ There is a large variety of clouds, but only two main shapes: fluffy, heaped 'cumulus' that form clouds when air moisture billows upwards; and flat 'stratus' clouds that form when a layer of air cools down enough for its water content to condense.

❍ Strong updraughts create huge cumulonimbus, or thunder, clouds. Cumulonimbus thunder clouds are the tallest clouds, often over 10 km high.

❍ Cumulus clouds are fluffy white clouds. They pile up as warm, moist air rises. Once the air reaches about 2000 m, the air cools to the point where water vapour condenses and clouds are able to form.

❍ Stratus clouds are vast shapeless clouds that form when a layer of air cools to the point where moisture condenses. They often bring long periods of light rain.

Different types of cloud in the sky form at different heights. Clouds are made of tiny droplets of water or ice.

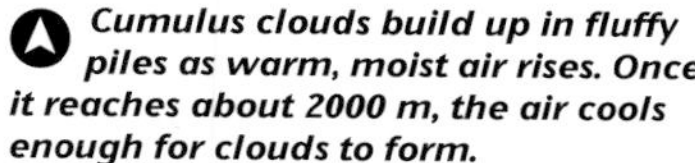

Cumulus clouds build up in fluffy piles as warm, moist air rises. Once it reaches about 2000 m, the air cools enough for clouds to form.

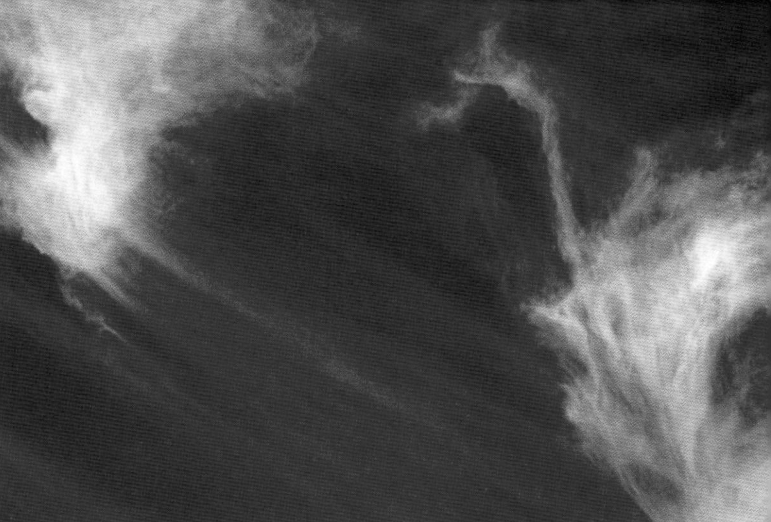

Feathery cirrus clouds high up in the sky are a clear warning that a warm front is on its way, bringing steady rain. When there is a warm front, a cold front is likely to follow, bringing heavy rain, strong winds and perhaps even a thunderstorm.

❍ Cirrus clouds are wispy clouds that form so high up they are made entirely of ice. Strong winds high up blow them into 'mares' tails'.

❍ Hailstones form when water droplets freeze inside a storm cloud then grow as more water freezes around them.

❍ The highest clouds are the rare 'mother of pearl' nacreous clouds, which can be found at 24,000 m.

❍ The lowest clouds are stratus clouds, from 1100 m to ground level.

❍ Contrails are trails of ice crystals left by jet aircraft.

Mist

Like clouds, mist is billions of tiny water droplets floating on the air. Fog forms near the ground. Meteorologists define fog as a mist that reduces visibility to less than 1 km.

Rain clouds

Rain starts when water drops or ice crystals inside clouds grow too large for the air to support them. Cloud drops grow when moist air is swept upwards and cools, causing lots of drops to condense. This happens when pockets of warm, rising air form thunderclouds. In the tropics raindrops grow in clouds by colliding with each other. In cool places, they also grow on ice crystals.

Types of cloud

Cirrus	Feathery white clouds
Cirrocumulus	Small patchy white clouds
Cirrostratus	Thin white sheets of clouds
Cumulus	White puffy clouds
Stratus	Low grey clouds
Nimbus	Dark heavy rain clouds

Weather

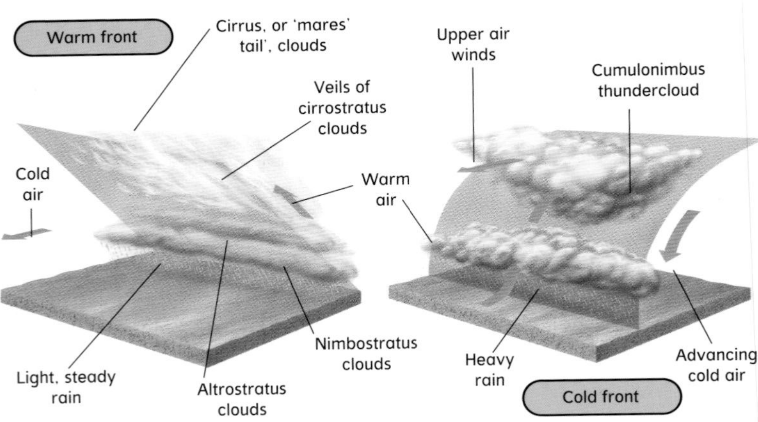

At a warm front, warm air rises over cold giving rain. At a cold front, cold air pushes warm air upwards giving heavy showers.

A satellite view of a large hurricane approaching Florida, USA. The yellow eye is the centre of the storm.

Amazing

There have been many reports of frogs raining down from the sky. This is probably caused by a tornado sucking up frogs from ponds and streams then dropping them from clouds like rain.

The more of the Sun's energy there is in the air, the windier it is. This is why the strongest winds may blow in the warm tropics.

Winter weather is cold because the days are too short to give much heat. The Sun always rakes across the ground at a low angle, spreading out its warmth. Black ice forms when rain falls on a very cold road. Rime is a thick coating of ice that forms when moisture cools well below 0°C before freezing onto surfaces.

A flood is when a river or the sea rises so much that it spills over the surrounding land. Small floods are common – big floods are rare. So flood size is described in terms of frequency. A two-year flood is a smallish flood that is likely to occur every two years. A 100-year flood is a big flood that is likely to occur once a century. A flash flood occurs after a small stream changes to a raging torrent after heavy rain in a dry spell. Even when no one drowns, a flood can destroy homes and wash away soil from farmland, leaving it barren.

Rainbow mnemonic

Richard **O**f **Y**ork **G**ave **B**attle **I**n **V**ain

Red, Orange, Yellow, Green, Blue, Indigo, Violet

10 types of lightning

Anvil
Ball
Bead
Cloud to air
Cloud to cloud
Cloud to ground
Forked
Ribbon
Sheet
Staccato

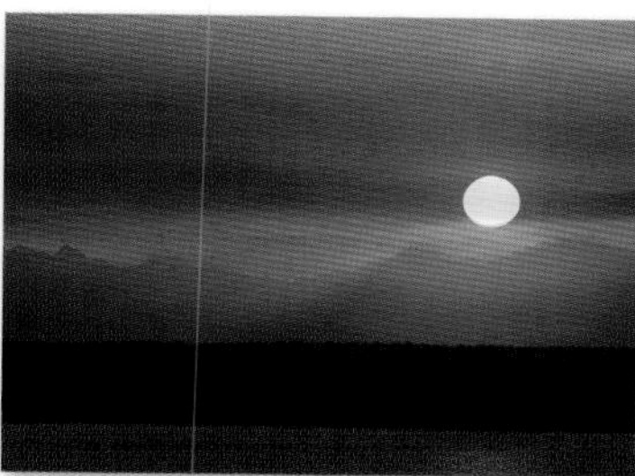

Without sunshine, the Earth would be cold, dark and dead.

A tornado starts deep inside a thundercloud, where a column of strongly rising warm air is set spinning by high winds roaring through the cloud's top. As air is sucked into this column, or mesocyclone, it corkscrews down to the ground.

Fresh snow can contain up to 90 per cent air, which is why snow can actually insulate the ground and keep it warm, protecting plants beneath.

Hailstones can be as big as melons. These chunks of ice can fall from thunderclouds. The biggest ones ever fell in Gopaljang, Bangladesh, in 1986 and weighed 1 kg each.

A drought is a long period when there is little or no rain. During a drought the soil dries out, streams stop flowing, groundwater sinks and plants die. Drought bakes the soil so hard that it shrinks and cracks. It will no longer absorb water even when rain comes.

Rainbows are caused by sunlight passing through falling raindrops. The water acts like a glass prism, splitting the light. White light is made up of seven colours – red, orange, yellow, green, blue, indigo and violet – so these are the colours, from top to bottom, that make up the rainbow.

Beaufort Scale

		Wind speed
0	Calm	under 2 km/h
1	Light air	2–5 km/h
2	Light breeze	6–11 km/h
3	Gentle breeze	12–19 km/h
4	Moderate breeze	20–29 km/h
5	Fresh breeze	30–39 km/h
6	Strong breeze	40–50 km/h
7	Moderate gale	51–61 km/h
8	Fresh gale	62–74 km/h
9	Strong gale	75–87 km/h
10	Storm	88–101 km/h
11	Violent storm	102–116 km/h
12–17	Hurricane	117 km/h and above

Climate

The nearer a place is to the Equator, the warmer the climate tends to be. The effect is to give the world three broad climate bands which fall either side of the Equator: the warm tropics, the cold polar regions, and a moderate 'temperate' zone in between.

❍ Climates are warm near the Equator, where the Sun climbs high in the sky. Tropical climates are warm climates in the tropical zones on either side of the Equator. Average temperatures of 27°C are typical.

❍ The climate is cool near the Poles, where the Sun never climbs high in the sky. Average temperatures of –30°C are typical.

The warmth of a region's climate depends on how close it is to the Equator. But oceans and mountain ranges have a huge influence too, so the pattern of climate is complicated, with many local variations.

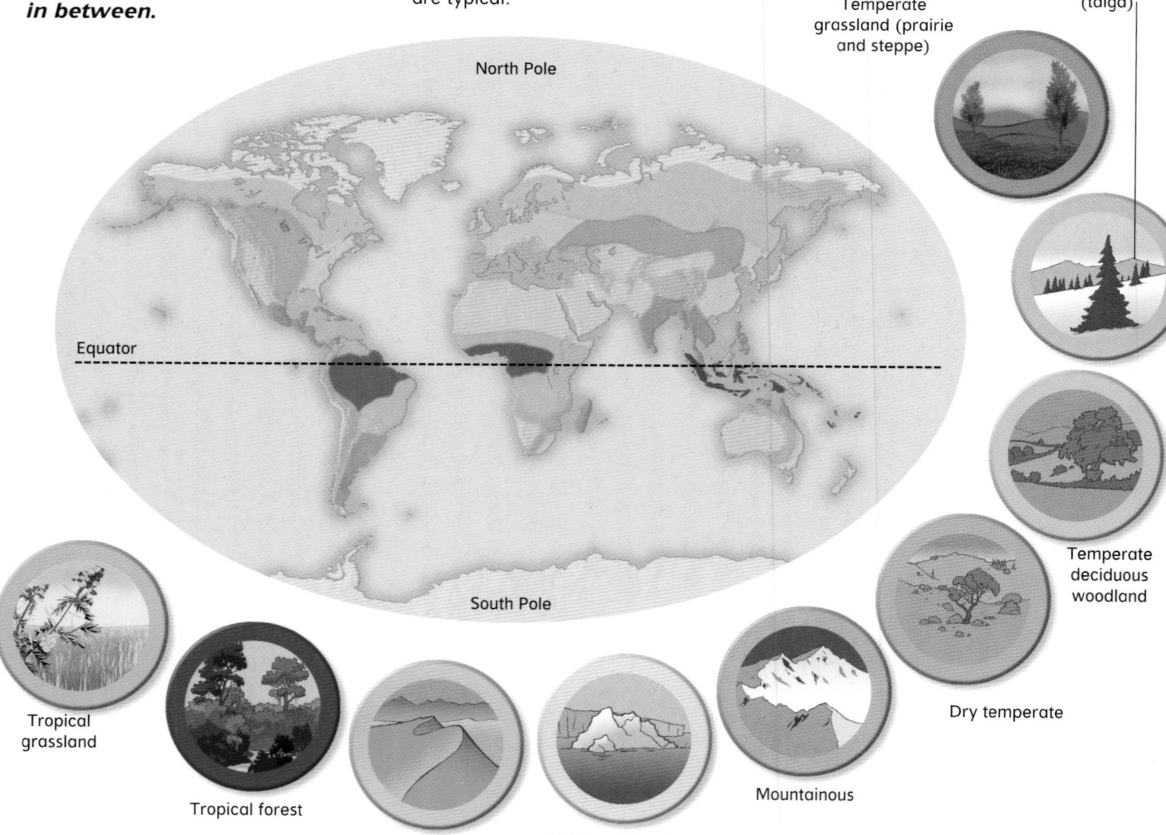

Monsoons

A monsoon climate is a climate with one very wet and one very dry season. This climate is typically found in countries such as India and Southeast Asia. Hot air rising over the land pulls in warm moist winds off the sea bringing heavy rain. Then the winds change, blowing cool dry weather from the mountains.

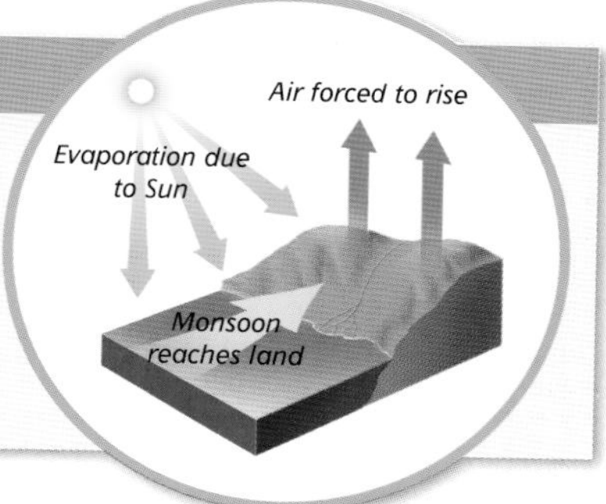

Amazing

Volcanic eruptions can send enough dust into the atmosphere to change the world's climate for a short time. After Mount Pinatubo erupted in the Philippines in 1991 many parts of the world had cooler weather in 1992.

- Antarctica has the coldest climate. It is so cold that almost nothing grows there and nobody lives there permanently.

- Temperate climates are mild climates in the temperate zones between the tropics and the polar regions. Summer temperatures may average 23°C, and winter 12°C.

- An oceanic climate is a wetter climate near oceans, with cooler summers and warmer winters.

California, USA, may have looked something like this 18,000 years ago when it was on the fringes of an ice sheet.

- A continental climate is a drier climate in the centre of continents, with hot summers and cold winters.

- One of the most equable climates in the world is Quito in Ecuador. It rarely drops below 8°C at night, nor rises above 22°C during the day, and 100 mm of rain falls reliably each month of the wet season.

- One of the world's wettest places is Tutunendo in Colombia, which gets about 11,700 mm of rain every year.

Tropical habitats

Some tropical places are warm and dry, including hot deserts such as the Sahara; some are warm and wet. Where it is wet, it tends to be very wet indeed, since the warm air takes up huge amounts of moisture. Large thunderclouds often build up in the morning heat, then unleash torrents of rain in the afternoon. Steamy rainforests flourish in this hot, moist climate.

Global Warming

Global warming is the general increase in average temperatures around the world. This increase has been about 0.8°C over the last 100 years. Most scientists now think that global warming is caused by human activities, which have resulted in an increase in the Earth's natural greenhouse effect. Humans have added carbon dioxide gas to the air by burning coal, oil and gas at an increasing rate in the demand for electricity and car travel.

Increase in global temperatures may turn some places into deserts, while others could become wetter as well as hotter.

The greenhouse effect keeps the Earth warm by trapping heat.

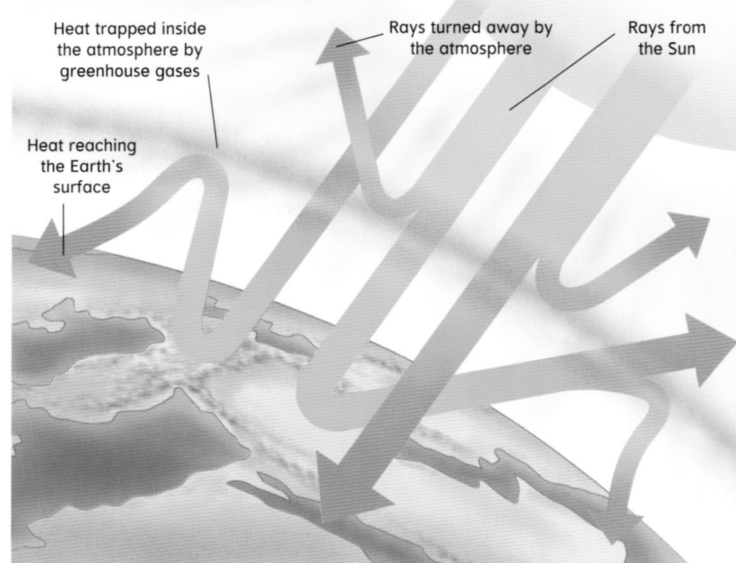

❍ The greenhouse effect is the way that certain gases in the air – notably carbon dioxide – trap some of the Sun's warmth like the panes of glass in the walls and roof of a greenhouse.

❍ When heat from the Sun reaches the Earth, some of it penetrates the atmosphere and reaches the ground. Much of this heat is then reflected back into space. Certain gases in the air trap heat reflected from the ground.

❍ In the past, this natural 'greenhouse effect' has kept the Earth comfortably warm.

❍ The gases pumped into the air by the burning of coal, natural gas and oil in factories and cars, for example, have trapped much more heat.

❍ Scientists believe that this is causing global (worldwide) warming of the climate, which could have devastating effects in years to come.

Amazing

The greenhouse effect keeps the Earth at a reasonable temperature. Without any greenhouse effect the average temperature would be 33°C lower and the Earth would be covered in ice. It would be lifeless.

The lush vegetation of the world's rainforests absorbs carbon dioxide from the atmosphere. When the rainforest is cut down and burnt, not only does it stop absorbing, but the burning releases even more carbon dioxide to add to global warming.

Cattle contribution

Cattle produce large amounts of methane gas digesting their food as they graze. This methane gas is an effective greenhouse gas. Rice fields also produce high levels of methane. It is estimated that methane is responsible for up to 15 per cent of global warming.

- Global warming is bringing stormier weather by trapping more energy inside the atmosphere.
- Many experts have predicted that there will be a 2–4°C rise in average temperatures over the next 100 years.
- Global warming may melt much of the polar ice caps, flooding low-lying countries, such as Bangladesh.
- Many countries have agreed to try and reduce global warming by limiting the amount of carbon dioxide their factories and vehicles produce.

Hole in the ozone layer

Life on Earth depends on the layer of ozone gas in the air, which shields Earth from the Sun's ultraviolet (UV) rays. In 1982 scientists in Antarctica noticed a 50 per cent loss of ozone over the Antarctic every spring. The loss of ozone is caused by manufactured gases, notably CFCs (chlorofluorocarbons), which drift up through the air and combine with the ozone. CFCs were used in many things, from refrigerators to aerosol sprays. CFCs were banned in 1996, and the hole is starting to mend. The levels of ozone are now monitored by satellites looking down from space.

Greenhouse gases

Carbon dioxide Normally balanced – animals breathe it out but plants use it up. Increased by burning fuels in vehicles, factories and power stations

Water vapour Naturally present in the atmosphere

Methane From animal waste, swamps, oil and gas rigs – increasing

Nitrous oxide From car exhausts and chemical fertilizers – increasing

CFCs Used in fridges, aerosols and foam packaging – now mostly banned

Resources

The Earth has many natural resources that sustain life. The planet has air, water, forests, minerals and a range of environments that living things can use.

❍ Some of these resources, such as the Sun's energy, are in practice limitless.

❍ Others are renewable, such as plants, which means that they can be regrown.

❍ We cut trees for firewood and timber to make homes and furniture.

❍ But some, like coal and oil, are non-renewable resources. Once used, they are gone for ever.

❍ Fossil fuels are oil, coal and natural gas. Fossil fuels were made from the remains of plants and animals that lived millions of years ago. The remains were changed into fuel by intense heat and pressure.

❍ Coal is made from plants that grew in huge warm swamps 300 million years ago in the Carboniferous Period.

❍ Oil and natural gas were made from the remains of tiny plants and animals that lived in warm seas.

❍ Metals, like coal, are mined from deep underground, but most have to be extracted from rock by fierce heating in a furnace with other chemicals.

The Earth's surface contains an enormous wealth of mineral resources, from clay for bricks to precious gems, such as rubies and diamonds.

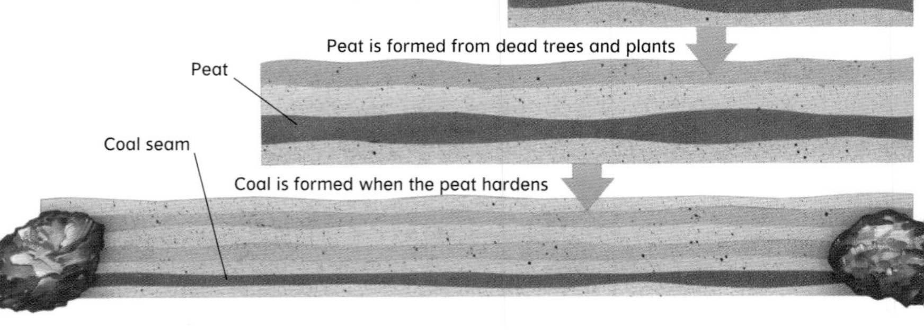

This diagram shows how coal seams are formed over millions of years. Much of the coal lies deep beneath rock layers, called strata. The pressure of the topmost layer squeezes the layers below, turning sand and mud into hard rock, and plant remains from peat into coal.

Oil is an extremely valuable natural resource that we use in our homes and for transport. It is found deep in the ground or below the seabed, pumped out by oil rigs that float in the sea, anchored to the seabed.

- Ores are the minerals from which metals are extracted. Bauxite is the ore for aluminium; chalcopyrite for copper; galena for lead; hematite for iron; sphalerite for zinc.
- Bulk materials, such as cement, gravel and clay, are taken from the ground in huge quantities for building.

Amazing

Almost all energy on Earth came originally from the Sun. Coal and oil were made from the bodies of living plants and animals that grew using the Sun's energy.

Recycling

To save resources, much of our 'rubbish' can be recycled – used again – in a variety of ways. Materials, such as glass, paper and metals can be treated and processed in a factory to be reused in the same form.

Wind power

Wind power is one method of generating electricity without using up precious resources. The wind is a renewable resource because in many parts of the world it seldom stops blowing. Wind turbines with spinning blades are grouped in wind farms, which supply electricity to the grid system.

Managed forestry means replacing trees that are cut by loggers with new saplings (young trees) that will grow and ensure the forest survives.

Maps and Mapmaking

Geographers (scientists who study the Earth and its features) rely on maps. A map is a small picture of a large area, and is drawn to scale. For example, 1 cm on the map might represent 1000 km of land on the ground.

Amazing

Satellites are now used to make very accurate maps, providing pictures of remote areas that are difficult to get to. They can accurately measure the heights of mountains and the depths of the oceans.

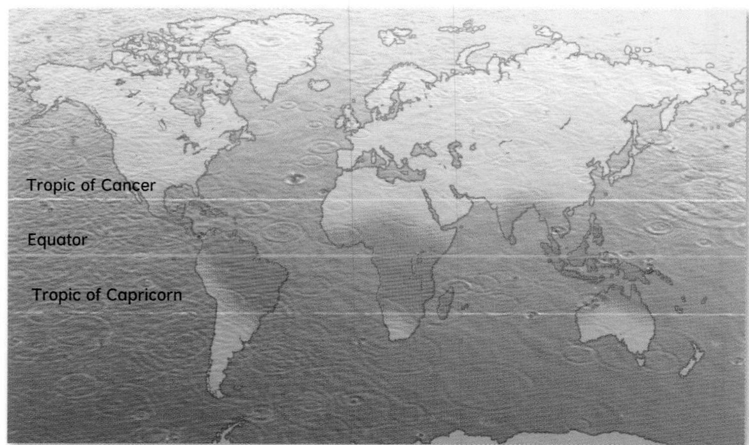

The Equator is an imaginary line around the middle of the Earth, with the tropics north and south of it.

The first reasonably accurate maps were made in Europe in the 1500s.

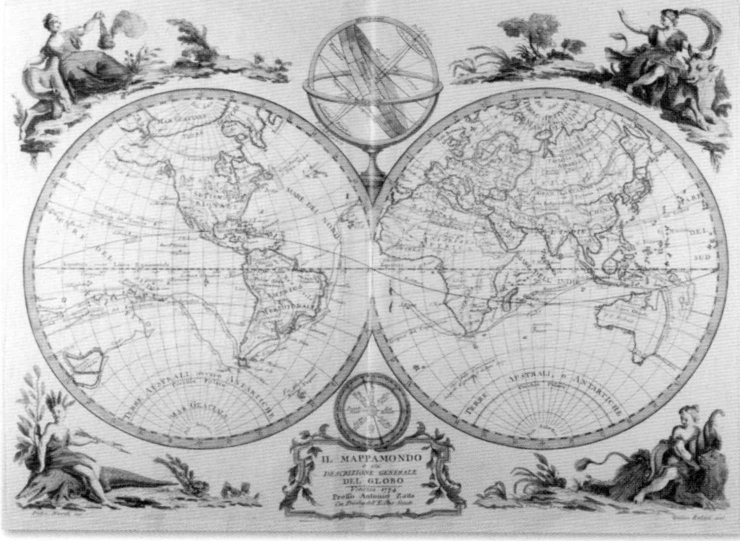

- Early navigators used a sextant to measure the height of the Sun above the horizon to help them work out latitude. Finding longitude became possible in the 1750s with the invention of accurate clocks for use at sea.

- Lines of longitude are drawn from north to south, while lines of latitude are drawn from east to west. These imaginary lines make it easier to locate any spot on the map.

- A flat map of a sphere like the Earth cannot be accurate unless certain adjustments are made. If you peel an orange carefully, you will discover that the peel won't lie flat on a table without breaking (see Mercator maps box).

- Maps are drawn such that one feature (such as land area) is accurate, but another feature (for example, shape) less so. These different ways of mapmaking are known as projections.

- The Equator is the line of 0° latitude.

Mercator maps

One map projection is named Mercator after a Flemish mapmaker named Gerardus Mercator (1512–1594). This projection shows the correct direction between two points, because the lines of latitude and longitude are correct. It makes landmasses look wrong though – Greenland looks the same size as North America, which is actually really much larger. If the Earth were an orange and could be 'unpeeled', this is what you would see. The curved surface cannot be transformed into a flat map unless some features are distorted.

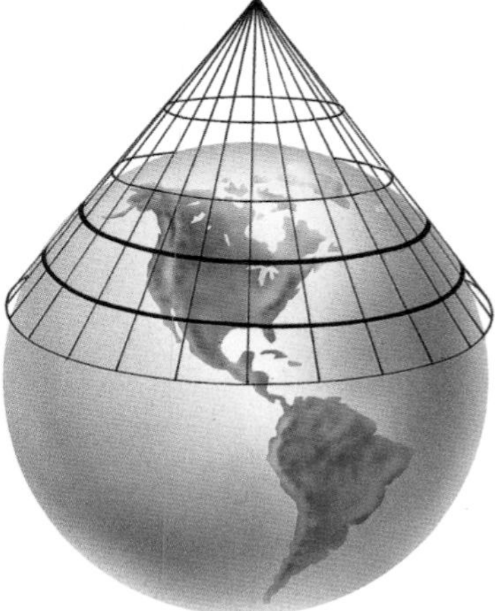

A conic projection of a globe projects the lines of latitude and longitude into a cone shape, which can then be flattened to give a picture of the wide landmasses, such as North America, as accurately as possible.

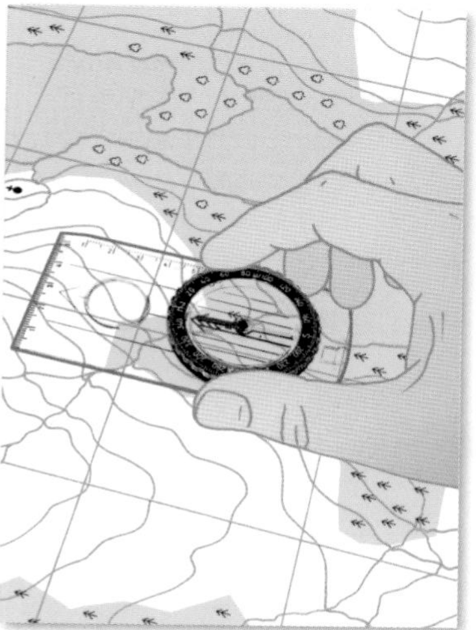

❍ The northern region is the Tropic of Cancer, the southern region is the Tropic of Capricorn.

❍ About 5000 years ago people in Egypt and Babylonia made drawings to show who owned which bit of land and where rivers were. The oldest map in existence is a clay tablet found in present-day Iraq, which has what may be a river valley scratched on it.

The spinning Earth acts like a magnet. At the centre of the Earth is liquid iron. As the Earth spins, it makes the iron behave like a magnet with a North and South Pole. These act on the magnet in a compass to make the needle point to the North and South poles.

❍ The line of 0° longitude runs through Greenwich in London, England, and is known as the prime meridian.

❍ The tropics are the regions of the Earth that lie immediately north and south of the Equator.

Global positioning systems

Global positioning system (GPS) satellites in orbit around the Earth can inform travellers where they are, to within a few metres. The satellites send out radio signals that are picked up by a computer on an aeroplane, ship or car; three or more 'fixes' give a precise position.

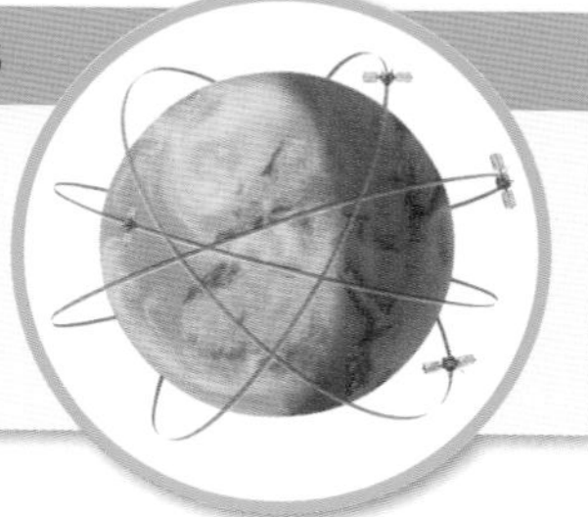

Glossary

Abyssal plain The broad plain on the deep seabed, 5000 m down and covered in ooze.

Atmosphere The thick layer of gases surrounding the Earth.

Aurora Spectacular displays of coloured lights in the night sky above the North and South poles.

Black smoker Chimney-like vent on the deep oceanbed churning out superheated water that looks black because of the minerals dissolved in it.

Chlorofluorocarbons (CFCs) Man-made chemicals that damaged the ozone layer in the atmosphere.

Climate Weather conditions over a long time period, e.g. deserts have a very dry climate and rainforests a very wet climate.

Continental drift The process whereby continents move slowly around the world, over millions of years.

Continental shelf A wide strip of seabed surrounding a continent or land mass. The sea here is much shallower than in the middle of the ocean.

Core The dense hot centre of the Earth.

Crater A circular rocky shape surrounding a hollow often found at the top of a volcano or left after a volcano has erupted.

Crevasse A deep crack in a glacier.

Crust The solid outer shell of the Earth, varying from 5 to 80 km thick.

Deciduous Trees that drop their leaves in winter and grow new ones in spring.

Deforestation Clearing a forest by cutting down the trees without replacing them. The cleared area is often used for farming.

Delta A flat piece of land, which has built up from material such as silt that has been deposited by a river as it flows to the sea.

Earthquake A brief, violent shaking of the Earth's surface, typically set off by the movement of tectonic plates.

Element A material made of only one type of atom. There are more than 100 elements on Earth.

Epicentre The place on Earth's surface directly above an earthquake's centre. This is where most damage occurs.

Equator An imaginary line around the middle of the Earth dividing it in two equal halves.

Erosion The gradual wearing away of land and rocks, usually by heat, wind, rain, ice, rivers or waves.

Eruption The explosion of a volcano when it throws out rocks, lava, ash and gases.

Fault A fracture in rock where one block of rock slides past another.

Firn Snow that has been packed down hard to make the ice in a glacier.

Fold mountains Mountains formed when the Earth's crust is squeezed into folds by the collision of two tectonic plates.

Fossil The preserved remains of a creature or plant long dead, usually turned to stone.

Fossil fuels Fuels such as coal, oil and gas made from the remains of plants and animals that have been gradually squashed beneath the ground for millions of years.

Geologist A scientist who studies the structure of the Earth.

Geyser A fountain of hot water and steam that shoots out of a hole in the ground. The water is heated by hot underground rock.

Glaciation The moulding of the landscape by glaciers and ice sheets.

Global warming The gradual increase in temperature of the Earth.

Gravity The pulling force that holds down everything on the Earth and stops it floating away.

Greenhouse effect The way certain gases in the atmosphere trap the Sun's heat like the panes of glass in a greenhouse.

Hemisphere Half of the Earth. The Southern Hemisphere is the half south of the Equator.

Hot spot A place where hot molten rock from the Earth's mantle pushes up through the crust to form volcanoes.

Ice age A long cold period when huge areas of the Earth are covered by ice sheets.

Iceberg An enormous chunk of ice broken from the end of a glacier or ice cap and floating in the sea.

Igneous rock Rocks created as hot magma from the Earth's interior cool and solidify.

Latitude Distance in degrees north or south of the Equator. Lines of latitude are imaginary lines round the Earth parallel to the Equator.

Lava Hot molten rock emerging through volcanoes, known as magma when underground.

Longitude Distance round the world measured in degrees from a north to south line through Greenwich, England. Lines of longitude are imaginary lines between the North and South poles.

Magma Hot molten rock in the Earth's interior. It is known as lava when it emerges onto the surface of the Earth.

Mantle The warm layer of the Earth's interior below the crust. Every now and then parts of the upper mantle melt to form magma.

Meander A bend or loop in a river.

Metamorphic rock Rocks created by the alteration of other rocks by heat or pressure.

Methane A gas given off by rotting material and animals passing wind that adds to the greenhouse effect.

Mid-ocean ridge A ridge along the middle of the sea floor where tectonic plates meet.

Mineral A material (not living) found naturally in the Earth. Rocks mostly contain a mixture of minerals.

Monsoon A season with heavy rain and winds that happens in southern Asia including India.

Moraine Sand and gravel deposited in piles by a glacier or ice sheet.

Oasis An area in a desert where there is water, and plants can grow.

Oceanic trench A deep underwater trench formed where one tectonic plate is pushed or subducted under another.

Ore Rock that contains a useful material like a metal. Metals and other materials are extracted from ore that has been dug out of the ground.

Ozone 'hole' Part of the ozone layer over the Antarctic with much less ozone than normal. The 'hole' appears each spring.

Ozone layer A layer of ozone (a form of oxygen gas) high in the stratosphere that protects us from the Sun's radiation.

Pangaea A single huge continent that scientists think existed millions of years ago before it split up into the continents of today.

Planetesimal One of the small lumps of rock circling the early Sun which later clumped together to form the planets.

Poles The North and South poles are the two points on Earth's surface furthest away from the Equator.

Precipitation Rain, snow or hail falling from clouds in the sky.

Projection A way of flattening out the Earth's round shape to draw it as accurately as possible on a flat map.

Seamount A mountain under the sea.

Sediment Small particles of sand and rock that are carried along by fast flowing water in rivers. They are dropped when the river slows as it reaches a lake or the sea.

Sedimentary rock Rock made from sand, mud and remains of creatures laid down underwater and gradually squashed into hard rock.

Seismologist A person who studies earthquakes.

Silt Fine grains like sand and clay carried by rivers and dropped when the flow of water slows at a river mouth.

Stalactite Stone column hanging from the roof of a cave, slowly built up by dripping water.

Stalagmite Stone column growing up from the floor of a cave, slowly built up by water dripping onto the ground.

Strata Layers of sedimentary rock.

Subduction The bending of a tectonic plate beneath another as they collide.

Tectonic plate The 20 or so giant rock slabs that make up the Earth's surface.

Tides The regular rise and fall of the sea along the shore caused by the pull of the Moon and Sun's gravity.

Tremor A shaking movement of the Earth's surface that is usually caused by an earthquake.

Tributary A smaller river or stream that joins a larger river.

Tropics Regions of the Earth on either side of the Equator with a hot climate.

Tsunami A giant wave moving out in all directions from an undersea earthquake or volcano.

Weathering The breakdown of rock when exposed to the weather.

LIFE ON EARTH

Origins of Life

Life began on Earth a very long time ago. The earliest fossils (remains) of life that have been found are of simple single-celled creatures called bacteria. They are about 3.5 billion years old. It is thought that these microscopic creatures are the ancient ancestors of all life on Earth.

The 'panspermia theory' suggests that life did not begin on Earth but came from outer space on comets. Long ago, comets often crashed into the Earth's surface and some carried the chemicals that are essential to life.

The science of grouping living things is called taxonomy. It is important in many ways, for example when making a decision about which creatures today are the closest relatives of the dinosaurs.

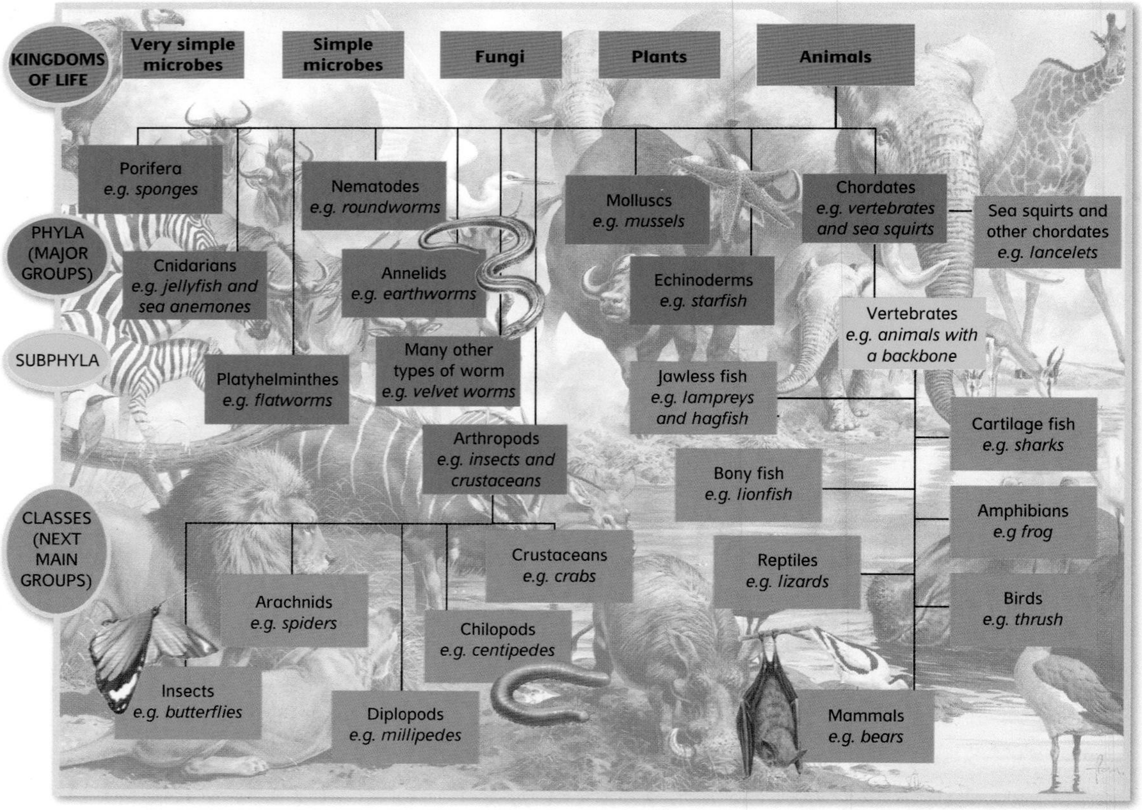

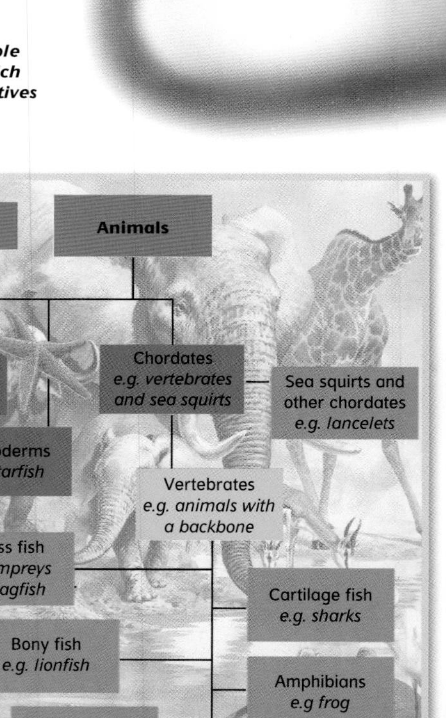

KINGDOMS OF LIFE

Very simple microbes

Simple microbes

Fungi

Plants

Animals

PHYLA (MAJOR GROUPS)

Porifera *e.g. sponges*

Nematodes *e.g. roundworms*

Molluscs *e.g. mussels*

Chordates *e.g. vertebrates and sea squirts*

Sea squirts and other chordates *e.g. lancelets*

Cnidarians *e.g. jellyfish and sea anemones*

Annelids *e.g. earthworms*

Echinoderms *e.g. starfish*

SUBPHYLA

Vertebrates *e.g. animals with a backbone*

Platyhelminthes *e.g. flatworms*

Many other types of worm *e.g. velvet worms*

Jawless fish *e.g. lampreys and hagfish*

Arthropods *e.g. insects and crustaceans*

Cartilage fish *e.g. sharks*

Bony fish *e.g. lionfish*

CLASSES (NEXT MAIN GROUPS)

Amphibians *e.g frog*

Crustaceans *e.g. crabs*

Reptiles *e.g. lizards*

Arachnids *e.g. spiders*

Birds *e.g. thrush*

Chilopods *e.g. centipedes*

Insects *e.g. butterflies*

Diplopods *e.g. millipedes*

Mammals *e.g. bears*

Amazing

Almost two million species, or types, of animal have been identified by scientists so far.

❍ Scientists do not agree about the way life began on Earth. Some believe that a mixture of chemicals was sparked into life by a source of energy, such as lightning. Others think that life first came to our planet from outer space, on a comet or by some similar means.

❍ However life began, it appears that early life-forms were very simple and remained so for an extremely long time. The first multi-celled creatures, such as sponges and jellyfish, did not appear until about 700 million years ago.

Corals may look like plants, but they contain many tiny animals called polyps.

Disappearing species

Many, many more species of animal have come and gone than are alive today. This reptile-like bird, *Archaeopteryx*, lived in the trees, hunting insects. It had feathers, and scientists believe it would have been able to fly quite well.

❍ Less than 600 million years ago life on Earth underwent an explosion in growth, and many new varieties of different animals and plants appeared in a relatively short time.

❍ Since this explosion in growth, animal and plant life has continued to develop and change (evolve) and has resulted in the huge variety of life that exists on our planet today.

❍ To make sense of the different types (species) of animals and plants on Earth, scientists put them into categories. They do this by looking at features that indicate past relationships, from DNA to skeletons.

❍ Life-forms are divided into groups or kingdoms, which are then split into smaller groups. The Animal Kingdom, for example, is divided into phyla (single: phylum) and each phylum is split into smaller groups.

❍ Animals or plants that are in the same group may share similar physical characteristics, such as appearance. They are grouped because they are closely related to one another, and have evolved from common ancestors.

Different species

Animals of the same species can only breed with one another. Dogs, for example, can breed with other dogs and they therefore belong to the same species. A dog cannot breed with a cat, and they are therefore different species. Each species is given a Latin name that is used by scientists all over the world, no matter what their own language. Humans belong to the species *Homo sapiens*, which means 'wise man'.

Numbers of species

1,300,000	Insects
400,000	Plants
85,000	Molluscs
60,000	Arachnids
32,000	Fish
26,000	Crustaceans
20,000	Roundworms
10,000	Birds
10,000	Reptiles
5600	Mammals

The Plant Kingdom

There are millions of different kinds of living things on Earth, so scientists group them to make them easier to study. The plant kingdom is one of the largest groups, and it includes more than 400,000 different kinds of plants.

These plants grow in damp, shady places. They do not make seeds or have vessels to carry water. Mosses can survive for weeks without water, then soak it up like a sponge when it rains.

There are probably more than one million different types of fungi, including mushrooms, toadstools, yeast and moulds. Fungi are not plants and do not have chlorophyll, but feed either from plants and animals, or from dead matter that has rotted in the soil.

Lichens can survive in many places where other plants would die, such as the Arctic, on mountaintops and in deserts. Some Arctic lichens are over 4000 years old.

Algae are simple organisms that live in oceans, lakes, rivers and damp mud. Algae vary from single-celled microscopic organisms to huge fronds of seaweed (brown algae) that can grow to over 60 m long.

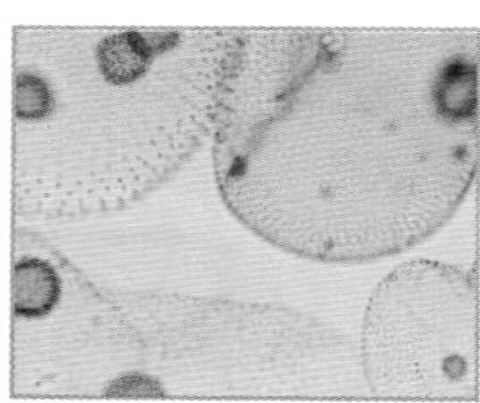

Phytoplankton is made up of tiny floating plants, such as diatoms, that live in water.

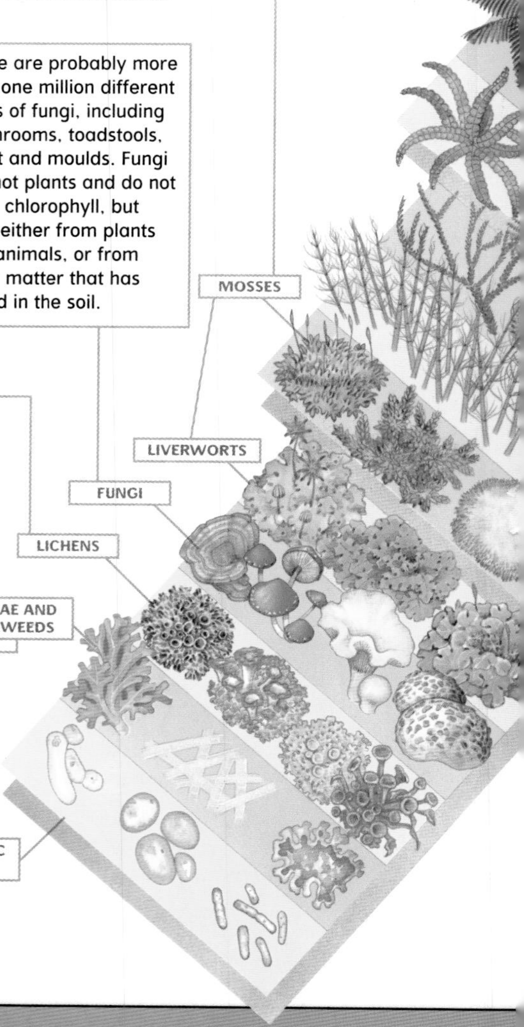

MOSSES

LIVERWORTS

FUNGI

LICHENS

ALGAE AND SEAWEEDS

MICROSCOPIC PLANTS

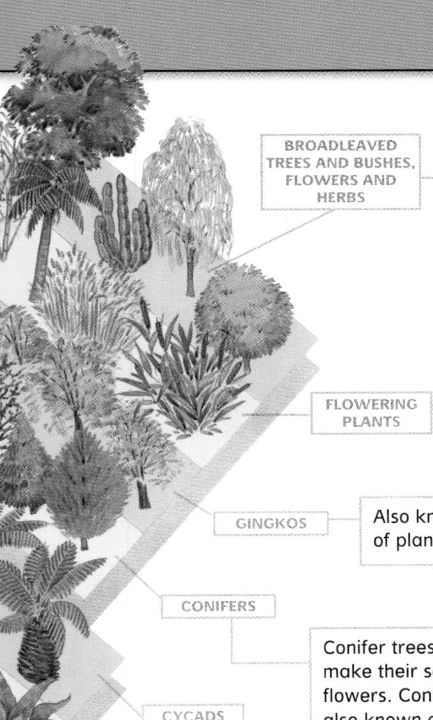

BROADLEAVED TREES AND BUSHES, FLOWERS AND HERBS

Trees, bushes, flowers and herbs that grow wide, flat leaves. Broadleaved trees can be evergreen or deciduous.

FLOWERING PLANTS

The flowering plant group contains more than 300,000 different species, including flowers, herbs, grasses, vegetables and trees (except conifers). Flowering plants are also known as angiosperms.

GINGKOS

Also known as maidenhair trees, gingkos are an ancient type of plant with fan-shaped leaves and fleshy yellow seeds.

CONIFERS

Conifer trees have needle-like leaves that make their seeds in cones rather than in flowers. Conifers, cycads and gingkos are also known as gymnosperms.

CYCADS

These are mostly short, stubby, palm-like trees. Some are thousands of years old. Cycads have fern-like leaves growing in a circle around the end of the stem. New leaves sprout each year and last for several years.

FERNS

Ferns live in damp, shady places around the world. They are an ancient group of plants and have been found as fossils in rocks 400 million years old. Coal is made largely of fossilized ferns, horsetails and club mosses.

CLUB MOSSES

HORSETAILS

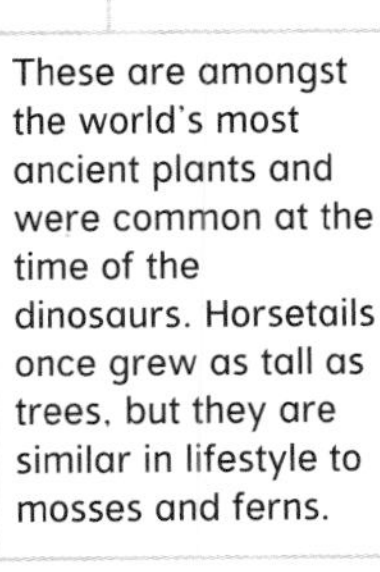

These are amongst the world's most ancient plants and were common at the time of the dinosaurs. Horsetails once grew as tall as trees, but they are similar in lifestyle to mosses and ferns.

Parts of a Plant

There are four major parts to a flowering plant: the roots, the stem, the leaves and the flower. Each part plays a vital role in keeping the plant alive and healthy.

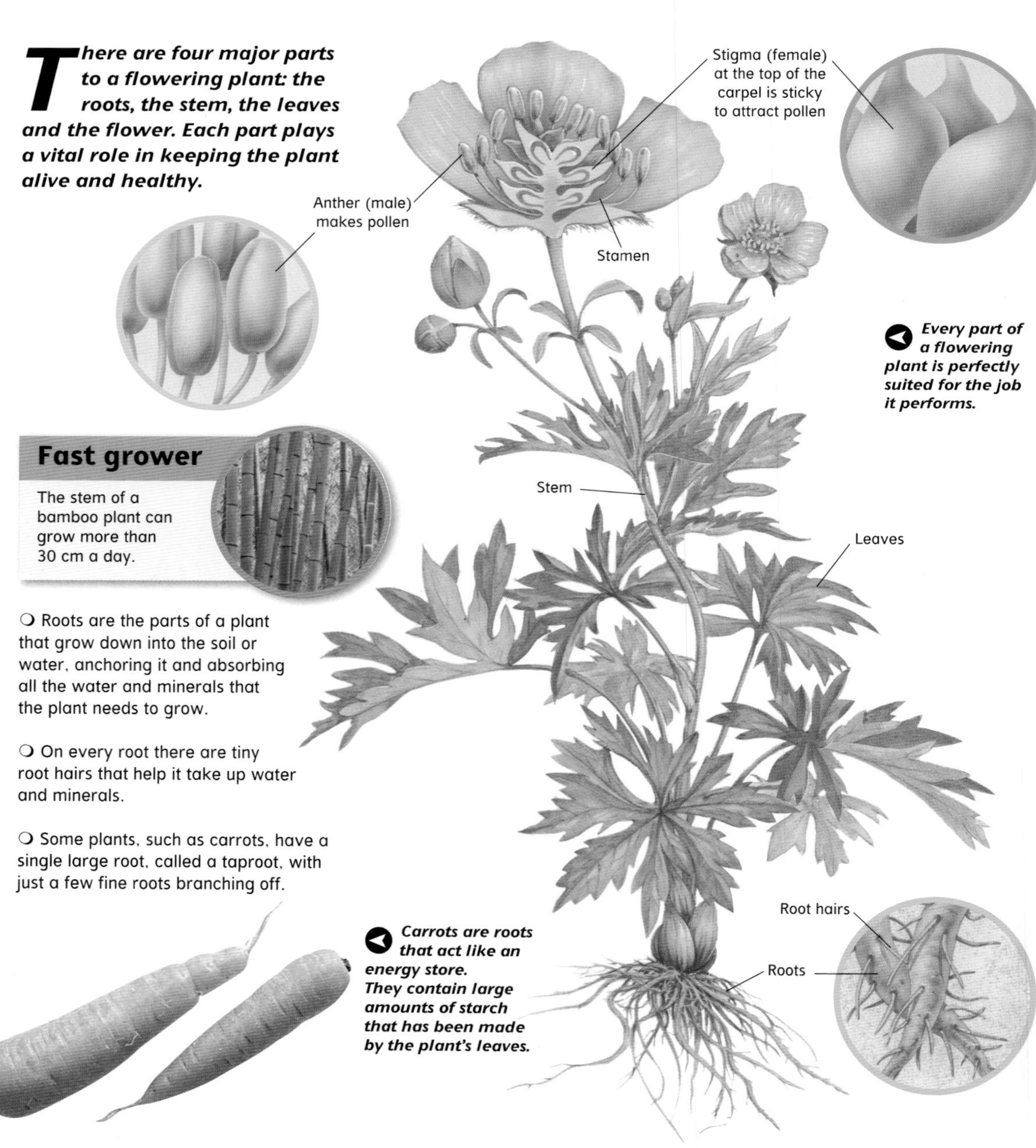

Every part of a flowering plant is perfectly suited for the job it performs.

Fast grower

The stem of a bamboo plant can grow more than 30 cm a day.

- Roots are the parts of a plant that grow down into the soil or water, anchoring it and absorbing all the water and minerals that the plant needs to grow.
- On every root there are tiny root hairs that help it take up water and minerals.
- Some plants, such as carrots, have a single large root, called a taproot, with just a few fine roots branching off.

Carrots are roots that act like an energy store. They contain large amounts of starch that has been made by the plant's leaves.

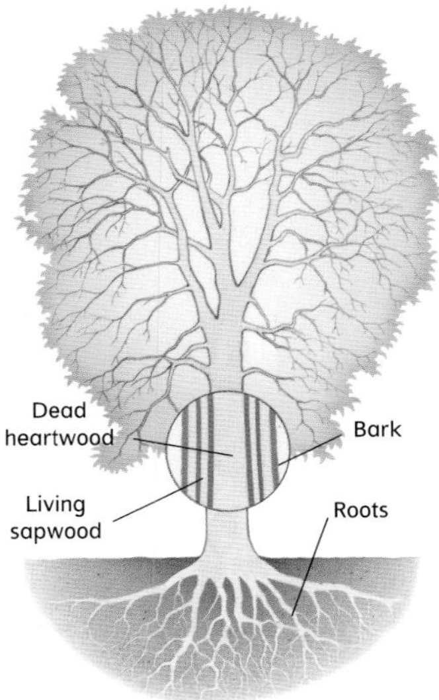

A tree trunk includes living sapwood, dead heartwood and a thick, protective layer of bark.

- Some plants, such as grass, have lots of small roots, called fibrous roots, branching off in all directions.
- The flowers are the plant's reproductive organs. The female flower parts are called carpels, and the male parts are the stamens.
- The stem of a plant supports the leaves and the flowers. It also carries water, minerals and food up and down between the plant's leaves and roots.
- Trees have one tall, thick, woody stem called a trunk. Trunks are at least 10 cm thick to help the tree stand up.

Amazing

There are thousands of poisonous plants around the world. Every part of the deadly nightshade is poisonous and eating a single berry can kill you.

Water carriers

If you break open a celery stalk you will see fibres sticking out of the end. These fibres are from groups of tubes, called xylem vessels, which carry water through the plant.

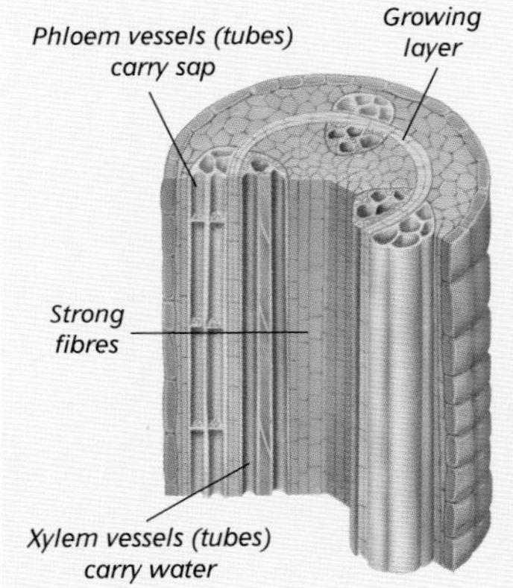

- Most desert plants have tough waxy leaves to cut down on water loss. They also have very few, or very small, leaves. For example, cactus spines are tiny leaves that lose very little water.
- The leaves of green vegetables are rich in many essential vitamins including Vitamin A, Vitamin E and folic acid (one of the B vitamins).
- Root vegetables are parts of a plant that grow underground in the soil.
- Turnips, rutabaga, beets, carrots, parsnips and sweet potatoes are the actual roots of the plant. Potatoes and cassava are tubers or storage stems.

Plants in the desert are specially adapted so they can survive for months, or even years, without rain.

Food Factory

Unlike animals, plants are able to make their own food. Each green plant is a remarkable chemical factory, taking in energy from the Sun and using it to combine carbon dioxide, from the air, with water to make sugary food. This process is called photosynthesis.

❍ Plants are made from tiny blocks of living matter called cells. The surface of a leaf is made from flat cells that are transparent to allow sunlight through.

❍ Most plant leaves contain a chemical called chlorophyll. This traps the energy in sunlight. During photosynthesis, plants spread out their leaves so the sunshine can reach as much chlorophyll as possible.

Life-giving plants

After great activity, the body breathes faster and deeper, to replace the oxygen used by the muscles for energy. The oxygen in the air, on which we depend for life, was mostly made by plants during photosynthesis.

Record plants

Tallest sunflower	7.76 m
Slowest-growing tree	White cedar, 10.2 cm in 155 years
Longest seaweed	Giant kelp, 60 m
Oldest plant	Creosote plants and bristlecone pines, over 10,000 years
Largest seed	Giant fan palm, weighs up to 20 kg

Sun's rays carry light energy to leaf

Photosynthesis, as shown in this tulip plant, is a process whereby simple chemicals are changed into food using sunlight.

Carbon dioxide is taken from air into leaves

Oxygen is given off from leaves

Stem

Bulb

Roots

Amazing

All green plants make sugar. Much of the sugar we eat comes from sugar cane, which is a tropical grass.

While a poppy is growing towards sunlight, the plant uses food that is made in its leaves. Without heat and light energy from the Sun, there would be no life on Earth.

❍ The leaf draws in air, which contains the gas carbon dioxide, through holes called stomata. It also draws up water from the ground, through the stem and leaf veins.

❍ When the Sun is shining, chlorophyll soaks up its energy and uses it to split water into hydrogen and oxygen. The hydrogen combines with carbon dioxide to make sugar and the oxygen is released through the stomata.

❍ Sugar is transported around the plant to where it is needed. Some sugar is burned up instantly, leaving carbon dioxide and water. This process is called respiration.

❍ Some sugar is combined into substances called starches, which are easy for the plant to store. The plant breaks these starches down into sugar again, when it needs fuel.

❍ Unlike other living things, plants cannot move to find sunlight – but they can grow towards it. Plant stems have tips that are sensitive to light to ensure that they grow in the right direction.

This is a hugely magnified slice through a leaf, showing the different layers. Leaves are thin and flat so they can catch the maximum amount of sunlight. The flat part of a leaf is called a blade, the stalk is called a petiole.

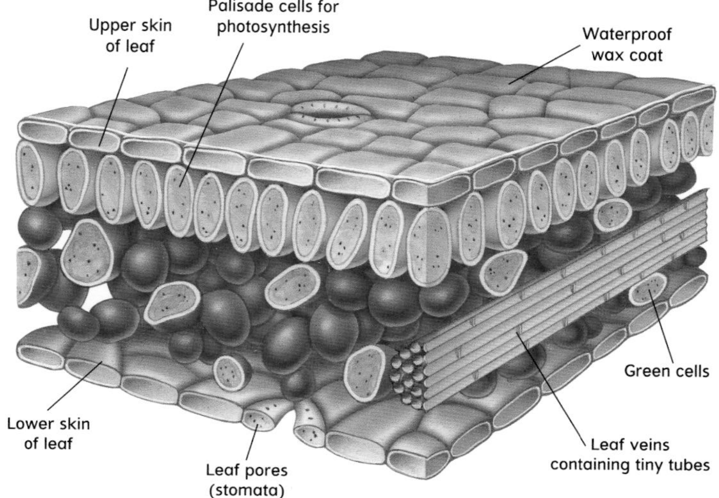

Sugar producers

Together all of the world's plants produce about 150 billion tonnes of sugar each year by photosynthesis.

Plant Reproduction

Every flowering plant has a life-cycle. It begins when a seed germinates, and continues as the new plant grows and forms flowers. The flowers are pollinated, and in turn, produce their own seeds.

Biennial plants take two years to grow from seed to a mature plant. The part-grown plant must be able to survive through a cold or dry season, then it continues to grow and change the year after and makes flowers and seeds.

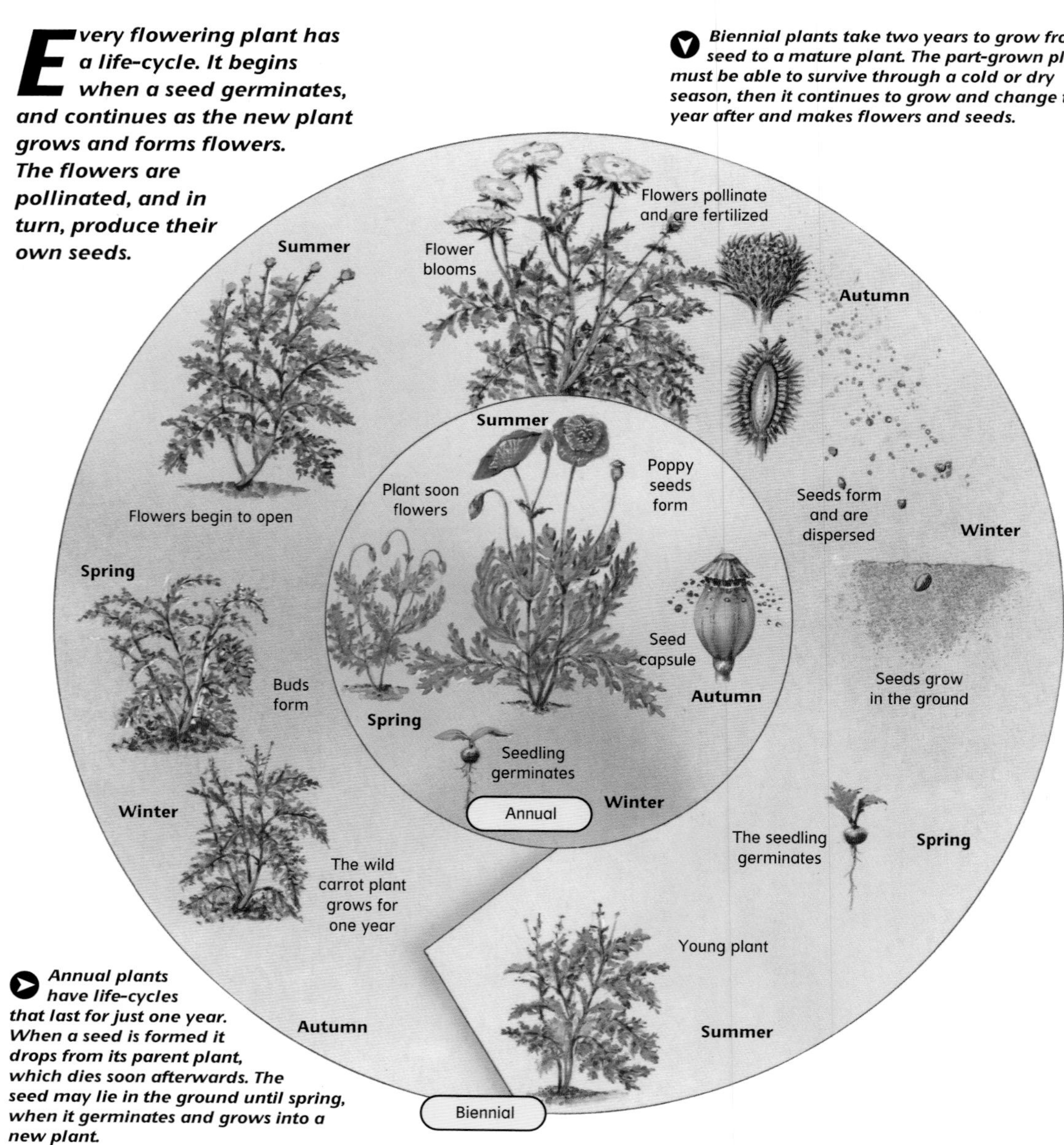

Annual plants have life-cycles that last for just one year. When a seed is formed it drops from its parent plant, which dies soon afterwards. The seed may lie in the ground until spring, when it germinates and grows into a new plant.

Daisy

The name 'daisy' comes from 'day's eye' since these eye-like flowers open by day and close up at night.

❍ Some flowers have both male parts, called stamens, and female parts, called carpels. Seeds for new plants are made when pollen grains from the stamens join with eggs inside the carpels.

❍ The carpel contains the ovaries, where the flower's eggs are made. A carpel usually looks like a short, thick stalk in the centre of a flower. The top of the carpel is sticky. This part is called the stigma.

❍ Stamens normally appear as spindly stalks that surround the carpels. Pollen is made in the anthers, at the top of the stamens.

❍ Before a flower can make seeds, it must be pollinated. The pollen has to be transferred to the stigma of another flower of the same type. This process is called pollination.

Amazing

Orchids produce the world's smallest seeds. A single gram of orchid seed contains an unbelievable 900 million seeds.

Pollen grains reach an ovule by travelling down a pollen tube. In some flowers, pollen tubes can be more than 10 cm long and grow in one or two days.

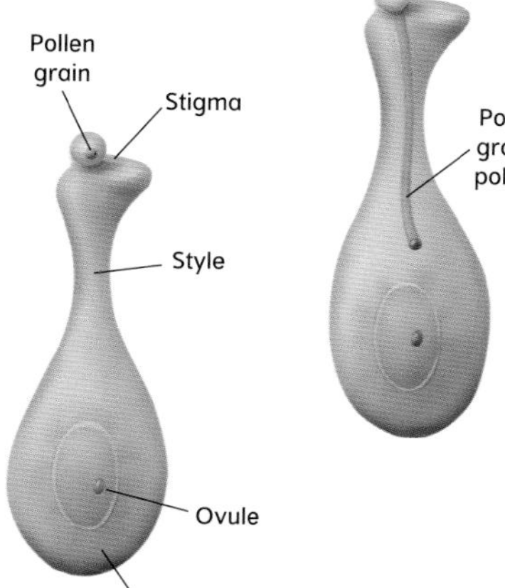

❍ There are several ways in which pollen can travel: it can be carried by insects or other animals, by wind or by water. Flowers that are pollinated by animals often have bright colours to attract insects. Wind-pollinated flowers are often dull in colour.

❍ When a pollen grain lands on a stigma it grows a long, thin tube that reaches down into the ovary. Inside the ovary are one or two egg-shaped ovules. The pollen tube seeks out an ovule to fertilize.

❍ After fertilization, the ovule turns into a seed and the ovary turns into a fruit. Meanwhile, parts of the flower, such as the petals and stamens, fall away.

❍ The fruit may swell up and become brightly coloured and juicy, so it gets eaten – or it may dry up and form 'parachutes' or 'wings' in order that it can be carried away by the wind to grow into a new plant.

❍ Inside a seed a plant embryo (the beginnings of a plant) is waiting to grow. The seed contains a store of food to help this growth.

❍ When the seed settles in the soil it takes in water, swells up and breaks open so the new plant can grow out. This process is called germination.

Recycling seeds

When an animal eats the seeds in a sweet, juicy fruit they are not entirely digested. Instead, they leave the animal's body in the droppings, so the seeds have a supply of manure to help the new plants grow.

Plant families

Angiosperms	Have enclosed seeds and easily seen flowers
Gymnosperms	Wind-pollinated, 'naked seeds' in cones
Pteridophytes	Simple plants, such as ferns, horsetails and clubmosses
Bryophytes	Liverworts and mosses, the simplest true land plants
Algae	Most live in water – they range from single-celled diatoms to giant seaweeds

How Plants Grow

When tiny plants start to grow they change food, stored in the seeds, into substances that build their roots, stem and leaves. If seeds are kept in warm conditions, such as a greenhouse, the changes take place quickly and the seeds soon sprout.

Spores

Spores are special cells of some plants that grow into new organisms. In plants such as ferns, mosses and in fungi, spores develop directly into a new plant, called a gametophyte.

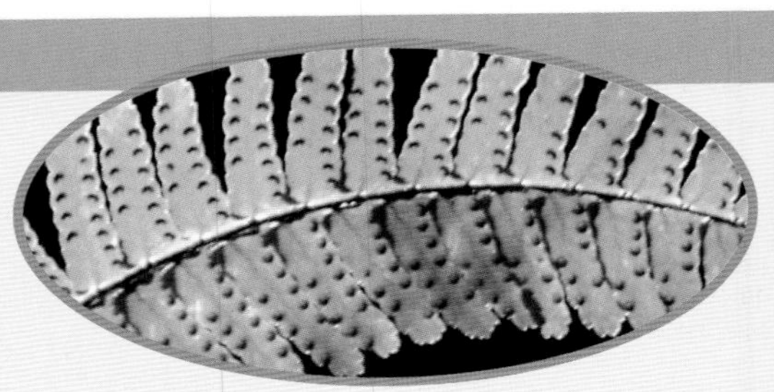

Stages of germination of a bean seed as it grows from a seed into a plant.

1. The seed lies dormant until conditions are right

2. The seed sends a root down and a shoot up

3. The shoot bursts into the air and grows cotyledons (seed leaves)

4. The stem and roots grow longer, and the plant soon begins to grow new leaves

Amazing

Rice grains are seeds of a type of grass. They are a popular source of food and more than 6000 tonnes of rice is eaten every second worldwide.

Coconuts are the fruit of the coconut palm tree. The seed is contained in a brown woody shell called a husk.

❍ Not all seeds germinate in the same way. Coconuts, for example, often fall into the ocean and may be swept away, eventually washing up on another warm beach where they can grow into new coconut palms.

Super giants

Tallest grass	Bamboo	25 m
Tallest cactus	Saguaro	18 m
Biggest fern	Norfolk Island tree fern	20 m
Tallest tree	Coast redwood	115 m
Longest leaf	Raffia palm	20 m
Heaviest pine cone	Coulter pine	4 kg

❍ A seed does not always sprout as soon as it forms. It may spend some time before germination, being inactive or dormant.

❍ An embryo inside a seed contains a cotyledon (seed food store) that is protected by the testa (a seed's tough outer casing). As the plant increases in size the seed case breaks open.

❍ The young plant that grows out of a seed is called a seedling.

❍ The root is the first part to appear and it grows downwards. Later, the shoot appears and grows upwards.

❍ The shoot grows towards the light, so its first leaves can make food by the process of photosynthesis.

Plants can even get all their needs – sunlight and water – in a crack in a pavement as rainwater carrying minerals seeps in.

This bristlecone pine from the USA has a long lifespan because it grows very slowly and in cool, dry areas, such as Nevada, Utah and California.

Trees grow tall as they compete for space and light. Branches spread out so that their leaves can reach the sunlight needed for photosynthesis. Deciduous trees lose their leaves in the winter and plants living beneath them often bloom in spring when most light reaches them.

❍ Once the store of food in the seed has been used, the plant relies on photosynthesis. The roots absorb water and minerals and grow strong enough to keep the plant anchored in the soil.

How old is a tree?

If a tree is sawn across you can see the annual growth rings. These show how much the tree has grown each year; new rings are made just beneath the bark and the oldest rings are found at the centre of the trunk. Counting the rings gives the age of the tree.

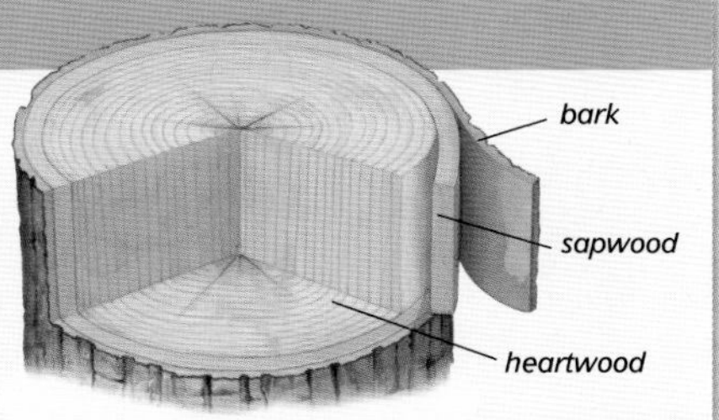

❍ There are two kinds of trees: evergreen, which hold onto their leaves all year round, and deciduous, which usually lose their leaves in autumn and grow new ones in the spring.

❍ Wood is a particularly long-lasting and tough plant material. Woody plants can live for a long time. The bristlecone pine of North America is one of the oldest species of tree in the world – some may be 10,000 years old.

❍ When trees grow together in large groups they form forests. There are three main types of forest: coniferous, temperate and tropical. Each kind of forest grows in different places, depending on weather conditions. Coniferous forests, for example, grow where winters are long and cold.

Plants on our Planet

Plants are vital to life on our planet because they make oxygen and help provide food that animals and people eat. Plants also provide us with useful materials, such as wood, cotton, paints, rubber and medicines.

This illustration shows the typical sequence of events in a grain farmer's year, from ploughing and sowing the seed through to harvest the following autumn.

Harvest time in late summer when the wheat is harvested

A few days after harvesting, the soil is cultivated to get rid of unwanted weeds

The seeds sprout before winter sets in, but don't begin to ripen until the following spring

After cultivation, the soil is prepared by ploughing and harrowing

About six weeks after the harvest, seeds are sown in the prepared soil

Wood

Every year the world uses 3 billion cu m of wood – a pile as big as a soccer stadium and as high as Mount Everest (8848 m).

❍ Plant leaves, stems, flowers and sap have been used since earliest times for medicinal purposes and, even today, plant-based remedies are popular across the world.

❍ Since about 3000 BC rice has been cultivated, and it is now the basic food for about half of the world's population. Rice grows in purposely flooded areas, called paddies.

Flower meanings

Basil	Hatred
Cactus	Maternal love
Daffodil	Deceit
Daisy	Affection
Geranium	Melancholy
Honeysuckle	Bonds of love
Hyacinth	Benevolence
Larkspur	Levity
Laurel	Glory
Lavender	Distrust
Lily	Pride
Lily of the valley	Return of happiness
Narcissus	Selfishness
Nettle	Cruelty
Rose	Beauty
Saffron	Abuse
Snowdrop	Consolation
Sunflower	False riches
Tulip	Declaration of love
Weeping willow	Sadness

❍ Wood was probably the first material from a plant to be used by people. It was used to make shelters and weapons. About 5000 years ago people began to weave cotton – a fibre that grows on the seeds of the cotton plant – to make clothes.

❍ The first crops were probably root crops like turnips. Grains and green vegetables were probably first grown as crops later.

❍ Corn was probably first grown about 9000 years ago from the teosinte plant of the Mexican highlands.

❍ Farmers usually put fertilizers on their fields to improve the soil. While the plants are growing they are treated with chemicals to prevent disease and insects from destroying the crop.

❍ Rubber comes from the sap of rubber trees. Natural rubber is very soft, but it can be toughened by adding chemicals. This is called vulcanizing.

❍ Algae may be tiny, but they are a vital food source for many creatures, from shrimps to whales, and they provide most of the oxygen that water creatures need for life.

Healing plants

For almost 50,000 years people have used plants to treat illness. Aspirin, for example, was originally made from willow bark. Many modern medicines are still made from plants.

Rose hips, from the dog rose, were used to boost the immune system and ward off colds

The bitter-tasting century plant was once used to help people with fevers and digestion problems.

Amazing

Bacteria in flooded rice fields produce methane gas that scientists believe may add to the problem of global warming.

Rice is grown in paddies. Once the grains of rice have been harvested, the plant stalks can be used to make mats, hats and shoes.

The Animal Kingdom

There are millions upon millions of different kinds, or species, of animals. They can be divided into two large groups: the invertebrates and the vertebrates. Invertebrates, such as worms and insects, do not have backbones. Vertebrates, such as lizards, birds and humans, do have backbones.

Worms are long, wriggling tube-like animals. The bodies of earthworms are divided into segments.

Snails and slugs are small, squidgy, slimy, soft-bodied crawling creatures. They belong to a group of animals called molluscs.

Crabs and lobsters are part of an enormous group of shelled invertebrates called crustaceans.

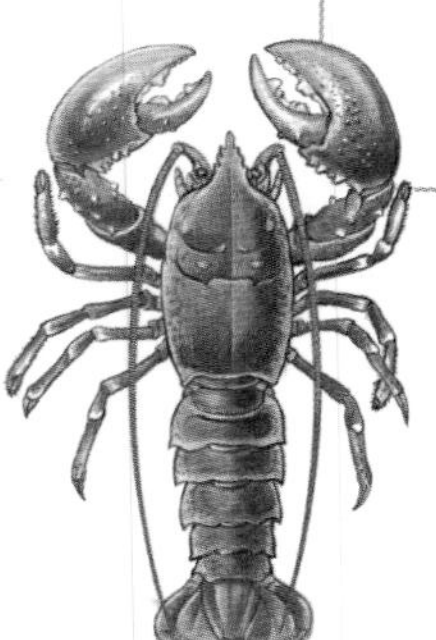

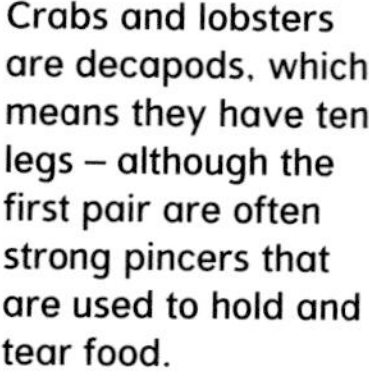

Crabs and lobsters are decapods, which means they have ten legs – although the first pair are often strong pincers that are used to hold and tear food.

Octopuses and squid belong to a group of molluscs called cephalopods. They are sea creatures with eight arms, or tentacles.

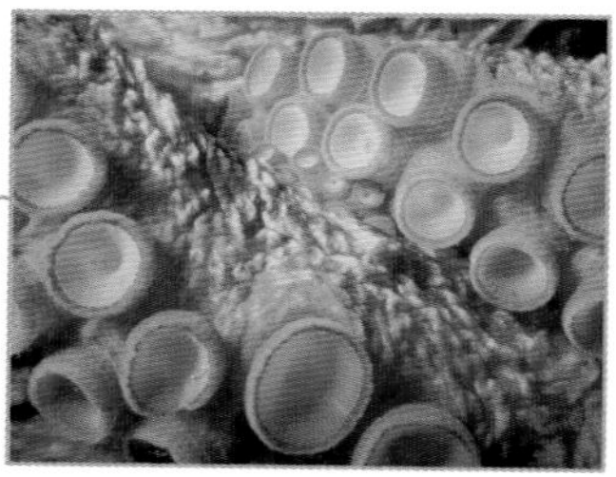

Spiders are small scurrying creatures which, unlike insects, have eight legs not six, and bodies with two parts not three.

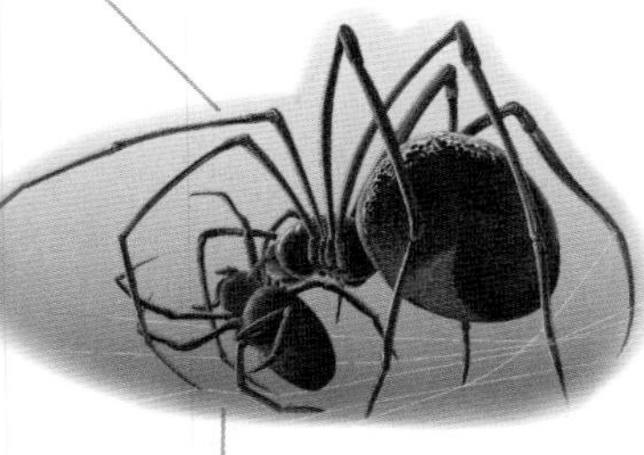

Spiders belong to a group of 60,000 creatures called arachnids, which also includes scorpions, mites and ticks.

Insects may be tiny, but there are more of them than all other animals put together – over 5 million species.

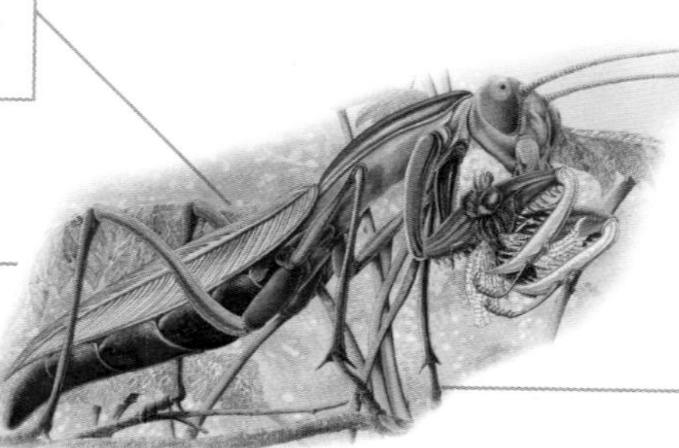

Flies, butterflies, moths, beetles, grasshoppers, dragonflies, fleas, earwigs, ants, bees and wasps are all types of insect.

Insects have six legs and a body divided into three sections: the head, thorax (middle) and abdomen.

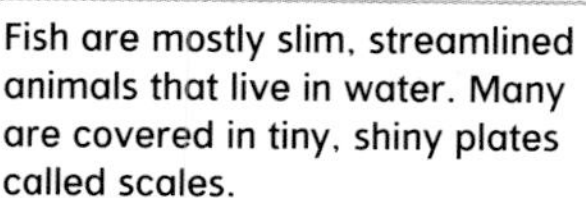

Fish are mostly slim, streamlined animals that live in water. Many are covered in tiny, shiny plates called scales.

Amphibians live both on land and in water. They include frogs, toads, newts and salamanders.

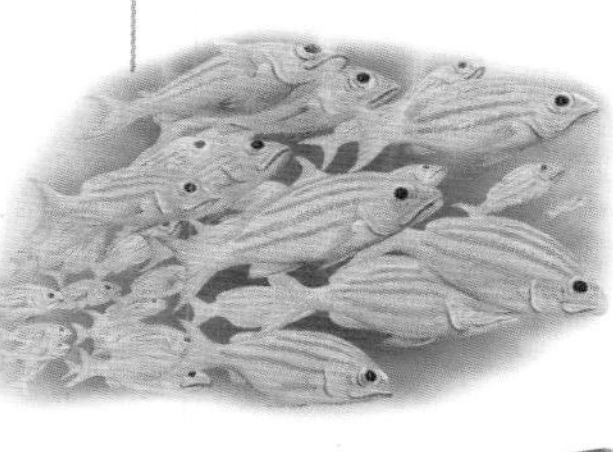

Frogs and toads begin life as tadpoles, hatching into water from huge clutches of eggs called spawn.

Most fish have bony skeletons and a backbone but sharks have skeletons of rubbery material called cartilage.

Reptiles are scaly-skinned vertebrates that live in many different habitats, especially warm places.

Crocodiles, alligators, lizards, snakes, turtles and tortoises are all types of reptile.

Mammals have furry bodies and feed their young on milk.

Not all birds can fly, but they all have feathers.

Instead of teeth, birds have a hard beak or bill.

Unlike humans, birds do not give birth to babies. Instead they lay eggs.

Mammals are able to keep their body temperature constant, which means that they can survive in very hot or very cold weather.

Record-breakers

Tallest land mammal
Giraffe

Largest animal
Blue whale

Heaviest land mammal
African elephant

Largest fish
Whale shark

Largest land carnivore
Polar bear

Largest feline
Siberian tiger

Largest deer
Alaskan moose

Largest rodent
Capybara

Largest butterfly
Queen Alexandra's Birdwing

Largest bird
Ostrich

Longest snake
Reticulated python

Smallest horse
Falabella

Smallest bird
Bee hummingbird

Fastest land mammal
Cheetah

Slowest land mammal
Three-toed sloth

Most poisonous fish
Stonefish

Most poisonous snake
Gaboon viper

Most poisonous jellyfish
Australian sea wasp

Loudest insect
African cicada

Invertebrates

Invertebrates, despite their size, are a very important group of animals. They are found all over the world, in many different habitats, especially oceans. They account for 97 per cent of all animal species.

❍ Insects were among the first creatures to live on land – nearly a quarter of a billion years before the first dinosaurs – and the first to fly.

❍ An insect's body is encased in such a tough shell (its exoskeleton) that it has no need for bones. Insects grow by getting rid of their old exoskeleton and replacing it with a bigger one. This is called moulting.

Amazing

You can teach an octopus to count to five and identify different shapes. It is also capable of opening closed jars to retrieve food, such as small crabs, inside.

❍ Jellyfish are sea creatures with bell-shaped, jelly-like bodies and long stinging tentacles. The bell of one giant jellyfish was found to measure 2.29 m across, with tentacles over 36 m long.

❍ At least 300,000 species of beetle have been identified. They are found worldwide, except in the oceans. They have a pair of thick, hard front wings, called elytra, which form an armour-like casing over the beetle's body.

❍ Coral reefs are the undersea equivalent of rainforests and teem with shrimps and other sea life. The reefs are built by invertebrates called polyps.

❍ Octopuses belong to a family of sea molluscs called cephalopods. An octopus has a round, soft, boneless body, three hearts and eight long tentacles that are covered in suckers.

❍ Snails and slugs are gastropods. Gastropod means 'stomach foot' and these animals seem to slide along on their stomachs. Most gastropods live in the sea, for example, limpets and whelks.

❍ Spiders are hunters and most of them feed mainly on insects. They have eight eyes, but most have poor eyesight and hunt by feeling vibrations with their legs. Many of them use silken webs to catch their prey.

Tropical coral reefs are the habitat of an amazing range of marine plants and creatures. Over millions of years the polyp skeletons pile up to form huge wall-like structures called reefs. One such reef, the Great Barrier Reef, can be seen from space. It is over 2000 km long and is the largest structure ever built by living creatures.

Intriguing insects

The average lifespan of a dragonfly is a few days.

The praying mantis is born with one ear.

A cockroach can survive for up to a week minus its head.

The greatest insect leaper is a type of froghopper – it can jump 100 times its own body length.

A caterpillar has over 2000 muscles in its body.

The butterfly was originally called a flutterby.

You are more likely to be bitten by a mosquito if you have blonde hair, wear blue clothes and eat bananas.

The hum of a housefly is usually in the key of F.

The heaviest insect in the animal kingdom is the Goliath beetle weighing over 110 g.

Breeds of tropical cockroach can travel 50 times their body length in the space of a second, equivalent to an athlete running 100 m in one second.

❍ Despite their name, starfish are not fish but belong to a group of sea invertebrates called echinoderms. They have five strong 'arms' that they use to prise open their prey. They eat shellfish, such as oysters.

Long jumpers

Grasshoppers are insects with powerful back legs, which allow them to leap huge distances. Some grasshoppers can leap more than 3 m.

Useful invertebrates

Invertebrates play an important role in the survival of all animals. Many of them are food for other animals, such as birds and reptiles. Insects, such as bees, wasps and butterflies (such as this monarch butterfly), pollinate flowers. Without them plants, including those we eat, would quickly die out.

❍ Many invertebrates are parasites; this means that they live on or in other animals' bodies. Tapeworms live in animals' guts and eat their food. Other invertebrates spread diseases. Mosquitoes, for example, carry malaria.

Insects

The caterpillars of death's head hawk-moths reach 12.5 cm when fully grown and make a clicking sound if they are disturbed.

Horse flies are among the fastest flying insects, reaching maximum speeds of 39 km/h. Unlike most other flies, their flight can be silent, allowing females to sneak up on their prey.

If the Bhutan glory butterfly is disturbed it quickly opens and shuts its wings, exposing its bright orange markings.

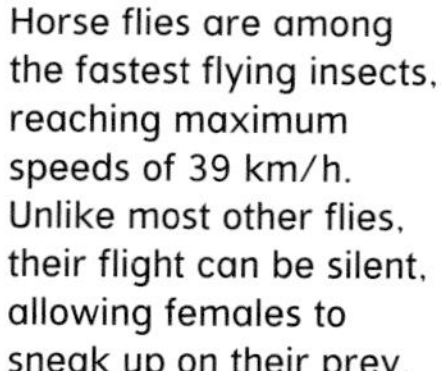

Insect-like springtails are also called snow fleas as they can survive extreme cold, and are active even in freezing weather.

Spittlebug nymphs produce 'cuckoo spit' by giving off a sticky liquid and blowing this into a frothy mass of white bubbles. As well as hiding the nymph from predators, these bubbles also protect the young bug from the drying effects of the Sun.

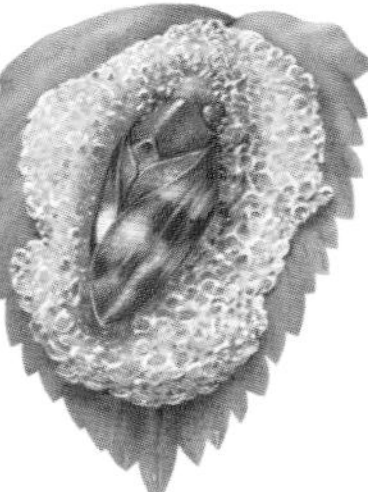

Water boatmen are not buoyant enough to float, so when they stop swimming, they sink to the bottom. This is useful because they feed on the bottom of ponds, canals and ditches, using their shovel-like front legs to scrabble up food.

How Animals Move

Movement defines what an animal is. Creatures travel to find food and shelter and avoid predators. Most land animals, from bugs to bears, use their legs for moving, or locomotion. Others fly, crawl on their bellies, wriggle, swing, slide, swim or slither.

❍ Burrowing animals use various methods of movement. Moles shovel soil using their powerful front legs. Earthworms contract their muscles to make their bodies hard so that they can force their way between grains of soil.

Amazing

Bears are one of the few animals to walk on the soles of their feet, like humans.

❍ Monkeys move through trees by swinging from their arms. A gibbon's arms are twice as long as its legs and it has hook-shaped hands to hang from the branches.

❍ Movement through water is much more difficult than movement through air – it needs extra muscle power. More than four-fifths of a fish is muscle.

❍ The African fringe-toed lizard has to dance across the hot sand in the desert to keep its feet cool.

❍ Hummingbirds and nectar-sipping bats flap their short, broad wings quickly, almost 100 times a second, so they can hover. An albatross, however, soars on the winds above the ocean, and can travel for many kilometres without flapping its wings once.

Cheetahs are the world's fastest land animal. Within two seconds of starting, a cheetah can reach speeds of 75 km/h, reaching a top speed of about 105 km/h. Their spines are so bendy that they can bring their hind legs forward between their front paws when they run. Unlike most cats, they do not have retractable claws on their feet. When they run, their claws stick into the ground like the spikes on an athlete's shoes.

Fast flier

Fastest of all animals is the peregrine falcon, which has been recorded travelling at 270 km/h when it dives or 'stoops' to catch its prey.

Fastest land animals

Cheetah	105 km/h
Pronghorn antelope	90 km/h
Springbok	80 km/h
Ostrich	70 km/h
Racehorse	70 km/h

The slowest mammal is the three-toed sloth, which has an average speed of 0.16 km/h

The paws of big cats have soft pads that are surrounded by tufty fur to muffle the sound of every footstep. Each claw on this lion's paw is curved and very sharp.

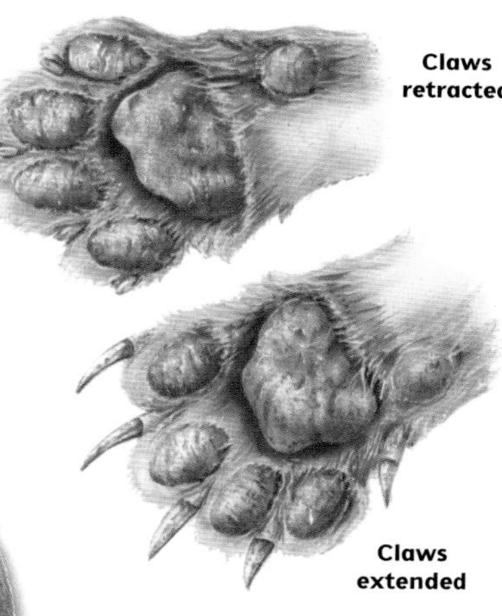

Muscles

Muscles get shorter, or contract, and pull different body parts to allow movement. In vertebrates the muscles are joined to bones, which make up the skeleton, as seen here in the bear. In insects and spiders the muscles are joined to a hard outer body casing (an exoskeleton).

The earthworm wriggles between soil grains, munching humus as it tunnels. The stiff hairs along its body help to grip the sides of the burrow, so the worm can thrust forward its front end to move onwards.

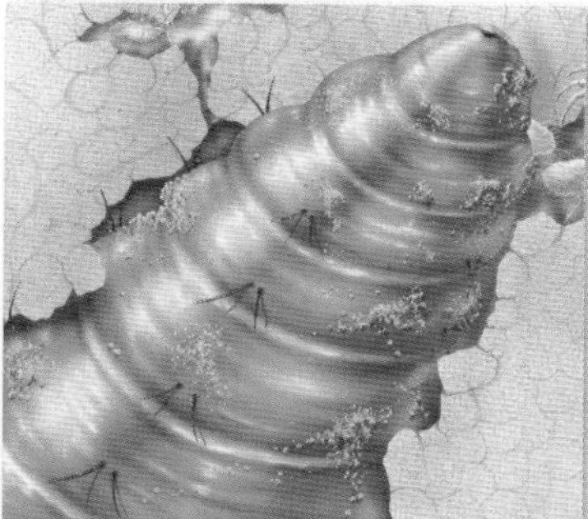

- Fliers and swimmers both use broad pushing surfaces – wings through air, and fins, flippers and tails through water. These surfaces produce propulsion (forward movement). Other body parts control steering and slowing down.
- Water is very dense so streamlining (a smooth body shape) enables fish, dolphins, seals and other sea creatures to easily move through it.
- One of the most adaptable movers has no limbs at all. The golden tree snake can slither fast, swim well, burrow, climb trees and even launch itself from a branch, and flatten its body, to glide for many metres.
- Jellyfish float about freely, moving by squeezing water out from beneath their bodies. When a jellyfish stops squeezing, it slowly sinks.
- To escape a predator, the ostrich can hurtle over the African grasslands at 70 km/h – as fast as a racehorse can run. If it tires it can still deliver a massive kick with its muscular legs.
- Penguins can leap high out of the water to land on an ice bank, but on land they can only waddle clumsily or toboggan along on their bellies.

Cat landings

Some cats spend a lot of their time in trees. When a cat, such as this caracal, falls out of a tree, it can twist its body round so that it lands on its feet.

1. The caracal may lose its footing as it chases prey along branches

2. It has a superb sense of balance and quickly begins to right itself

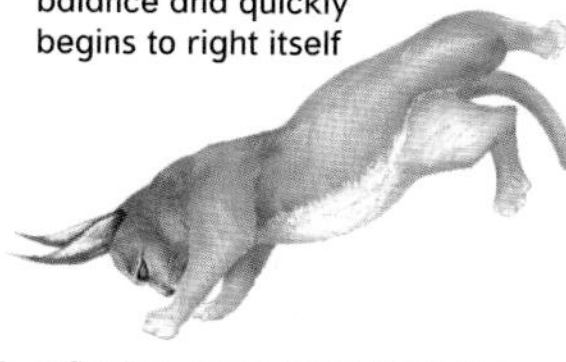

3. A flexible spine helps the falling caracal twist its body

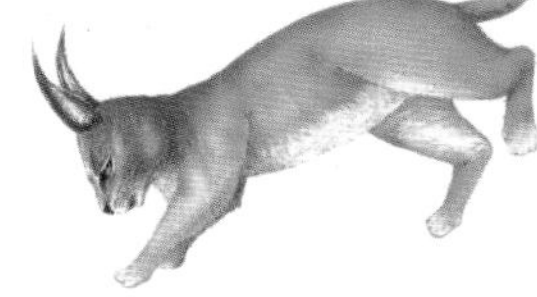

4. Cats' muscles are very strong and their joints are very flexible so they can absorb the shock of hitting the ground with a soft landing

Fish

Fish were the first vertebrate (backboned) animals to evolve on Earth, over 500 million years ago. They breathe using gills instead of lungs and their bodies are usually covered in scales. Fish live in freshwater (lakes and rivers) or salty water (sea and oceans). A few species can live in both types of water.

Some fish pack so closely in a shoal, that they are almost touching. They twist and turn as one whirling mass. This confusing sight makes it difficult for a predator to pick out and attack a single individual.

Amazing

Sharks' skeletons are made of rubbery cartilage – most other kinds of fish have bony skeletons.

- There are over 32,000 species of fish. Fish are cold-blooded vertebrates that breathe through gills – rows of feathery brushes inside each side of the fish's head.
- To get oxygen, fish gulp water into their mouths and draw it over their gills. As water passes into the gills it is cleaned by sieve-like structures and the oxygen passes into the fish's blood.
- Salmon are river and sea fish that are caught or farmed in huge quantities for food. All salmon are born in rivers and lakes far inland, then swim downriver and out to sea. Years later they return to their birthplace to spawn (lay eggs).
- Deep-sea anglerfish live deep in the ocean where it is pitch-black. They lure prey using fishing-rod-like spines with lights at the tip.
- Sharks have a reputation as the most fearsome predatory fish of the seas, but they are not the world's most dangerous animals. Each year, many more people are killed by poisonous snakes, tigers, elephants, hippos and crocodiles.

Freshwater fish

Rivers, lakes and other freshwater habitats are home to all sorts of fish, including bream and trout. Some fish feed on floating plant matter, while others take insects from the surface of the water. Pikes, such as this northern pike, are the sharks of the river – deadly hunters that lurk among weeds for unwary fish, rats and birds.

Biggest fish

The world's biggest fish is the whale shark, which can grow to over 12 m in length. Unlike most other sharks, the whale shark eats plankton and is completely harmless.

- Gulper eels can live more than 7500 m deep in the Atlantic Ocean. Their mouths are huge to help them catch food in the dark deep water. They can swallow fish that are larger than themselves.

- Nearly 75 per cent of all fish live in the seas and oceans. The biggest and fastest fish, such as swordfish, live near the surface of the ocean, far from land. They often migrate (travel) large distances to spawn or find food.

- Flatfish start life as normal-shaped fish, but as they grow older, one eye slowly slides around the head to join the other. The pattern of scales changes so that one side is the top, the other is the bottom.

- Many colourful fish species live in warm seas around coral reefs. They are often very bright, which makes them instantly recognizable to their own kind.

The world's biggest predatory, or hunting, fish is the great white shark. It measures up to 6 m in length and weighs more than 1 tonne. It has 50 or more teeth and each one is 6 cm long. The teeth are slim and razor-sharp like blades to 'saw' lumps of food from its victim. Sometimes they snap off but new teeth are always growing just behind, ready to move forward and replace them.

- Rays have flat diamond-shaped bodies. They mostly live on the seafloor, feeding on oysters and other shellfish.

Sea creatures

Dolphins always sleep with one eye active.

The pupil of the octopus's eye is rectangular.

The starfish has no brain and can turn its stomach inside out.

Oysters change sex annually.

Large electric eels can produce shocks in excess of 650 volts of electricity.

The heart of a shrimp is located in its head.

The seahorse is the world's only male species of animal that can become pregnant.

Sharks

Cleaner wrasse gather around the mouth and gill slits of this white-tip reef shark.

The epaulette shark can leave the water and move over dry land. It drags itself between rock pools using its strong pectoral fins.

The sand tiger has a huge appetite for many kinds of prey.

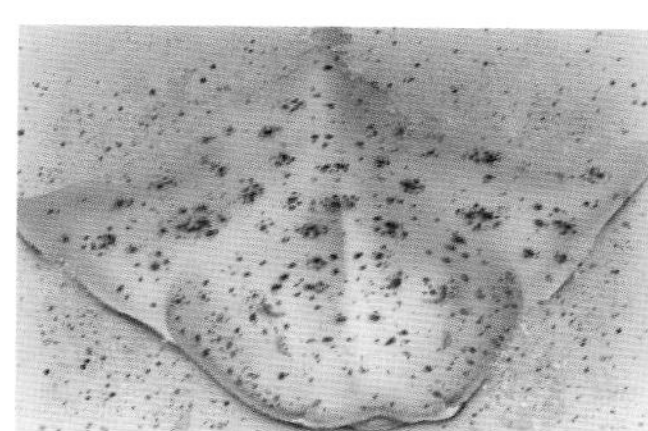

The angel shark has a wide flat body the same colour as sand. It lies in wait on the seabed for prey.

How Animals Feed

Animals that mainly eat other animals are called carnivores. Some are active predators that hunt down prey, while others use stealth or ambush methods. More than three-quarters of all animals in the world are herbivores (plant eaters).

❍ Meat eaters range from killer whales and sharks in the sea, big cats and wild dogs on land, and eagles and hawks in the air, to much smaller – but equally deadly – shrews, bats, frogs, dragonflies, spiders and even sea anemones.

❍ Some animals that may not seem to be carnivores actually are. A starfish might prey on a shellfish that is clamped to a rock, and spend most of a day prising it off and devouring the flesh.

The leopard has a very varied diet that ranges from dung beetles to large mammals, such as this gazelle, which should provide the cat with enough food for two weeks. Leopards drag their prey up into trees where it is out of the reach of other hungry predators and scavengers. They have large heads and powerful jaws to kill and take apart their prey.

Super-eater

An elephant can consume over 200 kg of food daily – the weight of three average-sized adult people.

The giraffe feeds by using its very long, black, powerful tongue to grasp twigfuls of leaves, pulling them into its mouth. It jerks its head away and the teeth strip leaves from the branch. The giraffe can extend its tongue by as much as 45 cm to gather shoots and leaves from branches. As the world's tallest animal, a male measures nearly 6 m to the horn-tips, it is able to reach the uppermost branches when feeding.

Vicious eaters

Many carnivores have bodily weapons to jab into their prey, wound and tear it apart to eat. These include strong, sharp, pointed teeth of sharks, alligators and big cats, fang-like mouthparts in spiders, sharp beaks of birds of prey, and claws of many birds and mammals.

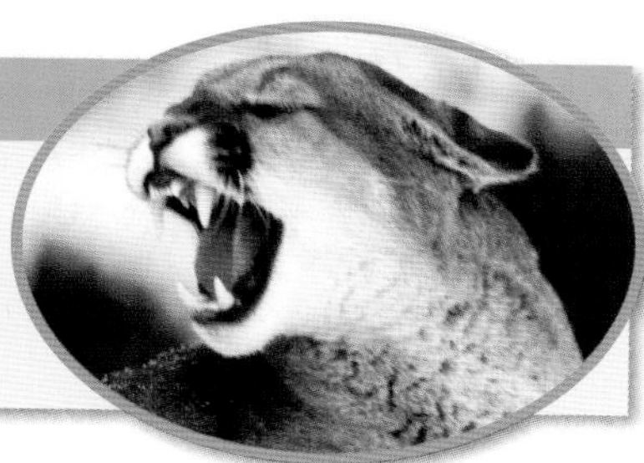

Amazing

Wild horses and ponies can graze for up to 16 hours daily on grass, flowers, fruits and berries.

❍ Rodents, such as rats, mice and squirrels, use their long, continuously growing front teeth to crack open the toughest seeds and nuts. Parrots achieve the same effect using their sharp and powerful bills.

❍ Foods such as flesh, blood and eggs, contain large amounts of nourishment and energy compared to plant foods, so carnivores can spend much less time eating than herbivores do.

Rather than spinning a web to catch its prey, the spitting spider squirts a glue-like chemical from its fangs, which turns into sticky threads as it flies through the air and traps the spider's victim.

❍ In any habitat, there are always more herbivores than carnivores, as the carnivores must feed on the plant eaters. Plant eaters range from elephants and hippopotamuses to many kinds of bugs, beetles, moths and caterpillars.

❍ Deer, most gazelles, giraffes and the black rhino are browsers, eating leaves from trees and shrubs. Zebras, cattle and the white rhino are grazers, eating leaves or grasses from the ground.

❍ The open ocean contains billions of microscopic animals and plants, called plankton. Plankton is eaten by whales and fish, and also by tiny animals, such as copepods, that are then eaten by larger animals.

❍ As darkness falls, birds of prey, such as hawks, rest while owls come out of tree holds, cliff crevices or quiet buildings. These nocturnal hunters catch a range of prey from beetles and mice to young rabbits and squirrels.

Amphibians

Amphibians first appeared on land around 370 million years ago. They spend at least part of their lives in water and even when they are on land they usually prefer damp habitats. Frogs, toads, newts and salamanders are amphibians.

Amazing

Not all tadpoles are left to fend for themselves. The male green poison-dart frog looks after the eggs while they develop on leaf litter, and then gives the tadpoles a piggy-back to the nearest pool of water.

➤ ***There are about 4800 species of frog and toad. Frogs are superb jumpers with long back legs to propel them into the air. Most also have suckers on their fingers to help them land securely on slippery surfaces.***

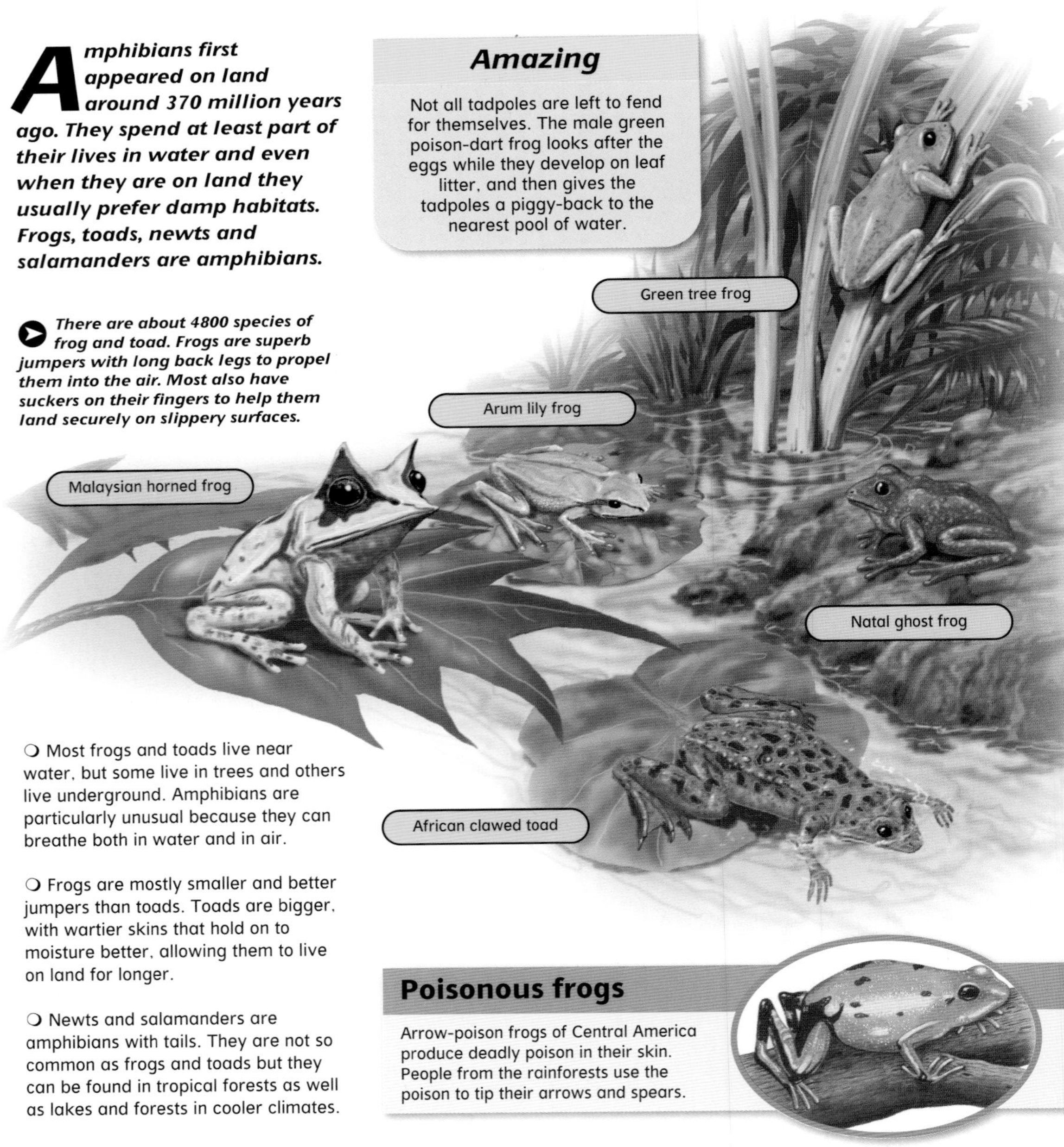

❍ Most frogs and toads live near water, but some live in trees and others live underground. Amphibians are particularly unusual because they can breathe both in water and in air.

❍ Frogs are mostly smaller and better jumpers than toads. Toads are bigger, with wartier skins that hold on to moisture better, allowing them to live on land for longer.

❍ Newts and salamanders are amphibians with tails. They are not so common as frogs and toads but they can be found in tropical forests as well as lakes and forests in cooler climates.

Poisonous frogs

Arrow-poison frogs of Central America produce deadly poison in their skin. People from the rainforests use the poison to tip their arrows and spears.

Kicking to swim

Many frogs move by leaping, which enables them to escape from predators quickly. They have toes that are joined with flaps of skin, called webbing, to make a broad surface area for kick swimming.

❍ Newts and salamanders tend to be well camouflaged, with patterns and colours that enable them to hide. However, some species are brightly coloured, often to indicate to predators that they are toxic (poisonous).

❍ Frogs and toads are meat eaters, or carnivores. They catch fast-moving insects by darting out their long, sticky tongues.

❍ The Goliath frog of West Africa is the world's largest frog, growing to more than 25 cm long. The biggest toad is the cane toad of Queensland, Australia – one weighed 2.6 kg and measured 50 cm in length with its legs outstretched.

❍ Amphibians have moist skin, which they normally keep covered in mucus to prevent it from drying out. Many amphibians are patterned or coloured so they can hide from predators. This is called camouflage.

❍ Although most amphibians prefer to stay near water, or in a wet habitat, there are some species of toad that manage to survive in deserts. They coat themselves in a thick layer of mucus and burrow underground during the hottest, driest spells of weather.

❍ Some amphibians are able to breathe through their thin skin. Oxygen from the air passes directly into their bloodstream.

❍ Some salamanders are lungless. They absorb oxygen through their skin and the lining of their mouth. This means the skin must always stay moist. If it dries, oxygen cannot pass through.

1. Frog spawn floats on top of freshwater

2. Tadpoles hatch from the eggs

3. Tadpoles grow legs and change into froglets

4. The froglet loses its tail and grows into an adult frog

Toads hibernate on land during the winter

Newts swim by lashing their tails

Amphibians go to water when it is time to lay their eggs. Females usually lay their eggs in or near a pond or stream. Most frogs lay between 1000 and 20,000 eggs in a mass of jelly. This large cluster of eggs is called spawn. Like many amphibians, frogs go through different stages before becoming adults. This change is called metamorphosis.

How Animals Breed

Breeding or reproduction – making more of the same kind – is essential for all living things. Some animals can reproduce by themselves, but others need a mate. Some animals lay eggs, others give birth to live young.

Some sharks lay eggs. Each egg has a strong case with the developing embryo inside. The case, known as a 'mermaid's purse', has long threads that stick to seaweed or rocks. This cat shark embryo develops slowly. At 50 days it is smaller than its store of food, the yolk. It gradually develops and finally hatches eight months later.

❍ Small and simple creatures may reproduce asexually. This means that they clone themselves by simply growing identical offspring as 'stalks' on their own bodies.

❍ Most animals reproduce sexually, when a male and female mate. The male's sperm joins with (fertilizes) the female's eggs.

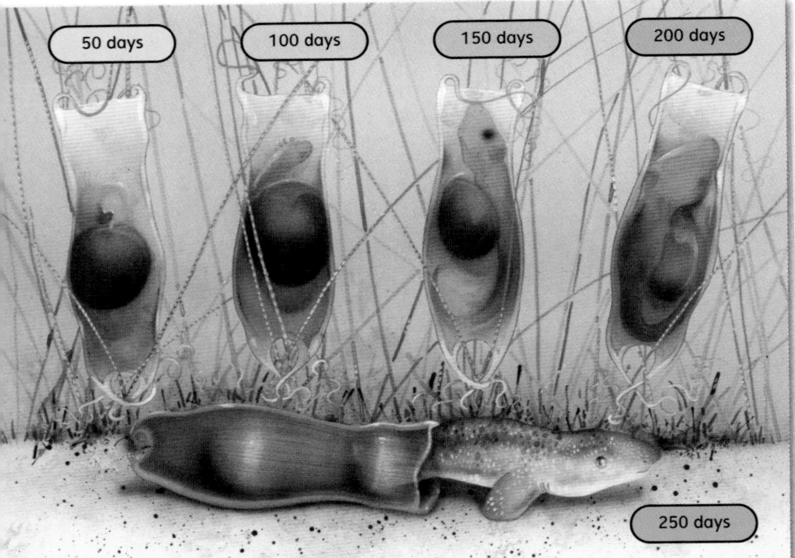

Mating alone

Some aphids, flatworms, leeches and other smaller animals reproduce by parthenogenesis. This means that they can make eggs and produce offspring without a male's sperm. If a female stick insect reproduces by parthenogenesis her offspring will all be female; if she mates with a male her offspring will be a mixture of males and females.

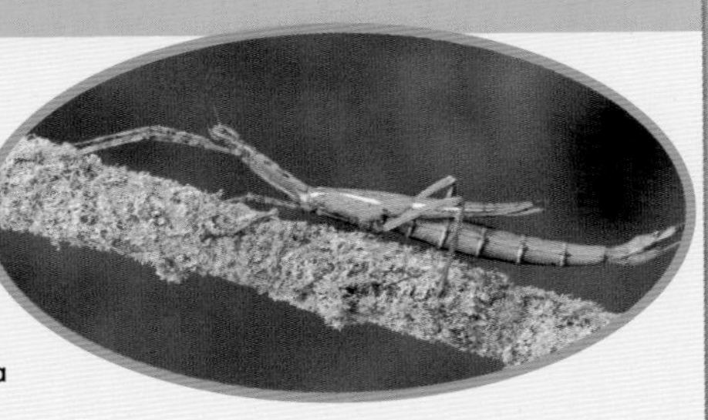

Young animals

Antelope	Calf
Badger	Kit
Bat	Pup
Bear	Cub
Beaver	Kitten
Camel	Calf
Cat	Kitten
Cod	Codling
Cow	Calf
Cranefly	Leatherjacket
Crocodile	Crocklet
Deer	Fawn
Dog	Puppy
Duck	Duckling
Eagle	Eaglet
Eel	Elver
Elephant	Calf
Fish	Fry
Frog	Tadpole
Giraffe	Calf
Goat	Kid
Goose	Gosling
Hamster	Pup
Hare	Leveret
Hawk	Eyas
Hippopotamus	Calf
Hog	Shoat
Horse	Foal
Jellyfish	Ephyra
Kangaroo	Joey
Lion	Cub
Llama	Cria
Mosquito	Nymph
Ostrich	Chick
Otter	Whelp
Owl	Owlet
Oyster	Spat
Pig	Piglet
Pigeon	Squab
Pilchard	Sardine
Rabbit	Kit
Rhinoceros	Calf
Sheep	Lamb
Snail	Spat
Spider	Spiderling
Squirrel	Kitten
Swan	Cygnet
Tiger	Cub
Whale	Calf
Zebra	Foal

❍ Animals that live in water often reproduce by simply releasing their eggs and sperm into the water, and leaving fertilization to chance. This is called external fertilization.

❍ On land, a female and male animal usually mate when the sperm pass into the female's body to fertilize the eggs. This is called internal fertilization.

❍ Courtship is an essential part of male and female animals getting together to mate. Animals use courtship to check that a possible mate is fit, healthy and strong; this means that their offspring will have a better chance of survival.

❍ For some animals breeding depends on owning a territory. This is an area that the animal occupies, and defends from intruders. Usually males defend a territory and perform courtship displays.

Amazing

The tadpole of the South American frog is three times bigger than the adult. Unlike most living things, it actually gets smaller as it grows.

❍ The female Nile crocodile lays her eggs in nests that she digs in sandy riverbanks. She covers the eggs to keep them at a steady temperature. When the babies hatch they make loud piping calls and the mother digs them out and carries them to the river, one by one.

❍ Larger animals, such as elephants and apes, usually produce just one offspring at a time and care for it over several years.

Putting on a show

A peacock is chosen by a female (peahen) according to how magnificent his brightly coloured tail feathers are, and how proudly he displays them.

Many male birds, such as frigatebirds, put on amazing courtship displays as they puff out their bright-red throat pouch to attract a mate. These birds can form colonies of thousands of pairs during breeding time.

❍ The great grey slugs of Europe court by circling each other for over an hour from a branch, before launching themselves into the air to hang from a trail of mucus. They then mate for seven to 24 hours.

❍ Birds of prey, such as kestrels, eagles and hawks, only lay a few eggs at a time. This makes them vulnerable to human egg collectors – one reason why some become endangered species.

Many animals mate with different partners each year, either one or several. However, some larger birds, such as swans, are monogamous – they mate for life. Each spring, pairs of swans renew their relationship by twining their necks together and calling to each other. A female swan lays up to eight eggs, which she cares for until they hatch, then both parents look after them.

Reptiles

It is believed that reptiles evolved from amphibians, around 340 million years ago. While amphibians have bare skins and lay their eggs in water, reptiles have a scaly skin and lay their eggs on land. They include lizards, snakes, crocodiles, alligators, tortoises and turtles.

❍ Reptiles are cold-blooded, but this does not mean that their blood is cold. Cold-blooded animals cannot keep the temperature of their bodies steady; it changes according to the temperature around them. They control their temperature by moving between hot and cool places.

Lizards cannot control their own body heat, and so rely on sunshine for warmth. This is why they live in warm climates and bask in the sun for hours each day.

Amazing

A 4–5 m long African rock python was once seen to swallow an entire 60 kg impala, a kind of antelope, whole – horns and everything.

Pythons are tropical snakes that live in moist forests in Asia and Africa. They are the world's biggest snakes, rivalled only by giant anacondas. Pythons are one long tube of muscle, well able to squeeze even big victims to death. They usually eat animals about the size of domestic cats, but occasionally they go for really big meals, such as wild pigs and deer.

Crocodiles

Crocodilian species lived alongside the dinosaurs 200 million years ago, and have changed very little since that time. Crocodiles are hunters that lie in wait for animals coming to drink at the water's edge. This dwarf crocodile, measuring only 1.5–2 m in length, is one of the smallest crocodiles. It is so small that a frog, fish or baby water bird is more than enough of a meal.

❍ Reptiles bask in the sun to heat their blood. When they are warm, reptiles' bodies work more efficiently and they can hunt for food. For this reason reptiles are often less active at cool times.

❍ A reptile's skin looks slimy, but it is dry and, unlike an amphibian's skin, it retains moisture well. Reptiles can live in very hot, dry places.

❍ Although reptiles grow for most of their lives their skin does not, so they slough (shed) it every now and then.

Chameleons can look forwards and backwards at the same time, as each of its amazing eyes can swivel in all directions independently of the other. A chameleon's tongue is almost as long as its body, but is normally squashed up inside its mouth. It feeds on insects and spiders, hunting them in trees by day.

Huge appetite

The Komodo dragon of Sumatra is the biggest lizard, weighing up to 150 kg. It can catch deer and pigs and swallow them whole.

❍ Lizards move in many ways; they can run, scamper, slither and even glide. Their legs stick out sideways rather than downwards.

❍ Most lizards lay eggs, although a few give birth to live young. Mother lizards do not look after their young.

❍ Crocodiles, alligators, caimans and gharials are large reptiles that form a group called crocodilians. There are 12 species of crocodile, eight alligators and caimans and two species of gharial.

❍ Constrictors are snakes that squeeze their victims to death before swallowing them whole. They have special jaws that allow their mouths to open wide, and can spend days digesting a meal.

❍ Two kinds of venomous snake are dangerous to humans: vipers and elapids, such as cobras and mambas. In India, snakes kill more than 7000 people every year.

Tortoises and turtles are like armoured tanks – slow but well protected by their shells. The hawksbill turtle lives in warm seas all around the world. Its beautiful shell means that it has been hunted so much that it has nearly died out.

Dinosaurs

For about 160 million years dinosaurs were the most successful land animals on Earth. There were giant land dinosaurs that were much bigger than elephants. Enormous flying reptiles took to the air and reptile monsters ruled the oceans.

Amazing

Scientists study fossilized animal dung called coprolite to find out what ancient animals ate.

Some dinosaurs, such as* Maiasaura *were careful parents. They made nests, guarded their eggs against predators and stayed with the young until they were able to fend for themselves.

Spinosaurus

Ankylosaurus

Spinosaurus *preyed on weaker dinosaurs, but some victims put up a fight, like this* Ankylosaurus.

❍ Dinosaurs dominated the land from about 225 million to 66 million years ago. This period is known as the Age of the Dinosaurs or the Mesozoic Era.

❍ No one knows exactly how dinosaurs evolved, or what type of animal they evolved from. It is thought that they probably evolved from a group of small two-legged reptiles.

❍ Birds evolved from dinosaurs and so are regarded as living members of the dinosaur group.

❍ Much of the information we have about dinosaurs comes from fossils. These are the remains of once-living things that have been preserved in rocks and turned to stone, over millions of years.

❍ When animals are fossilized their soft tissues (such as muscle or skin) are rarely preserved. Hard tissues, such as bones, teeth and claws, are much more likely to be preserved.

Studying dinosaurs

Palaeontologists are people who study fossils. They study fossilized dinosaur remains and modern reptiles, birds and mammals, to try and understand how dinosaurs may have lived.

Very big dinosaurs

	Weight	*Length*
Argentinosaurus	70 tonnes	30 m
Brachiosaurus	50 tonnes	26 m
Diplodocus	15 tonnes	30 m
Spinosaurus	12 tonnes	15 m
Tyrannosaurus	6 tonnes	12 m

Dino defences

Plant-eating dinosaurs were preyed on by the fierce meat eaters, but they had effective defences in the form of armour plating, shields, spikes and club-tails. Neck frills and horns protected the slow-moving Ceratopsians or 'horn-faced' dinosaurs from predators' teeth.

Styracosaurus *was one of the largest of the Ceratopsians*

Chasmosaurus *had frilled horns with bony centres that weighted heavily on the neck*

Triceratops *had large bumps called tubercules scattered among its scales*

❍ Dinosaurs laid eggs, like most other reptiles. There is evidence that some dinosaurs protected their eggs and looked after their young when they emerged from eggs.

❍ Some dinosaurs, such as *Velociraptor*, were fierce hunters who preyed on other dinosaurs. Others, such as *Diplodocus*, were plant eaters. It is now believed that *Tyrannosaurus rex* was both a predator and a scavenger; it hunted but also ate animals that had died naturally or been killed by another hunter. It had both monstrous jaws to rip off large chunks of flesh and sharp, savage claws.

➤ ***Dinosaurs were all land-living reptiles. They are divided into two groups, Ornithischians and Saurischians, according to the shape of their skeletons. Ornithschians had hips shaped like birds' hips, while Saurischians had hips shaped like reptiles' hips.***

What happened to the great dinosaurs?

The most likely explanation for the extinction of non-bird dinosaurs is a comet, asteroid or meteorite hitting Earth. There have been other extinctions in Earth's history, but the disappearance of the non-bird dinosaurs around 66 million years ago was a cataclysmic event. Dust-clouds flung up by the impact caused climate change: plants died, eggs failed to hatch and mature animals died of starvation or cold.

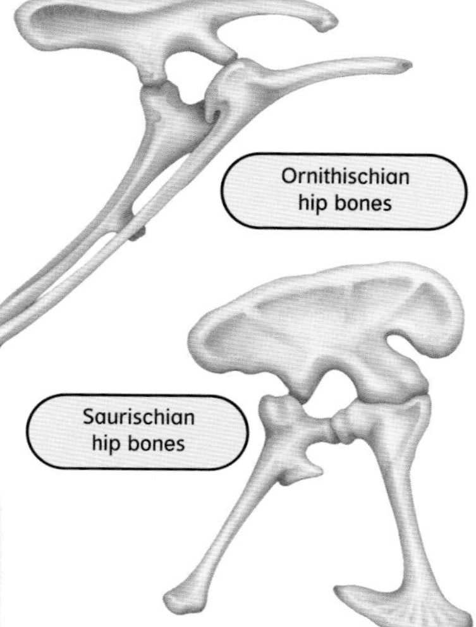

❍ Amongst the biggest land animals of all times were prehistoric reptiles, such as *Argentinosaurus* and *Brachiosaurus*. These 50-tonne reptiles were as big as houses.

❍ Dinosaurs were well-equipped for both defending themselves and attacking others. Some had horns on their heads; others had spikes or bony plates on their tails and spines. Meat-eating dinosaurs had large, pointed teeth with serrated edges for slicing through flesh.

❍ Dinosaurs lived on land, but other giant reptiles lived in the air and the seas. Plesiosaurs lived in the oceans and used paddle-shaped limbs to swim. They had large bodies, long necks and small heads. Pterosaurs were flying reptiles with beaks and large bat-like wings.

Meaning of prehistoric reptile names

Brachiosaurus	Arm lizard
Diplodocus	Double beamed
Ichthyosaurus	Fish lizard
Pterodactylus	Wing finger
Scelidosaurus	Limb lizard
Stegosaurus	Roof lizard
Triceratops	Three-horned face
Tyrannosaurus rex	Tyrant lizard king
Velociraptor	Speedy thief

Communication

Communication means passing on messages and information. Animals use sound, sight and movement to communicate, as well as a range of methods including scent, taste, touch and the emitting of electrical signals.

❍ Some messages are understood only by an animal's own kind, for example when a frog croaks to attract a female of the same species. Other messages can be understood by a wide variety of creatures – these are often about matters of life and death.

Animals often give a warning message. A skunk will wave its bold black-and-white tail to warn other animals to stay away. If they ignore this, the skunk raises its tail to release a foul-smelling spray. The fluid's strong smell irritates the victim's eyes and makes it hard for it to breathe.

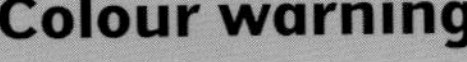

Colour warning

Yellow-and-black is one of the most common colour combinations to be used as a warning. It tells predators that an animal is venomous or tastes foul. Spiders, wasps, frogs (like this arrow-poison frog) and snakes all use this code. After an animal has had an unpleasant encounter with another bearing these colours, it will avoid others with this colour combination in the future.

Hornet (model)

Hornet moth (mimic)

Some insects pretend to be what they're not – especially other insects. The hornet moth is a mimic of the hornet. A hornet has a very painful sting and few other creatures dare to try and eat it. The hornet moth is harmless but few other creatures dare to eat it either.

❍ One method of communication is widely understood in the animal world – rearing or puffing up to make oneself appear bigger. This type of threatening behaviour makes other animals think twice before attacking. Cobras, for example, raise their heads, spread their hoods and hiss at an attacker. A scared or angry cat hisses and spits while its hair stands on end.

❍ The male orang-utan burps to warn other males to keep away.

❍ Honeybees indicate to each other the site of a rich food source, such as nectar-laden flowers, by 'dancing'. The bee flies in a figure of eight and shakes its body to indicate the direction of the food source.

Brain power

	Brain weight
Sperm whale	7800 g
Dolphin	1700 g
Human	1400 g
Camel	680 g
Giraffe	680 g
Horse	530 g
Cow	500 g
Chimpanzee	420 g
Lion	240 g
Baboon	140 g
Sheep	140 g
Dog	72 g
Kangaroo	56 g
Racoon	39 g
Cat	30 g
Porcupine	25 g
Rabbit	12 g
Owl	2.2 g
Rat	2 g
Frog	0.1 g

❍ Wolves are intelligent animals that communicate with body language. They use facial expressions and howl at each other. The howls of a hunting pack of wolves can be heard for about 10 km, telling other wolves to keep their distance. Coyotes use their ears and mouths to express feelings and will bare their teeth to show fear and anger.

❍ Sudden danger needs a short, sharp message to warn others in the group. Rabbits thump the ground and many birds make a loud 'seep' or 'tic' noise. Meerkats will give a shrill shriek, while the first beaver to notice a predator nearby will slap its flat tail hard on the water's surface.

The male white rhinoceros sprays urine to mark his home range. The centre of his territory needs to be marked in this way to a distance of about 1 sq km. Scent has an advantage over sights or sounds – it lasts after the sender has gone. Foxes, sheep and other animals spray strong-smelling urine or leave droppings around their territory. This gives information about the age, sex and health of the animal.

Amazing

Lemurs have different calls to warn members of their troop whether danger is coming from above, along the ground, or is hidden in the undergrowth.

Cobras raise their heads, spread their hoods and hiss at an attacker. The extended hood reveals a pattern that is on the rear of the hood, but shows through the stretched skin and thin, see-through scales. Some cobras spit, spraying venom out of tiny apertures in their fangs. The venom does not kill but can cause blindness.

Identifying strangers

Wolves and wild dogs smell each other's rear ends so if they find droppings later they will know if a pack member left them, or a stranger.

❍ Crows use at least 50 different croaks to communicate with each other. Crows from one area, though, cannot understand those from another.

❍ A gorilla named Coco was trained so that she could use over 1000 different signs to communicate. She made the signs with her hands and each sign stood for a word. Coco called her pet cat 'soft good cat cat' and herself 'fine animal gorilla'. Using sign language, she took an IQ test and scored 95.

❍ Many insects communicate using the smell of chemicals called pheromones, which are released from special glands. The tropical tree ant uses ten different pheromones, combining them with different movements to send 50 different kinds of message.

❍ Female glow worms communicate with males through a series of flashes.

Birds

Birds evolved from dinosaurs and are regarded as living dinosaurs. The earliest known bird fossil is 150 million years old. Known as* Archaeopteryx*, it had feathers and large eyes, like a bird, but it also had a reptile-like snout and teeth.

Chickens

All domestic chickens are descended from the wild red jungle fowl of India. They were first tamed 5000 years ago, and there are now more than 200 different breeds.

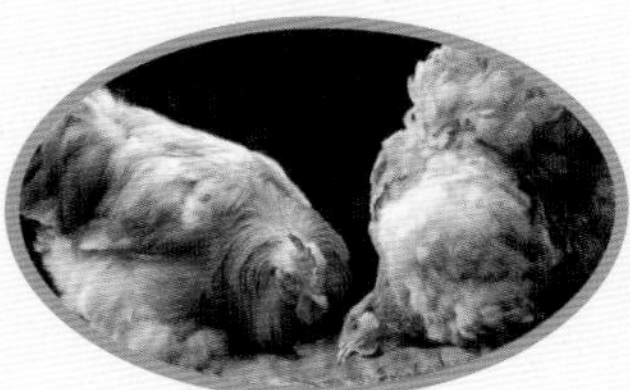

❍ Birds have four kinds of wing feather – large primaries, smaller secondaries, coverts and contours. Every kind of bird has its own formation, pattern and colour of feathers, called its plumage.

❍ Feathers are light, but they are linked by hooks called barbs to make them strong enough for flight. Birds fly in two ways – by gliding with still wings or by flapping their wings up and down.

❍ All birds lay hard-shelled eggs, in which their young develop. If a mother bird had young that developed inside her body instead, she would be too heavy to fly.

❍ Owls are nocturnal birds and hunt by night. They have huge eyes that allow them to see in almost pitch darkness, and their hearing is four times sharper than a cat's.

❍ Penguins cannot fly, but they are superb swimmers. They use their wings as flippers to push them through the water and steer with their webbed feet. Their feathers are waterproofed with oil and they have thick layers of fat to survive at temperatures of –60°C.

❍ Swifts are among the fastest-flying birds. Spine-tailed swifts from eastern Asia have been recorded flying at 120 km/h. They can fly for thousands of miles without stopping, and use their short, gaping bills to catch insects on the wing.

❍ Flightless birds include ostriches, emus and kiwis. The emu is the biggest living bird, towering up to 2.75 m in height and weighing more than 150 kg.

The lungs and heart take up much of a pigeon's chest. The digestive, excretory and reproductive systems fill the rear part of the body.

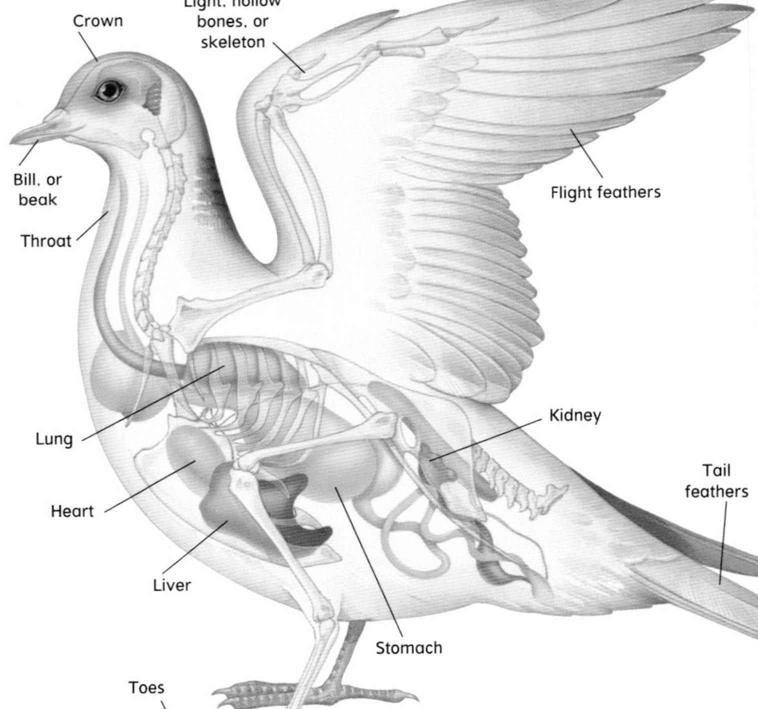

10 flightless birds

Calayan rail • Cassowary • Emu
Kakapo • Kiwi • Ostrich • Penguin
Rhea • Steamer duck • Weka

❍ Birds of rivers and lakes include birds that dive for fish (such as kingfishers), small wading birds (such as avocets and curlews), large wading birds (such as herons and flamingos) and waterfowl (such as ducks and geese).

❍ A game bird is a bird that is hunted for sport, for example pheasants, grouse and partridges. They spend most of their time on the ground looking for seeds. They only fly in emergencies.

❍ Migration is when animals move from one place to another to avoid the cold or find food and water. Migrating birds are often brilliant navigators. Bristle-thighed curlews, for example, find their way from Alaska to tiny Pacific islands 9000 km away.

Perching birds

More than 70 per cent of all bird species – over 5000 species altogether – are perching birds or passerines, for example sparrows and starlings, and this song thrush shown here. They have feet with three toes pointing forwards and one backwards, to help them cling to a perch. Most build small, neat cup-shaped nests and they sing a sequence of musical notes.

All birds have wings of varying shapes. They beat them to improve the airflow past their wings, thus helping them to fly. Wings are the birds' front limbs. Birds that soar in the sky for hours, such as hawks and eagles, have long broad wings. Small fast-flying birds, such as swifts, have slim, pointed wings.

In an eggshell

A bird's egg protects the developing chick inside. The yellow yolk in the egg provides the chick with food while it is growing. Layers of egg white, called albumen, cushion the chick and keep it warm, while the hard shell protects it. The shell is porous so that the chick can breathe.

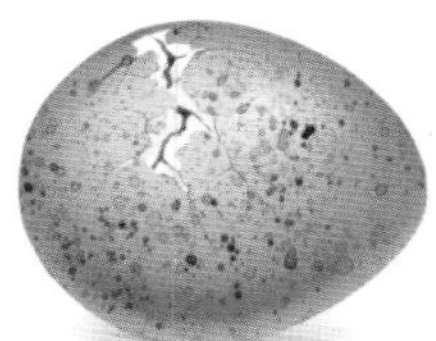

1. The chick starts to chip away at the egg

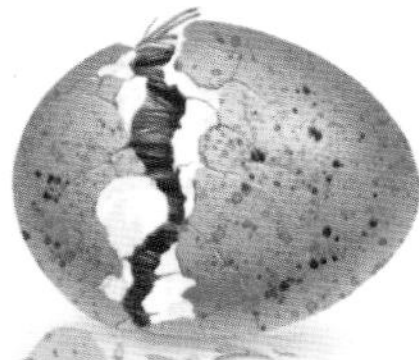

2. The chick uses its egg tooth to break free

3. The egg splits wide open

4. The chick wriggles free. Its parents will look after it for several weeks until it can look after itself

❍ Eagles are among 300 species of raptor (birds of prey). Birds of prey include kestrels, falcons, buzzards and vultures. Most are hunters and feed on birds, fish and small mammals. Most kill with their talons rather than their bill.

Amazing

Ostrich eggs are the largest eggs in the world and would take 40 minutes to hard-boil.

Bird oddities

Emus are unable to walk backwards.

The bones of a pigeon weigh less than its feathers.

There are more chickens in the world than people.

The elf owl is able to catch prey in its feet as it flies.

Mammals

There are about 5600 species of mammals alive today that are probably descended from reptiles. Humans are also mammals. They have hairy bodies, a large brain and special mammary glands for feeding their young with milk.

The duck-billed platypus lives along rivers and billabongs. At night it noses in the mud for worms, shellfish and other small animals. The male has a spur on his rear ankle, which he uses to jab venom into his enemies.

Prolific breeders

One single rabbit could have more than 33 million offspring in just three years, if they all survived to breed.

❍ There are two main mammal groups: the placentals and the marsupials. Animals in these groups give birth to live young. A third group, the monotremes, lay eggs. The duck-billed platypus and echidnas are all monotremes.

❍ When marsupials are born they are undeveloped and small. They usually move into a protective pouch for months, feeding from a teat.

❍ Giraffes are the tallest mammals, growing to more than 5 m. Their height allows them to reach and eat the leaves, twigs and fruit at the tops of trees.

❍ Apes are our group in the animal world. The great apes are gorillas, chimpanzees, orang-utans and humans. Gibbons are called lesser apes. Apes have long arms, and fingers and toes for gripping. They are clever and can use sticks and stones as tools.

❍ All mammals have three tiny bones in their ears that transfer sound vibrations to the inner ear from the eardrum.

❍ Bats are the only flying mammals. Most bats feed on insects or fruit, but vampire bats feed on blood, sucking it from animals, such as cattle and horses.

❍ Tigers and lions are the biggest members of the cat family, weighing up to 230 kg. Male lions may be as long as 3 m. Lions usually live in grasslands or scrub, in families (prides).

❍ Mammals have a variety of teeth shapes: chisels for gnawing, fangs for fighting and killing prey, sharp-edged slicers and flat-topped crushers.

❍ Whales, dolphins and porpoises are large mammals called cetaceans that live mostly in the sea and ocean. Dolphins and porpoises are small whales. The blue whale is the largest creature ever and can grow to be more than 30 m long.

❍ Elephants are the largest living animals on land – they can be as tall as 4 m and weight up to 10 tonnes. They are intelligent animals, with the biggest brain of all land animals. They have very good memories.

Newborn kangaroo

When they are first born, kangaroos are naked and look like tiny jellybabies with two arms. They haul themselves up through the fur on their mother's belly and into her pouch. Here the baby kangaroo (called a joey) sucks on teats and grows for six to eight months.

Amazing

Bats that hunt at night do not need to use their eyes. Instead, they find prey by echo-location: they make high-pitched squeaks and use the echoes to find their way in the dark.

The cat family

The snow leopard has thick fur and can survive extreme cold. Its grey coat helps to camouflage it in snow.

The caracal lives in dry places. Its gold colour makes it difficult to spot among the brown plants and sandy soil. It can jump four times its own body length.

The puma is a great athlete. It has long hind legs packed with muscles.

Jaguars can feed on turtles because they have large, heavy teeth and immensely powerful jaws.

Lions live on vast grasslands called savannah. Their pale fur blends in with the dried grasses of the open plains.

The world's most mysterious cat is the clouded leopard. It sleeps all day and only hunts at night.

Record-breaking mammals

Tallest land mammal	Giraffe	up to 6 m
Largest mammal	Blue whale	up to 33.5 m
Heaviest land mammal	African elephant	more than 6 tonnes
Fastest land mammal	Cheetah	105 km/h
Slowest land mammal	Three-toed sloth	crawls at 2 m a minute

Animals in Danger

In the next few hours, somewhere in the world, a species of animal will become extinct – disappear and be gone for ever. The species may be a rare kind of bird or mammal, or an insect, such as a beetle.

The dodo lived on the island of Mauritius in the Indian Ocean until European sailors arrived in the 1500s. Sailors killed the birds for food, and rats and cats ate the eggs. By 1680 the dodo was extinct.

❍ The biggest threat to animals is the destruction of their habitat. For example, this occurs when a forest is cut down for timber or when houses, factories or roads are built through the countryside.

❍ Tigers are often killed for their teeth, which are used in eastern medicines, and for their luxurious fur by people who enjoy hunting wildlife. Tigers are a threatened species, which means that they are at risk of extinction.

❍ As people in poor countries struggle to feed themselves, some turn to hunting wild animals, or sell them as pets or to eat. This trade affects apes, monkeys, tropical birds, lizards and snakes.

Back from the brink

The giant panda now lives only in south and west China. There are fewer than 2000 left in the wild but numbers are slowly increasing. There are many species that may disappear from the planet – for ever – before we have discovered them. It is estimated that there are seven to nine million different species of animal on Earth, but scientists have not named even two million yet.

Amazing

In prehistoric times several mass extinctions happened. The largest extinction took place 252 million years ago when about 96 per cent of living things vanished. The mass extinction of 66 million years ago saw the disappearance of the big dinosaurs.

The rare river dolphins of the Amazon, Ganges and other great waterways face grave problems. Their survival is threatened by water pollution from chemicals and competition with fishermen for food. They also have to avoid boats with propellers that may harm them and engines that disrupt their sound-sonar communication system. The baiji (also known as the Yangtze River dolphin) is already extinct.

10 species near extinction

The IUCN currently categorizes more than 4500 species as 'Critically Endangered' on its Red List. For species such as these ten, time is running out:

1. Brown-headed spider monkey
2. Pygmy three-toed sloth
3. Seychelles sheath-tailed bat
4. Spoon-billed sandpiper
5. Liben lark
6. Ploughshare tortoise
7. Bizarre-nosed chameleon
8. Fiji crested iguana
9. Rio Pescado stubfoot toad
10. Singapore freshwater crab

❍ Great white sharks are caught so often, both for 'sport' and because they are sometimes considered a threat to the safety of human swimmers, that they are now in danger of becoming extinct.

❍ The North American bison had a narrow escape. Two hundred years ago millions of bison wandered the Great Plains, but hunters in the 1800s killed most of them and by 1881 only 551 were left. Now protected, numbers have increased and there are more than 500,000 in the USA and Canada.

When an animal such as the golden lion tamarin's natural habitat disappears it has nowhere to find food or breed, so its numbers decline until it dies out altogether. Animals at risk can be bred in captivity.

Disappearing forests

Nearly half of the world's tropical rainforests have been destroyed over the last 50 years to clear the way for farmland or buildings.

❍ Power stations and vehicles send fumes up into the air; factory pipes pour poisons into rivers, lakes and seas; pesticides and herbicides (insect and weed killers) wash off farmland into water supplies. These factors all affect the natural environment, for the worst.

❍ Well-run zoos and wildlife parks are extremely valuable for conservation (saving wildlife for the future). Animals can be studied safely and bred in these places and will, hopefully, one day be released back into the wild.

❍ In many parts of the world animals will remain under threat, particularly in areas where humans live in poverty. It is difficult for poor people to look after their own wildlife when they are struggling to survive.

❍ Eco-tourism can help share the wealth of the world more evenly. People pay to see rare animals in their natural habitats, through such activities as going on safari. Money raised from these schemes can be used to support local people and conservation projects.

The Human Body

There are more than seven billion human bodies in the world, and each one of them has unique characteristics. Inside, however, they are all made and work in much the same way.

The body's biggest internal organ is the liver.

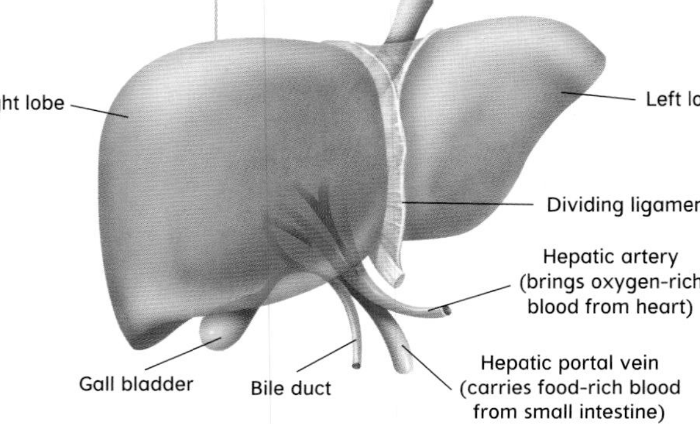

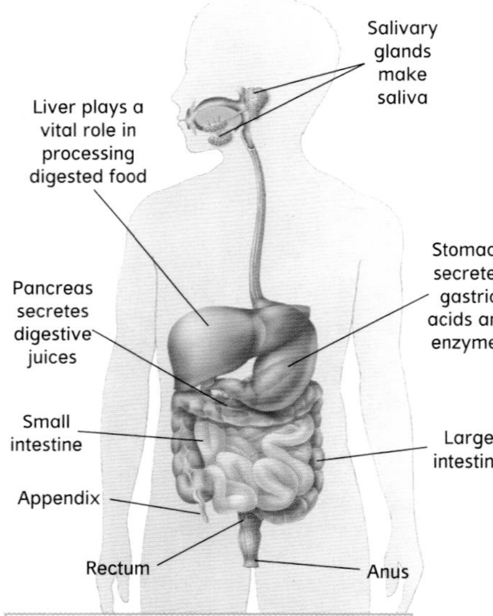

The digestive system is a passageway looped and coiled within the body. Foods passing along the tract are broken down and digested.

Cells are the body's building blocks. They vary in size and shape, according to the job that they do. Different organelles (special parts of a cell) keep it working properly.

Mitochondria 'power stations' change chemical fuel supplied by the blood as glucose into 'energy packs' of the chemical ATP

Endoplasmic reticulum, the main chemical factory where proteins are built under instruction from the nucleus

Ribosomes, individual chemical assembly lines where proteins are put together from basic chemicals called amino acids

Nucleus, the cell's control centre sending out instructions via a chemical called messenger RNA whenever a new chemical is needed

Lysosomes, the cell's dustbins, breaking up any unwanted material

Golgi bodies, the dispatch centre where chemicals are bagged up inside tiny membranes to send where needed

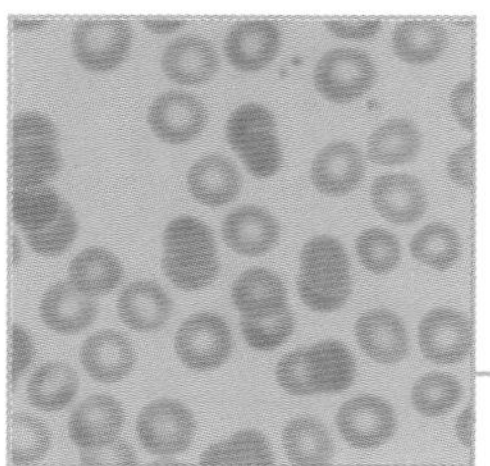

The whole body contains more than 100 billion billion cells.

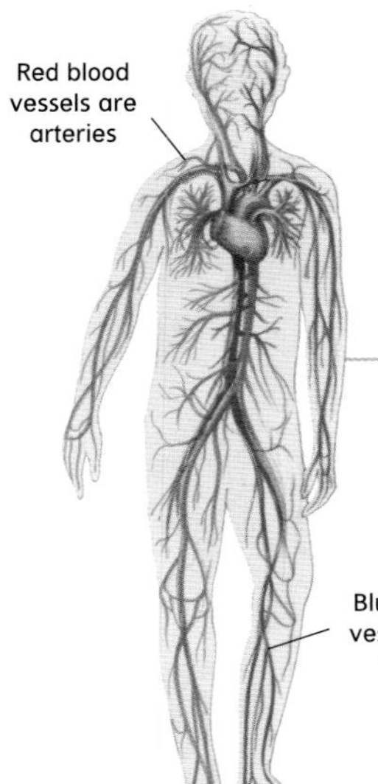

Tissues are groups of cells that are all similar and work to do a particular job. Brain cells, for example, make brain tissue.

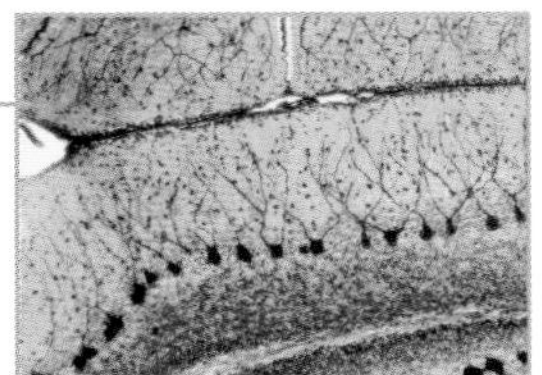

The outer layer of the skin is called the epidermis. It is hard-wearing and tough. Below the epidermis is the dermis. This skin layer contains the cells that sense touch, heat, pain and movement. Hair grows from its root, which is found in the skin's dermis. This cross-section of skin, hugely magnified, shows all these parts.

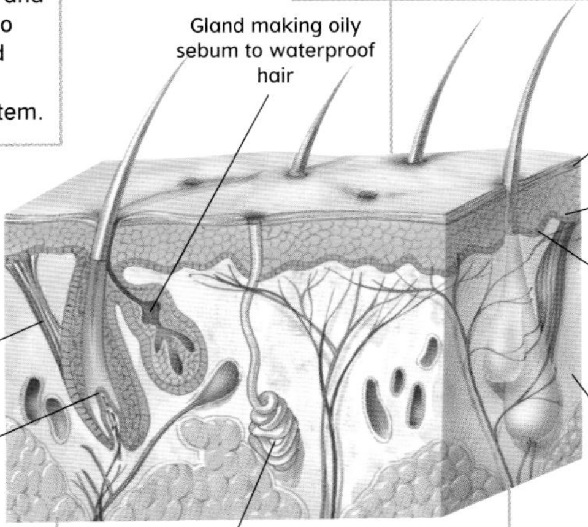

The heart, blood vessels and blood all work together to transport gases and food around the body. They make the circulation system.

Gland making oily sebum to waterproof hair
Keratin layer
Epidermis
Basal layer where new cells grow
Dermis
Hair erector muscle
Hair follicle (root)
Sweat gland

A nail has its root under the skin and grows along the nail bed, which is the skin underneath it. The paler crescent-like area is the lunula or 'little moon'. Nails grow about 0.5 mm a week.

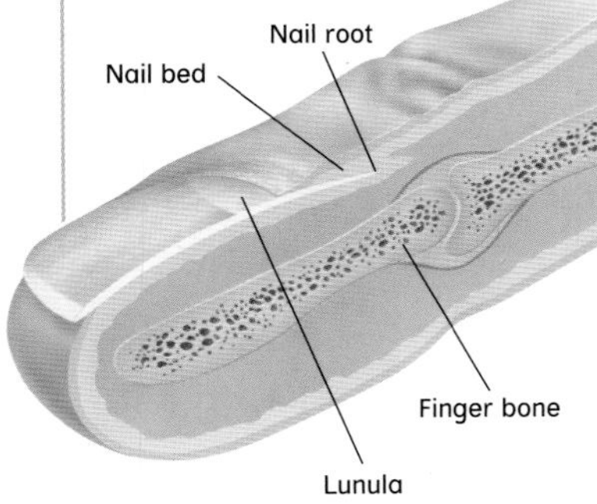

Fingernails and hair are both made from a protein called keratin. A hair is alive and growing only at its root, down in the base of the follicle. The shaft that sticks out of the skin is dead and is made of flattened cells stuck firmly together. An average person has between 100,000 and 120,000 hairs on the scalp.

Skin is the body's protective coat. It shields the body from infection, protects organs and tissues from damage, and helps the body maintain a constant and steady temperature.

Humans have...

206 bones

300 bones as babies

33 vertebrae

An average pulse rate of 70 to 80 beats a minute

8000 taste buds on the tongue

230 joints

100,000 hairs on an average scalp

23 pairs of chromosomes

365 acupuncture points

32 teeth in a full adult set: 12 molars, 8 pre-molars, 4 canines and 8 incisors

Bones and Joints

Bones provide the strong framework that supports the whole body and holds its parts together. All of the bones together are called the skeleton, and this gives protection to organs, such as the brain, as well as providing an anchor for muscles.

The 206 bones of the human skeleton includes 32 bones in each arm, 31 in each leg, 29 in the head, 26 in the spinal column and hips and 25 in the chest.

Skull bones

The skull, or cranium, is the hard bone that protects the brain. It is made up of 22 separate bones, cemented together along rigid joints called sutures.

Bones contain threads of the tough, slightly bendy substance called collagen. It also has hard minerals, such as calcium and phosphate. Together, the collagen and minerals make a bone strong and rigid, yet able to bend slightly under stress. Bones have blood vessels for nourishment and nerves to feel pressure and pain. Inside the tough casing of most bones is a soft, jelly-like core called the marrow, which can be either red or yellow.

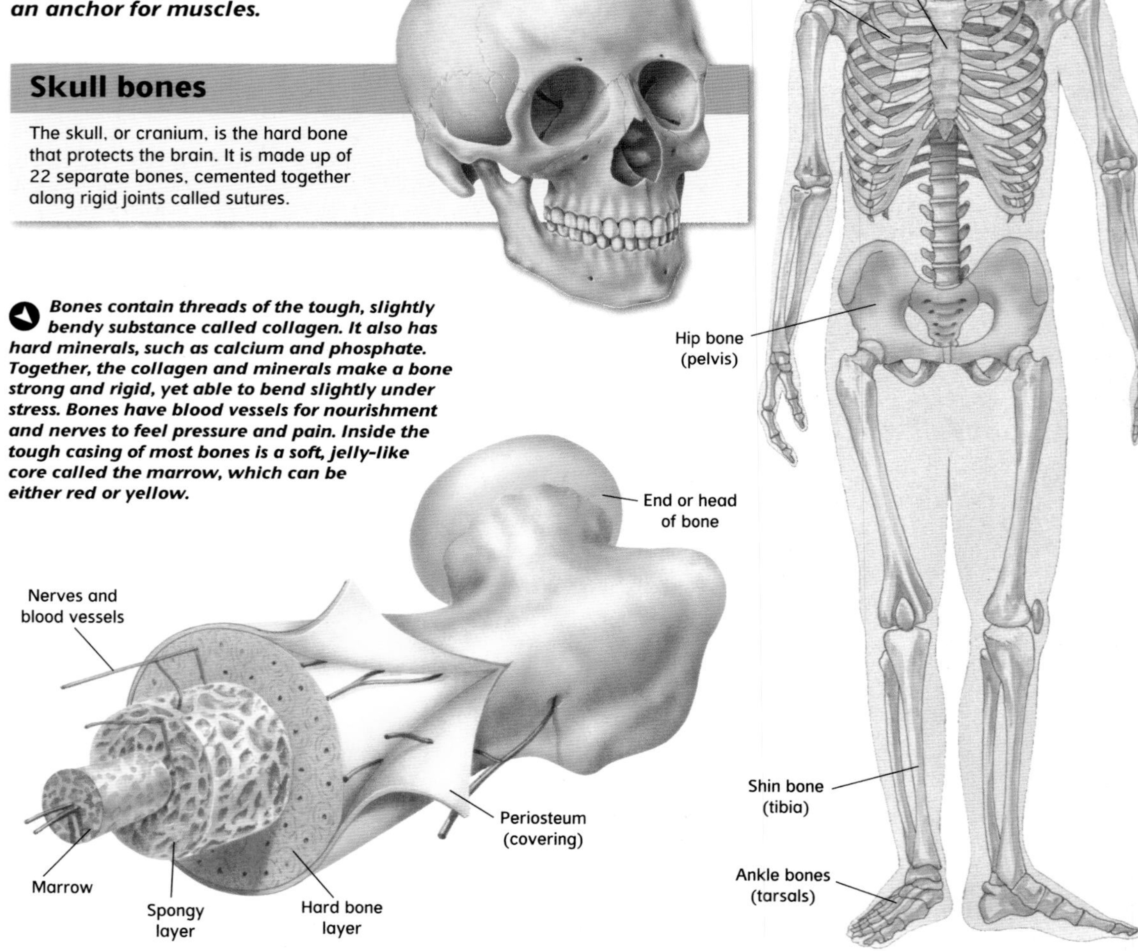

❍ An adult's skeleton has 206 bones, joined together by rubbery cartilage. A baby's skeleton has 300 or more bones but some of these fuse (join) together as the baby grows.

❍ Most women and girls have smaller and lighter skeletons than men and boys. Women's pelvises, or hip bones, are bigger than men's because the opening has to be wide enough to allow a baby to be born.

❍ Weight for weight, bone is five times stronger than steel, but bones are so light that they only account for 14 per cent of body weight.

❍ Marrow is the soft, jelly-like tissue in the middle of certain bones. It contains special cells that make new blood cells – up to three million per second.

❍ Body joints are places where bones meet. Most joints allow bones to move. There are several different kinds of joints, such as synovial joints that allow movement, and suture joints that do not.

❍ Synovial joints are found throughout the body, especially in the shoulder, elbow, hip and knee. These allow various kinds of movements, depending on their design. The elbow and knee are hinge joints, which allow only a to-and-fro movement. The shoulder and hip are ball-and-socket joints, which enable more flexibility, such as twisting.

Bone facts

The upper arm bone is called the humerus or, jokingly, the funny bone.

The smallest bones are the three tiny ossicles inside each ear.

The longest bone is the thigh bone or femur, making up about one-quarter of the body's total height.

The broadest bone is the hip bone or pelvis.

Most people have 12 pairs of ribs, but about one person in 500 has 13 or 11 pairs.

X-rays

In 1895 the German physicist Wilhelm Rontgen discovered X-rays and how they pass through flesh, but not through bone. X-rays are invisible waves of energy (called electromagnetic radiation). Doctors use X-rays to examine bones without the need for surgery.

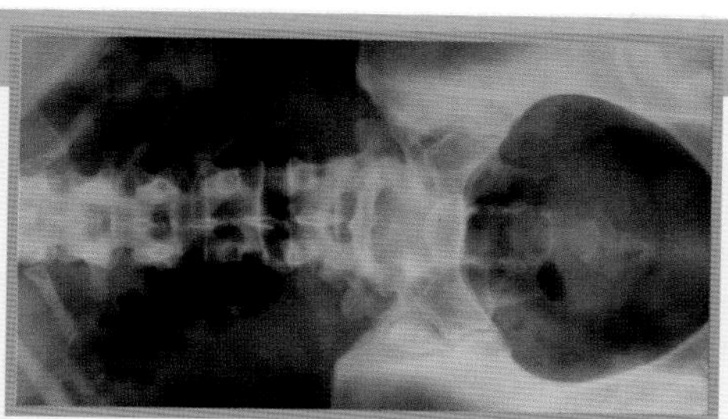

❍ Cartilage is a tough but flexible material that is used in many joints to cushion the bones against impact. It gives strength to the skeleton but allows movement. Unborn babies' skeletons are mostly made of cartilage that eventually hardens to bone.

❍ The backbone, or spine, extends from the base of the skull down to the hips. It is not a single bone, but a column of drum-shaped bones called vertebrae (single: vertebra).

❍ The backbone supports the body and contains and protects the spinal cord, which carries messages between the brain and parts of the body. The cord is about 45 cm long, and 31 pairs of main peripheral nerves branch from it.

❍ Tendons are cords that tie a muscle to a bone, or a muscle to another muscle. They are made from collagen. Ligaments are strong cords of tough collagen and stretchy elastin that strengthen joints.

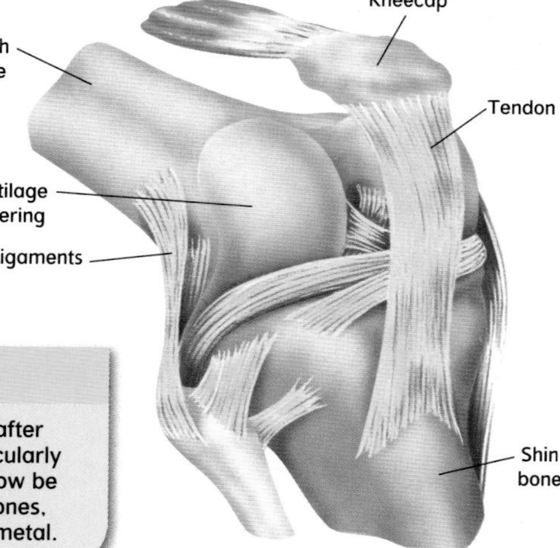

Strap-shaped ligaments criss-cross the outside of the knee joint to hold the bones in place.

Amazing

Joints can break down after many years of use, particularly the hip joint. Joints can now be replaced with artificial ones, made from plastics and metal.

Muscles and Moving

Every movement, every breath, every mouthful you chew – all of these actions and more are carried out by the body's muscles. By working together, the body's muscles carry out thousands of different activities every day.

❍ Muscles are special fibres that contract (shorten) and relax (lengthen) to move parts of the body.

❍ Voluntary muscles are those that you control by thinking, such as moving an arm. Involuntary muscles are those that work automatically, such as those that move food through your intestine.

❍ There are about 640 voluntary muscles in the human body and they make up over 40 per cent of the body's entire weight. Men usually have more muscle than women.

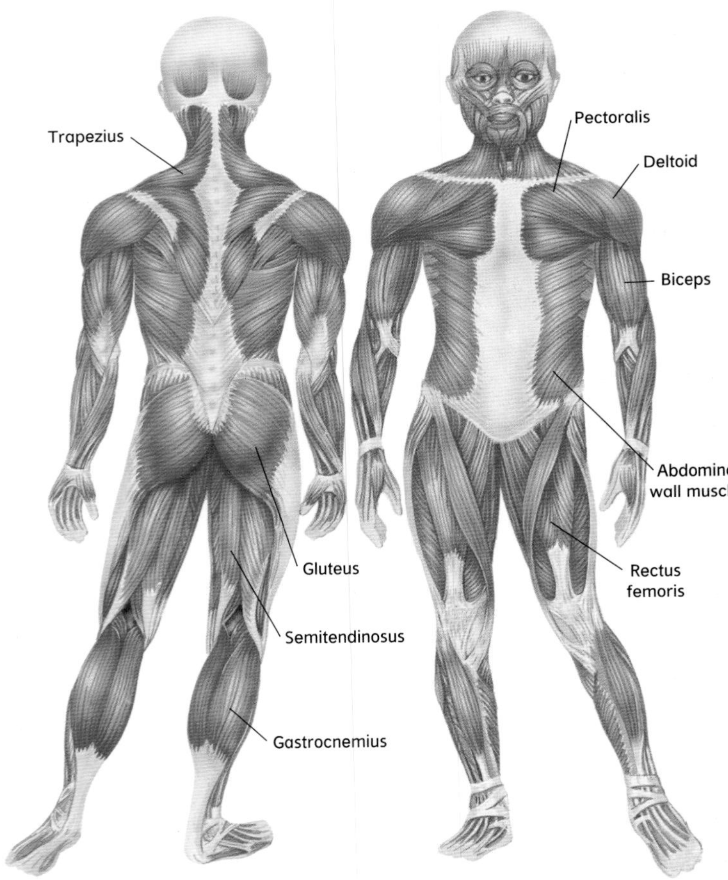

The muscles shown here are just beneath the skin. They are called superficial muscles. Underneath them is another layer, the deep muscle layer. In some areas there is an additional in-between layer, the medial muscles.

Working together

Muscles are controlled by the brain, which sends messages to them along string-like nerves. When a muscle contracts for a long time, its fibres 'take turns'. Some of them shorten powerfully while others relax, then the contracted ones relax while others shorten, and so on.

❍ Most muscles are firmly anchored at both ends and attached to the bones either side of a joint, either directly or via tough fibres called tendons.

Muscle power

An elephant has an estimated 40,000 muscles in its trunk.

The tongue is the only muscle in the human body not attached at both ends.

Each eyeball is moved by six slim, ribbon-like muscles that are the fastest-acting in the body.

The longest muscle in the human body is the sartorius, on the inner thigh.

The strongest muscle in the human body is the masseter, at the back of the jaw.

Pulling together

If all of the muscles in your body could pull together, they would have enough combined strength to lift a bus.

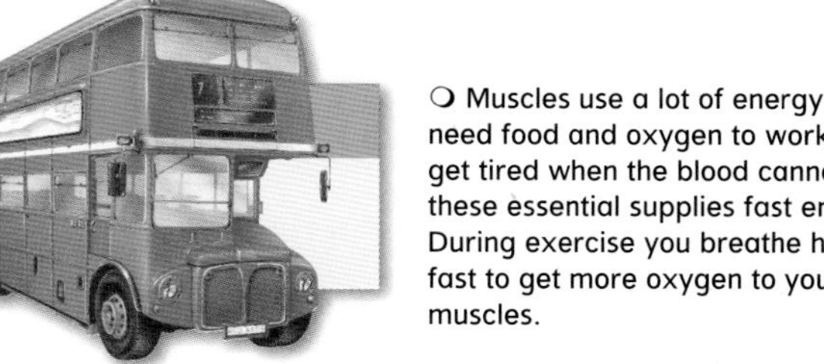

❍ Most muscles are arranged in pairs because although muscles can shorten themselves, they cannot forcibly make themselves longer. So the flexor muscle that bends a joint is paired with an extensor muscle to straighten it again.

❍ The brain controls muscles by sending nerve signals along nerves to the muscles, telling them when to contract, by how much and for how long. We learn to do many activities, such as walking, when we are young and they soon become automatic – this means we can do them without having to think about them.

Most muscles are arranged in opposing or antagonistic pairs to pull a bone one way and then the other, like the biceps and triceps in the upper arm.

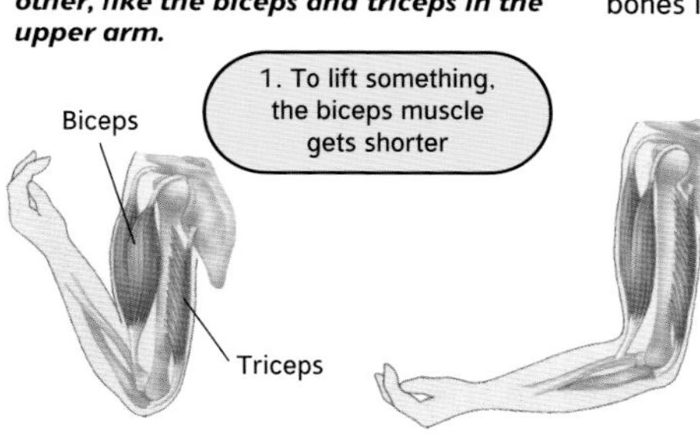

Inside a muscle are bundles of myofibres, each about as thick as a human hair. Every myofibre is made of even thinner myofibrils, which contain numerous strands of the substances actin and myosin. These slide past each other to make the muscle contract.

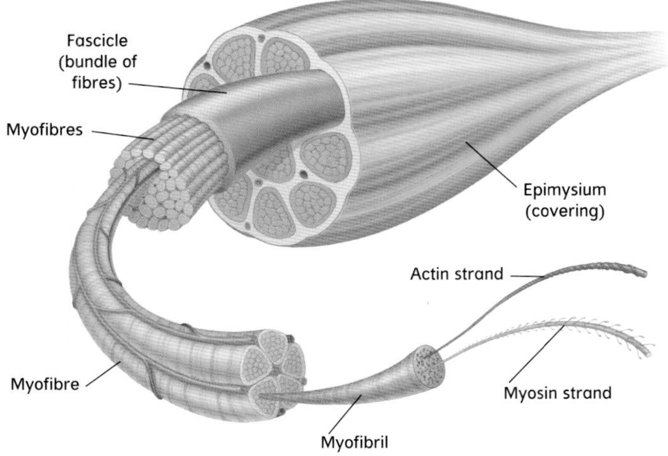

❍ Muscles use a lot of energy, and they need food and oxygen to work. Muscles get tired when the blood cannot bring these essential supplies fast enough. During exercise you breathe hard and fast to get more oxygen to your muscles.

❍ The body's smallest muscle is the stapedius. It is about the same size as this letter 'I' and is attached to the tiny bones in the ear that enable us to hear.

❍ The body cannot make new muscles, but the ones it has can grow. Exercise can make muscles grow larger and more efficient.

❍ The heart muscle is a unique combination of skeletal and smooth muscle. It has its own built-in rhythm of contractions of 70 beats a minute, and special muscle cells that work like nerve cells for transmitting the signals for waves of muscle contraction to sweep through the heart.

Amazing

The body's biggest muscles are the ones you sit on – the gluteus maximus muscles in the buttocks.

Lungs and Breathing

The human body is constantly active, even when it appears to be at rest. One process that never stops, day or night, is breathing. Breathing is concerned with the movement of two gases (oxygen and carbon dioxide) into and out of our bodies.

Breathing muscles

At rest, half a litre of air passes in and out of the lungs each time you breathe. Breathing uses the sheet-like diaphragm below the chest and the strip-like intercostals between the ribs. To breathe in, both muscle sets contract. The diaphragm changes from a domed shape to a flatter shape, pulling down the bases of the lungs. The intercostal muscles force the ribs up and out pulling on the lungs. Both these actions stretch the spongy lungs to suck in air. To breathe out, both muscle sets relax. The stretched lungs spring back to their smaller size, blowing out air.

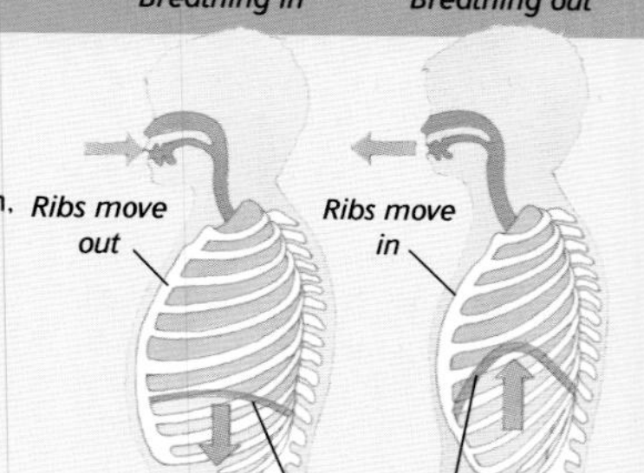

Muscles in wall of bronchus

Air space inside bronchus

Right bronchus

Windpipe

Upper lobe of left lung

Upper lobe of right lung

Right lung

Left bronchus

Left lung

Space for heart

Middle lobe of right lung

Lower lobe of right lung

Lower lobe of left lung

View along inside of bronchus

◀ Air flows to and from the lungs along the windpipe, which branches at its base into two bronchi, one to each lung. The heart fills the scoop-like space located between the lungs. Breathing in is called inspiration and breathing out is called expiration. No matter how much you breathe out, about 0.5 litres of air stays in your lungs.

❍ You breathe because every single cell in your body needs a continuous supply of oxygen to burn glucose, the high-energy substance from digested food that cells get from blood. As the cells burn glucose they make carbon dioxide, a waste gas.

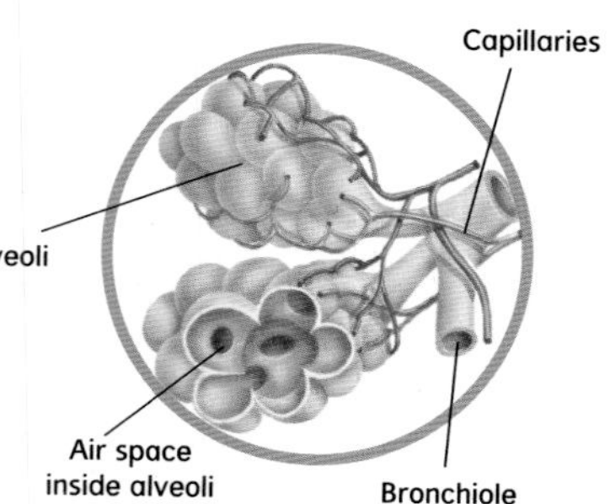

▶ The bubble-like alveoli are in groups or bunches at the ends of the narrowest air tubes. They make up about one-third of the space taken up by the lungs.

Breathe in, breathe out

If you live to the age of 80 you will have taken well over 600 million breaths.

❍ Scientists call breathing 'respiration'. Cellular respiration is the way that cells use oxygen to burn glucose.

❍ When you breathe in, air rushes in through your nose or mouth, down to your windpipe and into millions of tiny branching airways in your lungs.

❍ The two biggest airways in the lungs are called bronchi (single: bronchus), and they branch into smaller airways called bronchioles. At the end of each bronchiole are bunches of minute air sacs called alveoli (single: alveolus).

❍ Huge quantities of oxygen seep across the cell walls of the alveoli and into the blood. Carbon dioxide moves from the blood into the alveoli and can then be breathed out.

❍ The surface of the airways is protected by a slimy film of mucus that gets thicker to protect the lungs when you have a cold.

❍ Half a litre of air passes in and out of the lungs each time you breathe. Deeper breathing can increase this by up to six times!

❍ A yawn is an extra-deep breath that brings in more oxygen. It may prepare the body for action, rather than showing that a person is bored, but no one really knows why we yawn.

There are two vocal cords that are found in the voice-box in the neck. Each one sticks out from the sides as a flexible flap. The vocal cords have a triangular-shaped gap between them for normal breathing (top), and move almost together for speech (bottom).

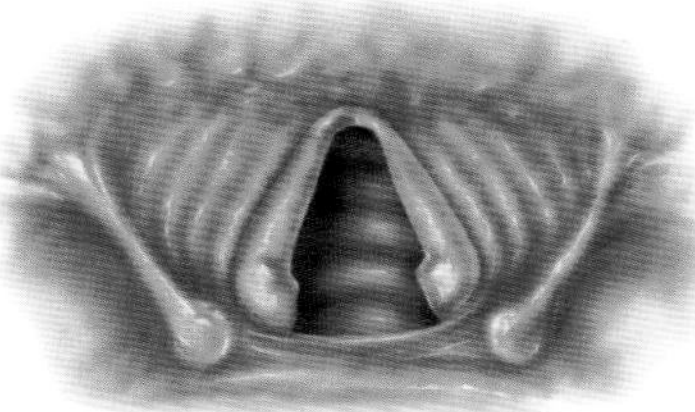

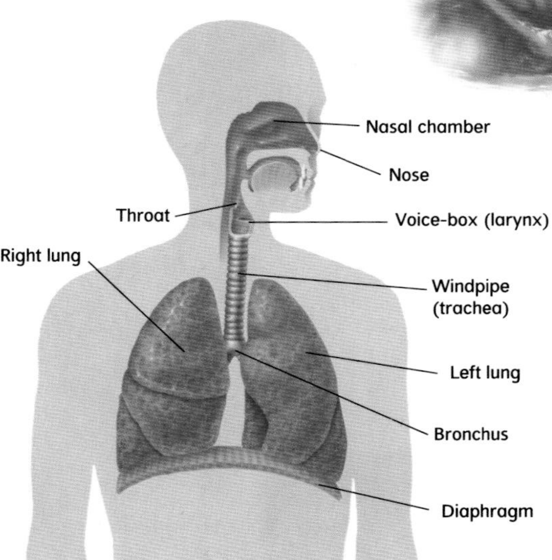

The respiratory system includes the parts of the body specialized to take in oxygen from the air. Some parts have other uses too, such as smell in the nose and speech in the voice-box (larynx).

Amazing

Some people open their mouths to yawn so wide when they yawn forcefully that they dislocate or 'detach' their jaws and cannot close the mouth again. One theory is that yawning happens when the body has been still for a time, breathing shallowly, so more oxygen is needed.

Eating and Digestion

The human body needs food and water. Food provides substances that are essential for the body to grow and repair itself. It also provides energy for life itself. Water is needed for the body to carry out all of its processes and has to be continually replaced.

The digestive system includes the mouth, teeth, tongue, throat, gullet, stomach, the small and large intestines, which together form a long tube, the alimentary canal (digestive tract or gut), the liver and the pancreas.

Amazing

When your stomach is empty it holds barely 0.5 l, but after eating a big meal it can stretch to more than 4 l.

Semi-digested food moves from the stomach to the small intestine, which is 6 m long, but tightly coiled. Here enzymes are added to the food, breaking it down so it can be absorbed. The intestine wall is covered with finger-like projections, called villi, which increase the surface area.

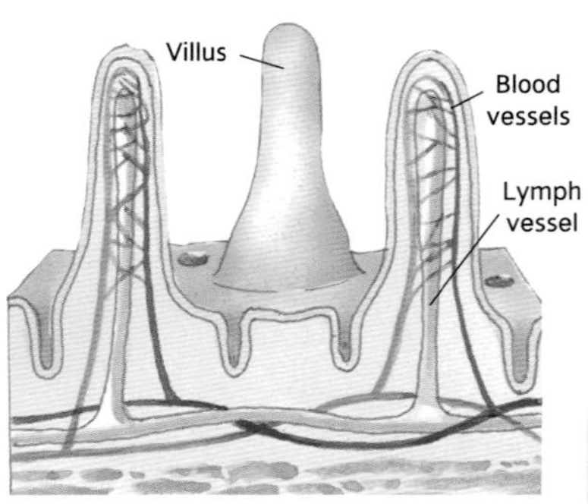

Water for life

Your body is mainly made of water – more than 60 per cent. You can survive for possibly weeks without food, but only a few days without water.

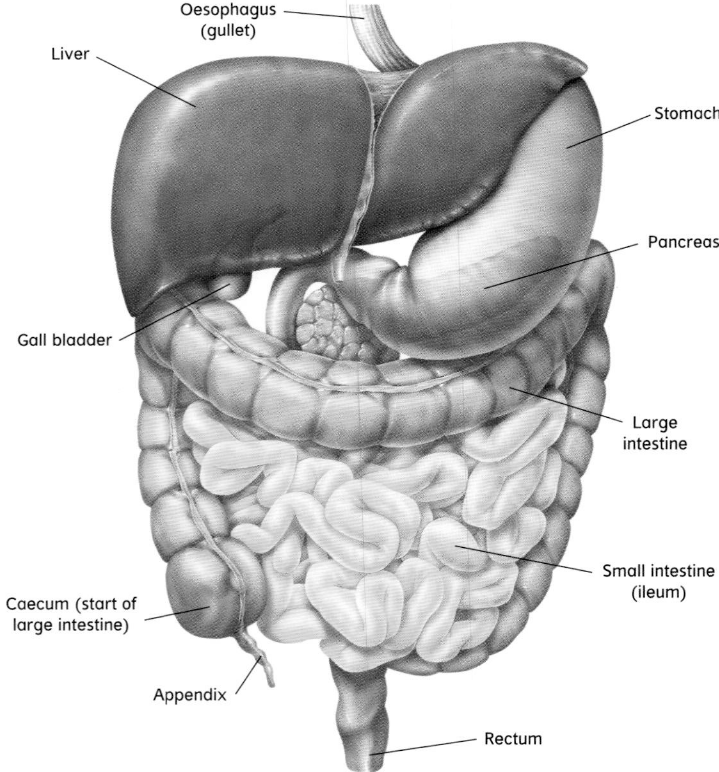

Digestion timeline

0 hour	Food is chewed and swallowed.
1 hour	Food is churned with acids and juices in the stomach.
2 hours	Partially digested food begins to flow into the small intestine for further digestion and absorption.
4 hours	Most food has left the stomach and passed to the small intestine.
6 hours	Leftover and undigested foods pass into the large intestine, which takes the water and returns it to the body.
10 hours	Leftovers begin to collect in the last part of the system, the rectum, as faeces.
16–24 hours	Faeces pass through the last part of the system, the anus, and out of the body.

❍ Digestion is the process by which your body breaks down the food you eat into substances that it can absorb (take in) and use.

❍ Your digestive tract is basically a long winding tube called the alimentary canal, or gut. It starts at your mouth and ends at your anus. If you could lay your gut out straight it would be six times as long as you are tall.

❍ When you eat you chew your food to break it into small lumps. They are coated in saliva (spit), which softens the food with special chemicals called enzymes.

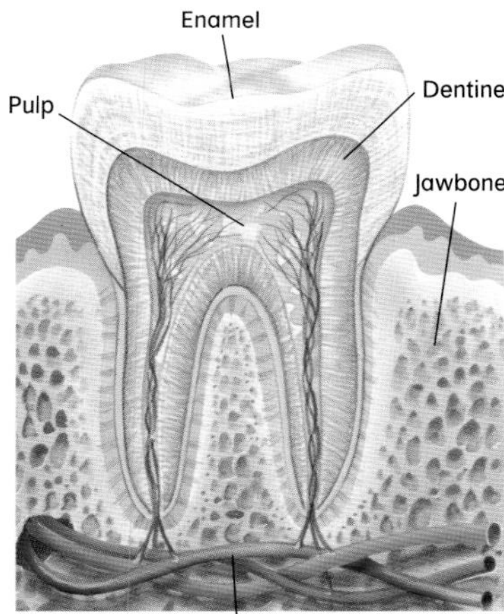

In each side of the jaw, the adult set of teeth includes two incisors at the front for biting, one taller canine for tearing, and two broad premolars, plus three wider molars for crushing and chewing. In the centre of a tooth is a soft pulp of blood vessels and nerves. Around this is tough dentine. On the outside of the top part, the crown, is even harder enamel. The roots fix the tooth into the jawbone.

The kidneys, ureters, bladder and urethra form the urinary system. The kidney has two layers – the cortex and medulla. The space where urine collects is the renal pelvis. Blood enters each kidney and filters through over a million nephrons (filtration units). The body has two kidneys, placed on either side in the small of the back.

❍ When you swallow, food travels down your oesophagus and into your stomach where more enzymes work on it and it is broken down into a mush called chyme. From here it travels into your small intestine.

❍ Chyme is further broken down by enzymes in your small intestine and the goodness is absorbed across the intestine wall into blood vessels that transport it around the body. Waste moves into the large intestine.

❍ Waste products and food that you cannot digest are pushed out of the large intestine through the anus when you go to the lavatory. This is called excretion.

❍ Nutrients from your food are taken to your liver to be turned into glucose, the main energy-giving chemical for body cells. The liver helps keep levels of glucose steady in the bloodstream.

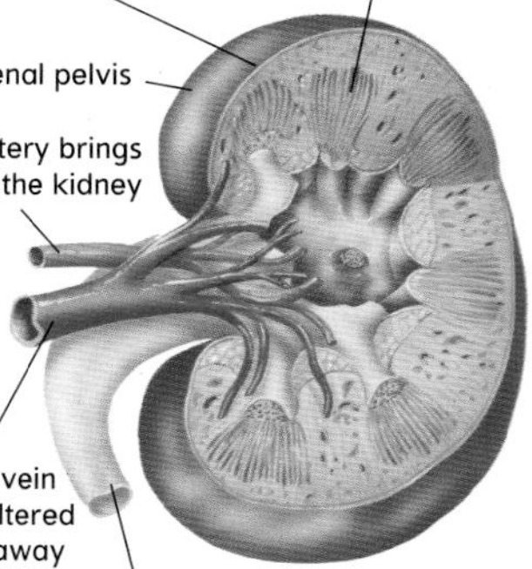

Outer layer, or cortex, contains capsules of nephrons

Inner layer, or medulla, contains tubules of nephrons

Renal pelvis

Renal artery brings blood to the kidney

Renal vein takes filtered blood away from the kidney

Ureter takes urine to the bladder

❍ Your body needs a balance of different food types to work properly. Carbohydrates, proteins, fat, fibre, vitamins and minerals are all essential for a healthy body.

❍ Kidneys are the body's filters. They take goodness and water out of the blood, and return them to the body while removing excess water and waste products. This excess water and waste is sent to the bladder, where it is stored as urine.

Hormones

The process of digestion is, like other body processes, controlled by hormones. These are natural chemicals that work to keep the body in harmony. Hormones are made in special places called endocrine glands and they travel all round the body in the blood. Female and male bodies have much the same hormone-making glands, except for the reproductive parts – ovaries (seen here) in the female and testes in the male.

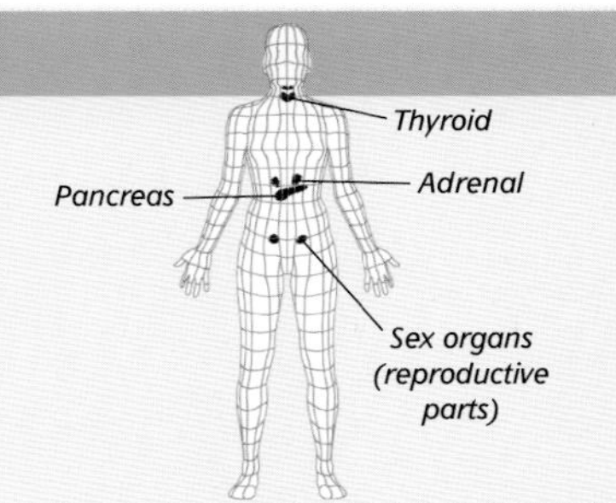

Heart and Blood

The circulatory system is a complex network of blood vessels, such as arteries, veins and capillaries, and the heart. These all work together to transmit blood to every part of the body, bringing oxygen and nutrients and removing waste products.

❍ Blood is the reddish liquid that circulates around your body. It carries food and oxygen to your body cells and removes waste. It also carries hormones and special cells that fight infections.

❍ The heart is a muscular bag that never stops pumping blood round the body. It is divided into two pumps. The right pump sends blood to the lungs, to collect oxygen. It returns to the heart, where the left pump sends it to the rest of the body.

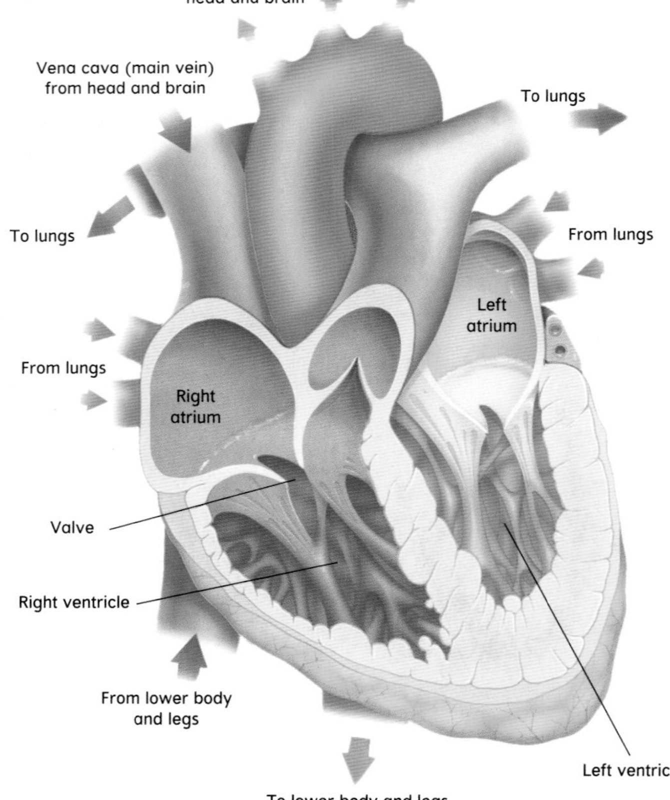

Taking your pulse

Your pulse is the powerful high-pressure surge, or wave, that runs through your body and vessels every time the heart pumps blood out. You can feel your pulse by pressing two fingertips on the inside of your wrist, below your thumb.

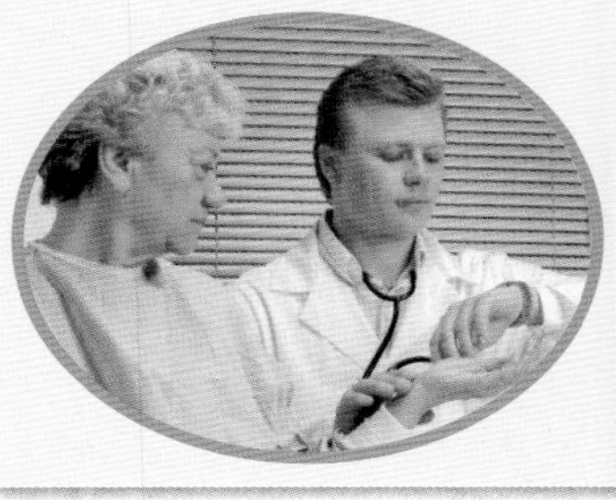

Inside the heart are four chambers. On each side are an upper atrium, which receives blood from the veins, and the lower thick-walled ventricle, which pumps it out into the arteries. One-way valves make sure blood flows in the correct direction.

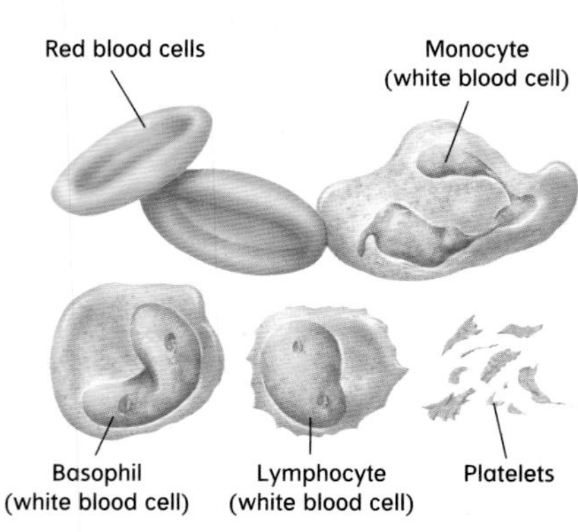

Blood is made up of red cells, white cells and platelets, all carried in a liquid called plasma. Red cells cannot change their shape, but the various white cells can, to enable them to attack germs invading the body.

Amazing

At any given moment about 65 per cent of all the body's blood is in the veins, 25 per cent in the arteries, 5 per cent in the capillaries and 5 per cent in the heart.

A blood vessel wall has several layers and blood itself contains different types of cells. Red cells are the most numerous and have a rounded, dished shape. White cells can change their shape as they surround and attack germs. Platelets are much smaller, resembling pieces of cells.

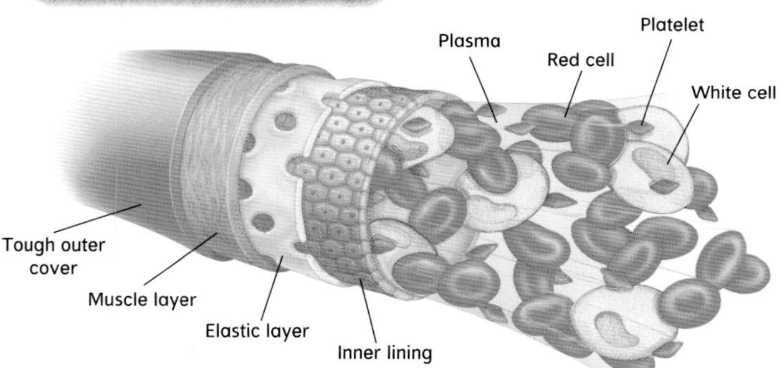

❍ White blood cells are essential in the fight against infection. There are different types of white blood cell and they work together to kill invading organisms, such as viruses or bacteria.

❍ Arteries are tube-like blood vessels that carry blood away from the heart. Most arteries contain blood that carries oxygen to the body parts.

❍ Veins are blood vessels that carry blood back to the heart. Most veins carry blood that has had the oxygen and nutrients removed. It contains carbon dioxide, which is released into the lungs.

❍ Capillaries are the smallest of all your blood vessels. They are only one cell thick, so chemicals can easily pass through them and into your cells. The largest capillary is still thinner than a human hair.

❍ Your blood has two main types of cell, white cells and red cells. It also contains platelets, which help to form blood clots to stop any bleeding. Blood also carries substances that fight infection and hormones.

❍ Red blood cells are button-shaped and they contain a red protein called haemoglobin. This protein combines with oxygen to carry it around the body. In each red blood cell there are about 250 million haemoglobin molecules.

Arteries carry blood away from the heart. They have thick walls to withstand the surge of high-pressure blood with each heartbeat. Capillaries are the smallest blood vessels, less than 1 mm long and far too thin to see. Oxygen and nutrients seep from blood through their walls into surrounding tissues. Veins are wide, thin-walled and floppy and take blood back to the heart.

Body full of blood

The amount of blood in your body depends on your size. An adult weighing 80 kg has about 5 l of blood, a child weighing 40 kg has half that amount.

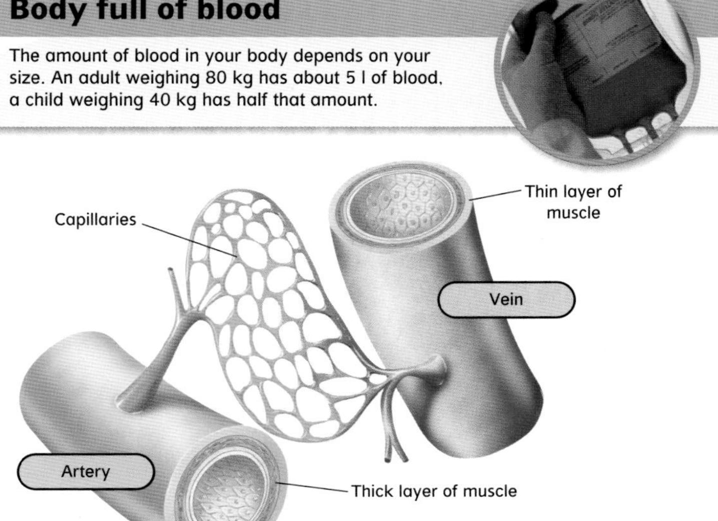

The Nervous System

The nervous system is your body's control and communication system. It is made up of nerves and the brain. It is your nervous system that controls everything you do, everything you see and everything you feel. It is the body's central 'computer'.

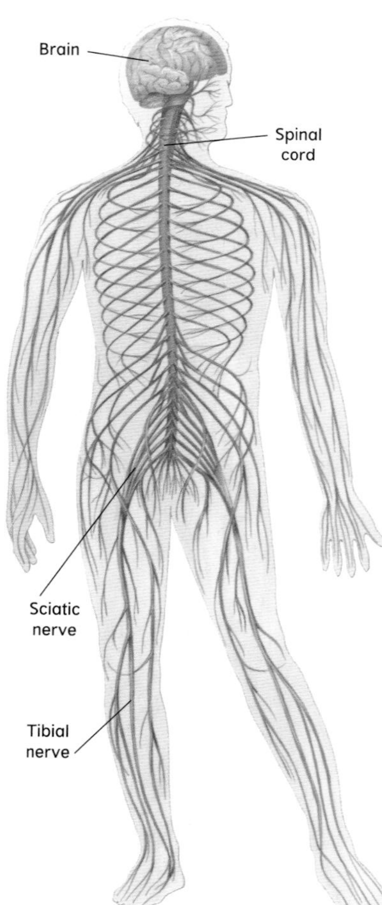

❍ Nerves are your body's hotlines, carrying instant messages from the brain to every organ and muscle – and sending back an endless stream of data to the brain about what is going on both inside, and outside, your body.

❍ Nerves are made of very specialized cells called neurons. Neurons are spider-shaped, with lots of branching threads called dendrites and a winding tail called an axon. An axon can be up to 1 m long.

❍ Neurons link up, like beads on a string, to make up your nervous system. Nerve signals are electrical pulses and they travel down neurons at great speed – up to 100 m each second.

❍ Sensory nerves carry information to your brain about your body's experience of the world. Eyes, ears, tongue and nose all have sensory nerves. Your skin is covered with sensory nerve-endings, called receptors.

Amazing

The left half of your brain controls the right-hand side of your body, and the right half of your brain controls the left-hand side of your body.

Nerves branch from the brain and spinal cord to every part of the body. All nerve signals are similar, but there are two main kinds, depending on where they are going. Sensory nerve signals travel from the sensory parts (eyes, ears, nose, tongue and skin) to the brain. Motor nerve signals travel from the brain out to the muscles, to make the body move about.

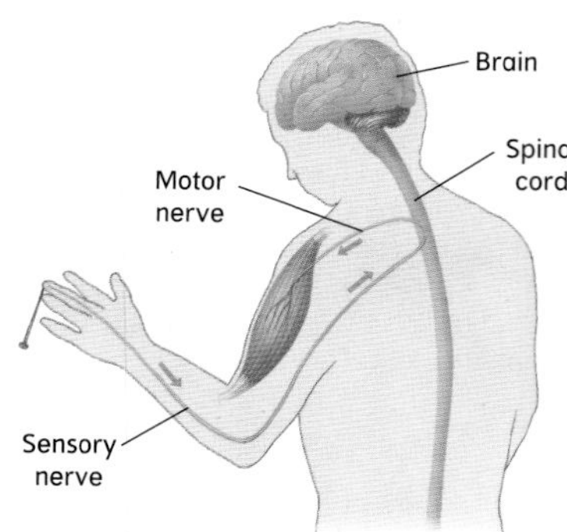

If you touch a sharp pin, a message goes along a sensory nerve to your spinal cord. A motor nerve moves your hand away at once. This immediate response is called a reflex action. The message carries on to your brain, which knows about the pain after your hand has moved, so then you feel it.

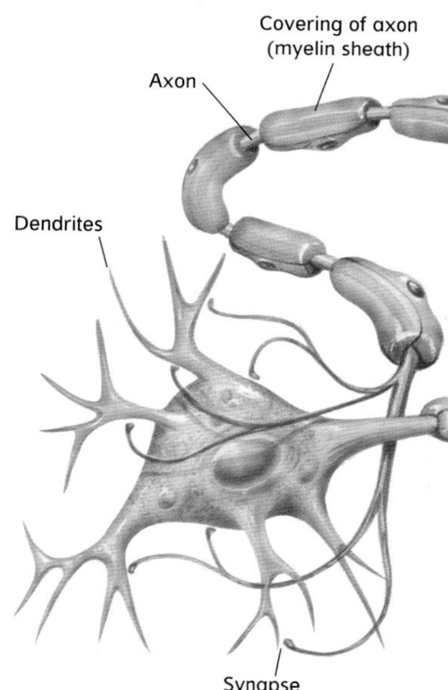

❍ Information about light, taste, touch, heat, smell and sound are all sent to the brain where it is processed.

❍ The brain is an extremely complicated organ, and we are slowly learning about how it works. Nerves from around the body bring information to the brain, where it is stored (as memory) and acted upon.

MRI scanners

Brain and nervous tissue do not show up well on X-rays, so doctors use special scanning equipment to investigate these areas. MRI (Magnetic Resonance Imaging) scans are commonly used in hospitals to examine brains for possible injuries and damage.

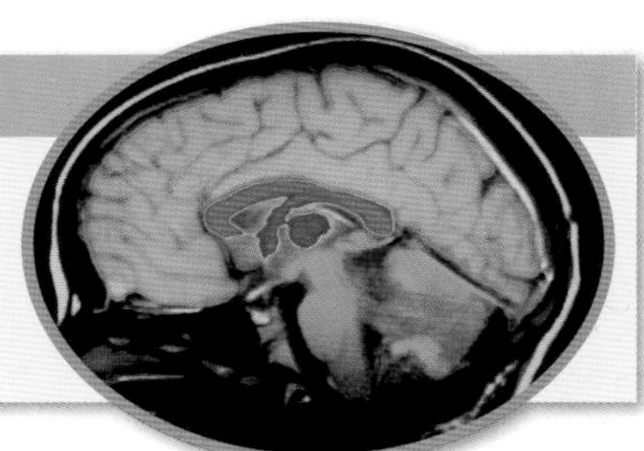

Nerve cells

There are hundreds of billions of nerve cells in the body. The brain alone contains 100 billion nerve cells.

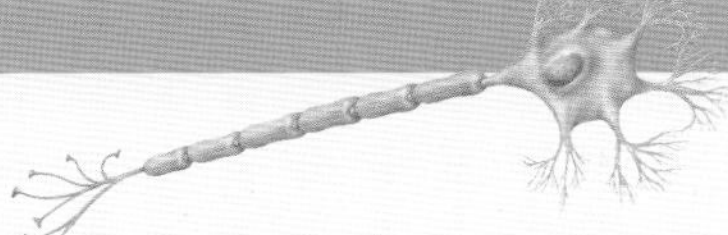

About nine-tenths of the brain is the large dome of the two cerebral hemispheres. The outer cerebral cortex is where conscious thoughts happen.

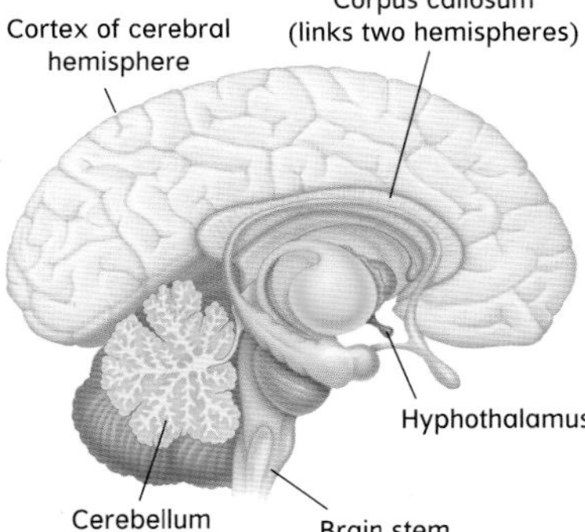

The brain and nerves are made of billions of specialized cells, nerve cells or neurons. Each has many tiny branches (dendrites) to collect nerve messages, and the axon or fibre is a longer, thicker branch that passes on these messages.

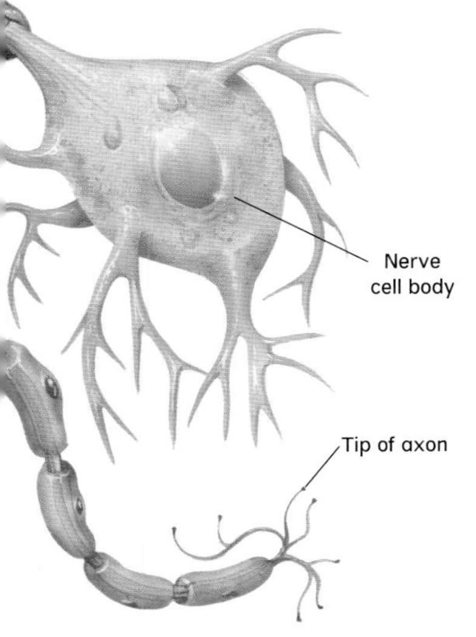

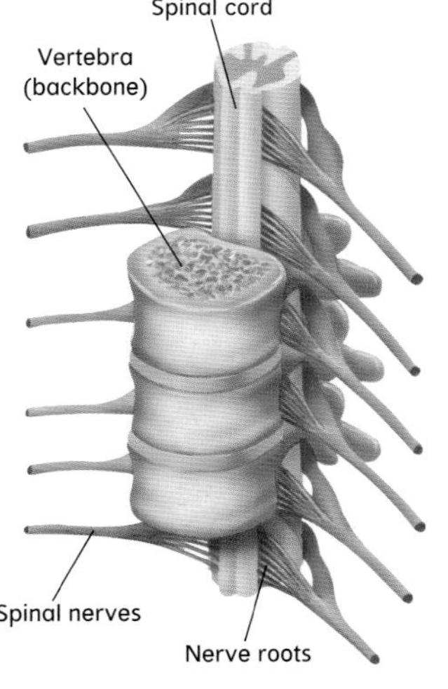

The brain is 'wired' into the body by the spinal cord. It extends from the base of the brain down inside the backbone (spinal column). Thirty-one pairs of nerves branch from it on each side out into the body. The spinal cord is protected inside a tunnel, which is formed by a row of holes through the vertebrae (backbones).

❍ The brain is divided into different regions, which perform different tasks. They are all linked and work together.

❍ The hypothalamus and brain stem are involved with automatic processes, such as breathing and digestion. The cerebral cortex is involved in thinking, decision-making and learning.

❍ The brain sends messages out to the muscles via motor nerves. The nerves instruct the muscles to contract and relax. The cerebellum coordinates all your muscles so they produce smooth, flowing movements.

Reproduction

In the beginning, a human body starts as a single cell, which is a fertilized egg. This egg grows, over a period of about nine months, into a baby that is ready to be born. A newborn baby needs constant care to survive.

❍ The process of making a new human being is called reproduction. Humans are mammals and reproduce in a very similar way to other mammals; they give birth to live young and feed them with milk that is made in special glands in the mother's body.

❍ A baby grows from an egg cell that has been fertilized by a sperm cell. Egg cells are made by females, in special egg-making places called ovaries. Every month a woman's body instructs an egg to ripen, ready for fertilization.

❍ Sperm cells are made by a man's body, inside special sperm-making places called testes. Millions of sperm cells are made every day and they are stored inside a coiled tube called the epididymis. Unused sperm are reabsorbed by the body.

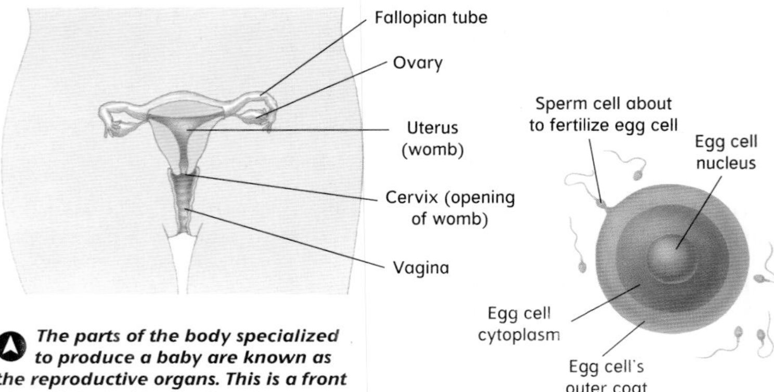

The parts of the body specialized to produce a baby are known as the reproductive organs. This is a front view of the inside of a female reproductive system showing the two ovaries and fallopian tubes, which join to the uterus. In the woman, egg cells are contained in the two ovaries. Each month the menstrual cycle causes one egg to ripen and pass along the oviduct into the womb, where a sperm cell may join with it.

The female egg cell passes along the woman's fallopian tube. At fertilization, tiny sperm cells swarm around the egg until one sperm manages to push its head on to the surface of the egg. The sperm head and egg membrane join, and fertilization takes place.

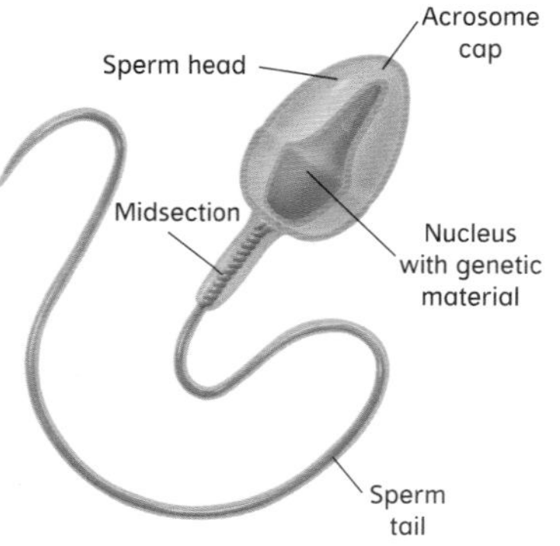

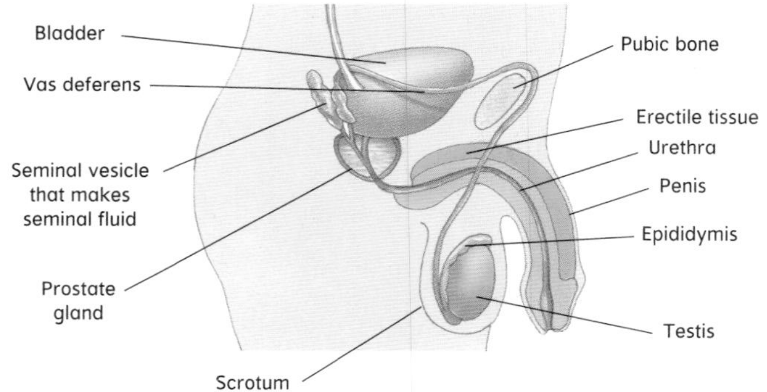

A mature sperm cell consists of a head, where genetic information is stored, a midsection and a tadpole-like tail, which allows it to swim rapidly towards the female egg cell.

This is a side view of the inside of the male reproductive organs. In a man, sperm are made in the two testes. During sex they pass along the vas deferens tubes, which join and continue as the urethra, to the outside.

❍ During sexual intercourse (sex), sperm cells enter the woman's vagina and may meet up with an egg. If a sperm enters the egg, and joins with it, then the egg is fertilized and might grow into a baby.

❍ A fertilized egg cell implants in the woman's womb. This is the place where babies grow during pregnancy.

❍ The fertilized egg divides into two, then each new cell divides again and this continues until lots of new cells have been created. The cells grow and become specialized: some become brain cells, some muscle cells. Each has a role to play in the new body.

Life begins when the fertilized egg divides into two cells, then four, eight, and so on. After a few days there are hundreds of cells, and after a few weeks, millions. These cells build up the various body parts. An unborn baby develops 'head-first', starting with the brain and head, then the main body, then the arms and legs. At first, the tiny baby has plenty of room in the womb and can float about freely. But as it grows it becomes cramped and has to bend its neck, back, arms and legs.

Ultrasound scans

Pregnant women can find out how their babies are growing, and check they are well by having ultrasound scans.

❍ During pregnancy, the baby is fed through a special tube called the umbilical tube. The tube is connected at one end to a placenta – a blood-rich collection of tissue on the womb wall – and to the baby's abdomen at the other.

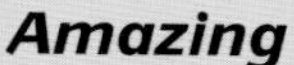

Amazing

Every single person is unique. Not just because of genes inherited from parents, but because experiences and learning change us.

❍ When the baby is ready to be born the mother begins 'labour'. During this process her body prepares itself to deliver the baby. The mother's womb has to push the baby out with strong muscular contractions. Once born, the umbilical cord is cut and the baby breathes on its own.

DNA – the structure of life

Children often look like their parents because all of our cells, including egg and sperm cells, contain DNA (deoxyribonucleic acid). DNA holds information about special structures called genes. Genes make us tall or short, fair or dark, healthy or likely to get particular illnesses and so on. Genes are passed on to children through sexual reproduction. Half of your genes are from your mother and half from your father. No one has the same mix of genes except identical twins. Inside each single cell of your body, there are over 20,000 individual genes.

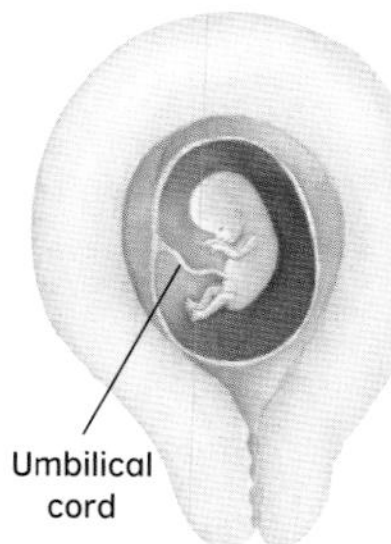

Two months
All main body parts are formed and baby is now called a foetus

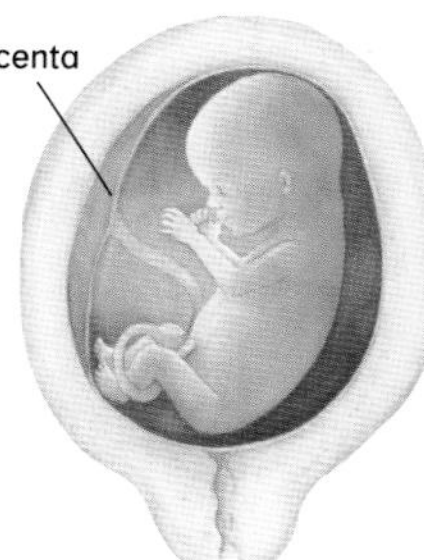

Three months
First hairs grow on skin

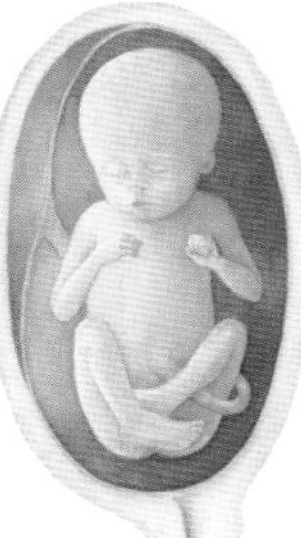

Five months
Hands and fingers can grip the umbilical cord

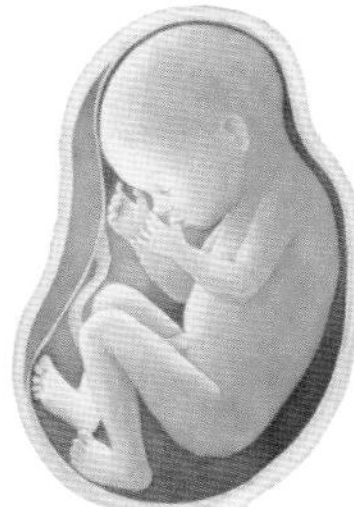

Seven months
Eyelids open, body is slim and skin wrinkled

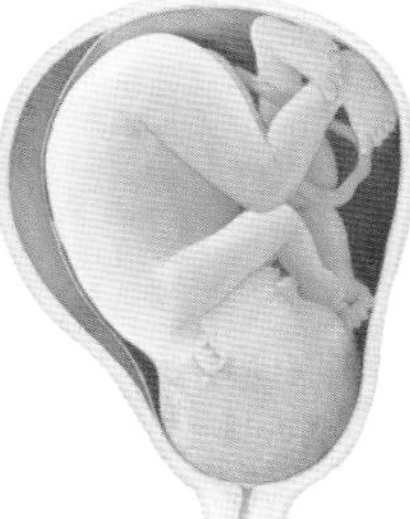

Nine months
Baby has 'turned' and is head-down, ready to be born

Glossary

Alveoli Microscopic air spaces inside the lungs, with more than 300 million in each.

Annual A flowering plant that completes its life-cycle in one year.

Anther The tip of a stamen, where pollen is made.

Artery Blood vessel leading away from the heart.

Biennial A flowering plant that takes two years to complete its life-cycle.

Bladder A bag-like organ in mammals that stores substances such as urine.

Broadleaved tree A tree that grows leaves that are wide and flat. It may be an evergreen or deciduous tree.

Camouflage Pattern or colour that blends in with the surroundings.

Capillary Tiny blood vessels.

Carbon dioxide A gas that plants need to photosynthesize, and that animals and plants make as a waste product from respiration.

Carnivore Animal that mostly or totally eats meat.

Carpel The female part of a flower.

Cartilage A rubbery or gristly substance that is similar to bone.

Cell The basic building block of animals and plants. The cells have different shapes to perform different tasks to keep the plant or animal alive.

Chlorophyll Chemical found in green plants essential for photosynthesis.

Chromosomes Lengths of the genetic material DNA that have been coiled up very tightly to resemble microscopic threads.

Clones Living things that have identical genes.

Conifer Trees and other plants that produce cones, not flowers.

Cortex The outer region or layer of a body part such as the kidney, brain or lymph node.

DNA Deoxyribonucleic acid, a chemical that makes up the instructions or genes for how a living thing grows and functions.

Deciduous Plants or trees that lose their leaves in autumn.

Digestion The process of taking in the goodness from food.

Endangered An animal or plant species that is in danger of becoming extinct.

Enzyme A chemical substance that causes other chemical reactions to occur, or speeds them up.

Evergreen Plants that keep their leaves all year.

Evolution The gradual process by which animals and plants adapt and develop to survive in a changing world.

Excretion Removal of wastes, by-products and other unwanted substances from the body – by the excretory or urinary system.

Exoskeleton The tough outer coat of an insect or similar invertebrate.

Extinction When an animal or plant species completely dies out.

Fertilization The process by which a male sex cell and a female sex cell join together, for example sperm and egg in mammals, pollen and ovule in flowering plants.

Fossil The process by which remains of an animal or plant become preserved as rock, over millions of years.

Genes Instructions or information, in the form of the chemical DNA, for how a living thing develops, grows and functions.

Germination The process by which a seed begins to produce a seedling.

Gills Organs used for breathing (respiration) by many animals that live in water, such as fish.

Glucose A type of sugar that is used as an energy supply by plants and animals.

Habitat The place that an animal or plant lives.

Herbivore An animal that eats mainly or only plants.

Hormone A chemical substance that is transported around a plant or animal to make an organ or tissue respond in a particular way.

Hydrogen Gas that combines with oxygen to make water.

Invertebrates Animals without backbones.

Joint The place where two or more bones or other skeletal parts meet.

Ligament Strong and flexible tissue that joins bones.

Lung Special organ used for breathing by animals that breathe on land (and mammals that live in water).

Marrow Soft, jelly-like substance in the middle of many bones, which makes new cells for the blood (red marrow) or stores energy and nutrients as fat (yellow marrow).

Migration Regular large-scale movement by animals to find better conditions, such as food or weather.

Mimicry When one animal looks like another (the model) to gain an advantage, for example pretending to be a poisonous animal when it is not itself poisonous.

Neurons Nerve cells, specialized to receive and pass on information in the form of tiny electrical signals called nerve impulses.

Nocturnal Active at night rather than during the day.

Nucleus The central region or control centre of a cell, containing the genetic material DNA.

Organ A collection of tissues that perform a particular job, for example lung, stomach or heart.

Organism Any living thing.

Ovary Place where eggs are made in females.

Ovule An egg.

Oxygen A gas that animals breathe. It combines with hydrogen to make water.

Perennial A plant that lives for many years.

Photosynthesis Process by which plants combine carbon dioxide with water to make food, using sunlight as a source of energy.

Plankton Tiny animals and plants that drift in the water of seas, oceans and large lakes.

Plasma The liquid part of blood without the microscopic cells (red cells, white cells and platelets).

Pollen Tiny capsules made by the stamens containing male cells. To reproduce, plants must pass pollen between flowers. Pollen is carried by the wind or other insects to other plants.

Pollination The process by which pollen is transferred to the female part of a flower.

Predator An animal that preys on (hunts) other animals, the prey.

Prey An animal that is hunted by another, the predator.

Reproduction The process of creating new life, or offspring.

Respiration Breathing; also releasing energy from food and gases.

Sap The food-containing liquid that moves through the roots and stem of a plant.

Seed A capsule, which forms from the ovule after fertilization, and contains a tiny plant with a foodstore.

Sepal A small leaf that forms part of the covering of the flower bud.

Species A type of animal or plant, the members of which can breed with each other but not with other species.

Spore A tiny seed-like capsule made by non-flowering plants such as mosses and also fungi.

Stamen A male part of the flower that bears the anther containing pollen.

Stem Part of the plant that supports the leaves and flowers and carries water and minerals and food made in the leaves to other parts of the plant.

Stigma The top of the carpel.

Stomata Tiny holes in a leaf through which gases can pass.

Synapse The junction or connection between two nerve cells or neurons.

Temperate forest A forest that grows in a region with warm summers and cool winters.

Tendon Special tissue that connects muscles to bones.

Territory An area or place where an animal lives and feeds, and which it defends by chasing away others of its kind.

Tissue A collection of similar cells that perform a particular task.

Tropical rainforest A forest that grows where the weather is always hot and wet.

Vein Main blood vessel or tube that carries blood towards the heart.

Vertebrate An animal with a backbone.

HISTORY

The Ancient World

Once people started to farm the land they roamed and settled in villages, and the population in certain areas began to grow – sometimes rapidly. Villages grew into towns, and towns developed into cities. Leaders of hunting bands became chiefs of their villages and towns; the strongest chiefs became kings, ruling not just their own areas but also other settlements. These powerful rulers created the world's first empires.

c.200,000 years ago fully modern humans evolved in Africa. They then spread out to the rest of the world. Other forms of human gradually died out.

c.9000 BC Wheat was cultivated in northern Mesopotamia, the area between the rivers Tigris and Euphrates, in West Asia. The availability of water and

c.90,000 BC →

Stone Age man

c.3100 BC In Britain, the first stage of building Stonehenge began.

c.2334–2279 BC Sargon, one of the earliest conquerors in world history, ruled Mesopotamia. He founded the Akkad dynasty and brought parts of Syria, Turkey and western Iran under his control. Sargon was the first leader to organize a formal military force.

c.3100 BC →

Stonehenge

c.2200 BC Egypt was weakened by crop failure and social upheavals, which led to the decline of the Old Kingdom, followed by a period of disorder, when Egypt split into several small kingdoms.

c.2000 BC The Mesoamerican Olmec civilization developed and flourished in the lowland gulf coast of southern Mexico. Olmecs built cities and made advances in commerce and the arts.

c.1279–1213 BC Rameses II or Rameses the Great was pharaoh of Egypt. He built the remarkable Temple of Abu Simbel in Aswan as well as other temples, forts and palaces across Egypt.

c.1000 BC Iron became a popular metal in Europe and western Asia as people gained experience in heating, melting and forging techniques.

c.800 BC Greece revived after a period of decline known as the Dark Ages.

c.605–562 BC Nebuchadnezzar II reigned over Babylon. He attacked Judah and captured Jerusalem. Various building projects were undertaken in Babylon during his reign, including the construction of the Hanging Gardens of Babylon, considered in ancient times to be one of the Seven Wonders of the World.

508 BC The nobleman Cleisthenes reformed the government of Athens so that it had a democratic government.

499–449 BC Greece and Persia were engaged in a series of battles, which are collectively referred to as the Greco–Persian Wars. The wars ended after the Greek city-states managed to expel the Persian armies.

431–404 BC The Peloponnesian War began when Athens broke a treaty with Sparta. All Greek cities took sides in the conflict that spread to include Sicily and other islands. The Peloponnesian War weakened the Greek cities and ruined their economy.

c.1279 BC

c.97–30 BC The reign of Emperor Sujin marked the start of documented Japanese history.

31 BC After a series of civil wars, Octavian, the nephew of Julius Caesar, defeated the murderers of his uncle. Instead of becoming dictator, Octavian assumed the title Augustus and used his wealth and influence to reform the government of Rome. He was later recognized as the first emperor of Rome. The Roman Empire included large parts of Europe and Asia, northern Africa and the Mediterranean islands.

31 BC →

Jesus Christ

c.AD 30 Jesus Christ was crucified on the hill of Golgotha in Jerusalem. His teachings later formed the basis of the Christian religion.

c.AD 100 The Mesoamerican Olmec civilization began to decline.

AD 117–138 Roman emperor Hadrian took control of the empire and reformed the government of the provinces.

AD 180–192 Roman emperor Commodus ruled during this period. His cruel reign marked the beginning of the Roman Empire's downfall.

c.AD 200 The Bantu people, descendents of the Neolithic Nok

development of irrigation techniques led to the decline of hunter-gatherer societies and an increase in settled agricultural communities that reared domestic animals. Dogs were among the first animals to be domesticated.

c.7400–6700 BC The people of Mexico began forming agricultural communities and grew vegetables such as pumpkins and gourds.

c.7000–5000 BC In China, small agricultural settlements developed. People cultivated rice and made simple pots and baskets.

c.6000 BC A primitive agricultural settlement that grew wheat developed at Mehgarh, west of the Indus Valley. This area later became a part of the Harappan or Indus Valley civilization.

c.6000 BC The aboriginal people of northern Australia made rock paintings of fish and crocodiles and other animal life.

c.3100 BC Menes, also known as Narmer, a king from Upper Egypt, unified Lower and Upper Egypt to form one kingdom. He made Memphis, near modern-day Cairo, his capital. Menes is considered to be the first Egyptian pharaoh.

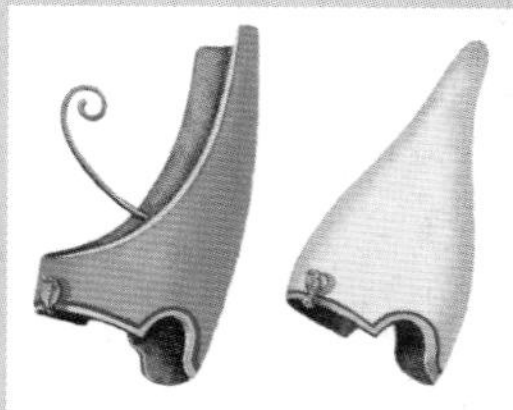

Crowns of Egypt

c.1700 BC The Minoan civilization began to flourish on the island of Crete. The Minoans were famous seafarers who traded across the Mediterranean Sea.

c.1600 BC Egypt was united again under the rulers of Thebes, a city in Upper Egypt. The country became prosperous and grew to rule many neighbouring areas.

Abu Simbel Temple

c.1500 BC People sailing in large canoes migrated to the Micronesian and Polynesian islands for the first time. They formed farming settlements raising pigs, yams and other foodstuffs.

c.1300 BC The Mycenean civilization in Greece began to decline. The Myceneans fought the war against Troy, a city in what is now Turkey, and lived in a series of small city states.

Nebuchadnezzar II

336 BC Alexander the Great, King of Macedonia, forced all the Greek states to accept him as their overlord. He then invaded the Persian Empire. He defeated the Persians in the Battle of Gaugamela. This defeat brought about the fall of the Persian Empire.

330 BC The Greek culture came to western Asia with Alexander's conquest of these areas. The style of Greek culture spread by Alexander and his followers is known as Hellenistic.

Alexander the Great

218 BC The two most powerful states in the western Mediterranean – Rome and Carthage – began the Second Punic War. At first the Carthaginian general Hannibal defeated the Romans, but the war ended with the humiliation of Carthage at the Battle of Zama in 202 BC.

149–146 BC The Third Punic War between Rome and Carthage resulted in the destruction of Carthage and led to Roman control over the western Mediterranean.

49 BC The very successful Roman general Julius Caesar was appointed Dictator of Rome and began to reform the corrupt government system. However, his enemies arranged his murder in 44 BC.

people from west Africa, migrated into central and southern Africa.

c.AD 224–651 The Iranian Sasanid dynasty ruled over Persia.

AD 306 As commander of the Roman Armies in Britain, Constantine the Great defeated his rivals and was made emperor by the Roman troops in Britain. He later converted to Christianity – the first Roman emperor to do so.

c.AD 372 The Huns, who had migrated from Central Asia to Europe, drove the Ostrogoths and Visigoths from Ukraine. The Goths fled into Roman territory, becoming a constant source of trouble to the Romans.

AD 406 The Germanic tribes of Vandals, Alans and Sciri crossed the Rhine. This event marks the collapse of Roman power.

AD 410 The Visigoths, led by Alaric, invaded Italy and sacked (burned and looted) Rome.

c.AD 440 The British hired Germanic mercenaries to replace the Roman army. The mercenaries later revolted.

AD 455 Vandals sacked Rome again. In AD 476, the Western empire finally collapsed.

Emperor Constantine

The Fertile Crescent

About 10,000 years ago people living across a wide area of the Middle East began to live as farmers. They planted seeds that grew into crops and kept domestic animals to provide milk and meat. The lands where these people lived included Egypt, the valley of the Tigris and Euphrates rivers and the Indus Valley. This area is known as the Fertile Crescent. It was here that the first towns and cities were built by early farmers.

❍ The first great civilization was that of the Sumerians, who farmed irrigated land by the Euphrates *c.*5000 BC and lived in mud-brick houses.

❍ About 3000 BC, a civilization developed from small farming communities in the Indus valley in Pakistan.

❍ Indus cities were carefully planned, with straight streets, bath-houses and big granaries (grain stores).

❍ By 1750 BC, the Indus civilization had declined. It finally vanished with the arrival of the Aryans *c.*1500 BC.

❍ Only when Hammurabi became king in 1792 BC did Babylon become a powerful city. In his 42-year reign, Hammurabi built a huge empire.

❍ Babylon was surrounded by walls 26 m thick – faced with blue bricks, decorated with dragons, lions and bulls.

Wealthy Assyrians strove to outdo each other with elaborate clothing and luxurious houses.

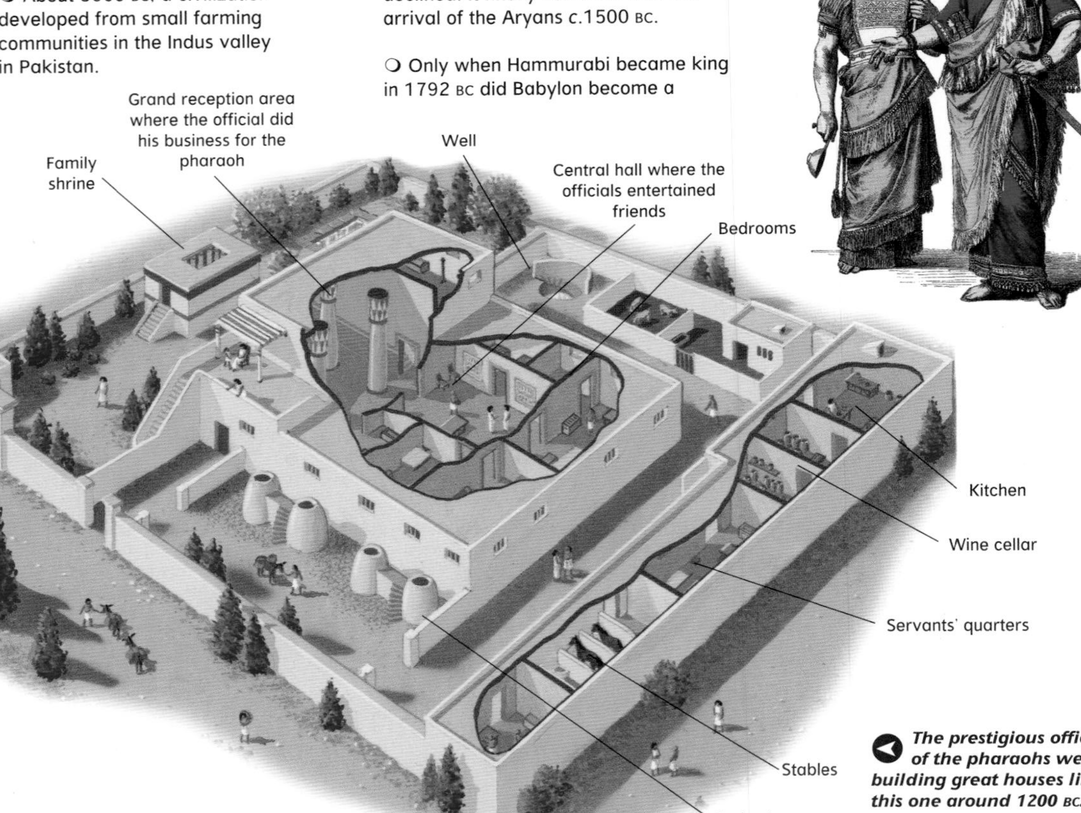

The prestigious officials of the pharaohs were building great houses like this one around 1200 BC.

Darius the Great ruled Persia from 522 until 486 BC.

❍ The grandest gate was the Ishtar Gate, which opened on to a paved avenue called the Processional Street.

❍ The Assyrians were ruthless warriors who fought with bows, iron swords, spears and chariots. They built up an empire covering all of Mesopotamia and Egypt by about the year 1100 BC. It was destroyed by the Persians in 612 BC.

❍ The Persian Empire reached its greatest extent around 490 BC under Darius I, who called himself Shahanshah ('King of kings').

❍ Pharaohs were the kings of ancient Egypt. They were also High Priest, head judge and commander of the army.

❍ There were 33 dynasties (families) of pharaohs, beginning with Menes around 3100 BC and ending in 30 BC.

Pharaohs were the rulers of ancient Egypt. The word 'pharaoh' means great house. Egyptians thought of the pharaoh as both the god Horus and the son of the sun god Re. When he died he was transformed into the god Osiris, father of Horus. Since he was a god, anyone approaching him had to crawl. Here the pharaoh is holding the symbols of his rule, the hook and flail. Workers used these tools to separate grain from the stalks.

❍ Egyptians believed that everyone had three souls: the ka, ba and akh. For these to flourish, the body must survive intact, so the ancient Egyptians tried to preserve their dead bodies as well as they could.

Amazing

In 521 BC several men claimed the throne of Persia. Instead of fighting each other, the men decided that whoever's horse neighed first would be king. Darius won.

River Nile

The Nile is the longest river in Africa, and its waters made farming possible for the people of hot, dry Egypt. Every year the Nile floods, as snow melts in mountains to the south raising the level of the water. As it floods, the river spreads fertile mud, which enables farmers to grow plentiful crops. The Egyptians sailed along the Nile to reach other farms and towns.

Gilgamesh

The *Epic of Gilgamesh* was composed around 2000 BC. It tells the tale of Gilgamesh (right), a powerful and oppressive king in ancient Sumeria. When his people pray for help, the gods create Enkidu, who meets Gilgamesh in battle. But the two become friends and share many adventures. The poem includes an account of a great flood, which has been likened to the Bible story of Noah.

The people of Mohenjo-Daro used ox-drawn carts. However, these would have been very slow and they probably relied on the river as their main source of transportation.

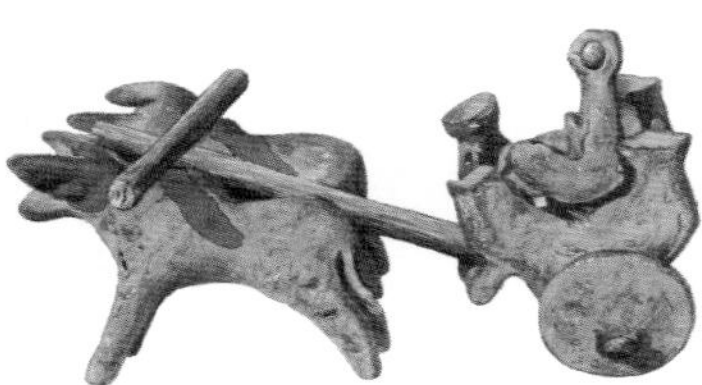

Ancient Greece

Greek civilzation grew out of the earlier cultures of Minoan Cretians and the Myceneans – a race of people who lived in what became Greece. By about 800 BC, the ideas of Greek scholars started to spread throughout the ancient world. Ancient Greece was divided into small, self-governing city-states – the most powerful of which were Athens and Sparta.

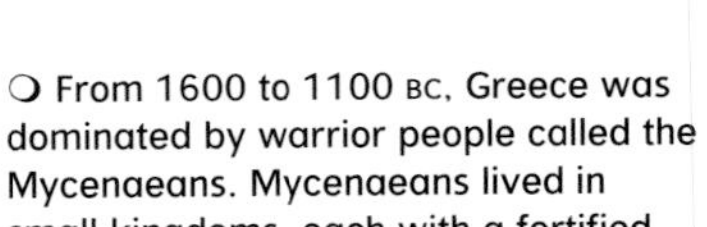

❍ From 1600 to 1100 BC, Greece was dominated by warrior people called the Mycenaeans. Mycenaeans lived in small kingdoms, each with a fortified city.

❍ The early Greeks held four major athletic events. These were the Olympic, Pythian, Isthmian and Nemean Games.

❍ Ancient Greece was not a single country, but a collection of independent cities or city-states, called polis (plural poleis). There were hundreds of poleis. The largest were Athens and Sparta.

The Greek epic poems* Iliad *and* Odyssey *are the principle sources for the story of the Trojan War. It is thought that they were composed in the second half of the 8th century BC, by the Greek poet Homer. During the war the Greeks trick the Trojans using a gigantic wooden horse.

The* Venus de Milo *was found on the Aegean island of Milos in AD 1820. It was carved in Greek Antioch (now in Turkey) c.150 BC and shows the goddess of love, Aphrodite.

❍ The great thinkers of Greece were called philosophers. The three greatest were Socrates, Plato and Aristotle.

❍ Greek mathematicians such as Euclid, Appolonius, Pythagoras and Archimedes worked out the basic rules of maths that are still used today.

❍ In ancient Greece, there were thousands of sculptors, architects, painters, dramatists and poets.

Famous people and their horses

Alexander the Great is known to have had a favourite horse, Bucephalus, but many other rulers had trusty steeds, too.

Alexander the Great	*Bucephalus*
Ulysses S Grant	*Cincinnati*
Duke of Wellington	*Copenhagen*
Richard the Lionheart	*Fauvel*
Caligula	*Incitatus*
Buffalo Bill	*Isham*
Buddha	*Kanthaka*
Stonewall Jackson	*Little Sorrel*
George Washington	*Magnolia*
Napoleon Bonaparte	*Marengo*
Robert E Lee	*Traveler*
General George Custer	*Vic*
Richard III	*White Surrey*

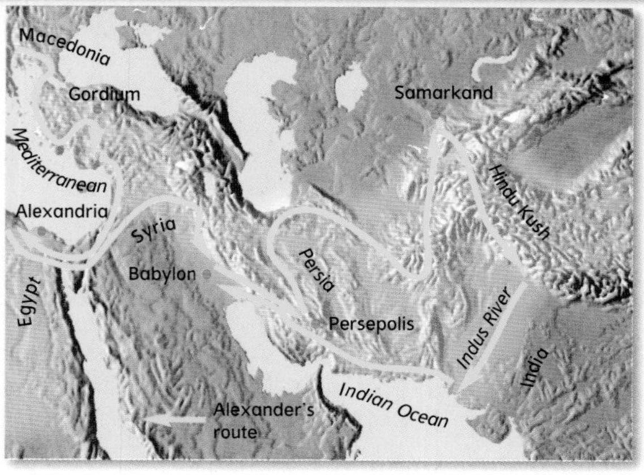

Alexander the Great was a young Macedonian king who united the Greek city-states, then led them on a vast invasion that created an empire that stretched from Greece to India.

- A Tragedy is a grand drama doomed to end unhappily for the hero.
- Greek gods included Apollo the god of light, Demeter the goddess of crops, and Artemis the goddess of the Moon.

Amazing

The city of Sparta had the finest army in ancient Greece. The Spartans believed they could defeat any army that outnumbered them by four to one – and they usually did.

Grand statue

The Parthenon was the most splendid temple in Athens, which was the leading city-state in ancient Greece. During the 400s BC, the Athenians built temples and shrines to the gods on a hill called the Acropolis. The Parthenon was more than 70 m long and about 18 m high, and was built to house a magnificent 12-m tall statue of Athene, goddess of wisdom and guardian of Athens, made of gold and ivory.

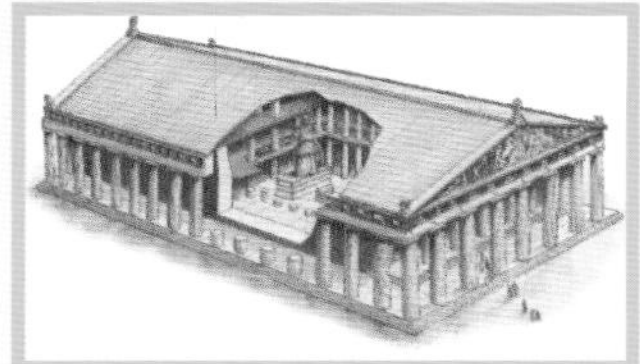

Formal drama was developed in ancient Greece in the 5th and 6th centuries BC. Huge audiences watched plays in open-air arenas.

The Seven Wonders of the World

The Tomb of King Mausolus – at Halicarnassus

The Statue of Zeus – at Olympia

The Pyramids at Giza – in Egypt

The Hanging Gardens of Babylon

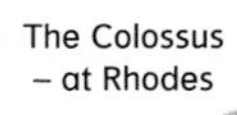

The Colossus – at Rhodes

The Temple of Artemis – at Ephesus

The Lighthouse – at Alexandria

30 words derived from the Greek language

Alphabet	Asteroid	Amnesia
Bicycle	Category	Chaos
Dinosaur	Dynasty	Echo
Economy	Gorilla	Gymnasium
Harmony	Hymn	Hysteria
Idea	Mania	Mechanic
Monarchy	Nemesis	Ocean
Orgy	Panic	Parallel
Problem	Rhinoceros	Sarcasm
Statistic	Telephone	Zodiac

Early money

Coins were first used by the Lydians (who lived in what is now Turkey) some time before 600 BC. The Greeks quickly adopted the use of coins for shopping and business. This one shows the head of Alexander.

The Roman Empire

The Roman Empire was the greatest the world had ever seen at that time. By the first century AD, Roman rule extended over much of Europe, North Africa and the Near East. The Romans took their way of life and government wherever they went. They used their skills of developing central heating and running water and introduced their food and language (Latin) to every country they conquered.

❍ According to legend, Rome was founded in 753 BC by the twin boys Romulus and Remus, who were said to have been brought up by a she-wolf. By 550 BC, Rome was a large city that was ruled by Etruscan kings. In 509 BC, the Roman people drove out the kings and formed themselves into an independent republic.

❍ In the 400s and 300s BC, Rome extended its power all over Italy, by both brute force and alliances. By 130 BC, Rome had built a mighty empire stretching from Spain to Turkey and along the North African coast.

Roman gladiators trained to fight in the arena. Roman rulers staged lavish and often bloodthirsty entertainments to keep the people amused. Gladiators fought one another or wild animals. There were various types of gladiator – the netman wore hardly any armour, and his weapons were a net and a trident (three-pointed spear).

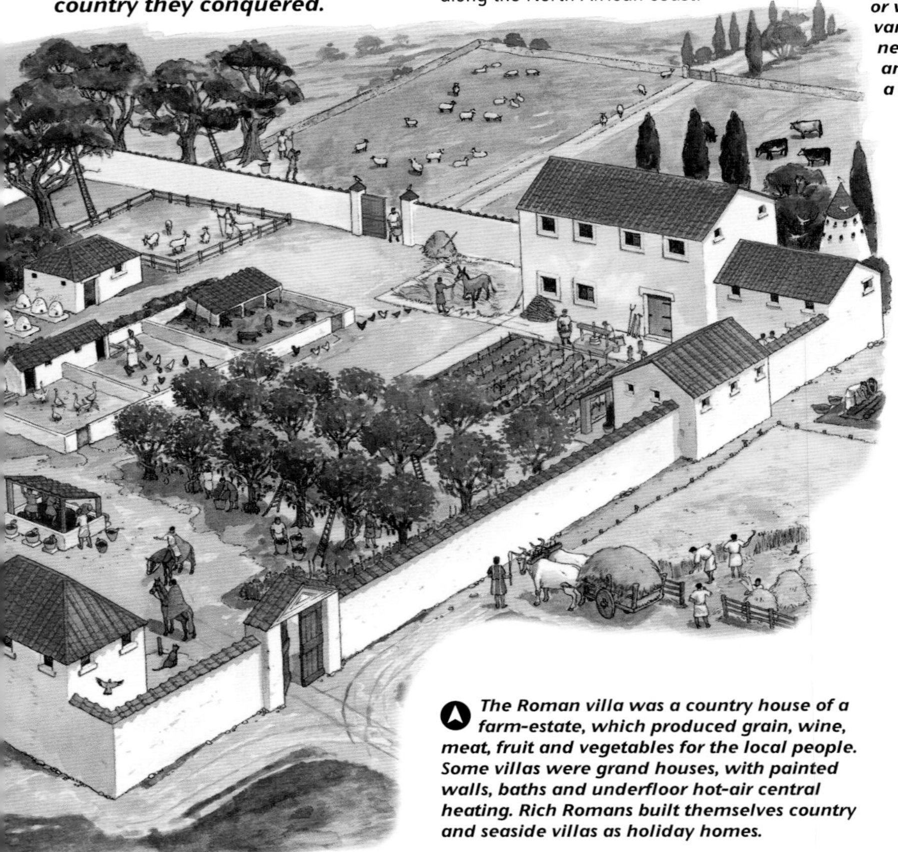

❍ Two popular generals, Pompey and Julius Caesar, used their armies to take over Rome and suspend the democratic, but corrupt, government of the Republic. Once in power, Caesar restored order and passed laws to reduce people's debts. Caesar was made dictator and ruled Rome without the Senate.

❍ In 44 BC, a man called Brutus killed Caesar to restore the government of the Republic – but Caesar's place was taken by another general, Octavian, Caesar's adopted son. By 27 BC, Octavian was so powerful that he is recognized as the first Roman emperor. He took the name Augustus, which means 'Exalted One'.

The Roman villa was a country house of a farm-estate, which produced grain, wine, meat, fruit and vegetables for the local people. Some villas were grand houses, with painted walls, baths and underfloor hot-air central heating. Rich Romans built themselves country and seaside villas as holiday homes.

🅐 ***Roman towns were the biggest and most sophisticated the world had seen. There were blocks of flats, called Insulae, as well as luxurious houses.***

❍ The bath houses (thermae) were places where people came to sit around and dip into hot and cold baths in magnificent surroundings.

❍ After the death of Emperor Marcus Aurelius, in AD 180, Rome was plagued by political struggles. The Praetorian Guard (the emperor's personal soldiers) chose or deposed emperors at will, and there were 60 emperors between AD 235 and 284 alone. The Empire was beset by famine, plague and invasion.

Amazing

In AD 100 over a million people lived in Rome, the largest city on Earth. But plagues and wars meant that by AD 650 there were only 10,000 people left in the city.

Vast Empire

At its greatest, the Roman Empire ran from Britain in the west, as far as Africa in the south and Babylon in the east. This map shows the Roman Empire in brown and the roads that they built in black.

Fearsome army

The Roman army was well trained and better disciplined than the enemies it faced. The best Roman units were the legions of about 5000 foot-soldiers, who went into battle throwing spears and then rushed in behind their shields using short, stabbing swords. Roman soldiers were trained to march all day, build roads and forts, and swim rivers. Roman officers were usually politicians. The testudo formation (right) proved itself highly effective for Roman foot soldiers.

Roman and Greek gods

God of	*Greek*	*Roman*	*Goddess of*	*Greek*	*Roman*
Agriculture	Cronus	Saturn	**Agriculture**	Demeter	Ceres
The dead	Thanatos	Mors	**The dawn**	Eos	Aurora
Fire	Hephaestus	Vulcan	**Flowers**	Hestia	Flora
Love	Eros	Cupid	**Health**	Hygeia	Salus
The sea	Poseidon	Neptune	**Hunting**	Artemis	Diana
Sleep	Hypnos	Somnus	**Love**	Aphrodite	Venus
The Sun	Helios	Sol	**The Moon**	Selene	Luna
War	Ares	Mars	**Motherhood**	Rhea	Ops
Wine	Dionysus	Bacchus	**Peace**	Irene	Pax
The woods	Pan	Silvanus	**Victory**	Nike	Victoria
Messenger of the gods	Hermes	Mercury	**Wisdom**	Athene	Minerva
King of the gods	Zeus	Jupiter	**Queen of the gods**	Hera	Juno

❍ Roman roads were built by the army to make sure that troops on foot and supplies in wagons could be moved quickly around the Empire. Many Roman roads can still be seen today.

❍ In AD 410, Visigoths led by Alaric invaded Italy and sacked (burned and looted) Rome. In AD 455, Vandals sacked Rome again. In AD 476, the Western empire finally collapsed.

China and Japan

The first farming communities in China were formed about 7000 BC. The Chinese civilization developed separately from other early civilizations and had a quite different culture. By 221 BC, all the Chinese were living under the control of a single emperor. Chinese technology and culture spread gradually to nearby lands. Around 300 BC, the Japanese began to farm their land and adopted skills from the Chinese.

- Early Chinese emperors are known of only by legend. Huang-Ti, the Yellow Emperor, was said to have become emperor in 2697 BC.
- The Shangs were the first definitely known dynasty of emperors. They came to power in 1750 BC.
- After 246 BC, Qin emperor Zheng expanded the empire and called himself Shi Huangdi, First Emperor. He had the 4000 km long Great Wall built to protect his empire from nomads from the north.

Amazing

Shi Huangdi was buried with an army of 6000 life-size clay soldiers, called the Terracotta Army when found in 1974. Certain parts of the tomb are said to be booby-trapped and have not been opened.

- In 210 BC, the small Han kingdom was ruled over by Liu Bang. Liu Bang was a poor villager who had come to power as the Qin Empire broke down. In 202 BC, Liu Bang proclaimed himself to be the first Han emperor and took the name Gaozu.
- Han cities were huge, crowded and beautiful, and craftsmen made many exquisite things from wood, paint and silk. Sadly, many of these lovely objects were destroyed when Han rule ended.
- By AD 200, the Han emperors were weakened by their ambitious wives and eunuchs (guardians). Rebellions by a group called the Yellow Turbans, combined with attacks by warriors from the north, brought the empire down.

Shinto priests believe that all things that inspire awe – from twisted trees to dead warriors – have kami (spirits).

The great tomb of the Terracotta Army (or Warriors) is located near Xi'an, central China. In their underground chambers, the life-size figures are arranged in precise military formation.

Early clocks

Mechanical clocks were invented by the Chinese in AD 723, which was 600 years earlier than Europe. This is Su Sung's 'Cosmic Engine', an amazing 10 m high clock built at Khaifeng in AD 1090.

Confucius believed that court officials should not plot for power but instead study music, poetry and the history of their ancestors.

❍ Around 660 BC, Jimmu Tenno, the legendary first emperor of Japan, established power in Yamato.

❍ From AD 250–710, the Yamato dynasty dominated Japan. Right up to today, Japanese emperors claim to be descended from the Yamato. The Yamato, in turn, claimed to be descended from the Shinto sun-goddess, Amaterasu.

❍ Shotoku Taishi (AD 574–622) was a young regent for old Empress Suiko. He gave Japan organized, Chinese-style government and promoted both Buddhism and Confucianism.

Great Wall of China

Although today's brick and stone wall dates from the AD 1400s, the Great Wall of China was first built of earth bricks in 214 BC, under Shi Huangdi.

❍ Shinto or 'way of the gods' has been Japan's main religion since prehistoric times. It gained its name during the 6th century AD, to distinguish it from Buddhism and Confucianism.

The Shang emperors were warriors. Their soldiers fought in padded bamboo armour.

The wisdom of Confucius

Never contract friendship with a man that is not better than thyself

The strength of a nation derives from the integrity of the home

Everything has beauty, but not everyone sees it

Silence is a friend who will never betray

Never give a sword to a man who can't dance

You cannot open a book without learning something

A journey of a thousand miles begins with a single step

The cautious seldom err

When anger rises, think of the consequences

It is better to light one small candle than to curse the darkness

If we don't know life, how can we know death?

To lead uninstructed people to war is to throw them away

When prosperity comes, do not use all of it

Real knowledge is to know the extent of one's ignorance

To know what is right and not to do it is the worst cowardice

Ignorance is the night of the mind, but a night without moon or star

The father who does not teach his son his duties is equally guilty with the son who neglects them

An oppressive government is more to be feared than a tiger

To see and listen to the wicked is already the beginning of wickedness

A man who has committed a mistake and does not correct it, is making another mistake

The Barbarians

After about AD 350 the ancient civilizations began to suffer problems caused by crop failure, disease and economic decline. Uncivilized tribes attacked the weakening empires, looking for easy plunder and wealth. The old empires collapsed in the face of the attacks from these barbarians who could neither read nor write. Civilization was close to collapse as warfare spread rapidly and the population of the world declined suddenly.

❍ The Goths were German peoples divided into Ostrogoths in the east, near the Black Sea, and Visigoths on the Danube. It was the Visigoths who, under their king Alaric, took Rome in AD 476.

❍ The Vandals were a German tribe who took over Spain and North Africa in about AD 380. They gave us the word 'vandal' for destructive troublemakers.

❍ The Huns were nomadic Mongols from eastern Asia who arrived in Europe AD c.370, driving everyone before them, until they were finally defeated in AD 455. The most feared Hun was their king, Attila.

Amazing

The barbarian wars caused massive bloodshed, starvation and hardship. It is thought the population of the former Roman Empire may have fallen by 50 per cent.

❍ In AD 330 Constantinople (now Istanbul in Turkey) became the capital first of the Roman Empire and then the Byzantine or Eastern Roman Empire. It was the centre of Western civilization for a thousand years.

❍ The Byzantine Empire was under constant attack from tribes of barbarians, but it held out behind its massive defensive walls.

❍ When barbarians attacked, generals from Italy were sent to reorganize local defences. In some areas, power fell into the hands of local men like the British king, Vortigern (AD 425–50).

❍ Vortigern invited Anglo-Saxon warriors from Germany to help him against the invading Picts. But these men soon rebelled and defeated Vortigern. Thousands more Anglo-Saxons came to settle in Britain, becoming the English.

❍ In 318 the Chinese emperor Liu Yuën died. While his heirs fought for power, barbarians poured into China. All the cities north of the Yangtse River were destroyed. Not until 507 were the barbarian invasions halted in China.

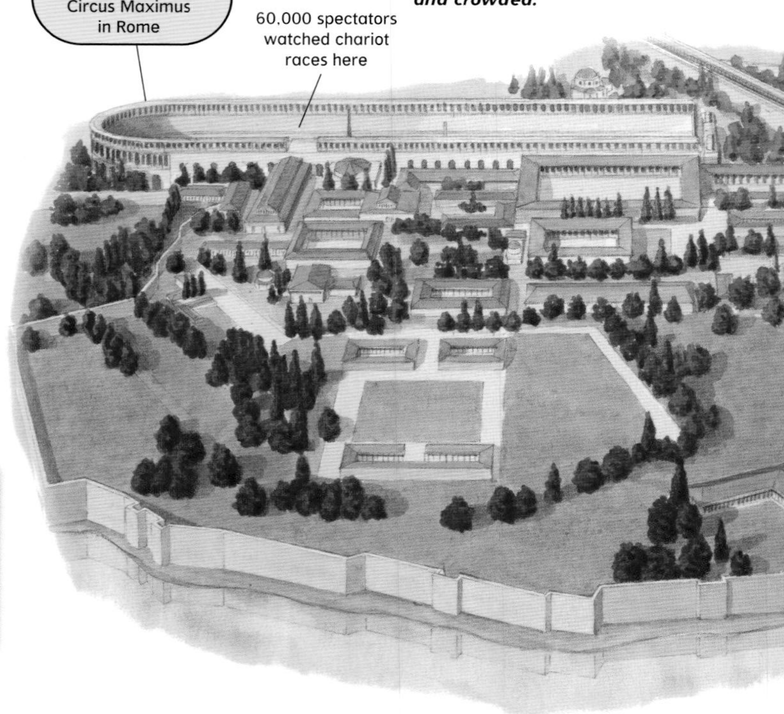

At its height, Constantinople was graced by some of the ancient world's most magnificent buildings. This picture shows the tranquil palace quarter. The rest of the city was noisy and crowded.

❍ In 457 the Ye Ta, or Hephtha, barbarians invaded Persia. They massacred thousands of people and captured the cities of Merv and Herat.

❍ In 475 the warrior Mehiragula led a group of tribes into India. For 50 years these tribes looted India. Then they fell back over the mountains to the north.

❍ By about 550 the main barbarian invasions had come to an end. Apart from China, most of the old empires had been swept away. New kingdoms and nations had come into existence.

The Hagia Sophia, now a museum, is the world's oldest Christian cathedral

Anglo-Saxon villages were made from materials such as wood, thatch and wattle (woven branches).

Gothic leader

Alaric was the great Gothic leader who took Rome in 410. He looted the city but spared the churches. Alaric planned to settle in Africa, but a storm forced him to stop at Cozenza in southern Italy, where he died.

In 1939, the burial ship of the overlord Raedwald (died 625) was discovered at Sutton Hoo in East Anglia. This helmet is one of the treasures it held.

Justinian I

Justinian I was the greatest Byzantine emperor, although his general's secretary, Procopius, described him as 'a demon incarnate'. He ruled with his beautiful former actress wife, Theodora. Justinian relied on her for support and advice, and it was she who changed laws to improve the lives of women and the poor.

New States

After about AD 550 the barbarian tribes stopped moving constantly in search of plunder and loot. They settled down to live as farmers and traders. Slowly the population began to grow once again as migrations of entire peoples came to an end. However, the old empires and civilizations had been destroyed or badly damaged. New kingdoms and states emerged from the chaos, and new ways of life were established.

❍ Chinese emperor Yang Di was murdered by one of his 3000 mistresses in AD 618. His minister Li Yuan seized power to found the Tang dynasty. Under the Tang trade grew, China became rich and the arts and sciences flourished.

❍ By AD 800, the Tang dynasty was breaking up. Order was restored in AD 960, when the Song family began to rule from the city of Kaifeng. The Song lasted until AD 1276, when the Mongol Kublai Khan conquered China.

❍ The Muslim religion began when the prophet Mohammed left Mecca in AD 622. The Muslim Arabs conquered Iraq (AD 637), Syria (640), Egypt (641) and Persia (650). By AD 661, their empire stretched from Tunisia to India. Its capital was at Damascus.

❍ The Fujiwaras were the family who dominated Japan for five centuries from the 7th century AD. In 858, they married into the Imperial family. Fujiwara power peaked with Michinaga (966–1028).

❍ The Angles, Saxons and Jutes were peoples from Denmark and Germany who invaded Britain and settled there between AD 450 and 600. Each tribe had its own kingdom, yet by 600 most of these people thought of themselves as English.

The Vikings' wooden ships, called longships, are masterpieces of boat-building – light and flat-bottomed enough to sail up shallow rivers, yet seaworthy in the open ocean.

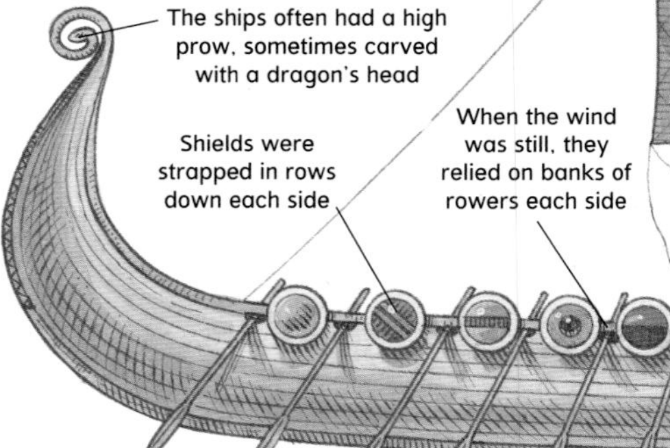

This enamel and gold jewel was found near Athelney. It is inscribed with the words 'Aelfred me ech eh t gewyrcan' – Old English for 'Alfred ordered me to be made'.

Amazing

The Vikings were the first seamen able to navigate out of sight of land. They used the stars and a primitive type of compass to find their way across the open ocean.

First New Zealanders

No human set foot on New Zealand before around 800 years ago. The first settlers in New Zealand were Polynesians known as Maori. The Maori came to New Zealand by canoe, from islands in the Pacific. The Maoris lived mostly near the coast.

Not all Vikings were pirates. At home, they were farmers and fishermen, merchants and craftworkers. Many went with the raiders and settled in the north of France, in northern England and in Dublin.

❍ The Vikings were from Norway, Sweden and Denmark. Between AD 800 and 1100, they raided the coasts of northwest Europe in their longships, searching for plunder to carry away.

❍ In AD 563, what is now Scotland was four kingdoms: the Scots in the west; the Picts in the north; the Britons in the southwest; and English in the east.

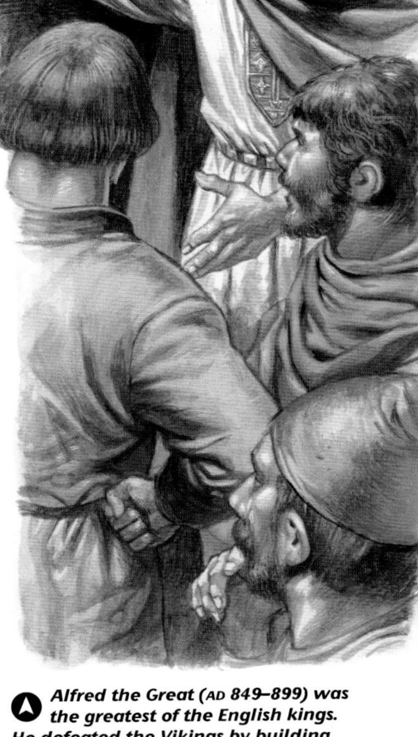

Alfred the Great (AD 849–899) was the greatest of the English kings. He defeated the Vikings by building forts, reorganizing the army and building England's first navy.

Viking voyages

This map shows some of the amazing voyages made by the Vikings, and their dates, with their Viking names.

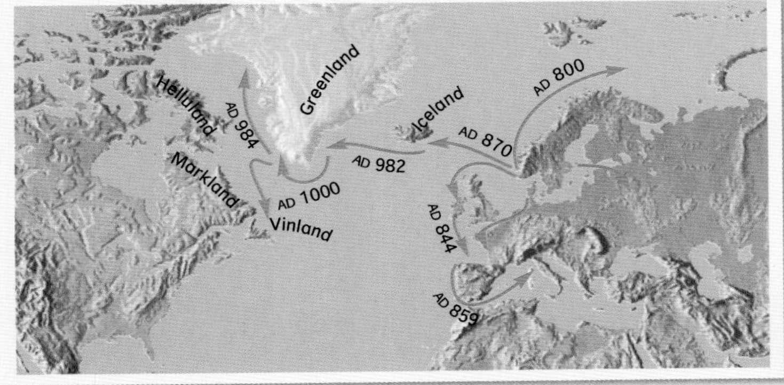

Viking weaponry included a spear, knife and protective shield. Vikings held their weapons sacred.

Feudal Europe

By about* AD *800 most of Europe was dominated by a new social system: feudalism. Land was owned by kings, who let it to nobles and knights in return for those men serving in the army or other government positions. The nobles let the land to peasants who farmed it. The peasants gave produce and some of their labour to the nobles. Each person in society had rights and duties that they owed to other people. Only a few, such as merchants or priests, lived outside the system.

❍ The Magyars were a people who lived near Russia's river Don. In 889 AD, led by the legendary king Arpad, the Magyars moved into Hungary.

❍ For 100 years, much of England was lost to the Vikings, but Alfred the Great's son Edward and his daughter Aethelflaed won back England by 918.

❍ In the 900s and 1000s, many people fought to be king in Scotland, which was gradually becoming united as one country. King Duncan I was killed by his general, Macbeth. Macbeth was later killed by Malcolm III.

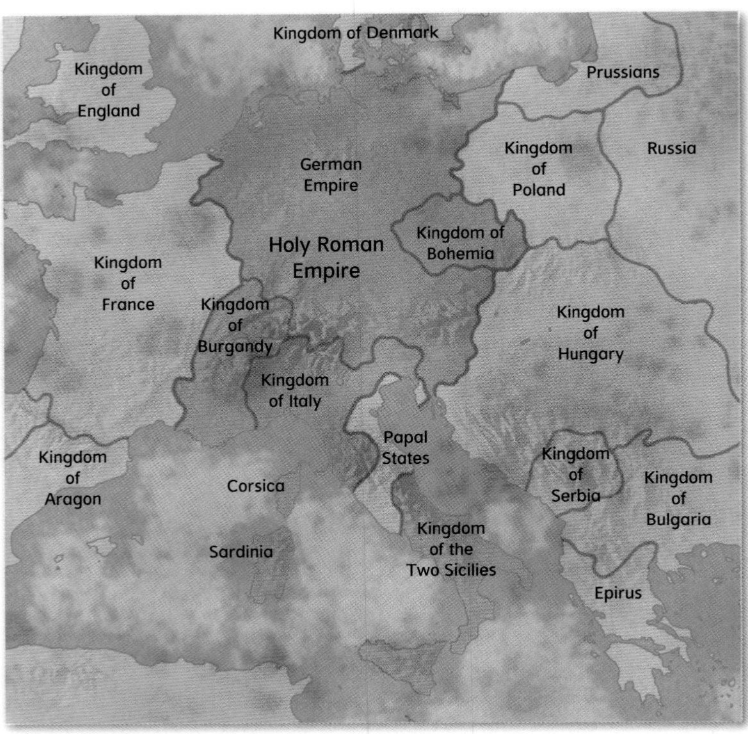

In 1250 the Holy Roman Empire extended from the North to the Mediterranean Sea (highlighted in brown). The Papal states (yellow), separated the Kingdom of the Two Sicilies, which also belonged to the Emperor.

Amazing

Knights had special designs, called coats of arms, painted on their shields and jackets so that they could recognize friend from foe in battle. Each knight had a different design.

Magna Carta

England's King John signed Magna Carta (Great Charter) – a list of rights requested by barons who felt that John was ruling badly. In 1215, they forced the king to put his seal (sign) to the Charter and promise to obey the rules within. Ever since, Magna Carta has been seen as a landmark in the development of modern government.

Knights practised fighting at special events called tournaments. Thousands of people watched famous knights.

❍ Duke William of Normandy invaded England in 1066, believing that King Edward had promised him the throne. The English chose Harold Godwinson to be king, but William killed Harold at the Battle of Hastings.

❍ The Holy Roman Empire lasted until 1806. It began in AD 800 when Pope Leo III gave King Charlemagne of the Franks, the title of the old Roman Empire.

❍ The Hundred Years' War was fought between France and England, from 1337–1453. The war was caused by disputes over land in France.

Suit of armour

Ailettes	Small square shields protecting the shoulders
Aventail	Chainmail bib protecting the neck
Bascinet	Type of helmet
Beaver	Cup-shaped piece protecting the chin
Besagew	Small round plate protecting the armpits
Cervellaire	Skull cap
Chamfron	Metal plate protecting the head of a horse
Colf	Hooded chainmail protecting the head
Couter	Rounded cup protecting the elbow
Cuirass	The part of the armour that comprises the breastplate and backplate
Gauntlet	Large glove
Gorget	Metal plate protecting the neck
Grille	Metal visor protecting the face
Pauldron	Metal plate protecting the shoulders
Poleyn	Cup-shaped piece protecting the knee
Rerebrace	Metal plates protecting the upper arms
Sabaton	Armour for the feet
Surcoat	Cloth covering worn outside a suit of armour
Tasset	Metal plate protecting the hips
Vambrace	Rounded iron armour protecting the lower arms

Medieval monasteries

Monasteries played a key role in medieval life in Europe, reaching a peak in the 1200s. Most monasteries had a church called an abbey, some of which are among the greatest medieval buildings. Like most English monasteries, the great 12th-century Cistercian monastery at Tintern in Wales (seen here) was destroyed by Henry VIII.

❍ The English won most battles during the Hundred Years War, but the French won the war because they had three times the resources.

❍ The Crusades were wars fought for control of Jerusalem and the Holy Land. When the Turks prevented Christian pilgrims visiting Jerusalem, the Pope called the First Crusade in 1095. The Crusaders gained control of the Holy Land and kept it for about 200 years.

❍ When Pope Gregory XI died in 1378, there was a Great Schism (split) in the Church. In 1417, the Great Schism was ended but the dispute had weakened the Church's authority fatally.

The greatest knight of the war was Edward the Black Prince (1330–1376), hero of the Battles of Crécy, Poitiers and Navarette.

Indian Empires

The great subcontinent of India was almost cut off from other areas by the high Himalaya Mountains. The peoples of India developed their own cultures and ways of life. Throughout Indian history, powerful rulers have tried to unite the area into a single empire. Some of these empires were larger or lasted longer than others, but always the tendency for different areas to break away caused the collapse of even the strongest empire.

❍ In 321 BC, the first great Indian empire was created by Chandragupta Maurya (*c*.325–297 BC). Its capital was Pataliputra on the Ganges.

❍ The Mauryan Empire at its peak included most of modern Pakistan, Bangladesh and India – except for the very southern tip.

❍ The most famous of the Mauryan emperors was Chandragupta's grandson, Asoka (*c*.265–238 BC).

❍ Asoka's men dug wells and built reservoirs all over India to help the poor. They also provided comfortable rest-houses and planted shady banyan trees for travellers along the new roads.

❍ The Hindu and Buddhist religions both began to develop and flourish during the great Gupta period.

❍ Hindu mathematicians developed the decimal system (counting in tens) that we still use today.

❍ Gupta power collapsed by about AD 500 under repeated attacks by Hun people from the north.

❍ Akbar (1556–1605) was the greatest of the Mogul emperors – conquering most of India and setting up a highly efficient system of government.

❍ Aurangzeb (1618–1707) was the last great Mogul ruler. He inspired rebellion by raising taxes and insisting on a strict Muslim code.

The first Mogul emperor was Babur (1483–1530), who invaded India on swift horses that completely outran the Indians' slower elephants. Babar founded the Mogul dynasty that was to dominate northern India for more than 200 years.

Mogul emperor Humayun remained ousted from the throne for 15 years before he could reassert his authority.

Amazing

Prince Gautama Siddhartha left his luxurious home and beautiful wife in Nepal to lead a life of poverty. He later founded the Buddhist religion and lived to be 80 years old.

The Moguls, or Mughals, were a family who ruled most of northern India from 1526. The Mogul Empire reached its peak under Shah Jahan (1592–1666), when many magnificent, luxurious buildings were built – most notably the Taj Mahal, built as a tomb for his favourite wife. According to legend, Shah Jahan cut off the hands of the craftsmen involved in the construction of the Taj Mahal so that they could not make such a monument again.

Stupas

During Asoka's reign, stupas – domed shrines said to contain relics of the Buddha – were built all over India.

The Guptas

The Guptas were a family of rulers who reigned in northern India from AD 320–c.500. This was one of India's golden ages, with writing, sculpture and other arts at their peak. The Hindu and Buddhist sculpture and painting of the Gupta period has been the model for Indian art down the centuries.

Buddhist shrine in Thailand, Asia. The various statues of the Buddha, or the enlightened one, as Prince Gautama Siddhartha became known, each gives a different gesture and stands or sits in a special way to emphasize one of the key teachings of the Buddhist religion.

Medieval Asia

For six centuries from AD 618 China was unified, rich and powerful under first the Tang Dynasty, then the Song dynasty. Chinese culture dominated neighbouring peoples, such as the Thais, Tibetans and Japanese and, at times, the Chinese emperor claimed to rule these areas as well as China itself. Then, in 1206, the barbarian tribes of Central Asia were united under the Mongol leader Genghis Khan. Within a few years the Mongols had devastated Asia, conquering vast areas and slaughtering millions of people.

❍ In earlier times, only aristocrats tended to hold key posts in government, but under the Song, anyone could enter for the civil service exams. Competition to do well in the exams was intense, and the main yearly exams became major events in the calendar.

❍ Under the Song, the Chinese population soared, trade prospered and all kinds of advances were made in science and technology – from the invention of gunpowder and the sailors' compass to paper and printing. Technologically, China was about 500 years ahead of Europe.

❍ By 1275, Hangzhou was the world's largest city, with a population of a million. Its warm climate encouraged a lively, leisurely lifestyle. The city was full of luxury shops, bars, restaurants, tea-houses and clubs where girls sang.

Mongol horsemen swept into Russia, crushing resistance and conquering a huge area that extended almost as far north as the Arctic Ocean.

Chinese porcelain and pottery is famous for its beauty and delicacy, and the perfection of the covering glaze. It reached a peak in the Ming era (1368–1644).

Amazing

When Genghis Khan conquered northern China he turned the farmland into pasture for his horses. Almost 20 million Chinese were killed before he changed his mind.

Genghis Khan

Of all the conquerors in history, few were more feared than 13th-century Mongol leader Genghis Khan, whose name means 'lord of all'.

❍ Often, people went out to stroll in the gardens by the West Lake or lazed over long meals on the lake's numerous floating restaurants. On the four islands in the lake there were gardens, statues and temples.

❍ Genghis Khan's horsemen conquered a vast empire stretching across Asia from China as far west as the Danube River in Europe. He destroyed cities and massacred thousands, yet under his rule trade prospered and all beliefs were tolerated.

Mongol feats

Genghis Khan led an army of 250,000 men and more than one million horses.

Heavy catapults for sieges were carried in sections on ox carts and put together.

Mongol soldiers lived on a diet of smoked sheepmeat and dried milk.

Soldiers were armed with bows, swords, axes and lances (long spears) with hooks for unseating enemy riders.

The Mongol Empire was the largest continuous land empire of all time.

Philosophers would travel from far away to talk to Genghis Khan about religion.

Samurai

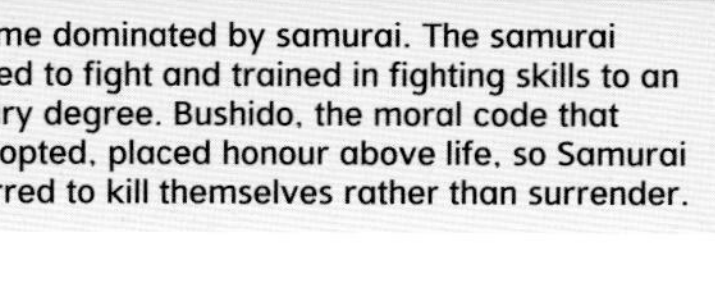

Japan became dominated by samurai. The samurai warriors lived to fight and trained in fighting skills to an extraordinary degree. Bushido, the moral code that Samurai adopted, placed honour above life, so Samurai often preferred to kill themselves rather than surrender.

❍ Genghis's horse archers could kill at 180 m while riding at full gallop. They once rode 440 km in just three days.

❍ After Genghis Khan died, his son Ogodai ravaged Armenia, Hungary and Poland.

❍ Genghis Khan's grandson – Kublai Khan – conquered the rest of China in 1265 and made himself the first of a line of Mongol emperors of China called Yuans. The Yuans lasted until 1368. Kublai Khan created a grand new capital called Ta-tu ('the Great Capital') – now Beijing. Kublai Khan adopted Chinese ways of government and ruled with such efficiency that China became very rich.

❍ In 1185, the Japanese nobleman Minamoto Yoritomo crushed the rival Taira clan and made himself ruler of Japan as sei-i-dai-shogun which means 'barbarian-conquering great general'.

❍ Warrior shoguns ruled Japan until the mid-1800s. The shoguns claimed to be acting on behalf of the emperor, but in reality they ruled for themselves and their supporters. The emperors lived in luxurious palaces, but had no real power.

▼ ***When the Mongol Khans seized China from the Song, they made a new capital in the north at Beijing. At its centre lies a walled area containing the emperor's palaces. It is called the Forbidden City because only the emperor and his servants could enter it.***

People first reached North America, crossing a land bridge from Asia and travelling on foot and by boat, 15,000–20,000 years ago. They gradually spread across the continent. The great civilizations of the Americas were in Central America (around Mexico) and in South America (in Peru), where people built large cities. Much of this culture was destroyed by European invaders in the 1500s.

❍ People began farming in Central America about 9000 years ago, almost as long ago as in the Middle East.

❍ Between 1200 and 400 BC, the Olmec culture developed in western Mexico. The Olmecs had a counting system and calendar, but no writing system, so little is known about them.

❍ The Maya built cities such as Tikal (Guatemala). Each Mayan city had a tall pyramid-shaped temple in the centre, with open courts around it. The Maya studied the Moon, Sun and stars and had a number system based on 20.

❍ Mayans traded far and wide. After about 1200, Mayan civilization broke up and the cities were abandoned.

Amazing

Aztec priests sacrificed humans by cutting out their hearts with a stone knife. They aimed to lift the heart up to the sun god while it was still beating.

❍ Aztecs and other peoples of Central America sacrificed human victims in order to seek the favour of their gods. The Aztec people worshipped the Sun, and believed that unless they regularly offered human victims to the Sun god, then he would abandon them and their crops would fail.

The serpent was one of 20 creatures that gave its name to a day on the Aztec farmers' calendar. The Aztecs had two calendars: one for religious ceremonies, with 260 days, and another of 365 days, like ours, but with eight months, not 12.

From AD 100 to 700, America's first true city developed at Teotihuacán, with vast pyramids and palaces. Teotihuacán may have been the world's biggest city in AD 300, with a population of more than 250,000 people. Spanish conquerors destroyed Teotihuacán and built a new city, now Mexico City.

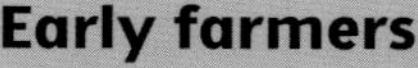

Early farmers

The first farming villages in the southwest were those of the Anasazi, Mogollon and Hohokam peoples and dated from AD 100. They lived either in caves or in underground 'pit houses' carved into the desert rock. About AD 700, the Anasazi began to build large stone villages called pueblos, which is why from this time they are also called Pueblo Indians.

❍ Religion was so important to the Aztecs that they went to war to capture prisoners to be sacrificed to the gods.

❍ The Aztecs did not use animals to carry loads or pull carts. They carried heavy loads on their backs or in canoes.

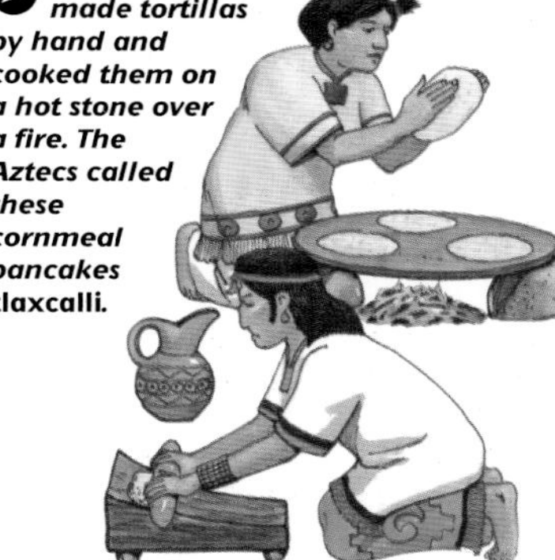

Aztec women made tortillas by hand and cooked them on a fire. The Aztecs called these cornmeal pancakes tlaxcalli.

Olmecs

The Olmecs carved huge heads from basalt with enormous skill – apparently with only stone chisels, since they had no metal. The Olmec heads consist of huge blocks of volcanic rock that weigh up to 14 tonnes. The area identified as the source of the Olmec boulders lies in the Tuxtla Mountains over 160 km away. No one knows how they were moved.

The Mayans began building large pyramids with small temples on top between 600 BC and AD 250. The Mayan pyramid at Chichén Itzá is in the Yucatán.

Exploration of the Americas

	Explorer	*Nationality*	*Work*
1492–1504	Christopher Columbus	Italian	Working for the Spanish, Columbus arrived in the Americas while trying to find a route to China. He made four voyages to the Caribbean and South America
1518–1521	Ferdinand Magellan	Portuguese	Explored the straits through South America that still bear his name, as well as much of the coast of South America
1519–1528	Hernan Cortés	Spanish	Explored most of Mexico and conquered the mighty Aztec Empire
1531–1541	Francisco Pizarro	Spanish	Explored the Andes Mountains of Peru, conquering the Inca Empire
1607–1611	Henry Hudson	English	Explored the northeast coast of North America, including Hudson Bay, which is named after him
1534–1537	Jacques Cartier	French	Sailed up St Lawrence River and founded French colonies

New Learning

From about 1350, scholars in Europe began to translate and copy books written by ancient scientists and historians. These books showed people that many of the things believed in the Medieval period were wrong. Exciting new theories and discoveries were written about and discussed. This period in European history is called the Renaissance, which means 'a new birth'. In the years after 1450, equipped with the new ideas of the Renaissance, Europeans had a huge cultural and scientific influence on the rest of the world.

❍ By the 1400s, kings relied on full-time soldiers paid with money. Kings turned to merchants to pay for their armies, so merchants gained power. The Italians invented banks to give loans to kings and merchants.

❍ Trading towns began to thrive across western Europe in the 1300s and 1400s – Antwerp, Flanders, Bruges, Bristol, Norwich, York, Florence, Venice, Milan and many others. Trading towns grew powerful and some had self-rule.

Amazing

Michelangelo became the greatest artist of the Renaissance, but he started his career carving fake ancient Roman statues and selling them for cash.

❍ Artists in the Renaissance, inspired by classical examples, began to portray people and nature realistically rather than as religious symbols. In the 1400s brilliant artists like Donatello created startlingly realistic paintings and sculptures. The three greatest artists of the Renaissance were Michelangelo, Raphael and Leonardo da Vinci.

❍ The Renaissance saw some of the world's greatest artistic and architectural masterpieces being created in Italian cities such as Florence and Padua.

❍ A spur to the Renaissance was the fall of Constantinople in 1453. This sent Greek scholars fleeing to Italy, where they set up academies in cities like Florence and Padua. Renaissance ideas later spread to northern Europe.

The ancient Italian city of Padua is full of masterpieces of Renaissance building and art, including paintings by Giotto and sculptures by Donatello.

❍ The Medici family of Florence in Italy were one of the richest and most powerful families in Europe between 1400 and 1700. The Medicis's fortunes began with the bank founded by Giovanni de' Medici in 1397. The bank was a success and the Medicis became staggeringly rich.

❍ The most famous Medici was Lorenzo (1449–1492). Under him, Florence became Europe's most spectacular city, full of great works of art and home to many artists.

This marble sculpture called David was made by Italian artist Michelangelo (1475–1564).

Renaissance warfare

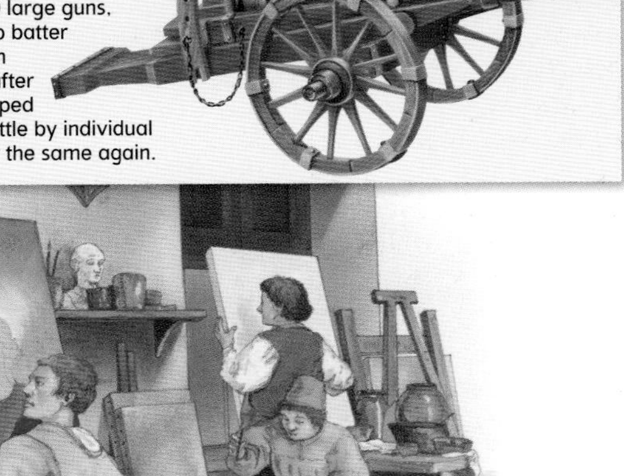

Not all the new discoveries of the Renaissance were to do with arts and sciences. Warfare was revolutionized by adapting the Chinese invention of gunpowder to the new concept of the gun. From about 1460 large guns, called cannons, were used to batter down castle walls and smash apart town defences. Soon after this, small guns were developed that could be carried into battle by individual soldiers. Warfare was never the same again.

Older artists took on apprentices in their studios so the younger generations of Renaissance artists could learn from them.

Positions held in Henry VIII's household

Clerk of the Green Cloth
Clerk of the Poultry
Clerk of the Spicery
Falconer
Gentlemen of the Privy Chamber
Groom of the Privy Chamber
Marshall of the Hall
Master of the Children
Master of the Jewels
Minstrel
Officer of the Confectionery
Officer of the Vestry
Page of the King's Chambers
Purveyor of Ale
Purveyor of Sea Fish
Sergeant of the Bake House
Squire for the Body
Sergeant of the Larder
The King's Barber
Wardrober of the Robes
Yeoman of the Cellar
Yeoman of the Pastry

King Henry VIII

The Renaissance reached England during the reign of King Henry VIII (ruled 1509–1547). When he came to the throne Henry was handsome and athletic, spoke several languages, played the lute and was keen on the new ideas of the Renaissance. He employed clever ministers such as Cardinal Wolsey and Thomas Cromwell. As he grew older, Henry was prone to savage tempers, ill health and he became very fat. He married six times, divorcing two wives and having two others executed.

Age of Explorers

B*y about 1430, Europeans were building new types of ship that could sail through rough weather and carry enough food and drink for long voyages. Merchants were keen to find routes to rich nations such as India, China and the Spice Islands. They hoped to become wealthy by trading with these countries.*

Amazing

Many men died on voyages of discovery. The first voyage around the world set off in 1519 with five ships and 230 men. Only one ship and 18 men survived the journey.

❍ Sailors were sent out to find routes across the seas. Sometimes they discovered what they were looking for, but sometimes they accidentally found completely different countries instead.

❍ Many voyages were encouraged by Portugal's Prince Henry the Navigator (1394–1460), who set up a school for navigation skills at Sagres.

❍ In 1488, Bartholomeu Dias sailed right round Africa into the Indian Ocean.

❍ One of the greatest voyages was in 1492 when Christopher Columbus set out across the Atlantic. He hoped to reach China but found the Americas.

❍ Within half a century of Columbus's voyage, the Spanish had conquered all the lands from California to Argentina.

Most of the explorers of the 1400s and 1500s sailed in a type of ship called a caravel. These were 30 m long and could cope with the roughest seas.

❍ By the Treaty of Tordesillas (1494) Portugal and Spain divided new discoveries along a line about 2000 km west of the Cape Verde Islands.

❍ Thousands of Spaniards went to live in America in the 1500s, creating Spanish-style cities such as Cartagena in Colombia and Guayaqil in Ecuador.

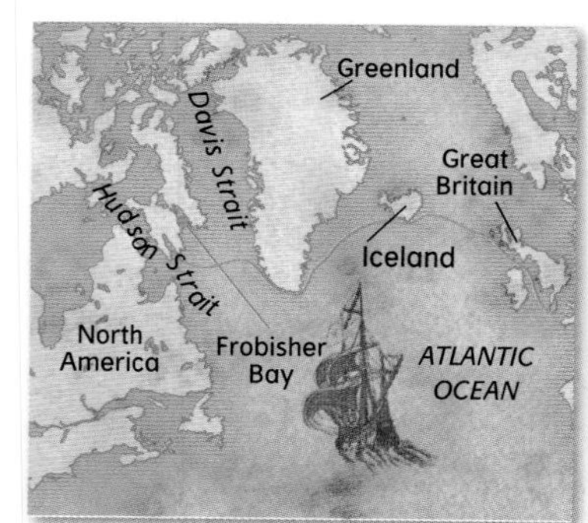

Exploring the northeast coast of Canada, Martin Frobisher discovered the bay that bears his name, Frobisher Bay.

The voyages of Portuguese navigator Vasco da Gama to India laid open the sea route to the East from Europe and helped Portugal to establish a flourishing trade. In 1497, Vasco da Gama sailed round Africa to Calicut in India, and returned laden with spices and jewels.

- In 1553 English traders arrived in Nigeria to trade in gold and ivory.
- In 1569 Flemish cartographer Gerardus Mercator introduced the Meracator Projection map, still used today for navigational chart making.
- In 1580 the English explorer Francis Drake returned to Portsmouth after having sailed around the world.

Sailors and ships

Sailor	Ship
Roald Amundsen	*Fram*
Christopher Columbus	*Santa Maria*
Captain James Cook	*Endeavour*
Charles Darwin	HMS *Beagle*
Francis Drake	*Golden Hind* (originally *The Pelican*)
Ferdinand Magellan	*Victoria*
Walter Raleigh	*The Ark*
Robert Falcon Scott	*The Discovery*
Ernest Shackleton	*Endurance*

Christopher Columbus

Columbus had three ships – the *Santa Maria*, *Nina* and *Pinta*. Columbus persuaded King Ferdinand and Queen Isabella of Spain to pay for his voyage. He set sail on 3 August 1492 and sailed west into the unknown for three weeks, by which time the sailors were ready to mutiny with fear. On 12 October, a lookout spotted the Bahamas. Columbus thought he was in the Indies (hence the 'West Indies'). He called the natives Indians. Columbus left 40 men on a large island that he called Hispaniola and went back to Spain a hero.

In 1534 French explorer Jacques Cartier (1491–1557) was commissioned by Francis I, king of France, on an expedition to North America, with the chief aim of finding spices, which were extremely precious at this time, as well as gold.

In the course of his four voyages across the Atlantic, Christopher Columbus (1451–1596) explored much of the Americas. However, his original plan was to find a westward sea course to the East.

Ferdinand Magellan

Ferdinand Magellan was the first navigator to sail across the Pacific from east to west. In 1519–1522, Magellan's ship *Victoria* sailed across the Atlantic, round the southern tip of South America, across the Pacific and back round Africa to Spain. Although this Portuguese explorer was killed in the Philippines, his crew and ship went on to complete the first round-the-world voyage.

Religion and Wars

In the early 1500s, many people in Europe were starting to question the teachings of the Catholic Church. They were angered by the excessive power of church leaders and the life of idleness that many monks seemed to lead. Many critics were especially annoyed by the huge amounts of money the Church made by selling 'indulgences' – a pardon for sin bought with cash. People who protested against the Church were called 'Protestants'. Eventually some Protestants left the Catholic Church to set up their own churches, which followed a reformed style of Christianity. This movement became known as the Reformation.

❍ In the 1500s the Roman Catholic church was determined to fight against the Protestant Reformation and other threats. Their fight is called the Counter-Reformation. In 1534, St Ignatius Loyola founded the Society of Jesus (Jesuits) to lead the Counter-Reformation.

❍ Investigative bodies called Inquisitions were set up to seek out and punish heretics – anyone who held views that did not agree with the Catholic Church's.

Amazing

In 1547 the English had to be Protestants under Edward VI, in 1553 they were Catholic under Mary and in 1558 they had to be Protestant again under Elizabeth I.

❍ From 1483, the Spanish Inquisition became a byword for terror, swooping on suspected heretics – Protestants and Jews alike – torturing them and burning them at the stake.

Thomas More (1478–1535) was executed when he refused to acknowledge Henry VIII as head of the English Church.

Martin Luther

Martin Luther (1483–1546) was the monk at Wittenberg University, who earned a reputation for his great biblical knowledge. His radical views sparked off the great Reformation, which divided Christians in Europe into Catholics and Protestants. Luther attacked the sale of indulgences by Pope Leo X, who was selling them by the score to raise money to build St Peter's Church in Rome. In 1517, Luther nailed a list of 95 grievances on the door of Wittenberg Castle's chapel, hoping to start a debate. His action resulted in him being expelled by the Church in 1521. Other more extreme rebels joined the cause, such as John Calvin (1509–1564) and Ulrich Zwingli (1484–1531), and the movement gathered pace across northwest Europe.

Elizabeth sent troops to Holland to help Protestants against the Spanish rulers, and secretly urged Francis Drake to raid Spanish treasure ships. In 1588 Spain sent an Armada to invade England. Elizabeth proved an inspiring leader and the Armada was repulsed.

Mary, Queen of Scots

Mary I (1542–1587) was the Catholic queen of Scotland held captive in England by Elizabeth I for 19 years, then beheaded. Mary was next in line to the English throne after Elizabeth. Many Catholics felt she was first in line, since they did not recognize Henry VIII's marriage to Anne Boleyn. Elizabeth's spy-master, Walsingham, trapped Mary into going along with a secret plot by Babington. Mary was found guilty of treason and beheaded at Fotheringay in 1587.

- In the St Bartholomew's Day massacre in 1571, up to 30,000 French Protestants, called Huguenots, were killed on the orders of the Catholic queen Catherine de' Medici.

- Many English Protestants were burned in Catholic Queen Mary's reign, earning her the name 'Bloody Mary'. Later, English Catholics, such as Edmund Campion (1540–1581), were killed in Protestant Queen Elizabeth I's reign.

- Catholic houses in England in the late 1500s had hiding places for priests called 'priest holes'.

- The battle between Catholics and Protestants created many victims and many martyrs as they were persecuted in the late 1500s.

- In Germany, a terrible Thirty Years War was started in 1618 as the Catholic-Protestant rivalries flared up.

- Russians were Christians of the Eastern Church ruled from Constantinople. Constantinople had become the second focus of Christianity when Rome fell to barbarians in the AD 400s.

- When Constantinople fell to the Turks in 1453, Ivan III called for Moscow to be the Third Rome. He married a Byzantine princess, and his grandson Ivan IV took the title czar after the Roman caesars.

Elizabeth I was daughter of Henry VIII and his wife Anne Boleyn, who was beheaded when Elizabeth was three. A brilliant scholar, Elizabeth was fluent in many languages by the time she was 12. She became queen in 1558, when her half-sister Mary died. At once Elizabeth strengthened the Protestant Church of England by the Act of Supremacy in 1559. She was expected to marry but she remained single, earning her the nickname 'The Virgin Queen'. Elizabeth's reign is famed for the poetry and plays of men like Spenser, Marlowe and Shakespeare.

Beyond Europe

During the period 1400 –1600 many different parts of the world began to make contact with each other. Sometimes the contact was a disaster – spreading deadly diseases or starting vicious wars. Other contacts were peaceful and profitable, with merchants swapping goods and ideas that benefited everybody. During these upheavals, some advanced European countries began to build empires in other parts of the world, but many countries remained independent of Europe.

❍ Hernán Cortés (1485–1547) was a Spanish soldier and explorer who landed in Mexico with only 500 men in 1519. Perhaps thinking that Cortés was the god Quetzalcoatl, the Aztec leader Moctezuma let Cortés take him prisoner and become ruler in his place.

❍ The Incas were South American people who created a remarkable empire in the Americas in the 1400s.

❍ The Incas began as a tribe in highland Peru, but in 1438 Pachacuti Inca Yupanqui became their Sapa Inca (king) and they built a huge empire in an amazingly short time.

❍ Francisco Pizarro (c.1478–1541) reached Peru when the Incas were hardly over a civil war between the Inca Atahualpa and his brother. The Incas, terrified of Pizarro's horses and guns, were easily slaughtered. Pizarro took the capital, Cuzco, in 1533.

❍ When the first European colonists arrived in North America, there were one and a half million Native Americans living in North America. There were hundreds of tribes in North America, each with its own language.

❍ The first successful English colony was set up at Jamestown, Virginia on 24 May 1607, with 104 colonists. Many of the Jamestown colony died in 'the starving time' of winter 1609.

Aztec conqueror

When Hernán Cortés landed in Mexico in 1519 he was treated like a god by the Aztecs. The Aztecs believed that the bearded Cortés was their god, known as Quetzalcoatl, returned to them. Their calendar told them it was a special year and so they welcomed Cortés and his army, even though they were terrified of the Spaniard soldiers' guns and horses. Within two years, Cortés had conquered Mexico.

Until Europeans arrived, Native Americans travelled around mainly on foot or by canoe. The Europeans introduced horses in the 1700s – and the indigenous population quickly became skilled riders.

❍ Toyotomi Hideyoshi (1536–1581) was the great Japanese shogun who unified Japan under his rule. Hideyoshi proved himself a brilliant general in a series of wars with rival generals. After defeating his enemies, he kept warriors and peasants separated as classes.

Native Americans wore clothes of buckskin (tanned deer hide). They adorned the costume with eagle feathers, which had special significance.

Thanksgiving

In 1620, 102 'Pilgrims' arrived in America from Plymouth, England, in the *Mayflower* and set up a colony near Cape Cod. They survived, with help from Wampanoag Native Americans. In November 1621 the Pilgrims invited the Wampanoags to celebrate their first harvest. This first Thanksgiving Day is now celebrated every year in the USA on 25 November.

At its height the Inca empire stretched from northern Ecuador to central Chile. Machu Picchu was the Incas' last mountain stronghold in Peru. It was unknown to outsiders until rediscovered by an American archaeologist in 1911.

Amazing

In 1539, a Spanish friar in Mexico heard about a city named Cibola, far to the north. Many men explored vast areas to find the city, but Cibola did not exist.

1600–1800

After the year 1600 the rate of progress began to speed up. Important new inventions and new ideas were developed. Mostly these led to people leading longer and healthier lives, but some people thought their traditional ways of life were under threat. There were uprisings and wars as people sought to adapt to the new realities of life. European countries with effective weapons continued to conquer other countries to build up empires.

1600 The British East India Company is formed and, over the next 250 years, becomes one of the most powerful commercial enterprises of its time. Most of its business is based in India, where it gains governmental and military authority.

1600 Tokugawa Ieyasu establishes himself as ruler of Japan after defeating many rivals for the throne in the Battle of Sekigahara.

1603 Queen Elizabeth I of England dies. On her deathbed she indicates that she wants the Protestant King James VI of Scotland to rule England after her. James becomes King James I of England. Although he rules both kingdoms, the two countries retain separate parliaments, legal systems and finances.

1618 Roman Catholics of Bohemia shut down Protestant chapels.

1600

1642 Tibet is formed as a religious state under the leadership of Ngawang Lobsang Gyatso, the fifth Dalai Lama.

1644 The Manchurians establish the Ch'ing dynasty, the last of the great Chinese dynasties. They later extend the boundaries of their kingdom to include Tibet, parts of Mongolia, Nepal and Turkistan.

1646 The parliamentary forces of Oliver Cromwell defeat King Charles I's army, forcing the monarch to surrender and end the Civil War.

1648 The Peace of Westphalia ends the Eighty Years War between the Spaniards and the Dutch, and the Thirty Years War between Germany, France and Sweden. About a third of the population of Germany die in the war.

Oliver Cromwell

1648 Charles I is arrested by the English Parliament for signing a secret treaty with the Scots. He is tried for treason against England, found guilty and beheaded the following year. The parliamentary leader Oliver Cromwell becomes 'Lord Protector' of England and rules with the aid of Parliament and the army.

1660 After the death of Oliver Cromwell, Charles II, eldest son of

1642

Bank of England

1694 The Bank of England is established in London. The bank introduces reforms that give England the world's first modern finance system, allowing the government to borrow money and thus be more stable than most others.

1695 The war between the League of Augsburg and France continues with France destroying Brussels, and England capturing Namur from France.

1695 Ottoman (Turkish Empire) Sultan Ahmed II dies and his nephew Mustapha II ascends the throne in his place. Mustapha II then renews the war against the predominantly Christian Austria.

1696 The English Parliament passes a new Navigation Act, which forbids the English American colonies from exporting goods directly to Ireland or Scotland.

1696 John III Sobieski, king of Poland, dies. Frederick, the elector of Saxony, is elected to the Polish throne the following year. He assumes the name of Augustus II and rules for 37 years. Augustus' invasion of Livonia starts the Second Northern War. During Augustus II's reign, Poland begins to decline from the position of a major European power and eventually becomes a protectorate of Russia.

1694

1701 English agriculturist and inventor Jethro Tull revolutionizes farming by the invention of the horse-drawn hoe and seeding drill. He also stresses the use of manure and the importance of breaking-up the soil into small particles.

1709 Englishman Abraham Darby discovers that iron ore can be smelted using coke, to produce pig iron. He demonstrates that coke is superior in cost and efficiency, by establishing furnaces that are much larger than is possible with using charcoal as fuel. Iron becomes much cheaper to produce and is a key factor in the Industrial Revolution.

1723–1790 Scottish philosopher and economist Adam Smith lives during this period. He is the author of *An Inquiry into the Nature and Causes of the Wealth of Nations*, which becomes a very important work in the field of economics.

1745 Charles Edward Stuart, also known as Bonnie Prince Charlie, leads the second Jacobite revolt. Although initially successful in capturing the English towns of Carlisle, Preston and Manchester, he is defeated in the Battle of Culloden. The uprising is known as 'The 45'.

1757 In India, Bengal comes under British rule when forces of the East India Company, led by Robert Clive, defeat Siraj ud-Daula, the Nawab of Bengal, in the Battle of Plassey. The battle marks the first stage in the British conquest in India.

1764 English inventor James Hargreaves develops the spinning jenny, recognized as one of the first mass-production industrial machines.

1701

King James I

violating the rights that have been afforded to them by the late Holy Roman emperor Rudolf II. Angry Protestants throw two of Prague's governors from a window in Hradcany Palace. This incident, which is referred to as the 'Defenestration of Prague', leads to the Thirty Years War, which is fought between France, Sweden, Spain and the Holy Roman Empire, among other countries. The war devastates central Europe.

1626 French colonizers settle in Madagascar and begin to drive out the Hovas who had been on the island for 600 years.

1629–1722 A series of weak rulers leads to the decline of the Safavid dynasty of Persia (now Iran). Its end comes when the Ghalzai Afghans invade Persia and occupy the city of Kandahar.

1636 The Japanese people are forbidden from travelling abroad by the country's shogun (military leader). This begins an increasing policy of isolation by the Japanese that would last over 200 years.

1641–1652 Buryat Mongols from Lake Baikal are defeated and brought under the control of the Russians. This marks the end of the Mongols as a power in Asia.

Charles I's execution

Charles I, is crowned king of England after agreeing to accept key concessions to Parliament. England returns to peace as a constitutional monarchy.

1661 Louis XIV gains complete control of France after the death of his dominating prime minister, Cardinal Mazarin. The king decides not to appoint a new prime minister. Instead, he strips the nobles and all regional councils of their rights and political influence, concentrating all the power in his own hands.

1675 Native tribes in New England gather together under the leadership of King Philip – whose original name was Metacomet – to raid 52 settlements. They kill almost 600 colonists in a revolt against being forced to pay an annual tribute (tax) to the English settlers.

1680 Ietsuna, the Japanese Tokugawa shogun, dies and is succeeded by his brother Tsunayoshi. He promotes neo-Confucianism and his reign is considered one of the most peaceful and prosperous in Japanese history.

1683 An Ottoman attack on Vienna fails due to German and Polish troops coming to the aid of the city. Viennese bakers invent a new pastry to celebrate: the croissant.

1696 Spaniards establish a colony at Pensacola in Florida.

1697 Charles XI of Sweden dies. His son Charles XII succeeds him. He promotes important domestic reforms. His disastrous invasion of Russia, however, marks the end of Sweden's status as a major power. Charles was shot dead in battle in 1718.

1697 The Ottoman Turks, led by Sultan Mustafa II, face a crushing defeat in the Battle of Zenta against Austria. This victory makes Austria the leading power in central Europe.

1697 The War of the League of Augsburg ends after 11 years with the Treaty of Ryswick.

1698 The London Stock Exchange is established. Although other European cities like Antwerp have organized trading houses, the exchange at London is the first of its kind in the world.

1698 The first steam engine is designed and made by English engineer Thomas Savery. The engine is made to pump out water from coal mines, though the idea is later adapted to other purposes.

Iron Bridge

Bonnie Prince Charlie

1775 The American War of Independence begins with a fight between the British forces and the local militia at Concord in Massachusetts. France later joins the war on the side of the American colonies against Britain.

1783 The American Congress declares the end of the War of Independence and the continental army is disbanded.

1783 French brothers Joseph-Michel Montgolfier and Jacques-Étienne Montgolfier develop the first hot-air balloon. Their balloon rises to a height of 1000 m and remains aloft for ten minutes. Next, they send a sheep, a rooster and a duck as passengers. The first manned flight takes place on 21 November when Francois de Rozier and the Marquis d'Arlandes fly over Paris.

Montgolfier balloon

Expanding World

In 1600 much of the world remained unexplored. Across the Pacific Ocean were vast areas of ocean and thousands of islands that were occupied by Polynesian and Melanesian peoples, but which had not been contacted by any ships. Australia and New Zealand were equally isolated from the outside world. Over the following two centuries, all these lands would be reached by outsiders.

- In North America there were six kinds of tribal area: the Southwest, Great Plains, Far West Plateau, Northwest, Eastern Woodland and Northern.

- Southwest Native Americans like the Puebloans lived by growing corn, beans and squash.

- Plains tribes like the Blackfoot, Comanche and Cheyenne hunted buffalo on foot.

- In Woodland tribes like the Delaware, the men hunted deer and fished while the women grew crops.

- Plateau and Northwest Native Americans like the Nez Percé and the Kwakiutl lived by fishing and gathering berries. They are famous for their baskets.

- Northern tribes like the Cree lived mainly by hunting caribou.

- From 1500–1800, Europeans shipped 10–12 million black people as slaves from Africa to the Americas. A total of 40 per cent went to Brazil, 30 per cent to Cuba, Jamaica and Haiti, and 5 per cent to the USA.

- In 1642 Dutch explorer Abel Janszoon Tasman became the first European to reach Tasmania. He named it Van Diemen's Land, in honour of Anton Van Diemen, the governor-general of the Dutch East Indies (later called Netherlands Indies).

- 1768 the British navy asked English naval captain and explorer James Cook to go to the Pacific island of Tahiti, to make measurements and observations of the planet Venus passing in front of the Sun. During this Pacific expedition, Cook visited New Zealand and found the Great Barrier Reef, off Australia.

Captain Cook

Cook took with him scientists and artists to study and record the plants, animals and peoples of the Pacific lands.

Although French missionaries managed to settle in parts of North America, French colonization of the region was not a success.

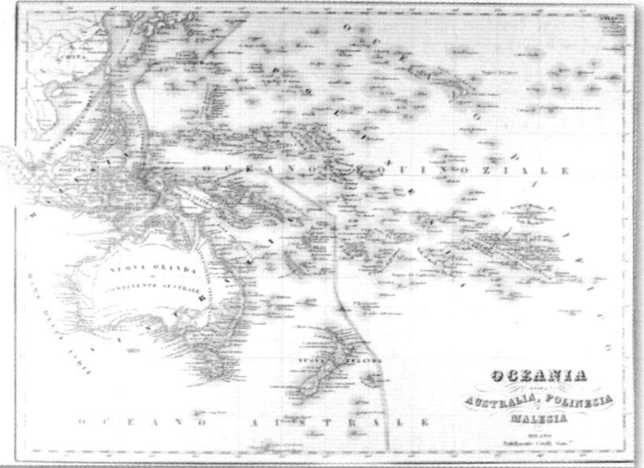

New Zealand (shown in the map) was called Aotearoa by the native Maori. Aotearoa means 'land of the long white cloud'.

Amazing

A myth persists that the word 'kangaroo' means 'I don't know' in the Aboriginal language, and that this was the result of a misunderstanding between Captain James Cook and the local he asked. Later language studies have proved this to be false.

Fighting for independence

In 1764–1765, British Prime Minister Grenville brought in three new taxes – the Sugar Tax on molasses, the Quartering Tax and the Stamp Tax. Colonists tolerated sugar and quartering taxes, but the Stamp Tax provoked riots, such as the Boston Tea Party, when crates of tea were emptied into the Boston harbour. Delegates from nine colonies met in New York to demand a say in how they were taxed. A Congress of delegates from all the colonies except Georgia met to demand independence, and appointed George Washington to lead an army to fight their cause. In 1776, the colonists drew up a Declaration of Independence, written by Thomas Jefferson. The British recognized independence in 1783, and in 1787 the colonists drew up a Constitution to lay down how their Union should be run. In 1789, George Washington was elected as the first president of the United States of America and the capital city was later named after him.

In 1772 Cook was sent back to look for the unknown continent that many still believed was in the south. On this voyage he sailed all the way around Antarctica, but it wasn't explored until 1820, 50 years later.

In southern USA many African slaves were field hands, picking cotton. Many tried to escape or protest, but they were in a minority – and there was no chance of a revolution like that led by Toussaint l'Ouverture (below) in Haiti.

American War of Independence

1765 American colonies object to the Stamp Act passed by British Parliament

1774 Boston Tea Party – American colonists throw chests of taxed tea into Boston harbour

1775 American troops fire on British troops at Lexington

1776 Second Continental Congress issues the Declaration of Independence

1778 France sends help to the American colonies in their war against Britain

1781 British lose the Battle of Yorktown

1783 Treaty of Paris – Britain recognizes American independence

Asia in Decline

The most powerful and sophisticated civilizations on Earth for centuries had been in Asia. Persia, China, Japan, and the Mongols had dominated the world. However, after about 1600 the Asian countries began to decline. Their economies faltered, so they did not have as much wealth as before, and they failed to invent or adopt the technological advances that were taking place in Europe. In many areas corrupt government made progress difficult and made everyday life miserable. Europeans took advantage of this to conquer more lands and add them to their growing empires.

❍ In the 1600s, the Ming emperors of China were unpopular after three centuries in power. Rebellions became increasingly common.

❍ In 1644, the last Ming emperor hanged himself as the bandit Li Zicheng and his men overran Beijing.

❍ Guarding the Great Wall were Manchu troops, from Manchuria in the north. A desperate Ming general invited them to help get rid of Li Zicheng.

❍ The Manchus marched into Beijing and proclaimed their own king as the 'Son of Heaven' and set up the Qing dynasty of emperors.

❍ In time, the Qing adopted Chinese ways, and even Manchu civil servants had to learn the classic works of Confucius, just like the Chinese.

❍ In 1617 Mustafa I succeeded his brother Ahmed I to the Ottoman throne. He was deposed the very next year by the elite troops for his mental problems, but was restored to the throne in 1622. This marked the beginning of the decline in the power of the Ottoman emperor as power passed to bureaucrats and soldiers.

❍ In 1700 the Mogul Empire in India was weakened by continuous rebellions against the emperor Aurangzeb and his corrupt reign.

❍ In the 1700s, rebellions weakened the Mogul Empire in India. The French and British vied to gain control of the collapsing empire.

❍ In 1774, the Turkish Ottoman Empire was defeated by the Russians after a six-year war, and was forced to allow Russian ships to pass through the Straits from the Black Sea to the Mediterranean.

Amazing

In 1758, the Nawab of Bengal thanked Robert Clive by showing him a vast pile of gold and jewellery. He told Clive he could keep anything he could carry at one time.

➤ ***In 1757, 3000 British soldiers, led by the East India Company's Robert Clive, defeated an army of over 50,000 French and Indian troops at the battle of Plassey. After Clive's victory, the British gradually gained control over much of India through a combination of bribes, bullying and gaining well-placed allies.***

British rule lasted in India until 1947. British officials and their families moved to India during the period that is now referred to as the Raj. British rule was resented by many Indians. Hindus felt that the British were undermining their religion.

Mongol horsemen

For centuries the Mongol horse archers had been almost invincible in battle. The combination of speed and hitting power had been unchallenged. The Mongols defeated and ruled over many neighbouring peoples. However, they were easily beaten by Europeans armed with guns in a series of wars after 1600. Mongolia became divided between Russia and China.

Chinese Empire

Under the Manchu rulers, the Chinese Empire was larger than it had ever been. The Manchu insisted that only the Emperor could make decisions. The administration of the vast empire soon became slow and corrupt as local governors refused to take decisions on their own. High taxes stopped merchants from making money. Although it was large, the Chinese Empire gradually grew poorer and weaker. The emperors of China ruled over a glittering court. They wore robes of silk, such as this one decorated with dragons.

A Europe of Ideas

Europe became a hotbed of new ideas and inventions after about 1600. Books were now cheap and easy to print, so people could read about discoveries more quickly and easily than before. Exciting new concepts about government, religion and lifestyles swept across the continent. Some people wanted to adopt the new ideas, others preferred a traditional lifestyle. There were frequent disputes and arguments, which sometimes led to warfare. After 1750 ideas about democracy and human rights spread rapidly.

- The English Civil War (1642–1651) was the struggle between 'Cavalier' supporters of King Charles I and 'Roundheads', led by Oliver Cromwell, who supported Parliament.

- Many revolutionary groups emerged among poorer people, such as the 'Diggers' and 'Levellers'.

- The war turned against the royalists when the parliamentarians formed the disciplined New Model Army. Oliver Cromwell was put in charge of the cavalry.

- After defeating the royal army, Parliament began talks with the king to establish a new, more democratic system of government. However, King Charles I broke his promises and tried to recruit a new army. He was beheaded in 1649.

Peter the Great (1672–1725) was the greatest of all the Russian czars (emperors). He built the city of St Petersburg and turned Russia from an inward-looking country to a major European power. Most earlier czars had bushy, traditional Russian beards. Peter shaved his off, in the modern European style.

Charles II's rule coincided with the Great Plague and the Great Fire of London.

- The successful parliamentarian general Oliver Cromwell (1599–1658) became the leader of the Roundheads and signed Charles I's death warrant. In 1653, he made himself Lord Protector – England's dictator. Cromwell supported the policies of the Puritans, groups of strict religious leaders.

- The Restoration of Charles II as king was in May 1660. Charles II proved a skilful ruler, tactfully easing tensions between rival religious groups. He introduced democratic reforms and reorganized the finances of government to make it more efficient.

Civil War

The Civil War in England was caused by a quarrel between King Charles I and his parliament over royal powers, religion and taxation. The war was fought between 1642 and 1651.

The Hall of Mirrors in the Palais de Versailles, which is situated just outside Paris, France. The 17th-century palace was built by Louis XIV on the site of his father's chateau.

❍ The Age of Reason is the time in the 1700s when many people began to believe that all-important questions about the world could be answered by reason.

❍ The hero of the Age was Isaac Newton. His discovery of the Laws of Motion proposed that every single event in the Universe could be worked out mathematically.

❍ In France, the great ideas were worked out by philosophers like Rousseau and Voltaire. People discussed the ideas earnestly when they met at fashionable 'salons' (supper parties).

Battle of Culloden

Fought in April 1746, the Battle of Culloden was the last stand of Charles Edward Stuart (known as 'Bonnie Prince Charlie') to restore the Stuart monarchy in Britain. His highland army attempted to overthrow King George II, but it was beaten by the English army, which had many more men (9000 against 5000). Bonnie Prince Charlie had to flee into the hills before he eventually escaped by ship to France. The Stuart's hopes of regaining the throne had ended.

Famous books

1615 ***Don Quixote***
Spanish writer Miguel de Cervantes writes about an adventurous knight

1637 ***Discours de la Méthode***
French philosopher René Descartes writes: 'I think, therefore I am'

1653 ***The Compleat Angler***
English sportsman Izaak Walton writes the classic book about fishing

1659 ***Diary***
English civil servant Samuel Pepys begins his diary

1719 ***Robinson Crusoe***
English novelist Daniel Defoe's book about a shipwrecked sailor

1755 ***Dictionary***
Writer Samuel Johnson lists thousands of English words

1776 ***On the Wealth of Nations***
Adam Smith establishes economics as a science

1781 ***Critique of Pure Reason***
German Immanuel Kant argues that humans cannot understand everything

❍ Charles II was known as the Merry Monarch, because his love of partying, theatre, horse-racing and women was such a relief to the public after years of grim Puritan rule.

❍ Charles II had many mistresses, and the most famous of them was Nell Gwyn. Previously an orange-seller, she became the most famous and highest paid actress in Europe.

Amazing

Charles II of England thanked those who had helped him escape execution during the Civil War by giving them pensions. Some are still being paid to their descendants.

The Industrial Revolution

Beginning in about 1700, a dramatic change swept over Britain and changed the way people lived. Before this time most people had lived in the countryside, where they farmed the land and produced only a bit more food than they needed for themselves. As the changes occurred, people began to live in towns where they worked in factories, producing goods that were sold for cash. This process is called the Industrial Revolution. It began with changes to farming techniques in Britain, that gradually spread out across the world.

❍ Before the 1700s, farmland was mostly wide open fields, cultivated in narrow strips by peasants growing food for themselves, using traditional, manual methods.

British inventor Thomas Newcomen's (1663–1729) steam engine used atmospheric pressure and was a forerunner of James Watt's engine. Water was injected into a large metal cylinder that was filled with steam. This condensed the steam and created a vacuum. A piston was pushed to the bottom of the cylinder by the weight of the atmosphere, thus pulling up the pumps connected to the piston and raising the water.

Amazing

Until the Industrial Revolution most clocks had only hour hands. Minute hands were added so that people would know when to begin work exactly on time.

In 1764, Lancashire weaver James Hargreaves created the 'spinning jenny' to help cottage weavers to quickly spin wool or cotton fibres into yarn (thread) on lots of spindles at once, turned by a single handle.

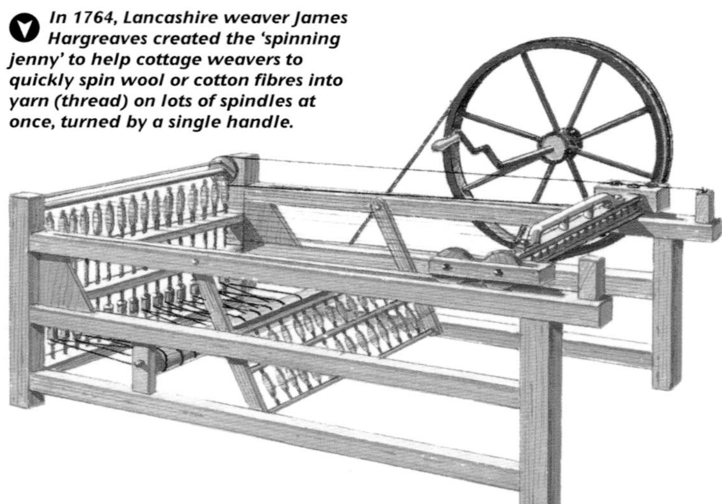

❍ Crop-growing was improved by techniques such as the four-field crop rotation system. The four-field system of 'Turnip' Townshend and Thomas Coke meant growing turnips, clover, barley and wheat in successive years so land was used all the time.

❍ Livestock farmers learnt how to breed cattle, horses and sheep to be larger, like Bakewell's Leicester sheep.

❍ The Farming Revolution created a pool of cheap labour, while the growth of European colonies created vast markets for things like clothing.

Water wheel

Sir Richard Arkwright's spinning machine was a 'water frame' that ran on water power. Arkwright had the machine set up at his cotton mill at Cromford in Derbyshire, England.

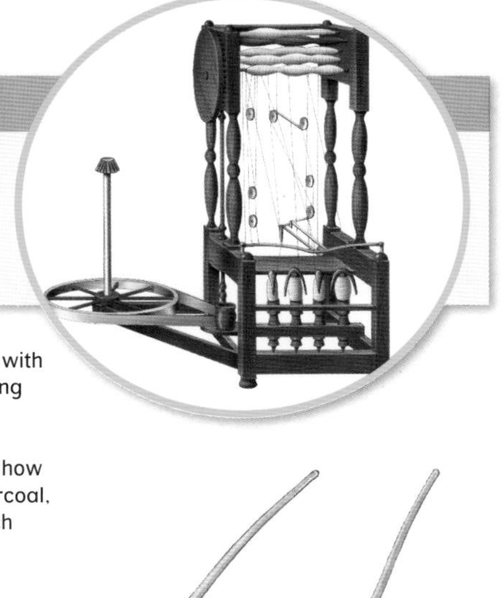

❍ The Industrial Revolution began with the invention of machines for making cloth, like the spinning jenny.

❍ In 1713, Abraham Darby found how to use coke, rather than wood charcoal, to make huge amounts of iron much more cheaply than ever before.

Side seed-box

Main seed-box

Coulter bar

Jethro Tull's seed drill made holes and planted seeds in them, dramatically speeding up the planting process for farm workers.

❍ The turning point was the change from hand-turned machines like the jenny to machines driven by big water wheels – like Arkwright's 'water (-powered spinning) frame' of 1769.

❍ In 1771, Arkwright installed water frames at Crompton Mill, Derby, and created the world's first big factory.

❍ In the 1780s, James Watt developed a steam engine to drive machines – and steam engines quickly replaced water as the main source of power in factories.

❍ In 1784, Henry Cort found how to remove impurities from cast iron to make wrought iron – and iron became the key material of the Industrial Revolution.

James Watt

Between 1764 and 1790 the Scottish inventor James Watt made a series of improvements to the design of the steam engine. Among the more important changes he made was to develop a rotary motion and a double-acting engine. Taken together these made steam engines far more powerful and reliable than before. They began to be used in large numbers in factories and mines, and to power ships and railway locomotives.

Revolutionary ideas

1701	**Jethro Tull**	Mechanical seed drill improves arable farming
1705	**Thomas Newcomen**	First steam engine
1713	**Abraham Darby**	Produces coke and uses it to smelt iron ore
1733	**John Kay**	Flying shuttle improves quality of wool and cotton cloth
1764	**James Hargreaves**	Spinning jenny improves quality of cotton thread
1769	**James Watt**	Announces improvements to Newcomen's steam engine
1769	**Richard Arkwright**	Water-powered frame for spinning cotton
1770	**Nicolas Cugnot**	First self-propelled road vehicle
1776	**Watt and Boulton**	First commercial steam engine using steam pressure alone
1777	**John Wilkinson**	First boat with an iron hull launched in Yorkshire, England
1779	**Samuel Crompton**	Spinning mule produces several cotton threads at once
1783	**Montgolfier Brothers**	First successful flight of a hot air balloon
1785	**Edmund Cartwright**	Power loom weaves cotton cloth at high speed
1804	**Richard Trevithick**	First successful steam-powered locomotive

The Age of Revolutions

In 1789 France exploded in revolution. People were no longer willing to live in poverty under a corrupt and dictatorial government and a lavish monarchy. The French Revolution was only the first of many other democratic and nationalist uprisings that swept Europe in the decades that followed. Later came a wave of Communist and Fascist revolutions, and more democratic uprisings. The pace of technological and industrial change continued to increase.

1789 The French National Assembly make the reformist nobleman Marquis de Lafayette commander of the National Guards and Jean-Sylvain Bailly the Mayor of Paris. The 'Declaration of the Rights of Man and of the Citizen' is made by the National Assembly to set out equal rights to all Frenchmen. Many areas of France collapse into violent anarchy.

1793 Louis XVI of France and his wife Marie Antoinette are accused of supporting foreign enemies of the new French Republic. They are tried, found guilty and executed.

1793 The Reign of Terror starts in France, during which thousands of people are declared enemies of the Revolution and are executed. At least 17,000 people are killed during this period.

1789

1852 Napoleon III, the grandson of Napoleon I, is elected to be the emperor of France. He is believed to be the first to lay the foundations for a family welfare system. During his reign, craftsmen and artists form associations to get finance for insurance.

1853 The Crimean War is fought between Russia and an alliance comprising the Ottoman Empire, the kingdom of Sardinia, Britain and France. The war is best known for the futile and almost suicidal charge of the Light Brigade of British cavalry. The war ends in defeat for Russia.

1857–1858 The Sepoy Mutiny among Indian troops in British service spreads rapidly to military stations all over northern and western India. It is eventually suppressed by British troops.

1852

Indian Mutiny 1857

1861 The American Civil War begins, with the Confederates making their first attack on Fort Sumter in South Carolina. The Confederate states break away from the United States of America to preserve their agricultural way of life, which is often based on slavery.

1865 In Virginia, Confederate general Robert E Lee surrenders to Union general Ulysses S Grant. The

17 December 1903 The American inventors and pioneers, Wilbur Wright and Orville Wright, invent the first powered flying machine.

6 October 1908 Austria announces its decision to make Bosnia-Herzegovina a part of the Austro-Hungarian Empire. This angers the Bosnia-Herzegovina natives and Serbia and the Ottoman Turks, who both want to control the disputed area.

February 1912 The Qing monarchy of China gives up their claim to the throne. The politician Yuan Shikai becomes head of the Chinese republic.

28 June 1914 Archduke Franz Ferdinand, heir to the throne of Austria–Hungary, is assassinated in Sarajevo by Gavrilo Princip, a Serbian activist from Bosnia-Herzegovina.

28 July 1914 The Austrian emperor Franz Joseph declares war against Serbia, starting World War I.

1 July–13 November 1916 Britain introduces the battle tank for the first time in the Battle of the Somme, an allied attack on German forces on the western front. The tanks can easily cross the muddy, uneven terrain, but suffer frequent mechanical failure. On 1 July 60,000 British soldiers were killed in just a few hours. This long and expensive battle ends with no clear result.

8 March 1917 Riots break out in St Petersburg. As soldiers join with the common people, a revolution against the monarchy begins to spread all over Russia. A provisional government takes power until elections can be held.

1903

1 October 1936 General Francisco Franco is declared the head of the nationalist forces in the town of Burgos. After winning a civil war, in which more than 500,000 people die, Franco becomes ruler of Spain in March 1939.

1 September 1939 World War II begins with the German invasion of Poland by Hitler's army.

1936

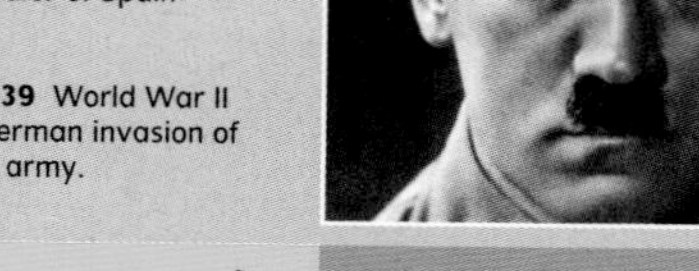

Hitler invades Poland 1939

3 September 1939 Britain and France declare war on Germany. Russia later joins the Allies against Germany.

7 December 1941 Japanese aircraft attack Pearl Harbor in Hawaii. The United States declares war on Japan.

6 June 1944 Allied Forces land on the Normandy coast in France on what is known as 'D-Day'.

30 April 1945 Nazi leader Adolf Hitler kills himself.

7 May 1945 Germany surrenders unconditionally to the Allied powers.

14 August 1945 Japan announces its surrender from the war.

4 April 1949 Belgium, Italy, Canada, the Netherlands, Portugal, Denmark, Britain, France, Iceland, Norway,

1804 Napoleon Bonaparte becomes emperor of France. Two years earlier, Napoleon had instituted a new constitution whereby he secured for himself the position of First Consul – for life.

1815 Napoleon is defeated in the Battle of Waterloo by a British army under the Duke of Wellington, aided by the Prussians. Napoleon is exiled to the island of St Helena.

1848 A series of revolutions starts in various parts of Europe, beginning with Sicily, and spreading to France, Germany and Austria. They are mostly unsuccessful in bringing about any political change, and are all eventually suppressed.

1848 The February revolution in France forces King Louis-Philippe to give up his throne and France becomes a republic.

American Civil War ends with the Confederate states being forced to rejoin the United States.

1870 German states led by Prussia defeat France in the Franco-Prussian War. Victory signifies the end of France's domination in Europe, and the beginning of a unified Germany, led by Prussia. The new state is dubbed the Second Reich.

1870 Napoleon III of France is forced to step down from the throne after losing the Franco-Prussian War. The Third French Republic is established.

1899–1902 British imperial forces defeat Boer settlers of South Africa after a long war that ends with the Treaty of Vereeniging, by which the Transvaal province and the Orange Free State become British colonies.

7 November 1917 The Bolsheviks, led by Vladimir Iilych Lenin, overthrow the provisional Russian government and establish the Communist Soviet Republic. During the Russian Civil War that follows, Lenin launches a campaign called 'Red Terror', which is aimed at eliminating his political opponents. He also launches a series of major economic reforms to meet Russia's pressing economic needs.

11 November 1918 Peace is declared and World War I ends.

1925–1927 Benito Mussolini, prime minister of Italy, passes laws to make himself dictator of Italy.

12 November 1927 After Lenin's death, the Soviet Communist Party expel Leon Trotsky. Joseph Stalin gains undisputed control of the Soviet Union.

2 August 1934 Nazi party leader Adolf Hitler assumes the title of Führer (leader) of Germany. He now has dictatorial (total) power over Germany and begins a rapid build-up of military power. Hitler wants to reclaim the lands that Germany had lost after being defeated in World War I. He uses the enlarged army and air force to bully Austria and Czechoslovakia into giving him what he wants.

Luxembourg and the United States form the North Atlantic Treaty Organization (NATO) to counter the the power of the Soviet Union.

October 1956 Hungarians revolt against Soviet rule, but the Russians suppress the uprising.

October 1962 United States President John F Kennedy discovers that the Soviet Union placed missiles in Cuba, aimed at United States cities. Following a tense confrontation, Russia removes the missiles.

10 March 1985 Mikahil Gorbachev becomes leader of the Soviet Union. His policy of modernizing the country leads to the break-up of the USSR.

10 May 1994 Nelson Mandela becomes the first black president of the Republic of South Africa.

11 September 2001 A group of Islamic extremists hijack four aircraft in the USA, crashing them into the World Trade Center in New York and the Pentagon building in Washington, killing more than 3000 people. Osama bin Laden, leader of the Al Qaeda terrorist group admits that he organized the attacks. US President George W Bush begins a worldwide campaign against terrorism.

19 March 2003 American and British air forces attack Baghdad, Mosul and Basra in Iraq. Soon after this the land forces conquer Iraq in a lightning campaign.

Europe in Revolution

France was one of the most powerful countries in the world, but years of incompetent government and expensive wars had made it almost bankrupt. In 1789 a revolution broke out that swept away the old monarchy and introduced a new republic. This led to war with the other monarchies in Europe. The French Revolutionary Wars would last until peace finally came in 1815. Later revolutions broke out in other countries to introduce democracy and human rights, but only some of them were successful.

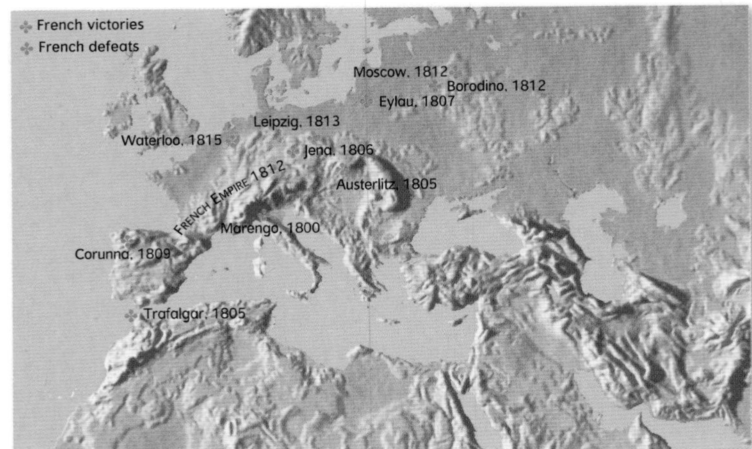

This map shows some of the major battles of the Napoleonic Wars.

❍ In 1789, France was bankrupt, and King Louis XVI summoned Parliament for the first time in 175 years.

❍ On 14 July 1789 the poor people of Paris, tired of debates, stormed the prison fortress of the Bastille.

❍ The French Parliament became the National Assembly. It adopted radical policies, such as ending serfdom. Many nobles fled the country in panic.

❍ French general Napoleon Bonaparte (1769–1821) set up a military government to bring order to France.

❍ By 1804, Napoleon's conquests had made him a hero in France, and he elected himself as Emperor Napoleon I.

❍ In 1805, Britain, Russia and Austria allied against Napoleon. Napoleon crushed the Austrians and Russians at Austerlitz. But in 1805 the British Admiral Nelson destroyed the French and Spanish fleet at Trafalgar.

Many nobles were sent to the guillotine and in 1793 King Louis XVI and his queen, Marie Antoinette, were themselves guillotined.

The French Revolution, combined with Napoleon's ambitious plans to conquer Europe, caused the outbreak of wars all over Europe.

Napolean retreats

Napoleon's retreat from Moscow in 1812 was one of the worst of all military disasters. The winter trek was so cold and food so scarce that only 30,000 of the original army of 695,000 that set out made it back to France alive.

Amazing

In 1848 Louis Napoleon, nephew of Emperor Napoleon, was elected President of France. In 1852 he made himself Emperor, just like his uncle.

- In 1812, Napoleon invaded Russia and captured Moscow, but then had to retreat in the bitterest winter.
- After the 1812 disaster, Napoleon's enemies forced him to abdicate and he was exiled to Elba.
- Napoleon escaped from Elba in 1815 to raise another army, but this was defeated by Wellington's armies at Waterloo, Belgium.
- The year 1848 saw revolutions break out across Europe – in France, Germany, Italy, Austria and Hungary.

Despite his extraordinary military resiliance, after his final defeat at Waterloo, Napoleon was banished by the British to the island of St Helena, where he died in 1821.

In 1860, the great hero Garibaldi led a rebellion and conquered all of southern Italy. In 1861, most of Italy was united under Victor Emmanuel. Venice was added in 1866 and Rome as capital in 1870. Garibaldi had landed in Sicily with just his thousand famous 'Red Shirts'.

Revolution

Simón Bolívar led the revolution against Spanish rule in New Granada. In 1819 revolutionary forces in South America defeated the Spanish army at the Battle of Boyaca. By 1828 nearly every country in Spanish America had become an independent republic, mostly with democratic constitutions and human rights well established in their systems of government.

- Many revolutionaries – often nationalists – were angry at repressive foreign governments in which too few had a say, and at the poverty suffered by ordinary people in the new cities.
- All but the new French Revolution were crushed – but the desire for change grew stronger over the century.
- In 1857 Count Cavour, prime minister of Piedmont, asked France for help with evicting the Austrians. Italy became united as one country, except for Rome, which was ruled by the Pope.
- After Napoleon's defeat in 1815, the new structure of Europe was decided at the Congress of Vienna, where the 1815 Vienna Settlement was signed by leading powers to prevent future territorial wars.

Europe Supreme

The booming populations, great wealth and many technological advances of Europe made this continent more powerful than any other in the 19th century. Several European countries used their power to build up large empires by conquering or taking over countries in other parts of the world. European factories dominated the world, while European ships carried trade between the nations. Later in the 19th century, America became wealthy and powerful, but could not yet rival Europe.

Amazing

The world's shortest war was fought between Britain and Zanzibar in 1896. The battle lasted just 38 minutes and ended with a complete victory for Britain.

- The British Empire began to build up in the 1600s, as British merchants started to extend their trading links throughout the world. The British won out over Dutch, Portuguese, French and Belgian rivals through the success of their navy and also their reasonably efficient colonial government.

- Britain gained control of India through the East India Company, between 1757 and 1858. In 1877, Queen Victoria was proclaimed Empress of India – the first time the word empire had been used in relation to the British possessions.

- In 1788, the British sent a fleet of 11 ships, carrying convicts, to start a prison colony in Australia. About 160,000 convicts were sent to Australia over the next 80 years, but by 1810 British settlers were also arriving voluntarily.

- In 1901, Australia became the independent Commonwealth of Australia, with its own parliament based at Melbourne.

- At its height the British Empire covered one fifth of the world and ruled one fifth of the total world population.

- After 1800, many Europeans wanted to explore the unknown interior of Africa in order to spread Christianity or to help combat the slave trade, run by Arab merchants. Some Europeans wanted to develop trade in products like minerals and palm oil.

- In the 1880s, Europeans competed fiercely for African colonies. This was called 'the scramble for Africa'.

- In some parts of Africa, colonial rule was established peacefully by agreement with the Africans.

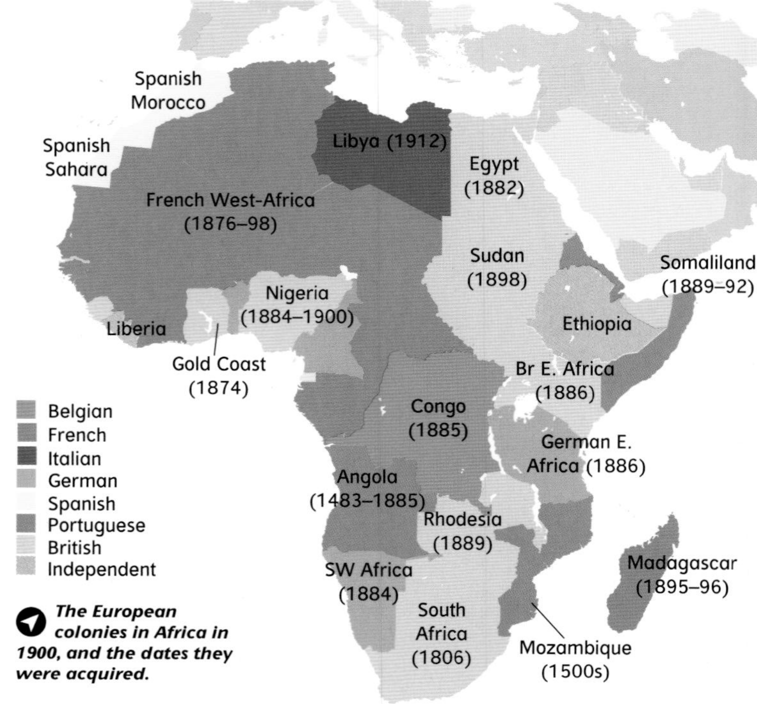

The European colonies in Africa in 1900, and the dates they were acquired.

This map shows the British Empire in the 1930s, when it was already beginning to shrink. Egypt was given some independence in 1922, when Sultan Ahmed became King Fuad I. Iraq gained a similar independence when amir Ahd Allah Faisal became King Faisal I in 1921.

In 1770, Captain James Cook landed on the east coast of Australia and claimed it for Britain. Eighteen years later, ships started to transport convicts there.

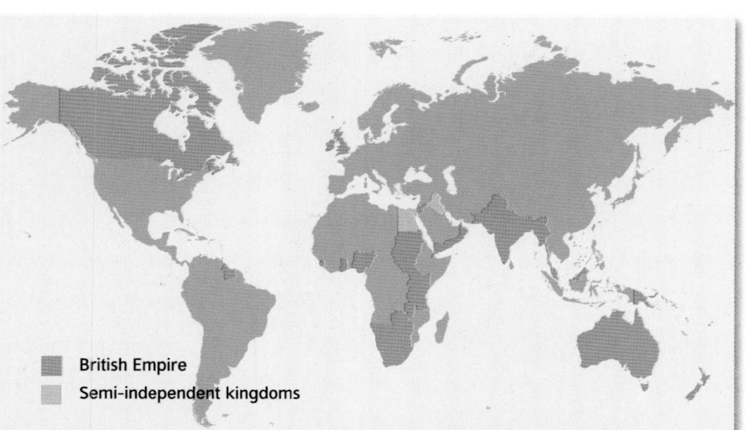

- In Nigeria and Ghana, the Africans fought hard against British rule, and in Tanzania and Namibia, they fought against German rule.

- Until 1900, the USA played little part in world affairs. Bismarck said, 'A special providence takes care of fools, drunkards and the USA'. But in 1898, the US battleship *Maine* was blown up off Cuba. Americans blamed the Spanish and in the war that followed, the USA easily defeated Spain. The USA then became more involved in world affairs.

Industrial power

In the late 1800s, the USA changed from a nation of farming pioneers and plantation owners to the world's biggest industrial powerhouse. American inventors and industrialists made products that changed the world – the typewriter (1867), the telephone (1876), the phonograph (1877) and electric light (1879). Then, in the early 1900s, Henry Ford pioneered the mass production of cars and made them affordable for millions of ordinary people.

Colonies in Africa in 1900

Belgium	Congo
Britain	Becuanaland, British Somaliland, Egypt, Gold Coast, Kenya, Nigeria, Nyasaland, Rhodesia, Sierra Leone, South Africa, Sudan, Uganda, Zanzibar
France	Chad, Djibouti, French West Africa, Gabon, Madagascar, Middle Congo, Shari Ubangi
Germany	Kamerun, Southwest Africa, Tanganyika, Togoland
Italy	Eritrea, Somaliland
Portugal	Angola, Guinea, Mozambique
Spain	Rio de Oro, Spanish Morocco, Spanish Sahara

World Wars

By 1914, Europe was divided into two armed camps as the empires and countries became rivals for power, territory and wealth. When the European states went to war in 1914, fighting spread rapidly across the world, involving many other countries. This World War ended in 1918 with the defeat of Germany, Austria and Turkey. The war was followed by economic hardship in many countries that had helped dictators to gain power. In Germany the dictator Adolf Hitler wanted to reverse the defeat of 1918. He invaded Poland in 1939, starting World War II, which would later involve more countries than World War I. When World War II ended in 1945, Europe was economically and physically ruined – millions had been killed.

❍ World War I was caused by the intense rivalry between European powers in the early 1900s. When Archduke Franz Ferdinand was assassinated in June 1914, Austria started a war with Serbia, and Russia came to Serbia's defence. Germany declared war on Russia and Russia's ally, France, on 3 August.

❍ As the Germans invaded France, they marched through Belgium, which brought Britain into the war. Soon a line of trenches, the Western front, stretched from the English Channel across to Switzerland. The opposing armies dug trenches – and stayed facing each other in much the same place for the whole four years of the war.

❍ The war also had an Eastern front, where the Central Powers (Austria and Germany) faced the Russians.

❍ In the Alps the Central Powers were opposed by Italy, while in Turkey, British and Anzac (Australia and New Zealand) troops fought the Turks.

❍ In 1917 the USA joined the Allies against the Central Powers, which precipitated the end of the war. At 11 o'clock on 11 November 1918, the Germans signed an armistice (peace).

Trenches were dug to protect the troops of the opposing armies from enemy gunfire. Conditions in trenches worsened incredibly quickly, and they soon became muddy hell-holes, which were filled with water, rats and disease. Soldiers had to eat, sleep and stand guard whilst ankle-deep in mud and filth.

The Battle of Britain began in the late summer of 1940. By October, the British had defeated the Germans and won this battle for the skies.

❍ After World War I, economic problems called the Great Depression spread across the world. In Germany 6 million people were out of work, and in 1933 enough people voted for the Nazi Party to make them the strongest party in parliament. Nazi leader Hitler made himself dictator of Germany.

❍ The Nazis prepared for war to give Germans *Lebensraum* ('living space'). In 1936, they marched into the Rhineland. In 1938, they took Austria, followed by Czechoslovakia. In 1939, Germany invaded Poland, which was allied to Britain and France. World War II had begun.

Sir Winston Churchill (1874–1965) was the British prime minister whose courage and inspiring speeches helped the British withstand the German threat. He received a knighthood in 1953.

U-Boats

German U-boats (submarines) were used during World Wars I and II to destroy warships and merchant ships belonging to the enemy.

Amazing

Britain's powerful warship HMS *Hood* had eight 38-cm guns and 60 other guns. It was sunk in May 1941 by a single shell from German warship *Bismarck*.

- After a lull, or 'Phoney War', the Germans quickly overran Norway and Denmark, then Luxembourg, the Netherlands, Belgium and France. By July 1940 only Britain and its empire was still at war with Germany.

- Italy joined the war on the German side, and Germany launched air raids on Britain to prepare for an invasion. This was the Battle of Britain. The British Royal Air Force won the battle, so Hitler called off the invasion of Britain.

Famous Quotes of Winston Churchill

I am easily satisfied with the very best

I have nothing to offer but blood, toil, tears and sweat

Russia is a riddle wrapped in a mystery inside an enigma

Before Alamein we never had a victory. After Alamein we never had a defeat

A lie gets halfway around the world before the truth has the chance to get its pants on

Never in the field of human conflict was so much owed by so many to so few

If you are going through hell, keep going

This is not the end. It is not even the beginning of the end. But it is, perhaps, the end of the beginning

USA enters the war

The Japanese attack on the United States fleet at Pearl Harbor, Hawaii, hastened the entry of the United States into World War II. American casualties included over 180 aircraft and more than 5000 lives, from the military and the civilian population.

- The USA joined the war when Japan bombed its fleet without warning in Pearl Harbor, Hawaii, on 7 December 1941.

- Germany, Italy, Japan and six other nations joined forces as the 'Axis'. Britain, the USA, USSR, China and 50 smaller countries formed the Allies. In 1942, the Allies halted the Axis in Africa, invading Italy in 1943 and France in 1944. Germany surrendered on 7 May 1945. Then the USA dropped atom bombs on the Japanese cities Hiroshima and Nagasaki. Japan surrendered on 2 September 1945.

- World War II (1939–1945) killed 22 million soldiers – compared to 10 million in World War I – and twice as many civilians, through starvation, bombings and massacres.

The Cold War

World War II left the USA and the Soviet Union as the two most powerful countries in the world. The Soviet Union thought that dictatorial Communism was the best way to run the world, while the USA believed in democracy and capitalism. Within a few years of the end of World War II the two powers had become hostile to each other. Other countries began to take sides in the dispute, and soon the world was divided into two opposing armed camps in a 'Cold War' – a conflict in which neither side actually declares war. In 1990 the Communist bloc began to disintegrate due to economic problems, thus bringing the Cold War to an end.

❍ The Cold War was fought using both propaganda and art and by secret means such as spies and secret agents.

❍ The Cold War thawed after 1985, when Soviet leader Mikhail Gorbachev introduced reforms in the USSR and began to co-operate with the West.

▲ In 1989, the Berlin Wall, which divided east and west Berlin, was pulled down. For many, the tearing down of the Berlin Wall marked the end of the Cold War. Communist governments across Eastern Europe gave way to democracy in the following months.

❍ Joseph Stalin (1879–1953) became dictator of the USSR after Lenin died in 1924, and remained so until he himself died, in 1953.

❍ Stalin used terror to wipe out opposition and ensure the revolution survived. Russians lived in fear of the secret police NKVD (later the KGB), and millions went to their deaths in the Gulags (prison camps).

❍ The USA and USSR waged an arms race to build up nuclear bombs and missiles one step ahead of their rival.

❍ Real war loomed when US president Kennedy threatened the USSR as it tried to build missile bases on Cuba in 1962.

Communism

Throughout the Cold War some people in the West supported Communism. The Argentinian Communist Ernesto 'Che' Guevara fought with the Revolution in Cuba and encouraged students and radicals throughout the capitalist world to join the Communist cause. He was killed leading a Communist uprising in Bolivia in 1967.

Amazing

When the Soviets took over Poland, they arrested anyone who had a telephone. They thought that only rich people who opposed Communism would own a phone.

❍ The republics within the USSR demanded independence too, and in 1991 the USSR was dissolved and replaced by a Commonwealth of Independent States (CIS).

Mikhail Gorbachev

Mikhail Gorbachev was born in 1933 and worked his entire adult life for the Communist Party in the Soviet Union. In 1985 he became the head of the Soviet Union, and was faced by massive economic and social problems. He tried to solve these problems within a Communist framework, but his reforms served only to unleash democratic forces that brought down the Communist regime.

❍ Gorbachev's reforms angered Communist Party leaders, who staged a coup and imprisoned Gorbachev, but he was freed and the coup was brought down by Boris Yeltsin, who became Russia's first president.

❍ In 2000, the Russians elected Vladimir Putin as president, a strong leader who they hoped would see them out of the crisis.

❍ Mao Zedong (1893–1976) led the communist takeover of China in 1949 and then ruled China as chairman of the republic. Chinese people hoped communism would end poverty and oppression. 'We have stood up', Mao said. The Communist Party continued to rule China into the 21st century.

❍ The Viet Cong started a rebellion in South Vietnam. They were supported by the Communist government of North Vietnam. In 1965, the USA began to bomb North Vietnam, while the USSR and China gave them arms. In 1975, the Viet Cong captured Saigon, the capital of the South, and the next year united North and South.

Fidel Castro was leader of Cuba from 1959 to 2011. He set up a one-party government to assume complete power.

Following the establishment of the People's Republic of China, Mao ordered the redistribution of land and the elimination of rural landlords.

End of Empires

African colony	*Date of independence*
Algeria	1962
Angola	1975
Benin formerly Dahomey	1960
Burkina formerly Upper Volta	1960
Burundi	1962
Cameroon	1960
Central African Republic	1960
Chad	1960
Ethiopia	1941
Gabon	1960
Gambia	1965
Guinea	1958
Guinea Bissau	1974
Ivory Coast	1960
Kenya	1963
Libya	1951
Madagascar	1960
Mali	1960
Mauritania	1960
Morocco	1956
Mozambique	1975
Niger	1960
Nigeria	1960
Rwanda	1962
Senegal	1960
Sierra Leone	1961
Somalia	1960
Sudan	1956
Tanzania	1964
Tunisia	1956
Uganda	1962
Zaire formerly Congo	1960
Zambia	1964

The Changing World

The collapse of the Soviet Union ushered in a period of rapid change that is still continuing. Many countries that had previously supported communism abandoned left-wing dictatorships when they were no longer subsidized by Soviet money and weapons. The more repressive of the right-wing governments also collapsed in the wave of changes. However, some countries took advantage of the changes to begin wars or to attempt to bully their neighbours, which resulted in a series of small-scale wars in many areas.

❍ In the 1970s and 1980s, opposition grew to the system of apartheid (or racial differentiation) in South Africa. Apartheid was supposed to allow the various peoples to develop their culture and exist economically separately within the one country, but in practice it was a racist system that discriminated against black people.

❍ In the 1980s and 1990s, economic failure brought down most Latin American dictators, including the generals Galtieri in Argentina (1983) and Pinochet in Chile (1990) who were both replaced by democratically elected presidents.

❍ On 2 August 1990 Iraqi forces made a surprise attack on Kuwait, which started the Persian Gulf War. The United States, NATO and Arab forces from several countries joined together to try to free Kuwait from Saddam Hussein and his army.

The European Commission building in Strasbourg. The Parliament is in Brussels. The Court of Justice is in Luxembourg.

❍ The Hubble Space Telescope was launched in 1990 by NASA. It orbits around the Earth at 600 km above the ground. Astronomers have used the telescope to obtain images of celestial objects and phenomena never before observed.

❍ On 1 July 1997, Hong Kong was handed over to China by Britain, ending more than 150 years of British control. It was made a special administrative region under the control of the Chinese government. Tung Chee-hwa was sworn in as Hong Kong's new leader.

Nelson Mandela

Nelson Mandela was imprisoned for 26 years for campaigning for the end of apartheid. Apartheid was a social system in place in South Africa that separated black and white citizens. Mandela was jailed in 1964 for being a senior member of the ANC (African National Congress). In 1990, South African president, F. W. de Klerk, released Mandela. In 1994, Mandela became the first black president of South Africa, and apartheid gradually began to break down. He died in 2013.

Amazing

In 1999 a worldwide scare began about the 'Millennium Bug' which was supposed to wreck computers at midnight on 31 December 1999. In fact nothing happened.

❍ On 11 September 2001, Islamic terrorists organized by Osama bin Laden's Al Qaeda organization flew hijacked airliners into the World Trade Center in New York and the Pentagon in Washington. This event sparked off a major campaign against terrorism led by US President George W. Bush.

❍ In 2002 the US attacked Afghanistan, bombing bases of the Islamic government and of Al Qaeda in the country. American-backed rebels took control of the country and closed down all terrorist bases. Osama bin Laden went into hiding but his organization continued to organize terrorist attacks. He was killed by US troops in 2011.

❍ On 4 April, 2003 American troops and tanks entered Baghdad, the capital of Iraq, and captured the airport. Hundreds of Iraqis fled the city. The next day, American and Kurdish forces jointly captured the Iraqi town of Mosul.

❍ On 4 January, 2004 *Spirit*, a six-wheeled robot made by the United States space agency NASA, landed on Mars.

❍ On 27 June, 2004 the American administration of Iraq ended and the governance of the country was given back to the Iraqis.

A ***In April 1945, 50 nations met at San Francisco to draw up the Charter for the United Nations. Poland signed it shortly after, to create the first 51 Member States of the UN. The UN peacekeeping force has been involved in keeping the peace in many places, including Somalia, Rwanda, Kosovo, Bosnia, Sierra Leone and East Timor.***

European Union

The European Union is an organization of European countries, with four governing bodies: the Commission, Council of Ministers, Court of Justice and Parliament. The Commissioners submit laws for the Council to make and put into effect. In 1999, the EU launched the euro, with the intention that it would become a single European currency. In 2004 the leaders of the European Union drew up a draft constitution that would change the EU from being an organization of independent countries to being a sovereign state in its own right. The move provoked controversy among those who preferred that the various member countries should remain independent states.

History Timeline

c.400,000 BC In Africa, *Homo erectus* are the first people to use fire.

c.9000 BC In what is now Iraq, the first farmers plant seeds of wheat and barley.

c.3100 BC Stonehenge is built in England.

c.500–350 BC The Greek Empire is at its most successful.

1438 In Peru, the Incas start to build their Empire.

c.AD 500 Teotihuacán, in Mexico, is the largest city in the world.

1250 The Mongols rule Southern Russia.

1492 In what is now the Caribbean, Columbus explored the West Indies.

1700s The Agricultural Revolution takes place in Britain.

1770 Captain Cook reaches Australia.

1805 Nelson defeats Napoleon at the battle of Trafalgar, off the coast of Spain.

c.2550 BC The pyramids at Giza are built in Egypt.

c.1200 BC The Phoenicians become successful sailors and traders in what is now Syria and Lebanon.

c.509 BC Rome, in Italy, becomes a republic.

c.AD 790 The Vikings begin raiding Europe.

1096 The Crusades begin in what is now Palestine.

1215 In England, Magna Carta is signed.

1519–1534 Spanish conquistadors conquer the Aztecs in Mexico.

1630s In Italy, Galileo proves that the Earth travels around the Sun.

1854–1869 The Suez Canal is built in Egypt.

1914–1918 World War I
1939–1945 World War II

1990 Space exploration continues. The Hubble telescope is launched by NASA.

Glossary

Agricultural Revolution The period of time from 1700 to 1850 during which methods of farming changed dramatically. This allowed fewer farmers to grow more food on the same area of land.

Allies Generally, allies are countries that join together to try to achieve a specific purpose. Sometimes one side in a war will be called the Allies, as were Britain, the USA, the Soviet Union and many other countries in World War II.

Anglo-Saxon The Germanic tribes who moved from Germany to Britain after the fall of the Roman Empire are known as the Anglo-Saxons. At first they were divided into a number of different kingdoms. They later became the English.

Apartheid A Boer word meaning 'separate development'. It was used to describe policies of the South African government that aimed to allow the different ethnic groups in the country to develop their culture, society and economy along paths separate from each other. In practice, the government was dominated by Afrikaans, who made sure that the Afrikaners got the best out of the policy.

Armada A large and powerful fleet of warships that sets out on a voyage to conquer another country.

Armour A layer of special clothing to protect a person in battle. Most armour was made of metal, but some was formed from leather, horn or wood.

Aztec A people who lived in what is now Mexico. They built up a large empire, but were conquered by the Spanish in the 16th century.

Bankrupt A person, organization or country is said to be bankrupt if it is unable to pay its debts when they become due.

Barbarian Peoples and tribes that are uncivilized or behave in an uncivilized way. The word comes from ancient Greek and means 'a person who cannot speak Greek'.

Blockade A blockade happens when one side in a war tries to stop food and other supplies from entering a fortress, city or even an entire country. It is usually hoped that a blockade will force the enemy to surrender without the need for serious fighting.

Boer A people living in South Africa who were descended from Dutch settlers who came to live there in the 16th and 17th centuries. They spoke Afrikaans, a language broadly similar to Dutch. The Boers are now called Afrikaners.

Byzantine The Eastern Roman Empire is known as the Byzantine Empire because it was based on the city of Constantinople, which had formerly been called Byzantine. The Empire lasted until 1453 when it was conquered by the Turks. Constantinople is now called Istanbul.

Caravel A type of ship used in Europe between about 1400 and 1600 that was small, but sturdy.

Charter A document issued by a king or other ruler that grants powers and rights to a group of people.

Civil war A civil war happens when the citizens of one country divide into two sides and fight each other.

Civilization People who live together in cities or towns and share a culture and way of life are said to form a civilization.

Cold war A cold war happens when two or more countries wage a campaign against each other without actually fighting. They may use propaganda, economic sanctions or threats instead of weapons. The struggle of the USA and its allies against the Soviet Union and its allies is sometimes called The Cold War, and lasted from 1947 to 1991.

Colony The first colonies were small groups of people who went to live in another part of the world while keeping their own laws and ways of life. Later the word came to mean any territory ruled by another country that was located a distance away.

Commonwealth A country in which the wealth of the nation is held in common for the good of all the people. Often the word is used to describe a state that is not a dictatorship.

Communism A system of government under which all economic power is held by the government on behalf of all the people. In theory this means that all people have equal wealth and rights, but most communist governments have been run as dictatorships.

Conquistadors Spanish soldiers who conquered areas of the Americas in the 16th and 17th centuries and who often stole gold and spread Christianity. Conquistador is Spanish for 'conqueror'.

Convict A person who has been sentenced to prison for a number of years.

Coup An illegal seizure of power by a group of people. The term is often used to mean a violent event in which the army or part of the army replaces the existing government with army officers.

Crusade A military campaign fought to protect Christian pilgrims or to extend lands for Christian rulers. A series of crusades were fought between the Christians of Europe and the Muslims during the 11th–15th centuries.

Czar From 1547–1917 the monarchs of Russia called themselves 'czar', which is the Russian for 'Caesar'. They did this to compare themselves to the emperors of ancient Rome. Czar is sometimes spelled 'tsar'.

Democracy A Greek word meaning 'people-power'. Generally, a democracy is a country in which all or most of the people have a say in how the government is run.

Depression A period of time during which there are economic problems and great poverty. Some depressions last only a few months, others may continue for years or even decades.

Dictatorship From ancient Rome meaning 'rule by speaking'. Generally a dictatorship is a country in which one person, or a small group of people, decide how the government is run.

Dynasty A family of rulers, kings or emperors. The history of some countries, such as China and Egypt, is divided into periods according to which dynasty was on the throne at the time.

Emperor Man who rules an empire. The word comes from ancient Latin and means 'victorious commander'.

Empire A territory in which members of one ethnic or national group rule over members of other ethnic or national groups.

Engine A machine that produces power to drive other machines. Engines may use one of several different sorts of fuel, such as coal, oil or gas.

Epic A long poem or book that tells the story of a hero or a group of heroes. An epic is usually based on fact, but has been much exaggerated to make it more exciting.

Etruscan A people who lived in central Italy about 2700 years ago. The Etruscans loved music and art, and were famous warriors. They were conquered by the Romans and lost their identity.

Explorer A person who travels to a place or area about which little is known by his own people, even if it is inhabited. Most explorers draw maps and write accounts of where they have been and what they have seen.

Felucca A boat used on the River Nile. It has a single triangular sail and a long, narrow hull.

Fertile Crescent An area of land reaching from Egypt, through the Middle East and along the valleys of the Indus and Euphrates rivers to the Persian Gulf. The people who lived in this area were the first in the world to learn how to grow crops and raise livestock.

Franks A tribe of Germanic people who invaded the Roman province of Gaul around the year AD 500. They took over the land and named it after themselves – France.

Fundamentalism A belief that one form of a religion is absolutely correct and that all other religions, or even forms of the same religion, are not only wrong but evil. Many fundamentalists attempt peacefully to convert others to their belief, but a few resort to violence or terrorism.

Gladiator A man in the ancient Roman Empire who was trained to fight wild animals or other gladiators to the death, in order to entertain a crowd of spectators.

Guerrilla This Spanish word means 'little war' and describes a military campaign during which no major battles take place. Instead the combatants attack each other's supply lines, communications and other small targets.

Guillotine This famous machine was designed to drop a heavy, sharp blade on to the neck of a condemned person. The blade sliced off the head instantly, so this was considered a painless and humane way to kill somebody. It was used to kill thousands of people during the French Revolution.

Hippodrome A horse race-course surrounded by banks of seating. The word comes from ancient Greek and means 'horse area'.

Holy Roman Empire An empire covering much of modern Germany and parts of Austria, Poland and nearby countries. The empire was usually weak as the nobles did not always do as the emperor instructed.

Inca A powerful people who lived in the Andes. The Inca Empire was conquered by the Spanish in the 16th century.

Indulgences Pieces of paper sold by the Catholic Church during the Middle Ages. The Church claimed that the indulgence cleansed the soul of the person to whom they were sold and allowed them to enter Heaven.

Industrial Revolution The dramatic change in the way industry was organized between 1700 and today. The Industrial Revolution saw the development of mass production using fewer workers to operate machines in factories, increasing productivity.

Knight In medieval Europe, a man who held land from a king or noble and, instead of paying rent, agreed to fight in an army.

Latin America Parts of the Americas where the inhabitants speak languages descended from Latin, mostly Spanish or Portuguese. Area covers most of South and Central America.

Legend A story that is passed on from generation to generation. Legends claim to be historical accounts of real events, but are often changed and confused as time passes.

Legion A unit in the army of ancient Rome. Each legion contained about 5000 infantry and 200 cavalry, plus officers and engineers. Only citizens of Rome could join a legion.

Manchu A people who live in the province of Manchuria in northeastern China. The Manchu ruled all China from 1644–1912.

Maori The people who lived in New Zealand before it was discovered by Europeans. The Maori were divided into many different tribes. Maori still live in New Zealand today.

Minoan The people who lived in Crete more than 3000 years ago are known as Minoans after their legendary king, Minos. They were probably a group of Greeks. Their civilization ended around 1300 BC, perhaps after a volcanic eruption.

Missionary A person who seeks to convert other people to the religion in which he believes. Missionaries often travel to remote parts of the world to look for converts.

Mogul A people who ruled most of India from the 16th–19th centuries. The Moguls were Muslims, while most of the people they ruled were Hindus.

Monastery A religious institution in which monks live, dedicated to a life of prayer and learning. During the Middle Ages in Europe some monasteries owned vast estates and much wealth, and some monks led lives of scandal and luxury.

Mongol A tribe of nomadic horsemen who lived in what is now Mongolia and northern China. In the 13th century the Mongols were united with other nomads and set out to conquer surrounding lands.

Nazi A shortened name of the German 'National Socialist Workers Party', led by Adolf Hitler from 1921–1945. The Nazi Party wanted to restore the power of Germany by reforming society, building up its military and invading neighbouring countries.

Nomadic People who do not live in any one place, but who move from place to place. Some nomads follow a route each year between different places, but other simply wander wherever they think they should go.

Normans The Normans lived in what is now Normandy, northern France, in the 10th–13th centuries. They were descended from Viking settlers who arrived in the 9th century.

Olmecs The Olmec civilization prospered between c.1200–400 BC. The most important centre for Olmec culture was on the Mexican Gulf coast. The Olmec lived in small thatched houses near rivers, fishing in the rivers and farming the lands made fertile by the river floods.

Ottoman The dynasty that ruled the Turkish people until the early 20th century. During the 15th and 16th centuries the Ottomans built up a powerful empire that covered much of southeastern Europe, North Africa and the Middle East.

Peacekeeper A military force that is used to keep the peace between two other warring sides. Peacekeepers usually supervise agreements and may occupy disputed territory to stop either side gaining an advantage.

Philosopher A person who thinks about the meaning of life and ultimate reality. The word is Greek for 'lover of knowledge' and the first philosophers lived in ancient Greece.

Picts People who lived in what is now northern Scotland before around AD 900. The Picts were famous as horsemen. The word means 'painted man' and they got this name as they tattooed their skins. The Picts joined with the Scots to form Scotland before AD 900.

Pilgrimage A religious journey undertaken to reach a holy place or to meet a holy person.

Pirate A person who steals on the high seas. Often large numbers of pirates would use ships to attack other ships or coastal towns.

Pope The head of the Roman Catholic church and the bishop of Rome is known as the Pope. The first bishop of Rome was St Peter, appointed by Jesus Christ to lead the Christian Church. The popes claim that this makes them the most important of all the bishops.

Protestant A Christian who belongs to one of the various churches that were founded when their members protested against the corruption of the Catholic Church in the 16th century.

Quetzalcoatl The chief ancestral god of the Aztecs. The Aztecs believed that Quetzalcoatl would one day return to rule them with wisdom and justice.

Raj The period of time when the British ruled most of India. The word is sometimes used to mean the system of government used by the British in India.

Rebellion When a small group of people rise up against their rulers in protest against a specific problem or worry.

Redcoat British soldiers fighting between 1650 and 1890 were often called redcoats because they wore coats or jackets made of bright red woollen cloth.

Reformation A religious movement in western Europe which began in 1517 and lasted about 100 years. During this time many people left the Catholic church to join 'reformed' churches which opposed what they saw as the corruption of the Catholic Church.

Renaissance A period of European history between about 1350 and 1550 when scholars rediscovered ancient Greece and Rome writings as well as developing new ideas and artistic styles.

Republic A country which is governed without a king or emperor. Some republics are democracies, which are run by their people, while others are run by a small group of people. The word comes from ancient Latin and means 'in the name of the people'.

Revolution A rebellion that spreads to include a significant number of the people in a country and is usually directed against a wide range of problems and complaints. A revolution may overthrow the entire system of government in a country.

Samurai Japanese warriors who trained continually to become highly skilled with both weapons and religion. The samurai were officially abolished in the 19th century.

Scots A tribe of people from northern Ireland who settled in what is now southwest Scotland around the year AD 400. The king of the Scots later inherited the kingdom of the Picts to create Scotland as it is today.

Serfdom A form of social status, close to slavery. Serfs were forced to farm a particular piece of land for a landlord. However, they did have rights under the law and there was a system to protect them from cruelty, unlike slaves.

Shogun This Japanese word means 'military commander'. It is usually used to refer to the military dictators who ruled Japan on behalf of the Emperor between the 12th and 19th centuries.

Slave A person who is owned by another person. Usually slaves have no human rights at all, they are forced to work without pay and may be punished or even killed by their owner. Slavery is illegal in most countries today.

Submarine A ship able to move below the water as well as on the surface. Some submarines are used by scientists to study sealife, but most are naval ships designed to sink other ships or to launch missiles.

Terrorist A fighter who seeks to inspire terror in his enemies. In recent years the word has come to mean a fighter who attacks and kills civilians rather than enemy soldiers.

Testudo A formation used by the Roman Army in which the shield of each man overlapped that of the next man, providing defence against arrows and spears. The word means 'tortoise'.

Tlatoani The Aztec name for their ruler.

Toltecs Mesoamerican people who lived in and around Tula, a city in central Mexico. Their civilization existed from around AD 950 to AD 1150.

Tournament A contest organized in medieval Europe so that knights could compete in events that tested their skills with weapons.

Vikings The people who lived in Scandinavia about a thousand years ago. The Vikings were fearless warriors who attacked many countries in western Europe. They were also highly skilled traders and seamen who travelled vast distances in their ships. The Vikings were the first Europeans known to have reached the Americas.

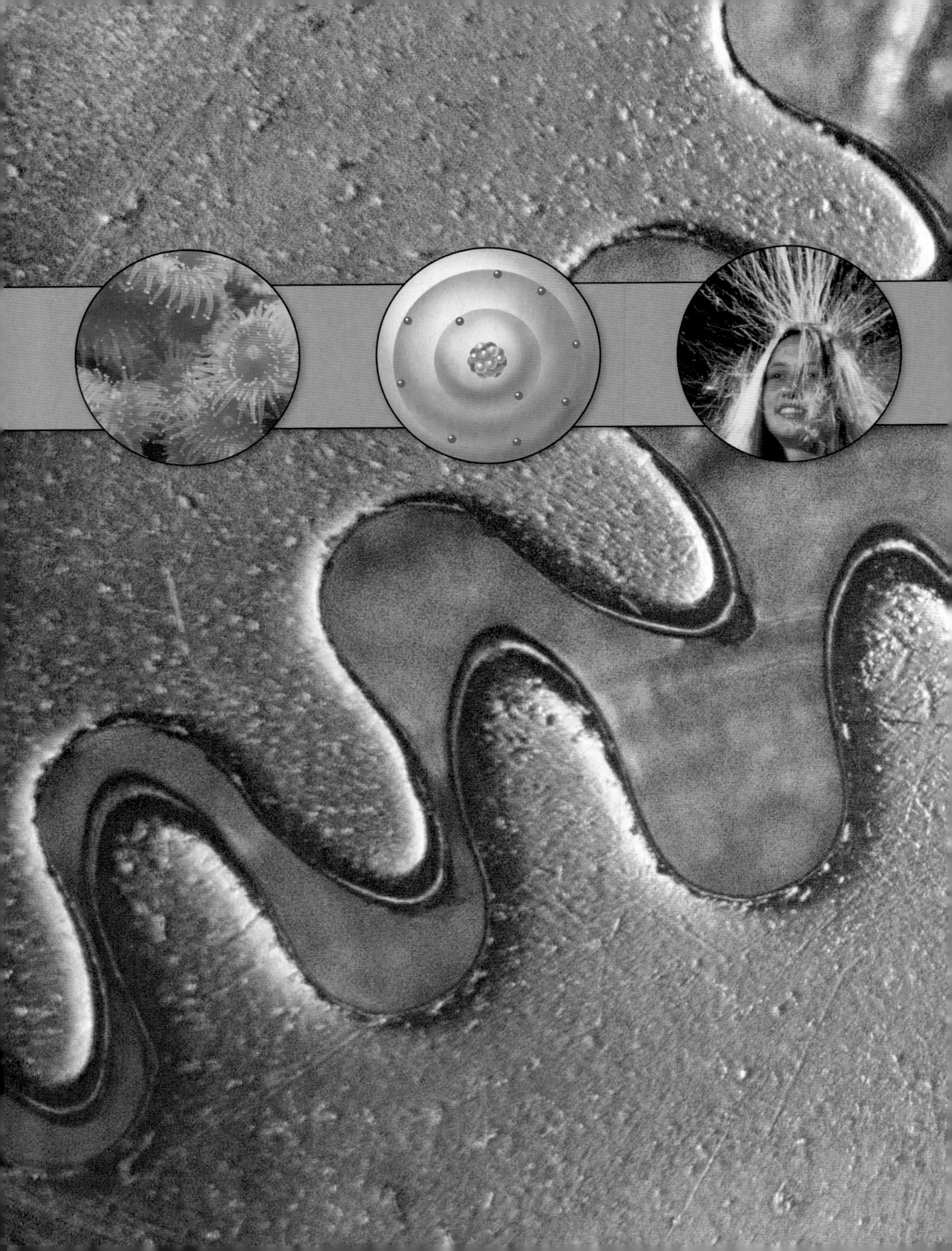

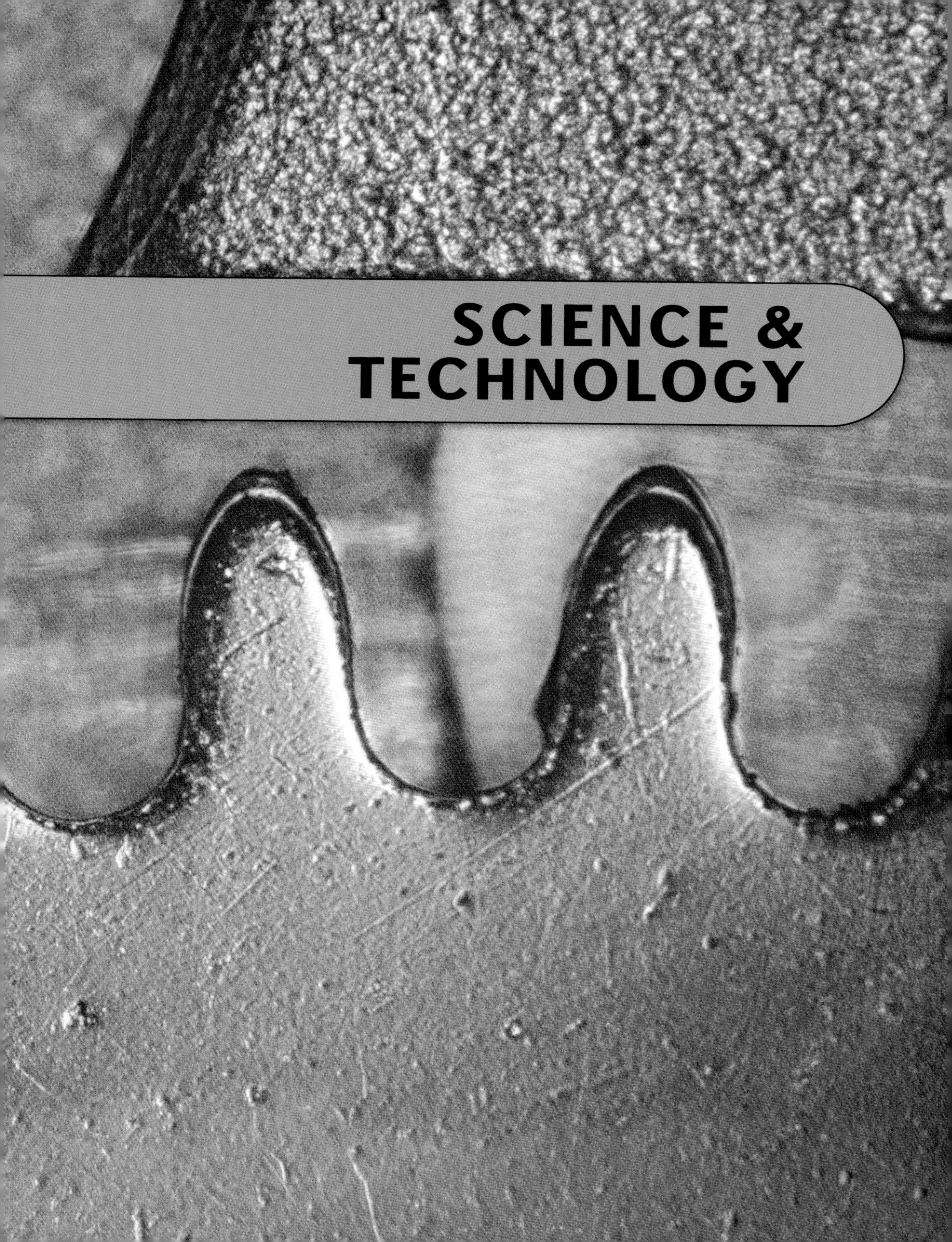

SCIENCE & TECHNOLOGY

Atoms and Molecules

Atoms are the tiny bits, or particles, that build together to make every known substance. A substance made of only one type of atom is called a chemical element. A molecule is two or more atoms bonded together.

❍ You could fit two billion atoms on the full stop after this sentence.

❍ Atoms are mostly empty space, dotted with a few even tinier particles called subatomic particles.

❍ In the centre of each atom is a dense core, or nucleus, made from two kinds of particle: protons and neutrons. Protons have a positive electrical charge, and neutrons none.

❍ Around the nucleus orbit negatively-charged particles called electrons.

❍ The number of protons, neutrons and electrons varies from element to element.

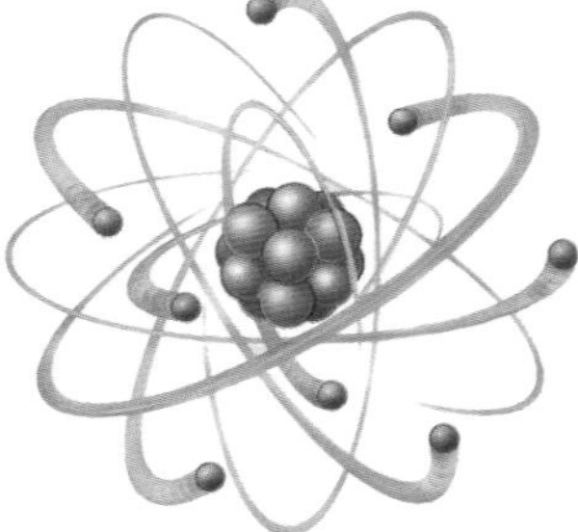

▲ The protons and neutrons in the nucleus of an atom are held together by a powerful force. When the nucleus is split, as happens in a nuclear reactor, huge amounts of energy are released.

❍ Atoms and molecules are held together by chemical bonds.

❍ The shape of a molecule depends on the arrangement of bonds that hold its atoms together.

▼ Inside an atom, electrons (blue) whiz around a dense nucleus of protons (red) and neutrons (grey). There is an equal number of negatively charged electrons and positively charged protons, so the atom has no overall charge.

Atom factfile

A typical atom measures about 0.2 to 0.3 nanometres across.

A nanometre is an incredibly small unit – one billionth of a metre. So 10 million atoms in a row would stretch just 2 mm!

The nucleus at the centre of an atom is tiny compared to the size of the atom as a whole.

If the whole atom were the size of a massive sports stadium, the outermost electrons would be whizzing around the farthest seats, and the nucleus would be the size of a human thumb in the middle.

In a solid substance, the atoms are about 0.3 nanometres apart, so their outermost electrons almost touch.

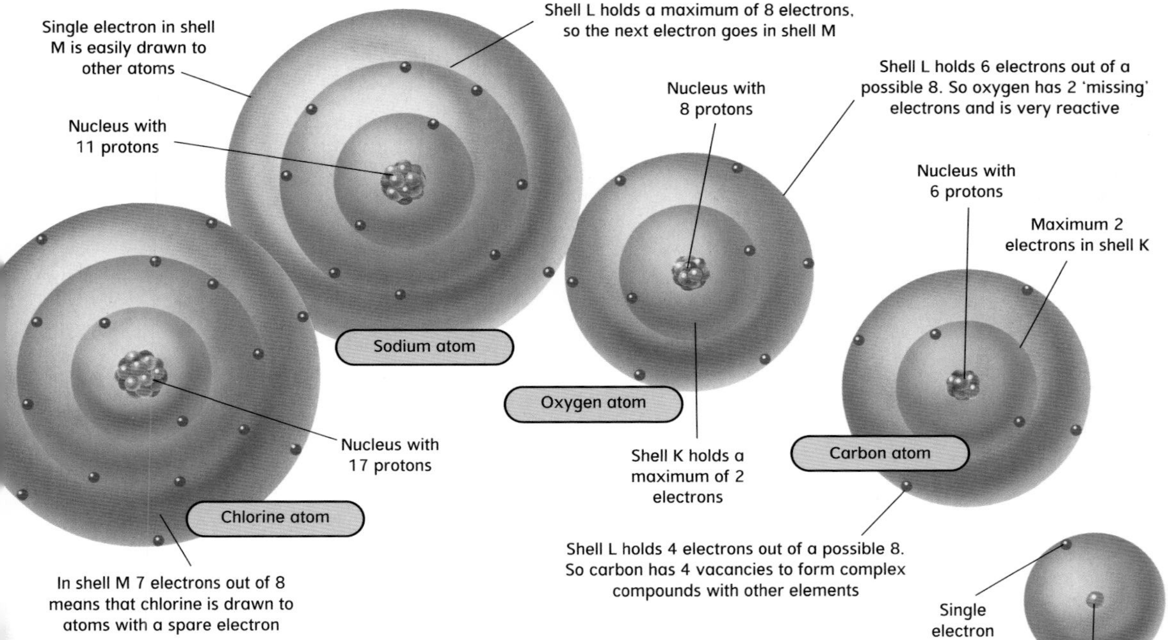

Single electron in shell M is easily drawn to other atoms

Shell L holds a maximum of 8 electrons, so the next electron goes in shell M

Nucleus with 11 protons

Sodium atom

Nucleus with 17 protons

Chlorine atom

In shell M 7 electrons out of 8 means that chlorine is drawn to atoms with a spare electron

Nucleus with 8 protons

Shell L holds 6 electrons out of a possible 8. So oxygen has 2 'missing' electrons and is very reactive

Oxygen atom

Shell K holds a maximum of 2 electrons

Nucleus with 6 protons

Maximum 2 electrons in shell K

Carbon atom

Shell L holds 4 electrons out of a possible 8. So carbon has 4 vacancies to form complex compounds with other elements

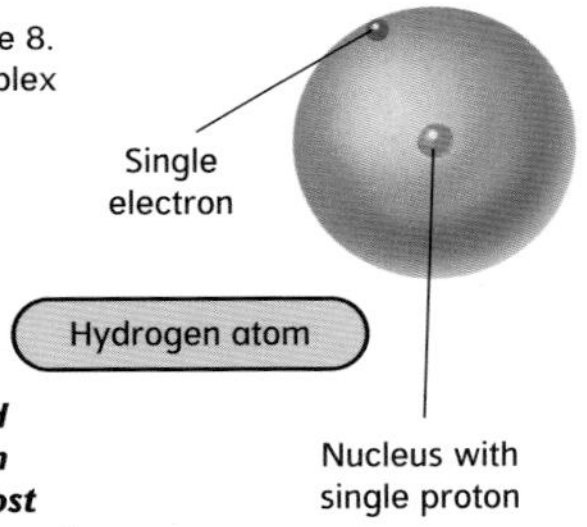

Single electron

Hydrogen atom

Nucleus with single proton

The electrons that orbit the nucleus of an atom are arranged in a series of layers called shells. Each shell can hold a maximum number of electrons. The innermost K shell can hold two electrons, the next L shell can hold eight, as can the M shell. The number of electrons in the outermost shell determines the chemical character of the element.

Amazing

Your body is made up of trillions of atoms. There is an abundance of oxygen, carbon, hydrogen and nitrogen, but there are also atoms of many other elements, including iron, tin, silver and even gold!

- Chemical formulas use numbers and symbols to show the atoms in a molecule.
- The formula for ammonia, a choking gas, is NH_3, because an ammonia molecule is made from one nitrogen (N) atom and three hydrogen atoms (H).
- Compounds only exist as molecules. If the atoms in a compound's molecules were separated, it would no longer be a compound, just atoms.

Simple hydrogen

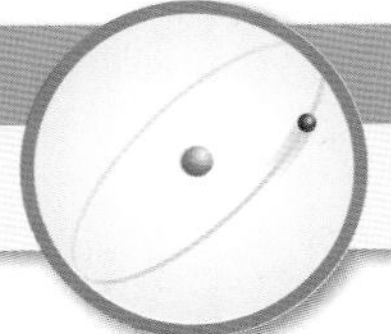

The simplest and lightest atom of all is hydrogen. It has just one proton as the nucleus and one electron going around it.

Molecules

Atoms usually bond together in groups to form combinations called molecules. For example, a carbon dioxide molecule (a waste product when we breathe out) consists of one carbon atom linked to two oxygen atoms. Carbon dioxide has the chemical formula CO_2. When carbon joins with only one oxygen atom, it forms carbon monoxide, with the formula CO.

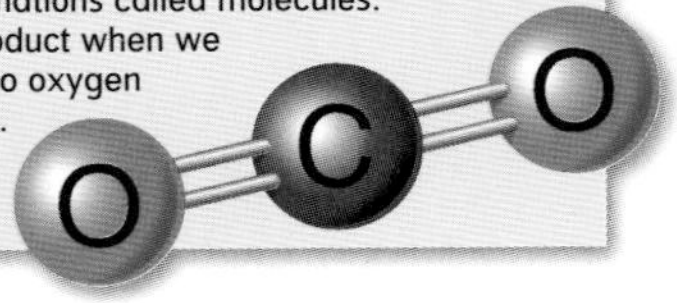

O C O

Solids, Liquids and Gases

Nearly every substance in the Universe is either a solid, a liquid or a gas. These are known as states of matter. Most substances can exist in all three states.

❍ There is a fourth, less common state of matter called plasma, which is a bit like a gas but full of charged particles called electrons and ions.

❍ Solids have strength and a definite shape. The molecules in a solid are firmly bonded together and locked into in a rigid framework.

Absolute zero

The lowest possible temperature is –273.15°C, known as absolute zero, at which atoms and molecules stop moving altogether. Scientists have come very close to achieving absolute zero in laboratories – within a millionth of a degree. There is no upper limit to temperature.

❍ In a solid the molecules vibrate on the spot. The hotter the solid becomes, the more they vibrate. If it gets hot enough, the molecules vibrate so much that the framework breaks down and the solid melts and becomes a liquid.

❍ A liquid has a fixed volume and flows and takes up the shape of any solid container into which it is poured.

❍ A liquid flows because its molecules are less firmly bonded than those of a solid. The molecules in a liquid are not locked together, and can slide over each other without breaking away.

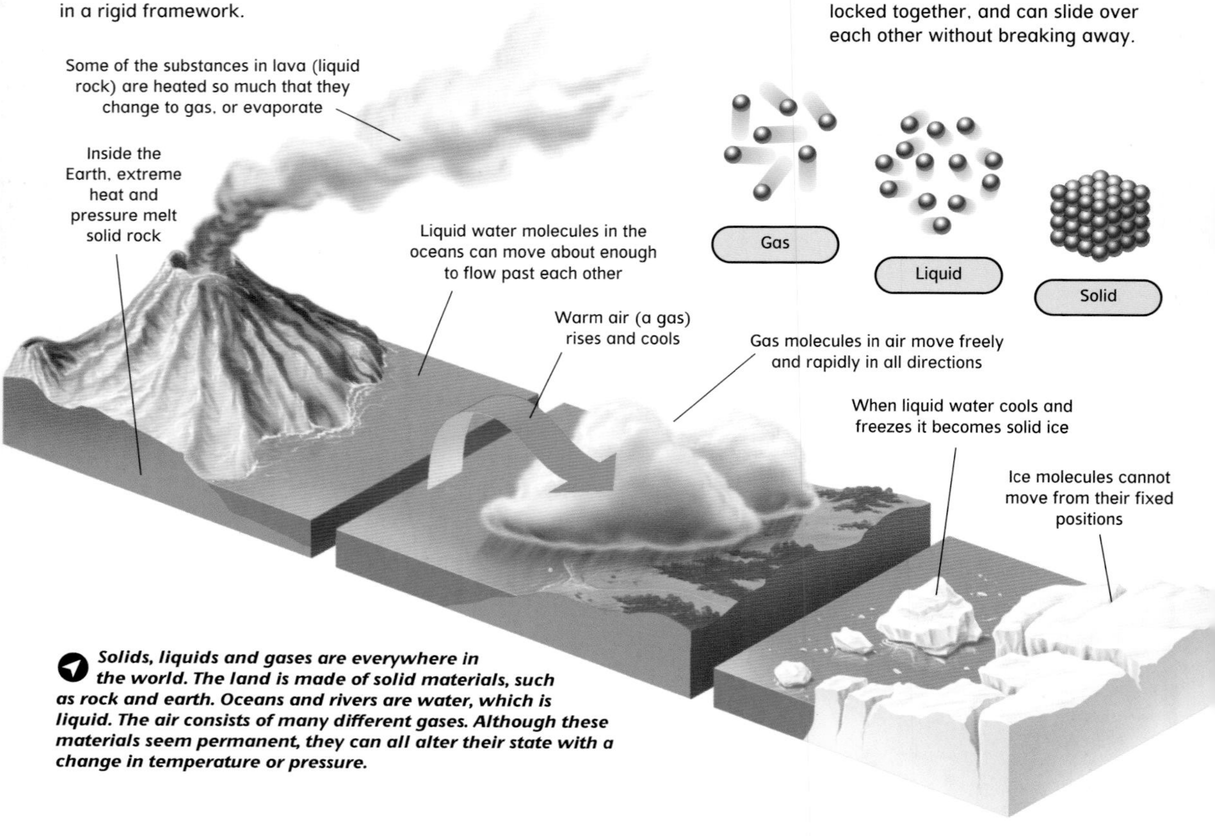

Solids, liquids and gases are everywhere in the world. The land is made of solid materials, such as rock and earth. Oceans and rivers are water, which is liquid. The air consists of many different gases. Although these materials seem permanent, they can all alter their state with a change in temperature or pressure.

Amazing

Reducing the pressure on a liquid lowers its boiling point. On high mountains the air pressure is much less than at sea level, and the boiling point of water can be as low as 70°C.

Water, like all liquids, takes the shape of whatever it is poured or flows into.

❍ A gas, such as air, does not have any shape or fixed volume. Its molecules move too quickly for any bonds to hold them together, and the gas will spread out to fill any container it is put into.

❍ When a gas cools, its molecules slow down until bonds form between them to create drops of liquid. This process is called condensation.

❍ A substance can change state by gaining or losing energy.

Liquid elements

Only two elements are liquid at room temperature:

Mercury (Hg) Bromine (Br)

Four others are liquid at just above room temperature:

Gallium (Ga) Caesium (Cs)
Francium (Fr) Rubidium (Rb)

❍ The melting point of tungsten metal is 3410°C. Its boiling point is 5900°C – about as hot as the surface of the Sun.

❍ The boiling point of the gas helium is –268.9°C, the lowest of any element.

The particles in solid chocolate gain energy as they are heated. They break away from each other as the solid melts.

Melting and boiling points

The temperature at which a substance melts from a solid to a liquid is called its melting point. The highest temperature a liquid can reach before turning to a gas is called its boiling point. Each substance has its own melting and boiling point. Water melts at 0°C and boils at 100°C. When a gas cools down enough, it condenses to a liquid, such as when steam turns to water. When a liquid cools down enough, it turns solid or freezes, such as when water turns to ice.

The Periodic Table

Elements are the simplest possible substances. There are over 100 elements, each of which is composed of its own unique type of atom. The Periodic Table is a chart that shows the similarities and differences between elements.

❍ The Periodic Table arranges all the elements in order of their atomic number – the number of protons (positively charged articles) in their atoms – starting with hydrogen at 1.

❍ Atoms usually contain the same number of electrons (negatively charged particles) as protons. So the atomic number also indicates the number of electrons in the atom.

❍ The vertical columns in the periodic table are called groups. The horizontal rows are called periods.

Amazing

In the 5th century BC Empedocles, a Greek philosopher, proposed that all matter was made from four elements – air, fire, water and earth. Not until the 17th century was the true nature of elements realized.

❍ Each group is made up of elements with the same number of electrons in the outer shell of their atoms, so they all behave in a similar way chemically.

❍ Each period begins with an alkali metal (which has one electron in its outer shell) on the left and ends with a noble gas (which has eight electrons in its outer shell) on the right.

Increasing electrons

The number of electrons in the atom's outer shell goes up one by one across each period.

Chemical symbol — Atomic number indicating number of protons in atom's nucleus

6 C Carbon 12.01

7 N Nitrogen 14.01

Atomic weight — Name of element

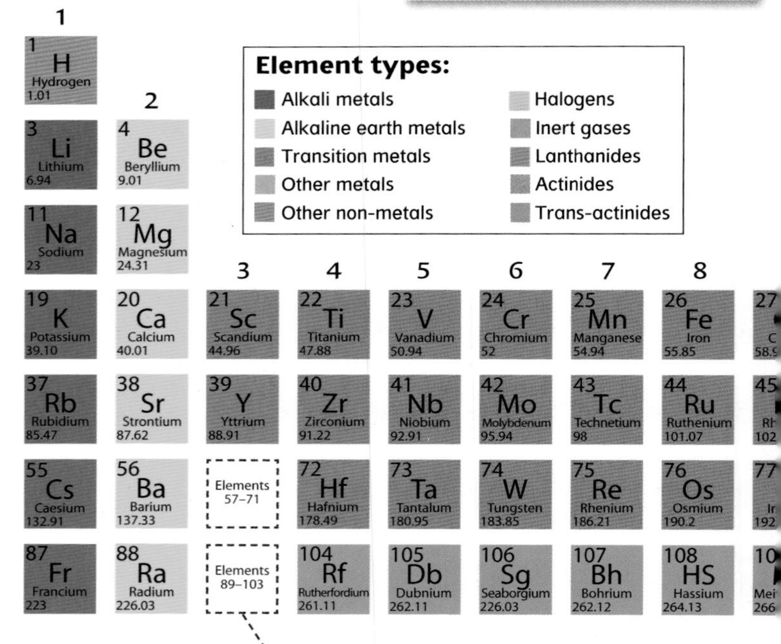

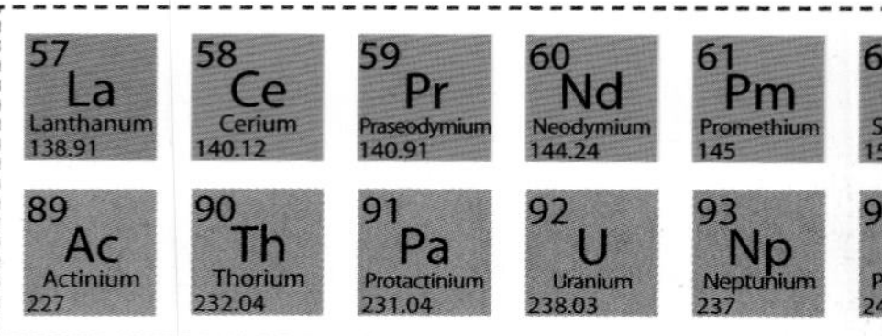

➤ ***As you move along a horizontal row in the Periodic Table the atomic weight of the elements increases. The lightest elements are upper left, the heaviest ones are lower right. The different colours represent elements with similar properties. Most of the elements are metals.***

❍ Scientists give each element a symbol. This is usually the first letter of its name, such as O for oxygen or C for carbon. If two or more elements begin with the same letter, a second small letter may be added. So hydrogen is H, and helium is He.

❍ Only a few elements, such as gold, copper and silver, can be found naturally in their pure state.

Noble gases

The elements in Group 18 (far right) of the periodic table are a very special group. They are extremely stable and unreactive. They are called the noble gases, because they stay 'noble' (apart from) other chemicals and rarely form compounds. Noble gases such as argon and krypton are used in lightbulbs, because they are unreactive and will not burn out the filament – the thin, coiled wire inside the bulb. Neon is used to make neon lights for the same reason, because it can glow brightly without reacting.

11	12	13	14	15	16	17	18
							2 He Helium 4
		5 B Boron 10.81	6 C Carbon 12.01	7 N Nitrogen 14.01	8 O Oxygen 16	9 F Fluorine 18.998	10 Ne Neon 20.12
		13 Al Aluminium 27	14 Si Silicon 28.1	15 P Phosphorus 31	16 S Sulphur 32.1	17 Cl Chlorine 35.45	18 Ar Argon 39.95
29 Cu Copper 63.55	30 Zn Zinc 65.39	31 Ga Gallium 69.72	32 Ge Germanium 72.61	33 As Arsenic 74.92	34 Se Selenium 78.96	35 Br Bromine 79.9	36 Kr Krypton 83.8
47 Ag Silver 107.87	48 Cd Cadmium 112.41	49 In Indium 114.82	50 Sn Tin 118.71	51 Sb Antimony 121.75	52 Te Tellurium 127.6	53 I Iodine 126.9	54 Xe Xenon 131.29
79 Au Gold 196.97	80 Hg Mercury 200.59	81 Ti Thallium 204.38	82 Pb Lead 207.2	83 Bi Bismuth 208.98	84 Po Polonium 209	85 At Astatine 210	86 Rn Radon 222
111 Rg Roentgenium 272	112 Cp Copernicum 277	113 Nh Nihonium 286	114 Fl Flerovium 289	115 Mc Moscovium 290	116 Lv Livermorium 293	117 Ts Tennessine 294	118 Og Oganesson 294

64 Gd Gadolinium 157.25	65 Tb Terbium 158.93	66 Dy Dysprosium 162.5	67 Ho Holmium 164.93	68 Er Erbium 167.26	69 Tm Thulium 168.93	70 Yb Ytterbium 173.05	71 Lu Lutetium 174.97
96 Cm Curium 247	97 Bk Berkelium 247	98 Cf Californium 251	99 Es Einsteinium 252	100 Fm Fermium 257	101 Md Mendelevium 258	102 No Nobelium 259	103 Lr Lawrencium 262

❍ Most substances are made of two or more elements combined together chemically in a compound.

❍ Although there only about 100 elements, they can combine in so many different ways that they produce many millions of compounds.

❍ The same combination of elements, such as carbon and hydrogen, can often react together to form a range of different compounds.

❍ About 20 of the most recently identified elements were created artificially by scientists. These elements do not occur naturally.

❍ Artificially created elements are often very unstable and last for only a fraction of a second before they break down.

❍ New elements get temporary names from their atomic number. So the new element with atomic number 116 was first called ununhexium. *Un* is the latin word for one; *hex* is latin for six. In 2012 it was given the name Livermorium.

❍ Scientists have made three atoms of element 118, which may be a solid.

Chemicals and Materials

Compounds are substances formed when the atoms of two or more elements join together. The properties of a compound are usually very different from those of the elements it contains.

❍ Compounds are different from mixtures. In a mixture, elements are combined loosely, but in a compound they are joined together chemically, and can only be separated by chemical reaction.

❍ Every molecule of a compound contains exactly the same combination of atoms.

❍ A compound's scientific name usually gives a clue to its components. Common salt, for example, is sodium chloride, indicating that it is made up of the elements sodium and chlorine.

The substance called acetone, also known as propanone, is commonly used in nail varnish remover. Each molecule of acetone has three carbon atoms (orange), one oxygen (pink) and six hydrogen (light green). It is written as the formula CH_3COCH_3.

Metals

Three out of four elements are metals. Most metals are shiny, hard substances that ring when you hit them. They are mostly tough, yet can often be easily shaped – either by hammering or by melting into moulds. This makes metals good for making everything from spoons to space rockets. Metals are rarely pure. Most occur naturally in the ground in chemical compounds called ores, and the metal must be extracted by heating and other processes. Even then, metals usually contain some impurities. Sometimes impurities are added to create an 'alloy', which gives the metal a particular quality. Carbon is added to iron to make an incredibly tough alloy called steel.

❍ The chemical formula of a compound summarizes which atoms its molecules are made of. The chemical formula for water is H_2O, because each water molecule has two hydrogen (H) atoms and one oxygen (O) atom.

❍ Natural materials are found around us, as part of nature, rather than being artificial or manufactured.

Metals are excellent conductors of heat, which is why a hot drink soon warms a metal spoon.

❍ Wood is an abundant natural material that is important in making furniture and utensils, as well as structures such as houses and bridges.

❍ Various kinds of rock and stone are also widely used, especially in the construction of larger buildings.

Amazing

One gram of gold can be drawn out into a thin wire 2.4 km long.

❍ Natural fibres, such as cotton, are woven into fabrics for clothes, curtains and other items.

❍ Glass is among the most useful of all materials. Various types of glass are made by heating the natural substances of sand (silica), limestone and soda-ash with other ingredients.

❍ Bulletproof vests are woven from an immensely strong material called Kevlar, which can withstand the impact of bullets. Kevlar threads are stronger than steel, but very light.

❍ Composites are combinations of different materials. A composite combines the best features of each of its constituent materials.

Common compound

Citric acid, found in lemon juice, is a compound of hydrogen, oxygen and carbon mixed with water.

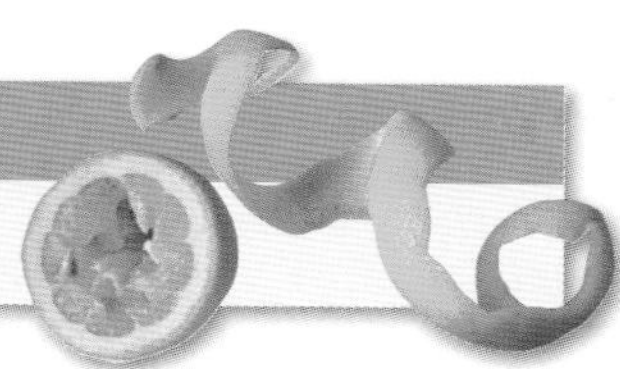

When atoms join by covalent bonds, they share pairs of electrons. In this type of bonding an atom, with room in its outermost shell for an extra electron, gains such an electron by 'sharing' it with another atom. Each atom gains a shared electron which bonds it to the other atom.

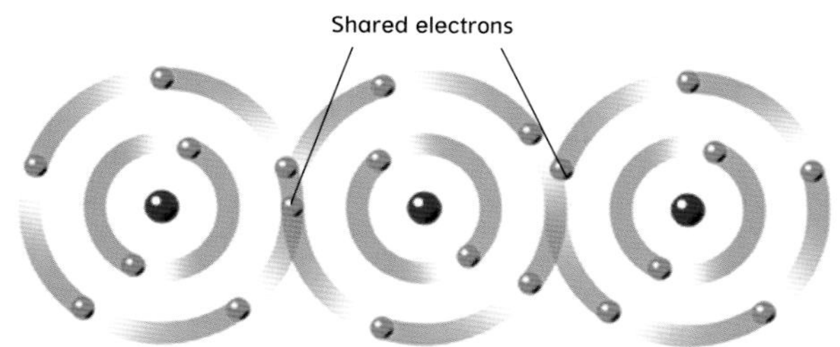

Ionic bonding involves the movement of one or a few electrons in the outermost shell. The electron jumps across to another atom that has a space in its outermost shell. The atom that has lost the negative electron now has a positive charge; the one that gains has a negative charge. When atoms have charges, they are called ions. Ions of different charges, positive and negative, attract and bond to each other.

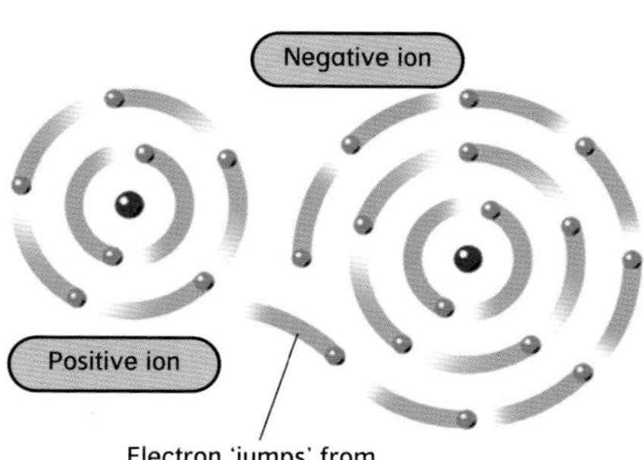

Chemical names for everyday items

Common name	Chemical name	Common name	Chemical name
Antifreeze	Ethylene glycol	**Laughing gas**	Nitrous oxide
Asbestos	Magnesium silicate	**Lime**	Calcium oxide
Aspirin	Acetylsalicyclic acid	**Mothballs**	Naphthalene
Baking powder	Sodium bicarbonate	**Plaster of Paris**	Calcium sulphate
Bleach	Sodium hypochlorite	**PVC**	Polyvinyl chloride
Carbolic acid	Phenol	**Rust**	Iron oxide
Caustic soda	Sodium hydroxide	**Salt**	Sodium chloride
Chalk	Calcium carbonate	**Saltpetre**	Potassium nitrate
Chloroform	Trichloromethane	**Sand**	Silicon dioxide
DDT	Dichlorodiphenyltrichloroethane	**Talcum powder**	Magnesium silicate hydroxide
Dry ice	Solid carbon dioxide	**TNT**	Trinitrotoluene
Epsom salts	Magnesium sulphate	**Vinegar**	Acetic acid
Fool's gold	Iron pyrites	**Vitamin C**	Ascorbic acid
Heavy water	Deuterium oxide	**Washing soda**	Sodium carbonate

Carbon Chemicals

Carbon is a very special element. The hardest known substance, diamond, is a form of carbon, as is coal and the graphite ('lead') in pencils. Carbon forms compounds easily because of its atomic structure.

❍ Compounds are either organic (they contain carbon atoms) or inorganic.

❍ There are many millions of known carbon compounds.

❍ Pure carbon occurs in four natural forms: diamond, graphite, soot and charcoal. There is also a special manufactured form called fullerene. Graphite can be stretched out into long fibres called carbon fibres.

❍ Carbon fibre has four times more tensile strength than steel. It can be mixed with plastic resins to make strong, light composite materials.

Amazing

Scientists have suggested that some planets orbiting distant suns could be made largely of carbon, with atmospheres rich in carbon dioxide, liquid hydrocarbon seas, graphite crusts and layers of diamond many kilometres thick.

❍ Fullerenes are molecules containing at least 20 carbon atoms linked together in a ball shape.

❍ Plastics are made from carbon compounds with small molecules (mainly consisting of carbon and hydrogen atoms) that link up to form long chains.

Oils are organic liquids that burn easily and do not dissolve in water. Crude oil, or petroleum, is made mainly of hydrocarbons. These are compounds containing only hydrogen and carbon atoms, and are by far the largest group of carbon compounds. Crude oil formed from underground and undersea sediments provides over half the world's energy needs and is extracted by oil rigs erected in the sea. The oil is broken down into simpler substances in an oil refinery.

❍ The small molecules are called monomers, and the long chains are called polymers. Different plastics are created using different monomers.

❍ The plastic polythene is made by making thousands of ethene monomer molecules link up into polymer chains. Ethene is derived from petroleum.

Diamonds are forever

Diamond, made of carbon atoms linked together in a rigid structure, is the hardest naturally occurring material.

Complex organic compounds are often made by mixing together two or more compounds so that a chemical reaction can take place. This can be done on a small scale in a laboratory.

❍ Plastic's durability makes it hard to dispose of, so scientists have developed types that can be degraded (broken down) by light or bacteria. However, the world still faces increasing problems with plastic waste.

All living things are based on carbon compounds. Over 90 per cent of all compounds are organic.

In some plastics, the chains are tangled together to make them strong yet flexible. These are ideal for making items such as parachutes, which need to be strong enough to support weight and yet flexible enough to glide in the air.

❍ Most carbon atoms have existed since the beginning of the Earth and, through a process called the carbon cycle, circulate continuously through animals, plants and the air.

❍ The leaves and stems of every plant are built largely from a natural material called cellulose. Like plastic, cellulose is a polymer – a long chain of carbon-based molecules. Plants put these chains together from sugar molecules called glucose, which they make with carbon dioxide from the air and water, using energy from the Sun.

Carbon chains and rings

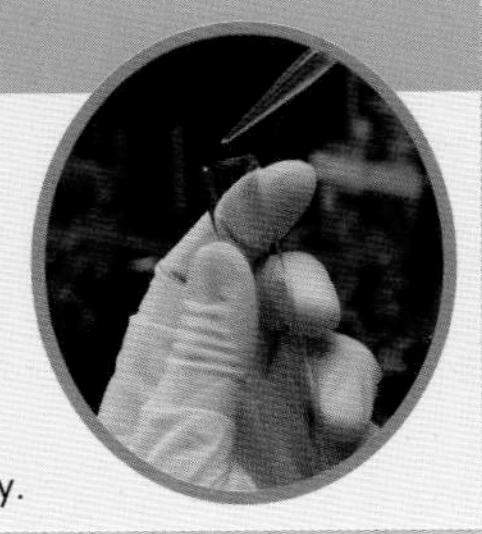

Carbon has an almost unique ability not only to form compounds with other elements, but also to join together with other carbon atoms as well to form complex chains and rings. Complex carbon chain and ring molecules are the basic chemicals that life itself depends on. For example, the proteins from which the body is built are all carbon compounds. There is such a huge variety of carbon compounds that there is an entire branch of chemistry, called organic chemistry, devoted to their study.

Electricity and Magnetism

Electricity is one of the most useful of all forms of energy. Electricity is closely linked with magnetism – the invisible force between magnetic materials. When electricity moves, magnetism is created. When magnets move, electricity is created.

Amazing

Static electricity was discovered in the 6th century BC by the ancient Greeks, who realized that amber (fossilized tree sap) will attract light objects when it is rubbed with wool or cloth.

❍ Electricity is the movement or flow of the tiny parts of atoms called electrons, which have an electric charge.

❍ Magnetism is the invisible force between materials such as iron and nickel. Magnetism attracts or repels.

❍ A magnetic field is the area around a magnet inside which its magnetic force can be detected.

The magnetic field around a bar magnet is invisible but these imaginary lines show its extent.

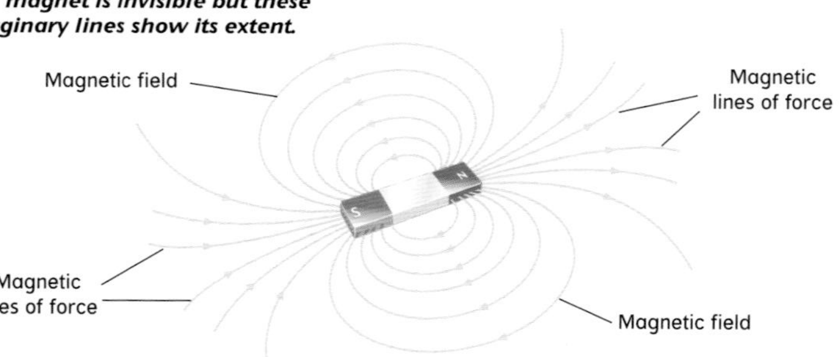

❍ A magnet has two poles: a north pole and a south pole.

❍ Like poles (e.g. two north poles) repel each other; unlike poles (e.g. a north pole and a south pole) attract each other.

❍ Electrons move easily through materials called conductors.

Electrons jump from atom to atom in conductor

Sheath or cover

❍ Metals are particularly good conductors – especially copper and gold, which are used for the wires and connectors in electric circuits.

❍ Electric current only flows if it has a pathway or circuit of conductors from its source and back again.

❍ Materials that are poor conductors of electricity are called insulators. Plastic and rubber are good insulators.

❍ Batteries change chemical energy into electrical energy. The links or bonds between atoms in chemical substances contain energy. As these break down in a chemical reaction, their energy passes to the electrons in the atoms and makes them move.

❍ DC is direct current electricity and AC is alternating current electricity. Direct current electricity flows steadily in the same direction. Alternating current electricity rapidly changes direction, flowing first one way and then the other.

An electromagnet can lift a car into the air by attracting the iron-based steel of the car's body.

❍ The Earth is a giant magnet. If a magnet is left to move freely, the Earth's magnetic field ensures that it always points with one end aimed at the North Pole and the other at the South Pole.

❍ When an electric current flows through a wire, it produces a magnetic field around the wire. The magnetic field is stronger when the wire is coiled around a piece of iron. This 'electric magnet' is called an electromagnet.

Electricity produced by generators in power stations travels as a current through power lines to our homes. Inside the power lines, millions of electrons jump between atoms in the conducting wires.

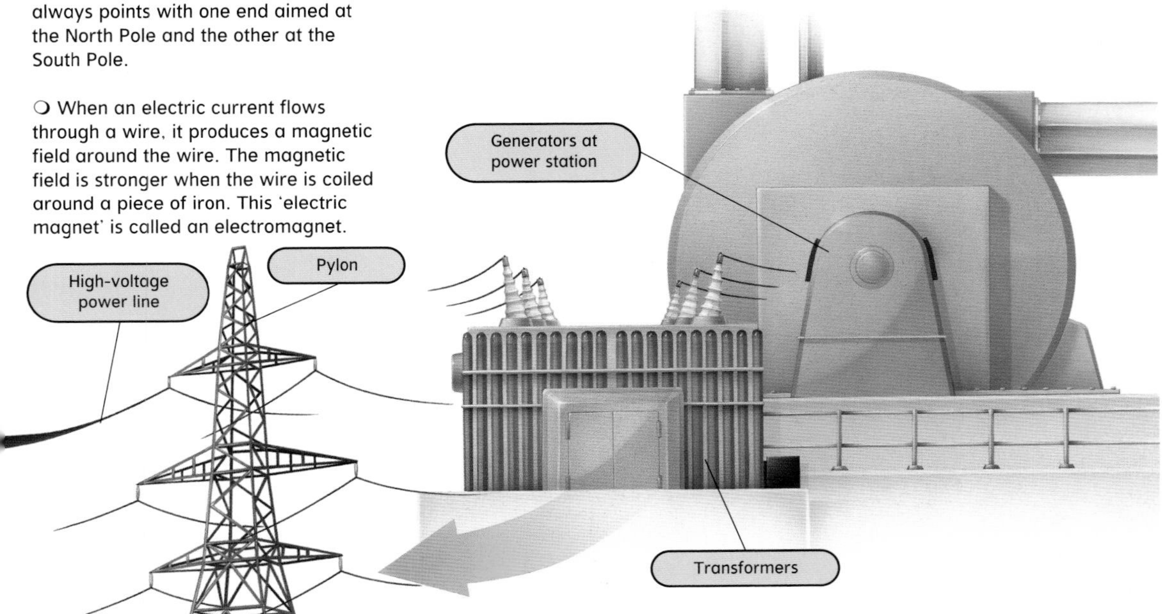

Natural electricity

Lightning is the sudden release of a giant charge of static electricity that builds up inside storm clouds.

Static electricity

Electrons are negatively charged particles. When two materials rub together, electrons may transfer from one material onto the other. The material that gains extra electrons becomes negatively charged, and the material that loses electrons becomes positively charged. This is called static electricity, because the charges on the materials do not move – they are static (stationary). Like charges repel each other, while unlike charges attract. Static electricity can cause your hair to stand up on end.

How long?

Using the same amount of electricity, these gadgets would run for the following times:

'Instant' hot-water shower	10–15 min
Electric heater (convector)	1 hr
Hair-dryer on maximum setting	1–1 hr 15 min
Washing machine	2 hr
Large freezer	3 hr
Standard television	3–5 hr
Electric blanket	6 hr
100-watt lightbulb	10 hr
Electric shaver	70 hr

Energy

It takes energy to make something happen. Energy is not just the light that comes from the Sun, or the heat that comes from a fire. In science, energy is the ability or capacity to do work, or to cause change.

❍ Energy comes in many different forms, from the chemical energy locked in sugar to the mechanical energy in a speeding train.

❍ Potential energy is energy stored up ready for action – as in a squeezed spring or a stretched piece of elastic.

❍ Kinetic energy is energy that something has because it is moving, such as a rolling ball or a falling stone.

❍ Food is a store of chemical energy, and when eaten can be used to power the movements of the human body.

When something is lifted, it stores the energy that is used to lift it as potential energy.

Amazing

A supernova explosion – the violent death of a massive star – produces more energy in its first 10 seconds than the Sun will have done during its entire 10 billion year lifetime.

❍ Energy transfer is the movement of energy from one place to another, such as heat rising above a fire or a ball being thrown.

❍ Energy conversion is when energy changes from one form to another, for example when wind turbines generate electric power.

❍ Other forms of energy include heat, electricity, sound and electromagnetic radiation.

❍ Light is a type of electromagnetic radiation, as are microwaves, radio waves, X-rays, ultraviolet, infrared and gamma rays.

Wind turbines convert the kinetic energy of moving air into electricity. The wind obtains its energy in the form of heat from the Sun. In fact nearly all the energy we use on Earth, in one form or another, comes from the Sun. Wind turbines generate their energy in a sustainable way, without using up valuable fuel resources.

Measuring energy

The main unit for measuring both energy and work is the joule (J).

An older unit was the calorie, which was used to measure heat energy and the chemical energy contained in foods.

One calorie equals 4.2 joules, and one kilocalorie or kcal (also written as 'Calorie' with a capital 'C') equals 4200 joules (4.2 kJ).

A 20-watt lightbulb requires 20 joules of electrical energy per second.

A typical lightbulb left on for 24 hours takes about 1.5 million joules.

A split-second bolt of lightning releases 5000 million joules.

A large earthquake releases about 5 billion joules in just a few seconds.

For a split second, as runners move away from the starting blocks, they accelerate faster than a sports car. They convert chemical energy into muscle power to produce kinetic energy. At the end of a race, runners quickly lose their kinetic energy and come to a halt.

❍ An average person needs 5 million to 10 million joules of energy from food each day to stay active and healthy.

❍ Energy is more concentrated in some foods than others. For example, 30 g of butter gives the same amount of energy as 500 g of peas.

❍ Nuclear energy is created in reactors inside nuclear power stations, nuclear-powered submarines, some spacecraft, and also in nuclear explosions. It is called nuclear energy because it comes from the nucleus of an atom.

❍ Walking needs about five times as much energy as sitting still. Running needs about seven times more energy.

❍ Energy can never be created or destroyed – it can only be changed from one form to another. So all the energy in the Universe has always existed, no matter what form it is in now.

Spacecraft energy

About 100 billion joules of energy is needed to launch a spacecraft.

Power stations

Power stations are giant energy converters – they convert chemical or nuclear energy in a fuel into heat. The heat generated by power stations is transferred to water, changing it into steam. The kinetic energy of the steam makes a turbine spin. The rotational (spinning) energy of the turbine drives a generator, which converts the rotational energy into electrical energy for us all to use. The steam escapes from large concrete chimneys.

Force and Motion

Forces are pushes and pulls. They change the speed, direction or shape of things. Some forces act only when things touch each other, such as kicking a football. Other forces, including gravity and magnetism, act at a distance.

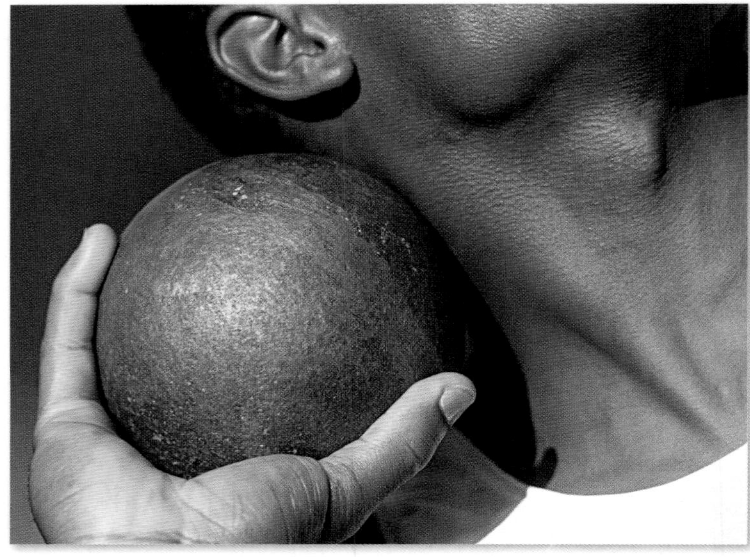

An object's mass makes it resist a force that tries to change its state of motion. This resistance is known as inertia. The more mass an object has, the greater is its inertia. The iron shot (ball) that athletes throw when they put the shot has a large mass, so it takes a lot of muscle power to overcome its inertia.

- Force is measured in newtons (N). One newton is the force needed to speed up a mass of 1 kg by 1 m/sec every second.

Before Newton, no one knew why things fall to the ground or why planets go round the Sun. According to legend the answer came to him while sitting in an orchard. As an apple fell nearby, he wondered if the apple was not simply falling but was being pulled down by an invisible force. From this simple idea, Newton developed his theory of gravity – a universal force that tries to pull all matter together.

- Everything that is standing still has inertia, which means that it will not move unless forced to.

- Everything that moves has momentum – it will not slow down, speed up or change direction unless forced to.

- When something moves there are usually several forces involved. When you throw a ball, the force of your throw hurls it forwards, the force of gravity pulls it down and the force of air resistance slows it down.

Newton's Laws of Motion

The Laws	*Examples*
1. An object keeps moving in a straight line in the same direction (or keeps still if it's already still), unless a force acts on it.	A spacecraft heading into outer space will keep going straight unless pulled by gravity towards a planet, or its engine fires to change its direction.
2. A force makes an object change its movement in the direction of the force, with an acceleration (increase in speed) that depends on the size of the force.	Kick a football and it changes from being still to moving in the direction of the kick. Apply more force, which means a harder kick, and the ball gains speed faster and goes farther.
3. For every action caused by a force, there is an equal and opposite reaction.	The engines of a jet-car blast hot gases backwards, which is the action. The reaction is to push the car forwards.

❍ The direction and speed of movement depend on the combined effect of all the forces involved – this is called the resultant force.

❍ A force has magnitude (size) and works in a particular direction.

❍ A force can be drawn on a diagram as an arrow called a vector. The way that the arrow points represents the direction of the force. The length of the arrow shows the force's strength.

Flea acceleration

A jumping flea can accelerate at up to 140 g (140 times the acceleration of gravity towards Earth), or 50 times the acceleration of a space shuttle taking off.

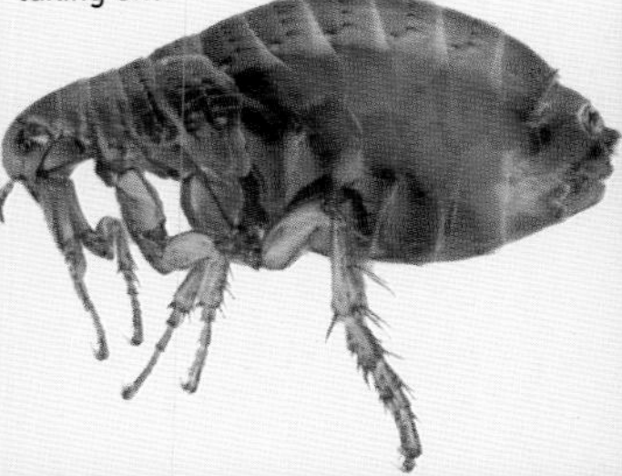

Moving force

To start moving, a skater uses the force of his muscles to push against the ground. As he or she pushes, the ground pushes back with equal force.

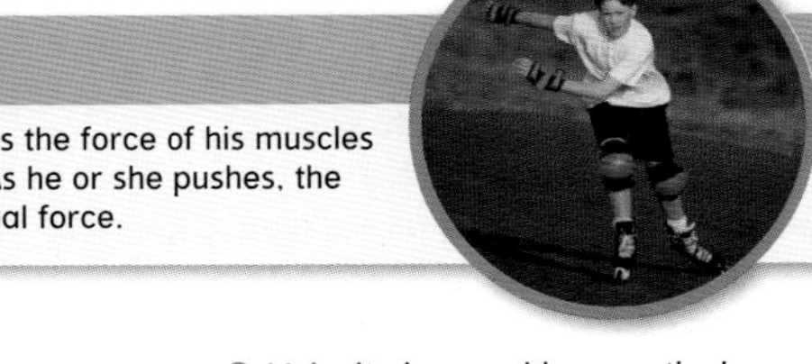

❍ Friction is the force that acts between two things rubbing together. It stops them sliding past each other.

❍ Drag is friction between air and an object. It slows a fast car, or any aircraft moving through the air.

The leverage of the bow string helps an archer to bend the bow so far that it has tremendous power as it snaps back into shape.

❍ Velocity is speed in a particular direction. Acceleration is the rate at which an object's velocity changes.

❍ Every movement in the Universe seems to be governed by physical laws. These laws were explained by scientists such as Isaac Newton and Albert Einstein.

❍ A force that misshapes material is called a stress.

Amazing

A space rocket taking off from the Earth's surface would have to achieve a velocity of more than 40,000 km/h in order to escape the force of Earth's gravity.

Heat and Temperature

Heat is the transfer or movement of energy from a hot substance which has more thermal energy to a cooler one with less energy. Temperature measures how hot or cold a substance is.

❍ Heat is not the same as temperature. Temperature is a measure of how fast molecules are moving. Heat is the movement of energy from a hot place to a cooler one.

❍ When you heat a substance its temperature rises because heat makes its molecules move faster.

❍ When objects heat up they expand because their molecules vibrate more and move further apart. When objects cool down, they contract because the molecules vibrate less and move closer together.

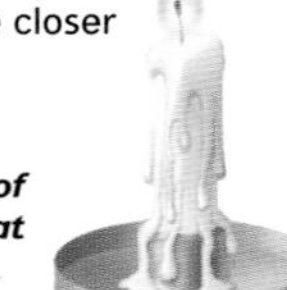

Radiation is one of the ways that heat spreads from a flame.

Amazing

The temperature of the Big Bang, the explosion that created the Universe some 13 billion years ago, was more than 10 billion billion billion°C.

A refrigerator is a heat pump – it pumps heat energy from cold regions to hot ones, opposite to the way heat flows in nature.

❍ Heat always spreads out from its source. It heats up its surroundings while the source cools down.

❍ Every time energy changes from one form to another, some of it turns into heat, which then spreads to its surroundings.

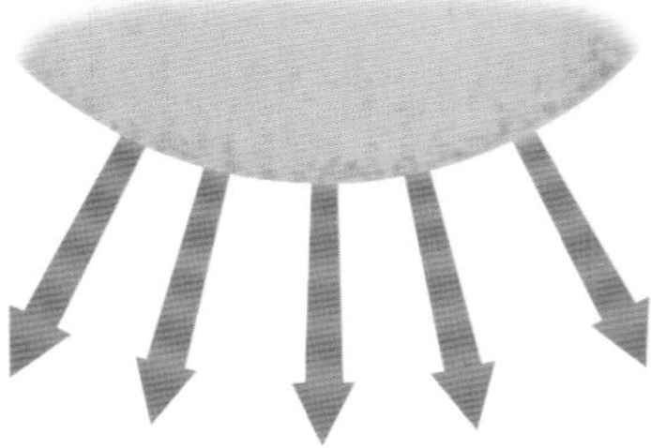

Radiation is rays of energy. The Sun's rays travel through space and reach us as heat and light energy.

❍ Heat moves in three different ways: conduction, convection and radiation.

❍ Conduction involves heat spreading from hot areas to cold areas by direct contact. It works a bit like a relay race. Energetic, rapidly moving or vibrating molecules cannon into their neighbours and set them moving too.

A bimetallic strip is used in a thermostat to respond to a change in temperature. It consists of iron and copper bonded firmly together. The strip bends when heated, because the copper expands more than the iron.

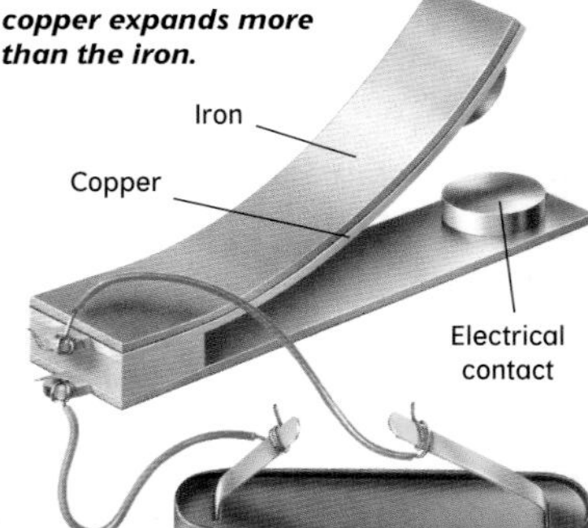

Trapped air

A hot-air balloon flies because the air trapped inside it is warmer (and thus less dense) than the surrounding air. The warm air floats upwards, carrying the balloon with it.

Centre of Sun

Inside lightning bolt

Centre of Earth

Lava from volcano

Oil in frying pan

Boiling water

Body temperature

Water freezes

Solid carbon dioxide ('dry ice')

15,000,000°C — 30,000°C — 6000°C — 1000°C — 200°C — 100°C — 37°C — 0°C — –78.5°C — Absolute zero –273.15°C

There is no limit to how hot things can become. The hottest ever temperature achieved in a laboratory was 4 trillion°C. At the other extreme scientists have come close to reaching –273.15°C, the lowest temperature limit, absolute zero.

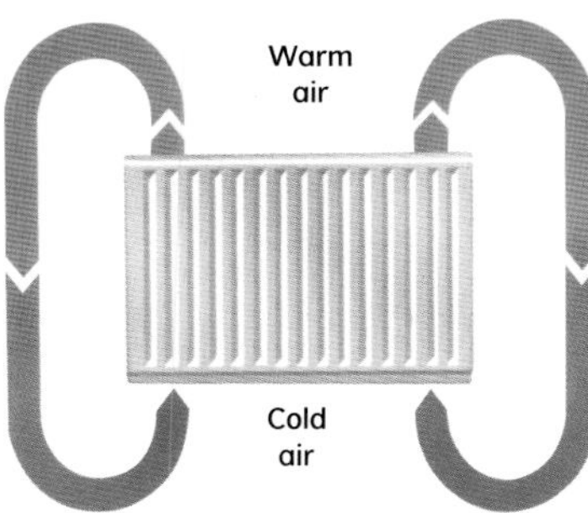

Air warmed by a radiator gets lighter and rises. Cold air moves in from below to replace it, and this is heated up too.

❍ Radiation is the spread of heat as heat rays – that is, invisible waves of infrared radiation.

❍ Convection is when warm air rises through cool air, like a hot-air balloon.

❍ Convection currents are circulation patterns set up as warm air (or liquid) rises. Around the column of rising warmth, cool air sinks to replace it at the bottom. So the whole air turns over like a fountain.

❍ The coldest temperature possible is absolute zero, or –273.15°C, when molecules stop moving.

Thermometers

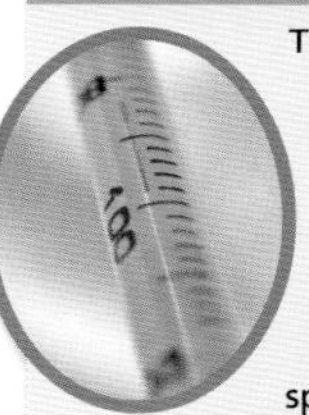

Temperature is measured by a thermometer. When a thermometer is dipped into something hot, a liquid (usually mercury or alcohol) inside the thermometer heats up and expands. The liquid spreads out along a channel in the thermometer with a scale which indicates the temperature of the liquid.

Temperature conversions

Fahrenheit to Celsius
subtract 32, multiply by 5 and divide by 9

Celsius to Fahrenheit
multiply by 9, divide by 5 and add 32

10°C = 50°F
20°C = 68°F
30°C = 86°F
40°C = 104°F
50°C = 122°F

Absolute zero –273.15°C = –459.67°F

When wood or coal is burnt on a fire, a chemical reaction starts that releases energy stored in the fuel. Flames are the area where substances in the fuel combine with oxygen in the air to release energy as heat and light.

Light

Light is energy that we can see with our eyes. It is one of the forms of energy known as electromagnetic radiation, which also includes X-rays, microwaves, radio waves, infrared and ultraviolet.

❍ For some purposes scientists view light as a continuous form of energy that moves in up-and-down waves. For other purposes, they view it as units of energy called photons. This is known in science as the 'wave-particle duality' of light.

❍ Although we are surrounded by light during the day, very few things give out light. The Sun and other stars and electric lights are light sources, but we see most things only because they reflect light. If something does not send out or reflect light, we cannot see it.

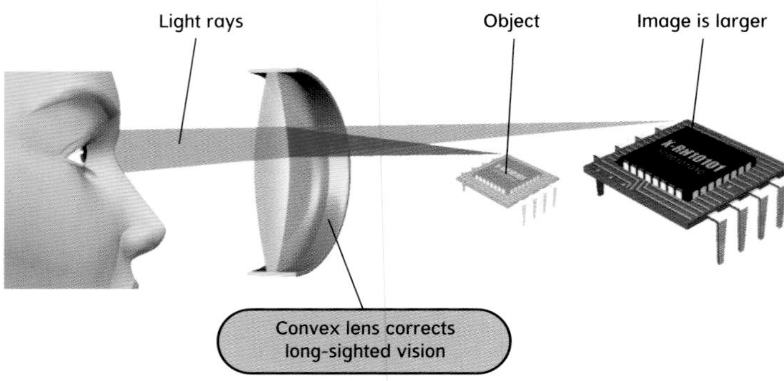

❍ On a sunny day 1000 billion photons fall on a pinhead every second.

❍ Light travels in straight lines. The direction can be changed when light bounces off something or passes through it, but it is always straight. The straight path of light is called a ray.

❍ When the path of a light ray is blocked altogether, it forms a shadow. Most shadows have two regions: the umbra and penumbra. The umbra is the dark part where light rays are blocked altogether. The penumbra is the lighter rim where some rays reach.

❍ When light rays hit something, they bounce off, are soaked up or pass through. Anything that lets light through, such as glass, is transparent. If it mixes the light on the way through, such as frosted glass, it is translucent. If it stops light altogether, it is opaque.

❍ When light strikes a surface, some or all of it is reflected. Most surfaces scatter light in all directions, and therefore all you see is the surface. But mirrors and other shiny surfaces reflect light in exactly the same pattern in which it arrives, so you therefore see a mirror-image.

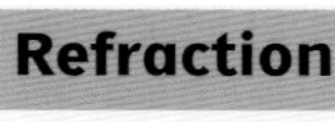

Refraction

Refraction makes a straw look bent. It is not really bent – the light rays bend when they pass through the water.

➤ ***Light bounces or reflects off very smooth surfaces, in the same pattern and at the same angle as the rays hit the surface. This produces what we call a mirror-image. In this mirror-image, left and right are reversed. So in a mirror, we do not see our faces as other people see them.***

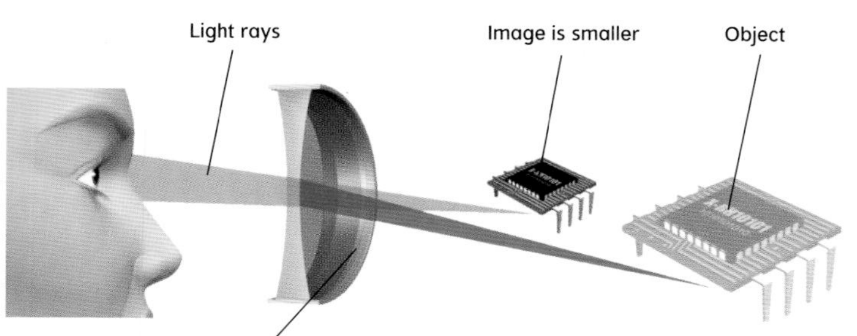

Concave lens corrects short-sighted vision

Glass lenses are shaped to bend light rays in a particular way. Convex (outward-curving) lenses are fat in the middle and thin at the rim. Light rays passing through a convex lens bend inwards, so they come together or converge. Concave (inward-curving) lenses are thin in the middle and thick around the rim. Light rays passing through a concave lens are bent outwards, so they spread.

❍ The emission of light by hot objects is called incandescence. Electric lightbulbs are incandescent – their light comes from a thin tungsten wire, or filament, that glows when it is heated by an electric current.

❍ Fluorescent lights have a gas-filled glass tube coated on the inside with powders called phosphors. Electricity passing through the gas in the tube causes it to emit invisible ultraviolet (UV) rays. The UV rays hit the phosphors and make them glow, or 'fluoresce'.

Colours

When we see different colours, we are seeing different wavelengths of light. Sunlight appears colourless but it is called white light, which is actually a mixture of all colours. When it hits raindrops in the sky it can be split up into all the different colours to form a rainbow. They are split because the raindrop refracts (bends) each wavelength of light differently, fanning out the colours in a particular order, from red (the longest waves) at one end, to violet (the shortest) at the other.

Amazing

It takes 4.3 years for light from Alpha Centauri, the nearest star to the Sun, to reach the Earth.

❍ In neon lights, a huge electric current makes the gas inside a tube electrically charged, causing it to glow.

Gas mixtures in neon lights glow different colours. Pure neon glows red.

Speed of light

The speed at which light travels depends on the medium through which it passes:

Vacuum	299,792 km/sec
Air	299,700 km/sec
Water	225,000 km/sec
Window glass	195,000 km/sec
Decorative glass (lead crystal)	160,000 km/sec
Diamond	125,000 km/sec

Sound

Most sounds you hear, from the whisper of the wind to the roar of a jet, are simply moving air. When any sound is made it makes the air vibrate, and these vibrations carry the sound to your ears.

❍ The vibrations that carry sound through the air are called sound waves, which move by alternately squeezing air molecules together and then stretching them apart.

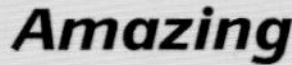

Amazing

Using only echolocation, bottlenose dolphins in captivity can distinguish between a tangerine and a small metal ball of the same size from a distance of 113 m.

❍ Sound waves travel faster through liquids and solids than through air because the molecules are more closely packed together in liquids and solids.

❍ We cannot see sound waves in the air, but we can see big vibrations in solid objects that produce sounds, such as loudspeakers or engines.

❍ We can also see the ripples on a liquid, such as water, through which sound passes.

The loudness (volume) of a sound depends on the energy of its sound waves. Loudness is measured on the decibel (dB) scale. Each rise of 10 dB represents a ten-fold increase in sound energy. For example, 60 dB represents ten times more sound than 50 dB. The quietest sounds we can hear, such as the ticking of a watch, are about 10 dB. Conversation varies between 40 and 60 dB.

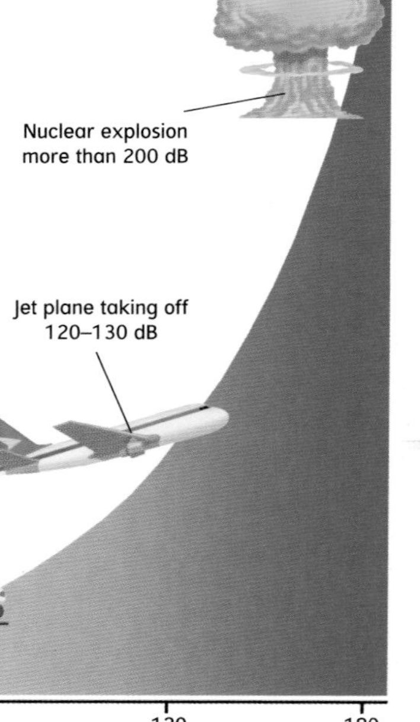

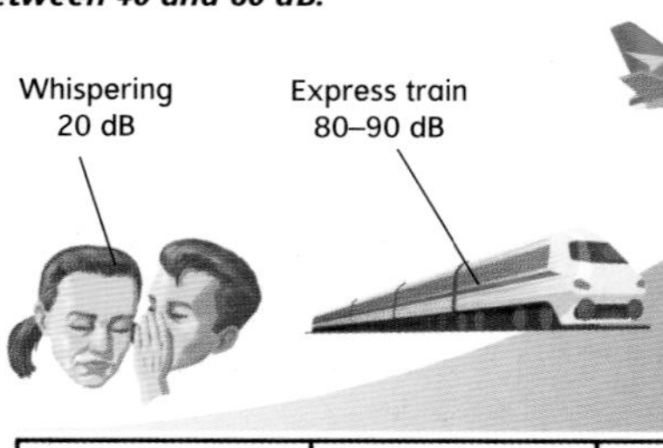

0 40 80 120 180

Decibels

Military aircraft are built to perform in extreme circumstances and they are usually much noisier than civilian aircraft of comparable size – but the military also have the quietest planes. Stealth aircraft, such as this US B-2, have specially silenced engines to reduce their chances of being detected.

Mach

A supersonic jet plane flies faster than sound. Its speed is given as a Mach number. The Mach number is the speed of the plane divided by the speed of sound in the air the plane is flying through. Mach 1 is the speed of sound, Mach 2 is twice the speed of sound.

Using echoes

Whales and dolphins make high-pitched sounds that bounce off the seabed. The echo that returns to the whale or dolphin helps it to find food.

A bat's squeaks and clicks are mostly ultrasonic – too high for our ears to detect. The sounds reflect from objects nearby and the bat works out whether the echoes indicate leaves and twigs to be avoided when flying or prey to be caught. This system is called echolocation, and it allows the bat to fly and feed – even in total darkness.

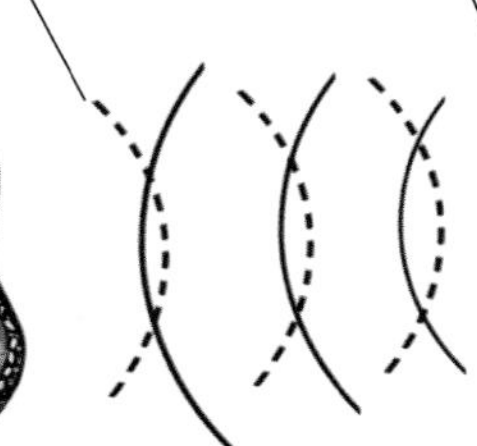

❍ Since sound involves motion, it is a type of kinetic energy.

❍ Sounds can be soft or loud, high-pitched or low-pitched. It all depends on the energy and frequency of the sound waves.

❍ Big, energetic waves move your eardrums a long way within the ear and sound loud. Small, low energy waves sound quieter. Loudness (volume) is measured in decibels (dB).

❍ The pitch of a sound depends on the frequency of the sound waves (the number of waves that reach your ears every second). The greater the frequency, the higher the pitch of the sound. Frequency is measured in hertz (Hz); 1 Hz is one wave per second.

❍ Sounds that are too loud can damage the ears. Sounds of 130 dB or over are painful, and prolonged exposure to sounds of upwards of 90 dB can cause deafness.

❍ Sound travels a million times more slowly than light, which is why you hear thunder after you see a flash of lightning, even though they both happen at the same time

❍ An echo is the reflection of a sound. You hear it a little while after the sound is made.

❍ Acoustics is the study of how sounds are created, transmitted and received.

❍ The highest sound the average human can hear is 20,000 Hz; the lowest is 20 Hz.

Speed of sound

Sound can travel through any medium except a vacuum. It generally travels faster through liquids than gases, and more rapidly through solids than liquids. Its speed is measured in m/sec.

Beryllium	12,890 m/sec
Aluminium	6420 m/sec
Stainless steel	5790 m/sec
Copper	4760 m/sec
Brick	3650 m/sec
Gold	3240 m/sec
Lead	2160 m/sec
Water, sea (20°C)	1531 m/sec
Water, distilled (20°C)	1497 m/sec
Mercury	1450 m/sec
Hydrogen	1284 m/sec
Cork	500 m/sec
Air (20°C)	343 m/sec
Air (0°C)	331 m/sec
Oxygen	316 m/sec
Carbon dioxide	259 m/sec

Air and Water

Air and water are the two most important substances in the world. Without them, life on Earth would not exist. Air provides living creatures with the oxygen they need to breathe.

- The air is a mixture of gases, dust and moisture.
- Water is a compound made of two hydrogen atoms and one oxygen atom. It has the chemical formula H_2O.

Amazing

Bacteria have been found alive in the air at an altitude of over 10 km, carried to that height by strong winds. Some scientists think that bacteria may even be able to survive in space.

Antoine Lavoisier (1743–1794) was a brilliant French scientist who is regarded as the father of modern chemistry. He was the first person to realize that air is essentially a mixture of two gases: oxygen and nitrogen. Lavoisier also discovered that water is a compound of hydrogen and oxygen.

Plants and animals interact with each other in regions called ecosystems. Plants need water to grow and survive. Rainforests receive a lot of rain annually, and so are abundant with plant life and animals. In an ecosystem, each organism (living thing) is dependent on the other organisms living there. Plants are the primary producers in any ecosystem, using the energy of sunlight to convert carbon dioxide and water into carbohydrates, and giving off oxygen as a waste product.

The atmosphere – the blanket of air that surrounds the Earth – is about 100 km deep. The atmosphere gets thinner with altitude.

- Earth is the only known planet with running water. In fact, three-quarters of the Earth's surface is covered by oceans.
- Water is the only substance that can exist as a solid, a liquid and a gas at normal temperatures. Water melts at 0°C and boils at 100°C.

The liner* Titanic *was said to be unsinkable, but when an iceberg breached her hull and let in water to replace the air, she sank like a stone.

2017 hurricanes

Since 1953, hurricanes are given personal names that are revised every six years by the World Meteorological Organization.

Alberto	Helene	Oscar
Beryl	Isaac	Patty
Chris	Joyce	Rafael
Debby	Kirk	Sara
Ernesto	Leslie	Tony
Florence	Michael	Valerie
Gordon	Nadine	William

Things float because of the upward pressure of the water, which is why you can lift quite a heavy person in a swimming pool. This loss of weight is called buoyancy. Buoyancy is created by the upward push, or upthrust, of the water. When you float in the water you will sink until your weight is exactly equal to the upthrust of the water, at which point you float.

❍ Water is one of the few substances that expands as it freezes, which is why pipes burst during cold weather.

❍ When an object is placed in water, its weight pulls it down. At the same time the water pushes back with a force called upthrust, which is equal to the weight of water displaced (pushed out of the way).

An iceberg is a huge chunk of ice that has broken away from a glacier. Only the tip of an iceberg is visible above the ocean's surface. The rest of the ice (up to 90 per cent) is submerged.

Combining substances

A remarkable property of water is its ability to make solutions with other substances. A solution is formed when a substance is added to a liquid and instead of just floating in the liquid, the substance breaks up entirely, so that its atoms and molecules completely intermingle with those of the liquid. This happens when instant coffee is added to water. The substance dissolved is called the solute; the liquid is called the solvent.

❍ An object will float if its weight is equal to or lighter than the upthrust of the water. This is called buoyancy.

❍ The buoyancy of water reduces a swimmer's body weight by 90 per cent.

Floating ice

Ice is less dense than water, which is why ice forms on the surface of ponds and why icebergs float.

❍ Objects that are less dense than water float; those that are more dense sink.

❍ Although steel is denser than water, steel ships float because their hulls are full of air. They sink until enough water is displaced to match the weight of steel and air in the hull.

❍ People float because their lungs contain air, and because body fat is less dense than water (bone and muscle are denser).

❍ About 2 per cent of the world's water is frozen in ice caps and glaciers.

Early Inventions

Karl Benz and his wife Berta were the German creators of the first successful petrol-driven car in 1885. At the age of 16, Karl Benz dreamed of 'a unit that could supplant the steam engine'. Karl and Berta Benz began developing their own car in the 1870s, while trying to earn money from a tinmaking business. By 1880, they were so penniless they could barely afford to eat.

Hammocks were used by Central American peoples 1000 years ago. They were introduced to ships in the 1590s to make sleeping easier at sea.

Englishman John Harrison's 1759 version of the chronometer (the 1735 version is shown here) won a £20,000 prize. The prize had been devised by the British government in 1714 to promote research into the development of accurate timekeeping devices for use by navigators at sea.

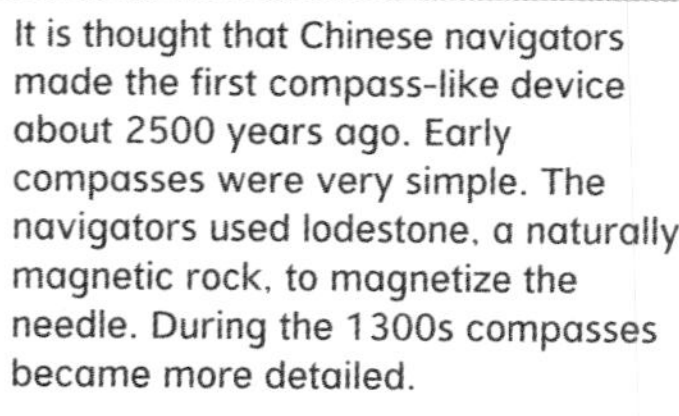

It is thought that Chinese navigators made the first compass-like device about 2500 years ago. Early compasses were very simple. The navigators used lodestone, a naturally magnetic rock, to magnetize the needle. During the 1300s compasses became more detailed.

Rocket, a famous early locomotive built by English engineers George and Robert Stephenson, won the world's first locomotive speed trials in 1829.

France's Montgolfier brothers developed the first hot-air balloon. It was first launched in 1783.

Fireworks were invented by the Chinese about 1000 years ago, after the invention of gunpowder. Original Chinese fireworks were only one colour, yellow. However, new ingredients, such as copper and sodium, were added in the 19th century to make a greater range of colours possible. The most popular form of firework, the rocket, is pushed high up into the sky by the jet of hot gases thrown out behind it when it burns rapidly.

The ancient Egyptians made sundials more than 3000 years ago. The marks showed hours. The length of the hours varied with the seasons, but people were used to such an idea and called them 'temporary hours'.

The science of vibrating strings was first worked out by Pythagoras, a Greek mathematician and philosopher, 2500 years ago.

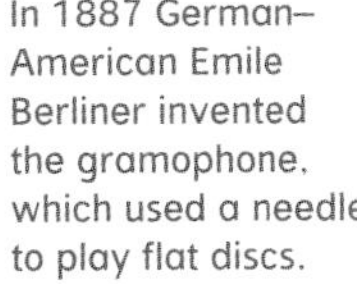

In 1887 German–American Emile Berliner invented the gramophone, which used a needle to play flat discs.

Many early boats, like this Welsh coracle, were made by stretching animal skins over a wooden frame.

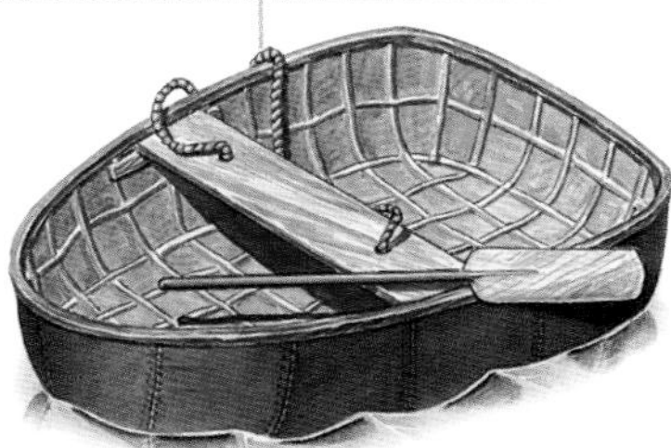

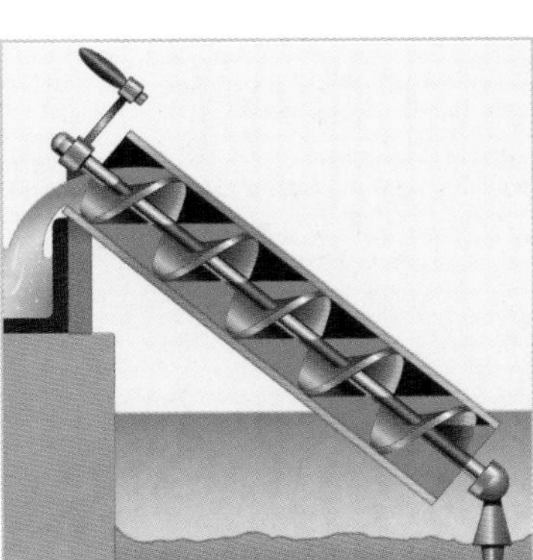

Archimedes' screw is a simple device for raising water. Devised by Archimedes, a mathematician and inventor of ancient Greece, Archimedes' screw scoops up water using a helical device that turns inside a tube. It is still used in the Middle East.

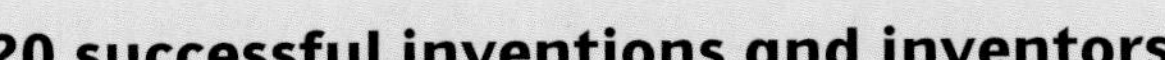

20 successful inventions and inventors

Year	Invention	Inventor
1595	Microscope	Zacharias Janssen
1620	Slide rule	William Oughtred
1709	Piano	Bartolomeo Cristofori
1798	Vaccination	Edward Jenner
1800	Electric battery	Alessandro Volta
1816	Stethoscope	Rene Laennec
1843	Typewriter	Christopher Sholes
1853	Glider	George Cayley
1866	Dynamite	Alfred Nobel
1870	Celluloid	John W Hyatt
1879	Cash register	James Ritty
1882	Electric fan	Schuyler Skatts Wheeler
1884	Fountain pen	Lewis Waterman
1885	Petrol motorbike	Gottlieb Daimler
1888	Ballpoint pen	John Loud
1894	Diesel engine	Rudolf Diesel
1908	Cellophane	J Brandenburger
1928	Sliced bread	Otto Rohwedder
1939	Electronic computer	John Atanasoff

Machine Power

A machine is a device that makes a task easier to do. There are two forces involved in every machine: the 'load' (weight) that the machine has to move, and the 'effort' used to move the load.

Amazing

One of the world's biggest machines is the Bagger 288 Excavator in Germany. It weighs in at more than 45,000 tonnes and is 95 m tall.

❍ There are six types of simple machine – the inclined plane (slope or ramp), lever, wedge, pulley, screw and the wheel and axle. More elaborate machines, such as cranes, are made up of combinations of these simple machines linked to other mechanical components.

Inclined plane

Pulleys

➤ ***An escalator combines the advantages of a pulley system and an inclined plane to carry passengers smoothly to the top. The steps are designed to swivel past each other as they go around the pulleys.***

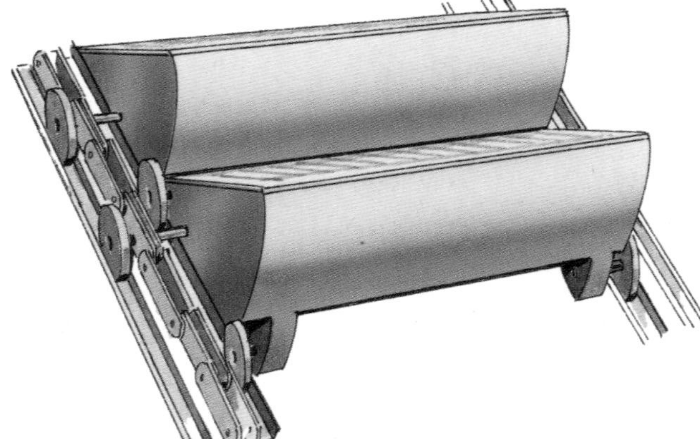

❍ Mechanical advantage tells you how effective a machine is. It is calculated by dividing the load by the effort.

❍ Work is done when a force moves an object and energy is converted from one form to another. The amount of work done is the effort multiplied by the distance through which the load moves.

❍ Power is the rate at which work is done or energy changed from one form to another.

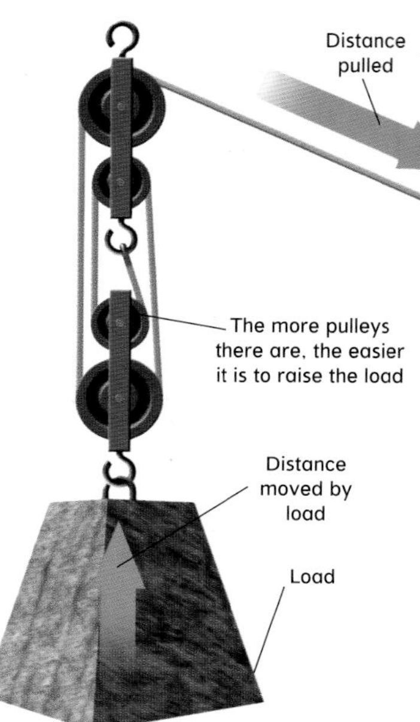

▲ ***Using a set of pulleys, or block and tackle, considerably decreases the amount of effort needed to lift a load, but proportionately increases the distance over which the effort must be applied.***

❍ A pulley is a grooved wheel around which a rope passes to move a load.

❍ A single pulley alters the direction through which the effort is applied, so by pulling downwards on the rope a load can be moved upwards.

Machine efficiency

Efficiency is how much work you get out of a machine compared to the energy you put into it. It is usually expressed as a percentage.

Aeroplane engine	10%
Steam locomotive	10%
Car petrol engine	22%
Steam turbine	30%
Diesel engine	35%

A wheel and axle can reduce friction (resistance) between a load and the surface over which it moves. Pushing a load up a ramp, or inclined plane, is easier than lifting it vertically. The shallower the slope of the ramp, the less effort is required, but the further the load has to move.

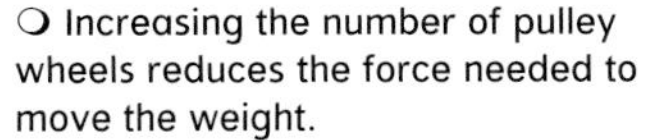

❍ Increasing the number of pulley wheels reduces the force needed to move the weight.

❍ The inclined plane, or ramp, is a sloping surface that reduces the effort needed to raise a load.

❍ A wedge is a moving inclined plane. An axe head is a wedge that magnifies force and makes it possible to split logs with little effort.

❍ A screw thread is an inclined plane wrapped around a shaft. Turning the screw moves it forward with more force than the effort used to turn it.

❍ Gears are pairs of toothed wheels (cogs) that intermesh and turn together to transmit or change force and motion.

❍ When an axle turns a wheel, the rim of the wheel turns with less force but travels a greater distance. Conversely, turning the wheel rim moves the axle a shorter distance but with more force.

❍ A lever is a bar that moves round a pivot (the fulcrum) and uses turning force to make it easier to move a load.

Nutcracker

A nutcracker is a pair of levers. The fulcrum is the hinge between the levers. Squeezing the nutcracker applies force (the effort) to the levers and breaks the nut (the load).

Changing energy

A waterwheel changes the kinetic energy of running water into useful mechanical energy. This can be harnessed to drive machines such as millstones, which grind grain into flour.

A big cog (gear wheel) turns a smaller cog with less force but greater speed. A small cog turns a larger cog with greater force but more slowly. The gear ratio is the number of times that the wheel doing the driving turns the wheel being driven.

A screwdriver used to prise the lid from a can of paint acts as a simple lever. The fulcrum is the rim of the can, the load is the lid, and the wrist provides the effort.

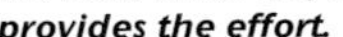

Construction

It was once thought that all prehistoric humans lived in caves. We now know that some cave 'dwellings' were actually used for religious rituals, and that some of the earliest dwellings were houses constructed from wood, leaves, grass and mud. All traces of these have long since vanished.

❍ Early mudbrick houses dating from at least 9500 years ago are found in Anatolia (modern Turkey).

❍ Pyramids are huge monuments with a square base and triangular sides that taper to a point at the top. They were built by ancient peoples in many parts of the world – including Egypt, Iraq, Peru and Mexico – as tombs or temples, and sometimes as a combination of the two.

Amazing

The Boeing Company's aircraft assembly plant at Everett, Washington, USA, has the largest capacity of any building in the world, with a total volume of 13,300,000 cu m.

❍ The tallest pyramid is the Great Pyramid at Giza in Egypt, built for the Pharaoh Khufu around 2550 BC. This was once 147 m high, but is now only 140 m, because some of the upper stones have been lost.

The world's biggest free-standing arch is the 192 m high Gateway to the West arch in St Louis, Missouri, USA.

❍ The Romans were among the first to use round arches, so round arches are called Roman or Romanesque arches.

❍ Roman arches were built from blocks of stone called voussoirs. They were built up from each side on a semi-circular wooden frame (later removed). A central keystone (wedge) was slotted in at the top to hold them together.

Eiffel Tower

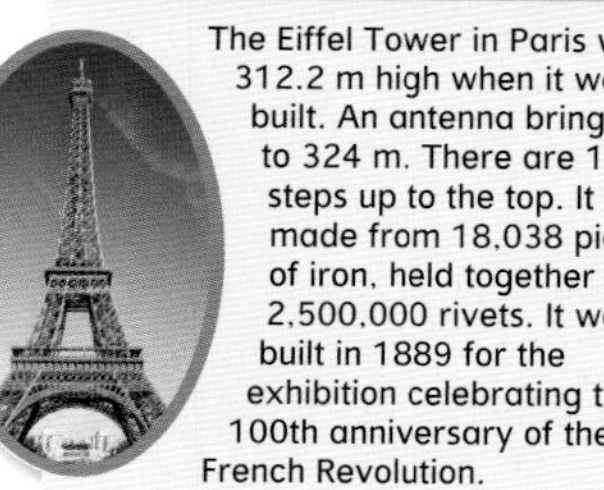

The Eiffel Tower in Paris was 312.2 m high when it was first built. An antenna brings it up to 324 m. There are 1665 steps up to the top. It was made from 18,038 pieces of iron, held together by 2,500,000 rivets. It was built in 1889 for the exhibition celebrating the 100th anniversary of the French Revolution.

❍ Pointed arches were first brought to Europe from the Middle East by Crusader knights in the 1100s. They were used in churches, and become part of the gothic style of architecture.

❍ The first skyscrapers were built in Chicago and New York in the 1880s.

❍ A crucial step in the development of skyscrapers was the invention of the fast safety lift by American engineer Elisha Otis (1811–1861) in 1857.

❍ Hong Kong in China has more skyscrapers than any other city in the world.

❍ At 570 m long, Prague Castle in the Czech Republic is one of the biggest ancient castles in Europe, having been started in around 880. It is probably also the oldest surviving.

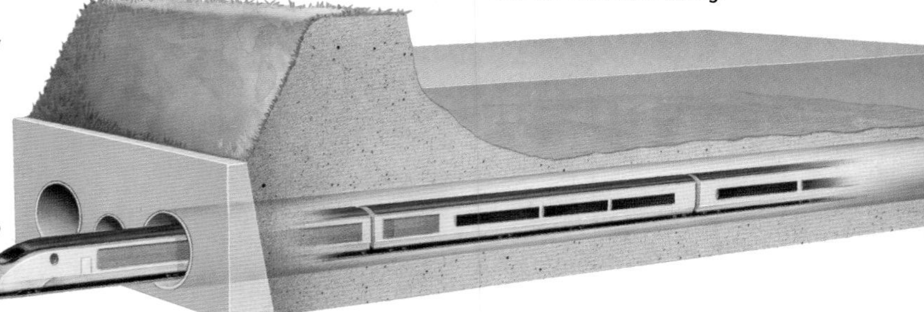

The longest tunnels so far built are sub-sea rail tunnels that have a three-tube structure, with two large tunnels carrying the tracks separated by a smaller service tunnel for maintenance work.

Buildings or bridges erected on soft ground are supported by posts called piles. Usually made of steel or concrete, the piles are driven firmly into the ground by pile-drivers. Pile-drivers wind up a heavy weight called a pile hammer inside a frame, then drop it on the head of the pile to bash it into the ground.

Leaning Tower

The Leaning Tower of Pisa in Italy is a 55 m high belltower or 'campanile'. Building began in 1173, and it started to lean as workers built the third storey. It is now tilting 3.9 m away from the perpendicular.

Deeper tunnels need to be bored out. Tunnels through soft rock or soil are dug with a powerful cutting machine called a shield. The shield's rotating cutting head is kept on a straight course by lasers. Ring-shaped steel and concrete supports are put in place to prevent the tunnel caving in again.

Tallest buildings

1. **Burj Khalifa** Dubai, United Arab Emirates 828 m
2. **Shanghai Tower** Shanghai, China 632 m
3. **Makkah Royal Clock Tower Hotel** Mecca, Saudi Arabia 601 m
4. **One World Trade Center** New York, USA 541 m
5. **CFT Finance Centre** Guangzhou, China 530 m
6. **Taipei 101 Tower** Taipei, China 509.2 m
7. **Shanghai World Financial Centre** Shanghai, China 492 m
8. **International Commerce Centre** Hong Kong, China 484 m
9. **Petronas Towers** Kuala Lumpur, Malaysia 452 m
10. **Zifeng Tower** Nanjing, China 450 m

Note: figures exclude masts

❍ Horseshoe arches are used in Islamic buildings all round the world.

❍ The world's biggest dam is the 540,000,000 cu m Syncrude Tailings Dam in Canada. The world's tallest dams are Jinping, China (305 m high) and Nurek,Tajikistan (300 m high).

A tall structure, such as a skyscraper, must have deep foundations (the part below ground) to support its height, made of massive concrete or steel piles sunk into the ground. The walls and floors are then attached to a skeleton of steel girders and beams.

Bridges

The first bridges were probably logs and vines slung across rivers to help people across. Clapper bridges are ancient bridges in which large stone slabs rest on piers (supports) of stone.

Arch bridge

The Ponte Vecchio in Florence, built in 1345, is one of the oldest flattened arch bridges in Europe.

❍ The Romans were among the first to use bricks in bridges. The Alcántara bridge over the Tagus River in Spain is made of stone covered with brick, and was built around AD 100.

❍ Long brick bridges could be made with a series of arches linked together. Each of these arches is called a span.

❍ Roman arches were semi-circular, so each span was short. Chinese arches were flatter, so they could span greater distances.

❍ Rope suspension bridges have been used for thousands of years. One of the first to use iron chains was the Lan Jin Bridge at Yunnan in China. It was built in AD 65.

❍ The first all-iron bridge was built at Coalbrookdale, England, across the River Severn. It was designed by Thomas Pritchard and built in 1779 by Abraham Darby.

For wide or deep channels, a suspension bridge, with a span of up to 1991 m, is often used. The deck (such as a roadway) is held up by steel cables hanging between tall towers. These cables are held in concrete blocks at both ends of the bridge. The deck may be supported by a framework to stop it swaying too much in the wind. The weight of the deck is transferred to the vertical cables over the towers and to the concrete blocks at either end.

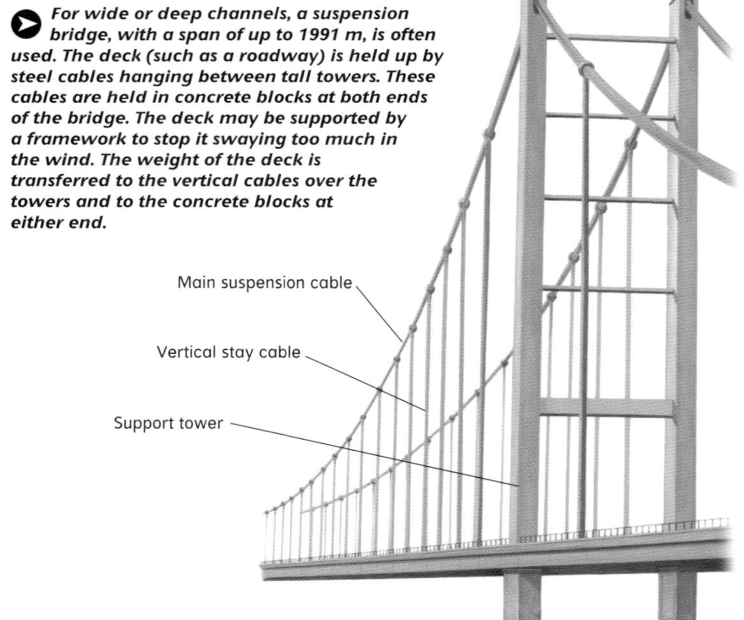

The first step in bridge-building is to build the piers and abutments. To erect piers in the water, a steel wall or shuttering is built on the riverbed. The water is then pumped out while the pier is built, before the walls can be removed, and the spans laid between the piers.

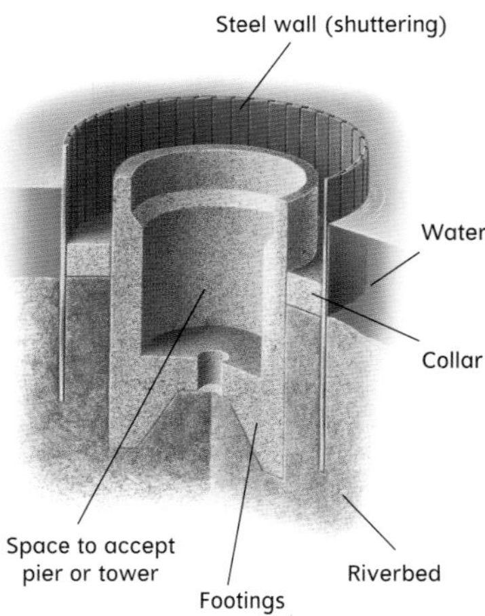

❍ The Millau viaduct in France is the world's tallest road bridge. It stands at over 343 m high. This is even higher than the Eiffel Tower.

Longest bridges

Steel-Arch

1	Chaotianmen, China	552 m
2	Lupu, China	550 m
3	Bosideng, China	530 m
4	New River Gorge, USA	518 m
5	Bayonne (Kill Van Kull), USA	510 m

Cable-Stayed

1	Russky, Russia	1104 m
2	Sutong, China	1088 m
3	Stonecutters, Hong Kong	1018 m
4	E'dong, China	926 m
5	Tatara, Japan	890 m

Suspension

1	Akashi-Kaikyo, Japan	1991 m
2	Xihoumen, China	1650 m
3	Great Belt, Denmark	1624 m
4	Yi Sun-Sin, S. Korea	1545 m
5	Runyang, China	1490 m

Golden Gate Bridge

The Golden Gate Bridge spans the entrance to San Francisco Bay in California, USA. The roadway is 67 m above the water, although this varies according to the tide. The bridge has 6 lanes for traffic and can also carry pedestrians and cyclists across. The bridge was opened to public traffic on 28 May 1937.

❍ In the early 1800s Scottish engineer Thomas Telford built superb iron bridges, such as Craigellachie over the Spey in Scotland (1814). He built one of Europe's first iron chain suspension bridges over the Menai Straits in Wales in 1826.

Most bridges are now built of concrete and steel. These are some of the main kinds. The longest are normally suspension bridges, usually carrying roads, but Hong Kong's 1377-m long Tsing Ma takes both road and rail.

Amazing

An average of 274,000 vehicles per day used the San Francisco Oakland Bay Bridge in 1996, which works out at an astonishing 100 million vehicles per year!

❍ In 1940 the Tacoma suspension bridge in Washington, USA, was blown down by a moderate wind just months after its completion. The disaster forced engineers to make suspension bridges aerodynamic.

❍ Aerodynamic design played a major part in the design of Turkey's Bosphorus Bridge (1973) and the Humber Bridge in England (1981), for a while the longest bridge at 1410 m.

❍ London Bridge was dismantled and reconstructed stone by stone in Arizona, USA, as a tourist attraction in 1971.

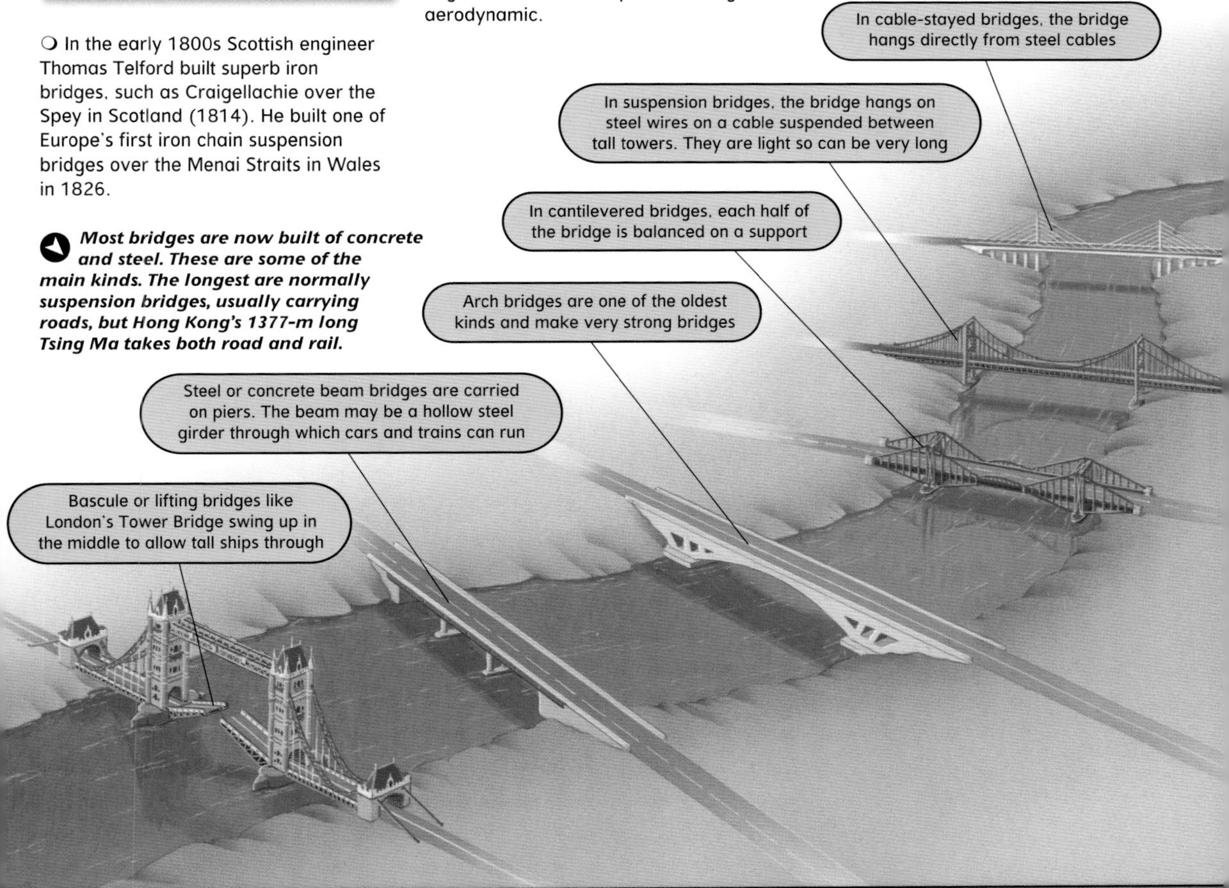

History of Rail Transport

On 15 September 1830 the world's first major passenger railway opened between Liverpool and Manchester in England. By 1835 there were over 1600 km of railway in the USA. In Britain railway building became a mania in the 1840s.

Amazing

Indian Railways had nearly 1,600,000 staff in 1997, making it the world's largest employer.

❍ In 1831 the *Best Friend* started a regular train service between Charleston and Hamburg, South Carolina, in the USA.

❍ On 10 May 1869 railways from either side of the United States met at Promontory, Utah, giving North America the first transcontinental railway.

❍ Steam locomotives get their power by burning coal in a firebox. This heats up water in a boiler, making steam. The steam drives a piston to and fro and the piston turns the wheels via connecting rods and cranks.

Track controllers use a 'block' system to stop a train entering a block of track that already has a train on it. Some routes in Europe and Japan use Advanced Train Protection (ATP), where the cab picks up signals from the track telling the driver what speed to travel. If the driver fails to respond, the train slows automatically. In the US, they have developed Advanced Train Control Systems (ACTS), which relies on satellites and other high-tech links. Signals can also warn train crews of hazards on the track.

❍ The *Flying Scotsman* was a famous loco designed by Sir Nigel Gresley (1876–1941). It pulled trains non-stop 630 km from London to Edinburgh in under eight hours.

❍ The diesel engines in diesel locomotives do not drive the train wheels directly. The engines generate electricity providing power to the electric motors that drive the wheels.

❍ The first practical electric trains date from 1879, but they only became widespread in the 1920s.

❍ The first monorail was built in Russia in 1820 but did not survive long. The Cheshunt monorail, built in 1825, was the first monorail to carry passengers.

This is a typical British diesel-electric locomotive from the 1960s. It has a cab at both ends so that it can be operated in either direction. This is one of the older generation of diesel-electrics that use DC (direct current) generators. DC generators give a current that flows in only one direction. Most newer engines take advantage of electronic devices called rectifiers to use the current from an AC (alternating current) generator. An AC generator gives a current that swaps direction many times a second. The rectifiers convert this into a direct current. AC generators are far more powerful and efficient.

Fastest train

The fastest recorded conventional train speed is 574.8 km/h by France's TGV in April 2007.

Bullet train

Japan's Shinkansen 'bullet train' was the first of the modern high speed electric trains, regularly operating at speeds of more than 220 km/h.

❍ The heaviest trains ever pulled by a single locomotive were 250-truck trains that ran on the Erie Railroad in the USA from 1914 to 1929. They weighed over 15,000 tonnes.

❍ Magnetic levitation or maglev trains do not have wheels but glide along supported by electromagnets.

❍ A maglev is proposed in Japan to take passengers from Tokyo to Nagoya and may be operational by 2025.

❍ Since 2000 the 240 km/h tilting train the *Acela Express* – Washington to Boston – is the USA's fastest train.

❍ The longest train was a 7.3-km, 660-truck freight train that ran from Saldanha to Sishen in South Africa, on 26 August 1989.

❍ The Trans-Siberian Express takes a week to go right across Russia and Siberia, from Moscow to Vladivostok.

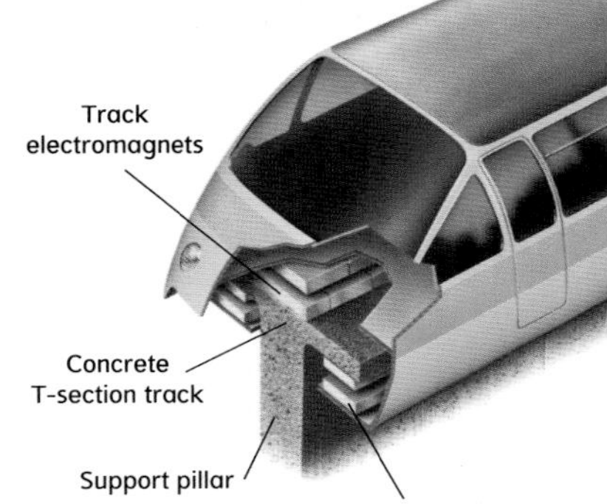

Test maglev train systems operate in China, Japan, Germany and the USA.

❍ Stretching for an incredible 9288 km, the Trans-Siberian Express is the world's longest train route.

❍ The world's first underground was the cut-and-cover Metropolitan Line in London, opened on 10 January 1863, using steam engines.

❍ New York City has the world's largest subway network, but unlike London's most of it is quite shallow. The first line opened on 27 October 1904.

Diesel engine in which diesel fuel is squeezed inside cylinders until it bursts into flame. The expansion of the fuel as it burns provides the engine's power

Fuel tank carrying diesel fuel. Because a diesel train carries its fuel on board, it is entirely independent, unlike electric locomotives

Switches are used to automatically change the direction of a train.

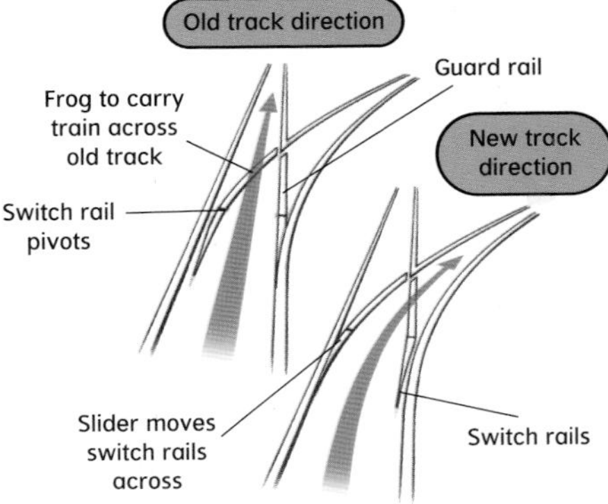

Longest metro systems

	Route (km)	No. of stations	Year opened
1 Seoul, South Korea	940	617	1974
2 Shanghai, China	488	303	1995
3 Beijing, China	456	270	1989
4 London, UK	402	270	1863
5 New York, USA	369	468	1904
6 Moscow, Russia	317	190	1935
7 Tokyo, Japan	310	290	1927
8 Madrid, Spain	284	294	1919
9 Paris, France	218	200	1900
10 Hong Kong, China	218	152	1979

History of Road Transport

By 1904, the layouts of cars were starting to resemble those of modern vehicles, with an engine at the front, the driver and steering wheel on one side, a petrol tank at the back, a shaft to drive the wheels and so on.

❍ Early cars were 'coach-built', which meant they were individually built by hand. This made them the costly toys of the rich only.

Mini car

The 1959 Mini, designed by Alec Issigonis, set a trend in small car design, with the engine mounted across the car driving the front wheels.

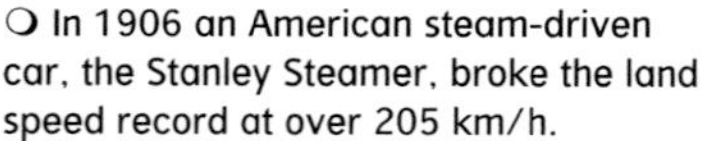

❍ In 1906 an American steam-driven car, the Stanley Steamer, broke the land speed record at over 205 km/h.

❍ The first petrol-engine motorbike was built by Gottlieb Daimler in Germany in 1885.

❍ The first car for ordinary people was Ford's Model T. The Ford Company built their 10 millionth car in 1924 and produced their 50 millionth car in 1958.

❍ The Model A Ford sold one million within 14 months of its launch in December 1927. The Ford Escort of 1980 sold one million in just 11 months.

❍ In 1905 the first motor buses ran on New York's 5th Avenue. In 1928 the first transcontinental bus service crossed the USA.

Brake calliper

Brake fluid under pressure in brake pipe pushes on piston

Brake pads press on brake disc to create friction, thus slowing down wheel

Piston presses two brake pads together

Brake piston

Stopping a fast-moving car demands great force. When the driver presses the brake pedal, brake fluid is forced through narrow pipes to cylinders on each wheel. The pressure of the fluid presses special pads – brake pads – against the brake discs on the wheels, which slow it down by friction. Many cars have ABS (anti-lock braking systems) where a computer applies the brake automatically within a split second and prevents the car's wheels from locking up and the car from skidding to a halt.

Amazing

The world's oldest known timber track roadway is the Sweet Track in England's Somerset Levels. Built in the 3800s BC, it ran for 2000 m across the marsh, and was made of oak plants supported by ash poles.

❍ The first car speed record was achieved by an electric Jentaud car in 1898 at Acheres near Paris. Driven by the Comte de Chasseloup-Laubat, the car hit 63.14 km/h. Camille Jenatzy vied with de Chasseloup-Laubat for the record, raising it to 105.85 km/h in his car *Jamais Contente* in 1899.

❍ In 1911 the governing body for the land speed record said that cars had to make two runs in opposite directions over a 1 km course to get the record.

❍ On 15 October 1997 a British jet car called *Thrust SSC*, driven by British fighter pilot Andy Green, broke the sound barrier for the first time. In two runs across Nevada's Black Rock desert it hit over 1220 km/h.

❍ The Mercedes Benz 300SL of 1952 was one of the first supercars of the post-war years, famous for its stylish flip-up 'Gullwing' doors.

First on the road

Steam coach	Trevithick, Britain	1802
Steam dredger	Evans, USA	1805
Gas carriage	Brown, Britain	1820s
Petrol car	Benz, Germany	1885

❍ The Aston Martin DB6 was the classic supercar of the late 1960s, driven by fictional spy James Bond.

❍ In 1861 French father and son Pierre and Ernest Michaux stuck the pedals directly on the front wheel to make the first successful bicycle, nicknamed 'boneshaker'.

❍ In 1874 Englishman H. J. Lawson made the first chain-driven bicycle. This was called a 'safety bicycle'.

❍ In 1885 John Starley made the Rover safety bicycle in England. Air-filled tyres were added in 1890, and the modern bicycle was born.

❍ More people in China cycle today than in the rest of the world put together.

Donald Campbell took on the record-breaking mantle of his father – and the* Bluebird *name for his car. On 17 July 1964, Campbell's* Bluebird *hit a world record 644.96 km/h on the salt flats at Lake Eyre in South Australia. At one moment he hit over 716 km/h – faster than any wheel-driven car has ever been. The total weight of the car was 4354 kg.

Simple cogs reverse the direction of rotation

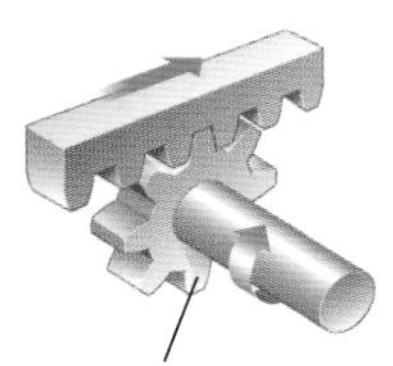

Rack and pinion change the rotation to a sliding motion

Bevels move the direction of rotation through a right angle

Worm gears change the motion to a slower, stronger rotation at right angles

Gears are used to modify rotation – either the speed, as in the link between an engine and wheels, or the direction.

Juggernauts

Big trucks are sometimes called 'juggernauts'. The word comes from Jagannath, a form of the Hindu god Vishnu. A statue of the god is annually carried in procession on a large chariot in Puri, Orissa, India.

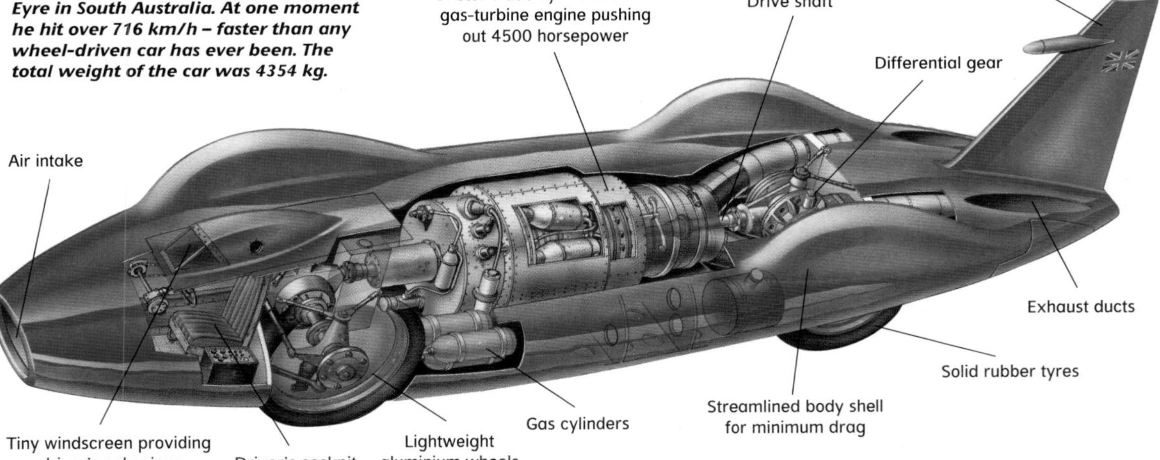

History of Water Transport

The ancient Egyptians made ships by a process of interlocking planks of wood and lashing them together with rope. Wooden sailing boats have been used for the last 4000 years.

❍ Sailors used to be called 'tars', after the tarpaulins used for making sails. Tarpaulin is canvas and tar.

Amazing

The world's smallest submarine, the Water Beatle, measures 2.95 m long, 1.15 m wide and 1.42 m high. Built by Englishman William Smith, it can dive to 30.5 m and stay submerged for four hours.

❍ Sailors' lavatories on old ships were simply holes overhanging the sea and were referred to as 'heads'.

Hydrofoils

By lifting themselves out of the water and almost flying across the surface, hydrofoils achieve very high speeds.

Surface-piercing hydrofoil | *Fully submerged hydrofoil*

❍ In 1807 American Robert Fulton made the first steam passenger boats, running 240 km up the Hudson River from New York.

❍ Early steamships were propelled by paddles, but in 1835 Swede John Ericsson developed a screw propeller. In 1845 a screw-driven boat won a tug-of-war with a paddle steamer.

❍ In 1843 British engineer Isambard Kingdom Brunel launched the first iron ship to cross the Atlantic, the *Great Britain*.

❍ In 1858 Brunel launched *Great Eastern*, the biggest ship of the 19th century, 211 m long and weighing 30,000 tonnes.

Hovercrafts, or 'air-cushion' vehicles, use a huge fan to blow air downwards and lift the craft above the water.

❍ The great age of ocean liners lasted from the early 1900s to the 1950s.

❍ The *Titanic* was the largest ship ever built at 46,329 tonnes when launched in 1911 – but it sank on its maiden (first) voyage.

❍ The *Queen Elizabeth* launched in 1938 was the largest passenger ship ever built – 314 m long and 83,673 tonnes. It burned and sank during refitting in Hong Kong in 1972.

❍ Navies of the 21st century have five main classes of surface warship: aircraft carriers, cruisers, destroyers and frigates, corvettes.

❍ The 332.9 m-long US aircraft carriers *Nimitz, Dwight D. Eisenhower, Carl Vinson, Abraham Lincoln, John C. Stennis, George Washington, Harry S. Truman, Theodore Roosevelt* and *Ronald Reagan* are among the world's biggest warships.

Submarines

To gain weight for a dive, submarines fill their 'ballast' tanks with water. To surface, they empty the tanks.

❍ The first workable submarine was a rowing boat covered with waterproofed skins, built by Dutch scientist Cornelius van Drebbel in 1620.

❍ On 23 January 1960, the bathyscaphe *Trieste*, controlled by Swiss oceanic engineer Jacques Piccard, descended a record 10,916 m into the Mariana Trench in the Pacific.

❍ The world's busiest ports are Shanghai, Singapore and Hong Kong.

❍ The world's busiest canal is the Kiel in northern Germany, through which 45,000 ships a year travel from the North Sea to the Baltic. It reduces the distance of the journey around Denmark by over 480 km.

Sailing ships rely on wind power to drive them along and can sail in almost any direction except directly into the wind – because the wind not only pushes the sails but also sucks them. As the wind blows across the curve of the sail, it speeds up and its pressure drops, creating suction in the same way that an aeroplane's wings create lift. However, the sail must be kept at exactly the right angle. Sailors let the sail swing round until the angle is right then hold it taut (tight) with ropes.

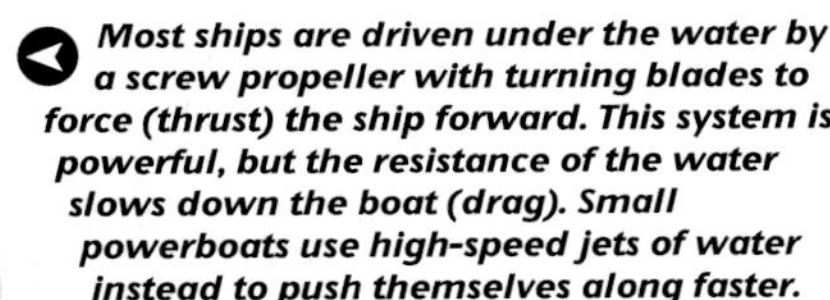

Most ships are driven under the water by a screw propeller with turning blades to force (thrust) the ship forward. This system is powerful, but the resistance of the water slows down the boat (drag). Small powerboats use high-speed jets of water instead to push themselves along faster.

Emergency signals

The following signals indicate an emergency at sea and a request for help:

1 Parachute flare or hand flare showing a red light
2 Rockets that throw off red stars at intervals
3 Smoke signals emitting large volumes of orange smoke
4 Signal by radio in the Morse Code group SOS or the spoken word MAYDAY (only used in life-threatening emergencies)
5 Slowly raising and lowering hands repeatedly
6 Continuous sounding of whistle or siren
7 Flames on the vessel (for example, from the burning of an oily rag)
8 Flying the International Flag code signal NC
9 Flying a square flag with a ball above or below it
10 An ensign (flag) flown upside down
11 A coat or article of clothing on an oar or mast

History of Air Transport

An aircraft's wings are lifted by the air flowing above and beneath them as they slice through the air. The amount of lift depends on the angle of the wing and its shape, and also how fast it is moving through the air.

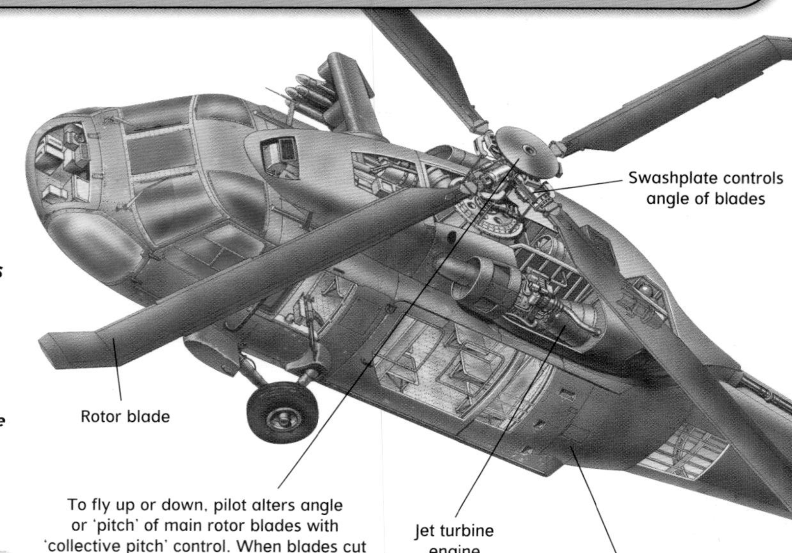

A helicopter's rotor blades are really long, thin wings. The engine whirls them round so that they cut through the air and provide lift just like conventional wings. But rotor blades are also like huge propellers, hauling the helicopter up just as a propeller pulls a plane.

Amazing

The first controlled, powered flight was made by American Orville Wright in 1903. His plane, the *Flyer*, travelled just 36 m!

- The first jet engines were built at the same time in the 1930s by Hans von Ohain in Germany and Frank Whittle in Britain – though neither knew of the other's work.

- Turbojets are the original form of jet engine. Air is scooped in at the front of the engine and squeezed by spinning 'compressor' blades. Fuel sprayed into the squeezed air in the middle of the engine burns, causing the mixture to expand dramatically. The expanding air not only pushes round turbines, which drive the compressor, but also sends out a high-speed jet of hot air to propel the plane. This high-speed jet is noisy but good for ultra-fast warplanes and supersonic aircraft.

The four-engined Boeing 747 flies at 10,000–13,000 m, well above most storms, and it can fly non-stop from New York to Tokyo.

- Turboprops are turbojets that use most of their power to turn a propeller rather than force out a hot air jet.

- Turbofans are used by most airliners because they are quieter and cheaper to run. In these, extra turbines turn a huge fan at the front. Air driven by this fan bypasses the engine core and gives an extra boost at low speeds.

- The age of jet air travel really began with the American Boeing 707 and Douglas DC-8 of the late 1950s.

- The four-engined A380 jet can fly 15,000 km non-stop at speeds of up to 900 km/h. Two-engined jets like the Boeing 777 can now also fly these distances.

Rocket launch

Only powerful rockets can give the thrust to overcome gravity and launch spacecraft into space. They fall away in stages once the spacecraft is travelling fast enough.

❍ In 1936 German designer Heinrich Focke built an aircraft with two huge variable pitch rotors instead of wings and achieved a controlled hover. In 1939, German Anton Flettner built the first true helicopter.

Because the top of the wing is curved, air pushed over the wing speeds up and stretches out. The stretching of the air reduces its pressure. Underneath the wing, air slows down and bunches up, so air pressure here rises. The wing gains 'lift' as the wing is sucked from above and pushed from below.

Drag
Lift
Trailing edge
Thrust
Weight
Spar
Flap
Aileron
Leading edge
Tip

Tail rotor drive shaft

Supersonic planes travel faster than the speed of sound (about 1220 km/h at sea level at 15°C), but hypersonic aircraft travel five times faster. Experimental hypersonic aircraft, like this Boeing X-51A, are already being built and tested.

❍ The world's first airport was College Park in Maryland USA in 1909. Many early airports, such as Berlin's, were social centres, attracting thousands of visitors and sightseers each year.

❍ The world's largest airport is King Fahd in Saudi Arabia. It covers 780 sq km. The USA's biggest is Denver. Europe's biggest is Paris's Charles de Gaulle.

Early planes

Most early planes were biplanes (double-wingers) or even triplanes (triple-wingers). Biplane wings were strong because struts and wires linked the small, light wings to combine their strength. In the years after World War I, huge biplane airliners were built including the Handley Page Heracles of the 1930s.

❍ On 20 March 1999 Bertrand Piccard of Switzerland and Brian Jones of Britain completed the first round-the-world hot-air balloon flight.

❍ The first human parachute drop was made by Jacques Garnerin from a balloon over Paris in 1797.

❍ Modern hang-gliding began with the fabric delta (triangular) wing design developed by the American Francis Rogallo in the 1940s.

Busiest airports

	No. of passengers handled each year (millions)
Atlanta	95
Beijing Capital	84
London Heathrow	72
Tokyo Haneda	69
Chicago O'Hare	67
Los Angeles	67
Dubai	66
Jakarta	62
Paris Charles de Gaulle	62
Dallas/Fort Worth	60

Computers

At the heart of every computer is a powerful microchip called the central processing unit (CPU). The CPU works things out, within the guidelines set by the computer's operating system (basic working instructions).

Computers have come a long way since 1823 when English mathematician Charles Babbage invented the first type of computer – the 'difference engine'. It proved too complex to complete and in 1834 Babbage began constructing his 'analytical engine' in which data was fed into the engine by punched cards. The results were designed to be printed out. Though it was never built in full, as it would have been the size of a small train, Babbage's idea helped others to invent the first practical computers.

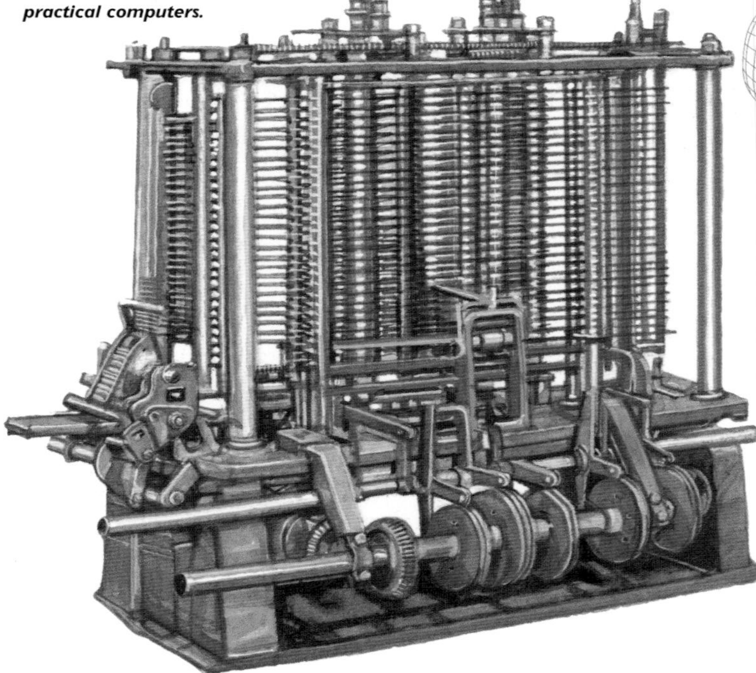

Amazing

The world's most powerful computer is Tianhe-2, installed at the National Supercomputing centre at Guangzhou, China. It is designed to be able to carry out 54,900 trillion calculations a second.

- A microchip is a slice of a semiconductor material such as silicon. 'Micro' means that all the components and connections of the integrated circuit on the chip are microscopic in size.

- Information is fed into the CPU as patterns of millions of tiny electrical signals per second.

Computers can sometimes fool us into thinking something is real using virtual reality (VR) systems. VR sends data (information) to our senses that closely mimic real scenes or events. In the VR tennis game below, pressure and flex (bending) sensors in the glove detect wrist, hand and finger movements and send signals to a computer. The computer analyses these movements to determine if the player had moved in the correct way to hit the 'virtual' ball, which can only be seen through the eyepieces.

- The microcircuits in the CPU analyse or process the signals and 'decide' what to do according to a set of rules built into the circuit design. The results are fed out as more electrical signals to various other parts of the computer.

- RAM (random-access memory) consists of microchips that receive new data and instructions when needed.

- The circuit can be made up of thousands of individual components. The components, such as switches, resistors, capacitors and transistors, are connected by wires or metal strips on the circuit board.

Computer hygiene

Electronic components must be made in extremely clean conditions. A few specks of dust could get inside the components and ruin the manufacture of microchips and electrical circuit boards.

❍ In general, computing ability doubles in speed and power every 18 months. This is called Moore's law, named after Gordon Moore who suggested it would happen in 1965.

❍ Some microprocessors can handle billions of bits of data every second.

Microchips

Microchips and other components are connected by inserting their metal 'legs' into sockets.

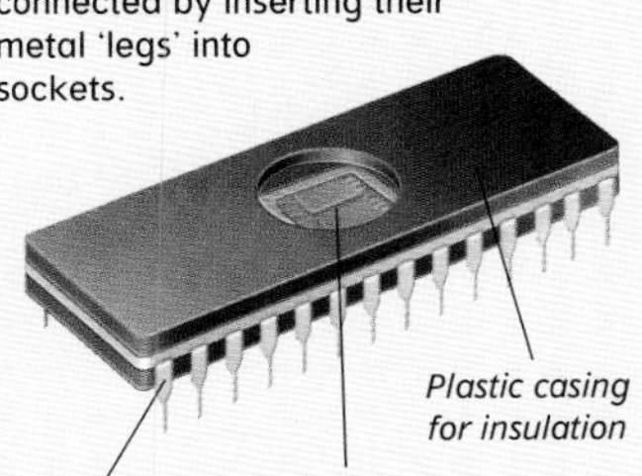

❍ Computers store information in bits (binary digits), either as 0 or 1.

❍ The bits 0 and 1 are equivalent to the OFF (0) and ON (1) of electric current flow. Eight bits make a byte.

The latest personal computers (PCs) are flat-screened. A liquid crystal display (LCD) produces images on a flat screen by using electric current to control the path of light through liquid crystals and coloured filters. The mouse and keyboard are connected by a short-range wireless system.

Computer abbreviations

AAC	Advanced Audio Coding
AGP	Accelerated Graphics Port
AI	Artificial Intelligence
AMD	Advanced Micro Devices
API	Application Programming Interface
BASIC	Beginners All-Purpose Symbolic Instruction Code
BBS	Bulletin Board System
CAD	Computer Aided Design
CPU	Central Processing Unit
DOS	Disc Operating System
FAQ	Frequently Asked Questions
GIGO	Garbage In Garbage Out
HTML	Hypertext Markup Language
HTTP	Hypertext Transfer Protocol
ICT	Information and Communications Technology
LAN	Local Area Network
MMU	Memory Management Unit
PC	Personal Computer
RAM	Random-Access Memory
ROM	Read Only Memory
WAN	Wide Area Network
WAP	Wireless Application Protocol
WYSIWYG	What You See Is What You Get
WWW	World Wide Web

Transistors are electronic switches. They are made of materials called semiconductors that change their ability to conduct electricity. In the early 1970s, the CPUs or microprocessor chips inside the first home computers contained about 8000 transistors each. By the early 21st century, several billion transistors can be found in the same-sized chip, working a thousand times faster than the first ones.

Telecommunications

Telecommunications is the transmission of sounds, words, pictures, data and other forms of information by electronic means. In order to function, every telecommunication system needs three things: a transmitter, a communications link and a receiver.

❍ Transmitters can be telephones or computers with modems. They change the words, pictures, data or sounds into an electrical signal and send it. Similar receivers pick up the signal and change it back into the right form.

Amazing

FLAG (Fibre-optic Link Around the Globe) is a submarine telephone cable that runs for 28,000 km from Japan to the UK. FLAG links many countries in Europe, Africa and Asia via the Mediterranean, the Indian Ocean and the South China Sea. The cable can support 600,000 simultaneous telephone calls.

❍ Telecommunications links carry the signal from the transmitter to the receiver in two main ways. Some give a direct link through telephone lines and other cables. Some are carried on radio waves through the air, via satellite or microwave links.

❍ Telephone lines used to be mainly electric cables, which carried the signal as pulses of electricity. More and more fibre optics are used, which carry the signal as coded pulses of light.

❍ Single-mode fibres are very narrow and the light bounces very little from side-to-side. These fibres are suitable for long-distance transmissions.

❍ The largest cables can carry hundreds of thousands of phone calls or hundreds of different television channels.

❍ Microwave links use very short radio waves to transmit telephone and other signals from one aerial to another. The signals travel between the aerials in a straight line.

Mobile phones

Mobile or cell phones use low-power radio waves to send messages. Areas across the world are divided into many small sectors called cells, each with an antenna that picks up signals from phones and sends them out. Because there are so many antennae spread across the world, millions of people can use mobile phones at once.

Broadcast communications satellites send radio signals direct to many receivers over a wide area, for radio programmes and television channels.

Communications satellite

Broadcast radio signals

Domestic satellite TV dish

Radio receiver

Radio lingo

A	Alpha	N	November
B	Bravo	O	Oscar
C	Charlie	P	Papa
D	Delta	Q	Quebec
E	Echo	R	Romeo
F	Foxtrot	S	Sierra
G	Golf	T	Tango
H	Hotel	U	Uniform
I	India	V	Victor
J	Juliet	W	Whisky
K	Kilo	X	X-ray
L	Lima	Y	Yankee
M	Mike	Z	Zulu

Wi-Fi networks

Wi-Fi networks are wireless local area networks that allow laptops, smartphones, video games consoles, printers and other devices to be linked. Wi-Fi provides access to computer networks anywhere within given locations, even in the open air. Radio waves carry signals between the components so there is no need for connecting wires. Wi-Fi networks may cover university campuses, whole towns or city centres.

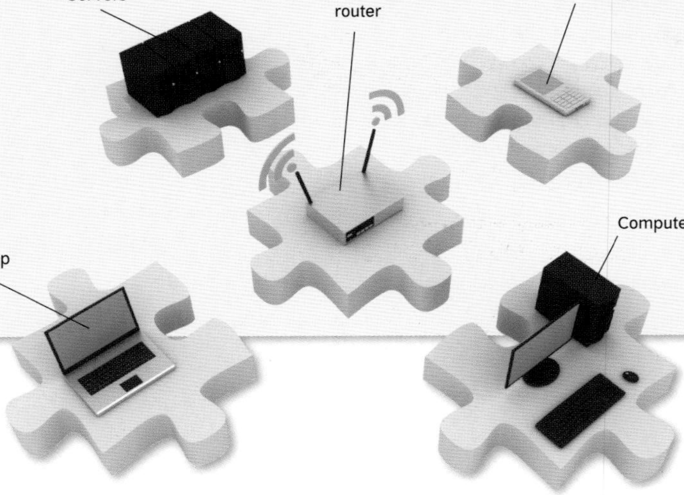

Servers

Wireless router

Mobile phone

Computer

Laptop

❍ Communications satellites are satellites orbiting the Earth in space. Telephone calls are beamed up on radio waves to the satellite, which beams them back down to the recipient, in the right part of the world.

❍ Most calls across the ocean go by undersea cable which is faster and cheaper than a satellite and can carry more calls.

❍ Most of the 1100 working satellites circling the Earth in space are used for telecommunications. Communications satellites use a special 'geo-stationary' orbit, which ensures that they are always in the same place above the Earth's surface.

❍ E-mail is a fast and convenient system for transmitting messages and files. The message is typed on a computer, smartphone or similar device, and is sent to the recipient's e-mail address. The message is stored until the recipient logs in to receive it.

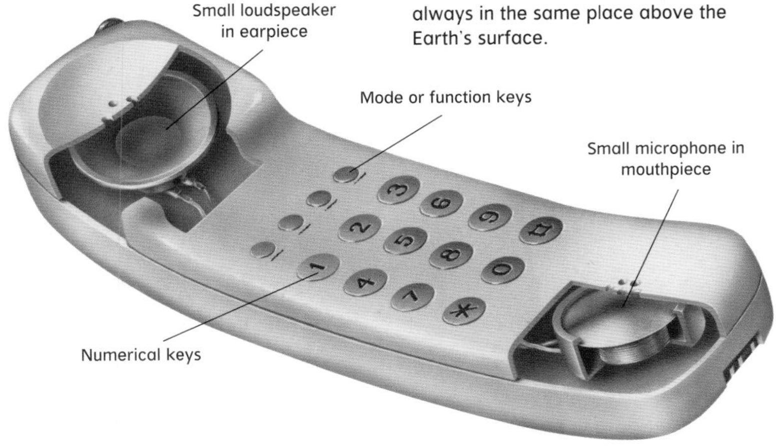

Small loudspeaker in earpiece

Mode or function keys

Small microphone in mouthpiece

Numerical keys

Telephones convert sound into an electrical signal. When you speak into a phone, the vibrations of your voice move a tiny microphone that alters an electrical current in strength. This creates an electrical signal, which is sent to the receiving phone. In the receiver the varying signal works a loudspeaker, which vibrates the air and recreates the sound of your voice. Today, many signals are sent as pulses of laser light along special glass threads called optical fibres. Signals are also sent as radio waves or microwaves through the air, or bouncing off satellites in space.

The Internet

The Internet is a vast network linking millions of computers around the world. The Internet began as a limited network called ARPAnet for the US military in 1969, was widened to research centres in the 1970s, taken up by businesses in the 1980s, and opened for public access in the 1990s.

❍ A hyperlink is a fast link between pieces of information on the Internet.

Amazing

In 2000 the 'I Love You' computer virus caused chaos on millions of computers across the globe. It deleted files and sent valuable information, such as passwords, to its home site in the Philippines.

❍ The World Wide Web is a network of hyperlinks – it's a way of navigating to the data in sites on all the computers linked to the Internet.

❍ The World Wide Web was invented in 1989 by Englishman Tim Berners-Lee of the CERN laboratories in Switzerland.

❍ For the Internet a computer's output is translated into a form that can be sent by phone lines with a modem (short for modulator/demodulator).

The Internet consists of the global telecommunications network and all the computers that are connected to the network at any particular time. Web sites and web pages are often said to exist in 'cyberspace', because they have no physical existence. In fact, the various components of a web page (headings, text, pictures, etc.) may be stored on different computers that are thousands of kilometres apart.

Signals from individual transmitters are sent on from a telephone exchange or an Internet service provider

Computer data is translated by a modem into signals that can be carried along phone lines

TV and radio signals are either broadcast as pulses of radio waves, sent direct via cables or broadcast from satellites

Portable laptop computers can be either mains- or battery-operated, and are small enough that they can be used at various locations.

Computer games

Computer games become more realistic every year, with faster action and better graphics, as well as more imaginative challenges. Many games can be played live over the Internet with people anywhere in the world.

Games console feeds images to monitor

Hand console with controls

Take a tablet

A tablet device is a mobile computer that usually includes features such as a camera, microphone and touchscreen. More portable than a laptop but with a larger screen than a smart phone, tablets are a popular way to browse the Internet.

Communications travel via satellites and are beamed up-and-down from antenna dishes on ground

Many communications, such as mobile phone calls and e-mails, are sent on or relayed by satellites in space

Telephones link into phone network by a direct cable link. Phones link through the air to local relay towers by radio waves

- Computers access the Internet via a local phone line to a large computer called the Internet Service Provider (ISP).
- Each ISP is connected to an internet exchange point (IXP). There are many linked IXPs worldwide.
- Some links between IXPs are made via telephone lines, while others are made via satellite.
- Web pages are viewed using a piece of software called a browser. The browser allows the user to search the Internet to find information about almost anything.
- A plug-in is a piece of software that extends the capabilities of a browser – for example, by enabling greater control of privacy, or blocking advertisements.
- HTML stands for hypertext mark-up language – a series of symbols that tells browsers how to display the words and pictures on a web page.
- There are trillions of different pages on the web, and people find the pages they want by entering keywords into a search engine.
- A broadband connection gives high-speed Internet access and is always on. It can be over ten times faster than traditional dial-up access, which uses an ordinary telephone line.

What can you use the Internet for?

1. View pictures
2. Read text
3. Watch television and see movies
4. Have 'real-time' conversations with friends using audio software and web cameras (webcams)
5. Listen to sounds and music
6. Shop and buy products
7. Send messages by e-mail
8. Send files to other people by file transfer protocol (FTP)
9. Join newsgroups and e-distribution lists
10. Take part in live, on-line discussions

Audiovisual Technology

People love gadgets – they make life easier and more fun, and many are used for entertainment. The machines and gadgets we use to play audio (sound) and visuals (images) include TVs, computers and MP3 players.

❍ Most sound recording today is digital, which means that sound vibrations are broken into tiny electrical chunks.

❍ To make a digital recording a device called an analogue-to-digital converter divides the sound vibrations into 44,100 segments for each second.

❍ On a CD (compact disc) the pattern of electrical pulses is burned by laser as a pattern of pits on the disc surface.

A powerful microscope reveals the bowl-like pits and the flat areas between them in the surface of a CD.

Amazing

The first ever sound recording was made in 1877 by American inventor Thomas Edison. He recorded the words "Mary had a little lamb," on to tin foil using a device called a phonograph.

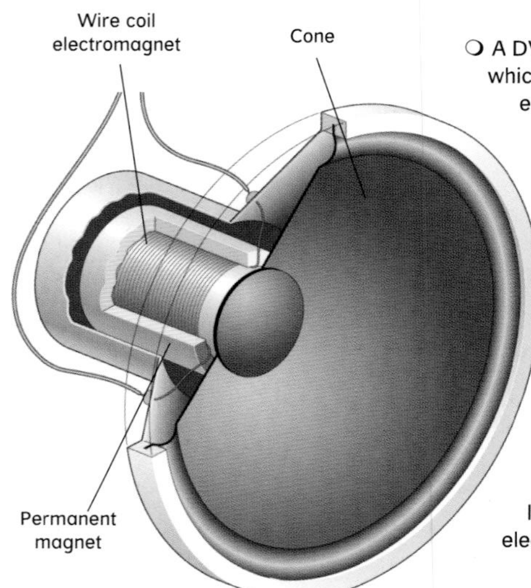

A loudspeaker converts a changing electric current into sound. Electrical signals flow through a wire coil and turn it into an electromagnet, which pushes and pulls against a permanent magnet to vibrate a cone and produce sound.

❍ In a CD there are over 3000 million pits in a spiral path or track about 5 km long. They can store about 70 minutes of high-quality music, over 700 megabytes (MB) of computer data or similar amounts of information.

❍ A DVD has more pits than a CD. The pits are smaller and arranged in different vertical layers.

Milestones

1936 First regular TV broadcasts in UK
1948 First LP discs produced
1951 First colour TV broadcasts in USA
1962 International relay of TV pictures by *Telstar* satellite
1964 Cassette tapes become available
1975 Flat liquid crystal display (LCD) TV screen developed
1977 Pocket TVs go on sale
1982 Compact discs widely available
1984 Camcorders introduced
1993 Computer videophones created
1996 DVDs introduced commercially
2008 Sales of LCD TVs surpass cathode ray sets worldwide
2009 USA conversion from analogue to digital broadcasting

❍ A DVD stores 4.7 gigabytes (GB) – which is equal to 4700 megabytes – enough for a full-length movie and its soundtrack. These pits are 'read' by a laser beam.

❍ Television relies on the photoelectric effect – the emission of electrons by a substance when struck by photons of light. Light-sensitive photocells in cameras work like this.

❍ Television cameras have three sets of tubes with CCDs (reacting to red, green and blue light) to convert the picture into electrical signals.

The iPod took little more than one year to develop, under the close eye of Apple chief Steve Jobs. It was launched in 2001 with the catchphrase '1000 songs in your pocket'. On 9 April 2007, it was announced that Apple had sold its millionth iPod, making it the biggest-selling digital music player of all time.

❍ Flat screens took over in the 1990s from older, heavier, box-like, glass-screen displays known as CRTs – cathode ray tubes, which used far more electricity than a flat screen.

❍ A plasma screen has millions of tiny cells (compartments), and two sets or grids of wire-like electrodes at right angles to each other.

❍ Each cell in a plasma screen can be 'addressed' by sending electric pulses along two particular electrodes that cross at the cell. The pulses heat the cell's gas into a form called plasma, causing an area of coloured substance (the phosphor) to glow, creating the displays we see on screen.

Millions of pulses every second at different 'addresses' all over the screen build up the overall picture.

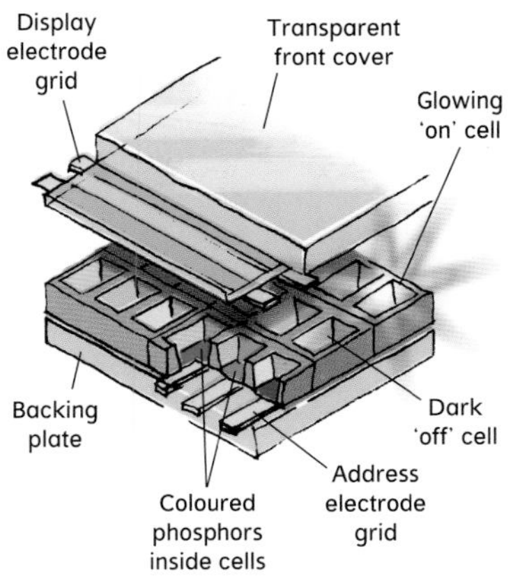

❍ In the past 20 years home cinemas have become bigger and better. The key parts are a widescreen display or television, a sound system with several loudspeakers, and the movie itself, on a DVD player or from an on-demand streaming service via the Internet.

❍ The wide screen format of home cinema televisions (16:9) has the correct proportions of width to height to fit neatly in our field of vision – the complete area that we can see with both eyes.

In a home cinema, audio information from the DVD or other source is fed into the sound system, which has controls such as volume (loudness), bass (deep notes), treble (high notes), balance (left or right speakers) and fade (front to rear speakers).

Camcorder

The camcorder is a personal movie camera and video recorder. Some easy-to-use models can now fit in the palm of the hand.

Laser beam

The amazingly intense light beam produced by a laser is used in a huge number of devices, from CD players to optical communications cables.

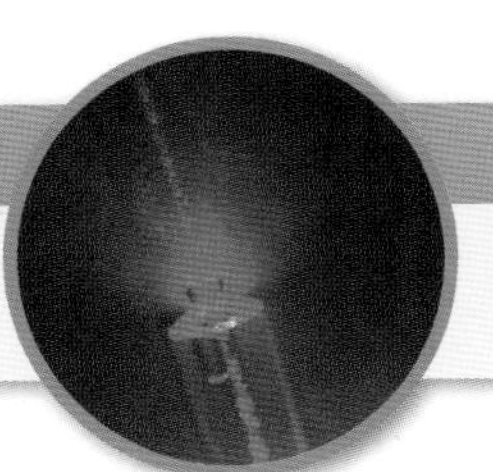

Power

Our world is driven by energy. Without energy the world would be dark, cold, still and silent. We use it in many forms, including movement, sound, chemical bonds, electricity, heat, light, waves and rays. Energy is needed to power thousands of devices and machines.

❍ Engines are devices that convert energy from fuel into movement.

❍ Engines that burn fuel to generate power are called heat engines. The burning is called combustion.

❍ An internal combustion engine, as used in a car, a jet or a rocket, burns its fuel inside the engine.

❍ In four-stroke engines, such as those in most cars, the pistons go up-and-down four times for each time they are thrust down by the hot gases.

❍ In jets and rockets, the engine produces hot gases which shoot out, pushing it forwards.

Oil refinery

In an oil refinery, crude oil is broken down into an enormous range of different hydrocarbons. Crude oil is separated by distillation into various substances, such as aviation fuel, gasoline and paraffin. As the oil is heated in a distillation column, a mixture of gases evaporates. Each gas cools and condenses at a different height into a liquid, or fraction, which is then drawn off.

❍ About 65 per cent of the world's electricity is thermal electricity, which is produced in power stations by burning coal, oil, and natural gas. Peat, alcohol, and biomass (firewood) are also used, but to a lesser extent.

❍ The other 35 per cent of the world's electricity is generated using nuclear energy, or by harnessing the energy of river water (hydro-electricity), sunlight (solar electricity), or the wind and tides.

❍ France is the most nuclear-electric country in the world – about 75 per cent of French electricity is generated in nuclear power stations.

Amazing

One kilogram of uranium can give the same amount of energy as 14,000 kg of coal.

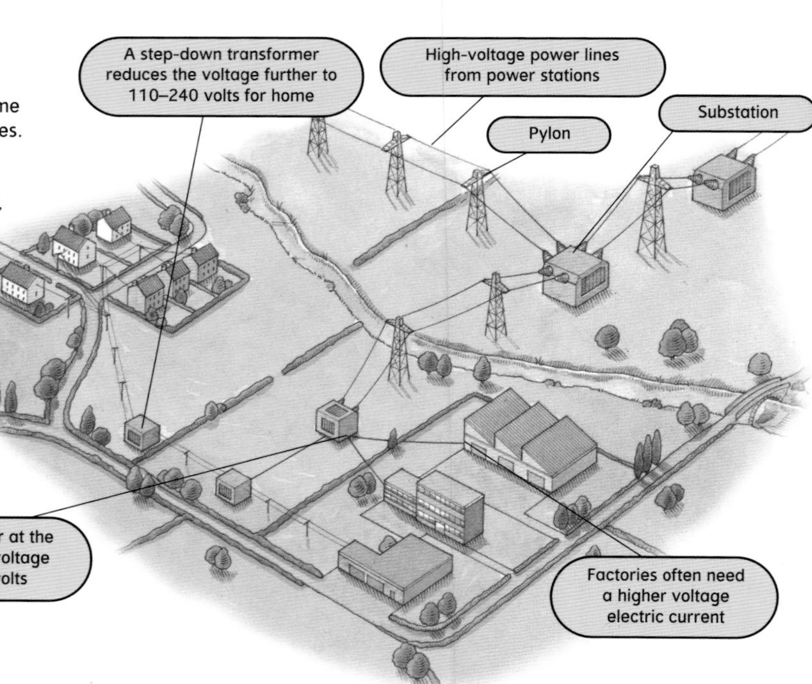

➤ ***Electricity is brought to homes and factories through a network of high-tension cables. Some cables are buried underground, some are suspended high in the air from metal towers called pylons.***

Common fuels

Common fuels we burn for energy include oil, coal and gas. These were formed by the fossilization of decayed plants and other life-forms long ago. Their energy came as light from the Sun. Oil and coal are extracted from deep in the ground, formed beneath rock layers.

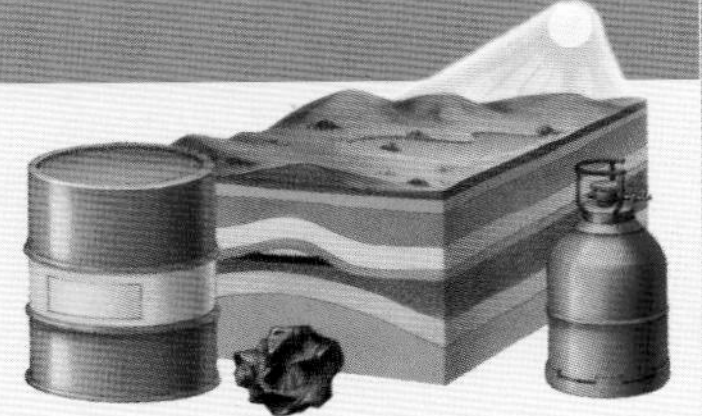

❍ In thermal power stations fuels are burned to make heat. The heat is used to boil water into steam, which blasts past the fan-shaped blades or rotors of a turbine and makes them spin. The turbine is linked to a generator. The spinning turbine rotates a magnetic field inside the generator, which makes electricity flow through a coil of wire around it.

❍ In hydroelectric power stations, running water spins the turbine blades.

❍ Electricity from power stations is distributed around a country in a network of cables known as the grid.

❍ Power station generators push out 25,000 volts or more. This voltage is too much to use in people's homes, but not enough to transmit over long distances.

❍ To transmit electricity over long distances, the voltage is boosted from 25,000 to 400,000 volts by step-up transformers. It is fed through high-voltage cables. Near its destination the electricity's voltage is reduced by step-down transformers at substations for distribution to homes, shops, offices and factories.

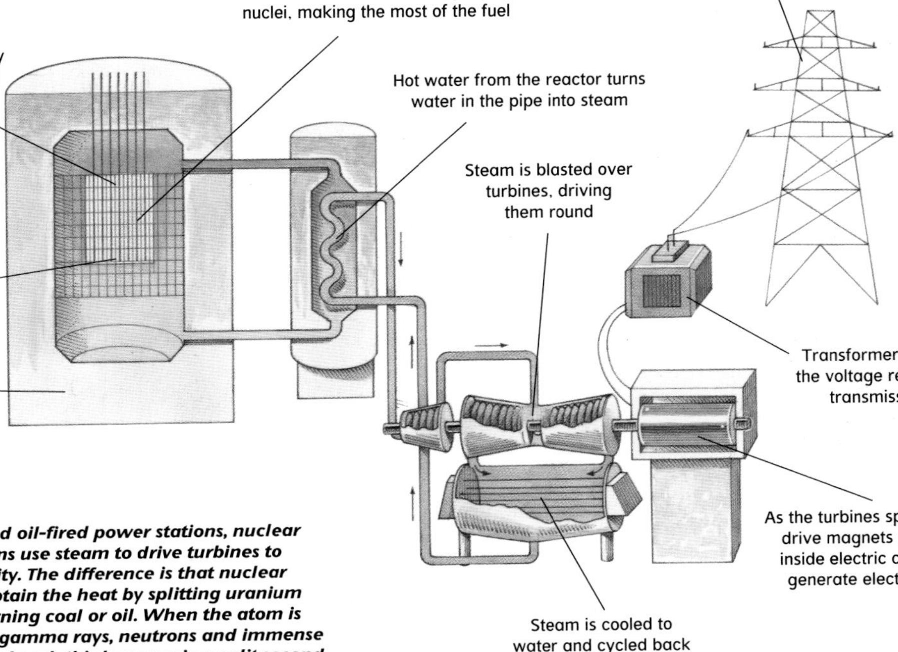

Control rods slow the process down by absorbing neutrons

A 'moderator' such as graphite slows down the neutrons so that they hit more nuclei, making the most of the fuel

Hot water from the reactor turns water in the pipe into steam

Electricity is distributed across the country through high-voltage power lines

Steam is blasted over turbines, driving them round

Uranium fuel rods give off heat

Concrete surrounds the reactor

Transformer boosts the voltage ready for transmission

As the turbines spin, they drive magnets round inside electric coils to generate electricity

Steam is cooled to water and cycled back to the reactor

Like coal- and oil-fired power stations, nuclear power stations use steam to drive turbines to generate electricity. The difference is that nuclear power stations obtain the heat by splitting uranium atoms, not by burning coal or oil. When the atom is split, it sends out gamma rays, neutrons and immense heat. In a nuclear bomb this happens in a split second. In a nuclear power plant, control rods soak up some of the neutrons and slow the process down.

Medicine

Technology is vital in many aspects of medicine today. Doctors can see inside the body using various kinds of scanners, or directly by looking through an 'endoscope'.

❍ An endoscope is a flexible tube that can be inserted into the body to view internal organs and achieve a more detailed and accurate diagnosis of a problem. Light to illuminate the interior of the body is carried to the tip of the endoscope along optical fibres.

Before an operation, patients are given anaesthetics, which either cause a loss of feeling in the body to numb the pain, or send them to sleep. English chemist Humphrey Davey noted the anaesthetic effects of nitrous oxide (laughing gas) in 1799, and in 1844 it was used by American dentist Horace Wells for tooth extractions. Later, other substances such as chloroform and ether were used. An operating theatre is kept extremely clean to prevent infection. Surgeons wear gloves, masks, hats and coats to avoid spreading germs through breathing and from cuts on the skin.

Amazing

Trepanning was an ancient practice that involved drilling a hole in the skull to relieve severe headaches, or release 'evil spirits' that were believed to cause mental illness. If the person survived, the bone eventually grew back over the hole.

❍ The natural background radiation you receive over a year is up to 100 times what you receive from a single ordinary chest X-ray.

PET scans

PET scans can show a living brain in action. This scan shows a monkey's brain from above.

A person's heart normally beats at about 60 to 100 times a minute but sometimes the rate becomes too fast or too slow. The rhythm can be corrected or steadied by a pacemaker, which was developed by Swedish doctor Ake Senning in 1958. The battery-operated pacemaker is connected to the heart and sends it timed electrical impulses to help it beat with a regular rhythm.

❍ Various complex scanners are used in medicine to give pictures of the inside of the body and help doctors diagnose problems. They include PET scanners, CT scanners and MRI scanners.

Doctors and diseases

Doctor	Specializes In
Cardiologist	Heart disease
Dermatologist	Skin
Gynaecologist	Female reproduction
Haematologist	Blood
Histologist	Cells and tissue
Nephrologist	Kidney
Neurologist	Nervous system
Ophthalmologist	Eyes
Otologist	Ear
Paediatrician	Children
Proctologist	Rectum and lower intestine

Disease	Affects
Athritis	Joints
Bursitis	Joints
Cirrhosis	Liver
Conjunctivitis	Eyes
Cystitus	Bladder
Dermatitis	Skin
Gingivitis	Gums
Glossitis	Tongue
Hepatitis	Liver
Meningitis	Brain
Phlebitis	Veins
Pneumonia	Lungs

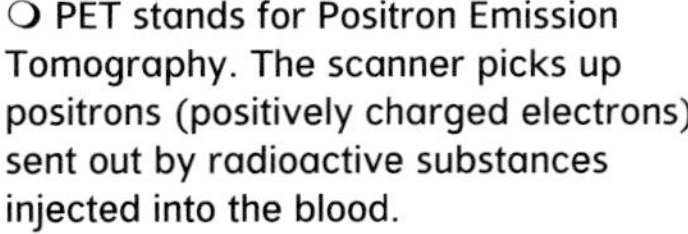

❍ PET stands for Positron Emission Tomography. The scanner picks up positrons (positively charged electrons) sent out by radioactive substances injected into the blood.

❍ CT stands for computerized tomography. An X-ray beam rotates around the patient and is picked up by detectors on the far side to build up a three-dimensional (3-D) picture.

❍ MRI stands for Magnetic Resonance Imaging. An MRI scan works like a CT scan but it uses magnetism, not X-rays. The patient is surrounded by such powerful magnets that all the body's protons line up.

❍ Genes are found in every living cell on special molecules called DNA (deoxyribonucleic acid). Scientists alter genes by snipping them from the DNA of one organism and inserting them into the DNA of another. This process is known as gene splicing.

X-rays

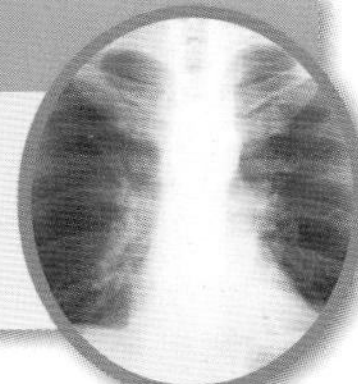

X-rays pass through most body tissues except bones, which show up white on medical X-rays.

❍ By splicing new genes into the DNA of bacteria, scientists can turn them into factories for making valuable natural chemicals. One protein made like this is interferon, a natural body chemical that protects humans against certain viruses. Enzymes for detergents and melanin for suntan lotion can also be made in this way.

❍ Gene therapy means altering the genes to cure diseases that are inherited from parents or caused by faulty genes.

Numbers and Shapes

Numbers are used for counting, calculating, and measuring quantities and sizes. Number symbols are also used for identification and to establish a sequence, as in the page numbers in this book.

❍ Throughout history people have used 10 as the basis for their numbers because we have ten digits (eight fingers and two thumbs) on our hands.

❍ More than 4000 years ago the ancient Egyptians had a number system that used just four symbols to write all the numbers smaller than 10,000. The symbols they used were for 1, 10, 100, and 1000. So 365 was written as 100+100+100+10+10+10+10+10+10 +1+1+1+1+1.

❍ Despite having such a cumbersome number system, the ancient Egyptians were able to calculate well enough to build the giant stone pyramids at Giza.

❍ The ancient Sumerians used a 10-based system that was similar to the Egyptian system, but the Sumerians also considered the number 6 to be important because 10 x 6 x 6 = 360, which is nearly the exact number of days in a year (365).

Amazing

The word 'plus' comes from the Latin word for 'more'. The symbol + was originally written on sacks and boxes that were overweight. The symbol – (minus) was written on those that were underweight.

❍ It is because of the ancient Sumerians that hours are divided into 60 (10 x 6) minutes, each with 60 seconds; and that a circle is divided into 360°.

Binary numbers

Computers and other electronic devices operate using the binary system of numbers that has just two symbols, 1 and 0. These two symbols correspond to an electronic switch being either on (1) or off (0). Binary numbers are difficult to read without a lot of practice. The number 10 is written in binary as 1010, 23 is written as 10111, and 55 is written as 110111.

❍ The ancient Romans had a number system that used seven letter symbols to write all the numbers below 10,000. The symbols they used were: I (1), V (5), X (10), L (50), C (100), D (500), and M (1000). So 365 was written as CCCLXV (100+100+100+50+10+5).

❍ The Mayans of Mexico used a base-20 number system 1500 years ago.

❍ Most Roman numbers were written by adding together smaller numbers like the Egyptians did, but some Roman numbers were written using subtraction instead. The number 4 was written as IV (5–1), 9 was written as IX (10–1), and 99 was written as IC (100–1).

❍ Roman numbers are still sometimes used to give the date at the end of a motion picture, for example MMV (2005).

Round the world

Many civilizations invented systems of numbers. Most ancient systems did not use the number zero. This made counting difficult. Arabic numbers are now the main system, because they are so easy to use.

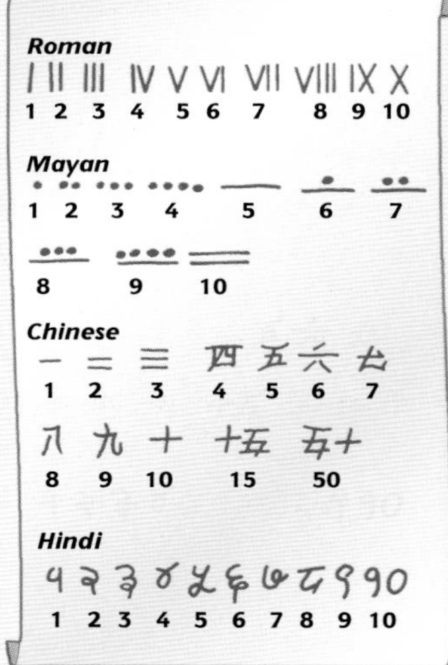

❍ The numbers we use today are based on Arabic numbers that were first used nearly 1500 years ago.

❍ The decimal system that is now used around the world was not possible until the Arabs invented a symbol for the number 0 (zero).

❍ The Arabs took the ancient Indian numbers for 1–9 and added the number 0 (zero), so that large numbers such as 500 and 1000 did not need their own special symbols.

Regular polygons

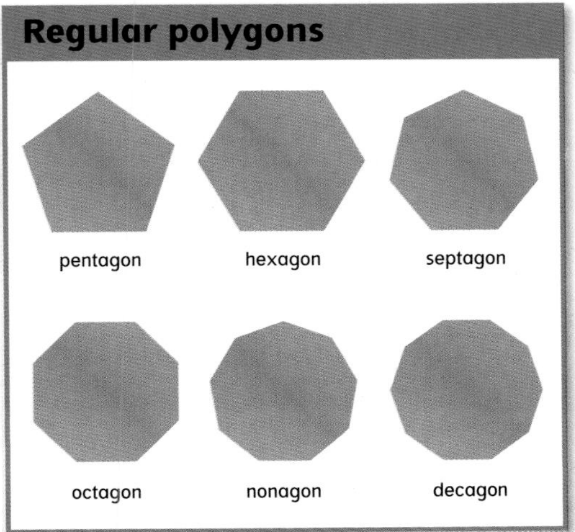

Regular polyhedrons

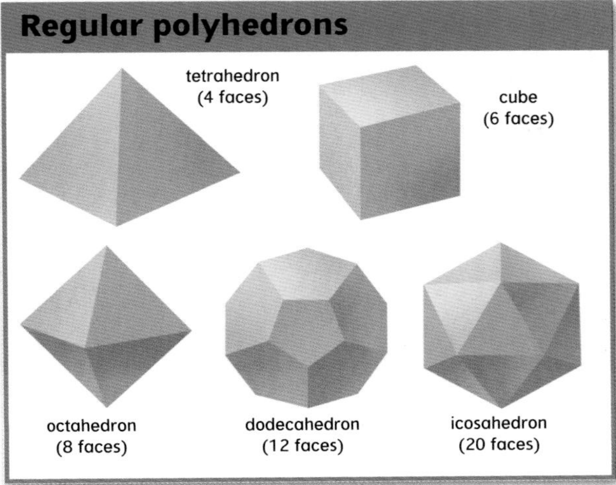

Areas of 2-D (flat or plane) shapes

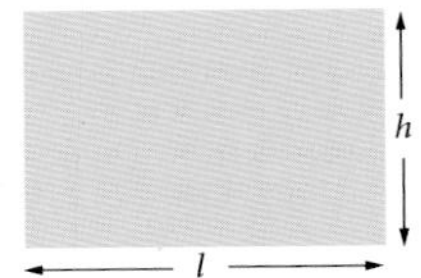

area of a **rectangle**
= length x height
$= l \times h$

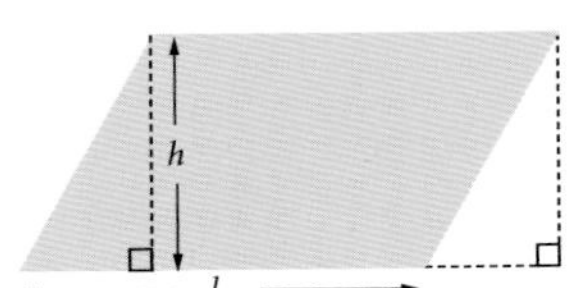

area of a **parallelogram**
= base length x right-angle height
$= l \times h$

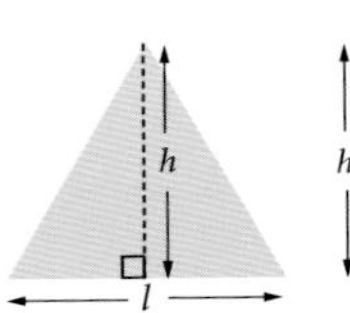

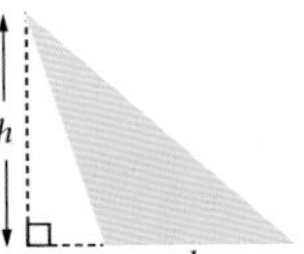

area of a **triangle**
= ½ base length x right-angle height
$= \frac{1}{2} l \times h$

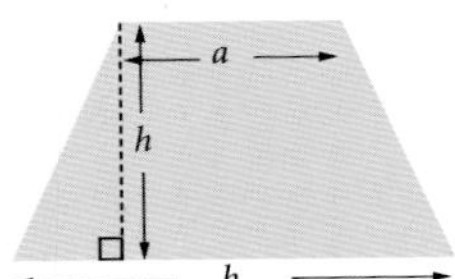

area of a **trapezium**
= ½ (sum of parallel sides) x right-angle height
$= \frac{1}{2}(a + b) \times h$

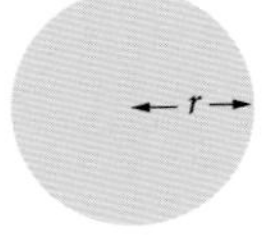

area of a **circle**
$= \pi \times \text{radius}^2$
$= \pi r^2$

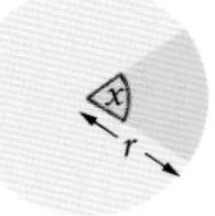

area of a **sector**
$= \frac{\text{angle of sector}}{360} \times \pi \times \text{radius}^2$
$= \frac{x}{360} \times \pi r^2$

Surface area of common 3-D shapes

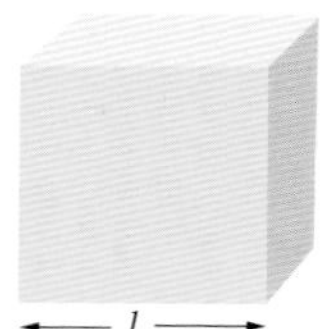

surface area of a **cube**
(faces are identical)
= 6 x area of each surface
= $6l^2$

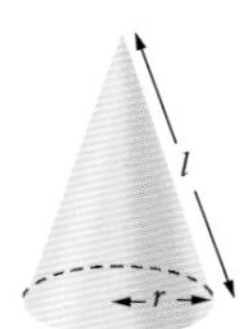

surface area of a **cone**
= area of a curved surface + area of base
= $\frac{1}{3}$ x π x (radius of cross section)^2 x slant height = $\frac{1}{3}\pi r^2 l$
= $\pi rl + \pi r^2$
= $\pi r(l + r)$

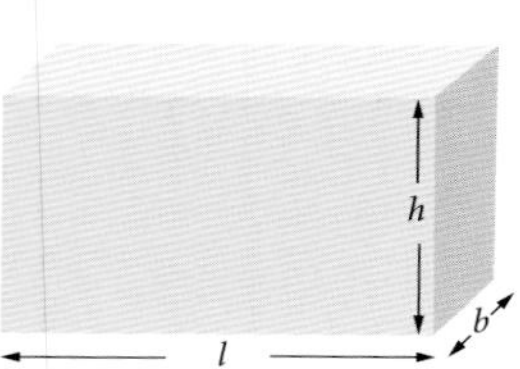

surface area of a **cuboid**
(opposite faces are identical)
= area of two end faces + area of two sides + area of top and base
= $2lh + 2hb + 2lb$
= $2(lh + hb + lb)$

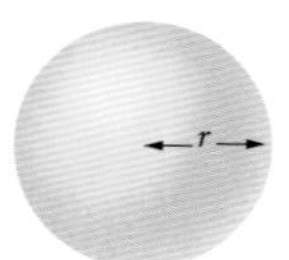

surface area of a **sphere**
= 4 x π x radius^2
= $4\pi r^2$

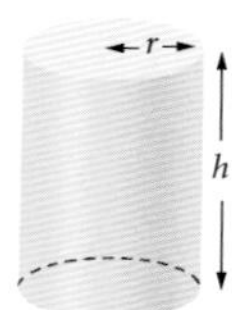

surface area of a **cylinder**
= area of a curved surface + area of top and base
= 2π x (radius of cross-section x height) + 2π x (radius of cross-section)^2
= $2\pi rh + 2\pi r^2$
= $2\pi r(h + r)$

Volume of common 3-D shapes

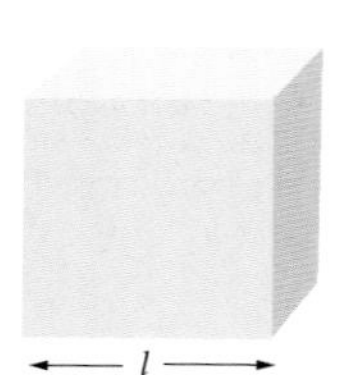

volume of a **cube**
= length^3
= l^3

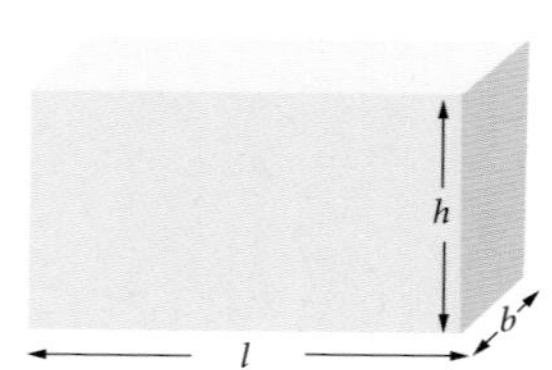

volume of a **cuboid**
= length x breadth x height
= $l \times b \times h$

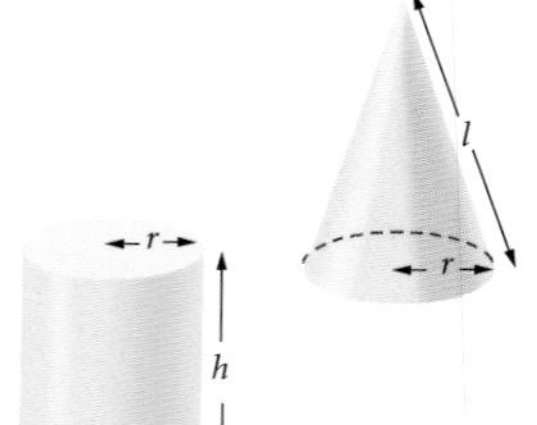

volume of a **cone**
= $\frac{1}{3}$ x (radius of cross-section)^2 x slant height
= $\frac{1}{3}\ r^2 l$

volume of a **cylinder**
= π x (radius of cross-section)^2 x height
= $\pi r^2 h$

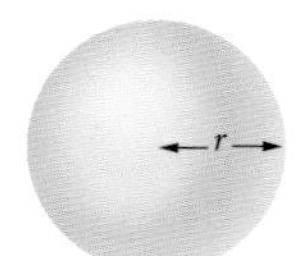
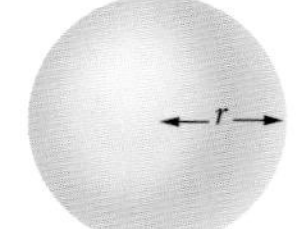

volume of a **sphere**
= $\frac{4}{3}\pi$ x radius^3
= $\frac{4}{3}\pi r^3$

Types of triangles

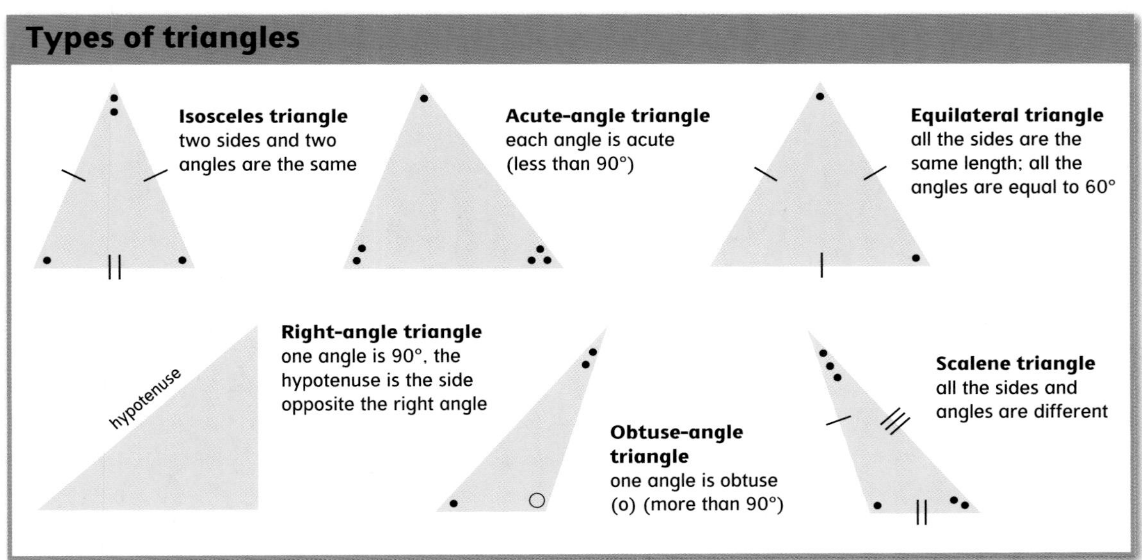

Trigonometry

For any right-angled triangle with angle u as shown the trigonometric ratios are:

$$\text{sine } u = \frac{BC}{AB} = \frac{\text{opposite}}{\text{hypotenuse}}$$

$$\cos u = \frac{AC}{AB} = \frac{\text{adjacent}}{\text{hypotenuse}}$$

$$\tan u = \frac{BC}{AC} = \frac{\text{opposite}}{\text{adjacent}}$$

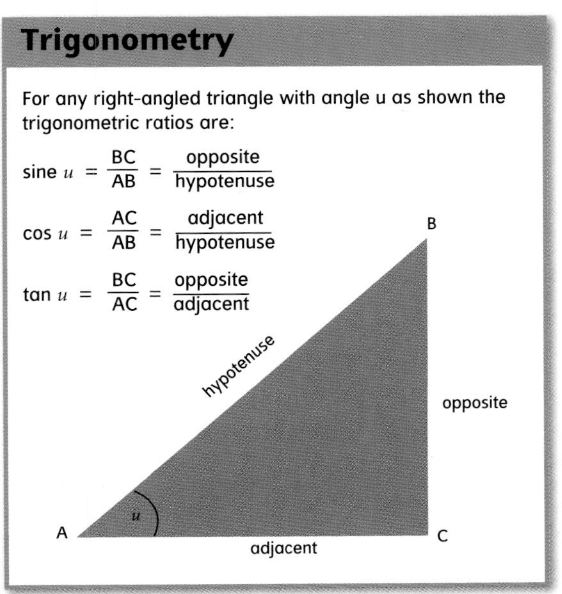

Pythagoras' theorem

Pythagoras' theorem $a^2 = b^2 + c^2$
i.e. the square of the hypotenuse is equal to the sum of the squares on the other two sides.

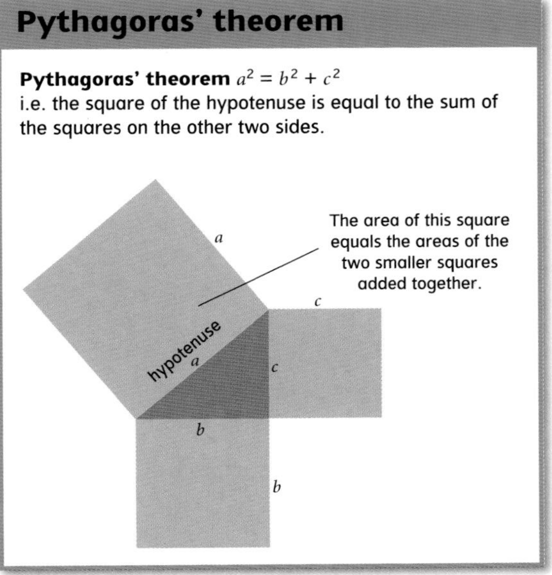

Glossary

Absolute zero the lowest temperature possible (–273.15° Centigrade).

Acceleration a change in velocity.

Air the mixture of gases that makes up Earth's atmosphere.

Alloy a type of metal made by adding other substances to a pure metal element.

Angle the relative position, measured in degrees (°), between two lines that meet or intersect.

Artificial manufactured or otherwise produced by human beings.

Atom the tiniest particle of any pure substance or chemical.

Bacteria single-celled organisms that live in a wide variety of environments, from hot springs to the human body.

Binary number a number written using just two symbols: 0 and 1.

Biplane an aircraft that has two wings, one above the other.

Boil to turn from a liquid into a gas.

Bond a close attachment formed by atoms and molecules.

CPU Central Processing Unit, the microchip that does most of the work in a computer.

Carbon an element that forms millions of compounds with other elements.

Carbon dioxide an invisible gas that is naturally present in air in small quantities.

Chemical formula a description of the number and type of atoms in a single molecule of a substance.

Circle a flat geometric shape in which every point around the edge is the same distance from the centre.

Circuit a pathway around which electricity flows.

Circumference the distance around the edge of a circle.

Compound a combination of two or more elements.

Conductor a material through which heat or electricity can flow.

DNA Deoxyribonucleic acid. DNA carries genetic information in the body.

Data information, usually expressed in electronic form.

Decibel the unit used to measure the loudness of sounds.

Diameter any line across a circle that passes through the centre.

Digital describes information that has been converted into binary numbers.

Electricity energy involving the flow of electrons through substances.

Electromagnetic radiation energy that travels as waves through space and matter.

Electron a subatomic particle that orbits the nucleus of an atom.

Element a pure substance that cannot be changed by chemical reactions.

Fax (facsimile) machine a device for sending written documents along telephone wires.

Freeze to turn from a liquid into a solid.

Friction the force that acts between two objects rubbing together.

Fulcrum the point on which a lever (a type of simple machine) pivots.

Gas any substance that flows and varies in volume to fit into a container.

Gene splicing the process of modifying DNA.

Heat the transfer of energy from a hot substance to a cold one.

Hydrogen the simplest element that is normally a gas. Hydrogen combines with oxygen to make water.

Insulator a material that resists the flow of heat or electricity.

ISP Internet Service Provider, a company that provides access to the Internet.

Internal combustion engine an engine in which the fuel burns inside the engine.

Jet engine an engine that blasts out hot gas to provide forward motion for aeroplanes.

Laser a device that produces very strong, amplified light of a particular wavelength.

Lever a simple machine that uses turning force to reduce the effort needed to move objects.

Light a form of electromagnetic energy that we can see with our eyes.

Liquid describes any substance that flows and has a fixed volume.

Machine a device that makes doing work easier.

Magnetic field the area around a magnet in which it exerts its force.

Magnetism an invisible force that attracts or repels magnetic materials, and which has electromagnetic effects.

Metal one of a group of elements with similar characteristics. Most metals are hard, have a shiny appearance, and are good conductors of heat and electricity.

Microchip a tiny electronic device that contains thousands of electrical circuits.

Modem (modulator/demodulator) a device that allows computers to send data along telephone cables.

Molecule two or more atoms held together by chemical bonds.

Mouse a device used to control the cursor on a computer screen.

Natural existing in nature without human assistance.

Neutron a subatomic particle without electric charge that forms part of the nucleus of an atom.

Noble gas one of the five gaseous elements that are almost totally unreactive.

Nucleus the central core of an atom.

Optical fibre a thin glass thread, along which light rays can pass. Optical fibres are used to transmit data in communications cables.

Organic chemistry the study of compounds that contain carbon.

Oxygen an element that is normally a gas. Oxygen is one of the components of air, and it is essential for living things.

Periodic Table an organized arrangement of chemical elements.

Plasma a substance that consists of electrically charged gas atoms.

Plastic an artificial substance made from crude oil.

Polymer a long chainlike molecule composed mainly of carbon and hydrogen atoms.

Proton a positively charged particle that forms part of the nucleus of an atom.

Radius the distance between the edge of a circle and the centre.

Rhombus a flat geometric shape that has four equal sides and two pairs of equal angles.

Right angle the relative position of two lines that meet or intersect at 90°.

Rocket a very powerful type of engine used in missiles and space vehicles.

Scanner a device that produces an electronic picture of something.

Shell one of the regions of space around the nucleus of an atom that is occupied by electrons.

Solid describes any substance that has strength and a fixed shape and volume.

Sphere a solid geometric shape in which every point on the surface is the same distance from the centre.

Square a flat geometric shape with four straight sides of equal length and four right angles.

Steam water in the form of a gas.

Steam engine a device that is driven by steam given off by boiling water.

Steel an alloy composed mainly of iron, together with a small amount of carbon. Other substances are also added.

Subatomic smaller than an atom.

Submersible small craft designed to operate underwater.

Temperature a measurement of how hot an object is.

Transparent allows light to pass through.

Trapezium a flat geometric shape that has four sides, two of which are parallel.

Triangle a flat geometric shape that has three straight sides.

Turbine a device that converts motion of a fluid into rotation.

Water a liquid that is a chemical compound of hydrogen and oxygen.

World Wide Web the part of the Internet available to public access.

X-rays high-energy radiation that can pass through skin and muscles.

ARTS & CULTURE

The First Artists

Many thousands of years ago, artists began to decorate the world in which they lived. There are many reasons why artists painted – personal, social, religious and magical. They also wanted to make their surroundings more interesting and more beautiful. Painting is clearly a natural instinct of human beings.

❍ The oldest-known works of art are small sculptures of bone and stone made in Europe around 38,000 BC. The most famous of these is the *Willendorf Venus*, found in Austria. It portrays a plump, semi-naked female figure, who was probably a fertility goddess.

❍ Many wonderful paintings, on rocks hidden deep inside caves, survive from around 40,000 to 15,000 years ago. They mostly show bison, deer and horses. These may have been holy animals that protected tribes of prehistoric people. Or they may have been painted by hunters, to give them magical power over their prey.

❍ The beauty of the natural world was the inspiration for many early artists. They created patterns and designs based on plants and living creatures.

The bright colours and varied shapes of flowers, birds and insects fascinated early craftworkers. They used dried plants, feathers and insect wings as raw materials, and created images of wild creatures to decorate their pottery, textiles, jewellery and stone carvings.

This dramatic picture of a bison, with head lowered ready to charge, was painted deep inside a cave at Lascaux, southern France, around 17,000 years ago. It was discovered by four French boys searching for treasure. Many more fine paintings, mostly of wild animals, have been found in caves nearby.

❍ Egyptians decorated mummies' tombs with wall-paintings, showing happy scenes in the afterlife. They believed that art had magic powers to help keep a dead person's spirit alive.

❍ For thousands of years, artists have created beautiful objects to honour dead ancestors. They have shaped containers for sacrifices (offerings) to ancestor spirits, and carved memorials recording ancestors' lives.

Amazing

Many murals (wall-paintings) were discovered in the Roman city of Pompeii, preserved under tonnes of ash from the eruption of Mount Vesuvius in AD 79.

❍ Much early art was made for use in religious ceremonies. Around 2000 years ago, Nazca artists in South America made pottery drums and played them to chants and dances.

Artists who came from many early civilizations, from South America to Siberia, made works of art to help dead people's spirits survive. The best known are ancient Egyptian mummies – dried-out, bandaged bodies, protected by beautifully decorated containers.

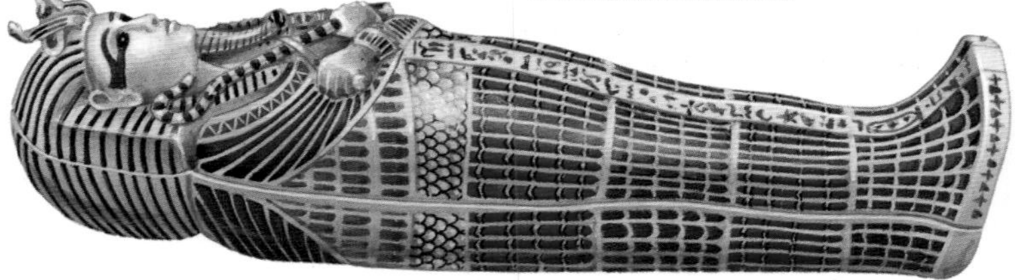

Pottery

For thousands of years, pottery has been beautifully painted with patterns and pictures, ranging from simple geometric designs to elaborate and complex scenes, including figures and landscapes. These Roman pots would have been used as kitchenware.

Square bronze vessels were used to offer food and drink to ancestor spirits in China over 3000 years ago. They were decorated with faces of 'taotie' – fierce monsters with claws and horns. Taotie may have originated as pictures of male ancestors but became monsters over time.

The Romans followed the Greek approach to sculpture, and many Greek sculptors went to work in Rome. This life-size sculpture of Augusto di Proma Porta can be seen today in the Vatican Museum, Rome, Italy.

❍ Gods and spirits feature in many early works of art. Long-haired nature-goddesses were pictured on statues, carvings and metalwork made by Celtic peoples living in Europe between around 800 BC and AD 100.

❍ Early Christian artists painted icons (holy images) of Christian saints. Worshippers believed that honouring these icons helped them to communicate with God.

Carefully planned

Ancient Egyptian artists, who worked between *c.*3100–30 BC, planned their tomb-paintings very carefully. First, they marked out the design on the tomb wall using a grid (pattern of squares) to help them. Then they sketched the outlines of human figures, plants and animals. Finally, they filled in the outlines with coloured paints.

Earliest art

c.38,000 BC	Small sculptures of stone and bone, Europe
c.38,000–15,000 BC	Many cave paintings, Europe
c.18,000 BC	Earliest-known pottery, China
c.10,000 BC	Rock-art pictures of human figures, Australia
c.8500 BC	Rock-art pictures of animals, North Africa
c.7000 BC	First copper jewellery, Middle East
c.6500 BC	First known woven cloth, Turkey
c.4800 BC	First engraved seals, used to stamp pictures on clay, Mesopotamia
c.4500 BC	First gold jewellery made, eastern Europe
c.3500 BC	Picture-writing invented, Mesopotamia
c.3000 BC	First jade jewellery made, China
c.2750 BC	First decorated bronze-castings, China
c.2700 BC	First silk made, China
c.2600 BC	Glass-making invented, Mesopotamia

❍ Between around 600 BC and AD 100, artists in ancient Greece and Rome created works of art portraying beautiful human bodies. Many of their greatest works show men and women naked, or wearing very few clothes. Artists often asked famous athletes to be their models, since they were fit, healthy and strong.

Old Masters, New Ideas

In Europe, from around AD 300, most art was based on Christian religious themes. But after around 1000 years, great changes took place in art and design. Artists began to copy ancient Greek and Roman works, and to observe the world around them with scientific curiosity. After another 500 years, fashions in art changed dramatically once again, as artists experimented with exciting new painting styles.

❍ Christian monks painted tiny, brilliant 'illuminations' (images) to illustrate religious books they had carefully written by hand. They were not just for decoration, but helped the reader to find particular passages of text faster.

In the 18th and early 19th centuries, artists in France were trained to paint in schools called academies. The teachers were often very gifted artists who could paint with technical brilliance, however the strict teaching rules of these schools tended to stifle personal flair. This meant artists who trained in them often produced technically correct but dull work.

❍ Monks did not try to make the people in their pictures look lifelike. Instead, they aimed to convey a religious message in their work.

❍ In medieval times most art was paid for by the Church but, during the Renaissance, rulers paid artists to work for them and preferred non-religious subjects for paintings, such as battles and Greek and Roman mythology.

❍ Artists in Italy were the first to study ancient Greek and Roman designs, from around AD 1300. Historians gave the art they created a new name, the 'Renaissance'. It meant the 'rebirth' of ancient civilization.

Amazing

In Medieval Europe, books were written out on vellum, a very fine kind of parchment made from the skin of a lamb, kid or calf.

Dutch painter Vincent van Gogh (1853–1890) was influenced by Impressionist painting techniques, but developed them in his own style. He created images, like this portrait of his friend, Dr Gachet, by using thick layers of oil paint, brushed onto canvas in swirling lines. This created striking images, and may have reflected Van Gogh's troubled mind.

Before the printing press was invented in the 1440s, manuscripts (handwritten books) were written out by monks. Their pages were decorated with beautiful small 'illuminations', or paintings. The early skills of European painting were learned by illumination. It could take a year to copy out and illuminate (illustrate) a medieval manuscript. For this reason, they were very valuable.

A ***A painting by Auguste Renoir (1841–1919). He tried to capture a lazy atmosphere and the relaxed feeling of friends sharing a meal. Renoir was an Impressionist and built up pictures using dabs of colour, rather than strong shapes and lines.***

❍ In France, around 1874, a group of artists pioneered a new painting style. They tried to convey their 'impression' of scenes, rather than create detailed copies. They experimented with ways of dabbing paint onto canvas to create movement, light and shade, and became known as the 'Impressionists'.

❍ The Impressionists painted using vibrant colours, rapid brush-strokes and swirls of paint. They painted outdoors to capture a sense of immediacy.

❍ Renaissance artists discovered 'perspective'. This is a way of painting that shows three dimensions on a flat surface. It transformed the way buildings, landscapes and crowds of people were portrayed.

❍ The best artists became known as 'Masters' or 'Old Masters'. They ran special 'academies' (schools) to teach students to paint and let them help in their studios.

Pointillism

Impressionist paintings inspired later artists to develop new techniques. They included Pointillism (painting with tiny 'points', of paint) to create fascinating 3-D effects without the use of hard line. This detail from a Pointillist painting, by French artist Georges Seurat (1859–1891), shows swimmers by a river on a sunny day.

❍ Around 1700, artists developed new painting skills. In 'Still Life' pictures, they copied flowers and animals in precise, realistic detail. They painted portraits that showed people's inner feelings as well as their outer appearance. With landscapes, they created dramatic effects of light and shade.

Leonardo da Vinci

The greatest Renaissance artists were not just painters and sculptors, but also gifted architects, engineers, poets and musicians. One of the most famous is the Italian Leonardo da Vinci (1452–1519). Although celebrated as a painter, he only completed about 25 paintings. He spent much of his time making drawings of his inventions – such as this flying machine, multi-barrelled guns, a parachute and even a tank.

European artists

1266–1337	**Giotto** Italian, his pictures showed people in a more lifelike way
1452–1519	**Leonardo da Vinci** Italian, painter, sculptor and architect, famous for the *Mona Lisa*
1475–1564	**Michelangelo Buionarotti** Italian, painted Rome's Sistine Chapel ceiling
1483–1520	**Raphael** Italian, famous for portraits of women and children, and biblical scenes
1541–1614	**El Greco** Spanish, painted many religious scenes
1606–1669	**Rembrandt von Rijn** Dutch, master of portraits
1775–1851	**J M W Turner** English, painted mostly landscapes
1776–1837	**John Constable** English, famous for his landscapes
1840–1926	**Claude Monet** French, Impressionist, famous for paintings of his garden and various landscape scenes
1853–1890	**Vincent van Gogh** Dutch, landscapes and portraits
1881–1973	**Pablo Picasso** Spanish, styles included abstract Cubism

Art Techniques

Artists use many different methods to create visual images and present important ideas. Whatever technique they use, they all hope to make us see the world in a new way – and to think about what we see.

Pottery (also called ceramics) is the art of making objects from clay. Wet clay is shaped by hand or by using a potter's wheel. Then it is dried, fired at high temperatures, cooled, and painted or covered with a glaze (thin layer of glass). This vase was made in ancient Greece around 400 BC.

A fresco is a picture painted directly on to fresh, wet plaster covering a ceiling or a wall. As the plaster dries, the paint bonds to it, creating an image. This is an Egyptian fresco.

Sculptors carve stone or mould clay to create statues and small figurines (model figures). This baked clay figure comes from the Bahia culture of Ecuador, South America, and is over 1500 years old.

Oil paints were invented in Europe around AD 1400. They could be blended smoothly together. This allowed artists to create subtle effects of light and shade, as in this painting by John Constable (1776–1837).

Watercolours are paints made of pigments (solid colours) mixed with water. They are used to create delicate, transparent 'washes' of colour on fine paper. This watercolour is by British artist Samuel Prout (1783–1852).

Since medieval times in Europe (c.AD 500–1500), coloured glass has been used to decorate churches and other buildings. Stained-glass windows are made from pieces of glass cut to shape then joined by strips of lead.

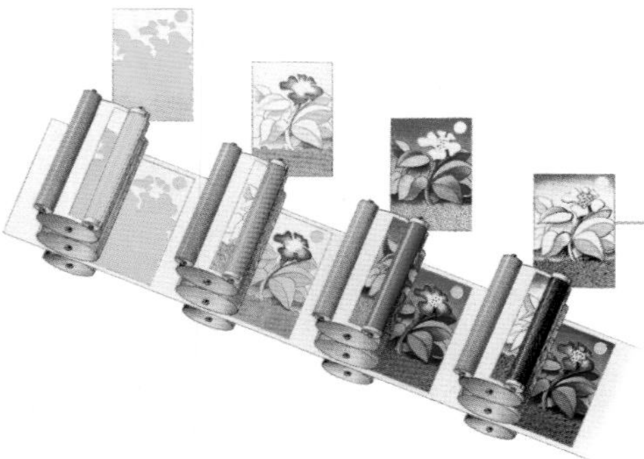

Lithography is a way of creating multiple copies of a picture. An image is drawn on stone with wax. Oil and water are poured over the stone. Ink runs off but sticks to the wax image. Sheets of paper are pressed on top of the stone. They pick up a layer of ink. Machines use a similar technique to print newspapers and magazines, but use curved metal rollers instead of a flat stone.

The technique of collage takes its name from a French word, *coller*, which means 'to stick'. To create a collage, artists glue scraps of paper, fabric and many other materials onto wood, canvas or paper, to make an attractive design.

Casting is a method of making metal objects. Ores (rocks containing metal) were crushed and baked to release the metal. This was melted, then poured into moulds. As the metal cooled, it hardened into the shape of the mould.

Illustration is the art of adding pictures to words on a page. Sometimes, illustrations give the reader extra information. Sometimes, they excite the imagination or create a special mood.

Amazing

Lithography was invented in 1798. French painter Henri de Toulouse-Lautrec (1841–1901) used lithography to create his famous posters.

The colour wheel

The three primary colours are red, yellow and blue. These can be mixed together to form orange, green and purple. On a colour wheel, one primary colour will appear opposite the mixture of the two other primary colours (for example, red will appear opposite green, which is a mixture of yellow and blue). These opposites are called complementary colours.

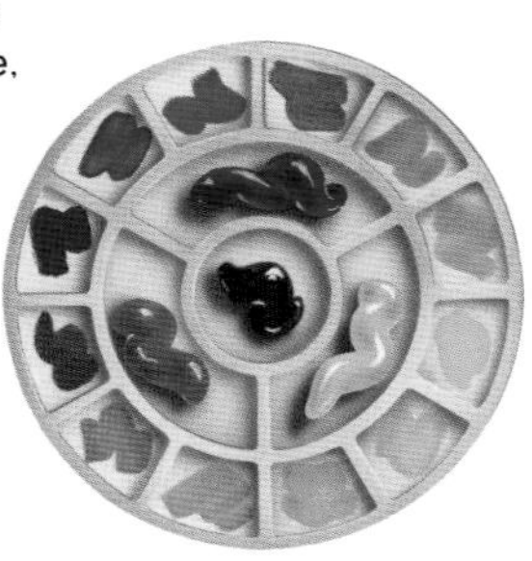

Making colours

In the past, the pigment (colour) of paints was taken from naturally occurring substances, such as extracts of plants. Today, many pigments are made using synthetic chemical dyes, such as the phthalocyanine, used to make phthalo green. Modern paints are manufactured in many shades based on mixing primary colours, as well as black and white. These can be mixed together to produce just about any colour found in nature.

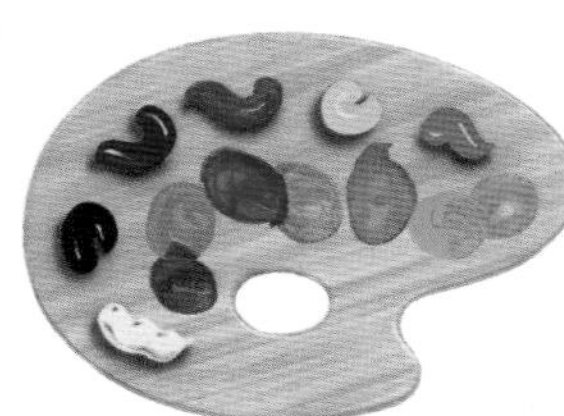

Art around the World

Art is important, all round the world. It can be amusing, entertaining, informative and inspiring. Or it can be threatening, disturbing and challenging. It can strengthen traditional values, spread new ideas, or preserve a treasured heritage from past times.

This totem pole comes from the northwest of North America. It is carved with images of totem (guardian) animals, together with the faces of dead ancestors. Both watch over living family members, and symbolize their importance. Only the wealthiest families could afford fine totem poles such as this one.

- The ancient Greeks were the greatest sculptors of the ancient world. They used sculpture to decorate their temples. The Greeks were experts at turning stone into life-like imitations of real people.

- Traditionally, Native Americans carved tall tree-trunks into towering totem poles, and stood them outside the homes of powerful families. They were signs of high rank, and records of family history. They were sometimes also thought to have protective powers.

- In Tibet, painted canvas cloths called *tankas* hang in Buddhist temples. They show gods, spirits and sacred symbols, and help Buddhist worshippers pray. The artists who create *tankas* follow strict rules and use traditional patterns and colours when composing their designs.

- The Inca civilization flourished in the Andes Mountains of South America around 500 years ago. Inca artists used gold and other precious metals to create statues of their gods, and fabulous jewellery worn by emperors, queens and priests.

Amazing

In Islam, it is forbidden to paint pictures of people or animals. So artists decorate mosques and holy books with beautiful and intricate geometric patterns.

Japanese art

Japanese artists are skilled at making woodblock prints. They carve their designs on to wooden blocks, which are covered in ink and pressed against paper. Some prints require 20 separate blocks, one for each colour.

❍ Muslim designers in North Africa, Central Asia, India, Southeast Asia and the Middle East use beautiful abstract patterns to decorate buildings, pottery, glassware and textiles. They blend Muslim holy designs, based on Arabic lettering, with local artistic traditions and techniques.

❍ Folk arts or ethnic arts are names given to art and crafts created by ordinary people. They include wood-carving, wall-paintings, basket-making, weaving and embroidery, and are often used to decorate homes, clothes and other everyday objects. Their designs and patterns may reflect religious beliefs, historic events or local wildlife.

❍ Powerful kings and queens are portrayed in art from many different lands. Royal portraits often show them wearing crowns, jewellery, or other symbols of wealth and power. In West Africa, rulers were traditionally portrayed seated on ancient sacred stools or thrones.

This mosque (meeting place for prayers) in Isfahan, Iran, is covered with patterned pottery tiles. Glazed tiles were generally used on the inside walls and floors of buildings. However, in Isfahan, tiles also cover the domes of the mosques. The bright-blue coloured tiles are also typically used for pottery made in the region.

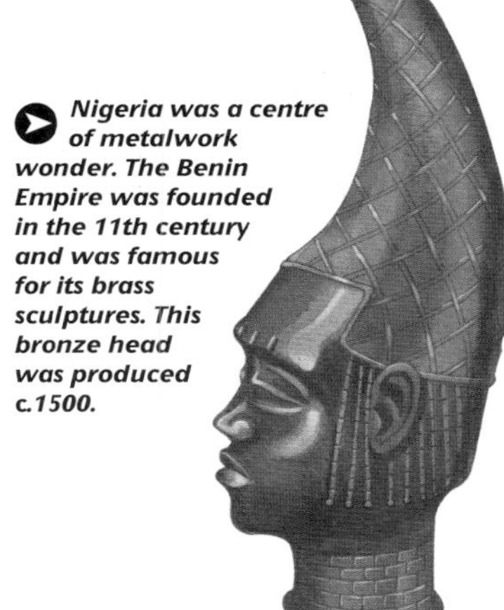

Nigeria was a centre of metalwork wonder. The Benin Empire was founded in the 11th century and was famous for its brass sculptures. This bronze head was produced c.1500.

Festival of lights

Diwali is the Hindu festival of lights. It celebrates the victory of good over evil, light over darkness and knowledge over ignorance. Houses and shops are decorated with small earthenware lamps, fuelled by mustard oil. Patterns called *rangoli* are traditionally drawn on houses and floors.

Modern Art

In the early 20th century, young European artists began to explore new ways of painting. They stopped trying to imitate the real world in their pictures. Instead, they experimented with colours and shapes to create powerful images that startled, and sometimes shocked, their viewers.

❍ Cubists painted pictures showing the world from several different viewpoints, all at the same time. Their pictures looked as if they were made out of jagged geometric shapes, blocks or cubes.

❍ The style of painting known as Expressionism began in Germany and France around 1905. Expressionists used strong colours, wild brush-strokes and distorted images to express powerful, anguished feelings.

❍ Abstract artists did not try to show people, places or things in their work. They arranged shapes and colours to create striking images.

This landscape painting by Spanish artist Juan Gris (1887–1927) was created in 1913 in typical Cubist style. It shows a view of houses, trees and fields split into angular shapes then rearranged. By painting with these Cubist techniques, the artist has managed to show three-dimensional space on the picture's flat surface.

❍ Early 20th-century artists were inspired by science and technology, especially photography. They were excited to find out about different styles of art from all round the world.

Expressionist painters often chose dramatic subjects for their pictures, or tried to show energy, movement, or dramatic action. This painting of stacks of corn, by Belgian Expressionist Constant Permeke (1885–1952), suggests the frantic movements of busy farmworkers at harvest time.

Amazing

The Spanish painter Salvador Dali (1904–1989) is famous for his strange, dreamlike paintings with oddly extended bodies, melting watches and half-open drawers set in desert landscapes.

Surrealism

During the 1920s, a group of European artists set out to paint images of the unconscious mind, creating bizarre, dreamlike pictures, often in lifelike detail. One of these 'surrealists' was the Belgian painter René Magritte (1898-1967), who enjoyed tricks and puzzles. His picture of a pipe was labelled 'This is not a pipe.'

The most famous 20th-century artist was Pablo Picasso (1881–1973). Born in Spain, he spent most of his working life in France. During his long career, he experimented with many exciting new artistic styles.

- After around 1950, the USA replaced Europe as the world centre of modern art. American artists pioneered huge paintings in bold bright colours, reflecting the vast American 'Wild West' landscape and dramatic modern American architecture.

- Other American artists copied techniques used in film and advertising to create multiple images. The most famous was Andy Warhol (1929–1987). His printed pictures of all kinds of objects, from soup-cans to movie stars, became known as Pop Art.

- Photographs were seen as a new kind of art by the late 20th century. Memorable images ranged from glamorous fashion shots to grim war scenes.

- Many artists design fashions, cars, furniture and also posters and logos. The best logos are simple but instantly recognizable.

- In the early 21st century, artists in Britain and Europe experimented with art that did not need pictures. They created 'installations', showing preserved dead animals or crumpled beds. Some people said that displaying objects in this way was a new kind of creativity, called Conceptual Art.

Computer art

Computers are powerful tools for artists. They can alter the shape, size, colour and content of images, at the click of a mouse. They can add special effects – bending and stretching features, adding 'soft focus' effects, or blurring and shading to make a photograph look like a painting. Computers also allow artists to combine multiple images to create home-grown cartoons or movies, and to add music or other sounds.

Modern artists

Alexander Calder (1898–1976)
American creator of mobiles

Christo (born 1935)
Bulgarian-born Belgian, famous for wrapping buildings and sections of coastline in plastic

Salvador Dali (1904–89)
Spanish Surrealist painter

Barbara Hepworth (1903–75)
British sculptor

David Hockney (born 1937)
British painter

Roy Lichtenstein (1923–97)
American pop artist

Henry Moore (1898–1986)
British sculptor

Piet Mondrian (1872–1944)
Dutch painter of abstracts

Gilbert and George (Gilbert Proesch born 1943 and George Passmore born 1942) British avant-garde artists known for their Performance Art

Andy Warhol (1928–87)
American painter and graphic artist famous for prints of soup cans and Marilyn Monroe

In the late 20th century, the focus of modern art shifted from Europe to the United States. A leading figure was Jackson Pollock (1912–56) who created large, abstract pictures by splashing paint onto a canvas laid on the floor – a style known as Abstract Expressionism.

Making Music

Many thousands of years ago, early humans discovered that certain objects – for example, hollow tree trunks, different kinds of stone, and the bones of large animals – made interesting sounds when struck. Gradually, they invented new kinds of instruments to make an exciting range of new and different sounds.

❍ Early people jangled small bones as rattles, made drums from animal skins and blew into hollow bamboo canes and bones to produce notes.

❍ Expert players taught other people the skills needed to make music. Instrumentalists and singers began to perform together.

❍ The oldest surviving instruments are a pair of flutes made from bird bone and mammoth ivory around 42,000 years ago in southern Germany. Tunes were played by blowing through the bones, just as with modern-day flutes.

The Aztec people, who ruled an empire in Mexico around AD 1400, made a drum. Aztec drums were used to accompany dancing at religious festivals, and to summon soldiers to fight in wars.

Aboriginal people have lived in Australia for at least 50,000 years. One of their best-known instruments is the didgeridoo – a long hollow tree-trunk, played by blowing. It makes a deep droning sound, that carries for long distances. Players use a technique, called 'circular breathing' to produce the drone continuously.

❍ Since prehistoric times, music has formed an essential part of many religious ceremonies. It can express hope and happiness, for example at a wedding, or echo the miserable cries of mourners at funerals. Many priests and priestesses were also musicians. They sang, chanted or played instruments to honour the gods.

Ancient Egyptians played bow-shaped harps at funeral ceremonies. The top of this harp is decorated with an image of Maat, the goddess of truth and justice who judged dead peoples' actions and decided their fate in the Afterlife.

❍ Until the 20th century, musical instruments were made of natural materials. Some, like rams-horn trumpets, were played almost unchanged. Others, like brass trumpets, fine violins (made of carved wood) or piano-keys (made of ivory) were carefully shaped by craft workers. In the 20th century, new, artificial materials, such as plastic and nylon, were used by instrument-makers to mass-produce instruments more cheaply than ever before.

Instrument inventions

c.4000 BC	Flute, harp, trumpet
3500 BC	Bells
AD 1500	Trombone
c.1545	Violin
1709	Piano
1821	Harmonica
1822	Accordion
1832	Modern flute
1840	Saxophone

This musician from the Andes region of South America is playing a set of wooden pan-pipes. In the late 20th century, haunting pan-pipe tunes from the high, remote Andes Mountains became popular worldwide.

The first instrument?

The Italian Luciano Pavarotti (1935–2007) was famous for his fine tenor (high male) voice. The oldest instrument of all is the human voice. From the beginning of human existence, human beings made calls to communicate (as do many other living creatures). Later, no one knows precisely when, they also began to sing, and speak separate words.

Amazing

The giant of the violin family is the double bass. Its four thick strings can be plucked or played with a bow. The deep sounds are amplified by the huge wooden sound box.

This Etruscan wall painting, made about 2500 years ago, shows a young man playing a double flute. The Etruscans lived in central Italy. Like other ancient Mediterranean peoples, they used music in religious ceremonies, as well as for entertainment.

- Pan-pipes have been popular for at least 3000 years. They are made of tubes, such as hollow plant-stalks, of different lengths fastened together. Players blow across the top of the tubes. Pan-pipes are named after the ancient Greek god, Pan, who lived in wild countryside. Greek legends told how he made the first set of pan-pipes, by binding riverside reed-stalks together.

- The first flutes were made of hollow bones. Later, they were made from wood. Ancient Greek and Italian flute players were very clever – they could play two flutes at the same time.

- Early instrument-makers were not afraid to think big. For example, the Japanese koto had strings 1.8 m long. It produced a loud, deep, humming sound. Musicians had to kneel on the floor to play it.

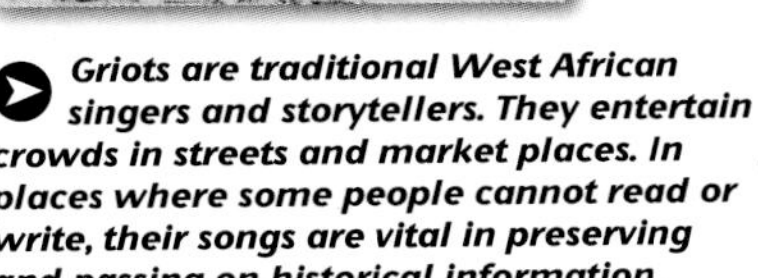

Griots are traditional West African singers and storytellers. They entertain crowds in streets and market places. In places where some people cannot read or write, their songs are vital in preserving and passing on historical information.

Musical notes

In medieval Europe, composers devised a way of writing music on parchment, so it could be read by other musicians. They invented a musical 'scale' based on a pattern of dots (or squares) combined with five horizontal lines. The shape and size of each dot indicated the length of each note. The position of each dot in relation to the lines showed its pitch. Today, a modern version of this notation is used all round the world. But traditional, local ways of writing music still survive.

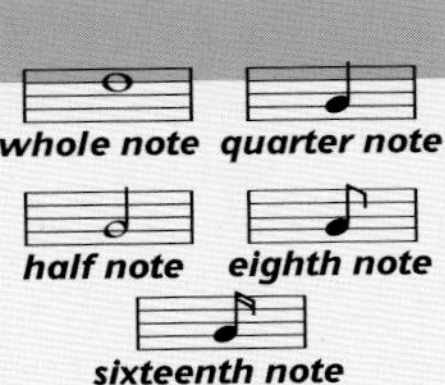

Classical Music

The music created in Europe between around 1600 and 1950 is often called 'classical'. It developed from chants, religious songs and instrumental pieces played in Christian churches from around AD 500.

❍ Church musicians tried to create a richer, more complicated sound by building better instruments, and finding new ways to use singers' voices. To write down their works, they began to use a musical scale that contained eight notes (still sung today; it begins, 'do, ray, mee').

❍ Church musicians were supported by rich people who paid them to write religious music. After about 1400, kings and other powerful people paid these composers to write non-religious pieces for them as well.

❍ Classical music developed still further once composers started to have their music printed, after around 1500. This meant that new compositions could easily be carried to performers in many different countries.

German composer Johann Sebastian Bach (1685–1750) wrote music to be played on organs and sung by church choirs. He also composed chamber music. He was musical director at the church of St Thomas in Leipzig, north Germany. Bach's works are still performed, and greatly admired, today.

Amazing

Mozart mastered his first piano piece before his fifth birthday, and in the space of just 30 minutes.

❍ Written or printed music was given a new name, a score. Each page showed all the parts played by different instruments, and performed by singers.

❍ Top classical composers became very famous, and attracted crowds of devoted fans. But people could never agree on which composer was best. Today, many music-lovers rank Johann Sebastian Bach (1685–1750), Wolfgang Amadeus Mozart (1756–1791) and Ludwig van Beethoven (1770–1827) among the greatest composers who ever lived.

❍ From around 1600, many classical composers wrote music for operas. These are plays in which a complete story is sung by actors and singers, accompanied by an orchestra.

Ludwig van Beethoven (1770–1827), who lived and worked in Germany, was the greatest composer of his day. He composed many passionate works for solo piano and for the orchestra. Extra players were needed to perform many of his compositions, which were considered very advanced and difficult for their time. Tragically, Beethoven went deaf and had to stop performing, but he went on composing until the end of his life.

Born in Austria, Wolfgang Amadeus Mozart (1756–1791) was a child prodigy who began composing when he was only five years old. Soon, he began to write concertos (pieces for solo instrumentalist plus orchestra), symphonies (works for full orchestra), church music, and operas. Mozart became famous throughout Europe, but died aged only 35, in poverty.

Richard Wagner (1818–1883) wrote the world's longest operas. Each one runs for over five hours. To stage them, Wagner built a huge opera house in his home town, Bayreuth, in Bavaria (southern Germany). He also founded an annual opera festival there that is still held today.

Conductor

The job of the conductor is to rehearse and direct the musicians. He or she shows them the speed and rhythm (often using a baton), and how to obtain the right balance in sound. Since the 19th century, great conductors have become classical music superstars, travelling all over the world to direct performances by top orchestras.

The symphony orchestra

The instruments of the symphony orchestra are arranged in groups in an arc in front of the conductor – strings at the front, then wind, and percussion at the back. The modern orchestra has about 100 musicians. Orchestras have four main sections: strings (violins, violas, cellos and double basses), woodwind (clarinets, flutes, oboes and bassoons), brass (horns and trumpets) and percussion (drums, cymbals and bells).

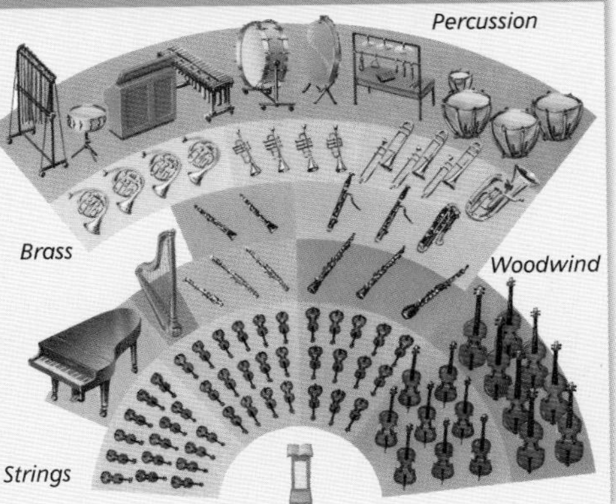

❍ Various new musical styles evolved during the 19th century. These included program music (a wordless composition in which the music tells a story) and orchestral and instrumental pieces with increasingly experimental and complex melodies and harmonies. Leading composers of this period include Schubert, Chopin and Liszt.

❍ In the early 20th century, composers began to experiment with new and different ways of writing music. One of the pioneers of this modern style was the Austrian composer Arnold Schoenberg (1874–1951). He abandoned the classical eight-note musical scale, creating an entirely new sound, called atonal music.

❍ A few years ago, many people thought that classical music had lost its popular appeal. But with the help of CDs, television, and music radio stations, a new generation of talented performers have found a fresh audience.

Great classical composers

Johann Sebastian Bach (1685–1750)	German composer
Ludwig van Beethoven (1770–1827)	German composer
Johannes Brahms (1833–1897)	German composer
Benjamin Britten (1913–1976)	British 20th-century composer
Frederick Chopin (1841–1904)	Polish composer
Edward Elgar (1857–1934)	British composer
George Gershwin (1898–1937)	American 20th-century composer
Edvard Grieg (1843–1907)	Norwegian 19th-century composer
George Frideric Handel (1685–1759)	German/British composer
Joseph Haydn (1732–1809)	Austrian composer
Wolfgang Amadeus Mozart (1756–1791)	Austrian composer, who wrote more than 40 symphonies
Franz Peter Schubert (1797–1828)	Austrian composer
Igor Stravinsky (1882–1971)	Russian 20th-century composer, most celebrated work was *The Rite of Spring*
Peter Ilyich Tchaikovsky (1840–1893)	Russian composer, famous for symphonies and ballet scores
Giuseppe Verdi (1813–1901)	Italian 19th-century opera composer
Richard Wagner (1818–1883)	German composer

Musical Instruments

The four main groups of instruments are called strings, woodwind, brass and percussion. Stringed instruments, such as violins and guitars, have strings stretched over a shaped hollow box. The strings produce a sound when they are rubbed with a bow or plucked by the fingers or a plectrum. Percussion instruments, such as drums or cymbals, make a sound when hit by sticks or fingertips. Woodwind and brass instruments are hollow tubes, made of wood or brass. Both are played by blowing. Players can open or close holes on the tubes to produce various notes.

Keyboards

Today, many instruments can be connected to electronic amplifiers, to make a much louder sound than was previously possible. For example, electronic keyboards have keys that look similar to a piano. But these produce a sound by sending an electric signal through an amplifier and loudspeakers. Keyboard players can also use electronics to change the type of sound they produce. By switching on electronic devices fitted to the keyboard, players can add 'special effects'.

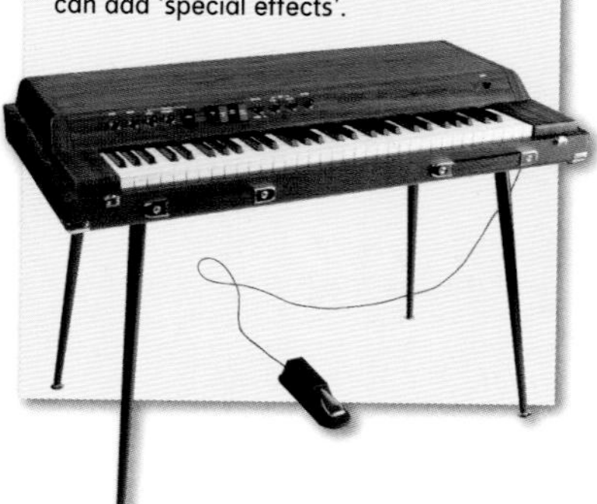

Strings

Woodwind

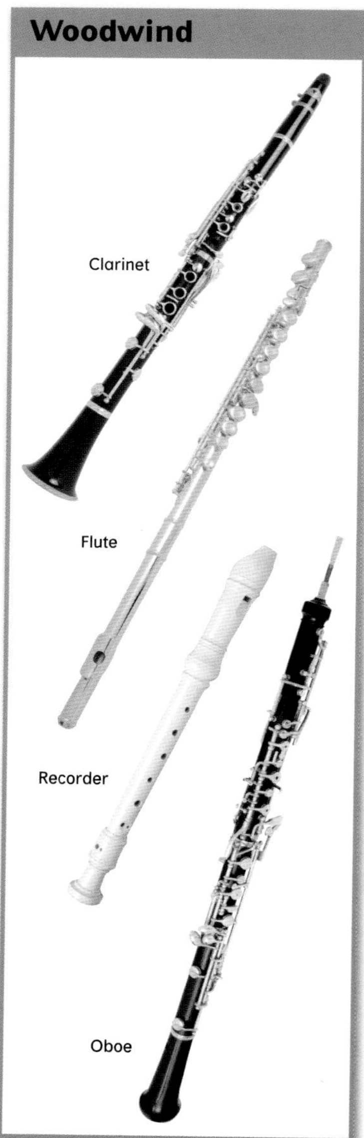

Brass

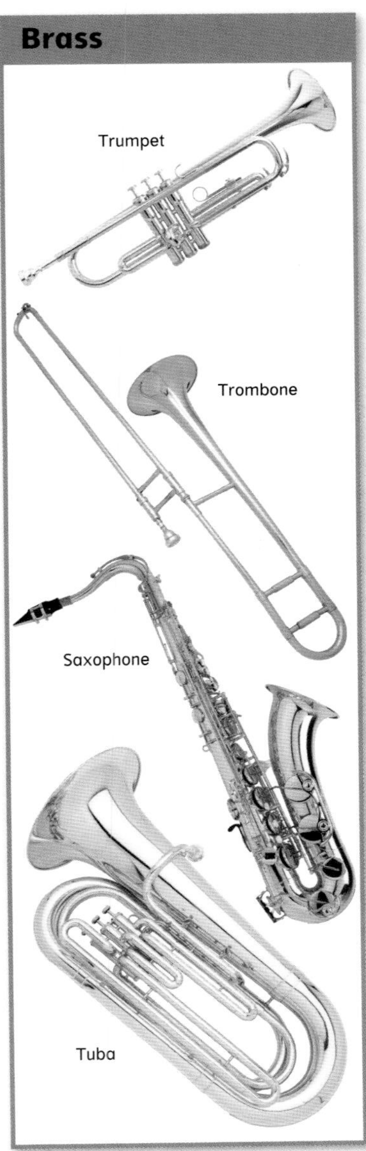

Percussion

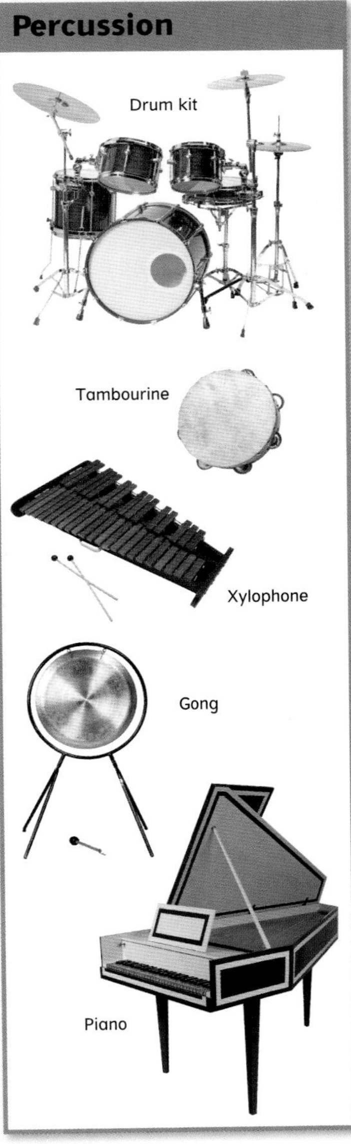

Piano

Pianos were invented in Europe in the early 1700s. Their name came from two Italian words: *piano* soft and *forte* (loud), because they could produce a very wide range of sounds, from quiet and gentle to very noisy. The first pianos were made of wood, but today most piano frames are made of metal. Old or new, all pianos produce sound in the same way. When the player presses a key with their finger, a set of levers moves a wooden hammer. This hits a wire and makes it vibrate to sound a note. The longer the wire, the lower the note that is played. Players can increase the sound made by the piano, or make each note last longer, by pressing pedals, connected to the wires by more levers, with their feet.

Amazing

An advantage of the keyboard is that players can accompany themselves as they sing. This is why many songwriters use the piano both to compose and perform.

Popular Music

There has always been popular music. But, until the 20th century, people could only hear popular tunes when musicians sang or played them 'live'. Sound recording, invented in 1878, changed the way people listened to music – forever.

One of the greatest jazz musicians was Louis 'Satchmo' Armstrong (1900–1971). He was a gifted trumpet player, who also pioneered 'scat' singing – a type of jazz performance in which the singer's voice is used like an instrument – and appeared in over 50 films.

❍ The first records, made from wax or plastic, let people hear their favourite music at home and in clubs and bars.

❍ Three of the most popular styles of 20th-century music were created by African–Americans in southern USA. Jazz music, played on brass and wind instruments, accompanied dancing and street processions. Soulful blues music told of love and suffering. Gospel music, performed by church choirs, combined hymn tunes with jazz and blues.

❍ Blues music, originally sung by African slaves, became popular among working people. Its energetic sound influenced rock and pop. Blues and jazz merged into R & B (rhythm and blues).

❍ In the 1950s, young musicians in the USA mixed White American country-and-western music with African-American rhythm and blues to create an exciting new sound – rock 'n' roll. Played on guitars backed by drums, rock 'n' roll's pounding beat made it great for dancing. Rock 'n' roll songs also put in words how many teenagers were feeling – they were bold, defiant, angry, sexy, anxious, happy and sad – sometimes all at the same time.

❍ In the late 1960s, bands started to mix rock 'n' roll, jazz and blues, amplified it electronically and created the style now known as 'rock'.

❍ Radio stations and record shops compiled charts of the most popular songs. Selling records became competitive between pop performers as they tried to get more publicity and enter the charts with bestselling records.

❍ In the 1990s record producers created a new phenomenon – girl and boy bands, advised by marketing experts. Some band members were not necessarily good musicians but the band's image was the main factor in selling records.

One of the greatest blues musicians was the guitarist B B King (1925–2015). Born in the southern US state of Mississippi, he began his career as a singer, but later became famous for his own special style of guitar-playing that influenced many younger musicians. His 1981 recording, 'There Must Be A Better World Somewhere', won international awards.

10 bestselling songs

1	**White Christmas**	Bing Crosby
2	**Candle in the Wind**	Elton John
3	**Silent Night**	Bing Crosby
4	**Rock Around the Clock**	Bill Haley and His Comets
5	**We Are the World**	USA For Africa
6	**If I Didn't Care**	The Inkspots
7	**Yes Sir, I Can Boogie**	Baccara
8	**My Heart Will Go On**	Celine Dion
9	**I Will Always Love You**	Whitney Huston
10	**All I Want For Christmas Is You**	Mariah Carey

The most famous rock 'n' roll performer was the American Elvis Presley (1935–1977) – known to his fans as 'the King'. Elvis became famous for his moody good looks, amazing stage clothes and provocative style of dancing, as well as for his singing. He became the first global rock music star. Thousands of screaming fans mobbed him whenever he appeared.

Reggae is a type of dance music from Jamaica, noted for its use of a heavy, offbeat rhythm. It was made world-famous in the 1970s by Bob Marley (1945–1981) and his group The Wailers. Reggae was one of the first alternative music styles to have a major impact on pop music.

Recorded music

The first machine to play recorded sound was the phonograph, designed by American inventor Thomas Edison in 1878. It used a stylus (needle) to draw sound waves on a spinning tinfoil (or wax) cylinder, then play them back through a horn. In 1887, German designer Emile Berliner invented the gramophone (right). It used a stylus to play sound recorded on flat wax discs.

The Beatles

The world's most successful recording group of the 1960s was the British band The Beatles. The 'Fab Four' were Paul McCartney (born 1942), John Lennon (1940–1980), George Harrison (1943–2002), and Ringo Starr (born 1940).

10 bestselling albums

1	***Thriller***	Michael Jackson
2	***The Dark Side of the Moon***	Pink Floyd
3	***Their Greatest Hits (1971–1975)***	The Eagles
4	***Back in Black***	AC/DC
5	***Saturday Night Fever***	Soundtrack album featuring The Bee Gees
6	***Rumours***	Fleetwood Mac
7	***The Bodyguard***	Soundtrack album featuring Whitney Houston
8	***Come on Over***	Shania Twain
9	***Led Zeppelin IV***	Led Zeppelin
10	***Bat out of Hell***	Meat Loaf

❍ By the late 20th century, CDs, pop videos, personal music players and the Internet had made popular music a multi-million dollar industry.

❍ By the year 2000, popular music had 'gone global'. 'World Music' from developing countries, especially Africa and the Caribbean, became popular with western listeners.

Amazing

The first popular singer to sell one million records was Italian tenor Enrico Caruso (1873–1921) who recorded passionate opera arias.

The Origins of Drama

Performing is very much a part of our lives. We all perform when we tell a joke or recount a story. Some people are especially good at performing and can hold an audience spellbound. For thousands of years, professional storytellers, actors, clowns, acrobats and dancers have earned a living by their skills.

❍ Early drama had a religious purpose. Kings, queens, priests and priestesses took part in holy rituals, acting out myths and legends about the gods.

❍ The first-known people to watch plays were the ancient Greeks. They gathered in large crowds on sloping hillsides to watch actors perform on level ground below.

❍ After around 500 BC, the Greeks began to build theatres. They arranged rows of stone seats in half-circle shapes, looking down on a stage called an orchestra.

Ancient Greek and Roman theatres were built in the open air. Actors performed in front of painted wooden scenery. This hid cranes or lifts that helped actors make dramatic appearances. Musicians stood nearby, playing music to accompany singing and dancing on stage.

In ancient Greece, all actors wore masks. They wore different masks for happy, fierce or sad characters. By changing them, actors could have many varied roles in the same play. Masks also helped audiences sitting at the back of large theatres, far away from the stage, see the actors' expressions. For this reason, they were made with deliberately exaggerated features, and often painted in bright colours. Some had hair or hats attached too.

❍ Ancient Greek plays were written for religious festivals in honour of the god Dionysus. Authors entered their plays in festival competitions. The winners had their plays performed.

❍ Greek actors were all men. The Greeks believed it was indecent for women to appear on stage. So young men and boys played women's roles.

❍ Greek actors spoke in verse and used mime. A 'chorus' (group) of singers and dancers commented on the events being acted.

❍ Greek drama was of two kinds: amusing comedies or serious, sad tragedies. 'Comic' and 'tragic' are terms still used to describe plays today.

Shakespeare

English poet and dramatist William Shakespeare (1564–1616) is one of the most famous and respected playwrights of all time. He wrote around 37 plays and hundreds of poems. Some of his plays are tragedies, for example *Romeo and Juliet* or *Hamlet*. Some are comedies, such as *A Midsummer Night's Dream*. Some are historical epics, like *Henry V*. Shakespeare worked as an actor, and ran his own theatre, called the Globe. Shakespeare's plays have been made into numerous films and translated into many different languages.

Ballad singers

Ballads are traditional songs that tell a story, often about the adventures of ordinary people. They were usually sung by one or two people, perhaps with guitars. Printed copies of the songs were often sold in the street.

❍ Medieval craft-workers presented open-air plays based on biblical stories. They acted out stories of Jesus Christ's life, from his birth to his crucifixion.

❍ In Tudor times (1485–1603), top playwrights, such as Shakespeare, trained troops of actors to perform their plays. Shakespeare also built an open-air theatre in London called the Globe.

❍ Medieval and Tudor kings employed 'jesters' to entertain in their courts. Jesters told jokes, performed tricks, sang and danced. If they were too rude they lost their jobs or were put in gaol.

Amazing

The first purpose-built theatre with a stage was built in Italy in 1618. It seated 3000 people but was almost completely destroyed during World War II.

Mime is a specialized kind of acting performed entirely without words. Mime artists use movements and gestures to indicate an imaginary world around them. The world's best-known mime artist is Frenchman Marcel Marceau (1923–2007).

❍ In medieval times, travelling poets, actors and minstrels entertained crowds in streets, at markets and fairs. They acted out stories about heroes, monsters and other traditional tales. They sang ballads telling of battles, love-stories and exciting adventures.

Famous playwrights

Aristophanes (c.445–385 BC) Greek, wrote comedies such as *The Frogs*.

Alan Ayckbourne (born 1939) British, prolific author of successful comedies of modern life, including *The Norman Conquests*.

Samuel Becket (1906–1989) Irish, wrote *Waiting for Godot*.

Anton Chekhov (1860–1904) Russian, wrote *The Cherry Orchard*.

William Congreve (1670–1729) English, author of *The Way of the World*, a comedy.

Johann Wolfgang von Goethe (1749–1832) German, playwright and scientist, his most famous work is *Faust*, in which a scholar sells his soul to the devil.

Henrik Ibsen (1828–1906) Norwegian, wrote *A Doll's House* and *Hedda Gabbler*.

Molière (Jean-Baptiste Poquelin) (1622–1673) French, wrote comedies including *The Misanthropist* and *The Miser*.

Eugene O'Neill (1888–1953) American, wrote *The Iceman Cometh* and other plays.

William Shakespeare (1564–1616) English, greatest dramatist whose plays include tragedies *King Lear*, comedies *Much Ado About Nothing* and histories *Julius Caesar*.

George Bernard Shaw (1856–1950) Irish, wrote *St Joan*, *Major Barbara* and other plays, usually from a satirical viewpoint.

Richard Brinsley Sheridan (1751–1816) Irish, wrote *The Rivals*, one of the most enduring comedies.

Sophocles (about 496–406 BC) Greek, wrote tragedies, including *Oedipus the King*.

Tom Stoppard (Thomas Straussler, b. 1937) Czech-born British writer, whose plays include *Travesties* and *Jumpers*.

World Theatre

Over the centuries, cultures all round the world developed their own distinctive forms of drama. In each country, drama was shaped by local beliefs, customs, myths, legends and living conditions. Everywhere, plays reflected the society in which they were performed.

❍ The south Indian tradition of theatre called Kathakali is at least 2000 years old. It was originally performed in temple ceremonies. The actors, dressed in rich costumes and dramatic make-up, act out stories from Hindu mythology. They use vivid facial expressions and elaborate arm and hand movements.

❍ In Japan, there are three traditional types of drama: Noh ('accomplished' plays), Kabuki (popular dramas) and Jojuri (puppet plays). Noh drama is the oldest. It originated around AD 1375, and is based on ancient Japanese literature. Each Noh performance contains five separate plays. Kabuki and Jojuri plays were first performed around 1700. They feature loud music, athletic dancing and spectacular costumes.

Noh actors are all men. They wear stiff, formal costumes, and heavy make-up. They chant their words, and use stately, stylized gestures to express their emotions. Their performances are accompanied by music on flute and drums.

Kathakli performers use intricate movements to express their devotion to the gods. Keeping the top half of their body still and balanced, they take tiny, rapid steps, making complicated patterns with their feet as they twirl round and round. As performers move, hundreds of tiny bells, worn round their ankles, create jingling music.

❍ Carnival was originally a religious festival, marking the beginning of the Christian fasting season, called Lent. Its name meant 'goodbye to meat'. People held parties, sang and danced as they used up all the rich foods in their homes, and prepared to eat only plain, simple meals for 40 days. Over the years, these celebrations became more elaborate. Today, carnival is celebrated in Europe and America with music, dancing, processions and actors dressed in the most amazing costumes.

❍ In many parts of the world, shamans (magicians, priests and healers) use drama, singing and dancing to try and persuade the unseen spirits they believe in to help and heal.

❍ Priests from the Hopi people, who live in the southwest of North America, dress up as Kachinas (ancestor spirits) to perform ritual dramas. They visit Hopi villages, dancing and singing, to bless them. Traditionally, Hopi people believe this will help make the rain fall, and encourage their food crops to grow.

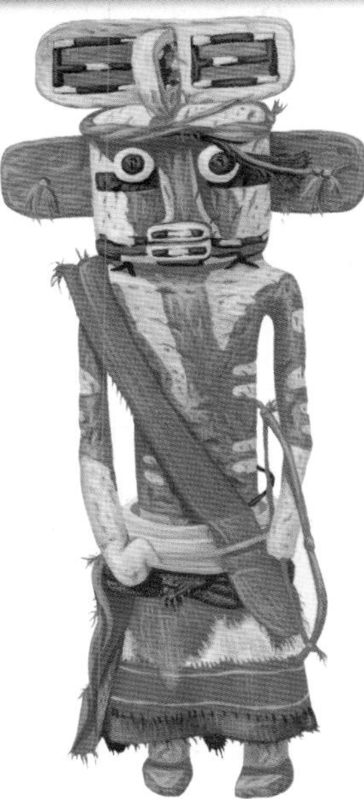

This Kachina (spirit figure) is made from natural materials: clay and plaited maize straw. According to Hopi legends, there are 335 different Kachinas. Each has its own special character and appearance.

❍ During the 18th and 19th centuries, lively, colourful shows that combined singing, dancing, loud music, clowning, acrobatics and mock battles were a popular form of entertainment in China. They became known as Beijing Opera.

The circus

The name 'circus' originated in ancient Rome. Originally it referred to a curved arena, where chariot races took place. Around 1700, European showmen used the name to describe shows by performing horses. After around 1800, other performers, such as acrobats, lion-tamers and clowns, started to take part in shows as well.

Amazing

In 1924 over 16,700 people packed into a big top in Kansas, USA, to see the Ringling Brothers and Barnum & Bailey Circus.

This shaman from West Africa is completely hidden by his costume of woven grass. Shamans put on disguises to help communicate with nature-spirits, and ask them to use their magic powers.

In Indonesia, shadow-puppets perform after dark from behind a brightly-lit screen. The puppets are cut out of sheets of leather, and moved by long sticks held by a dalang (puppet-master).

Punch and Judy

Punch and Judy is a puppet show, performed at English fairgrounds and seaside resorts. Characters include Punch (a clown), his wife Judy, their dog, their baby, a crocodile and a policeman. Punch and Judy stories range from funny and silly (stealing sausages) to cruel and violent (murder!). They are based on old, traditional drama, first performed for adults. This originated in Italy around 1500, where it was known as *Commedia dell'Arte* (Comedy of the Arts).

Modern Theatre

Until the late 19th century, most plays described dramatic historical or mythological events, or made fun of the way powerful people lived. But after around 1850, writers began to create dramas about the modern, everyday world, using situations that audiences might recognize from their own lives. Styles of acting changed as well, from loud and exaggerated to quieter, more lifelike, words and movements on stage.

Marie Lloyd (1870–1922) was a music-hall star, famous for her sometimes suggestive, witty, cheerful, songs. In the late 19th and early 20th centuries, music halls had twice-nightly shows of about 20 turns (acts) including conjuring, telling jokes, reciting monologues and dancing. Many top performers were women.

- In the 18th and 19th centuries, actors had to perform in huge, crowded theatres or noisy music halls. They had no microphones or electronic amplifiers to help them. So they shouted – or spoke in very loud, strong voices – and used grand, dramatic gestures to catch the audience's attention. This was called 'barnstorming' because travelling actors often performed in barns during the 19th century.

- The Norwegian playwright Henrik Ibsen (1828–1906) was the first major dramatist to write about the problems of modern society. Later, 20th-century writers copied his ideas.

- The Russian actor and director Constantin Stanislavsky (1863–1938) revolutionized the way many plays were performed. He encouraged actors to think and feel like the characters they were playing, rather than just pretend to experience emotions on stage. This is called 'method acting'.

- Many 20th-century playwrights aimed to spread a political message. For example, in Soviet Russia (1917–1989), the government paid actors to put on plays that praised Communist society.

- In Europe and the USA, many playwrights portrayed depressing or violent scenes from modern life. A few wrote plays that seemed to be nonsense. By shocking their audiences, these writers hoped to make people think, and maybe change society.

- Directors in the 20th century borrowed ideas from traditional theatre, especially ancient Greece and Japan, and copied circus skills. They changed theatre layouts and created 'theatre in the round' by seating the audience on all sides of the stage. They used the latest technology to produce dramatic lighting effects and astonishing scenery.

- After 1950, directors staged 'modern dress' versions of ancient masterpieces. They showed how old plays can still be relevant to the modern world. They also presented old works in new, fresh ways, by adding singing, music or dancing.

Props

Any moveable object, such as a gun, used by actors in stage or screen performances is called a 'prop' (short for 'property'). It is the job of the assistant stage manager (in a theatre) or continuity staff (on a film set) to make sure that all props are in the right place at the right time.

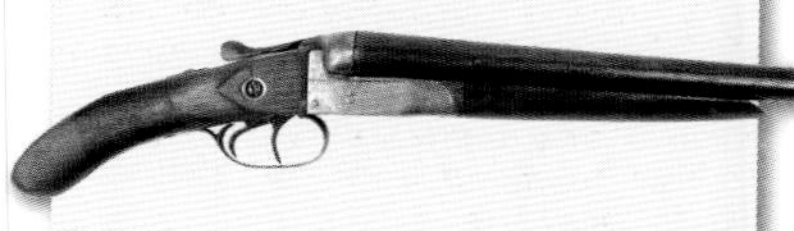

Amazing

The Reduced Shakespeare Company is famous for performing the entire catalogue of Shakespeare's works – 37 plays, and 154 sonnets – in just 97 minutes.

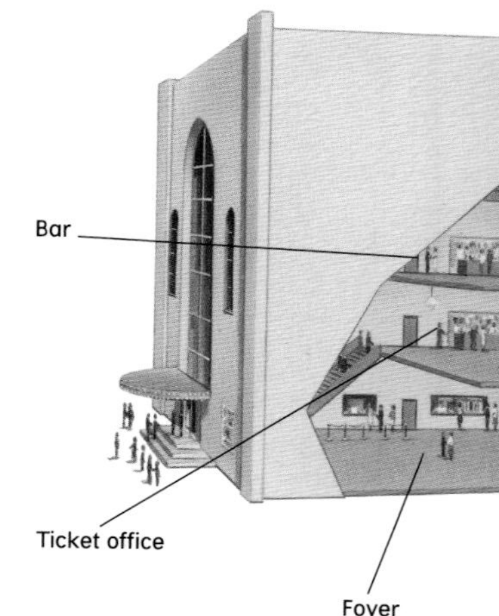

▲ *Many new theatres are modern-looking buildings, like the National Theatre in Ghana, Africa. The architecture of this building helps to create a national centre for the performing arts.*

'Kitchen sink' drama

In the mid 20th-century, British and American writers experimented with new kinds of plays about ordinary peoples' lives. Known as 'kitchen sink dramas', these plays described life in the raw, and often reproduced unhappy or unpleasant situations on stage. Their scripts included slang, swearing, quarrels and sometimes fights. Actors wore drab, everyday clothes instead of glamorous theatrical costumes, and were encouraged to speak in rough regional accents, rather than the refined, polished speech taught at traditional drama schools. One of the best-known kitchen-sink dramas, *Look Back in Anger*, by British writer John Osborne (1929–1994) caused outrage when it was first performed in 1956. Osborne (right) and his fellow-dramatists were nicknamed 'Angry Young Men'.

❍ Today, audiences can choose from an amazing variety of performing styles and plays. Playgoers might enjoy realistic dramas showing a 'slice of life' or they may like light-hearted comedies, passionate romances, charming fantasies, bitter tragedies, well-known classics or controversial new works.

▼ *A big theatre is a highly complex building. The audience sees only a small part of it as they enter through the foyer and find their seat in the auditorium. Behind the stage, which is in the middle of the building, are large areas used for storing scenery, wardrobe rooms for storing costumes, dressing and make-up rooms, rehearsal areas and a canteen for the actors and stage crew.*

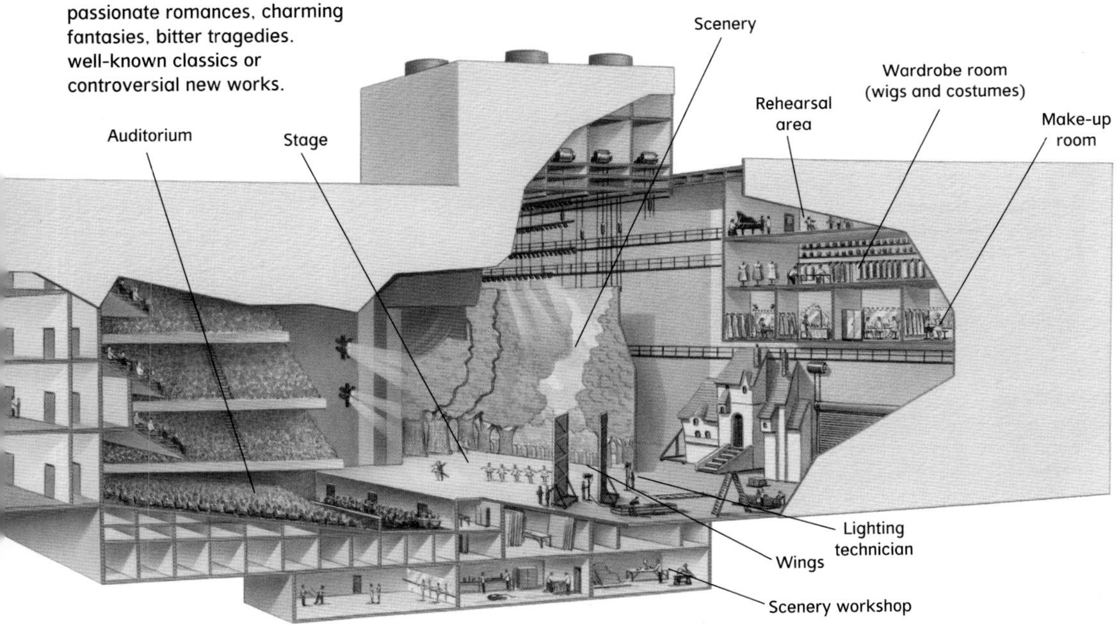

Moving to Music

Dance is one of the oldest of all the performing arts. Originally, everyone took part, moving to music made by singing, clapping hands or beating sticks and stones. But before long, the best dancers began to attract an audience. Other people stopped what they were doing to watch them perform.

This wall-painting, from the tomb of an Egyptian scribe c.1360 BC, shows musicians playing for dancers at a royal feast. The girl on the right is plucking a harp, while her companion strums a lute (an instrument rather like a guitar). Egyptian musicians also played flutes, drums and tambourines.

❍ Some of the first dances were performed for special occasions such as weddings, or at harvest-time. Dancers jumped and ran around to show their joyful feelings. Often, they sang and shouted at the same time.

❍ Early dancing was often very energetic. The best dancers could leap high, walk on their hands, and turn cartwheels and somersaults.

❍ Dancers often began to train at an early age. Young girls were sent to Hindu temples in south and east Asia when they were around five years old. They learned very graceful, complicated movements, and how to wear elaborate costumes. They were said to give their best performances when they were around 12 years old.

❍ Traditional dancers tried to change the weather. In Japan, for example, rain-dancers made rapid movements and chanted words to encourage rain to fall and crops to grow. In South America, they shook rattles that sounded like raindrops on leaves.

❍ Many dances had a religious purpose. For example, in Australia aboriginal people danced to try to bring themselves closer to nature-spirits. As they danced, they copied the movements of wild animals or birds.

A young girl takes part in an ancient religious dance at a Hindu temple in Bali, Indonesia. Her performance includes elegant hand movements and tiny running steps that make her look as if she is gliding across the floor. Nearby, a gamelan (an orchestra of metal gongs) plays a beautiful tune to accompany her dance.

Amazing

The Inuit of Canada and Greenland perform a traditional dance to the beat of a large, caribou-skin drum. The dances often act out a story, told in the singing, usually about hunting or animals.

❍ In North Africa and the Middle East, Sufis (a group of Muslim mystics) danced to worship God. They chanted God's name to rhythmic music and clapping, and began to turn round and round in a trance-like state. They forgot the everyday world around them, and instead concentrated all their thoughts on heaven.

Wearing long, traditional robes and tall felt (pressed-wool) hats, a group of Sufi men from Turkey begin their solemn religious dance. Turkey was home to the most famous community of Sufi dancers. They became known as the 'whirling dervishes'.

❍ Many African traditions tell how the spirits of dead ancestors can protect their living descendants, frighten enemies, drive out demons and keep harmful spirits away from houses and fields. Dancing often forms part of ceremonies designed to please the ancestors, and summon their power.

❍ Vigorous dances helped fighting men build up courage and team spirit before a battle, or celebrated victories after battle. African warriors, and Cossacks from Russia, became especially famous for their dancing skills.

Ghost dancers

In the late 19th-century, Native American warriors joined the 'Ghost Dance' movement to try to save their homelands. Before fighting against US government troops, farmers and settlers, they sang, danced and put on magical 'Ghost Shirts'. They believed these would all help protect them from bullet wounds.

These folk dancers are from Brittany, a region in northwest France. They are wearing traditional costume, including caps made from lace – a local craft speciality. Dances from Brittany feature fast, neat footwork, and are often accompanied by bagpipes, accordions, fiddles and drums.

This rain-dancer from northern Japan is wearing a kimono (a long robe) and broad-brimmed hat. Hats like this were traditionally worn by farmers working in the fields, to keep their head and shoulders dry in wet weather. The hat is trimmed with a fringe that looks like falling rain.

Cossack dancers

A Cossack dancer from Ukraine leaps high in the air, showing off his agility. Cossacks were famous for their bravery and horse-riding skills, and the men traditionally expressed their warlike energy in dramatic dances.

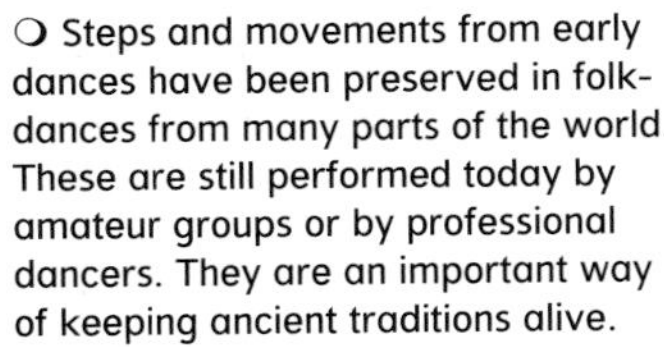

❍ Steps and movements from early dances have been preserved in folk-dances from many parts of the world. These are still performed today by amateur groups or by professional dancers. They are an important way of keeping ancient traditions alive.

Ballet

***B**allet originated in Italy and France about 300 years ago in stage performances that told stories through music and movement. Until around 1900, most dancers performed in a strict 'classical' style. Since then, some dancers have chosen new styles, such as jazz ballet and modern dance that allow them to move more freely.*

❍ In classical ballet, all movements are planned and rehearsed in great detail. Dancers must develop great strength and control of their bodies, and learn how to dance on the tips of their toes.

❍ Classical ballet became an international success after the first performance of *La Syphide* in 1832. In this ballet, based on a Scottish folk-story, a peasant leaves his bride to follow an enchanting female spirit. She is a symbol of perfect happiness, which he can never possess.

❍ In the 19th century, large theatres were built in many European cities to house companies (teams) of the very best dancers. One of the most famous ballet theatres, the Bolshoi in Moscow, Russia, opened in 1856. Its dancers became famous for their daring feats on stage, and still attract large audiences today.

❍ All ballet dancers use their technical skills to create an artistic interpretation of music. They have to try to convey thoughts and feelings through movement and sound, and the results can be powerfully dramatic.

❍ Modern ballet was developed by an American dancer, Isadora Duncan (1875–1927). She invented a new way of dancing, inspired by ancient Greek styles. Like the ancient Greeks, she performed barefoot in flowing robes, and used wild, free movements to express her feelings on stage.

These dancers are performing a dramatic* pas de deux *(dance for two). Dances like this are very popular in most classical ballets. All classical ballet relies on close partnerships between male and female dancers. They have to trust each other completely in order to perform daring, complicated moves.

Isadora Duncan, pictured in one of her favourite costumes, which were inspired by voluminous ancient Greek clothes. Compare what she is wearing with the more traditionally-dressed ballet dancer shown below-left. Classical ballet steps would not be possible in Isadora's clothes.

❍ Dancers trained in modern ballet often perform in musicals and other stage shows. Although their dances may look easy, and are often comical, they still involve a great deal of practice and technical skill.

❍ Female ballet dancers wear slippers of thin satin, with padding in the toes. In 1948, a pair of ballet slippers featured in a successful film, *The Red Shoes*. It told the story of a girl who became obsessed by ballet-dancing.

Amazing

Leading ballerinas put such a strain on their shoes during performances that they will often wear out two pairs of shoes in a single night.

Ballet positions

In classical ballet, all movements made by male and female dancers begin and end in one of five positions. These originated around 1700, probably as a way of making dancers' feet look elegant. Each foot position is accompanied by a special way of holding the arms, from the simplest and most relaxed (1) to the most difficult and strenuous (5).

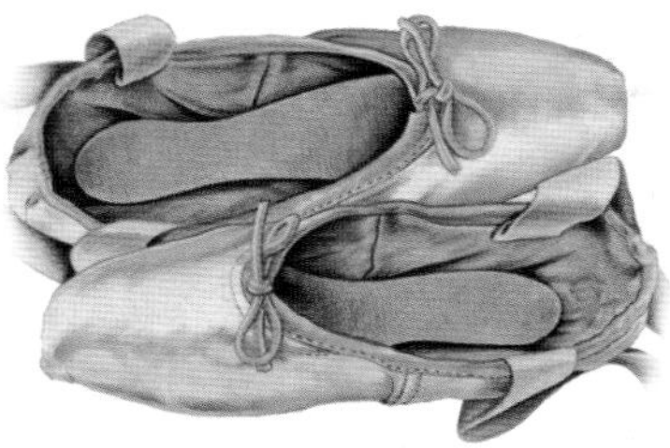

The famous Bolshoi Ballet was founded in Moscow as a dance school in 1773. The Bolshoi Theatre was built in 1856. The ballet school is famous for the athletic skills of its dancers, and its large-scale performances, such as the 1907 ballet **Les Sylphides**, *originally choreographed by Mikhail Fokine (1880–1942).*

Balanced on **pointes** *(the tips of her toes) this dancer makes ballet-dancing look light and effortless. Her sleeveless* **tutu** *(frock) with its tight bodice, low neck, and short, transparent skirt, stiffened to stand away from the body, is designed to show off her slim, elegant limbs and graceful movements.*

Stravinsky

Ballet pioneer Sergei Diaghilev asked some of the leading young composers of his time to write music for his new ballets. They included fellow-Russian Igor Stravinsky (1882–1971). Stravinsky's brilliant compositions included *Firebird* (based on a Russian folk-tale) and *Rite of Spring* (based on ancient, pagan Russian dances). They created great excitement when they were first performed.

The Russian Vaslav Nijinsky (1890–1950) was one of the most celebrated ballet dancers of all time. He became famous for his dancing with the Ballets Russes. Roles included **L'Aprés-midi d'un faune** *('A faun's afternoon') in 1912. His career was cut short when he became mentally unwell in 1919.*

❍ The other great pioneer of modern ballet was Russian company manager, Sergei Diagilev (1872–1929). He commissioned new music, and combined this with dances that used bold, dramatic movements. This new style of dancing shocked many audiences.

❍ Russian dancer Vaslav Nijinsky wore a skin-tight costume to perform his most famous role. Here, he is standing in a twisted position, with his knees bent and his arms held stiffly by his sides. Movements like this were a complete change from the smooth, poised steps of classical ballet.

Classical ballet steps

Arabesque	Balanced on one leg with the other leg extended behind
(en)Arriere	Backward step
(en)Avant	Forward
Ballone	A broad leap with a kick
Cote	To the side
Etendre	To stretch
Glissade	A gliding step
Grand jete	A long jump
Pirouette	Spinning on one foot
Plie	Bending at the knees
Sissone	Jumping from both feet to one foot
Temps leve	Leaping in the air from one leg

Dance

Ballet performances are still popular worldwide. So are many folk-dances. But new forms of dancing are developing all the time. They are based on the kinds of music people like to listen to and the ways they choose to entertain themselves.

❍ Dancers perform at weddings and parties, in bars and clubs and at open air venues. Their lively movements, combined with cheerful music, create a feeling of celebration and encourage everyone watching to relax and have a good time.

❍ Dance is also an important part of many stage entertainments, such as British pantomime or Chinese Beijing Opera. In both, dance is used to show the character of heroes and villains, to create tender love-scenes, or add extra interest to the plot.

❍ In many countries, people perform traditional dances to entertain tourists and display their local culture. Dancers wear traditional dress, and move to music performed on traditional instruments.

❍ At carnival time, in South America and Europe, dancers wearing fantastic costumes lead crowds of merry-makers to sing and dance through city streets.

❍ Among young people, many new styles of dancing developed in the late 20th century. Most were closely linked to popular music. In the 1950s, dancers 'jived' to rock and roll. In the 1960s, they danced the 'twist' to pop music played by The Beatles. In the 1970s, they 'pogoed' to raw, rebellious sounds played by punk rock bands.

Dressed in a bright and beautiful costume, this African entertainer performs an energetic, high-stepping dance to the beat of a goatskin drum. Behind her, fellow-dancers, wearing face-paint, leopard-skins and ankle decorations, join in.

Stars of Beijing Opera – a traditional Chinese entertainment that combines words and music with dance – perform a daring acrobatic feat. These dancers have spent many years training to develop their skills. They need strong muscles, very flexible bodies and excellent balance.

❍ Breakdancing is a dynamic and very acrobatic style of dance that is part of hip-hop culture. It emerged gradually out of the hip-hop movement in the South Bronx of New York City, USA, during the late 20th century.

Ballroom dancing

In 19th-century Europe, dances and balls gave young men and women a rare opportunity to meet. They learned formal dances, such as the waltz or the polka. The tango is a racier and more daring type of ballroom dancing that developed in Argentina in the early 1900s.

This dancer is performing at the world-famous Rio carnival in Brazil. Originally, carnival was a Christian festival held at the beginning of Lent, a period of fasting in February or March. The word carnival means 'farewell to meat'. People held special meals so that they could eat up all the meat that was forbidden in Lent. During carnival time normal life is suspended and the daily worries are forgotten for as long as the festival lasts.

Breakdancing involved much more energetic movements than previous dance styles, and greater use of the hands and body on the floor, with spinning and gymnastic floor movements. For greater ease of movement, and to look fashionable, break-dancers often wear clothing that is influenced by sportswear.

Fancy footwork

During the 1920s, a new dance called the Charleston caused a sensation. Invented by African–Americans in Charleston, South Carolina, USA, and danced to a jazzy rhythm, it featured fast, high-kicking, backward steps that made women's skirts fly high above the knees.

Popular dances

Dances	Examples
Country Dances (origins 16th–19th century Europe)	Reel, Jig, Circle Dance, Morris Dance
Ballroom Dances (origins 19th century Europe)	Waltz, Quadrille, Polka
Ragtime Dances (origins 20th century USA)	Foxtrot, Bunny Hug, Turkey Trot, Quickstep
Latin American Dances (origins 20th century African-Caribbean-American fusion)	Cha-cha-cha, Samba, Rhumba, Tango, Lambada

Amazing

On 24 May 1998, the greatest-ever number of tap dancers gathered for a single routine at the Stuttgart City Square, Germany – 6952 dancers tapped away for 2 min 15 sec.

❍ Dance can express joy at achievements of all kinds. Sportsmen and women dance with delight when they have won a race, or scored an important goal.

Words and Writing

Words have played a key part in the development of civilization. Spoken language, picture-symbols and written alphabets based on sounds have all been used to communicate ideas, beliefs, histories, technologies and laws. Just as importantly, they have also been used to educate and entertain.

❍ Stories were told for thousands of years before they were written down. They were memorized, then passed on from one generation to the next by word of mouth.

❍ Some of the earliest stories were epics – long tales, recited as poetry that told the adventures of revered heroes and leaders from the distant past. Other stories were based on religious beliefs, or gave a warning against possible dangers, or passed on a moral message.

❍ To hold listeners' attention, spoken tales were full of exciting events, strong characters, practical wisdom, humour, romance and suspense. Storytellers would sing, dance, use gestures and make dramatic sounds, to make their recitals even more entertaining.

❍ Many early stories aimed to give young people guidelines as to how they should behave. For example, epics about soldiers and knights taught young boys to grow up as fighters, and to be brave when in battle. They also encouraged adults who heard them to live up to the great exploits of the heroes in epic tales.

❍ Writing allowed stories and many other kinds of information to be stored and learned by others. It also made it much easier to send information from one place to another.

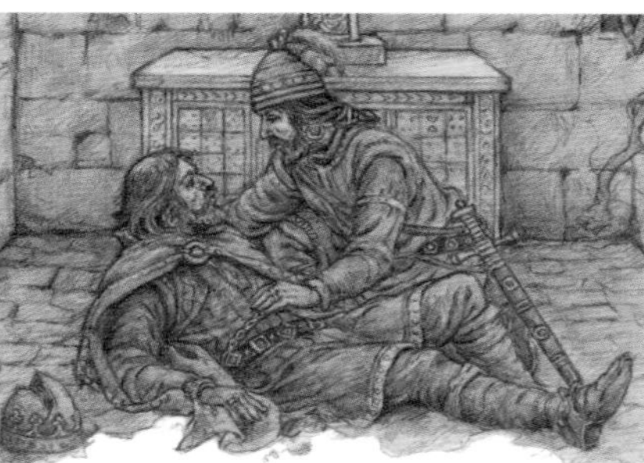

Ancient legends from Britain and France tell of King Arthur and his knights. These tales of heroic deeds, love and Christian values are not just exciting stories. First written down in medieval times, they may have been based on much older Celtic tales from England, Wales and France.

The Vikings of Scandinavia and Iceland told sagas – long, exciting tales of warriors that mixed legend with true history. The sagas were created by poets called skalds, who made a living by telling the tales as entertainment. The sagas were not written down until long after Viking times.

❍ The world's earliest writing was invented in Mesopotamia (now Iraq), around 3200 BC. At first, it was used to make lists, recording goods handed over to government tax-collectors, and stocks stored by merchants.

❍ Early writing used picture symbols. Each symbol stood for one item, such as a cow or a tree. Later, around 1000 BC, scribes in Phoenicia (now Syria and Lebanon) invented an alphabet – a system of writing in which each symbol stood for a separate sound. Today, most languages use alphabets. However, Chinese and Japanese languages both still use picture symbols.

Viking runes

There were 16 letters, called runes, in the Viking alphabet. They were used for labelling valuable items with the owner's name, recording accounts, keeping calendars and for sending messages. From top left, these symbols stand for the sounds: F U Th A R K H N I A S T B M L R

North-European legends told how Thor, the mighty thunder-god, rode angrily through the clouds, brandishing a great thunderbolt. Stories like this were entertaining. and they may also have helped to explain to early farmers how and why natural disasters, such as thunderstorms, took place, causing terrible damage to their crops.

The poem* Beowulf *was originally performed aloud. Set in 6th century Scandinavia, part of the story tells how the hero Beowulf dives into a lake to battle the monster Grendel's mother (shown above) in an underwater cave. Beowulf and his exploits are paralleled in other northern mythologies.

The ancient Egyptians invented a system of writing that used more than 800 picture symbols. It was called hieroglyphs, or sacred writing, because it was used to write religious texts on temple walls.

❍ Alphabets were simpler to use than picture-writing, and easier to learn. Instead of memorizing thousands of different picture-symbols, readers and writers only had to learn the sound of each letter of the alphabet. Most alphabets contained around 30. By combining these, they could produce the sound of each word.

Letters and characters

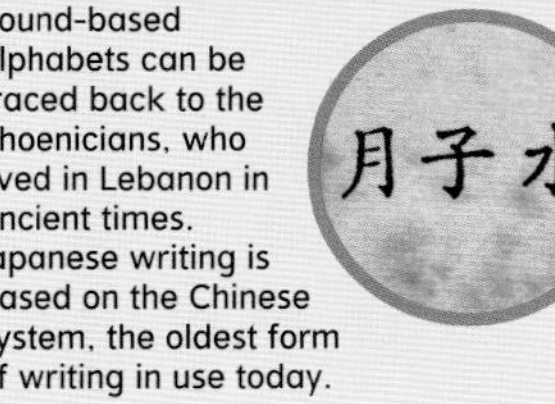

Sound-based alphabets can be traced back to the Phoenicians, who lived in Lebanon in ancient times. Japanese writing is based on the Chinese system, the oldest form of writing in use today.

Ancient legends from Japan tell the story of Susano, god of storms and seas. He was one of three children of Izanagi, the great father-god. One day, Izanagi decided to divide the world among his children, and gave all the seas to Susano. But Susano was not satisfied and quarrelled with his father, who banished him from heaven. Susano went to live in the Underworld, stealing a wife from an eight-headed dragon he met on the way.

Amazing

Sometimes, Viking runes were used to write messages in secret code, or even magic spells. These supposedly gave the objects they were carved on special power.

❍ Over the centuries, people have used many different writing materials. The first scribes (trained writers) in Mesopotamia used pointed sticks to make marks in wet clay slabs and cylinders. Ancient Egyptians made sheets of papyrus (an early kind of paper) from reed plants that grew by the River Nile. Chinese and Japanese people wrote with delicate brushes.

Scriptures and Sacred Writing

Originally, the word 'scripture' just meant 'writing'. But over the years, its meaning changed. Today, it is used to describe holy books from many different faiths. All round the world, believers rely on scriptures to teach and guide them. Scriptures tell millions of men, women and children how to worship, what to think, and how to live their lives. They inspire people to create great art or do brave and noble deeds, and comfort them when they face death, despair or disaster.

❍ Creation myths, preserved in many scriptures, offer answers to important questions, such as 'Who made us?' or 'How did we get here?'. The answers are often religious, involving a powerful god or gods. In most creation myths, the gods lay down holy laws for people to obey. These are often strict but give meaning and purpose to peoples' lives and reassure them that the world has an underlying order, and that nothing happens by chance.

For centuries hieroglyphs (Egyptian symbols that represented words) were a mystery. But in 1799 a stone was found near Rosetta, Egypt, that contained hieroglyphic, demotic, and ancient Greek scripts. By comparing them, scholars were able to work out what the hieroglyphs meant.

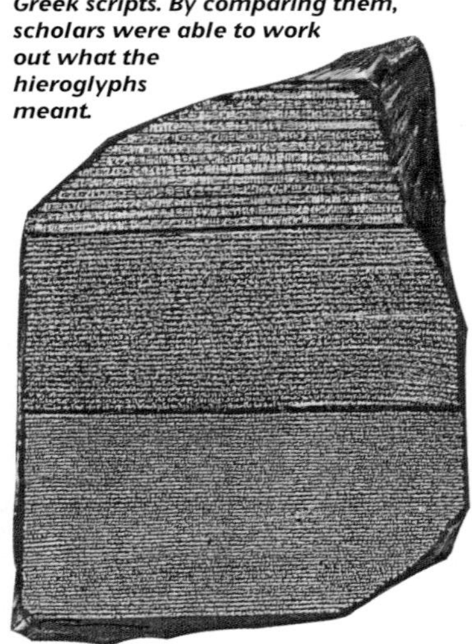

In some civilizations, the symbols used to write holy texts were also considered to be holy. For example, in ancient Egypt, picture symbols, which were known as hieroglyphs (holy writing), were used for writing gods' names and other religious words. The hieroglyphs were respected and feared, because people thought they shared the gods' powers.

❍ The Vedas (poems praising Hindu gods and goddesses) are some of the oldest holy scriptures to survive, dating from around 1500 BC. At first, they were memorized and passed on by word of mouth. Later, they were written down in the holy Hindu language, Sanskrit. Other Hindu scriptures include the Upanishads (teachings of religious leaders) and the Mahabharata and Ramayana (religious poems about the adventures of Hindu heroes and gods).

Most scriptures were first written down many hundreds of years ago. In times of danger they were hidden away for safety. About 2000 years ago, when ancient Romans occupied the Jewish homeland, Jewish people hid copies of their scriptures in pottery jars (right), and stored them in caves near the Dead Sea (now in Israel). These Dead Sea Scrolls were found again in 1947, and are some of the oldest-known scriptures to survive.

❍ Buddhist holy scriptures are called the 'Tripitaka' (Three Baskets) because they were originally written on palm leaves and stored in three baskets. In the first were rules on how Buddhist monks should live. Stories of the Buddha's life were stored in the second and Buddha's teachings of the right way to live were kept in the third basket.

❍ The world's first-known printed book is a Buddhist holy scripture, called the Diamond Sutra ('Precious Verse'), made in China around AD 800.

❍ Muslims believe that their scripture – the Holy Koran – contains the actual words of Allah (God). They believe that the text of the Koran was revealed to the Prophet Muhammad, who lived in Arabia from AD 570–632. Muslims respect and honour Arabic, the language in which it is written.

❍ *Tao-te Ching/Daode jing* (The Book of the Way and its Power) was written by Chinese religious teacher Lao-tzu around 400 BC. His book taught people to lead good lives. By doing this, they would be following a great power, called Tao (the Way).

The Sikh religion was founded in Punjab (now part of India and Pakistan) by Guru (wise leader) Nanak, in 1499. He preached purity, self-control, charity and tolerance. Followers of the Sikh religion are guided by the teachings of their holy scriptures, the* Guru Granth Sahib. *Copies of this book are handled with great reverence. In Sikh gurdwaras (temples), they are placed on a cushion, and covered with a cloth, to protect their pages. At night, they are carefully put away in a special room.

David and Goliath

Many scriptures contain stories about heroes who have fought for their religion. The Jewish Tenakah and the Christian Old Testament both describe how Jewish hero David fought bravely against the enemy giant Goliath to defend his people, their homeland, and their traditional faith. Goliath belonged to an ancient people, called the Philistines. Since the time David killed him, 'philistine' has been used to mean 'people who attack religion or culture'.

Amazing

Followers of Judaism, Christianity and Islam all respect the same scriptures and are sometimes known as the 'People of the Book'.

❍ The religious philosopher Confucius lived in China from 551 to 479 BC and taught people how to live in peace by practising five 'virtues': goodness, kindness, wisdom, modesty and trustworthiness. His teachings were written in a book called the *Analects* ('conversations') Many people in China and East Asia still follow his teachings.

St Paul (who lived around AD 60) was one of the first Christian preachers. He travelled to many parts of the Roman Empire, teaching the Christian faith. He also wrote Epistles (letters) to guide new Christian communities.

Words and pictures

Until the 20th century, many people could not read. So stories from many different holy scriptures were portrayed in religious art. In Christian countries, they were often painted on church walls, where worshippers could see them. This church wall-painting is from Ethiopia, one of the first African countries to make Christianity its official religion (AD 341).

Many Buddhist men and women decide to spend some time as monks or nuns, to learn more about their faith. This bhikkhu, or Buddhist monk, is studying holy scriptures.

Major world scriptures

	Religion	*Date first written down*
Veda	Hindu	c.1500 BC
Upanishads	Hindu	c.500 BC
Mahabharata	Hindu	c.400 BC–AD 400
Ramayana	Hindu	c.400 BC–AD 400
Tenakah	Jewish	c.1200 BC onwards
Torah		
Nevi'im (Books of Prophets)		
Ketuvim (Books of Histories)		
Talmud (writings of Jewish religious teachers)		c.AD 200–500
Tripitaka	Buddhist	c.386–349 BC
Bible		
Old Testament (the Jewish Tenakah)	Christian	c.1200 BC onwards
New Testament	Christian	c.AD 300 (as a collection)
Koran	Muslim	c.AD 632 (as a collection)

Poems and Novels

Poets have held a special place in society since ancient times. In each civilization, they have won praise for their special ways of seeing the world, as well as for their skill at creating word-patterns. Playwrights (since around 500 BC) and novelists (since around AD 1020) have also become famous for creating works that provoke, protest, inspire and amuse.

❍ We do not know the names of many early poets. The first well-known poet was a Greek, later called Homer. His epic stories, the *Iliad* (about war between Greeks and the city of Troy) and the *Odyssey* (about the travels of Greek hero Odysseus), were based on older traditions, and were first written down about 800 BC.

Haiku

'Breaking the silence of an ancient pond, A frog jumped into water... A deep echo.' Those words are a translation of a Japanese poem, known as haiku. Each haiku is very short. In its original Japanese, it has only 17 syllables (separate sounds). Haiku poems are often inspired by natural sights and sounds, and describe a moment of insight or understanding – or perhaps a glimpse of eternity.

❍ Homer may never have existed. He may have been a name given to a group of poets working in Greece to retell stories at the same time.

❍ One of the most famous episodes in Homer's epic poem, *Iliad*, tells how a wooden horse helped the Greeks to capture the enemy city of Troy. They built the huge horse outside the city walls, then pretended to go away. Curious to find out more, the men of Troy dragged the horse into their city. They were horrified when fully armed Greek soldiers leaped out from inside the horse, where they had been hiding, opened the city gates, and let the rest of the Greek army march in.

The* Rhymes of Robin Hood, *first written down around AD 1350, describe the adventures of an English outlaw hero who hid in the woods. With his band of merry men and girlfriend, Maid Marian, Robin Hood robbed the rich and helped the poor.

❍ Many popular poems tell stories in verse. Originally composed to be recited out loud, they feature dramatic characters, strong rhythms and catchy rhymes. One famous series of story-poems, about Anansi the spider, has travelled all round the world.

❍ Early poets also told tales of brave knights and noble ladies. Their poems were based on ancient folk-tales, that combined Celtic or Germanic legends with the Christian faith.

❍ In the past, poems were often very long, and followed various complicated rhyming word patterns. Today, many are short, and do not rhyme at all. Old or new, most poets share the same aim – to use language to say something new and memorable about the world.

❍ After around AD 1400, collections of stories became popular in Europe. They were called 'novels', from the Italian word *novella*, which means 'new things', or 'news'. By around 1700, novels had taken the form they still have today – a long, imaginary story with powerful central characters.

❍ Novels did not become popular until after AD 1700. But as more people learned to read, and public lending libraries opened, novels slowly attracted a much larger readership.

Amazing

When the first part of *Don Quixote de la Mancha* was published in 1605, it was a bestseller. It is said to be the first modern novel. It was written by Spanish author Miguel de Cervantes (1547–1616).

In the late 18th century, a group of British poets gathered in the Lake District of northwest England and wrote about their feelings for nature. Robert Southey (1774–1843), William Wordsworth (1770–1850) and Samuel Taylor Coleridge (1772–1834) became known as the 'Lake Poets'. They used poems about nature as a way of exploring their deepest feelings, and commenting on events in their world.

Elizabeth Barrett Browning (1806–1861) was one of the best-known poets in 19th-century Britain. She was celebrated for her tender, passionate love poems and her opinions about politics, slavery and women in society. Her second book of poetry, called, simply,* Poems*, won great praise when published in 1844.

❍ Novels do not have to tell of great events or adventures. Jane Austen (1775–1817) was a genius at portraying the lives of ordinary people in a carefully observed way and with wry humour. Her novels include *Sense and Sensibility*, *Emma* and *Pride and Prejudice*.

One of Britain's best-loved poets is John Keats (1792–1821). In 1818 and 1819, Keats produced a series of brilliant poems including 'Ode to a Nightingale', 'To Autumn' and 'The Eve of St Agnes'. However, he was already seriously ill with tuberculosis. In 1820, Keats left England to escape the cold weather. He died in Italy, aged only 25.

❍ Some of the most famous works of literature in the 19th and 20th centuries were written by adults for children. Their text was often combined with illustrations. Together, text and pictures created magical, imaginary worlds.

❍ Writers of the 19th century created books showing how new discoveries in science and technology might change the world. This kind of work has now developed into a special kind of literature, known as science fiction, or sci-fi. In recent years, fiction writers with expert scientific knowledge, such as Isaac Azimov (1920–1992) and Arthur C Clarke (1917–2008), have created complex but believable science-fiction adventures.

The adventures of shipwrecked sailor Robinson Crusoe on a tropical island, were described in a novel by English writer Daniel Defoe, published in 1719. Defoe based his book on the true story of Scottish sailor Alexander Selkirk, who spent five years alone on an island off South America.

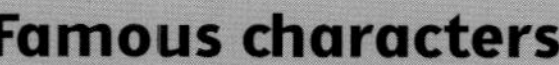

Famous characters

Several imaginary characters, invented by novelists, have become extremely well-known. A few people think that they once really existed. Quasimodo, a tragic figure who lived in cathedral bell tower, was created by French writer Victor Hugo (1802–1885) in his novel *The Hunchback of Notre Dame*. One-legged pirate Long John Silver, famous for his cry of "Yo Ho, my hearties!" appeared in *Treasure Island*, a novel by Scottish writer Robert Louis Stevenson (1850–1894). Brilliant detective Sherlock Holmes – together with his great friend, Dr Watson – starred in novels and short stories by Scottish doctor Sir Arthur Conan Doyle (1859–1830).

Printing and Publishing

Until around 500 years ago, there were very few books. Most were written by hand, and all were very expensive. But around AD 1440, a German inventor, Johannes Gutenberg, built a machine that could print books in large numbers. This revolutionized the way books were produced, and made them available, cheaply, to many more readers. Printed books remain an important source of information and entertainment in our world today. Hundreds of thousands of new titles are published every year.

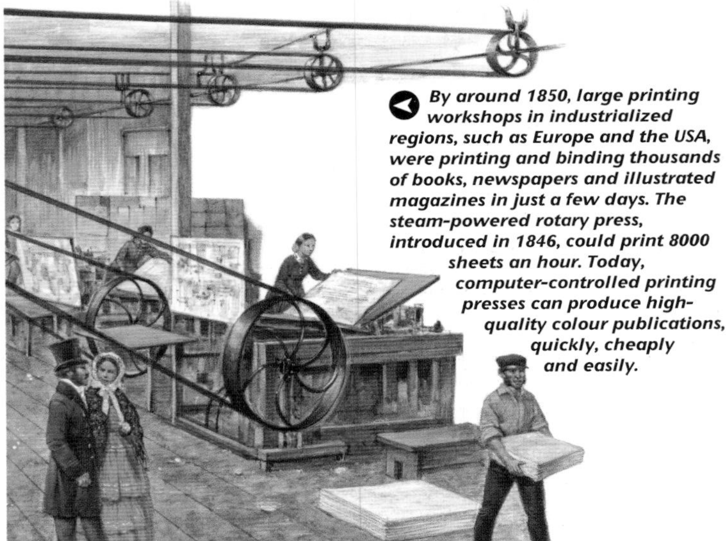

By around 1850, large printing workshops in industrialized regions, such as Europe and the USA, were printing and binding thousands of books, newspapers and illustrated magazines in just a few days. The steam-powered rotary press, introduced in 1846, could print 8000 sheets an hour. Today, computer-controlled printing presses can produce high-quality colour publications, quickly, cheaply and easily.

❍ Gutenberg's machine – called a printing press – used moveable type. Skilled workers assembled individual letters to make words and sentences, then locked these into place in a wooden frame called a 'forme'. They covered the forme with a thin layer of ink, laid a sheet of paper on top, pressed down hard with a wooden pad, removed the sheet (now covered with inky type, or letters) and hung it up to dry.

❍ Printing was not a new invention. The first printed pages were produced in China soon after AD 800. But the writing for each page was carved as a whole from a single wooden block. Gutenberg's moveable type was much easier, quicker and more flexible to use.

❍ Once printed books became widely available, after around AD 1600, more people learned to read (and write). To satisfy this mass-market, soon newspapers, pamphlets, posters and song-sheets were printed in large numbers.

The bestselling book of all time is the Bible. Over the centuries, about six billion copies of the Bible have been sold. The aim of most publishers is to create bestsellers.

Gutenberg printer

In about 1440 the German, Johannes Gutenberg, developed a way of printing using movable type. First he cast hundreds of individual metal letters in moulds. Then he arranged these letters into pages of text, which he printed on a press – a far quicker method than woodblock printing.

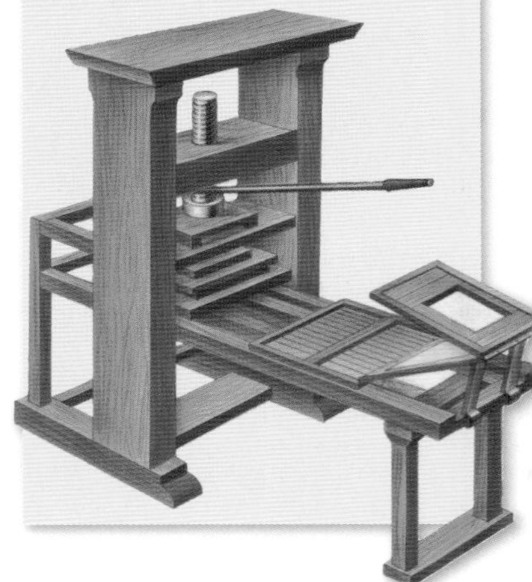

Some authors write books out by hand, others use a computer, and they often make many revisions along the way.

At the publisher, editors go through the author's text for content, clarity, consistency, and to check for mistakes. Designers plan how the pages will look – choosing the type size and style, and deciding on the layout (the positioning of text, and images if the book is illustrated).

Following the designer's instructions, an illustrator usually produces rough versions of images for approval, before creating the final finished pieces. These may be made by hand, created digitally using a software package on the computer, or be a combination of the two.

❍ Books, newspapers and magazines are produced by businesses known as publishing (or media) companies. They select the best books and articles from among those sent by authors to them, or commission specially written work.

❍ Authors are the starting point for most books – fiction or non-fiction. Before starting writing, they may spend many weeks researching a subject and making notes on how to shape the content of the book.

❍ Book illustrators are artists who specialize in turning ideas into visual images. They generally work on books of one particular kind, for example story-books or reference books. Specialist photographers also provide photos to use in books, to illustrate a particular point, or inspire a special mood.

❍ At a publisher's office, editors go through an author's text, correcting any errors, making suggestions for changes, and questioning anything that is not clear. They works closely with a designer, who plans how the finished pages of a book will look.

❍ Once the text and pictures are ready, the finished pages (prepared by a designer) are sent in electronic form to a reproduction house. There, they are made into colour film, or processed by special computers linked directly to colour printers. Modern printers are very fast, and usually print eight pages at a time on huge rolls of paper. The paper is then folded, cut, stitched and bound to produce a finished book.

❍ Finished books and magazines are stored in a publisher's warehouse. Bookshops and libraries order the titles they want from publishers.

Electronic books

E-books are downloaded from the Internet and read on a computer, a hand-held electronic device or on a smart phone. Today, there are many millions of books available on the Internet to download for a fee or without charge.

Amazing

The longest novel ever written was *A la Recherche du Temps Perdu* by Marcel Proust with an estimated 9,609,000 characters.

Newspapers today are printed on machines called web presses. Paper is fed from huge rolls through the press at a rate of up to 1000 m a minute. The pages are then folded and cut, ready for distribution.

Beginnings of Broadcasting

Over the last 100 years, broadcast media have spread news, views, arts, sports, music and drama worldwide. The first broadcasting system to be invented was radio. By the mid-1920s, there were more than 1500 licensed radio transmitters, and over 4 million radio receiver sets in peoples' homes.

Amazing

Today, smart phones and MP3 devices stream (continually transfer digitally) files of music, TV and radio broadcasts from the Internet.

Italian scientist Guglielmo Marconi pioneered the use of radio waves as a means of communication. He constructed his first radio apparatus in 1895. At first it was only used to transmit simple messages in Morse Code. But by 1897, Marconi was able to send long-distance messages by radio, over a distance of 19 km. In 1901, he made the first 'wireless' radio transmission across the Atlantic Ocean.

The radio was designed only to transmit simple messages, but in 1906 music was broadcast. By the time this picture was taken in the 1940s, many households in Europe and America had a radio. It was the most popular family entertainment before the arrival of television.

- Radio systems contain several separate elements. Microphones convert sounds into electrical signals (electromagnetic waves that move at the speed of light). Valves or transistors amplify (magnify) them. Transmitters send them out into the world. Aerials receive them, and carry them to more amplifiers. Then they pass to loudspeakers, tuning and volume controls in each radio.

- Early radio sets were huge and heavy, with massive wooden cases, wide loudspeakers, and fragile glass valves (electrical components that magnified sound) inside. The first portable radio receiver was made in 1923. Car radios were invented in 1929.

- By 1901, radio messages could be sent across the Atlantic Ocean. The first, experimental, music broadcast was made in 1906.

- By 1916, radio stations in Europe and the USA made regular broadcasts, playing 'concerts' of gramophone recordings, or live performances by musicians in radio broadcast studios.

- Radios were revolutionized in the late 1950s and 1960s when transistors (miniature switches and amplifiers) and microchips (tiny electrical circuits made of layers of silicon) were invented. Radios became smaller, lighter and easy to carry around.

- Television works by scanning images, converting them into electric signals and sending these along a cable or through the air on radio waves. A receiver collects the signals, turns them back into images and displays them on a screen.

Camcorders

Camcorders (video recorders) allow people to make their own films easily. The films have a special hand-held quality that is now sometimes imitated in Hollywood movies to mimic live reportage. They are also used by television reporters making live news broadcasts, and by reporters working in remote, war-torn areas where it is too difficult or dangerous to send a full camera and sound-recording crew.

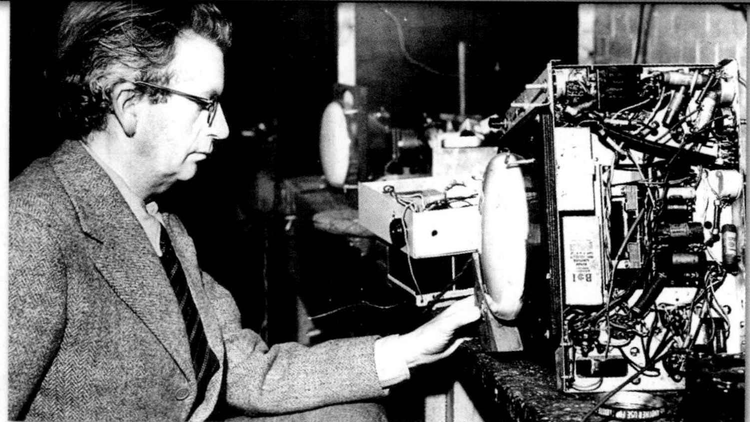

The British inventor John Logie Baird (1888–1946) gave the first demonstration of a television in 1925. His apparatus included a cookie tin and darning needles. The system remained basic until the 1950s. Broadcasts were in black and white, and usually performed live. Colour was introduced in 1953, but was only used widely from the 1960s.

❍ Several different television systems have been invented since 1925. Baird's system is no longer used.

❍ Outside broadcasts of sports events, church services and important royal occasions began in the 1920s and 1930s.

❍ In Britain, King George V gave the first royal Christmas broadcast by radio in 1932. This began a tradition that still continues today.

❍ The scientist who invented the first reliable television camera, in the 1930s, feared that television would become 'the biggest time-waster of all time'. He warned, 'Use it well.'

❍ The world's first regular television broadcasts were made in London by the British Broadcasting Corporation (BBC) in 1936 and 1937. Announcers wore formal evening dress to introduce the programmes.

❍ Colour television broadcasts began in the USA in 1951. Videotape recording of TV broadcasts was invented in 1956.

❍ In the USA, scientists made a broadcasting breakthrough in 1969 when their spacecraft sent back live pictures of the first person to walk on the Moon. The moonwalk pictures were shown on television all round the world.

❍ In 1979, Japanese businessman Akio Morita, head of the Sony Corporation, invented a battery-powered portable personal stereo cassette tape player. He called it a Walkman. Later broadcasting inventions include personal radios and CD players.

The first television broadcasts were made in 1929. Early sets were disguised as pieces of decorative furniture. By 1949, when this 'Predicta' set was made, television was still a rare and expensive luxury, but the design of the 'Predicta' was streamlined and modern, rather than functional and hidden away. Today, there are television sets in most homes in the developed world.

Broadcasting satellites

TV pictures and sound waves can be sent around the world. They are sent from one location up to satellites floating in space and transmitted to a receiver at another location. This means that live news pictures can be broadcast immediately from any trouble spots, making the world seem a smaller place. Global broadcasts mean viewers and listeners can now choose the latest international productions, instead of their own local or traditional media. Some people fear that this might weaken local cultures, or make them disappear completely.

Home Entertainment

Since they were first invented, radio and television have had an enormous impact on home entertainment. Broadcasting has created thousands of new jobs, from camera operators to newsreaders, and has allowed information to be accessible to millions of people as news, entertainment and education. Today, online broadcasts via the Internet keep people up-to-date with events, sports, music and celebrities, all round the world, 24 hours every day.

In the late 20th century, television presented classic dramas filming works of literature, such as **Pride and Prejudice** *by Jane Austen, to a vast new audience. Most of these costume dramas were made in Britain, and exported, with translated dialogue, to different parts of the world.*

Television

Although a trip to the cinema is still an exciting event, in the past 20 years home theatres have become bigger and better, seeking to replicate the big-screen experience for viewers without them having to leave the house. The key parts are a large, widescreen display, a sound system with several loudspeakers, and the movie itself, usually on a DVD player or via an Internet streaming device.

Before television sets became affordable in the 1950s, radio plays were popular home entertainment. In 1938, Orson Welles caused a sensation by broadcasting a science-fiction play. Called *War of the Worlds*, it described an invasion by aliens. It was so realistic that many listeners fled from their homes in terror.

Amazing

Jerry Seinfeld earned an estimated $267 million for the show *Seinfeld* in 1998 – the highest annual earnings ever by a television or film actor.

Since the 1960s, broadcasts on television have both entertained and informed audiences. Programmes about distant countries, exotic wildlife, art, archaeology and ancient monuments have all allowed audiences to view wonderful things that they might otherwise not have seen.

Today, many radio and television broadcasts can be seen and heard on computers, or downloaded on to personal media players using formats such as MP3. Most broadcasts are now also interactive. Broadcasters invite audiences to take part in favourite programmes by sending e-mails, joining in Internet debates, and even making their own programmes.

❍ Television has revolutionized political campaigns. Politicians who are skilled television performers have a better chance of winning elections.

❍ Television broadcasts of live music – from opera to rock festivals – bring pleasure to millions who cannot travel to concerts or buy tickets for live shows. However, some music fans say that watching television can never replace the thrill of being at a live performance.

❍ Television producers make serials that they can sell to as many TV networks as possible. These serials are then shown as repeats in later years to earn extra fees.

❍ Soap operas originated in the 1920s and 1930s as daytime radio broadcasts designed to appeal to housewives. They were sponsored by the makers of soap, and cosmetic products. They describe the daily lives of ordinary people – who lead extraordinarily eventful lives. Today, soaps are some of television's most popular television programmes.

❍ Fashions in broadcasting often lead to complaints, as programme-makers take part in ratings wars to attract the most viewers. This leads to popular programmes such as top reality shows being shown at the same time.

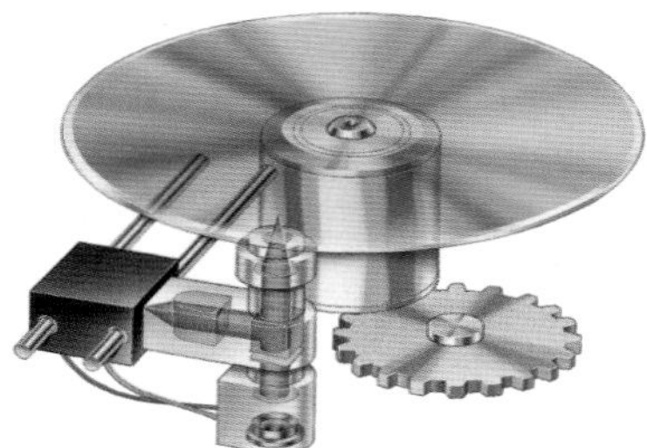

DVDs (Digital Versatile Discs) were developed from CDs (Compact Discs) in the late 1990s. Like CDs, they are made of plastic with a thin metal coating and read by laser-beams. Each DVD can store an enormous amount of data – words, music and very high quality images – in digital form. The first DVD recorders went on sale in 2000. Today, they have replaced video players for recording TV broadcasts and for showing movies in many homes.

❍ Telecommunications is the almost instantaneous transmission of sounds, words, pictures and information by electronic means. At present, TV, radio and phone links are all carried separately, but increasingly they will all be carried the same way. They will be split up only when they arrive at their destination.

This PlayStation portable (PSP) brought out in 2005 took game playing to new heights with the small handheld screen and controls. The graphics of the Ridge Racer game (above) were some of the fastest available on a portable device.

Videotape recording

Until videotape recorders were invented, viewers had only one chance to see a programme – at the time it was scheduled to be broadcast. The first videotape recording was made in 1956, but home video recorders and players were not available until 1972. Videos were a breakthrough in broadcasting, allowing viewers to watch what they wanted, at a time that they could choose.

❍ Video games originated in the late 1960s. Several different systems were invented, but all used a console that could be loaded with computer programs and linked to a TV set. These early games were revolutionized by the Game Boy, invented by Japanese company Nintendo in 1989. Each set had a tiny screen and console that could easily be carried around, and offered players many different adventure games and puzzles.

❍ Game Boy was followed by PlayStation, launched by Japanese electronics giant Sony in 1994. The games featured advanced graphics, realistic feedback, and fast, sensitive controls.

The First Films

Films are one of the world's youngest and most profitable art forms. The first film was shown to the public in 1895. By the 1930s, millions of people in Europe and North America were visiting the cinema every week. Today, DVDs (digital versatile disks) and other electronic media mean that people all round the world can watch movies whenever they like, at home.

❍ Today's film industry would not exist without three 19th-century inventions: photography, lantern-slide projectors and the zoopraxiscope.

❍ The oldest surviving photograph was taken in either 1826 or 1827. It was produced after spreading a mixture of chemicals on a glass plate, reflecting an image on to them, then exposing the plate to light.

Celluloid film

The cinematographe machine, invented by the Lumière brothers, worked by passing a continuous strip of film printed with photographic images in front of a bright light and a magnifying lens. This produced a large, moving picture on a screen. From around 1889, cinema films were made of celluloid – a kind of plastic manufactured from wood-pulp, acid and alcohol. Celluloid film was flexible and transparent – but also dangerously explosive! Many early films were destroyed when they caught fire.

❍ Early photographers discovered that by shining a light through finished glass-plate photographs, images could be projected onto another surface. They gave magic lantern shows, in which the audience sat in a darkened room and watched photos projected on to a wall.

Amazing

The first movie in Three-Color Technicolor was *Becky Sharp* (1935), starring Miriam Hopkins.

❍ In the 1880s, American Eadweard Muybridge (1830–1904) set up groups of cameras with threads attached to the shutters, so that dozens of photos could be taken in quick succession. Muybridge's aim was to study movement, but he realized that by showing his photos one after the other, very fast, he could produce pictures that appeared to move.

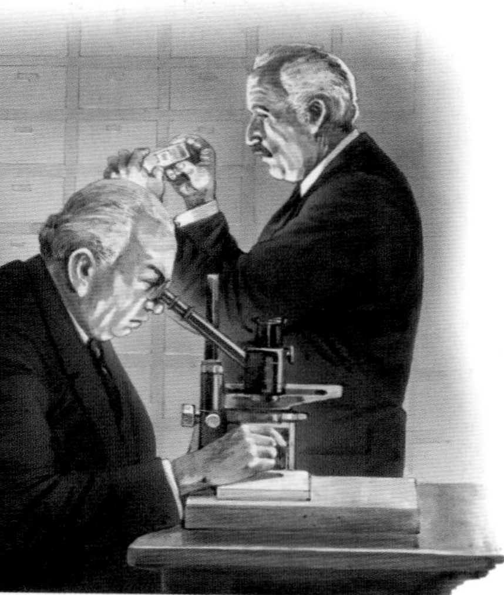

In France, two brothers, Auguste (1862–1954) and Louis Lumière (1864–1948) had the brilliant idea of combining a camera and a projector. In 1895, they perfected the cinematographe machine. It took pictures on a continuous strip of film, and replayed them on a screen. They had invented movies.

Charlie Chaplin (1889–1977) was one of the first, and most famous, movie stars. He began his career as a comedian in English music-halls, but moved to America, where he soon became a great success in early silent films. A brilliant mime, with great comic timing, he developed an instantly recognizable image, popular with fans all round the world. Dressed in a baggy suit and bowler hat, with a 'toothbrush' moustache, he made fun of cruel, silly or pompous people, and stood up for the powerless, ordinary 'little man'.

Movie sound

In the early days of cinema, film shows were accompanied by live performances of piano music, or by recorded tunes played on gramophones. In 1911, the Wurlitzer company in the USA began to make huge organs – known as 'Mighty Wurlitzers' – for cinemas, to provide loud, dramatic music, and many sound-effects, for films. The first film with a built-in soundtrack (recorded speech that was played at the same time as the film) was not produced until 1927.

❍ Muybridge invented a machine called a zoopraxiscope to show his moving pictures. It was made of a large hollow cylinder, which turned round and round. Images were pasted on the inside; as the drum turned, viewers could not see where one image ended and the next began. They blurred together and seemed to move.

❍ Also in America, Thomas Edison (1847–1931), helped by William Dickson, built a kinetograph – a very fast camera that could take 40 photos a second. They also designed a special machine, called a kinetoscope, for viewing kineotgraph film. Viewers looked down a pair of lenses – rather like binoculars – in a darkened booth.

❍ The earliest films were silent. Actors told the story in mime. This meant that performances could be enjoyed by audiences in many different countries. Film shows were usually accompanied by mood music, played in the cinema on a piano or organ.

❍ The first film with sound – known as a talkie – was produced in 1927. It was very successful with audiences, but disastrous for some movie stars. Although they were clever at movement and mime, they did not have pleasant speaking voices. They were replaced by actors who looked attractive and could also speak their lines well.

❍ Many of the first films were comedies. But, by the 1920s, dramatic adventure stories, historical epics and classics from world literature were also made into films.

Buildings, known as movie theatres or cinemas, were designed to house the large audiences who wanted to watch new films. Cinemas soon became a popular – and much cheaper – alternative to the theatre. Like music halls, they became favourites with ordinary people, as well as wealthy, well-educated theatregoers.

Film firsts

1927	**First 'talkie'**	*The Jazz Singer*
1928	**First film to win Best Film Oscar**	*Wings*
1937	**First feature-length Walt Disney animation**	*Snow White and the Seven Dwarfs*
1939	**First colour film to win Best Film Oscar**	*Gone With the Wind*
1939	**First African American to win an Oscar**	Hattie McDaniel (Best Supporting Actress for *Gone With the Wind*)
1940	**First film in stereosound**	*Fantasia*
1942	**First twins to win an Oscar**	Julius and Philip Epstein (Best Screenplay for *Casablanca*)
1948	**First British film to win Best Film Oscar**	*Hamlet*
1953	**First film to be released in Cinemascope**	*The Robe*
1963	**First African American to win a Best Actor Oscar**	Sidney Poitier for *Lilies of the Field*
1964	**First James Bond movie to win an Oscar**	*Goldfinger* for Best Effects and Sound Effects
1969	**First X-rated film to win Best Film Oscar**	*Midnight Cowboy*
1970	**First actor to refuse a Best Actor Oscar**	George C Scott for *Patton*
1974	**First sequel to win Best Film Oscar**	*The Godfather Part II*
1975	**First film released in Sensurround**	*Earthquake*
1976	**First woman to be nominated for Best Director Oscar**	Linda Wertmuller for *Seven Beauties*
1991	**First animated film to be nominated for Best Film Oscar**	*Beauty and the Beast*
1995	**First wholly computer-generated film**	*Toy Story*
2001	**First African American woman to win Best Actress Oscar**	Halle Berry for *Monsters Ball*

Making Movies

Making a film is a complicated and very expensive process. Visual images, spoken words, sound effects, music, studio sets, outside locations and action sequences all have to be very carefully planned and rehearsed, before shooting (photography) can start.

British director Sir Alfred Hitchcock (1899–1980) became known as the master of suspense, after he created many chilling horror movies. In the movie industry, a producer raises money to make a new movie and organizes the financial side of film-making, while the director is in charge of the more creative elements. The director tells the camera crews how to set up their cameras, and directs the actors to act the way the script is written.

On the set of **Lord of the Rings: The Fellowship of the Ring** *(2001). Producer Barrie Osbourne and Viggo Mortensen playing Aragorn check a take.*

❍ As well as having creative responsibility for the concept behind each film, directors are also responsible for writing, or checking, the script, directing the actors' speech and movement on the film-set, giving instructions to lighting and camera crews, checking on how each scene looks through the camera, and choosing the 'cut' (final selection of images) for each film.

❍ Many directors use a storyboard to work out how to shoot a film. This is a sequence of sketches that show roughly how each scene will look. This visual planning also helps to ensure that small details of costume or background remain the same from scene to scene throughout the filming.

Film lighting is a very skilled profession. The level of light on each film set, or in the open air, can affect the overall colour of the finished file. Lighting can also be used for dramatic effect, for example to create a stormy, threatening mood, or to suggest that characters are harmless.

❍ Lighting plays a major part in creating the look of a film, whether it's shot outdoors on location, or indoors on a studio set. Lighting can create cosy, gloomy, frightening or very dramatic effects.

Hollywood

In 1911, film-makers went to a remote settlement called Hollywood, near Los Angeles, to film westerns. Hollywood had a dry, scrubby landscape, very much like parts of the American Wild West. Within two years it had become the centre of American film-making and it has dominated the industry worldwide ever since.

❍ Sometimes film-makers build sets – life-like mock rooms, buildings, landscapes, fantasy environments or moving models of monsters. It is often cheaper, easier and visually more effective to film on location out in the real world.

❍ Once shooting has finished, each film has to be edited. Most directors shoot more material than they need. The final visual images are chosen by the director and a team of editors. They are then combined with a soundtrack of voices, music and sound-effects.

Completed films are marketed to the public. Big posters outside cinemas show dramatic scenes from each film or glamorous pictures of its stars. Directors and actors give interviews to press and TV journalists, or appear at film festivals and awards ceremonies.

Amazing

To add extra impact to their performances, Bollywood actors lip-synch (pretend to sing) the words of popular songs performed by expert musicians off-stage.

Clapperboard

A clapperboard is used in a movie or TV studio to mark the beginning or end of a take (a short section of movie). Details of each take are filled in on the clapperboard, which is held up in front of the camera before filming begins. Movies are not usually made in the order of a story. Director, scriptwriters, camera crew and actors work on the scenes in whatever order is convenient, for example when the actors are available or the weather is right. Several takes may be needed before a scene is filmed properly. The final takes are put together in order by an editor and, if necessary, cut to create the finished movie.

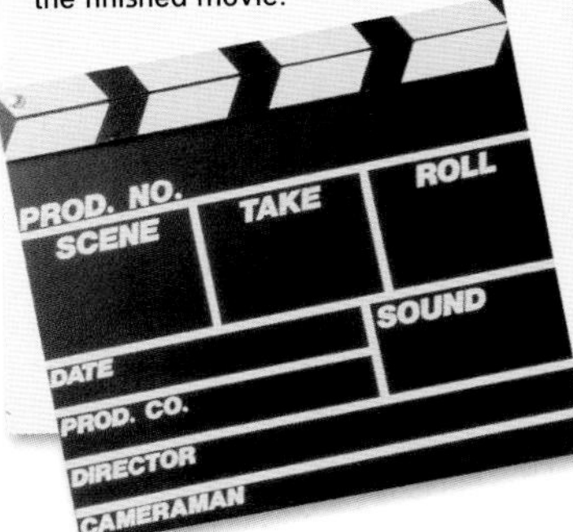

Bollywood films, made in Bombay, India, are lavish song-and-dance spectacles that tell exciting adventure stories or passionate tales of love. Male and female stars are chosen for their good looks, and attract vast numbers of fans. They use facial expressions, mime and dance to express powerful emotions.

Special Effects and Superstars

Throughout the 20th century, new technology helped film-makers create fantastic visions of reality. Colour photography made scenes on screen seem more dramatic and lifelike. Special effects and computer-generated images allowed directors to create visual impressions that could never exist in real life.

- All early films were shot (photographed) in black and white, although a few had faint colour added after shooting by technicians at film studios. The first full-colour movie, made using a process called 'Technicolor', was produced in 1935.

- Film-makers use models and computer technology to create stunning visual effects, such as earthquakes, floods, or invasions from outer space. Pioneered in the 1960s and 1970s, these SFX (special effects) are now extremely accomplished and realistic.

- From the 1930s to the 1950s, cowboy adventures, crime thrillers and wartime hero stories were popular, together with cartoons. In the 1950s and 1960s, light romances and historical epics were favourites with audiences. In the late 1960s and 1970s, many films began to feature the latest fashions in pop and rock music and dancing.

- Serious 'art' films, inspired by writers and philosophers, asked questions about the meaning of life. Many were made using experimental techniques in France and Scandinavia between 1950 and 1980.

- Since the early days of film-making, directors from many countries made films designed to make a political protest, or spread their political ideas. The most outspoken films were often banned by governments whose ideas were criticized in the film.

Amazing

Andy Serkis, who played the character of Gollum in *The Lord of the Rings* film trilogy, was ruled ineligible for an Oscar nomination because his onscreen character was computer generated.

Technology developed by scientists at the US government's National Aeronautics and Space Administration (NASA) helped create special effects for the action movie **Terminator 3: Rise of the Machines** *(2003). Engineers and film-makers relied on NASA robotics to design terrifying robot monsters that moved in a menacing way to threaten human heroes on screen. Since the mid-20th century, growing expertise in robotics and photography have raised expectations among film-goers. Viewers now expect robots to be slick, smart and extremely lifelike. Old-fashioned monsters that look homemade are no longer so appealing.*

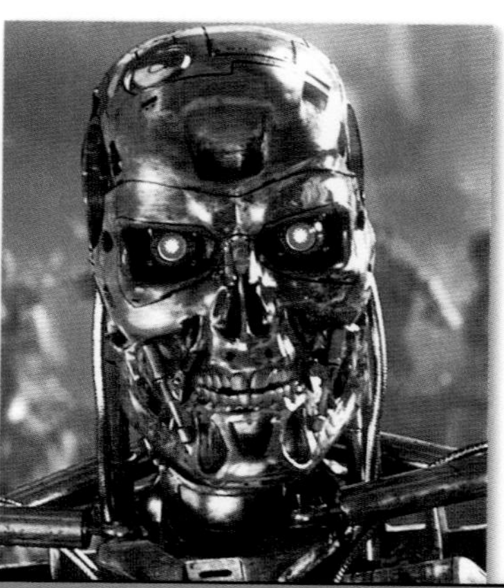

Superstars

Marilyn Monroe

Audrey Hepburn

Rudolf Valentino

Elizabeth Taylor

Boris Karloff (as Frankenstein's Monster)

Nicole Kidman

Tom Cruise

Samuel L Jackson

George Clooney

Nicholas Cage

Pioneered in* The Matrix *franchise (and seen here in this scene from* The Matrix Reloaded, *2003) the effect known as 'Bullet Time' has been used to create extraordinary action sequences. To achieve it, still cameras were arranged in a circle around the actors, then used to take photos in a carefully-timed sequence. When linked together, copied on to film, and played through a projector, the photos showed events happening in hyper-slow motion, or let viewers see the actors from front, back and sides, all at the same time.

Awards record

The Oscars are the gold-plated awards presented each year by the US Academy of Motion Picture Arts and Sciences. US actress, Katharine Hepburn (1907–2003), is the only actor to have won four Oscars.

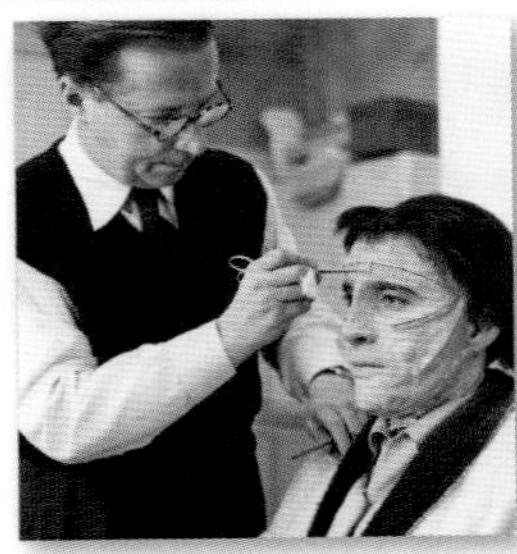

Film-makers use costumes and make-up to create a character's look. Dressing an actor can take hours and may include prosthetics (false body parts), and wigs as well as make-up effects. Shown here, the face of Frankenstein's monster in* Curse of Frankenstein *(1957) featured blisters and scars. Many effects can be added using computers.

Academy Award winners

Best actor

2002	Adrian Brody
2003	Sean Penn
2004	Denzel Washington
2005	Jamie Foxx
2006	Philip Seymour Hoffman
2007	Forest Whitaker
2008	Daniel Day-Lewis
2009	Sean Penn
2010	Jeff Bridges
2011	Colin Firth
2012	Jean Dujardin
2013	Daniel Day-Lewis
2014	Matthew McConaughey
2015	Eddie Redmayne
2016	Leonardo DiCaprio
2017	Casey Affleck

Best actress

2002	Halle Berry
2003	Nicole Kidman
2004	Charlize Theron
2005	Hilary Swank
2006	Reese Witherspoon
2007	Helen Mirren
2008	Marion Cottilard
2009	Kate Winslet
2010	Sandra Bullock
2011	Natalie Portman
2012	Meryl Streep
2013	Jennifer Lawrence
2014	Cate Blanchett
2015	Julianne Moore
2016	Brie Larson
2017	Emma Stone

❍ Modern film acting is very different to acting on stage. Actors use subtle changes of facial expression and small movements to show thoughts and feelings. Directors shoot actors' faces in close-up with high-powered lenses, allowing viewers to share each character's emotions.

❍ Leading actors cannot risk getting hurt in action scenes so directors hire specialist stunt actors to take their place. Male and female stunt actors are trained to crash cars, climb mountains, jump from moving trains or leap through fire, all as safely as possible, to avoid injury.

Animatronic techniques create special effects that would be impossible in real life. For example, in* Lord of the Rings: The Two Towers *(2002), the character of Gollum was made by filming a live actor's movements and combining them on computers with scanned images. When refined using 'morphing' software, this created a creature with unsettling traces of human behaviour.

Buildings Great and Small

Architecture is the art and science of designing buildings. Before starting each new project, an architect has to consider the purpose of the building, the site where it will stand, the money needed to pay for it, and the materials available. In the past, almost all big buildings were designed for rich and powerful people. They paid for fine palaces, temples, and tombs. Ordinary people built their own smaller, simpler shops, workplaces and homes. In each civilization, buildings for rich and poor reflected local beliefs and traditions, plus local environmental and climatic conditions.

Some of the very first homes were shelters of brushwood and branches, built inside caves or under overhanging rocks around 50,000 years ago. This stone house in Portugal makes use of the space underneath large boulders in the same way.

The trading town of Çatal Hüyük in Turkey dates from around 7500 BC. Its houses, made of sun-dried clay bricks, were built joined together, side by side. They had no windows. Access was through a trapdoor in the roof.

Stonehenge, in southwest England was built in phases between 3000 and 1600 BC. Its stones are arranged in circles around an open space. They align with the rising Sun at midsummer. Stonehenge may be a temple or observatory.

The ancient Egyptians built pyramids as tombs for important people, especially their pharaohs. The Great Pyramid, at Giza, built around 2560 BC, is the largest pyramid. It is over 148 m tall, and its base measures 230 m on each side.

The ancient Greeks and Romans built temples as homes for gods. They believed that the gods' spirits might live there. The Parthenon temple (of the goddess Athena, built in the 5th century BC) in Athens is the most famous Greek temple of all.

Water wheels were invented in the Middle East 2000 years ago. They were designed to carry water for drinking and to water crops. As the wheel turned, buckets dipped into a river and filled with water. Water was then poured into ditches.

The Colosseum was a vast amphitheatre (circular arena) in Rome, Italy. It was built of wood, concrete and stone by the ancient Romans around AD 80. It seated almost 50,000 spectators, who flocked there to watch gladiator fights.

This Buddhist pagoda at Pagan, Burma, is one of many holy temples built for King Anawrahata (ruled 1044–1077) and his family. Each layer of the pagoda represents a different stage in a human soul's journey towards nirvana (peace and blessedness).

This temple in Qufu City, in the Shandong province of China, was built in 1302 to honour the ancient Chinese philosopher, Confucius. Like many Chinese buildings, it has a wide, heavy roof, decorated with elaborate carvings.

The Forbidden City – a huge network of temples, palaces and gardens, built between 1421 and 1911 – lies within the Chinese capital, Beijing. This is the Temple of Heaven, where the emperor went every year to make sacrifices to the sky gods.

These onion-shaped domes decorate the roof of the Russian Orthodox Cathedral in Moscow, Russia. Like other cathedrals, it is cared for by a bishop (Christian leader). Each Christian country has cathedrals built in its own local style.

In regions with plentiful timber, such as Canada, Russia, and northern Europe, many traditional homes are built of wood – a cheaper material than imported brick or stone.

This stone-walled, straw-thatched house in Peru is built to a design used by the Incas, who ruled the Andes over 500 years ago. Like Inca houses, it has a walled courtyard. Many traditional building styles are hundreds of years old.

In crowded cities there is not much space for building, and houses are often several storeys high, closely packed together, to fit lots of people in one place. These tall merchants' houses in Amsterdam, in the Netherlands, were designed about 1650.

This house on the prairies (grasslands) of western USA is made of sods – slabs of earth with the grass roots attached. In the 19th century, migrant families that settled on the prairies could not afford expensive timber, bricks or stone.

The Potala Palace in Llasa, Tibet, is built of clay, bricks and stone. It is perched high on a cliffside for safety. First designed as a fortress between AD 1000–1500, the palace later became home to the Tibetan Buddhist leader, the Dalai Lama.

Mobile homes

Nomadic peoples, like the Mongols of Central Asia, live in homes that are easy to move. The Mongols take their gers – domed tents made of thick felt – with them when they go in search of new grazing land for their flocks.

Master masons

Castles were among the biggest buildings in the world before around AD 1500. The first castles were small and made of wood. After around 1100, they became splendid forts and homes, built of stone. By around AD 1500, there were over 20,000 castles in England, Wales, France, Spain and Germany.

Modern Architecture

Today, buildings are bigger, taller and more complex than ever before. Many also feature 'intelligent' computer-controlled systems to manage the environment inside.

❍ Modern architecture developed as a rebellion against cluttered, heavy and dull 19th-century designs. Most modern buildings have clean-cut lines, simple shapes and few decorative details.

❍ After around 1900, architects began experimenting with exciting new styles, including Art Nouveau, using flowing shapes inspired by nature. Arts and Crafts is based on traditional buildings. Art Deco is glamorous and streamlined. Functionalism is based on practical needs while Brutalism uses massive shapes. Modernism and High Tech uses new engineering.

Air-conditioned shopping malls have everything under one roof, including many shops, services and often a food hall. Architecture varies from one mall to another, however they are all similar. Critics say they are 'consumerist machines' lacking the social aspect of outdoor markets.

Some designers win fame for their personal style. The Spanish architect Antonio Gaudi (1853–1926) is famous for his original and unusual building designs. Most of his buildings are in the city of Barcelona in Spain. In an attempt to break away from historical styles, he used flowing curves in many of his buildings, which he decorated with brightly coloured ceramics or mosaics of glass.

❍ Architects used industrial technology to create the first modern buildings. Instead of old-style load-bearing walls, they constructed frames of strong steel girders (beams) to support the weight of floors, windows, roofs, ceilings and the people living or working inside. Buildings were 'clad' (covered) by thin 'skins' of clay tiles, concrete blocks, bricks, timber, metal, glass or stone.

Bridges are some of the biggest and most beautiful structures in the world. But their graceful curves and arches are the result of careful mathematical calculations, not simply artistic design. Their strength and safety are more important than their appearance.

At 828 m, the Burj Khalifa Dubai in the United Arab Emirates is the tallest structure in the world.

Skyscrapers

Steel-frame construction technology was first used to build 19th-century factories, then skyscrapers in the USA. The world's earliest skyscrapers were built in the 1880s in Chicago, USA, after a fire destroyed many old wooden houses. The first to be completed was the Home Insurance Building with ten storeys in 1883. Electricity-powered elevators (lifts) were invented to carry people to the upper floors. Nowadays many skyscrapers have more than 200 storeys.

- By the mid-20th century, many buildings were made of solid concrete poured into wooden moulds and reinforced (strengthened) by steel rods inside. Big dark grey concrete buildings were tough and often forbidding.

Amazing

Some skyscrapers sway in the wind. They are sometimes fitted with weights at the top that are moved from side to side to make the building lean into the wind – cancelling out the effect.

- Buildings in the 20th century were inspired by ideas of how people should live. Architects wanted to replace slums with bright modern buildings and create healthier environments. In wealthy countries, the standards of housing rose but in spite of modern architects' achievements, many ordinary people in poor countries still live in homes without sanitation or clean water.

- Top 21st-century architects win prizes for their designs. But some people blame them for wrecking cities with new developments that overpower older buildings nearby. Supporters of modern buildings admire architects' imagination, daring and skill.

The Opera House at Sydney, Australia, was designed by Danish-born architect Jorn Utzon. The Opera House stands on the edge of Sydney Harbour, so Utzorn based its design on curving ships' sails.

The Atomium

Modern engineering techniques have allowed architects to create exciting structures on a huge scale. The Atomium, shown here, was built for the international fair held in Brussels in 1958. It represents a giant model of an atom with nine huge steel balls rising to 120 m.

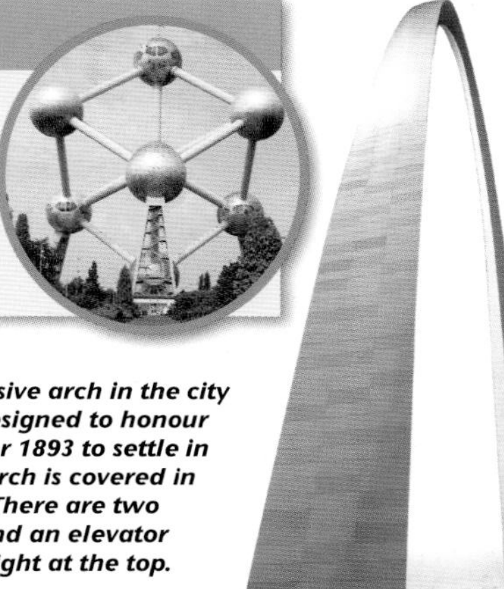

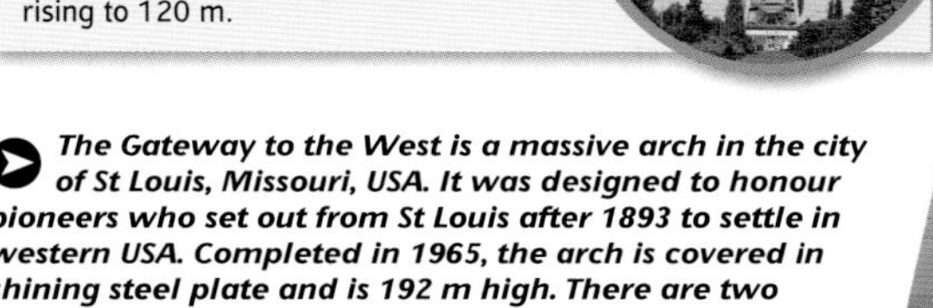

The Gateway to the West is a massive arch in the city of St Louis, Missouri, USA. It was designed to honour pioneers who set out from St Louis after 1893 to settle in western USA. Completed in 1965, the arch is covered in shining steel plate and is 192 m high. There are two theatres and a museum at the base, and an elevator takes visitors to an observation room right at the top.

History of Culture

The word 'culture' is often used to describe art forms that are enjoyed by only a few people – such as opera or ballet. But culture can mean much more than that. It can describe someone's upbringing and education, their religious faith, their community's traditions, and their nation's language, literature and art. It can also describe how a person lives, their political ideas, and how they identify themselves. Usually, culture refers to all these things together, and is used to describe a unique civilization of a particular time or people.

❍ Within each society or civilization, culture has many separate functions. It can amuse and entertain, or be thought-provoking. It can reinforce traditional values, or inspire people with unsettling new ideas.

❍ All around the world different cultures have developed special ceremonies to mark the important stages of each person's life. For example, new babies are traditionally welcomed with naming rituals. Older children take part in initiation ceremonies, which show they are leaving childhood behind and becoming young adults.

❍ In many cultures, marriages traditionally involve the bride moving home, and gifts of food or property to the newly-married couple. Almost everywhere they are an excuse for joyful celebrations.

❍ Often people are laid to rest with funeral prayers. Usually these express hope in a new life after death. In many cultures, dead family members are honoured with tombstones or similar memorials, while important, powerful people are commemorated by grand public monuments.

❍ National costumes are a symbol of pride, closely linked to local culture. People dress to conform to their cultural beliefs. Flesh-revealing clothes are unacceptable in certain cultures. Clothes reflect local climates and products (wool or silk) as well.

Many different faiths teach that men and women should be modestly dressed in public, and that they should wear special clothes when performing religious rituals, as a sign of respect. These Muslim women, who are on holy pilgrimage, have covered their heads and shoulders with a simple white garment. Jewish men also cover their heads and shoulders while reading from holy scriptures.

Amazing

The famous song 'Happy Birthday To You' generates over a million pounds in royalites every single year.

❍ Today many people work in food industries – farming, fishing or working in factories and supermarkets. Global distribution allows people in richer countries to eat foods from all over the world, but in poor regions some people starve. Natural disasters or too much or too little rainfall result in famines. Other countries can send emergency supplies to aid those people in need.

❍ People who belong to a particular faith use holy signs. For Christians, the cross is a holy sign. It reminds them of the wooden frame on which Jesus Christ was executed in about AD 30. Muslims use a crescent moon to symbolize Islam and Jewish people use a six-pointed Star of David.

Flags originated as banners, carried to help soldiers follow their leaders into battle. Now they are important national symbols, carried in processions at international events and flown on public holidays.

Clothes can reflect religious beliefs, wealth, occupation and status, as well as ethnic or national identity. This young Masai woman, from Kenya, East Africa, wears a traditional beaded collar. Her large metal earrings are a sign of wealth, and her beaded necklace will be individual to just her.

Depending on where they live or what they believe, people may prize some foods as delicacies, or refuse to eat them at all. For centuries, growing and catching food have been important occupations. Many people are also employed in food-based industries, such as driving refrigerated lorries or stacking fruit on shop shelves.

Birthday celebrations

People celebrate birthdays in different ways across the world. In Europe and America, birthdays are celebrated by offering gifts and cards, and by sharing a cake decorated with candles. Each candle stands for one year of the birthday person's age. It is considered good luck to blow them all out in one go.

Changing eating habits

Sharing a meal is one of the oldest pleasures known to civilized human beings. In many cultures, hospitality (offering food and drink) is a sacred duty. But in the 20th century new fast foods, such as takeaway burgers and fries, seemed likely to change these ancient cultural traditions in many parts of the world.

In many countries mothers are the head of the family. Many mothers work to support their children and also manage the home. Some companies provide childcare. To prevent overpopulation in China, the government made a law forbidding people to have more than one child. This has helped to slow down the population growth.

A Jewish bride and groom sip wine together during their wedding ceremony as a symbol of the joys and sorrows they will share together in the years ahead.

People in the armed forces and public services, such as police, wear uniforms as a sign of belonging and to encourage discipline and self-respect. Members of national or local sports teams show their loyalty to each other and are united by the same clothes.

Glossary

Abstract art Paintings that have no obvious similarity to real objects, made by arranging shapes and colours in a purely imaginary way, which may be hard to understand.

Alloy A metallic substance made from a mixture of two or more metals, or from a metal mixed with other non-metallic elements, examples being brass, bronze and steel.

Amphitheatre A circular or oval building that contains rows of seats rising from an arena, where performances take place for an audience.

Amplify To make louder. Sounds can be amplified by sound boxes or resonators, or electronically by turning them into electrical signals using a microphone, and passing the signals through an electronic amplifier into loudspeakers.

Animatronics The techniques of designing, building and operating life-like machines or robots that are worked by electronics, assisted by computers and controlled remotely, to mimic real people, animals or aliens.

Architect A person who designs buildings.

Art nouveau French phrase meaning 'new art', an elegant design style of natural flowing or swirling lines, fashionable at the beginning of the 20th century.

Atonal music A form of modern music composition where the notes or sounds are not arranged in the traditional order of scales and harmonies, but in a more abstract way.

Audition An interview to find suitable performers for roles in a play or musical performance. It usually involves candidates reading from a script, singing or giving a short performance, watched by the director.

Auditorium The main part of a theatre, cinema or public performance venue where the audience sits to view the stage. It may consist of a floor area, with seats called stalls, and layers called circles and balconies above, also with seats.

Bass The very low sounds or musical notes, played by large instruments such as a double bass or a tuba, or sung by a man with a very deep voice.

Baton A stick waved by the conductor of an orchestra to emphasize the rhythm and pattern of the music, so that everyone plays or sings the notes in the correct way at the correct time.

Biographies Accounts of a person's life, written or told by someone else.

Brass A shiny, yellowish metal that is an alloy, or mixture, of the pure metals copper and zinc. It is used to make wind instruments such as cornets, trumpets, trombones and horns, which form the brass section of an orchestra.

Broadcast To scatter or spread something over a wide area – today this word usually refers to the spreading of information, news or knowledge usually by radio or television.

Camera obscura A windowless room or box with a small hole in one wall, through which light passes from outside, to produce on the wall opposite inside, an upside-down (inverted) image of the scene outside.

Cast A list of characters in a play, opera or similar production, and the names of the actors who play them. Decisions by the director and others about which actor suits each role is called casting.

Celluloid An early synthetic plastic, used for billiard balls, dentures, combs and photographic film. It is highly flammable and has been replaced by less flammable cellulose acetate for movie film, but the term 'celluloid' is still used generally to mean movies or films in the cinema.

Ceramics Objects that are made by shaping and firing (heating) clay or similar materials, at very high temperatures, so they become hard and brittle.

Ceremony A formal act, convention or event carried out according to custom or traditional rules, usually performed to honour and continue some kind of past ritual, rite or anniversary.

Choreographer The person who decides which dance steps and movements should be used by people during a ballet, musical or similar production. The choreographer then instructs and directs the performance of the dancers.

Civilization A people, their society and culture that have developed in a social, political and technological sense, and are refined in interests and tastes.

Commission To order a picture or other piece of work to be created, often especially for and to the instructions of the person making the order. The person making the order will usually make a payment to the artist or whoever is completing the piece.

Cubism A 20th-century painting technique where the image is broken down into geometric shapes like circles, squares and cubes, which are then rearranged in the picture.

Cue Words or actions of a performer that alert other performers that it is their turn to speak or carry out certain actions.

Culture A way of life of a group of people who share certain customs, beliefs, technology and ideas. People who speak the same language may share the same culture (the Japanese, for example) but not necessarily.

Custom A traditional practice, usually established by a particular community of people.

Dialogue A conversation or discussion between two actors in a play or production, or possibly between two representatives of groups with different ideas.

Digital Digital sound is recorded, not as continuous up-and-down waves, but as codes of numbers or digits, which usually results in a clearer, purer, more accurate recording.

Engraving A printing technique where a pattern or image is cut, or engraved, into a metal or wooden plate. Ink is then rubbed on, and the plate is pressed onto paper to make an impression.

Epic A very long story, poem or tale, told in an elevated style, which relates many great and magnificent deeds, especially involving a hero or heroine.

Etching A printing technique where a pattern or image is cut into an acid-proof coating on a metal plate, and acid is applied that etches, or erodes, the image into the metal. Then the coating is removed and the plate is used to make prints.

Expressionism A style of drama, music or painting where the artist or performer tries to illustrate or express emotions and feelings, rather than real images of the actual world.

Fables Short stories, often based on animal characters, which teach lessons especially to children, to show them how they can lead better lives.

Folk dance The traditional dance of a group of people or a country. Its movements and steps are passed down from generation to generation, and dances are often performed in traditional costume.

Foyer The entrance hall of a theatre, cinema or performance venue, where the audience enters the building, perhaps meet in groups, and buy tickets, programmes, refreshments and merchandise. Also known as 'front of house'.

Fresco From the Italian word for 'fresh', a painting done on the plaster or render (coating) of a wall or ceiling using water-based paints, which are applied while the plaster is still wet.

Frets The series of small metal bars found on a fingerboard or fretboard of a stringed instrument, such as a guitar. When a string is pressed down onto a fret and made to vibrate, a certain note is played.

Guilds Associations often dating from medieval times, formed by craftspeople, traders or merchants engaged in a particular skill or occupation, to protect their work and maintain standards. Guilds usually provided apprenticeships to train young people.

Hieroglyphs The system of writing that uses small pictures to represent words, syllables, or sounds, and which was invented and used by, for example, the ancient Egyptians for religious scripts and texts.

Hit A song or a type of recording that is extremely popular, often selling many copies so that it enters the weekly bestseller charts or 'hit parade'.

Icons Sacred images from Christianity such as Christ, Mary, one of the saints or a scene from the Bible – sculpted or painted onto wooden panels and used as a centrepiece for prayer and worship.

Illuminations Paintings of characters, especially those made by medieval monks, to illustrate handwritten books, often to emphasize the first letter on a page.

Impasto A technique of applying oil or acrylic paint so thickly, with a brush or a palette knife, that the texture and thickness of the strokes remain in the paint.

Impressionism A technique developed by French artists in the 19th century, who painted very quickly outside, using tiny dabs of paint to give an idea of the subject, rather than a detailed and realistic image.

Jazz A form of popular music, originating from African Americans, often with a fast or syncopated rhythm, complicated musical pattern and tunes, and improvised (made up at the time) words.

Legend A popular traditional story or myth, about historical characters and past events, for which there is no modern proof that it is true.

Lithography A printing technique where an image is drawn in wax or oil onto a slab of stone or metal, and after treatment with chemicals such as acid and water, ink sticks only to the waxed or oiled areas and can then be transferred to paper.

Location A site outside a movie studio, where actors and crew film parts of a movie that need specialized backgrounds, scenery and real places or buildings.

Logo An emblem, design, or symbol used by an organization, which appears on things concerned with that organization, such as buildings, vehicles and clothing.

Manuscript The original handwritten (or more recently, typed) version of a book or document.

Mason A person who builds or works with stone.

Mass media The method by which information and news are communicated to the general public, usually by way of television, radio and the press.

Melody A sequence of musical notes that travel up and down the scales, usually producing a recognizable and pleasant tune.

Mosaics Decorative patterns or pictures made by arranging pieces of coloured glass, tiles or stones, often bedding them into cement or mortar to be firmly held.

Mural A painting made to decorate a wall, which may be applied directly to the surface such as the rock of a cave, or the plaster of a wall, or to canvas, which is then stuck onto the wall.

Music hall Usually a type of theatre or concert hall, in which musical entertainment can be seen.

Neoclassicism A late-18th century style of painting that tried to recreate the formal artistic glory or classical tradition of ancient Greece and Rome.

Nobel Prizes Six international awards given annually to people who have made great achievements in physics, chemistry, physiology or medicine, literature, economics and the promotion of peace. They are named after Swedish industrialist Alfred Nobel.

Opera A dramatic play in which the words are sung, accompanied by an orchestra. The play usually tells a story of great tragedy or love.

Oral culture Oral culture is passed on by speech, not by being written. In this way many of the world's epic tales, for example Homer's *Iliad* and *Odyssey* were told and retold by generations of Greeks before they were written down.

Patron A rich person, or benefactor, who pays, gives gifts to, or otherwise assists a poorer but talented person such as a musician, artist or composer.

Perspective The technique of illustrating the three-dimensional space of the real world on a two-dimensional flat surface such as paper, for example, by showing things farther away as smaller, and making horizontal lines of walls, buildings and fences lead away towards a single point on the horizon.

Pigment A chemical that gives colour to whatever contains it, for example, paints are made of finely ground crystalline pigments mixed with a base such as an oil.

Pioneer Someone who does things that no one has done before, such as exploring unknown lands, or developing new musical styles or playing techniques.

Porcelain A type of pottery invented in China more than 2000 years ago, made from fine, white clay and ground glass, to produce delicate, thin-walled, translucent (almost see-through) pieces of china.

Primary colours Red, yellow and blue pigments, from which all other colours can be made by mixing them – but which cannot be made by mixing other colours.

Projector A machine, such as a movie projector, that casts an enlarged image, either still or moving, onto a screen, wall or some other smooth surface.

Prose The ordinary form of written language composed of phrases, sentences and paragraphs, rather than broken up into lines or verses, as in songs or poems.

Quartet Any group of four. In music, the term usually refers to a group of singers, or musicians who play instruments from the same category, such as a string quartet.

Realism The 19th-century paintings of the real world, especially those of ordinary working people and their lives and hardships, which were subjects that previously had not been considered worthy of art.

Rehearsal Preparation for a public performance, such as playing a piece of music or acting in a play, by repeating and practising over and over again.

Renaissance 'Rebirth', the period in history after the medieval time of the Dark Ages, when European artists and scholars began to rediscover and extend the classical knowledge of ancient Greeks and Romans; it generally dates from about AD 1400.

Resonate When the vibrations of a sound produce further vibrations in nearby objects or air spaces, which enhance or amplify (make louder) the original sound.

Ritual A ceremony or event that is always carried out in the same way, according to strict rules.

Romanticism Early 19th-century paintings and literature that illustrate powerful feelings and emotions, often suggesting a sentimental ideal but unrealistic view of reality.

Scribe A person who writes. Long ago, when few people could write and there was no printing, scribes copied out important documents and books.

Scriptures The writings of a particular religion. For example, the scriptures of the Christian religion in the Bible.

Scroll A long piece of paper or parchment (dried animal skin used like paper), with writing on it, which is rolled up for storage.

Surrealism A 20th-century painting style with strange, bizarre, unreal, often dream-like images, which may be inspired by deep thoughts or the unconscious mind.

Symbolism An artistic style of the late 19th century where painters used symbols, or representations, to suggest ideas, which are inspired by the imagination rather than by reality.

Synchronized When things happen at the same time or in a set pattern. For example, in films, the sound recording runs alongside the film so that the actors' words are heard precisely when their lips move – words and movements are 'in synch'.

Synthesize To make artificially or put together from various sources. In music, the synthesizer is a machine that can make a huge variety of sounds electronically, which can resemble other instruments and even produce sound effects such as the wind, thunder and lightning.

Take Part of a scene with words and action, shot without interruption during filming in a scene from a movie.

Tapestry A thick piece of fabric on which a picture or pattern is created, either during the original weaving process, or by embroidery stitches added afterwards.

Textiles A term originally used only for cloth made by weaving (passing crosswise threads, or weft, between lengthways threads, or warp), but now used for fabric made by any different methods.

Theory A set or system of ideas or proposals, which tries to explain how something works or happens. Theories are tested by observing and doing experiments, to find out if they are true.

Tradition The passing on of the culture of a group of people from old to young, including their customs, stories, history and beliefs.

Tragedy A very sad event, such as an unhappy love affair or an appalling crime or a disaster. In theatre, the term refers to a play about a sequence of unhappy events which usually end for the worst.

Transmission The transferring or moving of something from one place to another. Nowadays the term usually refers to the sending out or broadcasting of the radio signals for a radio or television.

TV network A large group of broadcasting stations, operated by a single organization, which are linked so that they can send out, or broadcast, the same programmes over a large area, such as an entire country or continent.

Vibrations Regular, repeated, often rapid movements, to and fro. Musical instruments work by vibrating particles or molecules in the air, which are called sound waves and pass through the air to the ears.

Western movies Films about people exploring and settling in western North America, mainly in the 19th and early 20th centuries, especially people descended from the European arrivals in North America, their struggles against the elements and their dealings with the Native North American peoples (Indians).

Zoepraxiscope A device that gives the illusion of a moving image, when a series of pictures on the inside of a spinning cylinder are viewed through vertical slits in the cylinder.

Index

Page numbers in *italics* refer to illustrations

A

Aaron 83
aborigines 225
  dance 336
  music 322, *322*
absolute zero 254, 269, *269*, 308
abstract art 320, 366
Abu Simbel, Egypt 192, 193, *193*
abyssal plain 106, *106*, 128
AC/DC current electricity 262
acceleration 267, 308
acetone 258, *258*
Achernar 15
Aconagua, Argentina 98
acoustics 273
actors 330–331, *330–331*, 332, 354, 355, 358–359, *358–359*
Adams, John Couch 46
Adirondacks, USA 98
aerodynamics 291, *291*
  bridge construction 283
aerosols 123
Africa 86, *86*, 87, 90, *90*, 91, 216, 217
  art 319, *319*
  colonization 236–237, *236*, 241
  dance 336, 340, *340*
  deserts 110
  music 323, *323*
  tectonic plate 91
African clawed toad 156, *156*
African rock python 160
aftershocks 95
Age of Reason 229
Agricultural Revolution 230–231, *230–231*, *244*, 246
agriculture 123, 144, *144*, 145, *145*, 192–193, 194, 195, 212, 213, 222, *244*
air 29, 114, 274–275, *274–275*, 308
  hot-air balloons 268, *268*
  mountains 99
  pressure 115, *115*, 255
  radiators 269, *269*
  resistance 266
  transport 290–291, *290–291*
aircraft 117
  aluminium 82
  military 272, *272*
aircraft carriers 289
airports 291
Akashi-Kaikyo Bridge, Japan 282
Akbar 208
Akkad dynasty 192
Al Qaeda 233, 243
Alaric the Visigoth 193, 199, 202, 203
albatrosses 150
Alcántara Bridge, Spain 282
Aldrin, Buzz 62, 63, *63*
Aleutian Mountains 99
Alexander the Great 193, *193*, 196, 197
Alfred the Great 205, *205*, 206
algae 134, *134*, 141, 145
alimentary canal 181
alligators 160
alloys 30, 258, 308, 366
Alpha Centauri 271
Alpha stars 15, 16
alphabets 342, 343, *343*
altostraus clouds 118, *118*
aluminium 81, 82, 125
alveoli 178, *178*, 188
Amazon River 87, 103, 112
amber 82, 85, 262
America *see* Central America; Latin America; North America; South America; United States of America (USA)
American Civil War 232–233, *233*
American War of Independence 223, 225
amethyst 82, 83, *83*
ammonia 42, 44, 46
  molecules 253
ammonites 77, *77*, 85, *85*
amphibians 76, 147, *147*, 156–157, *156–157*
  reptiles 160
Amsterdam, Netherlands 361, *361*
anaesthetics 302
Anansi the Spider 346
Anasazi 213
ancestor worship 313, *313*, 332, 337
Andes 98, 99, *99*, 105, 112
Andromeda Galaxy 18, 19
Angel Falls Venezuela 103
angel sharks 153, *153*
angiosperms 135, 141
anglerfish 152
angles 305, *305*, 307, *307*, 308
Anglo-Saxons 202, 203, *203*, 246
  invasion of Britain 204
animals 73, 76, 114, 132, 146–147, *146–147*, 274
  brain weights 164
  caves 108
  communication 164–165, *164–165*
  deserts 111
  endangered species 170–171, *170–171*, 188
  fastest land animals 150
  feeding 154–155, *154–155*
  fossils 77, 84–85, *84–85*
  movement 150–151, *150–151*
  rainforests 112
  record-breakers 147
  reef formation 88
  reproduction 158–159, *158–159*
  rock formation 80
  seed germination 141
  trade 170
  young animals 158
animatronics 359, *359*, 366
Ankylosaurus 162, *162*
Annapurna 99
annual plants 140, 188
Antarctic Ocean *see* Southern Ocean
Antarctica 86, *86*, 87, 90, *90*, 91, 110, 121, 123
  Antarctic Treaty 87
  icebergs 101
  tectonic plate 91
Antares 15
antelopes 111
anthers 136, *136*, 188
antimatter 12, 68
ants 146
anus 181
anvil lightning 119
apartheid 242, 246
apes 159, 168
aphelion 29
Apollo missions 62–63, *62–63*
aquamarine 82, 83, *83*
Arabian Desert 110, 111
Arabian Sea 107
Arabic numbers 304, *304*
arachnids 146
Aral Sea, Asia 105
Archaeopteryx 77, *77*, 133, *133*, 166
archery 267, *267*
arches 280, *280*
  bridges 282, *282*, 283, *283*
Archimedes' screw 277
archipelagos 88, 89
architecture 196, 360–361, *360–361*
  modern 362–363, *362–363*
Arctic 86, 87, 88
  icebergs 101
  Institute Glacier, Antarctic 101
Arctic Circle 87
Arctic Ocean 106, 107
Arcturus 15
Argentina 75, 98, 242
argon 257
Aristophanes 331
Aristotle 196
Arkwright, Sir Richard 231
Armada, Spanish *218–219*, 219, 246
armies 192, 193, 214
  Roman 199, *199*
  Spartan 197
armour 207, 246
Armstrong, Louis 'Satchmo' 328, *328*
Armstrong, Neil 62, *63*
arrow-poison frogs 156, *156*, 164, *164*
art 312–321, *312–321*
  academies 314, *314*, 315
  earliest 312–313, *312–313*
  Europe 314–315, *314–315*, 320–321, *320–321*
  films 358
  modern 320–321, *320–321*
  royalty 319
  techniques 316–317, *316–317*
Art Deco 362
Art Nouveau 362, 366
arteries 173, *173*, 182, 183, *183*, 188
Arthur, King 342, *342*
artificial materials 308
artists 214, 215, *215*, 312–315
Arts and Crafts 362
arum lily frog 156, *156*
Aryans 194
asexual reproduction 158
Asia 86, *86*, 87, 90, *90*, 91, 98
  decline 226–227, *226–227*
  medieval 210–211, *210–211*
Asimov, Isaac 347
Asoka 208, 209
aspirin 145
Assyria 194, 195
asteroids 26, 31, 48, 49, 52–53, *52–53*, 68
  Asteroid Belt 52, 53, *53*
asthenosphere 78, *78*
Aston Martin cars 287
astrological signs 55, *55*
astronauts 62–63, *62–63*, 64, 65
astronomers 13, 15, 16, 23, 26, 28, 29, 37, 56, 57
astronomy 54, *54*, 242
Atacama Desert, Chile 110
Athelney treasure 204, *204*
Athens 196, 197
Atlantic Ocean 88, 103, 106, 107
atmosphere 68, 128, 272
  Earth 15, 30, 73, 76, 114–115, *114–115*
  Mercury 34
  Moon 32
  Neptune 46
  Uranus 45
  Venus 36
atolls 89, *89*
Atomium, Brussels 363, *363*
atoms 12, 13, 15, 68, 77, 252–253, *252–253*, 308
  atom bombs 15, 239
  compounds 258, 259
  electricity 252
  electrons 259, *259*
  elements 253
  molecules 258
  nuclear power 301
  Periodic Table 256–257, *256–257*, 309
Attila the Hun 202
Auckland, New Zealand 75
Augustus 192
Aurangzeb 208, 226
Aurigae constellation 15
Aurora Borealis 115, *115*
Austen, Jane 347, 352

Australia 75, 81, 86, *86*, 90, *90*, 91, 224, 225, 236, 237, *244*
deserts 111
Austria 222, 223, 232
music 324, 325
autumn 74
autumnal equinox 75
axis of the Earth 75, *75*
axles 278, 279
axons 184, *184*
Ayckbourn, Alan 331
Aztecs 212, 213, *213*, *245*, 246
music 322

B

B-2 stealth aircraft 272, *272*
Babbage, Charles 292
babies 175, 186–187, *186–187*, 364, 365
Babur 208, *208*
Babylonia 16, 127, 194
Bach, Johann Sebastian 324, *324*, 325
backbones 77, 175
bacteria 105, 132, 145, 183, 274, 308
Baffin Island 88, 101
Baird, John Logie 351, *351*
ball lightning 119
ballad singers 331, *331*
ballet 338–339, *338–339*
positions and steps 339
ballroom dancing 341, *341*
Baltic Sea 106
bamboo 136
Bangladesh 119, 123
banking 214
Bank of England 222, *222*
bankruptcy 234, 246
Bantus 192–193
barbarians 202–203, *202–203*, 246
new states 204–205, *204–205*
Barcelona, Spain 362, *362*
bark 137, *137*, 143, *143*
barnstorming 334
Barnum & Bailey Circus 333
barons 206
barred spiral galaxies 18, *18*
Barrett Browning, Elizabeth 347, *347*
basking 161
bath houses (thermae) 198
bathyscaphes 289
bats 108, *108*, 150, 154, 168, 169, 273, *273*
batteries 262
bauxite 82, *82*, 125
Bayeux tapestry 51, *51*
Bayreuth Festival, Germany 325
beaches, coral 89
bead lightning 119
beans 142, *142*
bears 150, 151, *151*
Beatles, The 329, *329*
Beaufort Scale 119
Becket, Samuel 331
Becky Sharp 354
bees 146, *149*
honeybees 164
Beethoven, Ludvig van 324, *324*, 325
beetles 146, 148
Beijing, China 75, 211
Beijing Opera 333, 340, *340*
Bek crater, Mercury's 35, *35*
belemnites 85
Benin 319
Benz, Karl and Berta 276
Beowulf 343, *343*
Bering Sea 107
Berlin Wall, Germany 240, *240*
Berliner, Emile 277, 329
Berners-Lee, Tim 294
beryl 82, *82*
Beta stars 15, 16
Bhutan glory butterfly 149, *149*
Bible 83, 195, 331, 345
bicycles 287
biennial plants 140, 188
Big Bang 12–13, *12–13*, 68, 268
Big Crunch 13
Big Dipper constellation 16, *16*, 17, *17*
Bin Laden, Osama 233, 243
binary numbers 304, *304*, 308
binoculars 17, 20
biosphere 30
biplanes 291, *291*, 308
bipolar 'butterfly' nebulae 23, *23*
birds 76, 84, 111, 147, *147*, 166–167, *166–167*
anatomy 166, *166*
Archaeopteryx 77, *77*, 133, *133*, 166
display 159, *159*
fastest flier 150
flightless 166
of prey 155, 159, 167
birthdays 364, 365
birthstones 82, 83, *83*
Bismarck 239
Bismarck, Otto von 237
bison 312
bits (binary digits) 293
black holes 18, 24–25, *24–25*, 68
Milky Way 20, *20*, 21
black ice 118
Black Prince 207, *207*
black smokers 107, 128
bladder 172, *172*, 181, 188
block printing 318, *318*, 348
block and tackle 278, *278*
blood 182–183, *182–183*
blue stars 14, 15
blues 328
Boeing aircraft 290, *290*, 291, *291*
Boeing Company plant, USA 280
Boers 233, 246
boiling point 255, 308
Bolivar, Simón 235
Bollywood 357, *357*
Bolsheviks 233
Bolshoi Ballet 339
bonds 252, 308
covalent 259, *259*
ionic 259, *259*
bones 174–175, *174–175*
fossils 76, 84, 85
Bonnie Prince Charlie *see* Stuart, Charles Edward
books 228, 229, 314
printing 348–349, *348–349*
Bootis constellation 15
boreholes into the Earth's crust 79
Borneo 88
Bosphorus Bridge, Turkey 283
brachiopods 85
Brachiosaurus 163
Brahms, Johannes 325
brain 177, 184–185, *184–185*
brakes 286, *286*
brass 326, 366
Brazil 109
Brazilian Coastal Range 99
breakdancing 340, 341, *341*
breathing 178–179, *178–179*
breeding *see* reproduction
brick 282
bridges 259, 282–283, *282–283*, 362, *362*
bascule 283, *283*
beam 283, *283*
cable-stayed 283, *283*
cantilevered 283, *283*
clapper 282
longest 282
piers 282, *282*
suspension 282, *282*, 283, *283*
brightest stars 15
bristlecone pines 143, *143*
Britain 204, 227, 232
Battle of Britain 238, *238–239*, 239
Industrial Revolution 230–231, *230–231*
world wars 238, 239
see also England; Scotland; United Kingdom (UK)
British Broadcasting Corporation (BBC) 351
British East India Company 222
British Isles 88
Britons, ancient 202
Brittany 337, *337*
Britten, Benjamin 325
broadband 297
broadcasting 328, 350–351, *350–351*
broadleaved plants 135, *135*, 188
bronchi 178, *178*, 179
browsers 297
browsing animals 155
Brutalism 362
bryophytes 141
Buddhism 201, 208, 209, *209*
art 318
scriptures 344, 345, *345*
Buenos Aires, Argentina 75
buildings 125, 259, 360–361, *360–361*, 362–363
construction 280–281, *280–281*
tallest 281
bulbs 138, *138*, 139
bullet-proof vests 259
buoyancy 275
Burj Khalifa, Dubai 363, *363*
Burney, Venetia 48
Bush, George W. 233, 243
bushes 135
butterflies 146, 149, *149*
bytes 293
Byzantine Empire 202, 203, 246

C

cables 294, 300, 301
cacti 137, *137*
Cage, Nicholas 358, *358*
calcium 81
calcium carbonate 108, 109
Calder, Alexander 321
calderas 93
calendars 75
Aztecs 212, 220
California, USA 87
Callisto 41, *41*
Caloris basin, Mercury 34
calving 101
Cambrian Period 76
camcorders 299, *299*, 350, *350*
camels 111
camouflage 188
newts and salamanders 157
Campbell, Donald 287
Bluebird 287, *287*
Campion, Edmund 219
Canada 81, 105, 216, *216*
canals
busiest 289
Mars 38
cane toad 157
Canis Major constellation 15
Canis Minoris constellation 15
cannons 215, *215*
Canopus 15
canyons 96, *96*, 97
Cape Verde Islands 216
Capella 15
capillaries 182, 183, 188
capitalism 240
caracals 151, *151*, 169, *169*
caravels 216, *216*, 246
carbon 82, 260–261, *260–261*, 308
carbon cycle 261
carbon dioxide 36, 73, 92, 114, 115, 138, 139, 188, 253, 308
breathing 178, 179
global warming 122
carbon fibre 260
Carboniferous Period 76, 124
Caribbean *244*
Caribbean Sea 107
Carinae constellation 15
Carnival 332, 340, 341, *341*
carnivores 154, 155, 157, 188
carpels 136, *136*, 137, 141, 188
carrots 136, *136*
cars 122, 123, 237, *237*, 286–287, *286–287*
engines 300

invention 276
Oakland Bay Bridge, San Francisco, USA 283
Carthage 193
Cartier, Jacques 217, *217*
cartilage 147, 152, 175, 188
Caruso, Enrico 329
Caspian Sea 105
Casseiopia constellation 16
cassette tapes 298
Cassini 42, 58, 59, *59*
casting 317, *317*
castles 361, *361*
Castro, Fidel 241, *241*
cat sharks 158, *158*
Catal Hüyük, Turkey 360, *360*
cathedrals 361, *361*
cathode-ray tubes 298, 299
Catholicism 218–219
cats 133, 151, 155, 164, 168, 169, *169*
cattle 123, *123*, 155
caves 108–109, *108–109*
paintings 109, *109*, 312, *312*
Cavour, Count 235
CDs (compact discs) 298, 329, 351
celery 137, *137*
cells 138, 188
anatomy 172, *172*
blood cells 182–183, *182–183*
sperm 186, *186*
celluloid 354, *354*, 366
cement 125
Cenozoic Era 76
Centauri constellation 15
centaury 145, *145*
Central America 193, 212–213, *212–213*, 220
central heating 198
central processing unit (CPUs) 292, 293, 308
cephalopods 146, 148
Ceres 48, 52, 53
Cervantes, Miguel de 346
CFCs (chlorofluorocarbons) 123, *123*, 128
chalcopyrite 125
chalk 80, 81, *81*
chameleons 161, *161*
Chandra X-Ray Observatory 21
Chandragupta Maurya 208
Chang Jiang river 103
Chaplin, Charlie 354, *354*
charcoal 260
Charge-Coupled Devices (CCDs) 56, 57, 68
Charlemagne 207
Charles de Gaulle Airport, Paris, France 291
Charles I 222, 223, *223*, 228
Charles II 222–223, 228, *228*, 229
Charleston (dance) 341, *341*
Charon 48, 49
Chasmosaurus 163, *163*
cheetahs 150, *150*
Chekhov, Anton 331
chemicals 81, 82, 258–259, *258–259*
bonds 252
elements 81, *81*
formula 252, 308
names for everyday items 259
Cheshunt monorail 284
chickens 166
chicks 167, *167*
children 364, 365
Chile 221, 242
China 75, 87, 91, 95, 215, 216, 222, *226*
ancestor worship 313, *313*
ancient 193, 200–201, *200–201*
barbarian invasions 202, 203
bicycles 287
block printing 348
clocks 201, *201*
Communism 241
compasses 276, *276*
fireworks 277, *277*
medieval 210–211
numbers 304, *304*
population 365
satellites 61
theatre 333
Ch'ing dynasty 222
chlorine 258
chlorophyll 138, 139, 188
Cho Oyu 99
chocolate 255
Chopin, Frederick 325
Christianity 192, 236, 313, 314, 332
drama 331
religious wars 218–219, *218–219*
scriptures 345, *345*
Christmas broadcasts 351
Christo 321
Christy, James 48
chromosomes 173, 188
chromosphere 28, *28*, 68
chronometers 276, *276*
chrons 76
Churchill, Sir Winston 239, *239*
chyme 181
Cibola 221
cinema 354–359, *354–359*
home entertainment 353, *353*
making films 356–357, *356–357*
special effects and superstars 358–359, *358–359*
circles 305, *305*, 308
circulatory system 173, *173*
circumference 30, 308
circus 333, 334
cirques 100, *100*
cirrus clouds 116, *116*, 117, *117*, 118, *118*
citric acid 259
civil wars 222, 223, 228, 232–233, 246
civilizations 193, 194, 195, 202, 246, 364, 366
Middle East 194–195, *194–195*
clapperboards 357, *357*
clarinets 326, *326*
Clarke, Arthur C 347
classical music 324–325, *324–325*
claws 77, 85
clay 125
cleaner wrasse 153, *153*
climate 120–121, *120–121*, 128
continental 121
forests 112–113, *112–113*
global warming 122–123, *122–123*
oceanic 121
climate change 121, 122–123, *122–123*
Clive, Robert 226, 227
clones 158, 188
Clooney, George 358, *358*
cloth 231
clothing 364–365, *364–365*
cloud to air lightning 119
cloud to ground lightning 119
clouded leopards 169, *169*
clouds 72, 116–117, *116–117*
appearance of Earth 31, *31*
Jupiter 40
Neptune 46
Venus 36
clowns 330, 333, *333*
clusters 68
galaxies 18
stars 15, 17
coal 122, 124, 260
seam formation 124, *124*
Coalbrookdale Iron Bridge, England 282
coats of arms 206
cobras 161, 164, 165, *165*
cockroaches 77
coconuts 142
cogs 279, *279*
coins 197, *197*
coke 222, 231
cold 87, 120, 121
planets 44
Cold War 240–241, *240–241*, 246
cold-blooded animals 160, 161
Coleridge, Samuel Taylor 347
collage 317, *317*
collagen 174
colonization 246
Africa 236–237, *236*, 241
India 222, 226, 227
North America 220, 221, 222, 223
Colorado River, USA 96, *96*
Colosseum, Rome 360, *360*
colour 119, 271
animal communication 164
gemstones 82
minerals 81, *81*
pigments 317, 368
primary colours 317, 368
sky 115
stars 14
Venus 37
wheel 317, *317*
Columbia Glacier, Alaska 101
Columbus, Christopher 216, 217, *217*, *244*
comets 26, 50–51, *50–51*, 68
Commedia dell'Arte 333
Commodus 192
Commonwealth 236, 240, 246
communications 294–295, *294–295*
animals **164–165**
Internet 296–297, *296–297*, 329, 350
communications satellites 60, 294–295, *294–295*, 296–297, *296–297*
Communism 233, 240, 241, 242, 246
compasses 276, *276*
composers 324–325, *324–325*
composites 259
compounds 258, 259, 308
carbon 260, 261
computer games 297, *297*, 353, *353*
computers 292–293, *292–293*
abbreviations 293
art 321
buildings 362
central processing units (CPUs) 292, 293
Internet 296–297, *296–297*, 329, 350
laptops 297, *297*
Millennium Bug 243
world's most powerful 292
Conceptual Art 321
condensation 255
conduction 268
conductors 258, *258*, 262, 308, 325, *325*
cones 306, *306*
Confucius 201, *201*, 226, 345, 361
Congress of Vienna 235
Congreve, William 331
conifers 76, 113, 135, 188
coniferous forest 143
conquistadors *245*, 246
Constable, John 316
Constantine the Great 193, *193*
Constantinople 202, *202*, 214, 219
constellations 16–17, *16–17*, 68
brightest stars 15
construction 280–281, *280–281*
continents 72, 86–87, *86–87*
climate 121
continental crust 78, *78*, 79
continental drift 90–91, *90–91*, 128
continental shelf 106, *106*, 128
contrails 117
convection 268, 269
currents 78
convicts 236, 237, 246
Cook, Captain James 224, *224*, 225, 237, *237*, *244*
Copernicus, Nicolaus 30

copper 125, 257, 262
coprolites 162
coracles 277, *277*
corals 133, *133*
coral reefs 88, 89, 148, *148*
corn 145
corona 28, *28*, 68
corries 100
Cort, Henry 231
Cortés, Hernan 220
cortex 185, *185*, 188
corundum 82
Cossacks 337, *337*
cotton 144, 145
cotyledons 143
country and western music 328
coups 241, 247
courtship 159
covalent bonds 259, *259*
coyotes 165
Crab Nebula 22
crabs 107, 146
crafts 319
Craigellachie Bridge, Scotland 283
cranes 278
Crater Lake, USA 105
craters 73, *73*, 128
lakes 105
Mercury 34
Meteor Crater, Arizona, USA 52, *52*
meteorite craters 53
Moon 32, 33
creation myths 344
crescent Moon 32, 33, *33*
Cretaceaous Period 76
crevasses 100, *100*, 128
Crimean War 232
crinoids 85
crocodiles 147, 149, 160, 161
Cromwell, Oliver 222, *222*, 228, *228*
crop production 145
crows 165
crude oil 260
Cruise, Tom 358, *358*
Crusades 207, *245*, 247, 280
crust of the Earth 72, 78, *78*, 79, 128
crustaceans 146
crystals 80, 81, 82, *82*
birthstones 83, *83*
Cuba 241
Cuban Missile Crisis 233, 240
cubes 305, *305*, 306, *306*
Cubism 320, *320*, 367
Culloden, Battle of 222, 229, *229*
cultures 214, 364–365, *364–365*, 367
cumulonimbus clouds 116, *116*, 118, *118*
cumulus clouds 116, *116*, 117, *117*
Cuquenan Falls, Venezuela 103
Curiosity rover, Mars 38, *38*
Curse of Frankenstein 359, *359*
cycads 135
Cygnus constellation 16, *16*
cylinders 306, *306*
cymbals 326
czars 219, 228, 247

D

Daimler, Gottlieb 286
daisies 141, *141*
Dalai Lama 222, 361
Dali, Salvador 320, 321
Dallol, Ethiopia 110
Damascus, Syria 204
dams 105, 281
dance 330, 336–341, *336–341*
ballet 338–339, *338–339*
popular dances 341
Darby, Abraham 222, 231, 282
Darius the Great 195, *195*
dark nebulae 22, 23
darkness 74, 119
data 184, 292, 293, 308, 353
Davey, Humphrey 302
David and Goliath 345, *345*
day 74, 75
de Medici, Catherine 219
Dead Sea, Israel 104, *104*, 105
Dead Sea Scrolls 344, *344*
Death Valley, USA 87, 110
death's head hawkmoth 149, *149*
decapods 146
decibels 272, 308
deciduous trees and plants 113, 128, 143, 188
decimal system 208, 304
deer 155
Defoe, Daniel 347
deforestation 113, *113*, 123, 128
Deimos 38, *38*, 39
Delta II rocket 25, *25*
deltas 103, 128
democracy 228, 240, 247
Denmark 89
depression, economic 238, 247
deserts 76, 86, 97, 110–111, *110–111*
largest 110, 111
mountains 98
plants 137, *137*
Devonian Period 76
Dhaulagiri 99
Diadectid fossil insect 91
Diaghilev, Sergei 339
diamonds 82, 83, *83*, 260
Dias, Bartholomeu 216
Dickson, William 355
dictatorships 193, 198, 228, 233, 238, 240, 242, 247
didgeridoos 322, *322*
diesel locomotives 284–285, *284–285*
digestion 180–181, *180–181*, 188
digital information 308
digital recording 298
dinosaurs 53, 81, 84, 148, 162–163, *162–163*
biggest 162
footprints 85, *85*
names 163
Diplodocus 163
discovery of planets 26, 27, 45
diseases, insects 149
distance of planets from the Sun 26, 27
Diwali 319, *319*
DNA (deoxyribonucleic acid) 187, 188, 303, 308
doctors 303
dodos 170, *170*
dogs 133, 154
dolphins 151, 153, 168, 170, *170–171*, 272, 273, *273*
Don Quixote 346
Donatello 214
double bass 323, 326, *326*
Doyle, Arthur Conan 347
drag 267
dragonflies 77, 146, 154
Drake, Sir Francis 216, 219
drama 196, 330–331, *330–331*, 332–333, *332–333*
ancient Greece 197, *197*
modern 334–335, *334–335*
world theatre 332–333, *332–333*
Drauchen-hauchloch 105
Drebbel, Cornelius van 289
drought 119
drums 322, *322*, 326
drum kits 327, *327*
dryness 87
duck-billed platypus 168, *168*
Duncan, Isadora 338, *338*
Dune of Pilat 97
dust 14, 15, 20, 22, 26, 72, 92, *92*, 114, 115, 121
Earth's formation 30
Saturn's rings 43, *43*
DVDs 298, 299, 353
dwarf planets 48–49
dynasties 193, 201, 208, 209, 247
China 200, 204, 210, 211, 222, 226, 232

E

e-mail 295
eagles 154
ears 168
sound 392–393, *392–393*
Earth 27, *27*, 30–31, *30–31*
ages of 76–77, *76–77*
appearance of 31, *31*
asteroid collision 31, 52, *52*, 53
atmosphere 114–115, *114–115*, 128
caves 108–109, *108–109*
climate 120–121, *120–121*, 128
compared to Mars 38
constellations 16, 17
continental drift 90–91, *90–91*, 128
core 30–31, *30–31*, 72, 78, *78*, 79, 128
deserts 110–111, *110–111*
distance from Sun 27, 29
driest place 110
earthquakes 94–95, *94–95*
forests 112–113, *112–113*
formation of 72–73, *72–73*
galaxies visible from 18, 19
glaciers 100–101, *100–101*
global warming 122–123, *122–123*, 128, 145
hottest place 110
interior of 78–79, *78–79*
islands 88–89, *88–89*
lakes 104–105, *104–105*
landscapes 96–97, *96–97*
magnetism 263
mountains 98–99, *98–99*
oceans 106–107, *106–107*
resources 124–125, *124–125*
rivers 102–103, *102–103*
seas 106–107, *106–107*
spinning 74–75, *74–75*, 127
and the Sun 29
surface of 72, 73, 78
and Venus 26, 37
volcanoes 92–93, *92–93*
weather 80, 118–119, *118–119*
wettest place 121
earthquakes 78, 79, 94–95, *94–95*, 128
aftershocks 95
Moment Magnitude Scale 95
tectonic plates 91
earthworms 150, 151, *151*
earwigs 146
East China Sea 107
eating 180–181, *180–181*, 365
echinoderms 149
echoes 273
echolocation 272, 273, *273*
eclipses 29, *29*, 68
lunar eclipses 32
ecliptic 30
eco-tourism 171
economics 222, 226
Great Depression 238
ecosystems 274
Ecuador 221
Edison, Thomas Alva 298, 329, 355
eels 153
eggs 85, 166, 167, *167*
dinosaurs 163
human reproduction 186, *186*, 187
Egypt 127, *237*
ancient 192, 193, *193*
astronomy 16, 54
dance 336, *336*
hieroglyphs 343, *343*, 367
music 322
numbers 304
pharaohs 194, 195, *195*
pyramids *245*, 360, *360*
ships 288
Suez Canal *245*
sundials 277, *277*

tomb paintings 312, 313, *313*
Eiffel Tower, Paris, France 280, *280*
Eighty Years War 222
Einstein, Albert 13, 267
El Greco 315
electric eels 153
electricity 12, 82, 122, 262–263, *262–263*, 264, 300, 308
black holes 24, 25, *25*
computers 292, 293
distribution 300, *300*, 301, *301*
household appliances 263
wind turbines 125, *125*
electromagnetism 262, *262*, 263
electromagnetic radiation 56, 264, 308
light 270
electronic books (E-books) 349
electrons 15, 262, 308
atoms 259, *259*
Periodic Table 256–257, *256–257*, 309
television 298, 299
elements 72, 81, *81*, 308
compounds 258, 259
liquid 255
Periodic Table 256–257, *256–257*, 309
elephants 77, 154, *154*, 155, 159, 168, 169, 176, 208
Elgar, Sir Edward 325
Elizabeth I 218, 219, *219*, 222
elliptical galaxies 18, *18*
emeralds 82, 83, *83*
emergency signals at sea 289
Empedocles 256
emperor penguins 87
emperors 247
China 200, 201, 204, 226, 227, *227*
India 208, 209, 226
Japan 193, 201, 204, 210
Rome 192, 193, 198, 199
empires 236, 241, 247
Austro-Hungarian 232
British 227, 236–237, *236–237*
Chinese 227
Holy Roman 206, *206*, 207, 247
Ottoman 222, 223, 226, 247
Roman 198–199, *198–199*
Empty Quarter (Rub'al-khali) 110
emus 166
endangered species 170–171, *170–171*, 188
endocrine glands 181, *181*
endoscopes 302
energy 12, 264–265, *264–265*
conversion 264
heat 264, 268–269, *268–269*, 308
light 264, 270
measuring 264
power 300–301, *300–301*
renewable 125, *125*
engines 190, 247, 300, 308
internal combustion 300, 308
steam 223, 230, *230*, 231, *231*, 284, 309
England 202, 203, 204, 205, 206
American colonies 220, 221, 222, 223
Civil War 222, 223, 228
Magna Carta *245*
Norman Conquest 207
Reformation 218, 219
trade 217
environments 124
enzymes 181, 188
eons 76
epaulette sharks 153, *153*
epicentres *94*, 95, 128
epics 196, 247, 342, 367
Gilgamesh 195, *195*
epochs 76
Equator 17, 30, 74, 75, 120, *120*, 128
latitude 126
equatorial bulge 75
eras 76
ergs 110
Ericsson, John 288
Eridani constellation 15
Eris 48
erosion 81, 84, 128
landscapes 96–97, *96–97*
escalators 278, *278*
Espelands Falls, Norway 103
ethene 260
Ethiopia 345
Etruscans 198, 247, 323, *323*
Euphrates River 194
Eurasia 86
tectonic plate 91
Europa 41, *41*
Europe 86, *86*, 87, 90, *90*, 91
art 314–315, *314–315*, 320–321, *320–321*
Enlightenment 228–229, *228–229*
feudal 206–207, *206–207*
Ice Age 101
maps 126, *126*
Renaissance 214–215, *214–215*, 249
revolution 234–235, *234–235*
world power 236–237, *236–237*
European Commission 242, *242*, 243
European Union 243
Evening Star *see* Venus
Everest 38, 98
evergreens 143, 188
forest 113
evolution 133, 188
dinosaurs 162
excretion 181, 188
exoskeletons 148, 188
exosphere 114, *114*
expanding Universe 12, 13
exploration 216–217, *216–217*, 224–225, *224–225*, 247
Americas 213, 217, 220
explosions 21
Expressionism 320, *320*, 367
extinction 170–171, *170–171*, 188
dinosaurs 163
mass extinction 170
eyes
corrective lenses 270–271, *270–271*
Sun damage 29

F

fabrics 259
factories 122, 123, 231, 236
Fahrenheit 269
famine 364
far side of the Moon 32
fault block mountains 98, *98*
fax (facsimile) machines 308
feathers 77, 166
ferns 76, 84, 135
Fertile Crescent 194–195, *194–195*, 247
fertilization 141, 188
external 159
feudalism 206–207, *206–207*
films 354–355, *354–355*
directors 356, *356*
lighting 356, *356*
making 356–357, *356–357*
marketing 357
special effects and superstars 358–359, *358–359*
fingernails 91, 173, *173*
fingers 77
fire 113, *113*, 269, *269*
fireworks 277, *277*
firn 100, *100*, 128
firs 113
fish 76, 84, 147, *147*, 148, 150, 151, 152–153, *152–153*
biggest 153, *153*
coral reefs 88
Dead Sea 105
shoals 152, *152*
FLAG (Fibre-optic Link Around the Globe) 294
flags 364, *364*
flash floods 118
fleas 146, 267, *267*
Flettner, Anton 291
flies 146, 149, *149*
flight 77, 150, 151
world's first powered 290
floating 275
floods 118, *118*, 195
global warming 123
Florence, Italy 214
flowers 76, 135, 136, *136*
meanings 144
fluorescent light 271
flutes 323, 326, *326*
Flying Scotsman 284
Focke, Heinrich 291
Fokine, Mikhail 339
fold mountains 98, *98*, 99, *99*, 128
folk art 319
folk dance 337, *337*, 367
food 264, 265, 364, 365, *365*
digestion 180–181, *180–181*
invertebrates 149
plants 144–145, *144–145*
Forbidden City, Beijing 211, 361, *361*
force 266–267, *266–267*
Ford, Henry 237, 286
foreshocks 95
forests 76, 112–113, *112–113*, 124, 143, 171, 189
fires 113, *113*
forked lightning 119
fossils 76, 77, 84–85, *84–85*, 128, 188
bacteria 132
continental drift 90, 91
dinosaurs 85, *85*, 162
fossil fuels 124, 301
index fossils 85
resin 82, 85
trace fossils 85
foxes 111
France 207, 218, 222, 223, 224
art 314, 315, 320
ballet 338
French Revolution 232–233, *233*, 234, *234*
Napoleonic Wars 234–235, *234–235*
nuclear power 300
satellites 61
world wars 238, 239
Francis I of France 217
Franco, General Francisco 232
Franks 207, 247
Franz Ferdinand, Archduke 232, 238
freezing 275, 308
frequency 273
frescos 316, *316*, 367
freshwater 104
birds 167
habitats 152
islands 89
friction 267, 279, 308
frigatebirds 159, *159*
fringe-toed lizards 150
Frobisher, Martin 216
frogs 147, 154, 156–157, *156–157*, 159
deserts 111
poisonous 156, *156*, 164, *164*
rain 118
fronts 117, 118
frost 97
frost shattering 96
fruit 141
fuels 124, 125, 300, 301
Fujiwara dynasty 204
fulcrum 279, *279*, 308
Full Moon 32, 33, *33*
fullerenes 260
Fulton, Robert 288
Functionalism 362
funerals 364
fungi 134, *134*
furniture 259

G

Gagarin, Yuri 65
galaxies 12, 13, 17, 18–19, *18–19*, 20, 21, 68
  black holes 24
  Local Group 19, 68
  NGC4438 25
galena 125
Galileo Galilei 41, *56*
Galileo space probe 52, 58, *245*
gall bladder 180, *180*
Gama, Vasco da 217, *217*
game birds 167
gamma rays 25, 264
Ganymede 41, *41*
Garibaldi, Giuseppe 235, *235*
Garnerin, Jacques 291
garnet 82, 83, *83*
gas giants 31
gases 12, 23, 24, 25, *25*, 26, 72, 73, 254–255, *254–255*
  Earth's atmosphere 114–115
  gas clouds 12, 13, 14, 20, 22
  greenhouse 122, *122*, 123
  natural 122, 124
  Sun 28
  volcanoes 92, *92*, 93
gastropods 148
Gateway to the West Arch, Missouri, USA 280, *280*, 363, *363*
Gaudi, Antonio 362
Gautama, Siddhartha 208, 209
gazelles 154, *154*, 155
gears 279, *279*, 287, *287*
Gemini 63
gemstones 82–83, *82–83*
generators 263, *263*, 301
genes 187, 188
  gene splicing 303, 308
  gene therapy 303
Genghis Khan 210, 211, *211*
geographers 126
geology 76–77
  geological column 76, *76*, 77
  geologists 76, 77, 90, 128
George V 351
geosphere 30
geostationary orbit 60, 68, 295
Germanic peoples 193, 202, 204
Germany 218, 219, 222
  art 320
  music 324, 325
  railways 284, *285*
  world wars 238, 239
germination 141, 142, *142*, 188
Gershwin, George 325
geysers 93, *93*, 128
giant pandas 170, *170*
gibbous Moon 33, *33*
Gibraltar 106
Gilbert and George 321
Gilgamesh 195, *195*
gills 152, 188
gingkos 135, *135*
Giotto 214, 315
giraffes 154, *154*, 155, 168
glaciers 30, 97, *97*, 100–101, *100–101*
  fastest flowing 101
  longest 101
gladiators 198, *198*, 247
glass 125, 259
  stained glass 316, *316*
Global Positioning System (GPS) 60, 61, 127
global warming 122–123, *122–123*, 128, 145
Glossopetris fern 91
glow worms 165
glowing nebulae 22, *22*
glucose 181, 188
Gobi Desert 111
Goethe, Johann Wolfgang von 331
Gogh, Vincent van 314, 315
gold 82, *82*, 217, 253, 257, 259, 262
Golden Gate Bridge, San Francisco, USA 283, *283*
golden lion tamarin 171, *171*
golden tree snake 151
Goliath frog 157
Gondwana 90, *90*
gongs 327, *327*
Gopaljang, Bangladesh 119
Gorbachev, Mikhail 233, 241, *241*
gorillas 165
Gospel music 328
Goths 193, 202
government 226, 228, 234, 235
grain farming 144, *144*
gramophones 277, *277*, 329, *329*
Grand Canyon, USA 39, 96, *96*
granules 29
graphite 260
graptolites 85
grass 137
grasshoppers 146, 149, *149*
grasslands 76
gravel 125
gravity 12, 15, 23, 72, 74, 107, 128, 266
  black holes 24
  Moon 33
  Sir Isaac Newton 266, *266*
  spacecraft 64, 65
grazing animals 155
Great Barrier Reef, Australia 89, *89*, 148, 224
Great Bear constellation 16, *16*
Great Britain *see* Britain
Great Dark Spot, Neptune 46, *46*, 47, *47*
Great Dividing Range 99
Great Dog constellation 17, *17*
Great Lakes, North America 104, 105, *105*
Great Nebula of Orion 22, 23, *23*
Great Pyramid, Giza, Egypt 280, *360*
Great Red Spot, Jupiter 40, *40*, 41
Great Schism 207
Great Wall of China 200, 201, *201*
great white shark 153, *153*, 171
Greece 93, 192, 193, *244*, 262, 314, 315
  ancient 192, 193, 196–197, *196–197*
  astronomy 16, 17, 21, 40, 44, 46
  drama 330–331, *330–331*, 334
  gods and goddesses 197, 199
  sculpture 313, *313*, 318
Green, Andy 286
green tree frog 156, *156*
greenhouse effect 122, *122*, 123
  Venus 36
Greenland 88, 89, 127
Greenwich, London, UK 127
Greenwich Mean Time (GMT) 75
Gresley, Sir Nigel 284
Grieg, Edvard 325
Grigg-Skjellerup Comet 50
griots 323, *323*
Gris, Juan 320
Guatemala 212
guerillas 247
Guevara, Che 240, *240*
guillotine 234
guitars 326, *326*
Gulf of Mexico 107
Gulf War 242
gulper eels 153
gunpowder 215
Gupta dynasty 208, 209
Guru Nanak 345
Gutenberg, Johannes 348
Gwyn, Nell 229
gymnosperms 135, 141

H

habitats 188
  destruction 170–171, *170–171*
Hadrian 192
haiku 346
hailstones 117, 119, *119*
Haiti 225
Hale Bopp Comet 50, 51
Halley, Edmund 51
Halley's Comet 50, *50*, 51
hammocks 276, *276*
Hammurabi of Babylon 194
Han dynasty 200
Handel, George Frederic 325
Handley Page aircraft 291
hang-gliding 291
Hanging Gardens of Babylon 192, 197, *197*
Hangzhou, China 210–211
Hannibal 193
'Happy Birthday To You' 364
Harappan civilization 193
Hargreaves, James 222, 230, 231
Harold Godwinson 207
harps 322, *322*
Harrison, John 276
Hastings, Battle of 207
Haumea 48
Hawaii 92, 93
  Ice Age 101
hawks 154, 155
Haydn, Joseph 325
heart 177, 182–183, *182–183*
  beats per minute 303
heartwood 137, *137*, 143, *143*
heat 74, 78, 79, 80, 82, 120, 121, 264, 268–269, *268–269*, 308
  Death Valley, USA 87
  Sahara desert, Africa 86
  stars 14, 15
  Sun 28
heaviest planet 26
helicopters 290–291, *290–291*
helium 12, 13, 15, 28, 42, 44, 46
  boiling point 255
Hellenism 193
hellodor 82
hematite 125
Henry the Navigator 216
Henry VIII 215, *215*, 219
  household staff 215
Hepburn, Audrey 358, *358*
Hepburn, Katherine 359, *359*
Hepworth, Barbara 321
herbivores 154, 155, 188
herbs 135
Herschel, Sir William 44, 45
hieroglyphs 343, *343*, 367
High Tech 362
hills 97, *97*
Himalayas 98, 99, *99*, 208
Hinduism 208, 209, 227, 319, 332, *332*
  dance 336, *336*
  scriptures 344
hippodromes 202, *202*, 247
hippopotamuses 155
history
  ancient world 192–193, *192–193*, 194–195, *194–195*
  Earth 73
  medieval 206–207, *206–207*, 210–211, *210–211*
  1600–1800 222–223, *222–223*
Hitchcock, Alfred 356, *356*
Hitler, Adolf 232, *232*, 233, 238, 239
HMS *Hood* 239
Hockney, David 321
Holland 219, 223
Hollywood, California, USA 356, *356*
Holy Roman Empire 206, *206*, 207
home entertainment 352–353, *352–353*
Homer 196, 346
homes 360, *360*
  wood 361, *361*
Homo erectus 244
Homo sapiens 133, *133*
Hong Kong 242, 280, 289
Hooke, Robert 40

Hopi 332
hormones 181, 188
horse flies 149, *149*
Horsehead Nebula 23, *23*
horses 155, 208, 220
famous owners 195, 196
horsetails 135
hot spots 79, 128
hot-air balloons 223, *223*, 268, *268*, 276, *276*
first round-the-world flight 291
hottest planet 27, 36
hours 74, 75, 304
houses 280, 360, *360*
ancient world 194, *194*
mud 361, *361*
Rome 198, *198*, 199, *199*
wood 361, *361*
hovercraft 288, *288*
HTML (hypertext mark-up language) 297
Huang-Ti 200
Hubble Space Telescope 23, 45, 46, 48, 61, *61*, 242, *245*
Hudson Bay, Canada 107
Hugo, Victor 347
Huguenots 219
humans 73, 76, 133, 168
atoms 253
body 172–173, *172–173*
bones and joints 174–175, *174–175*
eating and digestion 180–181, *180–181*
evolution 192
heart and blood 182–183, *182–183*
lungs and breathing 178–179, *178–179*
muscles and moving 176–177, *176–177*
nervous system 184–185, *184–185*
reproduction 186–187, *186–187*
rights 228
sacrifice 212, 213
Humayun 208, *208*
Humber Bridge, UK 283
hummingbirds 150
Hundred Years War 207
Huns 193, 202
hurricanes 118, *118*, 274
Huygens 59
Hyakutaye comet 50
hydro-electricity 300, 301
hydrocarbons 260
hydrofoils 288, *288*
hydrogen 12, 13, 15, 42, 44, 46, 73, 188, 253, 308
atoms 253
plants 139
hypocentres 94, *94*

I

Ibsen, Henrik 331, 334
ice 76, 86, 87, 96, 97, 123, 254, 275
black 118
clouds 116, 117
Europa 41
glaciers 97, *97*, 100–101, *100–101*
Greenland 89
Ice Ages 100, 101, 121, 128
icebergs 101, *101*, 128, 275, *275*
Saturn's rings 43, *43*
Iceland 88
icons 313, 367
igneous rock 77, 80, *80*, 128
Iguacu Falls, South America 87, *87*
Iliad 196, 346
illustration 317, *317*, 349
Impressionism 315, *315*, 367
incandescence 271
Incas 220, 221, *244*, 247
art 318
houses 361, *361*
index fossils 85
India 87, 90, *90*, 91, 95, 121, 216, 217, 287, 304
ancient 193, 208–209, *208–209*
barbarian invasions 203
Bollywood 357, *357*
colonization 222, 226, 227
Indian Mutiny 232, *232*
Indian Railways 284
satellites 61
tectonic plate 91
theatre 332, *332*
Indian Ocean 88, 89, 106, 107, 216
Indonesia 88, 93
shadow-puppets 333, *333*
Indricotherium 77, *77*
'indulgences' 218, 248
Indus Valley civilization 193, 194
Industrial Revolution 222, 230–231, *230–231*, 248
inertia 266
inflation 12
infra-red rays 264, 270
inorganic compounds 260
Inquisition 218
insects 76, 77, 84, 111, 146, *146*, 148–149, *148–149*
communication 164, *164*, 165
facts 148
fossils 85, 91
mimicry 164, *164*
installations 321
instruments, musical 322–323, *322–323*, *325*, 326–327, *326–327*
insulators 262, 308
internal combustion engine 300, 308
International Space Station (ISS) 65, 66–67, *66–67*
Internet 296–297, *296–297*, 329, 350
intestines 180, *180*, 181
Inuit dance 336
inventions 276–277, *276–277*
inventors 277
invertebrates 146, 148–149, *148–149*, 188
Io 41, *41*
ionic bonds 259, *259*
iPod 298, *298*
Iran 223
Iraq 127, 233, *237*, 242, 243, *244*
iron 30, 34, 72, 78, 81, 82, 125, 192, 253, 262
bridges 282
magnetic poles 127
Mars 38
smelting 222, 231
irregular galaxies 18, *18*, 19
irrigation 105
Islam 204, 208, 281, 345
dress 364, *364*
religious art 318, 319, *319*
scriptures 344
islands 88–89, *88–89*
biggest 88, 89
isoseismic lines 94, *94*
ISP (Internet Service Provider) 297, 308
Issigonis, Alec 286
Istanbul, Turkey 202
Italy 214, 233, 235
ballet 338
Renaissanca 315

J

Jackson, Samuel L 358, *358*
Jacobite rebellions 222, 229
jade 82
jaguars 169, *169*
James I and VI 222, 223, *223*
Jamestown, Virginia, USA 220
Japan 95, 220, 222, 223, 226, 232
ancient 193, 200, 201, *201*
art 318, *318*
dance 336, 337, *337*
legends 343, *343*
medieval 210, 211
music 323
poetry 346
satellites 61
theatre 332, *332*, 334
trains *285*
World War II 239
jaws 77
jazz 328, 367
Jefferson, Thomas 225
jellyfish 133, 148, 151
Jerusalem 192, 207
jesters 331
Jesus Christ 192, *192*
jet engines 272, 290, 300, 308
jewels 82, 217, 226
Jimmu Tenno 201
John, King 206, *206*
joints 174–175, *174–175*, 188
Jojuri drama 332
Jones, Brian 291
Jordan River 105
Judaism
dress 364
scriptures 344, 345
juggernauts 287
Julius Caesar 193, 198
Jupiter 26, 27, *27*, 40–41, *40–41*
core 40
distance from Sun 27, 40
Shoemaker-Levy Comet 51
Trojan asteroids 52
Jurassic Period 76
Justinian I 203, *203*

K

K2 *see* Tirich Mir
Kabuki drama 332, *332*
Kachinas 332, 333, *333*
Kalahari Desert, Africa 111
Kangchenjunga 99
Karachi, Pakistan 75
Karloff, Boris 358, *358*
Kathakali 332, *332*
Keats, John 347, *347*
Kennedy, John F 233, 240
Kevlar 259
keyboards 326, *326*, 327
Kidman, Nicole 358, *358*
kidneys 181, *181*
Kiel Canal, Germany 289
Kilauea, Hawaii 92, 93
killer whales 154
kinetic energy 264, 265, 273, 279
kinetographs 355
King, B B 328, *328*
King Fahd Airport, Saudi Arabia 291
kitchen foil 82
kitchen sink drama 335
kiwis 166
knights 206, 207, *207*, 248
Kohoutek comet 50, *50*
Komodo dragon 161, *161*
Konfuzi *see* Confucius
Koran 344
kotos 323
Krakatoa, Indonesia 93
Krubera Caves, Georgia 109
krypton 257
Kublai Khan 204, 211

L

labour 187
Lake Baikal, Siberia 104, 105
Lake Poets 347
Lake Titicaca, Peru 105, *105*
lakes 104–105, *104–105*
deepest 104
glacial 97, 104
highest navigable 105
islands 89
largest 105
oxbow lakes 102, *102*, 103
Lambert-Fisher Glacier, Antarctica 101
Lan Jin Bridge, Yunnan, China 282
landscapes 96–97, *96–97*
ocean bed 106, *106*
lantern-slide projectors 354
Lao-tzu 344
lapis lazuli 82
Large Magellanic Cloud 18, 19, 68
larynx 179, *179*
Lascaux caves, France 109, *109*

lasers 299, 308
Latin 16, 198, 257
Latin America 216, 220, 221, 235, 242, 248
latitude 126, 127, 129
laughing gas *see* nitrous oxide
Laurasia 90, *90*
lava 73, 80, *80*, 92, *92*, 93, *93*, 129
- crystals 82

Lavoisier, Antoine 274, *274*
Lawson, H J 287
Le Verrier, Urbain 46
lead 125
League of Augsburg 222, 223
Leaning Tower of Pisa, Italy 281, *281*
leap years 75
leaves 136, *136*, 137
- cells 138, 139, *139*

legends 198, 248, 368
legions 199, *199*, 248
lemurs 165
Lenin, Valdimir Ilyich 233, *233*
lenticular clouds 116
Leonardo da Vinci 214, 315
leopards 154, *154*, 169, *169*
levers 278, 279, 308
- leverage 267, *267*

Lhotse 99
lichens 134, *134*
Lichtenstein, Roy 321
life 30, 31, 274
- conditions on Earth 31, 73
- Europa 41
- Mars 38, 39
- origins 132–133, *132–133*
- plant life-cycles 140, *140*
- taxonomy 132, *132*, 133
- theories 133

lifts (elevators) 280
ligaments 175, *175*, 189
light 13, 15, 22, 74, 75, 139, 270–271, *270–271*, 309
- black holes 24, 25
- bulbs 271
- colour 119
- Earth 44
- Jupiter 41
- Moon 32, 33
- Uranus 44
- Venus 36
- years 13, 20, 21, 23, 68

lightning 119, 263, *263*
limestone 80
- cave systems 108, *108*

lions 168, 169, *169*
liquid crystal display (LCD) 293, *293*
liquids 254–255, *254–255*, 309
Liszt, Franz 325
literature 346–347, *346–347*
- famous characters 347
- publishing 348–349, *348–349*

lithography 317, *317*, 368
lithosphere 78, *78*
Liu Bang 200
liver 84, 172, *172*, 180, *180*, 181
lizards 77, 84, 147, 150, 160, *160*, 161
- biggest 161, *161*

Lloyd, Marie 334, *334*
lobsters 146, *146*
Local Group 19, 68
locomotives 284–285, *284–285*
- *Rocket* 276, *276*

lodestone 276
London Bridge, Arizona, USA 283
London Stock Exchange 223
London, UK 75, 101
longitude 126, 127, 129
longships 204–205, *204–205*
Look Back in Anger 335
Lord of the Rings
- *The Fellowship of the Ring* 356
- *The Two Towers* 359, *359*

Los Angeles, USA 75
loudness 272, *272*, 273
loudspeakers 298, *298*
Louis XIV 223
Love waves 79
Lowell, Percival 38
Lumière, Auguste and Louis 354, *354*
Lunar 9 62
lunar eclipses 32
lungs 178–179, *178–179*, 189, 275
Luther, Martin 218
Lydians 197
Lyra constellation 15
- Ring Nebula 23, *23*

Lystrosaurus 91

M

M80 (NGC 6093) 15
Maat Mons, Venus 37, *37*
Mach speed 272
machines 278–279, *278–279*, 309
- efficiency 278
- Industrial Revolution 230, *230*, 231, *231*

Machu Picchu, Peru 221, *221*
Madagascar 88
Magellan, Ferdinand 217
Magellanic Clouds 19, *19*, 68
maglev trains 285, *285*
magma 80, *80*, 91, 92, *92*, 93, *93*, 129
Magna Carta 206, *245*
magnesium 30, 81
magnetic fields 262, 263, 301, 309
magnetism 262–263, *262–263*, 309
- Jupiter 40
- Neptune 47
- Uranus 47

magnets 127
Magritte, René 321
Magyars 206
Maiasaura 162, *162*
main sequence stars 28
Makalu 99
Makemake 48
malaria 149
Malaysian horned frog 156, *156*
Maldives 89
mammals 76, 84, 147, 150, 168–169, *168–169*
- record-breaking 169

Mammoth Caves, USA 109
mammoths 84, 85, 322
Manaslu 99
Manchus 226, 248
Mandela, Nelson 233, 242, *242*
mantle of the Earth 72, 78, *78*, 79, 129
- continental drift 90, 91

manuscripts, illuminated 314, *314*, 367
Mao Zedong 241, *241*
Maoris 204, *204*, 225, 248
maps and mapmaking 126–127, *126–127*
- conic projection 127, *127*
- Mercator projection 127, *127*

Mara Valley Falls, Norway 103
marble 80
Marceau, Marcel 331, *331*
Marconi, Guglielmo 350, *350*
Marcus Aurelius 199
Mariana Trench 289
Mariner 35, *35*, 58
Marley, Bob 329, *329*
marriage 364, 365, *365*
marrow 174, *174*, 189
Mars 26, 27, *27*, 38–39, *38–39*
- compared to Earth 38
- Curiosity rover 38, *38*
- distance from Sun 27, 38
- landings 38
- space probes 58

marsupials 168
Martinqiue 93
Mary I 219
Mary, Queen of Scots 219, *219*
Masai tribe 365, *365*
masks 330, *330*
mass 15, 266
materials 258–259, *258–259*
mathematics 304
- ancient Greece 196
- area 305, *305*, 306, *306*
- calculating volume 306, *306*

Matrix Reloaded 359, *359*
matter 12, 24
- black holes 25, *25*

Mauna Kea, Hawaii 99
Mauna Loa, Hawaii 93
Maurya dynasty 208
Mayans 212, 213
- numbers 304, *304*

meanders 102, *102*, 103, 129
measuring
- energy 264
- force 266
- space and time 13

mechanical advantage 278
medicine 302–303, *302–303*
- plants 144, 145

medicine men *see* shamans
Medicis 214
Mediterranean Sea 106, 107
meerkats 165
Megazostrodon 77, *77*
Melanesia 224
melting points 255
Menai Straits Bridge, UK 283
Menes of Egypt 193, 195
Mercalli Scale 95
Mercator, Gerardus 127, 216
Mercedes Benz cars 286
merchants 206, 214, 216, 220
Mercury 26, 27, *27*, 34–35, *34–35*
- core 34
- craters 34, 35, *35*
- distance from the Sun 26, 27, 34
- sunrise and sunset 34
- volcanism 35, *35*

'mermaid's purses' 158, *158*
mesocyclones 119, *119*
Mesopotamia 192
- writing 342, 343

mesosphere 78, *78*, 114, *114*
Mesozoic Era 76, 162
Messenger 35, *35*, 58
metals 72, 81, 82, 124, 309
- metallurgy 192
- processing 258
- recycling 125

metamorphic rock 80, 129
metamorphosis 157
Meteor Crater, Arizona, USA 52, *52*
meteorites 30, 39, 52–53, *52–53*, 68
meteoroids 52, 53, 68
meteorologists 117
methane gas 39, 44, 46, 73, 123, 129, 145
metro systems 285
Mexico 212, 213, 220, *244*
Mexico City, Mexico 75, 213
mice 155
Michaux, Pierre and Ernest 287
Michelangelo Buonarotti 214, 315
- *David* 214, *214*

micro-organisms 76
microchips 292, 293, *293*, 309
micrometeoroids 62, 68
Micronesia 193
microprocessors 293
microwave background radiation 13, 68
microwaves 264, 270, 294, 295
migration 167, 189
militarism *see* warfare
Milky Way 15, 18, 19, 20–21, *20*, *21*, 68
Millau viaduct, France 282
mime 331, *331*
mimicry 164, *164*, 189
Minamoto Yoritomo 211
minerals 80, 84, 108, 124, 125, 129
- colour 81, *81*

Ming dynasty 210, 226
Mini car 286, *286*
mining 124
Minoans 193, 196, 248
minus 304

Mir 66, 67
mirrors 270, *270*
missionaries 224, 236, 248
Mississippi-Missouri river 103
mist 117
mitochondria 172, *172*
mobile phones 294, *294*
Model T Ford 286
modems 294, 309
Modernism 362
Mogul dynasty 208, 209, 226
Moguls 248
Mohenjo-Daro civilization 195, *195*
molecules 252–253, *252–253*, 309
  gases 254–255
  heat 268
  liquids 254
  solids 254, 255
  sound 272
moles 150
Molière 331
molluscs 85, 146
Moment Magnitude Scale 95
momentum 266
monasteries 207, 248, 314
Mondrian, Piet 321
Monet, Claude 315
money 197
Mongefossen, Norway 103
Mongols 202, 204, 210–211, *210–211*, 223, 226, 227, *244*, 248, 361, *361*
monkeys 150
monomers 260
monorails 284
Monroe, Marilyn 358, *358*
monsoons 121, *121*, 129
Montezuma 220
Montgolfier, Joseph-Michel and Jacques-Etienne 223, 276
Monument Valley, USA 110–111, *110–111*
Moon 31, 32–33, *32–33*, 72, 73, *73*
  craters 32, 33
  distance from earth 62
  formation 32, *32*
  landings 62–63, *62–63*, 351
  new 32, 33, *33*
  quarters of the Moon 33, *33*
  seas 32, 33
  solar eclipses 29, *29*
  tides 107, *107*, 129
moons (satellites) 68, 69
  Jupiter 40, 41, *41*
  Mars 38, *38*, 39
  Neptune 46, 47
  Pluto 48, *49*
  Saturn 42, 43
  Solar System 26, 27
  Uranus 44, 45, *45*
Moore, Gordon 293
Moore, Henry 321
Moore's law 293
moraine 97, 100, *100*, 129
More, Sir Thomas 218, *218*
morganite 82
Morita, Akio 351
Mortensen, Viggo 356, *356*
Moscow, Russia 75
mosques 319, *319*
mosquitoes 149
mosses 76, 134, *134*
mother of pearl clouds 117
moths 146, 149, *149*
motion 266–267, *266–267*
  Newton's Laws of Motion 266
motorcycling 286
moulting 148
Mount Everest, China/Nepal 38, 98
Mount Pelée, Martinique 93
Mount Pinatubo, Philippines 93, 121
Mount St Helens, Washington State, USA 93, 98
Mount Vesuvius 312
mountains 88, 97, 98–99, *98–99*, 120, 255
  glaciers 100, *100*
  highest 98, 99
  longest ranges 98, 99
  Moon 73
  rivers 102, *102*
  seamounts 106, *106*, 129
  undersea 88, 106, *106*
mouse, computer 293, 309
movies 354–359, *354–359*
  directors 356, *356*
  lighting 356, *356*
  making 356–357, *356–357*
  marketing 357
  special effects and superstars 358–359, *358–359*
Mozart, Wolfgang Amadeus *324*, 325
MP3-players 298, 350
MRI (Magnetic Resonance Imaging) scanners 185
mud 80, 84
Muhammad 204
mummification 312, *312*
murals 312, 368
muscles 151, *151*, 275
  body's biggest 177
  body's smallest 177
  brain 185
  breathing *178*
  humans 176–177, *176–177*
music 322–339, *322–339*
  ballet 338–339, *338–339*
  classical 324–325, *324–325*
  dance 336–337, *336–337*
  instruments 326–327, *326–327*
  music halls 334, 368
  notation 323, *323*, 324
  popular 328–329, *328–329*
  sound recordings 298
Muslims *see* Islam
Mussolini, Benito 233
Mutarazi Falls, Zimbabwe 103
Muybridge, Eadweard 354, 355
Myceneans 193, 196

N

nacreous clouds 117
Namib Desert, Africa 87, *87*
Nanga Parbat 99
Napoleon Bonaparte 233, 234–235, *234–235*
NASA (National Aeronautics and Space Administration) 54, 61, 242, 243, 245, 358
Natal ghost frog 156, *156*
Native Americans 220–221, *220–221*, 223
  drama 332, 333, *333*
  Ghost Dance 337, *337*
  totem poles 318, *318*
  tribes 224
NATO (North Atlantic Treaty Organization) 232–233, 242
natural materials 258, 259, 309
navies 289
navigation 126, 276
  satellites 60, 61
Nazcas 312
Nazism 238, 248
Near Earth Objects (NEOs) 52, 68
Nebuchadnezzar II 193, *193*
nebulae 17, 22–23, *22–23*, 68
  star formation 14, 22, 23
Nelson, Admiral Horatio 234, *244*
Neogene Period 76
neon 257, 271, *271*
Neptune 26, *26*, 46–47, *46–47*
  distance from the Sun 27, 46
  rings 46, *46*, 47
nerves 184–185, *184–185*
neurons 184–185, *184–185*
neutrons 252, 309
Nevada, USA 87
névé 100, *100*
New Guinea 88
New Guinea Range 99
New Horizons 58
New York, USA 75
New Zealand 75, 86, 93, 204, 224, 225, *225*
  Ice Age 101
Newcomen, Thomas 230, 231
newspapers 348, *349*
Newton, Sir Isaac 229, 266, *266*, 267
newtons (N) 266
newts 147, 156, 157
nickel 30, 72, 78, 81
night 74, 75
nightshade, deadly 137
Niijima 89
Nijinsky, Vaslav 339, *339*
Nile crocodiles 159
Nile River 103, 195, *195*
nimbostratus clouds 116, *116*, 118, *118*
nitrogen 30, 47, 114, 115, 253
nitrous oxide 123, 302
noble gases 257, 309
nobles 206
nocturnal creatures 155, 189
Noh drama *332*, 452
Nohoch Nah Chich cave system, Mexico 108
nomadic peoples 202, 248, 361, *361*
noon 75
Normans 248
North America 86, *86*, 87, 90, *90*, 91, 127
  colonization 220, 221, 222, 223
  history 220–221, *220–221*
  Ice Age 101
  tectonic plate 91
North Pole 75, *75*, 127
Northern Hemisphere 15, 16, *16*, 74, *74*, 115
Northern Lights 115, *115*
nose 179, *179*
novels 346–347, *346–347*, 349
nuclear
  power 265, 300
  reaction 14, 15, 28, 252
nucleus 172, *172*, 186, *186*, 189, 252, 253, 309
numbers 304, *304*
nutcrackers 279, *279*

O

Oakland Bay Bridge, San Francisco, USA 283
oases 111, 129
oboes 326, *326*
observatories 29, 56–57, *56–57*, 69
ocean liners 289
  Queen Elizabeth 289
  Titanic 274, *274*, 289
Oceania 86, *86*, 87
oceanic crust 78, *78*, 79
oceans 31, 73, 86, *86*, 90, 106–107, *106–107*
  climate 120
  depths 107
  habitats 152, 153
  Panthalassa 90, *90*
  trenches 91, 106, *106*, 129
octopuses 146, *146*, 148, 153
Odyssey 196, 346
Ohain, Hans van 290
oil 122, 124, 260
  refineries 260, 300, *300*
  rigs 125, *125*
oil paints 316, *316*
Old Masters 315
Olmecs 192, 212, 213, *213*, 248
Olympic Games 196
Olympus Mons, Mars 38
O'Neill, Eugene 331
opals 82, 83, *83*
opera 324, 325, 368
  Beijing opera 333, 340, *340*
Opportunity 38
optical fibres 294, 295, 309
optical telescopes 56
orbits 26, 69
  asteroids 52
  comets 50, 51
  dwarf planets 48

Earth 30
geostationary orbit 60, 68, 295
Jupiter 40
Mars 38
Mercury 34
Moon 32
Neptune 46
Pluto 48
retrograde 37, 45, 69
satellites 60, 61
Saturn 42
Venus 36
orchestras 325, *325*
orchids 141
Ordovician Period 76
ores *72*, 82, 125, 129
organic chemistry 261, 309
organic compounds 260, 261
organisms 134, 189
organs 172, *172*, 189
Orion constellation 15, 16
Great Nebula 22, 23, *23*
Horsehead Nebula 23, *23*
Ornithischians 163, *163*
Osborne, John 335, *335*
Oscars 355, 358, 359
ostriches 151, 166, 167
Ostrogoths 193
Otis, Elisha 280
Ottoman Empire 222, 223, 226, 248
ovaries 141, *141*, 186, *186*, 189
ovules 141, *141*, 189
owls 155, 166
oxbow lakes 102, *102*, 103
oxygen 30, 73, 76, 81, 114, 115, 189, 253, 309
algae 145
fish 152
human body 178, 179, 182, 183
plants 138, 139
oysters 82, 153
ozone layer 115, 129
global warming 123

P

pacemakers 303
Pacific Ocean 86, 106, 107, 224
coral islands 88, 89
Ring of Fire 93
tectonic plates 91
packaging 123
Padua, Italy 214, *214–215*
painting 196, 214
Pakistan 75
palaces 361, *361*
palaeontologists 162, *162*
Palaeozoic Era 76
Paleogene Period 76
Palestine *245*
pan-pipes 323, *323*
pancreas 180, *180*, 181, *181*
Pangaea 90, *90*, 129
panspermia theory 132
Panthalassa 90, *90*
paper 125
parachutes 261, *261*
first drop 291
parallelograms 305, *305*
parasites 149
parsecs 13, 69
parthenogenesis 158
Parthenon, Athens, Greece 197, 360, *360*
pas-de-deux 338, *338*
Pathfinder 39
Pavarotti, Luciano 323, *323*
peacocks 159, *159*
Pearl Harbor, Hawaii, USA 232, 239, *239*
pearls 82, 83, *83*
peasants 206
peat 124, *124*
Peking *see* Beijing, C
Peloponnesian Wars 192
penguins 87, 151, 166
pensions 229
People of the Book 345
perching birds 167
percussion 326
peregrine falcon 150, *150*
perennial plants 189
peridot 82, 83, *83*
perihelion 29
Periodic Table 256–257, *256–257*, 309
Periods 76
permafrost 85
Permeke, Constant 320
Permian Period 76
Perseus constellation 16
Persia 192, 193, 195, 223, 226
barbarian invasions 203
personal music players 329, 351
Peru 212, 221, 240, *244*
PET (Positron Emission Tomography) scans 303, *303*
Peter the Great 228
petroleum 260
pharaohs 194, 195, *195*
phases of the Moon 32, 33, 69
pheromones 165
Philippines 93, 121
philosophers 196, 229, 248
phloem vessels 137, *137*
Phobos 38, *38*, 39
Phoenicians *245*, 342, 343
phones 294–295, *294–295*, 296, 297
phonographs 237, 329
photoelectric effect 298
photography 320, 321
cinema 354–355, *354–355*
space probes 35, 39, 43
photons 270
photosphere 28, *28*, 69
photosynthesis 114, 138–139, *138–139*, 189
physics 25
phytoplankton 134, *134*
pianos 322, 327, *327*
Piazzi, Giuseppe 52
Picasso, Pablo 315, 321, *321*
Piccard, Bertrand 291
Piccard, Jacques 289
Picts 202, 205, 248
pigeons 166, *166*
pigments 317, 368
pike 152, *152*
piles (construction) 281, *281*
Pilgrim fathers 221, *221*
pilgrimages 249
pines 113
pirates 205, 249, 347
pitch 273
Pizarro, Francisco 220, *220*
planes *see* aircraft
planes, inclined 278, 279
planetary
nebulae 22, 23, *23*
rings 41, 43, *43*, 45, *45*, 46, *46*, 47, 69
planetesimals 72, 129
planets 14, 40, 69, 72
carbon 260
Solar System 26–27, *26–27*
see also individual planets
plankton 155, 189
plants 73, 76, 90, 119, 124, 125, 133, 134–135, *134–135*, 274
cellulose 261
deserts 111
Earth's atmosphere 30
families 141
giant 142
growth 142–143, *142–143*
human uses 144–145, *144–145*
medicine 144, 145
parts 136–137, *136–137*
photosynthesis 114, 138–139, *138–139*
poisonous 137
rainforests 112
records 138
reproduction 140–141, *140–141*
plasma 15, 254, 309
plasma screens 299, *299*
Plassey, Battle of 222, *226–227*
plastics 260, 261, 309
Plato 196
playwrights 330, 331, 348
Pleistocene Ice Age 101
plesiosaurs 163
Plough constellation 16, *16*, 17
plug-ins 297
Pluto 26, 48–49, *48–49*, 58
distance from Sun 27, 48
poetry 196, 346–347
Pointillism 315, *315*
Poland 223, 238, 240
polar regions 75, 87, 120, 121, 123
poles, magnetic 262, 263
politics 353, 358, 364
pollen 141, *141*, 189
insects 149
pollination 140, 141, 189
Pollock, Jackson 321, *321*
pollution 170
Polyakov, Valery 66
polygons 305, *305*
polyhedrons 305, *305*
polymers 260, 309
Polynesia 193, 204, 224
polyps 88, 133, 148
polythene 260
Pompeii 312
Pompey 198
Ponte Vecchio, Florence, Italy 282, *282*
Pop Art 321
popes 207, 235, 249
poppies 139, *139*
porcelain 210, *210*
porpoises 168
ports, world's busiest 289
Portugal 216, 217
Potala Palace, Tibet 361, *361*
potential energy 264
pottery 313, *313*, 316, *316*
poverty 170, 171, 363
power 300–301, *300–301*
nuclear 265, *265*, 301, *301*
stations 263, *263*, 265, 300
Prague Castle, Czech Republic 280
Precambrian Time 76
precipitation 116
predators 150, 151, 154, 189
birds of prey 155, 159, 167
great white shark 153, *153*, 171
Presley, Elvis 329, *329*
pressure 28, 30, 78, 80
air 115, *115*, 255
Jupiter 40
Saturn 42
Venus 37
prey 154, 189
Pride and Prejudice 352, *352*
prime meridian 127
printing 348–349, *348–349*
printing press 348, *348*
Pritchard, Thomas 282
Procyon 15
prominences 28, *28*, 29, 69
props 334, *334*
Protestantism 218–219, 249
proton-proton chain 15
protons 252, 253, 309
Proust, Marcel 349
Prout, Samuel 316
pteridophytes 141
pterosaurs 163
publishing 348–349, *348–349*
Puebloans 213, 224
pulleys 278, *278*, 279
pulse 182
pumas 169, *169*
Punch and Judy 333
Punic Wars 193
puppets 332, 333, *333*
Pushkin, Aleksandr Sergeyevich 347
Putin, Valdimir 241
putting the shot 266, *266*
pylons 263, *263*, 300, *300*
pyramids *245*, 280, 304
Egyptian 16, 54, 360, *360*
Mayan 213, *213*
Pythagoras 277
theorem 307, *307*
pythons 160, *160*

Q

Q-waves 79

Qin dynasty 200, 226, 232
quarks 12, 13
Quartenary Period 76
quartz 82
quasars 18, 24, 69
Queen Elizabeth 289
Quetzalcoatl 220, 249
Quito, Ecuador 121
Qu'ran *see* Koran

R

rabbits 165, 168, *168*
radar 69
radiation 22, 69, 268, 269, 270
radiators 269, *269*
radio 294, *294*, 328, 350–351, *350–351*
  home entertainment 352–353, *352–353*
  lingo 294
  telescopes 57, 69
  waves 264, 270, 295
radioactivity 77
radiometric dating 77
Raedwald of Anglia 203
rain 73, 87, 97, 121
  clouds 116–117, *116–117*
  dances 332, 336, 337, *337*
  deserts 110
  monsoons 121, *121*, 129
  mountains 98
  water cycle 103, *103*
rainbows 118, 119, *119*
rainforest 87, 112–113, *112–113*, 121
  global warming 123
Raj 227, 249
RAM (random access memory) 292
ramps 278, *278*, 279
Ramses II of Egypt 192
Raphael 214, 315
raptors *see* birds of prey
rats 155
Rayleigh waves 79
rays (fish) 153
receivers 295
recorders 326, *326*
records 328
  best sellers 328, 329
recycling 125
red giants 15, 28
red planet *see* Mars
Red Shoes 338
red stars 14, 15
reefs 88
  Great Barrier Reef, Australia 89, *89*
reflecting telescopes 56
reflection nebulae 22
reflections 270
Reformation 218, 249
refracting telescopes 56
refraction 270, *270*, 271
refrigerators 123, 268, *268*
reggae 329
religions 228, 312, 313
  drama 330, 331, 332, *332*
  music 322, 324
  symbols 365
  wars 218–219, *218–219*, 222–223
  writing 344–345, *344–345*
Rembrandt van Rijn 315
Renaissance 214–215, *214–215*, 249, 314, 315, 369
renewable energy 125, *125*
Renoir, Auguste 315
reproduction
  animals 158–159, *158–159*
  humans 186–187, *186–197*
  plants 140–141, *140–141*
reptiles 76, 90, 91, 147, *147*, 160–161, *160–161*
  amphibians 160
republics 249
  Roman 198
reservoirs 105
Reseu Jean Bernard caves, France 109
resources 124–125, *124–125*
respiration 139, 178–179, *178–179*, 189
resultant force 267
revolution 232–233, *232–233*, 249
  Europe 234–235, *234–235*
rhinoceroses 155, 165, *165*
rhombus 309
rhyme 346
rhythm and blues 328
ribbon lightning 119
rice 142, 144, 145
  growing 145, *145*
Rigel 15
right angles 305, *305*, 307, *307*, 309
rime 118
Ring of Fire, Pacific Ocean 93
Ring Nebula 23, *23*
Ringling Brothers Circus 333
river dolphins 170, *170–171*
rivers 76, 84, 102–103, *102–103*
  deltas 103, 128
  islands 89
  landscape formation 96, *96*, 97, *97*
  longest 103
  tributaries 102, 129
roads 199
  oldest 286
Robin Hood 346, *346*
robots 67
rock 30, 72, 73, 76, 80–81, *80–81*, 114, 259
  fossils 77
  gemstones 82–83, *82–83*
  interior of the Earth 78
  lava 73
  Mars 39
  oldest 81, 86, 87
  rock cycle 80, *80*, 81
  Saturn 42, 43
  volcanic bombs 92, *92*
  waterfalls 103, *103*
  weathering 81, 96, *96*
rock 'n' roll 328
Rocket locomotive 276, *276*
rockets 25, *25*, 35, *35*, 267, 290, *290*, 300, 309
  Space Shuttle 64–65, *64–65*
Rocky Mountains, North America 98, 99
rodents 111, 155
Rogallo, Francis 291
Rome, ancient 192, 193, 198–199, *198–199*, *245*, 314, 315
  astronomy 34, 36, 38, 40, 42, 48
  bridges 282
  drama 330
  gods and goddesses 199
  numbers 304, *304*
  population 199
  pottery 313, *313*
  Roman Empire 198–199
Rontgen, Wilhelm 175
roots 136, *136*, 137, *137*
  seedlings 142, *142*, 143
  vegetables 137
rose hips 145, *145*
Rosetta Stone 344, *344*
Rousseau, Jean-Jacques 229
rovers 38, 39, *39*
Rub'al-khali (Empty Quarter) 110
rubber 144, 145
rubidium 77
rubies 82, 83, *83*
runes 342, *342*, 343
running 265, *265*
Russia 75, 79, 87, 127, 206, 210, 223, 226, 242
  ballet 339
  Cold War 240–241, *240–241*
  Napoleon Bonaparte 235
  Peter the Great 228
  railways 285
  religion 219
  Russian Revolution 232–233
  satellites 61
  space exploration 59, 60, 61, 62, 66, 67
  theatre 334

S

S-waves 79, *79*
sagas 342
Sagittarius 21
Sahara desert, Africa 76, 86, 110, 111, 121
sailors 288, 289
sailors and ships, famous 217
St Bartholomew's Day massacre 219
St Paul 345, *345*
salamanders 147, 156, 157
saliva 181
salmon 152
Salt Lake City, USA 85
salt water 104, 105
Salyut 1 66
samurai 211, *211*, 249
San Francisco, USA 95
sand 80, 81, 84, 103
  dunes 110, 111, *111*
sand tiger sharks 153, *153*
sandstone 80
Santorini, Greece 93
sap 137, 189
sapphires 82, 83, *83*
sapwood 137, *137*, 143, *143*
Sarawak Chamber, Malaysia 109
Sargon of Mesopotamia 192
satellites (artificial) 60–61, *60–61*, 69, 123
  broadcasting 351, *351*
  communications 294–295, *294–295*, 296–297, *296–297*
  global positioning system (GPS) 127
  WMAP 54
Saturn 26, *26*, 42–43, *42–43*
  distance from Sun 27, 42
  moons 42, 43
Saturnalia 42
Saurischians 163, *163*
savannah 86, 112
Savery, Thomas 223
saxophones 327, *327*
Scandinavia 342, 343
scanners 302, 303, *303*, 309
Schoenberg, Arnold 325
Schubert, Franz Peter 325
science 214, 320
science fiction 347
scientific research, Antarctica 87
scientists 12, 13, 24, 25, 30, 79, 81, 85, 122
Scooter, Uranus 47
Scorpion constellation 17, *17*
Scotland 205, 206
  Jacobite rebellions 222, 229
  Scots 205, 249
screw propellers 288, *289*
screws 278, 279
scripts 334
scriptures 344–345, *344–345*, 369
sculpture 196, 214, *214*, 316, *316*
sea anemones 154
Sea of Japan 107
Sea of Okhotsk 107
seahorses 153
seals 151
seamounts 106, *106*, 129
seas 80, *80*, 84, 99, 106–107, *106–107*
  icebergs 101, *101*
  largest 107
  Moon 32, 33
  rivers 102, 103
  sea levels 88
  tsunamis 95, *95*
seasons 74, 112, 113
seconds 75
sediment 102, 103, 129
sedimentary rock 80, *80*, 81, 129
  fossils 84
seeds 76, 134, 135, 141, 189
  germination 142, *142*, 143
Seinfeld, Jerry 352
seismologists 95, 129
seismometers 95
Selkirk, Alexander 347
Senning, Ake 303
senses 184, *184*, 185
sepals 189
serfdom 234, 249
Serkis, Andy 358
Seurat, Georges 315

Seven Wonders of the World 192, 197, *197*
sexual intercourse 187
Seychelles 89
shadows 270
Shah Jahan 209
Shakespeare, William 45, 330, *330*
  the Globe 331
  Reduced Shakespeare Company 334
Shakta Pantujhina caves, Georgia 109
shale 80
shamans 332, 333, *333*
Shang dynasty 200, 201, *201*
Shanghai, China 289
shape of Earth 30
shapes 305–307, *305–307*
  calculating area 305–306, *305–306*
  calculating volume 306, *306*
sharks 147, 152, 153, *153*, 154, 171
  eggs 158, *158*
Shaw, George Bernard 331
sheet lightning 119
shellfish 76, 82
  ammonites 77, *77*, 85, *85*
  fossils 84
shells (atoms) 253, *253*, 309
Sheridan, Richard Brinsley 331
Shi Huangdi 200
shield volcanoes 93
Shintoism 200, *200*, 201
ships 204–205, *204–205*, 216, *216*, 236, 275, 288–289, *288–289*
  famous sailors and ships 217
  sailing 289, *289*
  warships 289
Shoemaker-Levy Comet 51
shoes, ballet 338, 339
shoguns 211, 220, 222, 223, 249
shooting stars 52, 69
shopping malls 362, *362*
Shotoku Taishi 201
Shrek 357
shrews 77, *77*, 154
shrimps 153
Sikhism 345, *345*
silicon 30, 81, 292
silt 84, 103, 129
Silurian Period 76
silver 82, *82*, 253, 257
Singapore 289
singing 322, 323
singularity 24, 69
Sirius 15
Sistema del Trava, Spain 109
Sistema Huautla caves, Mexico 109
sitars 326, *326*
size of
  Earth 27
  galaxies 18, 19
  Jupiter 26, 27, 40
  Mars 27, 38
  Mercury 27, 34
  Moon 32
  Neptune 27, 46
  Pluto 48
  Saturn 26, 27, 42
  Solar System 27
  stars 15
  Uranus 27, 44, 45
  Venus 26, 27
skeleton 174–175, *174–175*
skin 173, *173*
skull 174, *174*
  trepanning 302
skunks 164, *164*
sky 115
Skylab 66
skyscrapers 280, 281, *281*, 363, *363*
slavery 224, 225, *225*, 236, 249
sloughing 161
Slovakia 109
Small Magellanic Cloud 18, 19, 68
smell, animal communication 165
Smith, Adam, *The Wealth of Nations* 222
snails and slugs 146, *146*, 148, 159
snakes 147, 151, 160, 161, 165, *165*
  constrictors 161
snout 100, *100*
snow 87, 119, *119*
  glaciers 100
  snowflake crystals 101
snow leopards 169, *169*
soap operas 353
Socrates 196
sodium 258
sodium chloride 258
SOHO (Solar and Heliospheric Observatory) 29
solar eclipses 29, *29*
solar power 300
Solar System 18, 26–27, *26–27*, 69, 73
  formation 26, 68
solar wind 115
solids 254–255, *254–255*, 309
solutions 275, *275*
Song dynasty 204, 210
song thrushes 167, *167*
Sony 353
Sophocles 331
sound 272–273, *272–273*
  animal communication 164
  sound barrier 286
sound recording 298, *298*, 299, 328
  bestsellers 328, 329
  cinema 355, *355*
  radio stations 328
South Africa 242
South America 86, *86*, 87, 90, *90*, 91, 98
  ancient 192, 193
  dance 336
  history 220–221, *220–221*
  tectonic plate 91
South American frog 159
South China Sea 107
South Pole 75, *75*, 87, 127
Southern Cross constellation 17, *17*
Southern Hemisphere 16, 17, *17*, 74, *74*, 115
Southern Ocean 87, 106
Southey, Robert 347
Soviet Union (USSR) *see* Russia
Soyuz spacecraft 67
space 73, 114, 115
  exploration *245*
  probes 58–59, *58–59*, 69
    Mars 38, *38*, 39, *39*
    Pluto 49, 58
    Saturn *42*
    Venus 36, 37
  stations 66–67, *66–67*, 69
  telescopes 56, 69
    Hubble Space telescope 23, 45, 46, 48, 61, *61*, 242
'space race' 61
Space Shuttle 64–65, *64–65*, 69
space suits 62
spacecraft 265, *265*
  rockets 267, 290, *290*, 309
Spain 213, 217, 223
  General Franco 232
  Inquisition 218
  Latin America 216, 220, 221, 235
Sparta 196, 197
species 133, 146, 189
  endangered 170–171, *170–171*
  fish 152
  frogs and toads 156
  invertebrates 148
speed
  aircraft 290
  cars 286, 287
  Earth 74, 75
  light 12, 271
  planets 40, 42
  sound 272, 273
sperm 186, *186*
sphalerite 125
spheres 306, *306*, 309
Spice Islands 216
spices 217
spicules 28, *28*
spiders 146, *146*, 148, 154
spinal cord 185, *185*
spinning jenny 222, 230, *230*
spinning machines 230, *230*, 231, *231*
Spinosaurus 162, *162*
spiral galaxies 18, *18*, 19
Spirit 38, 243
spitting spiders 155, *155*
spittlebugs 149, *149*
sponges 133
spores 142, *142*, 189
spring 74, 107
springtails 149, *149*
Sputnik 1 60, 61, *61*
squares 309
squid 146
squirrels 155
staccato lightning 119
stacks 107, *107*
stained glass 316, *316*
stalactites 109, *109*, 129
stalagmites 109, *109*, 129
Stalin, Joseph 233, *233*, 240
stamens 137, 141, 189
Stanislavsky, Constantin 334
starfish 149, 153, 154
Starley, John 287
stars 12, 13, 14–15, *14–15*, 69
  black holes 24
  life cycle 15
  Milky Way 20, 21
  Northern Hemisphere 15, 16
  number of 15
  Southern Hemisphere 17
  swarms 15
static electricity 262, 263, *263*
statistics
  Earth 30
  International Space Station (ISS) 66
  Jupiter 41
  Mars 38
  Mercury 35
  Neptune 46
  Pluto 48
  Saturn 43
  Sun 28
  Uranus 45
  Venus 37
steam 92, 93, *93*, 309
  engines 223, 230, *230*, 231, *231*, 284, 309
  power stations 301, *301*
  steamships 288
Steamboat Geyser, Yellowstone Park, USA 93
steel 275, 309
stems 136, *136*, 137, *137*
Stephenson, George 276
Stevenson, Robert Louis 347
stick insects 158, *158*
stigmas 136, *136*, 141, *141*, 189
still life 315
stomach 180, *180*, 181
stomata 139, *139*, 189
Stonehenge, UK 192, *192*, *244*, 360, *360*
Stoppard, Tom 331
storms 121, 123
  Jupiter 40, 41
  Saturn 43
storyboards 356
storytellers 330, 342, *342*, 346–347, *346–347*
Strait of Gibraltar 106
strata 124, *124*, 129
stratosphere 114, *114*
stratus clouds 116, *116*, 117
Stravinsky, Igor 339
stress 267
stringed instruments 326
Stuart, Charles Edward 222, 229
stunts 359
stupas 208, 209
Styracosaurus 163
Su Sung 201
subatomic particles 252, 309
subduction 91, 129
submarines 239, *239*, 249, 265, 289
  world's smallest 288

submersibles 309
subtropics 86
subways 285
Suez Canal *245*
Sufis 336, 337, *337*
sugar 138
sugar cane 139
sulphur 81
sulphuric acid 36
Sumerians 194, 304
summer 74, 75, 87, 121
Sun 15, 26, 28–29, *28–29*, 69, 72, 73, 74, 75, 107, 114, 115, 120
core 28, *28*
distance from Earth 28
energy 124, 125, 138
formation 72
global warming 122, 123
position in galaxy 20, 21
radiation 268, *268*
rays 114, 115, 123
sunspots 29, 69
temperature 28, 29
winter 118
sundials 277, *277*
supergiants 15
supernovae 15, 22, 69, 264
supersonic aircraft 291, *291*
surgeons 302, *302*
Surrealism 321, *321*, 369
Surtsey Island, Iceland 88
Sutton Hoo treasure 203, *203*
swamps 76, 124
swans 159
Sweden 223
Sweet Track, Somerset, UK 286
Swift spacecraft 25
swifts 166
swimming 150, 151
swordfish 153
Sydney, Australia 75
Sydney Opera House, Australia 363, *363*
Sylphides, Les 338, 339
symphony orchestras 325
synapses *184*, 189
Syncrude Tailings Dam, Canada 281

T

tablet computers 297, *297*
Tacama Bridge, Washington, USA 283
tadpoles 157, *157*
South American frog 159
tails 77
Taj Mahal, India 209, *209*
talkies 355
Tambora, Indonesia 93
tambourines 327, *327*
Tang dynasty 204, 210
tankas 318
tanks 232
Tao-te-Ching 344
tap dancing 341
tapeworms 149
tarpaulin 288
Tasman, Abel Janszoon 224
Tasmania 224
Ice Age 101
taxonomy 132, *132*, 133
Taylor, Elizabeth 358, *358*
Tchaikovsky, Peter Illyich 325
Technicolor 354, 358
technology 226, 236, 320
buildings 362, 363
Industrial Revolution 222, 230–231, *230–231*
tectonic plates 91, *91*, 98, 129
earthquakes 94
teeth 77, 85, 168
extraction 302
human body 181, *181*
predators 155, *155*
rodents 155
telecommunications 294–295, *294–295*, 353
cable 294
computers 296
fibre-optics 294, 295
telephones 237, 240, 294–295, *294–295*, 296, 297
telescopes 52, 54, 56–57, *56–57*, 69
television 298, 299, *299*, 350–351, *350–351*
home entertainment 352–353, *352–353*
Telford, Thomas 283
temperate forest 143, 189
temperate zone 120, 121
temperature 120, 121, 268–269, *268–269*, 309
Africa 86, 110
Antarctica 87
Arctic Ocean 107
conversion 269, *269*
global warming 122–123, *122–123*
interior of the Earth 78, 79, 80
mountains 99
stars 14, 15
Sun 28, 29
temples
Buddhist 360, *360*
Chinese 361, *361*
Egyptian 192, 193, *193*
Greek 197, *197*, 360, *360*
Mayan 212
Roman 360, *360*
tendons 175, *175*, 189
tents 361, *361*
Teotihuacán *212–213*, 213, *244*
tephra 92, *92*
Terminator 3: Rise of the Machines 358, *358*
territories 159, 189
terrorism 233, 243, 249
testudo 199, *199*, 249
Tethys Sea 90, *90*
Thanksgiving 221
theatre 330–335, *330–335*
drama 196, 330–331, *330–331*, 332–333, *332–333*
layout 335, *335*
modern 334–335, *334–335*
theatre in the round 334
world 332–333, *332–333*
theory of relativity 13
thermometers 269, *269*
thermosphere 114, *114*
thermostats 268, *268*
Thirty Years War 219, 223
Thor 343, *343*
thunder 116, 117, 121
Tianhe-2 computer 292
Tibet 222
tides 107, *107*, 129
Tien Shan 99
tigers 170
Tigris River 194
timber 361, *361*
time 13
travel 25
zones 75, *75*
tin 253
Tintern Abbey, Wales 207, *207*
Tirich Mir 99
tissues 173, *173*, 189
Titan 43, 59
Titan III/Centaur 59, *59*
Titanic 274, *274*, 289
toads 147, 156–157, *156–157*
Tokugawa Ieyasu 222
Tokyo, Japan 75
Toltecs 249
tomb paintings 312, 313, *313*
topaz 82, 83, *83*
tornadoes 118, 119, *119*
tortoises 147, 160, 161
totem poles 318, *318*
Toulouse-Lautrec, Henri de 317
tourmaline 82
tournaments 207, *207*
Toussaint l'Ouverture, François Dominique 225
Tower Bridge, London, UK 283, *283*
Toyotomi Hideyoshi 220
trace fossils 85
trade 214, 216, 217, 236
Trafalgar, Battle of 234, *244*
tragedy 197, 369
trains 284–285, *284–285*
Rocket 276
Trans-Siberian Express, Russia 285
Transantarctic Range 99
transistors 293, *293*
transits of Venus 37
transmitters 294
transparency 309
transport
air 290–291, *290–291*
rail 284–285, *284–286*
road 286–287, *286–287*
water 288–289, *288–289*
trapeziums 305, *305*, 309
Treaty of Tordesillas 216
trees 76, 84, 85, 114, 124, 135, *135*, 188
forestry 125
forests 112–113, *112–113*
growth rings 143, *143*
Namib Desert, Africa 87, *87*
structure 137, *137*
trench warfare 238, *238*
trenches, ocean bed 91, 106, *106*
trepanning 302
triangles 305, *305*, 307, *307*, 309
Triangulum galaxy 19
Triassic Period 76
tributaries 102, 129
Tricertops 163, *163*
Trifid Nebula 22, *22*
trigonometry 307
trilobites 85
triplanes 291
Triton 46, 47, *47*
Trojan asteroids 52
Trojan Horse 196, *196*
trombones 327, *327*
tropical forests 86, 112–113, *112–113*, 143, 171, 189
tropics 86, 112, 113, 117, 121, 127, 129
storms 121
Tropic of Cancer 127
Tropic of Capricorn 127
wind 118
troposphere 114, *114*, 115
trucks 287
trumpets 322, *327*
trunks 137, *137*
Tsing Ma Bridge, Hong Kong 283
tsunamis 95, *95*, 129
tubas 327, *327*
tube worms 107
Tugela falls, South Africa 103
Tull, Jethro 222, 231
tungsten 255
tunnels 280, *280*
construction 281, *281*
turbines 301, *301*, 309
turbofans 290
turbojets 290
turboprops 290
Turner, J M W 315
turquoises 82, 83, *83*
turtles 147, 160, 161, *161*
Tutunendo, Colombia 121
typewriters 237
Tyrannosaurus rex 85, *85*, 163
Tyssestrengene, Norway 103

U

U-boats 239, *239*
UFO sightings 31
ultrasonic sound 273
ultrasound scans 187, *187*
ultraviolet rays 115, 123, 264, 270, 271
unconformities 77
underground railways 285
uniforms 364
United Kingdom (UK) 75
railways 284, 285
satellites 61
see also Britain
United Nations (UN) 243, *243*
United States of America (USA) 75, 85, 87, 127, 236
aircraft carriers 289
art 321
Civil War 232–233, *233*

Cold War 240–241, *240–241*
industrial power 237
popular music 328, 329
railways 284, 285
satellites 61
space exploration 58–59, 62–67
War of Independence 223, *225*
world wars 238, 239
Universe 12–13, *12–13*, 69
age of 12
brightest objects in 24
history 13
measuring 13
ununoctium 257
uranium 77, 300, 301
Uranus 26, *26*, 44–45, *44–45*
distance from Sun 27, 44
rings 45, *45*
urinary system 181, *181*
USS *Glacier* 101
Utigard falls, Norway 103

V

Valentino, Rudolf 358, *358*
valleys 97, *97*, 102, *102*
Vallis Marineris, Mars 39
Vandals 193, 199, 202
Vedas 344
Vega 15
vegetables 135, 137, 145
vegetation zones 112
veins 173, *173*, 182, 183, *183*, 189
vellum 314
Velociraptor 163
velocity 267
vents, volcanic 92, *92*
Venus 26, 27, *27*, 36–37, *36–37*
clockwise rotation 37
craters 36
day 37
distance from Sun 27
Mariner 35
Venus de Milo 196, *196*
Vercors caves, France 109
Verdi, Giuseppe 325
vernal equinox 75
Versailles, France 229, *229*
vertebrates 146, 147, 189
Vesuvius 312
video games 353
videotapes 353
Vietnam War 241
Viking 39, *39*, 58
Vikings 204–205, *204–205*, 206, *245*, 249
runes 342, *342*, 343
villi 180, *180*
violins 322, 326, *326*
virtual reality 292
viruses 183
Visigoths 193, 199, 202
vitamins 137
vocal cords 179, *179*
voice 323
volcanoes 73, *73*, 78, 79, *79*
biggest 93
earthquakes 94
eruptions 92–93, *92–93*, 121, 128
Io 41
island formation 88–89, *88–89*
Mars 38
Mercury 35
Moon 32, 33
most active 92
mountains 98, *98*
Ring of Fire 93
rock cycle 80, *80*
tectonic plates 91, 93
Venus 36, 37, *37*
Voltaire, François-Marie Arouet 229
Vortigern 202
Vostok science station, Antarctica 87
Voyager 42, 43, 44, 47, 58, 59, *59*

W

Wagner, Richard 325, *325*
walking 265
Walkmans 351
War of the Worlds 352
warfare 192, 195
Renaissance 215
trench warfare 238, *238*
Warhol, Andy 321
warships, world's biggest 289
Washington, George 225
Washington, USA 101
wasps 146, 149
water 12, 30, 72, 73, 80, 84, 114, 123, 124, 258, 274–275, *274–275*, 309
ancient Rome 198
cave formation 108–109, *108–109*
clouds 116–117, *116–117*
cycle 103, *103*, 104
deserts 110, 111
Europa 41
human body 180
hydroelectric power stations 301
lakes 104–105, *104–105*
landscapes 96–97, *96–97*
life on Earth 31
Mars 39
movement 150, 151
oceans and seas 106–107, *106–107*
rivers 102–103, *102–103*
transport 288–289, *288–289*
water boatmen 149, *149*
water vapour 123
watercolours 316, *316*
waterfalls 87, *87*
highest 103
Waterloo, Battle of 233, *233*, 235
waterwheels 279, *279*, 360, *360*
Watt, James 230, 231
wave-particle duality 270
waves 96
tsunamis 95, *95*, 129
weapons 205, *205*
weather 80, 118–119, *118–119*
clouds 116–117, *116–117*
troposphere 115
weathering 81, 96, *96*, 129
wedges 278, 279
weight of
Earth 28, 79
Jupiter 26, 40
Sun 28
weightlessness 66, 69
Welles, Orson 352
Wellington, Duke of 235
Wells, Horace 302
West Indies *244*
whale shark 153, *153*
whales 145, 154, 155, 168
wheels 278, 279
whirling dervishes 337, *337*
white dwarfs 15
white holes 25
white light 119

white stars 14, 15
Whittle, Frank 290
Wi-Fi 295, *295*
wildlife parks 171
Willendorf Venus 312
William I, the Conqueror 207
wind 80, 87, 96, 97, 115, 117
Beaufort Scale 119
Neptune 46
renewable energy 125, *125*
Saturn 42
tropics 118
turbines 264, *264*
Uranus 44
Venus 36
wings 167, *167*
winter 74, 75, 118, 120, 121
WMAP satellite 54
wolves 165, *165*
wood 143, 144, 145, 259
woodwind 326
words 342–343, *342–343*
derived from Greek 197
Wordsworth, William 347
work 278
working mothers 365
'world music' 39
World War I 232, 233, 238–239, *238–239*, *245*, 291
World War II 232, 238–239, *238–239*, *245*
World Wide Web 296, 297, 309
wormholes in space 25, *25*
worms 146, *146*
Wright, Orville and Wilbur 232, 290
writing 342–343, *342–343*, 346–347, *346–347*
publishing 348–349, *348–349*
religions 344–345, *344–345*

X

X-rays 15, 56, 175, *175*, 185, 264, 270, 303, *303*, 309
xylem vessels 137, *137*
xylophones 327, *327*

Y

Yamato dynasty 201
yawning 179
years 75
Yellow Emperor 200
yellow stars 15
Yellowstone Park, USA 93
Yeltsin, Boris 241
Yenisey River 103
Yosemite Falls, USA 103
Yuan dynasty 211

Z

Zanzibar 236
zebras 155
zero 304
absolute zero 254, 269, *269*, 308
Zeta Puppis 15
zinc 125
zircon 81, 82
Zodiac 55, 83
zoopraxiscopes 354, 355, 369
zoos 171

Acknowledgements

All illustrations are from the Miles Kelly Artwork Bank.

The publishers would like to thank the following sources for the use of their photographs:
(t = top, b = bottom, l = left, r = right, c = centre)

Cover (front) Science Photo Library, (spine) alexsvirid/Shutterstock, (back) David Ashley/Shutterstock

1 Eric Isselee/Shutterstock; 2–3 Adisa/Shutterstock; 52(t) Action Sports Photography/Shutterstock; 81(cl) Jeremy Horner/Shutterstock; 88(c) Yann Arthus-Bertrand/Corbis; 98(t) Martin M303/Shutterstock; 104(tr) Roger Tidman/FLPA; 113(tl) Michael and Patricia Fogden/FLPA; 123(tr) szefei/Shutterstock; 214–215(c) Yann Ar-thus-Bertrand/Corbis; 229(tl) Jose Ignacio Soto/Shutterstock; 267(l) Cosmin Manci/Shutterstock, (b) Photolibrary; 274(tr) Alexandr Zyryanov/Shutterstock; 288(b) Dave Turner/Shutterstock; 293(tc) Richard T. Nowitz/Corbis; 293(cr) Courtesy of Apple; 294(tr) Nokia; 295(tc) alexsl/iStockphoto; 297(tl) Courtesy of Apple, (tr) Sony Computer Entertain-ment; 318(br) Archivo Iconografico, S.A./Corbis; 320(tr) Moderna Museet Stockholm/Dagli Orti/The Art Archive, (bl) Constant Permeke Museum, Jabbeke/Dagli Orti/The Art Archive; 335(tr) pictorialpress.com; 349(tl) Radu Razvan/Shutterstock, (tc) rCarner/Shutterstock, (tr) Rawpixel.com/Shutterstock; 352(tr) Scanrail1/Shutterstock, (l) BBC/Pictorial Press, (br) Monkey Business/Fotolibrary; 353(bc) Sony; 356(tc) New World/Pictorial Press; 357(tl) DreamWorks/Pictorial Press, (bl) Rex; 358(bc) Pictorial Press; 359(tl) Warner Bros/Pictorial Press, (c) Hammer/Pictorial Press, (br) New Line/Pictorial Press; 362(tr) Matt Seaber; 363(tl) Typhoonski/Dreamstime

All other photographs are from:
Castrol, Corbis, Corel, digitalSTOCK, digitalvision, Hemera
ILN, NASA, PhotoAlto, PhotoDisc, PhotoEssentials, Stockbyte

Every effort has been made to acknowledge the source and copyright holder of each picture.
Miles Kelly Publishing apologizes for any unintentional errors or omissions.